Werner Hegemann and the Search for Universal Urbanism

Schlafwagenzug BERLIN—KÖLN
22 Uhr 40 aufgenommen.

Wo die langen Züge langer Wagen
hinter langen elefantengleichen Renn-
maschinen
kraftgeladen, ungeduldig, heimlich lauernd,
leise dampfend, leise zischend warten —

Wo die riesengroßen schwarzen Eisen-
Elefanten
ihre ungeheuren weißen Rüssel
schnaubend in die Lüfte werfen
und auch wohl wie siegestrunkene Trompeter
in die hochgeschwungenen Posaunen blasen,
brüllen, schreien oder aus der Tiefe grollenden
Gebrummes
wild losbrechen und sich zornig retten
in die Höhen zischenden Falsetts —

In dem großen internationalen Rennstall
tausendpferdiger Dampfmaschinen,
wo sich Renner aus Madrid und Warschau
und die Post vom goldenen Horn begrüßen —

In der himmelhohen, münstergleichen,
eisenstolzen, glasgedeckten Halle
stand mein Bett auf sechzehn Rädern,
weiß und friedlich,
und ich schlief.

Werner Hegemann
(„B. Z. am Mittag" Nr. 205)

Werner Hegemann and the Search for Universal Urbanism

Christiane Crasemann Collins

For Michelangelo Sabatino
with best wishes
for a bright future!
Christiane C. Collins
Spring 2007

W. W. NORTON & COMPANY
New York • London

To my sons

Nicolas and Luke Collins

and their families

Frontispiece: Poem by Werner Hegemann at the Berliner Railroad Station, 1928.

Printed in the United States of America
First Edition

For information about permission to reproduce selections from this book, write to Permissions, W. W. Norton & Company, Inc., 500 Fifth Avenue, New York, NY 10110

Book design by Abigail Sturges
Manufacturing by Quebecor World Fairfield
Production manager: Leeann Graham

Library of Congress Cataloging-in-Publication Data

Collins, Christiane Crasemann.
Werner Hegemann and the search for universal urbanism / Christiane Crasemann Collins.
p. cm.
Includes bibliographical references and index.
ISBN 0-393-73156-1.
1. Hegemann, Werner, 1881-1936. 2. City planners-Germany-Biography. 3. City planning-History. I. Title.

HT169.G3C637 2005
307.1'216'092—dc22
[B]

2004065436

W. W. Norton & Company, Inc., 500 Fifth Avenue, New York, N.Y. 10110
www.wwnorton.com
W. W. Norton & Company Ltd., Castle House, 75/76 Wells St., London W1T 3QT
0 9 8 7 6 5 4 3 2 1

Contents

Acknowledgments

The making of this book occurred in several stages. During my extensive involvement with the personage and oeuvre of Werner Hegemann I received encouragement and support from colleagues, friends, and family. To all I am much indebted, equally to those acknowledged in the notes, as well as to the many whose names are not mentioned.

Above all the three persons who triggered my interest in Werner Hegemann and contributed to the genesis of the book will always be remembered with profound gratitude. George R. Collins, Ida Belle Hegemann, and Robert C. Weinberg regrettably will not witness the culmination of our shared hopes.

A discussion of Werner Hegemann in the book on the Austrian city planner Camillo Sitte by G. R. and C. C. Collins, published in 1964/1965, caught the attention of architect and urban planner Robert C. Weinberg, who had befriended and aided the exiled Hegemanns in New York. Weinberg encouraged the Collinses to delve into Hegemann's work. When I took up Weinberg's suggestion, he generously donated to me the publications and documentation pertinent to Hegemann from his own library. Weinberg's gift greatly furthered my research and is an important part of the Christiane Crasemann Collins Collection.

In 1964 Robert Weinberg introduced me to Ida Belle Guthe Hegemann, who was living in Putney, Vermont. Hegemann's widow received me warmly as the "first" scholar interested in her husband's professional life. She generously shared her recollections and her husband's papers with me. She instructed her family that after her death, the Hegemann Papers should be deposited with me for the duration of my work. From 1983 on this important documentation has been crucial to the accomplishment and comprehensiveness of the book. The Hegemanns' daughter, Eva Maria Ladd, and her husband, Paul Ladd, offered unfailing hospitality. Manfred Hegemann combined patience with the book's lengthy progress and encouragement of its completion. My greatest debt of gratitude is to the Hegemann family for their trust and support during the entire process.

Subsequent phases of my research received exceptional assistance in America at the libraries of Columbia University, particularly the Avery Architectural Library; Cornell University; the Frances Loeb Library of the Harvard University Graduate School of Design; and the Ryerson & Burnham Libraries of the Chicago Art Institute. In Europe, the Berliner Staatsbibliothek, the Deutsches Literaturarchiv in Marbach, the Netherlands Architecture Institute in Rotterdam, and the Royal Library of Copenhagen all provided valuable archival material.

Professional and personal obligations delayed progress on the Hegemann project during the early phase. At that time Juanita Ellias and my research assistant, Jeannette Rausch, were a particular source of valued help and friendship. Concentrated work began in 1993 when I settled in West Falmouth, Massachusetts, with the Hegemann Papers, the C. C. Collins Collection, and my library in the tower of my old house.

Correspondence and travels to Buenos Aires and Europe complemented my own holdings. In Berlin I enjoyed the hospitality and friendship of my cousin Joachim v. Rosenberg. Deep gratitude also goes to Eva-Maria Barkhofen, director of the architecture division at the Berlinische Galerie for her knowledgeable encouragement and for organizing the recent transfer of the Hegemann Papers, now the Werner Hegemann-Archiv. (WHA) to her institution.

Among others abroad who shared information and provided helpful insights are Renate Banik-Schweitzer, Donatella Calabi, David R. Midgley, Riitta Nikula, Wolfgang Sonne, and Mark Swenarton. I am grateful for comments and suggestions from American colleagues, including Anthony Alofsin, Mardges Bacon, and Dietrich Neumann.

The end phase of the Hegemann project benefited from Allison B. White's editing of the manuscript and contributing to its literary readability. For her skill and friendship I am most appreciative. Susan Tallman gave invaluable counsel on the wording of the chapter headings. Many thanks are due to my patient computer consultant Michele Andolina, who helped with technological difficulties and advice, and to Pedro P. Silva for designing the jacket for the book.

Last but not least, I consider myself fortunate to have encountered the expert editorship of Nancy Green, who eagerly accepted the challenge of producing a book on a little-known individual written in the author's third language.

Preface

Intellectually rich and complex lives present enigmas for historians attempting to portray them. The options waver between adopting a linear structure, conceivably alien to the person described, or one that circles the maze and selectively offers insights into a jumble of contradictions and ambiguities. This latter type of assessment accommodates inconsistencies and prevents what might otherwise turn into a dull flatland coursed by a lifeline.

Certain segments of the study of Werner Hegemann benefit from a chronological narrative while others impede it. The Berlin years from 1922 to 1933 defy a sequential order; rather they profit from a hopscotch pattern of overlapping episodes. This assessment reflects the ambiguities and bewildering lacunae characteristic of Hegemann. His personal complexity resembles that of the modern city, to which he dedicated his lifelong attention. He advocated city planning as a science, a *Wissenschaft*, requiring the interaction of a range of disciplines. The city itself, however, represented more than a sum of functions and eluded scientific inquiry. Hegemann recognized it as an organic, evolving process, comprised of multiple elements that continuously blended and clashed, merging past, present, and future. In an endeavor to reconcile a rational scientific position with viewing the city as a cultural phenomenon in perpetual flux, he envisioned the present and future metropolis as a resilient synthesis of diverse elements responding to collective action.

In the Berlin of the 1920s, Hegemann excelled as a nonconformist critic and acquired a reputation as an adversary of modern architecture. Historians of the International Style perceived him as an awkward "other," easier to ignore than to scrutinize. Cognizance of the pluralism and the discords within Modernism aided the reemergence of interest in Hegemann. His position regarding modern architecture was anchored in his belief in the primacy of urban planning over the built environment and the city as a cultural and economic nexus. The modern canon's denial of history and its emphasis on the invention of a new style compromising an avowed functionalism and social commitment were anathemas to Hegemann.

Hegemann was not a practicing architect or planner, but an observant critic, who confronted contradictory trends with his own often ambivalent convictions and expressed them in his numerous publications. Singular episodes from his controversial presence as an architectural critic and political activist in Berlin illuminate the ferment of the Weimar years. His convictions were shaped by his travels as an intellectual ambassador between continents and the lively global exchange of ideas. It is ironic that his views collided with those of a movement designated as "international."

Hegemann's literary output emits his prescient awareness of the dangers inherent in the German propensity for heroic figures, which culminated in its fervent reception of the Führer. In his historic novels he debunked the hero myths of the "Great" Frederick II as presaging Hitler. Hegemann's hope for a peaceful transnational European culture clashed with the Nazi ideology of national identity and its opposition to otherness. During his years in Berlin, Hegemann's recognition of the linkage of hero worship, the mythology of sacrifice, militarism, war, and his pacifist convictions found rapport primarily among literary figures and social activists, but not architects.

Despite his premonition of the dangers of Nazism, Hegemann remained optimistic, adhering to his conviction that universal urbanism would lead to world peace. Universality for Hegemann signified a shared humanity that transcended the boundaries of nationality and region. He expressed this hope in 1936, shortly before his untimely death in exile: "The whole world could become engaged in internal improvements and urban rivalry to such an extent that, during the time required for carrying out the civic plans, international peace would rule and even become a permanent guest upon our planet."

Sources

Unusual circumstances made it possible to base research for this book chiefly on primary documentation in archives that had survived times of political upheaval. Absent from these were the archive and office papers at the Wasmuth Verlag in Berlin, including Werner Hegemann's correspondence as editor of *Wasmuths Monatshefte für Baukunst* and *Der Städtebau*, which were destroyed in World War II. Other resources were purged by the Nazis or eradicated by their threatened owners.

Sources used for this study have been noted in the acknowledgments, preface, and text of the book. In addition, however, some background identification seems warranted.

Ida Belle Hegemann, *The Family Saga*. Unpublished typescript. Approximately 325 pages, variously numbered. Written in Putney, Vermont, 1960s.

Hegemann's widow composed the narrative of their years together (1920–1936) for their children as a memoir of their parents' background, years in Europe preceding their exile, and their father's death. This major section of *The Family Saga* consists of long excerpts from the couple's daily letters, written during times apart, into which Ida Belle inserted her own recollections to fill in the gaps. She compiled the section about her husband's early years—before 1920—somewhat later, reconstructing his experiences from his diary, autobiographical notes, letters to his mother, and her conversations with his relatives. In an accompanying note dated 1968, she expressed her amazement that through all their moves, the confiscation of their property in Berlin, their exile, and changing residences five times in America, the bundles of documents, letters, diaries, and photographs remained intact. This material is referred to in this text as Hegemann Papers.

FS	Family Saga.
HP	Hegemann Papers.
WHA	Werner Hegemann-Archiv. In 2002 the Hegemann Papers were deposited at The Berlinische Galerie, Landesmuseum für Moderne Kunst, Photographie und Architektur.
CCCC	Christiane Crasemann Collins Collection. Comprises the author's material, presented to her by Robert C. Weinberg, including his correspondence pertaining to the completion of the volumes on *Housing* by W. Hegemann (1935–1937) and publications, photographs, and slides bought from Ida Belle Hegemann at the death of her husband in 1936. The CCCC also comprises both the author's correspondence and interview notes relating to her research on Werner Hegemann, Joseph Hudnut, Elbert Peets, the New School of Social Research, Columbia University, exile affairs in the Americas, and urbanism in South America.
FLLHGSD	Frances Loeb Library, Harvard Graduate School of Design.

Abbreviations in the text, captions, and notes in addition to those listed above:

WMB	*Wasmuths Monatshefte für Baukunst*
STB	*Städtebau, Monatshefte für Stadtbaukunst, Städtisches Verkehr–Park–und Siedlungswesen*
WMB/STB	*Wasmuths Monatshefte für Baukunst and Städtebau* (*WMB* and *STB* merged in 1931)

Translations are by the author unless otherwise indicated.

Werner Hegemann and the Search for Universal Urbanism

Fig. 1. Werner Hegemann portrait, ca. 1930. WHA

1. A Transatlantic Education

Prussia to Pennsylvania

Werner Hegemann's development as a planner began in Mannheim, Germany, on June 15, 1881. His career took him to many places and through distinct phases as a result of both circumstances and his unceasing drive. From early on he committed himself to the pursuit of overriding themes and endeavors, which can be synthesized as an "urban universality" benefiting humanity and world peace (Fig. 1).

Hegemann was the eighth of nine children—three of whom died in infancy—born to Ottmar Hegemann and Elise Vorster. His father owned a mirror and picture frame manufacturing business and the family was financially comfortable, but Ottmar and Elise's marriage was unstable; in 1895 the couple separated and the children were split up between them. Werner's childhood effectively ended, and he was sent to boarding school at Büdingen at age fourteen. When his classmates went to their families for vacations, Werner was obliged to stay at school because he lacked a proper home, and his earliest writings expressed his loneliness. Nevertheless, while at Büdingen he played the violin, wrote poetry, read voraciously, and met and made lifelong friends.

After two years at Büdingen, Werner transferred to the Gymnasium Plön in Holstein. During his summer vacation in 1897, at age sixteen, he took off walking alone to Copenhagen, where he happened upon a fare reduction by a shipping company and bought a $40 ticket to New York. On board ship he won $100 in a lottery, which he put to use in Manhattan for a few days of sightseeing before returning on the next boat back to Europe. This was the first of Hegemann's Atlantic crossings and marked the beginning of his countless travels to the far corners of the world.

Hegemann graduated from Plön with an Abitur certificate in February 1901, and with good grades in all but mathematics. After a visit to London, he entered the Königliche Friedrich-Wilhelm Universität in Berlin. He was warmly welcomed in the home of his mother's sister, Maria Vorster, or "Tante Ria," who was married to the architect Otto March. March took great interest in his nephew's education and encouraged his inclinations toward architecture, city planning, and history. He guided Hegemann toward investigating urban developments in America, especially the Greater Boston initiative, and recommended his nephew for the position of secretary for the exhibitions of 1910 in Berlin and Düsseldorf. These events (henceforth referred to as Berlin 1910 and Düsseldorf 1910) became determining factors for Hegemann's career and for city planning in general, drawing international attention to Berlin as a center for new ideas in urbanism.

The rapidly expanding cities in Europe and America claimed attention from a range of specialists with a variety of backgrounds and training. These authorities were frequently at odds with each other, debating which expertise was most vital for urban improvement. Was it transportation, sanitation, architecture, streets, or parks? Gradually the realization took hold that the complex problems of the modern metropolis called for a multidisciplinary approach. In Central Europe this conviction was stimulated by Camillo Sitte's landmark book, *Der Städte-Bau nach seinen künstlerischen Grundsätzen* (City planning according to artistic principles) (1889), which stressed the city as an evolving, organic totality composed of open spaces and streets enclosed by buildings. In America, urbanism developed tangential to the park and boulevard systems, envisioning a town–rural continuum initiated by Frederick Law Olmsted Sr. and his followers. However, it would be simplistic to trace city planning as a distinct field of knowledge to the influence of single individual such as Sitte or Olmsted. The city as a topic of intellectual inquiry demanded concern and intervention from practitioners across the disciplines. Where and how this new subject could be studied in all aspects remained unresolved for several decades. Even today, it has yet to find a comfortable niche in academic institutions, where it is shifted from schools of architecture to departments of political science, economics, and sociology.

Hegemann's educational wanderings reflect the complexities of city planning as a field of knowledge in the throes of defining itself. His interests lay in economics and history, studies that set him apart from his contemporaries. Perhaps his focus was a reason for his avoidance of the "Seminare für Städtebau" in Charlottenburg, which concentrated on urban design. The seminars were instituted around 1907, and are considered the first courses in city planning, although Theodor Goecke, Joseph Brix, and Felix Genzmer gave lectures on "Stadtbaukunst" at the Technische Hochschule in Charlottenburg in 1903.[1]

The summer of 1902 found the young Werner bicycling from Morocco to Tunisia and into the Sahara Desert, returning to Germany via Spain. He then proceeded to the University of Munich for a brief interlude, motivated by the reputation of the economist Lujo Brentano, under whom he would later work on his dissertation. Brentano was the cofounder of the Verein für Sozialpolitik (Association for Social Policy) and was considered a *Kathedersozialist* (ivory tower socialist). His commitment to the cause of workers and low-income housing deepened Hegemann's interest in the social, political, and economic implications of city planning. Encouraged by his mentor, Hegemann moved to Paris in search of Charles Gide's courses in *économie sociale* and similar subjects. He did not attend the Ecole des Beaux Arts, but studied at the Faculté de Droit de l'Université de Paris from 1903–04, where he enrolled in Gide's courses in *économie sociale*, and others such as *économie politique*, *histoire du droit et le droit constitutionel*, *histoire des doctrines économiques*, *économie politique*, and *science financière*. At the Sorbonne he sought out Henri Lemonnier's lectures on art history, the only courses he ever took in that subject; his impressive knowledge of art and architecture was derived from independent study and personal observation. Hegemann never had any professional training in architecture, nor did he develop a talent for drawing.

Hegemann's year in Paris left him with a profound and lasting affection for the city and French culture. Written responses to this early encounter with Paris have not survived, but the evocative impressions of his later travels bear comparison to those by the poet and celebrated flaneur Walter Benjamin.[2] During his year in Paris Hegemann became fluent in French and acquired a predilection for its literature. He often wrote in French in diaries and letters to his wife, Ida Belle. His initial stay in the city also provided him with the lifelong friendship of Pierre Lievre, and he stayed at his home during his later visits in Paris.

The young German absorbed the stirrings of great ferment in French urbanism—the Musée Sociale (Social Museum), an institute for the study of urban issues—and made contacts with those active in the charged atmosphere that led to the formation of the Société Francaise d'Urbanistes (SFU). The career of the urban historian Marcel Poëte (1866–1950) was just commencing, and Hegemann responded to his ideas when he mounted the Berlin 1910 exhibition.

Furthermore, Charles Gide and his *économie sociale* made a lasting impression on Hegemann, since their ideas converged with his own sociopolitical approach to city planning. In particular, André Gueslin's diagram of the major points of Gide's doctrine, "*Les grands courants de l'économie sociale*," contains numerous elements that Hegemann integrated into his urban pursuits. Among these were *socialisme*, *Christianisme social*, *solidarisme*, *liberalisme*, consumer cooperatives, and credit unions.[3] Throughout his life Hegemann acknowledged his indebtedness to Gide for stimulating his socialist leanings and his concern for housing. Of equal importance was Gide's suggestion that Hegemann study with Simon N. Patten (1852–1922) at the University of Pennsylvania in Philadelphia (the

Department of Economics later became the Wharton School of Economics). He followed Gide's advice and spent 1904–05 in the United States, the first of several long stays in this country.

Patten's innovative social theories merged with American Progressivism. His rejection of classic economic theory, which assumed that laissez-faire was an economic system without need of regulatory supervision, made Patten an outcast among his conservative colleagues. Patten's doubt that private and social interests worked hand in hand was prescient of John Maynard Keynes's premises. Patten expressed his ideas awkwardly in writing, but he was a charismatic teacher and his students were devoted to him; several became important in American planning, such as John Nolen, Benjamin C. Marsh, and Rexford G. Tugwell. Hegemann's contacts with them, renewed during later sojourns in the country, acquired lasting significance. This young generation eagerly accepted Patten's anti–laissez-faire message that deliberate intervention by the government was essential for urban and social progress, especially for long-range planning, and his recognition of the interdependency of economics and the social sciences.

Hegemann was captivated by these challenges when he set out on his *Wanderjahre* and found himself energized by the conviction that city planning required the political as well as social action exhorted by American reformers. Tugwell summarized Patten's "salient aspects of thought and achievement," which had drawn Hegemann across the ocean:

> His [Patten's] most characteristic contributions to economics were the evidence he presented in support of the economic interpretation of history, his distinction between the pain-deficit and pleasure-surplus stages in human progress, his insistence that there is no natural limitation on progress but that productive power is subject to the law of increasing rather than decreasing returns, his recognition that improvements in consumption may contribute to further progress quite as much as improvements in production, his emphasis on dynamic economics, his confidence in programs calling for the aggressive interference of government . . . and his confidence in cooperation and other forms of socialization.[4]

These ideas conveyed to Hegemann an interpretation of American democracy that differed from the preconceptions he had brought from Europe. Such ideas proved influential in reconciling his preference for public participation and debate with the demands for comprehensive planning on a regional scale.

Hegemann's formative years were impacted as much by his immersion in Progressivism and contacts with its advocates as by his choice of courses at the University of Pennsylvania, which centered on economics. In addition to Patten's lectures on the development of English thought, the courses included industrial processes, corporation finance, money, credit, and foreign exchange.

Following this academic track and to gain practical experience, Hegemann entered the Allgemeine Elsaessische Bank Gesellschaft in Strassbourg as a *Volontär* (unsalaried clerk) in August 1905. Simultaneously, he spent two semesters studying in the Faculty of Law and Political Science at the Kaiser-Wilhelms-Universität, also located in Strassbourg.

In the summer of 1906 Hegemann returned to the University of Munich, intent on completing his requirements and obtaining a doctorate in political science. He was reunited with Lujo Brentano and became acquainted with Walther Lotz. Hegemann's dissertation, *Mexikos Übergang zur Goldwährung: Ein Beitrag zur Geschichte des Mexikanischen Geldwesens (1867–1906)* (Mexico's transition to the gold standard: A contribution to the history of Mexico's financial system), was published in 1908 in a series on political economy edited by Brentano and Lotz. Hegemann dedicated his work to his wife, Alice Hesse, whom he had married in 1904; their daughter, Ellis, was born in 1906, while he was in Munich.[5] Hegemann and Alice Hesse were divorced in 1916 during his time in the United States (1913–21), and in 1920 he married Ida Belle Guthe in Ann Arbor, Michigan.

Hegemann's choice of studying Mexico's transition from the silver to the gold standard is somewhat baffling, and his dissertation remained an isolated event, although he frequently included it when listing his publications. Other than his later comments on the influence of Mayan buildings on the architecture of Frank Lloyd Wright, he did not pay any further attention to Mexico.

Boston 1915

At the age of twenty-seven and now a *Doktor*, Hegemann returned to Philadelphia in 1908. Perhaps on the recommendation of his acquaintances in that city, he briefly held the position of municipal housing inspector. Philadelphia became the stepping-stone for the unfolding of his career in urbanism and led to a sequence of events that proved crucial for Hegemann in particular and city planning in general. His well-connected uncle, Otto March, may have had a hand in guiding his steps from Philadelphia to Boston, via the First National Conference on City Planning in Washington, D.C. (May 21–22, 1909).[6]

By the end of the nineteenth century, the United States and Germany, and especially Boston and Berlin, were linked by their mutual interests in matters pertaining to the growth and administration of cities. Before World War I, American interest in city planning was stronger than in Europe, where the wave of *Amerikanismus* in the 1920s primarily focused on architecture rather than urbanism and social reform. Nevertheless, as Berliners were considering the possibilities of a Greater Berlin, with Otto March as one of the prime promoters, similar propositions in Boston drew notice.

Two Americans who published extensively on their impressions of Germany around the time of Hegemann's arrival in America were Sylvester Baxter and Frederic C. Howe, who advocated social reform rather than civic beautification. Baxter had studied in Leipzig and Berlin and later lived in Malden, Massachusetts as an author, poet, and literary scholar. He was the first to suggest the term "Greater Boston" and vigorously proposed what later evolved into the Metropolitan Park System.

In July 1909, Baxter published "The German Way of Making Better Cities," which expanded on an article by Cornelius Gurlitt, "German City Planning," that he had translated the previous year.[7] Baxter's article began euphorically: "In no other country has the art of city-planning been carried to so high a degree as in Germany to-day," and he went on to describe the discipline as "a conscious development . . . of well-considered attainment of definite ends deliberately aimed at." In his opinion the German term *Städtebau*, literally "town-building," was appropriate for this new art-*cum*-science in its most inclusive implications. He echoed Gurlitt's admiration for Camillo Sitte, but then turned to matters of administration and housing. The latter passages, especially those on land speculation in Berlin and mutual building societies, are strikingly similar to Hegemann's proclamations in 1912–13. Surprisingly, Hegemann had published little on this topic at the time of Baxter's article.

Another American who influenced Hegemann was Frederic C. Howe, whose remarkable career embraced municipal politics, social activism, journalism, and the writing of over a dozen books.[8] Howe studied history and political science in Berlin with von Treitschke in 1891, and returned to Germany several times, including a visit to the City Planning Exhibitions of 1910, which were organized by Hegemann. The two may have met at that time, and three years later as director of the People's Institute of New York, Howe invited the German urbanist to give a lecture tour.

Howe's background and interest in the city coincided with Hegemann's. In his autobiography Howe related that some time after 1901, while working in Cleveland for the socialist mayor Tom Johnson, "The possibility of a free, orderly, and beautiful city became to me an absorbing passion. Here were all of the elements necessary to a great experiment in democracy." He continued, "I had an architectonic vision of what a city might be. I saw it as a picture. It was not economy, efficiency, and business methods that interested me so much as a city planned, built, and conducted as a community enterprise. I saw the city as an architect sees a skyscraper, as a commission of experts plans a world's fair exposition. It was a unit, a thing with a mind, with a conscious purpose, seeing far in advance of the present and taking precautions for the future."[9] Howe viewed cities to be the social agencies for the betterment of life. The city became "the enthusiasm of [his] life;" he studied it and wrote numerous articles and books on it. Best known among his books on this topic is *The City: The Hope of Democracy*, first published in 1905; it is probable that Howe's manifesto-like tone and analysis of political and municipal systems influenced Hegemann's pamphlets *Für Gross-Berlin* of 1913. On the other hand, Howe's article, "City Building in Germany," reflected his encounter with the City Planning Exhibition in Berlin and events surrounding it that were intimately associated with Hegemann.[10] These publications are emblematic of the transfer and retro-transfer of international urbanism in its early stages. The interchange was furthered by conferences, meetings, and personal contacts among the pioneers in this new field of knowledge.

The emphasis on German precedents had provided an auspicious ambient for Hegemann's return to America in 1908. Young and unknown, he was not included in the program of the 1909 First National Conference on City Planning, which took place in Washington, D.C., although he likely attended this important event.[11] Frederick Law Olmsted Jr., who had recently returned from travels abroad, delivered the keynote address. In his introduction on "The Scope and Results of City Planning in Europe," Olmsted concluded that much could be learned from both European mistakes and successes. He reported extensively on the range of German city planning, which included building and zoning regulations and provisions for property owners to cede land for roads and other public uses.

Among the other speakers were John Nolen and Benjamin C. Marsh, the executive secretary of the Committee on Congestion of Population in New York.[12] Marsh had organized the so-called Congestion Show in New York, which was also displayed at the conference in Washington.

In an interview with Olmsted, Marsh, who had also recently returned from Europe, spoke of "great foreign cities" that had adopted city planning and had absorbed large surrounding areas. Among those he mentioned was Berlin, where discussions were taking place about incorporating thirty towns for the purpose of "a consolidation of outlying territory with the city proper." The conference program included a section on "Plans for the Enlargement of Berlin," listing the larger towns to be consolidated in Greater Berlin with their population figures, as well as the "Requirements of the contest for the development of Greater Berlin."[13] It is not clear whether these details were publicized in order to stimulate American planners to embark on comparable undertakings in their own country, or to elicit their proposals for the Greater Berlin competition. Planners were cautioned against an overemphasis of German models, particularly if they would lead to municipal and/or governmental control of comprehensive planning. Many feared that the search for civic improvements and urban progress implied socialism. A balance between American laissez-faire and comprehensive city planning was recommended.[14] Progressives such as Marsh, who advocated social reform, came mostly from New York and were edged aside by Olmsted, who preferred a more cautious approach.

Marsh was a student of Simon Patten and was influenced by Fabian socialist doctrines. He had traveled extensively in Europe, gathering information and contributions for the Congestion Show, on which he collaborated with the housing reformer Mary Kingsbury Simkhovitch, founder of the Greenwich House Settlement in New York City in 1902. Marsh blamed land speculation as the underlying cause of congested housing and unsanitary conditions, much as Hegemann did when he battled the *Mietskasernen* (rental barracks) in Berlin. The New York Congestion Show was cosponsored by the Municipal Art Society, which was interested in both civic beautification and urban planning as it affected social well-being. In the history of American planning the Congestion Show holds significance as the first exhibition on the city held in the United States.

Hegemann published two articles on "Die Ausstellung für Städtebau und städtische Kunst in New York" (The exhibition of city planning and municipal art in New York) in the journal *Der Städtebau* of October and November 1909, and he referred to the immediate transfer of the exhibit to Washington.[15] He described the vast halls of the Armory, and in a typescript, "Plans for City Planning Exhibitions" (1909), commented on the New York event and made recommendations for the Boston 1915 group.

Hegemann's articles, addressing a German audience, and Charles M. Robinson's July 1909 article were both critical of the arrangement of the displays in the Congestion Show, which the latter called "poorly planned and needlessly ineffective." Robinson's name is primarily linked to the "City Beautiful" movement, a phrase that he coined in 1903. But his concerns embraced more than the aesthetic, and he cited approvingly a sign in the exhibition: " . . . It is a City's Chief End to Provide the Best and Most Healthful Conditions for All Its Citizens, and to Do This It Must Have a Town Plan for the Whole City and an Efficient Administration."[16] In the exhibition's section on foreign cities, Robinson noted "the material on the enlargement of Berlin," which was shown in several plans and texts.

Hegemann was impressed by the Congestion Show, particularly the display of posters with informational texts and tables of statistics. He mentioned a large central space set aside for daytime and evening lectures. Recalling an earlier speech by Otto March delivered to the Ausschuss für Gross-Berlin, in which he warned of the enormous economic outlay and the efforts required to carry out the plans for Greater Berlin, Hegemann stressed the importance for urbanists to learn from the struggles toward comprehensive planning in both New York and Berlin. In this vein he wrote the two articles in *Der Städtebau* and singled out the alarming housing conditions in both cities. Presciently poised in New York for the forthcoming events in Berlin and their far-reaching implications, Hegemann recommended a comparable undertaking for Berlin: "An exhibition for Berlin similar to the New York City Planning Exhibition could surely offer Berlin much of interest, perhaps even something unexpected and provocative, and would captivate wide attention for these important matters, thereby stimulating public opinion in anticipation of the fundamental changes in the townscape and urban planning of Berlin, a delay of which will, in the opinion of experts, present an imminent danger for the capital city." Hegemann's awareness of the importance of exhibitions as vehicles for stimulating the engagement of citizens in urban concerns, which he convincingly articulated in his articles, became a determining factor in his career and led to his involvement in several major exhibitions. His analysis of the display in the Congestion Show is an early indication of his attention to presentation techniques designed to enhance the appeal of such events for the general public.

The 1909 First National Conference on City Planning in Washington brought representatives and trends together in a summit meeting at a time called "A Benchmark Year in the History of City Planning." This year saw the publication of Daniel H. Burnham's "Plan of Chicago," which alerted Europeans to the sophistication of American developments when it was shown in Düsseldorf and London the following year. Furthermore, a city planning course offered at Harvard by James Sturgis Pray was the first in the country and a significant step toward defining the new profession.

For Hegemann, now twenty-eight and embarking on a career in urbanism, it was an auspicious time to be immersed in the challenges in America. He was the only German to approach it so broadly. The dense web of experiences and events that constituted Hegemann's formative years culminated during his brief sojourn on the East Coast in 1909, which represented a turning point that brought clarification to his convictions and hopes that were later reinforced by his extended stays in the United States. A survey of his experiences and the individuals aiding them contributes to the understanding of his perceptions. Throughout his life, Hegemann recognized the significance of this era. He propagated the outlook he had gained in Europe and America and showed foresight when he chose to go to Boston, with its reputation as the "Athens of America." It was a decision that presaged promises beyond the *Boston 1915* movement and its connections to "Greater Berlin."

Among contacts predating Hegemann's arrival in Boston in 1909 was his acquaintance with John Nolen, whose preparation for his profession resembled Hegemann's own. Nolen's career began with several years of administrative duties at the adult extension division of the University of Pennsylvania. After travels in Europe, he entered the School of Landscape Architecture at Harvard, graduating in 1905. His professional life is emblematic of American urbanism's roots in landscape and open-space planning. Nolen's career was dedicated to drafting comprehensive plans and reports for a number of small- to medium-sized towns. His friendship with Raymond Unwin and his admiration for the garden city was comparable to Hegemann's, as was his missionary idealism, which perceived city planning as the physical replanning of society. Hegemann & Peets's residential developments in the Midwest and Pennsylvania from 1916 to 1921 reflected their admiration for Nolen. Hegemann also established lasting contacts with George B. Ford and his brother James. James Ford, a specialist in housing, directed the Museum of Social Ethics at Harvard and in that capacity contributed to the exhibitions in Boston and Berlin.

Boston 1915 was a six-year plan of civic improvement that set 1915 as the goal for achieving its ambitious program. It was conceived by Edward Albert Filene, a wealthy department store owner and progressive reformer.[17] Filene's father had emigrated from Germany in 1848, and his sons, Abraham and Edward, developed an unpretentious dry-goods store in one of Boston's mercantile landmarks. Conscious of his humble background, Edward Filene, who liked to be called "E. A.," devoted his energy and wealth to social betterment. Although a self-educated man from a Jewish family and lacking Brahmin credentials, Filene was highly respected in Boston. His conviction that the citizens' well-being was essential for economic progress won acclaim and support for the *Boston 1915* movement, and his status as one of the wealthiest and best informed men in the city aided its promotion.

Filene inspired and persuaded a group of professionals and prominent businessmen to carry forward an ambitious plan to bring together thirty-seven neighboring communities and small towns into a comprehensive metropolitan unit. The administrative structure of "Greater Boston" would then be empowered to carry out a range of social and civic endeavors that would bring prosperity and renown to the major city of New England.

Hegemann was particularly impressed by one unique feature of *Boston 1915*, which was the involvement of members of the cultural and financial elite who made up a reform movement motivated by the belief that it would benefit their own interests as much as the lives of the working people. *Boston 1915* was a compelling demonstration of the conviction that urban improvement and economic progress were linked to the betterment of all citizens, "regardless of race, color, or previous condition of servitude," as stated by J. Randolph Coolidge Jr. at the Washington, D.C. meeting. He noted that the *Boston 1915* movement "was not merely local, but rested on such broad principles of good citizenship as to be applicable in any city under a democratic form of government; its purpose being to organize, stimulate and direct the civic consciousness of citizens."[18]

In his autobiographical depictions, Hegemann exaggerated his involvement with *Boston 1915*, a movement that unquestionably had a profound impact on his convictions and career. Under the influence of the diverse ambitions and strategies of the movement, Hegemann's awareness of the scope of planning concerns expanded, and his interest in economics and housing became integrated into an evolving synthesis. An understanding of this phase of Hegemann's formative years sheds light on many decisions and principles of his later years.

Suggestions for the exhibition were made by Hegemann in a six-page unpublished essay, "Plans for City Planning Exhibitions" (1909).[19] The opening paragraph stated its objective: "The overwhelming problem of city planning has just entered the public consciousness and in the very near future the world is liable to be flooded with city planning exhibitions. One of the most pressing questions at present, therefore, is how to plan a city planning exhibit, how to make it dramatic, striking and conclusive for everybody." What followed was an analysis of installation and display techniques and spatial organization that might facilitate achieving this goal. From the beginning of his interest in exhibitions, their methodology, and their possibilities, Hegemann considered them vehicles to introduce city planning to a general public and to stimulate civic action. He perceived the exhibitions as a means for presenting an urban universality, rather than restricted features of the modern metropolis. This essay put forward the flaws in the presentation of material shown in New York. He primarily attributed these to the absence of a clear trajectory for visitors to follow. A specialist could deal with this, but the general public would be confused by the complexity without proper guidance. City planning exhibitions, he said, should represent an "efficient little course" or a condensed curriculum on the subject for casual students and nonspecialists, without overwhelming them with the multiplicity of elements to be considered.

Hegemann considered that international exhibits and those addressing local problems would differ in size and intent, but the techniques for effective presentation would be similar. Large signs, he said, should be required, as well as the publication of a directory, pamphlet, or catalogue with chapters corresponding to sections or rooms in the show. Plans, maps, drawings, photographs, and models would enliven the presentation of difficult and theoretical subjects. Hegemann recommended a comparative method, displaying the accomplishments in various localities side by side, a method that became a distinguishing feature of the international exhibitions he organized in Germany.

While Hegemann presumably composed this memorandum for the committee in charge of the Boston 1915 Exhibition, his motivations were broader. He may have had in mind Frederick Law Olmsted's hope for a wide exchange of "material illustrative of city planning" eventually leading to an exhibition. Beyond the application of his suggestions in America, Hegemann was already working on a framework for his expectations in Berlin.

Boston 1915 allowed Hegemann to interact with leading figures in American urbanism, notably Frederick Law Olmsted Jr., who enjoyed a prominent position in Boston. The son of the renowned landscape planner of New York's Central Park and the park systems in Boston and other cities, he differed from his "visionary" father by stressing planning as an ongoing procedure under the continuous oversight of experts, rather than an overall preconceived master plan.[20] Olmsted and Hegemann exchanged letters regarding the labeling of examples in the Boston 1915 Exhibition; in one letter Hegemann mentioned his prospects in connection with an exhibition on Greater Berlin. He also wrote about a previous conversation they had had concerning the possibility of Hegemann's subsequent return to Boston to "make comparative studies," not further specified in the letter.

During Hegemann's time in Berlin, some of their correspondence addressed matters of building regulations. Olmsted referred to a book-length study by Flavel Shurtleff on legal and administrative aspects of city planning and asked Hegemann to research how these were handled in Europe. In a letter to Thomas Adams in London, Olmsted mentioned that he and Raymond Unwin, Thomas Mawson, Patrick Geddes, and Hegemann "were all in touch with each other working on a possible international exchange of 'material illustrative of city planning'." In his letters to Hegemann, Olmsted wondered about aesthetic building regulations in Germany. In reply Hegemann reported on their application in various German cities he had visited in connection with his *Der Städtebau nach den Ergebnissen der allgemeinen Städtebau-Ausstellung in Berlin* (City planning according to the results of the universal city planning exhibition in Berlin) in 1911, also noting his intention of meeting Olmsted soon.[21] This fragmentary correspondence demonstrates that Hegemann embraced the contact with Olmsted and recognized him as a prominent authority among American urbanists, providing guidance and direction to a new generation.[22]

With its proximity to Harvard, Boston furthered Hegemann's desire to spend more time in America, a wish fulfilled in 1913 with the invitation for an extended lecture tour. The offer may have been prompted by Olmsted's international networking, deriving additional stimulus from Hegemann's rise to recognition for his role in the events in Berlin and Düsseldorf in 1910.

Hegemann was much impressed by Edward A. Filene's commitment to social reform and progress, and his enthusiasm and ability to initiate and organize the complex *Boston 1915* undertaking. Hegemann had comparable reactions to the ambience cultivated by the Bostonian elite, which dispelled European misconceptions of an American lack of sophistication. Upon returning to Europe in 1922, after an absence of nearly ten years, he interwove many Boston recollections into his fiction. In his 1924 novel *Deutsche Schriften*, he fashioned a composite portrait of one Manfred Maria Ellis, a member of the Boston Brahmin class. Occasionally he referred to the fictional Ellis as a character based on the socially prominent Philip Cabot, a member of the *Boston 1915* committees. On the other hand, Hegemann also created the character of Manfred Maria Ellis as his own alter-ego and, in a confusing fictional twist, claimed to have lodged in the home of "M. M. Ellis," or Philip Cabot, while working in Boston.[23]

An additional touch of poetic license is discernible in Hegemann's portrayals of his involvement with *Boston 1915*, notably with its exhibition, as he magnified his own role in his autobiographical notations, although it is not documented in other sources.

The *Boston 1915* movement was formally established on April 2, 1909, and proceeded to issue three promotional bulletins. No. 1, "What *Boston-1915* Is" explained "the gist of it" on the cover:

> A CITY MOVEMENT—bringing about co-operation of all people and organizations who are trying to do something for the improvement of Boston.
>
> A CITY PLAN—combining all the separate desirable plans for improvement into one general program which the people can understand and carry out.
>
> A CITY CALENDAR—setting dates ahead when different parts of that program can and ought to be finished.
>
> A CITY EXPOSITION—showing, year by year, the city's progress as made apparent in its factories, stores, public departments, institutions, city equipment and resources, homes and health, social and industrial relations—and exposition of the city itself in action—which not only shall give an accounting but shall be prophetic of
>
> THE CITY THAT IS TO BE.

No. 2, "What Is Said of *Boston-1915*," included an article from *The Survey*, entitled "Boston's Level Best," describing how *Boston 1915* was launched by 150 men at a dinner at the Boston City Club upon the initiative of Edward A. Filene, who became its chairman.[24] A directorate was formed and expanded the following year. The same article, under the heading, "Pulling Power of a Goal," observed that "the idea of an exposition in which the exhibits will be the things as they are in 1915 turns pride into a becoming civic force." This essay is followed by "Quotations from the Press," which included "things that have been said in Boston and various parts of the country about the *Boston-1915* movement."

It was presumably Filene, with his long experience in department store advertising, who was responsible for the effective promotion of *Boston 1915*. These efforts were closely observed and later employed by Hegemann in Berlin. *The "1915" Yearbook: A Directory of Information Concerning Boston and the Metropolitan District* proudly stated on the first page: "*Boston-1915* is a movement for making the most of Boston's possibilities. It makes no social, racial, religious or political distinctions. It proposes to bring mutual help and support to all men and women, and organizations working to benefit the city. . . . It is Your Opportunity."[25]

An illustrated monthly record of its achievements touted "New Boston" as "The Official Organ of *Boston-1915*."[26] On the basis of a successful first year, the "Foreword" proposed reaching a wider public in

Boston and in other cities and towns to inform them of the possibilities carried forward by the Greater Boston plan. The Boston 1915 Exposition was described as "one of the larger enterprises undertaken" and "most important" for presenting "the Boston-1915 idea visibly and concretely to those who exhibited and to those who came to see it."[27] *New Boston* noted that during six weeks "two hundred thousand people visited the Exposition, and opportunity was given to every school pupil to see it." This first issue of *New Boston* from May 1910 also published "Aim of the Exposition of 1915," which was written as an announcement prior to the event. It reported "the proposed Boston Exposition" to present "the best that is being done not only in the United States but all over the world," in civic developments. The exhibition was to include "charts, models, moving pictures, stereopticon lectures, etc." Hegemann's collaboration is not mentioned in these publications.

The much lauded exhibition took place from November 1 to 27, 1909 (later extended to December 11), in the vacant former building of the Museum of Fine Arts in Copley Square; the regular collections had been moved to the new museum on Huntington Avenue. The impressive High Victorian Gothic structure in Copley Square, later demolished, was an appropriate venue for the Boston 1915 Exhibition of 1909. *New Boston* featured a picture of the former museum with three large posters on the facade announcing the "'1915 Boston' Exposition" and noting dates and hours, and another placard stating "Special Attractions. Last Week. Closing Sat. Dec. 11."[28]

Thomas N. Carver of the Department of Economics at Harvard University was the author of the *Official Catalogue*.[29] His brief foreword states, "The people of Boston can have as fine a city as they want, provided they want it badly enough to be willing to pay for it. Nothing so good as a fine city is to be had for nothing." Hegemann cited Carver's introductory message in the *Catalogue* in connection with a description of *Boston 1915* in the first of his three volumes on *Housing*.[30] He considered the five-year plan to be an example of lasting value. Much later, in 1935, with a touch of nostalgia Hegemann commented on his own involvement with *Boston 1915* and its exhibition: "The author of the present volume had the privilege of suggesting and directing a city planning exhibition. It occupied during November, 1909, the large ground floor of the pseudo-Gothic Old Art Museum of Boston and has become the father of numberless [*sic*] similar and larger exhibitions; notably those of Berlin, Düsseldorf and London held in 1910."

The *Official Catalogue* does, indeed, list Werner Hegemann as one of three members forming the Exhibition Committee and in charge of "The Visible City." He was also on the City Planning Committee responsible for city plans, streets, parks, harbor, docks, transportation, housing, and public buildings. Among others this committee included Sylvester Baxter, Philip

Cabot, and Arthur A. Shurtleff. Hegemann's participation is substantiated by his draft of a proposal for the various types of public buildings to be shown in the category "The Visible City."[31] His manuscript, dated September 9, 1909, bears the note "Approved by E. A. [Edward A. Filene]." Further down on the page is an unsigned handwritten comment dated September 13, 1909: "A very good plan. Its success in the Exp. will depend on how definitely it shows 'the best things in the world' in each division, and especially how architecture is working for the masses (wage earners, etc.) = Architecture of schoolhouses for general use after school hours, etc., etc." The title page lists the architect Robert P. Bellows as "in charge," and these lines may be his. The proposal divides "public buildings" into a variety of structures, followed by a classification into eight subjects. Another category lists "elements of city life" and suggests placing each of the eight groupings into separate but adjacent rooms to aid circulation among the divisions. Hegemann also recommended that photographs be obtained from the Boston Public Library and Harvard University.

The exposure of Greater Berlin at the event in Boston promoted the future Berlin 1910 Exhibition and encouraged Americans to attend the event. Plans and diagrams of the present and future of Berlin, including "details of the great scheme" for Greater Berlin, were displayed in Room 3. The entrance hall and Rooms 2 and 3 of the exposition were devoted to city planning. Frederick Law Olmsted Jr. introduced this section of the *Official Catalogue* with a comprehensive report on the state of American city planning. Five subsections were devoted to selected cities, including Daniel H. Burnham and Edward H. Bennett's plan for Chicago, which was shown with fifty-nine "paintings" and drawings, noting the "cooperation" of Jules Guerin. On this occasion in Boston, Hegemann and a wider public saw these plans for the first time. Hegemann later tried without success to procure them for the exhibition in Berlin, but eventually obtained them for Düsseldorf, from where they were moved to London. In the section on foreign cities, the German zoning systems and building regulations were, according to Olmsted, "a matter of special interest to the modern city planner. . . . They do for the benefit of whole communities what the American real estate speculator often does for the benefit of himself and a small number of persons."[32]

The section on "Housing: Healthy Homes at Reasonable Rents for all the People," occupied two rooms. The introduction in the catalogue is signed by Philip Cabot, Chairman of the Housing Committee of Boston 1915. Cabot considered "the spread of congestion and the danger of conflagration" the greatest problem for Boston's housing situation, which was worse than that in New York. He noted the benefit of zoning as practiced in Germany, and workers' housing in England. Cabot saw the greatest promise in "the movement in England known as 'co-partnership in housing,'" because it solved the difficulties regarding the relationship of landlord and tenant. He explained in some detail how a co-partnership tenants' society could jointly purchase land to build houses. During his years in Berlin, Hegemann was an ardent promoter of these *Baugenossenschaften* and was on the board of one of the first in the city, called "Ideal."

The *Official Catalogue* also included a list of lectures, sometimes two or three a day, scheduled in the afternoons and evenings. Speakers on the opening night included Jane Addams of Chicago, Rabbi Stephen S. Wise of New York, and Daniel H. Burnham of Chicago. The range of the lecturers and the topics reflected the wide scope of Filene's ambitions for *Boston 1915*.

In June 1908, when he was beginning to formulate his considerations for *Boston 1915*, Filene invited Lincoln Steffens, the author and reformist journalist of muckraking fame, to study the city.[33] Steffens was known for his conviction that diagnosing and denouncing municipal abuses would lead to reform measures. The proposed book on Boston was never published, but Steffens included a chapter, "The Muck I Raked in Boston," in his 1931 *Autobiography*. Steffens perceived Filene to be an intellectual who got things done like a practical businessman. He was impressed when Filene asked him how he could achieve overcoming "the class, race, and religious differences that split up Boston" and that prevented the city from "acting as a unit on anything."

Steffens composed a "Preliminary Memorandum" of recommendations for Filene. It urged an exhibition and emphasized the need for "tangible symbols of improvements . . . the sooner you can get a graphic embodiment of everything you stand for, the better." Other recommendations by Steffens suggested advertising, specialized conferences, and the establishment of a civic museum: "If you are going to make Boston a leader along all lines, then you will want to bring here data, designs, city plans of other cities for basis of comparison . . . they could be built up into a growing collection, so that by 1915 you could have the best civic museum in the country." An elaboration of this "memorandum" was presented to the *Boston 1915* committee at its first meeting in March 1909. After the closing of the exhibition in December 1909 Filene wrote to Steffens that it had been a success and had attracted "200,000 [*sic*]" visitors. Steffens's social commitment, his manifesto-style of writing, and the suggestions he conveyed to Filene greatly influenced Hegemann's activism upon his return to Berlin.

During his stay in Boston Hegemann was actively engaged in gathering material to be shown together with the Greater Berlin competition entries. Some of these items derived from the exhibits in New York and *Boston 1915*. Another source mentioned in his memorandum was the Museum of Social Ethics at Harvard University. Hegemann saw this innovative institution as a valuable resource for expanding the scope of the exhibition in Berlin. The museum was established by Francis Greenwood Peabody, a Protestant theologian and Unitarian thinker who founded the

Department of Social Ethics at Harvard in 1906 in an attempt to bridge the gap between the theory and practice of ethics. On his travels Peabody became acquainted with the "social museums" already functioning in Europe, and in 1905–06 he was the first exchange professor from Harvard to lecture at the University of Berlin, moving in the circle that promoted the Greater Berlin idea.[34] The Social Museum at Harvard was inaugurated in 1906 upon Peabody's return from Europe. Comparable to a twentieth-century think-tank, the museum's purpose was "to promote investigations of modern urban conditions and to direct the amelioration of industrial and social life," especially in the congested cities. Peabody believed that "the Harvard Social Museum was the first attempt to collect the social experience of the world as material for university teaching, and to provide guidance for academic inquirers into the study of social progress."[35] Comparative study and inductive teaching methods were basic to the museum, which included a library and seminar rooms. Together with the Department of Social Ethics it focused on the problems of the modern city in all its manifestations. The Social Museum and its students became actively involved in Boston's civic life. Comparable to the better known Musée Social in Paris, it answered research questions and lent from its collections. It contributed to the Boston 1915 Exhibition, and Hegemann obtained material from it for display in Berlin.

At the time of Hegemann's stay in Boston, James Ford, brother of George B. Ford, taught in the Department of Social Ethics. They shared a strong interest in housing, and may have collaborated on an exhibition on "The Housing Problem," organized by James Ford at the Social Museum in 1911, which borrowed items from the Berlin event.[36] In 1916 Hegemann wrote to Ford applying for a position, presumably at the Social Museum.

Hegemann was keenly aware of the meaning of his transatlantic episodes. With the insight that is frequently heightened by a premonition of the end, he reminisced about them and the Boston 1915 Exhibition a year before his death. He wrote that he "conceived the hope of seeing the world conquered by the idea of a general house cleaning and rebuilding," and hoped that "the multiplication of city planning exhibitions would sooner or later advance the civic education and imaginative powers of our contemporaries to soon see every city in the world engage in working out a civic five-year plan similar to the one in Boston." In conclusion, he anticipated that "the whole world could become engaged in internal improvements and urban rivalry to such an extent that, during the time required for carrying out the civic plans, international peace would rule and even become a permanent guest upon our planet."[37]

Harboring these expectations, the pragmatic idealist Hegemann set out from Boston at the age of twenty-eight with an invitation to assume the position of *Generalsekretär* (secretary general) for the Universal City Planning Exhibition (Allgemeine Städtebau-Ausstellung) in Berlin.

2. A New Discipline

A Master Plan for "Metropolis"

In November of 1909 Hegemann left America for Berlin. The prospect of taking charge of the Allgemeine Städtebau-Ausstellung (Universal City Planning Exhibition) scheduled for the spring of 1910 put an end to his *Lehr-und Wanderjahre*, or formative years. The scope of his experiences was uncannily appropriate for the role awaiting him.

The coming three years of this Berlin period provided a stabilizing interlude of lasting importance. The youthful Hegemann was an open-minded and enthusiastic participant in events, and eagerly sought out a range of people. As secretary general of the exhibition he presented himself with mature confidence.

The Universal City Planning Exhibition, Berlin 1910, became the springboard for Hegemann's professional life, replete with diverse possibilities for finding his vocation. The exhibitions in Berlin and Düsseldorf were comparably pivotal for emerging city planning. The Greater Berlin competition, exhibition, and related events raised Berlin's stature internationally as a center for modern urbanism pointing toward the metropolis of the future. Hegemann was enthralled and motivated to pursue a career in this exciting new field.

The interplay between Hegemann and this stimulating atmosphere is intriguing. With unique prescience and energy he transformed his assigned position into that of a facilitator to advance innovative urban concepts, and the exhibitions constituted his prime challenge. They were significant for his involvement with visual presentation and were shaped by his attentive observations in America. He was arguably ahead of his time in exploring exhibition techniques as a means of clarifying theoretical concepts for specialists and the general public. Throughout his life he pursued this idea and often employed it in his illustrated lectures and publications. An avid photographer, he used his own slides in his presentations and developed an early interest in film, all of which he used to his advantage to call attention to the built environment.

Hegemann's interest in the visual was complemented by his facility for writing, demonstrated in numerous articles, pamphlets, essays, novels, and plays. His skill in disseminating information earned him the designation of "publicist." Considering the idealistic aim of his endeavors, this moniker connotes unmerited superficiality. A more appropriate term might be crusader, as he raised a general awareness of everything pertaining to the past, present, and future city. His ultimate goal was to empower a broad constituency to implement social progress and reform substantiated by his firm belief that these were irrevocably linked to city planning. These ideas and abilities, honed during his formative years, achieved maturity and practical application during this interval in Berlin.

Like other major European cities, Berlin had expanded haphazardly into contiguous areas, while its center had become increasingly strangled both physically and economically by the end of the nineteenth century. Realizing the urgency for long-term solutions, in December of 1905 the Vereinigung Berliner Architekten (Association of Berlin Architects, or VBA) initiated the formation of a steering committee to consider the development of a master plan for "Greater Berlin." A year later the Architektenverein zu Berlin (Architectural Association of Berlin, or AB) joined with the VBA in the publication of the competition program for the development of Greater Berlin.[1] The introduction to the program was signed by the steering committee, composed of seven representatives from each organization, with Hegemann's uncle, Otto March, as chairman. From the beginning March was a persuasive leader in these endeavors.

Nearly a century later the program for the international open competition continues to impress with its comprehensiveness and vision. In addition to addressing the administrative and urban integration of 176 communities and small towns spread over an area of 2,000 hectares (4,940 acres), the participants were instructed to consider transportation networks of roads, railroads, canals, and harbors, zoning regulations, and open space, including parks, parkways, sports facilities, playgrounds, and residential developments, particularly low-income housing.[2] Introducing this last element into the competition program, while innovative, was not unique. Ebenezer Howard's Garden City, with its emphasis on housing within a park-like setting, swiftly captivated worldwide attention and became a major attraction in the 1910 exhibitions. Even earlier, Arturo Soria y Mata's proposal for the Ciudad Lineal of the 1880s had integrated transportation and housing in an open-ended growth model and became a much debated rival for the size-limiting English invention.

The designation "greater" was also used by other cities, among them Greater London, "Gross" (*sic*) Barcelona, and Greater Boston. In each case the term signified the planning of a regional conglomerate that would forge a future metropolis. The case of Greater Boston, promoted by *Boston 1915*, lends itself particularly well to a comparison with Berlin for urban considerations and the link provided by Hegemann's presence when it was debated. There was, however, a notable difference between the strivings in the two cities. The initiative for a Greater Berlin came from a different sector than that propelling the *Boston 1915* movement. Civic efforts in the United States frequently originated with businessmen, such as Edward Filene in Boston, who recognized city planning as a means toward shaping the urban environment both economically and socially.[3] The steering committee for Greater Berlin, on the other hand, was formed by the architectural profession and initially had scant support from the business community and municipal authorities.

In retrospect, the arduous work by the Berlin steering committee was eclipsed by the competition which led to the City Planning Exhibition in Berlin in May–June of 1910 and its sequel, the International City Planning Exhibition in Düsseldorf the following September. The steering committee dedicated nearly two years to formulating the guidelines for the competition program, which were made public in 1907. Obtaining existing plans from each of the 176 communities, forestry departments, real estate holding companies, and numerous other entities proved to be a major task.[4] The awesome scope and seriousness of the undertaking were driven home by the accumulated documentation representing the localities to be integrated into the future Greater Berlin.

In 1911, when he was documenting the exhibitions that ensued from the Greater Berlin competition, Hegemann published a farsighted article, "Major town planning competitions and town planning committees."[5] Accordingly, "With the enormous development of modern cities since the mid-nineteeth century, a tradition of handling urban problems by means of competitions had evolved." He examined the causal link between various competitions and the development of city planning theories, comparing the events to teaching institutions dedicated to the subject, which as yet did not exist. By putting urban problems on their agenda, architectual conferences were also beginning to have an effect on city planning ideas. Hegemann concluded that although the Greater Berlin competition might not presently lead to practical results, the debate helped to clarify Berlin's formidable problems.

Contemporary publications on the Greater Berlin competition emphasized the signifcant role that architects, rather than engineers or "geometers," played in this initial phase. By contrast, nearly all previous plans for the towns to be included in the master plan had been drawn up by non-architects. As the competition program was finalized and the jury selected, the realization took hold that city planning on this scale involved teamwork and the expertise of a range of specialists, and that the discipline was a synthesis of many elements. The steering committee responded to this realization by engaging a wider range of professional expertise and establishing connections to municipal authorities. The unification of the communities and small towns depended on their own legally protected decision making. Eventually the steering committee established a *Zweckverband*, or local administrative union, that assisted in resolving difficulties between the state and the various municipalities and integrated them into the process.

Twenty-seven competition entries were received; six of these only addressed parts of the total area and were eliminated from final consideration. In his review of the Universal City Planning Exhibition, Raymond Unwin noted the process by which the competition entries were evaluated by an interdisciplinary jury composed of architects, engineers, surveyors, and members of municipal entities. The vast quantity of material was distributed among the members, who then reported to the entire jury.[6]

A detailed analysis of the competition entries in the light of future developments, their place within the history of Berlin, and the sporadic results of their suggestions will not be attempted. Our focus is the momentum generated by the Greater Berlin competition and the exhibitions of 1910 toward establishing city planning as a discipline with both a scientific and a humanistic base, comprehensive, yet not dependent on any one of the many components of this synthesis.

The outcome of the competition radiated beyond the city, throughout Europe, and to the Americas. Its renown was enhanced by the exhibitions, which showed the proposals within historical and geographic contexts. Town plans of earlier periods and recent achievements from Germany and abroad provided an overview of possibilities and opportunities for comparison.

Hegemann and the Invention of the City Planning Exhibition

In a 1916 letter-*cum*-curriculum vitae to James Ford in Cambridge, Massachusetts, when he had returned to the United States, Hegemann wrote that he had reported to Otto March on the New York Congestion Exhibition of 1909. He also mentioned his lengthy, two-part article in *Der Städtebau*, which contributed to the preparations for the City Planning Exhibition in Berlin and his appointment as its secretary general.[7]

Hegemann's review of the exhibition in New York makes frequent references to the movement for a Greater Berlin and the potential for staging an exhibition. It concludes with an impassioned call for civic action and stresses the importance of housing in modern planning:

> At the present moment, when the battle for the new Berlin, for Greater Berlin, has begun to capture the attention and public opinion has to be guided repeatedly and without respite toward these tasks until they are solved, right now is

> the moment to point out the connections between the unsavory predicaments of work performed at home and the unsanitary conditions of housing in Berlin—the same as in New York—and to stress the improvements, which might be achieved by implementing a modern city plan.

The relationship of the American precedents to the exhibitions in Berlin and Düsseldorf is notable.[8] Of the transatlantic influences frequently grouped under the term *Amerikanismus*, the links of 1909–1910 are of importance for their impact on international as well as American and German city planning. For American urbanism the exhibitions brought significant European recognition that furthered the importance of the new profession across the Atlantic.

Hegemann may have overstated his own role in his letter to Ford, which he composed to explore the possibilities of a position at Harvard. Of the exhibition in Berlin, he wrote that it was:

> the first public exhibition of the results of the international competition for a city plan for the Greater Berlin called by the combined efforts of the cities and counties of Greater Berlin. The work in connection with this exhibition brought me in continuous intercourse with the leading representatives of city planning thought in Europe. The success of the Berlin exhibition led to much of the material I had collected for Berlin being used again and amplified. Many of the city planning exhibitions of larger or smaller scale held since 1910 in so many European cities were directed either by myself (Düsseldorf, Frankfurt, Bremen) or by men or women [!] having worked under my direction.[9]

About the same time as the review of the Congestion Exhibition for *Der Städtebau* in 1909, Hegemann wrote a five-page report to the organizers of the Boston 1915 Exhibition. Under the title "Plans for City Planning Exhibitions," he gave detailed suggestions for a show that would address the local problems of a city, including recommendations on how to solve them. Special attention was called to the need for effective advertising and for a "pamphlet" summarizing the main themes of the presentation.[10]

While Hegemann used his time in New York and Boston to gather ideas and gain practical expertise, anticipating the task awaiting him, discussions regarding an exhibition had already begun in Berlin. In November 1909 *Der Städtebau* reported that under the chairmanship of Otto March, a committee was working on an exhibition in connection with the expected results of the competition for Greater Berlin.[11] The scope of the tentative program was comprehensive. In addition to the winning proposals, the program included a range of topics only recently considered integral components of modern city planning. Plans of major cities from Germany and abroad were listed, followed by a section on transportation. Next came a section devoted to the statistical and graphic display of economic and social matters pertaining to sanitation, health, social problems, housing density, mortality rates, employment, and building inspectors. The fifth section included layouts for suburbs, residential developments, garden cities, and industrial regions with workers' housing. Following that, parks, cemeteries, playgrounds, and sports facilities were grouped together. Designs and models were suggested for groups of buildings, such as hospitals, and for plazas and streets. A section for artistic embellishment included monuments, bridges, and fountains. The last item, simply called *Literatur*, gained much favorable comment in later reviews of the exhibit. It evolved into a substantial documentation on urbanism, a resource center available to the public for research and/or the purchase of material. Combined with the lecture series and guided tours, Literatur resembled an open university or seminar available to all—an incipient social museum.

Lectures and meetings held in conjunction with Berlin 1910 enhanced its impact. A newsletter enclosed in the periodical *Der Städtebau* announced two lecture series for May 1–21 and May 23– June 15.[12] Many German experts, such as Goecke, Stübben, Brinckmann, Genzmer, Muthesius, Südekum, and Jansen, were among the speakers, as well as Hegemann. The topics dealt primarily with German planning, with the exceptions of Eberstadt's talk on workers' housing in England and Germany, Muthesius's on the garden cities, and Hegemann's on American urbanism.

According to the newsletter, the steering committee had sent out over one hundred invitations asking for examples for inclusion in the exhibition. The requests went to European countries and to America. Eugéne Hénard made himself available to gather French material, and Raymond Unwin offered to gather British material. To facilitate the transport, particularly of large models, the Royal Railways Management of Berlin reduced the costs on their own railroads and persuaded others to do the same. The Hamburg-Amerika-Line provided assistance with shipping from overseas.

A five-year lead time, from 1905–10, allowed for the appraisal of the Greater Berlin competition entries and for arrangement of the actual show. This period also generated expectations for the event among the citizens of Berlin and the rest of Germany, as well as those in other countries. Response to the Universal City Planning Exposition was remarkable. Interest of the general public and Berliners concerned about the future of their city ran high, perhaps higher than anticipated. For city planners within Germany, visiting the exhibition and meeting with local and foreign colleagues were essential. It proved necessary to arrange guided tours prior to the scheduled opening hours for out-of-town groups and visitors from abroad. As secretary general, Hegemann welcomed guests, especially foreigners; during his travels he had acquired worldly polish aided by his fluency in English and French. Because no guestbook or attendance records survive, individual visitors can be verified only if they published on their experience or are mentioned in reports by others. A tentative list of urbanists from abroad includes: from the United States, Sylvester Baxter, Edward T. Devine, George B. Ford, Frederic C. Howe, and possibly John Nolen; from England, Stanley D. Adshead and Raymond Unwin, who arrived with a group of compatriots; and from France and Switzerland, Eugéne Hénard and Jeanneret/Le Corbusier. Others came from Scandinavia, including Bertel Jung from Finland; from the Netherlands, Hendrik Petrus Berlage; from Belgium, Marcel Smets; and from Spain, Cebriá de Montoliu.

The exhibition committee intended to present an international overview of historic and modern city planning, coupling urban heritage with future design possibilities. Also mentioned were a forthcoming publication, a *Städtebau-Handbuch* (Town Planning Manual) related to the show, and a program of lectures. These outreach aspirations, conceivably promoted by Hegemann, were certainly corroborated by the group in Berlin before his return in November 1909. At that time, the competition entries were being submitted and the City Planning Exhibition was at an early discussion stage under the guidance of a committee. Although he was not present during its initial planning, the program reflected Hegemann's exposure to American precedents and social progressivism. His articles and the report to Edward Filene substantiate this connection in the absence of more specific correspondence.

What were Hegemann's contributions to this state of affairs in Berlin, where experts from a variety of specialties and opinions had been debating the competition for Greater Berlin and how to present it to the world at large for several years? Undoubtedly his grasp of the importance of exhibitions to define and formulate city planning as a comprehensive discipline—a *Wissenschaft*—was a key contribution. He also understood the role of such events as catalysts for generating urban change and momentum by means of raising public awareness of a wide range of problems. He expressed these points emphatically in his publications, lectures, and decisions from the other side of the Atlantic and once he faced the tasks in Berlin.

Hegemann also procured American examples for a predominantly European show in Berlin, readied in barely six months between November 1909 and May 1910. Some of this material came from the Boston 1915 Exhibition, such as the display of Boston's "Emerald Necklace" of parks and parkways and that city's transportation network. He provided photographs, many his own, of Chicago's inner-city playgrounds and several plans by John Nolen. The plan for Chicago by Daniel H. Burnham and Edward H. Bennett, represented in Jules Guérin's exquisite drawings, had presumably not been shown in their originals in Boston. In Berlin 1910 they were displayed in large photographs. An exchange of letters between Hegemann and Burnham testifies to the latter's reluctance to authorize the original drawings to travel. After ironing out disagreements about safety and cost, the originals were, indeed, prominently displayed at the Düsseldorf Exhibition.[13] From there they journeyed to the Royal Institute of British Architects Town Planning Conference in London for its exhibition in October 1910, where they were celebrated as the centerpiece. In a review, S. D. Adshead commented that "a huge gallery was given up to the magnificent American drawings of Chicago and Washington, shown only in photographs in Berlin."[14] These photographs formed the core of Hegemann's pamphlet *Der neue Bebauungsplan für Chicago*.[15] In its opening paragraph he compared Chicago and Berlin:

> The efforts to arrive at a comprehensive master plan for the entire area of Greater Berlin have recently found an instructive example in Chicago. Chicago with its population of two million is appropriate to a certain extent for a comparison with the growth of Greater Berlin in the past half century, while older cities of millions, which culturally should preferably be compared with Berlin, have grown much more slowly.

Here, however, the comparison ended, and he waxed enthusiastic over the optimism and public pride that made Burnham's great plan possible. He admired the network of parks and parkways, taking full advantage of Lake Michigan, creating lagoons and water amenities. Held up as worthy models for Berlin and other European cities were Chicago's playgrounds with their field houses scattered throughout the city. Photographs of these, many taken by Hegemann during his visit to the city in 1909, were exhibited in Berlin 1910 and included in his *Parkbuch*.[16]

If Hegemann's title of *Generalsekretär* did not seem particularly promising as he entered the stage in Berlin, it did have lasting significance for him intellectually and for his reputation as an authority in a nascent discipline. Before he left Berlin again in 1913, his ideas gained cogency and breadth. He was able to verify by practical experience the impact of exhibitions, confirming their importance for informing the public of urban problems and possible solutions. The participatory engagement that reached beyond professionals increased the possibility of implementing city and regional planning. For Hegemann social activism and reform were closely linked to urban planning, and the exhibitions were central to developing these ideas. The organization and presentation of visual material accompanied by explanatory texts had captured his attention through the shows in New York and Boston. Both had opened his eyes to the possibilities of clarifying the diverse components of the built environment. Hegemann's exposure to American progressivism, now meeting up with European social concerns, convinced him of the need for a rational plan to be superimposed on laissez-faire endeavors, while allowing for citizen participation. The latter, being somewhat of a contradiction, would persist in his urban theories.

The Universal City Planning Exhibition took place in May and June of 1910 in the galleries of Königliche Akademische Hochschule für die Bildenden Künste (the Royal Academy for the Visual Arts) in Charlottenburg, then an independent town adjacent to Berlin and only later integrated into Greater Berlin (Fig. 2). The event is usually referred to as the "Berlin 1910 City Planning Exhibition" (Berlin 1910) because its genesis was the Greater Berlin concept. Today few photographs of the installation are extant in publications or archives.[17] The scant visual records and descriptions of visitors and reviewers confirm that the design of exhibitions was in its infancy. Compared to recent persuasive presentations of similarly recondite subject matters, the discrepancy between this unsophisticated installation in Berlin and the renown it achieved is astonishing. This status obviously derived from the exhibition's content and the novelty of showing city planning with a broad spectrum of subjects relating to the urban environment. The official guidebook included floor plans of the *Erdgeschoss* (ground floor) and the *Stockwerk* (first floor) with narrow corridors and few wide spaces.[18] An introductory note refers to the "not entirely favorable spatial layout . . . ," which did not permit "a coherent conceptual development." The awkwardness of the available spaces was frequently mentioned. Individuals in charge of the arrangement were Theodor Goecke, Walter Lehweiss, and Werner Hegemann, the *Generalsekretär*, noted in this order.

The floor plans in the guidebook indicate the location of the different urban categories, whose placement was frequently determined by their

Fig. 2. Plan of the Allgemeine Städtebau-Ausstellung in Berlin, 1910. FLLHGSD

ÜBERSICHTSPLAN

der

Allgemeinen Städtebau-Ausstellung.

Erdgeschoß.

GROSS-BERLIN.

GROSS-BERLIN

FRIEDHÖFE.

TOIL.

HOF

WIEN.

FRIEDHÖFE.

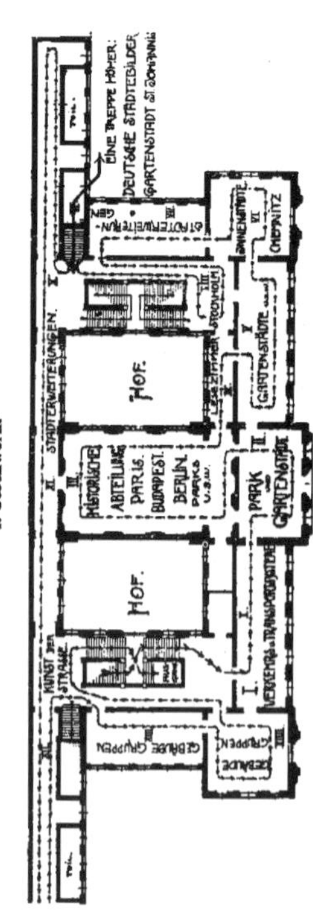

Fig. 3. Entrance Hall of the Berlin 1910 Exhibition. FLLHGSD

physical dimensions. For example, the large model of the 1858 expansion of Vienna, measuring 20 square meters (215 square feet), was installed prominently in the entrance hall, a space one would expect to be devoted to the competition entries (Fig. 3). Hegemann called the Vienna model gigantic, a *Riesenmodell*, and included a photograph of the entrance hall in his documentary volumes.[19]

An early eyewitness account was the review by Raymond Unwin, who visited Berlin 1910 as the official delegate of the Royal Institute of British Architects, which was contemplating an exhibition in connection with the impending Town Planning Conference for October 1910 in London.[20]

Unwin was widely known and respected, and his review remains one of the most perceptive of many contemporary opinions expressed by visitors from Germany and abroad. Unwin focused first on the model of Vienna, which was surrounded by drawings and photographs of the competition for redesigning the *Karlsplatz*. The capital of Austria shared the entrance hall with the competition entries for Greater Berlin, which were also displayed in two long corridors. The magnitude of the problems faced by Berlin, comparable to those of London, captured Unwin's attention, as did the process and the results of the competition for Greater Berlin. He related how the twenty-seven entries were evaluated by an interdisciplinary jury composed of members of municipal entities, engineers, architects, and surveyors. Unwin commented on the four winning entries in the order of their rating, noting that in all but one the professional team included engineers, economists, and transportation specialists in addition to architects. Unwin felt that Hermann Jansen's scheme, *In den Grenzen der Möglichkeit* (Within the boundaries of possibility), one of the two first prizes, fell short in addressing the connections between the railroad stations and instead proposed three separate railroad rings around the center of the city. Jansen's green belt, which was supplemented by additional open spaces carefully selected for their suitability, won Unwin's approval. Also valuable, in Unwin's opinion, were the five arterial roads that fanned out from the center of the city, providing access to future residential developments. Regarding the second first-prize entry by Brix and Genzmer, *Denk an künftig* (Consider the future), Unwin called attention to their recommendation for a railroad network extending through the entire city, especially from north to south. In the introduction to their published plan for Greater Berlin, Brix and Genzmer stated that "structural interventions in cities ought to respond to present needs, while fulfilling future demands."[21] Farsightedly they envisioned a regional master plan guiding development indefinitely under the jurisdiction of an empowered general commission.

According to Unwin, "the scheme by Professor Eberstadt [Eberstadt, Möhring & Petersen, third award] . . . [is] one of the most interesting, and clearly shows the value of the association of the economist or sociologist with the work of city development."[22] Eberstadt's recommendations were based on surveys, statistics, and economic factors. He was a well-known expert on housing, a subject on which he had pubished extensively. Eberstadt weighed his knowledge of the English cottage system against the German multi-storied blocks. The Eberstadt, Möhring & Petersen entry advocated a group of parks radiating from the center of the city to a surrounding green belt.

Unwin's review was dedicated primarily to urbanism, commenting only briefly on the architectural features of the prize-winning proposals. Surprisingly, he singled out the visionary skyscrapers by Bruno Schmitz, an early advocate of skyscrapers in Germany and winner of the fourth prize, with Otto Blum, Havestadt & Contag.[23] Unwin, who generally did not favor high-rise buildings, was intrigued by Schmitz's "fine architectural conceptions."

The number and size of models displayed in the exhibition impressed Unwin: "many of them [are] very beautifully made, and, beside their immense value for interesting the general public in the right methods of town development, their help to the expert is evidently thought by the Germans to be very considerable."[24]

In another article Unwin commented on matters of wider importance evoked by *Berlin 1910*, demonstrating a perceptive grasp of its significance.[25] He presented an overview of both the positive and problematic aspects of the city, emphasizing the urgency for the comprehensive approach that formed the basis of the Greater Berlin movement:

> It is particularly noteworthy that, although town-planning powers have been exercised for many years by the different municipalities around Berlin, for want of common action and a central body coordinating their work, many parts of Berlin, though well planned as isolated portions, have grown up with little more proper relation to the whole plan of the city than we find in the different areas of London.

Unwin was a forceful advocate for regional plans for Berlin, London, and other major urban centers. Addressing the problem of implementation, he stressed the "importance for securing the proper cooperation of all the different local authorities now possessing town-planning powers, and the co-ordination of their different plans under the guidance of some central body, either voluntary or statutory."

The variety of disciplines that entered into the solution of urban problems was highlighted by their interrelatedness and advanced an inclusive approach. Berlin 1910 brought together examples from a range of geographic regions and historic periods within the subject categories, inviting multiple comparisons and emphasizing similarities rather than differences. By de-emphasizing specific national aspects, the exhibition compelled the idea that city planning was a universal concern that crossed political boundaries, demanding an engagement of minds, efforts, and resources on a global scale. The visual orchestration furthered an auxiliary language and contributed to an understanding between the speakers of different languages and diverse, entrenched professions. The goal was to foster dialogue and teamwork.

It may seem excessive to read these lofty ideals into an exhibition briefly situated in inadequate quarters and to suggest that they were initiated by Hegemann. However, it is certain that he persistently pursued these concepts throughout his career, propagating them in subsequent exhibitions, publications, lectures, and in public and private actions. In the next decade, when Europe was torn asunder by war and strife, he increasingly advocated a "citizen of the world" brotherhood and pacifism fortified by a common language.

Considering the international interchange based on personal contacts, meetings, and publications that characterized city planning in the years prior to World War I, it is not surprising that Berlin 1910 had a lasting impact and generated many published commentaries. In addition to contemporary reviews from Germany, some of the most sagacious were penned by those who traveled from afar to join a confluence of urbanists for viewing and exchanging ideas. For a few weeks in Berlin a highly charged seminar on the broadest as well as the most specialized aspects of urbanism took place.

Although the sequel to Berlin 1910 in Düsseldorf in September 1910 bore the title Internationale Städtebau-Ausstellung, it did not generate the same international interest (Fig. 4), primarily receiving attention from within Germany. Perhaps urbanists were already focused on the Town Planning Conference in London, scheduled for October. A cluster of significant events made 1910 a landmark year for city planning. Stanley D. Adshead, writing on The Town Planning Conference, commented, "Town planners from all parts of the world met once more to improve an acquaintance which had been made during recent Town Planning tours, and at recent Conferences held in America, Berlin and Vienna. It was obvious from the commencement of the proceedings that *town planning is of all the arts an international one* [emphasis added]."[26]

Düsseldorf 1910 followed its predecessor in Berlin in many respects, but differed significantly in motivation and content. The city of Düsseldorf was chosen as a relevant location to hold the initial discussions of the Siedlungsverband Ruhrkohlenbezirk (Regional Plan for the Ruhr-Coal District, or SVR) and publicize its efforts. As an early example of an implemented comprehensive regional plan, the SVR has gained lasting importance from its official inception in 1920 to the present.[27] The ambitious open space component of the regional plan proved significant for Düsseldorf 1910 and coincided with Hegemann's interest in bringing

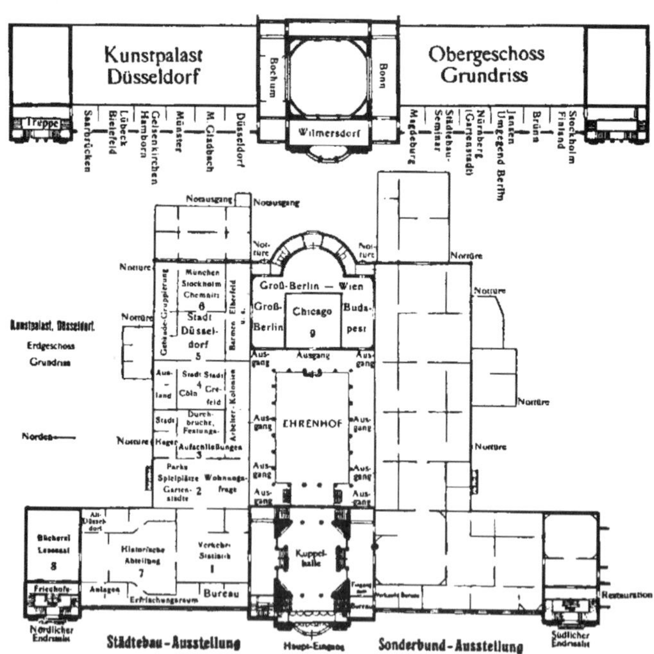

Fig. 4. Plan of the Internationale Städtebau-Ausstellung in Düsseldorf, 1910. FLLHGSD

American park and parkways accomplishments to the attention of German planners. It is thought that the large scale "green belt" of the SVR was influenced by the example of Boston, also greatly admired by Hegemann. He had obtained plans of the SVR from the Mayor of Essen for Berlin 1910, and early discussions of the regional plan may have been an incentive for choosing Düsseldorf as a focus for these farsighted schemes.

Düsseldorf 1910 became the occasion for forming a commission to discuss a "contiguous park plan [*Grünflächenplan*] for the city's administrative district," and Hegemann was asked to report on his observations in America.[28] As was his custom, his report was based on site visits to the area of the proposed SVR, which he compared to the accomplishments in Boston. He described the example of Greater Boston with its "system of public '*Grünflächen*' [to be] the most beautiful and oldest in existence." On the basis of his observations in Boston, Hegemann recommended aiming for a "*Grünflächen*-System" to be achieved over a period of time, with each town in the regional master plan contributing desirable parcels. The open space could encompass existing forests and facilities for active recreation and sports. It would be planned in relation to a vast traffic network that would make it accessible to the public.

The exhibition also presented an opportunity to announce a competition for a master plan of Greater Düsseldorf, for which the deadline was July 1912.[29] The jury of thirteen included Otto March, Theodor Goecke, and Hegemann from Berlin, Theodor Fischer from Munich, and Cornelius Gurlitt from Dresden, as well as several from Düsseldorf. The competition results, with additional material from other German cities, were shown at yet another exhibition, the "Cities Exhibition"of July–November 1912 in Düsseldorf.[30]

Hegemann added to Düsseldorf 1910 American material not previously exhibited in Berlin 1910, including university campuses. It is noteworthy that the original drawings by Jules Guérin for the Plan of Chicago (1909) by Daniel H. Burnham and Edward H. Bennett were shown on that occasion for the first time outside of the United States. Hegemann had been unable to procure them for Berlin 1910, where they were displayed in large photographs.

From Düsseldorf 1910, Guérin's drawings of the Chicago Plan traveled to London and became the star attractions at the Royal Academy. The guide to Düsseldorf 1910 listed eighteen drawings in the section "Special Exhibition of the City of Chicago, Burnham, D. H., Chicago."[31] The layout printed in the guidebook indicated that the Chicago drawings were displayed prominently in the central entrance hall at the Kunstpalast Düsseldorf. Hegemann's efforts to procure them had been justified. The adjacent halls were given over to the competition entries for Greater Berlin, Vienna, and Budapest, in spaces notably more suitable than those in Berlin 1910.

During the last week before the closing of Düsseldorf 1910 a conference took place, featuring a list of speakers and topics related to the exhibition. Its content was surpassed by the lectures addressing theoretical concerns at the "First Congress for City Planning, Düsseldorf 1912" in connection with the later exhibition, and the presentations were published.[32] Hegemann was instrumental in organizing and participating in both conferences. At the Congress of 1912, Robert Schmidt from Essen, the generator of the SVR, described the regional plan's "Modern urban structure" that combined industry with residential towns. Albert Südekum, Secretary of State from Berlin, spoke on "New versions of municipal constitutions and municipal administration in the United States." Hegemann's topic was one that had captured his attention in connection with the SVR and regional plans in general, "Open space in relation to housing in city planning." He regretted that urbanism was "still far removed from considering public needs as the basis of all planning," and the scarcity of parks and playgrounds, which he criticized vehemently in the pamphlets *Für Gross-Berlin*.

"The Task of Town Building Is an International One . . . and Every Nation May Contribute to Our Knowledge."

In the German language region the Berlin and Düsseldorf exhibitions of 1910 received a variety of reviews. Some discussed the competition entries and the future of Greater Berlin, while others gave overviews of the presentations. Still others used the competition and exhibitions to examine theoretical planning issues questioned since the late nineteenth century. These were also the ongoing topics of lectures and discussions during the formulation of the competition program, which continued in conjunction with the events. Some of the lectures were later published and reached a wider audience.

Two interrelated themes preoccupied the architectural and emerging planning professions. As mentioned earlier, the move toward Greater Berlin in 1905 was initiated by two architectural associations, Vereinigung Berliner Architekten (VBA) and Architektenverein zu Berlin (AB). When preparations for the Greater Berlin competition program got underway, the architects began to include other professionals, reluctantly yielding some of their *Städtebau* turf to less aesthetically oriented specialists. Of increasing concern was how individuals coming from diverse backgrounds could work together productively without competing. The dilemma of where to place urbanism and city planning—in the humanities or the social sciences, and whether they were "art" or "science" or a synthesis of both—was seriously debated. Another concern was the legacy of Camillo Sitte's appreciation of unplanned, evolving towns, and his concept of the primacy of urban space. Reconciling Sitte's principles with the progressive demands of the modern metropolis was a quandary. These questions were stimulated by the events leading up to 1910, and they are still relevant and worthy of consideration today. Ongoing discourses produce new insights but do not necessarily lead to conclusive answers.

Ernst Wasmuth Verlag of Berlin, the leading publisher for architecture, art, and city planning in Germany during the early twentieth century, produced the majority of publications related to the Greater Berlin movement and Berlin 1910.[33] Wasmuth was also the publisher of the first periodical exclusively devoted to city planning, *Der Städtebau; Monatsschrift für die Künstlerische Ausgestaltung der Städte nach ihren Wirtschaftlichen, Gesundheitlichen, und Sozialen Grundsätzen* (City planning; Monthly journal for the artistic design of cities according to economic, sanitary, and social principles), founded in 1903 by Camillo Sitte (1843–1903) and Theodor Goecke (1850–1919).[34] Sitte did not live to see the first issue, which appeared in January 1904. Goecke continued as editor until his death, remaining partial to the principles of his admired colleague and friend. A professor at the Technical University of Berlin-Charlottenburg, Goecke participated in the Seminar on City Planning, Charlottenburg. Begun in 1907 by Felix Genzmer and Joseph Brix, it was the first university-affiliated program in city planning.[35] In addition to his work as a teacher, editor, and author of books and numerous articles, Goecke was active as a professional planner. He was already an important figure when he joined the steering committee for Greater Berlin in 1905, and his opinions carried considerable weight.[36]

The widespread influence of Camillo Sitte's slender volume, *Der Städtebau nach seinen künstlerischen Grundsätzen* (City planning according to artistic principles), published in Vienna in 1889, continues to be discussed today.[37] Regard for Sitte's principles has persevered, especially as they meshed with those of the garden city and preservation movements. As much as he has been admired, Sitte has also been misinterpreted and ridiculed. In many instances this can be attributed to the distortion and misapplication of his principles by some of his followers. His critics have assailed the arbitrarily curved streets and the picturesque as prescriptions, considering them out of the context of Sitte's parameters. Of undeniably persisting value is his interpretation of the urban environment as an evolving cultural landscape. He considered its essence to be space rather than built volume, space being the determinant of urban experience.

The movement for Greater Berlin impelled a reconsideration of Sitte's influence and ideas, which were still eminent. As co-founder and editor of the journal *Der Städtebau*, Theodor Goecke became a key figure in this discourse and a gauge on which to observe change. This is particularly apparent in the editorials and articles he wrote for *Der Städtebau* from 1909 to

1911, in which he shifted from an aesthetic to a comprehensive, multidisciplinary concept of planning. With a remarkable about-face in his editorial of 1910, Goecke assured readers that the future exhibition would display the achievements of modern metropolises together with the results of the Greater Berlin competition.[38] This change in his approach is also reflected in his review of the report by Eberstadt, Möhring, and Petersen that accompanied their competition entry "*Et in terra pax*" and was published separately in an expanded version.[39] Goecke calls it "one of the most important publications on town planning in recent times," praising the authors' emphasis on housing as the basis of city planning.

Der Städtebau devoted a well-illustrated double issue to Berlin 1910.[40] According to Goecke, it was the first exhibit in Germany devoted exclusively to city planning; the "Städteausstellung" of 1903 in Dresden had included other topics. In Berlin, it was advantageous to consider a selection of projects from all regions and times related to the concept of Greater Berlin, expanded with housing, residential suburbs, park systems, and recreational open space. Goecke did not clarify the difference between the forward-looking inclusiveness favorably discussed in his review and the scope of the Dresden exhibition. Harking back to an editorial of the previous year, he referred, with a touch of nostalgia, to "the spirit of Camillo Sitte," whose portrait graced the review. He stated that the success of the exhibition testified to the artistic interpretation of city planning as the most comprehensive and impartially tolerant of diverse and practical demands. Goecke considered this to be the only appropriate way to involve the widest interests for the tasks of city planning while balancing the more specialized tendencies. Faced with the urgent need for a comprehensive approach underscored by the competition program, and now most vividly by the exhibition, Goecke reached out once more to Sitte's guiding principles. Although striving to be evenhanded, his review was somewhat slanted toward the Sittesque. Examples from the various categories were discussed and illustrated as he moved from transportation to parks and recreational open space. He devoted attention to recent park developments in Germany and England and singled out American park systems and playgrounds. Although Goecke did not mention him, Hegemann was particularly proud of his efforts in bringing this selection and other American examples to Berlin. They were later circulated as a separate exhibition with an accompanying pamphlet that included Hegemann's essay, "*Die Bedeutung einer neuzeitlichen Park-Politik*" (The significance of a modern park politic).[41]

The next topics in Goecke's review were garden cities and residential developments. This section of the exhibition, as well as the one on park systems, elicited the greatest interest from the general public. Ebenezer Howard's garden city concept, with its adaptations and variations, was visually displayed, contributing toward its worldwide spread. The section on urban housing represented a stark contrast. Among the town expansions Goecke noted, among others, projects by Otto Lasne, Karl Mayreder, Hermann Jansen, Karl Henrici, and Theodor Fischer, the last two being prominent followers of Sitte. Turning to examples from abroad, he cited Albert Lilienberg's development for Gotenburg. The category *Platz und Kunst auf der Strasse* (city square and art on streets) was dedicated to a wide range of picturesque design solutions. Many older historic town plans were shown under "Monumental Groupings." In closing his report, Goecke mentioned a collection of townscape photographs exhibited by A. E. Brinckmann and the postcards by Susanne Homann. This straightforward presentation acquainted *Der Städtebau* subscribers unable to travel to Berlin with this important event.

In tracing the reexamination of urbanism in the writings of the elder statesman Goecke, the first issue of *Der Städtebau* in 1911 is significant. The Introduction announced changes in editorial policy:

> Modern town planning requires the collaboration of vast independent specialties, art and technology, sociology, administration, and political science. Our periodical has taken on the task of furthering this new approach regarding town planning. The recent expansion of the journal signifies a new step en route toward making room for a comprehensive treatment of our subject.[42]

This expansion of the journal would feature a comprehensive yearly report by Rudolf Eberstadt (1856–1922) on city planning and housing literature. Eberstadt's background was in political economy—or Charles Gide's *economie sociale*—rather than architecture. He was internationally recognized as a housing specialist and received an award in the Greater Berlin competition. Eberstadt's advent as a regular contributor to *Der Städtebau* was a clear indication of the journal's altered direction and commitment to new trends.

The exhibitions in Berlin and Düsseldorf provoked a consciousness raising and reexamination of purpose within the professions of architecture and city planning, accompanied by changing demands on their professional associations and periodicals. The about-face at *Der Städtebau* was a representative example. The pride of these professionals, mixed with apprehension about losing their status and identifying their novel tasks reached beyond the VBA and AB to other organizations in Germany. The *Neudeutsche Bauzeitung* (New-German Building Journal) became the official publication of the Bund Deutscher Architekten (Association of German Architects, or BDA) with the first issue of Volume 6, 1910, now subtitled "Organ of the Association of German Architects."[43] The defensively worded editorial was devoted to the need for a clear definition of architecture as a noble, ideal calling.

> One cannot have a genuine calling to architecture, and still want to delegate the great architectural tasks of our time to others than those who have devoted themselves wholeheartedly to this art and to those among them from whom

> one can expect the worthiest artistic work. It is intolerable that the designation architect is mistakenly applied to those who have some other connection to the building trades, perhaps important to them and others, but who have no true vocation toward architecture. This would deny or disregard the value of this genuine relationship with art.

The review of Berlin 1910 in the *Neudeutsche Bauzeitung*, once it had become the official publication of the BDA, is important in light of the uneasy relationship architects had with recent tendencies in city planning. The lengthy essay by Walter Kornick was preceded by a preview in an issue that did not yet carry the subtitle "Organ des BDA."[44] The preview reported on the modest and brief opening ceremony on May 1 that featured Otto March's inaugural address, and related some first impressions. Kornick stressed the titanic tasks that must be overcome in order to resolve the urban problems of the modern metropolis, and he recommended that visitors view the competition entries last, regarding them as a crowning achievement. His lengthy review showed a plan of the expansion of Mannheim (Hegemann's native city) and several townscape views, interiors, and ground plans of churches in other German cities. This selection was somewhat unrelated to the displays and perhaps an attempt to appease architects.

Kornick's readable, ideologically balanced essay is, of all contemporary German reviews, the most often cited today. It combined comforting passages on the Sittesque qualities of older towns with discussions of housing and rent-versus-income statistics, and transportation in relation to industrial and residential developments. Considerable attention was devoted to the rehabilitation of inner cities and the artistic and historic considerations this demanded, emphasizing the role of architects in preserving the cultural heritage of towns. Kornick warned that introducing single architectural elements would not suffice to repair awkward urban contexts. Elaborating on the significance of the city planning exhibition in clarifying and refining the important role of the modern architect, Kornick stated:

> The city planning exhibition has shown us in a wealth of great and greatest, but also intimate building problems, what a vast area of activity is available to the modern architect. The demand that our present time requires truly educated architects, which is heard from here and there (off and on) from outside and from our own camp, has only received its well-defined meaning with the maturing of the city planning problem . . . .

In Kornick's view, architects needed to be trained in the practical and humanistic aspects of their profession to respond fully to the requirements of modern city planning and to understand contemporary socio-political tensions in order to represent them in the built environment. In the concluding passages of his essay, Kornick augured a salient concept of Hegemann's: the interdependency of architecture and planning.

It is surprising that Kornick did not mention Hegemann in his articles. Indeed, Hegemann's role in shaping the presentation of new concepts was seldom acknowledged by reviewers, a fact which may have prompted him to publish books and articles as vehicles for his multiple endeavors. Having obtained his doctorate in economics, Hegemann was an outsider to both architecture and economics, a perspective that may have reinforced his recognition of their interconnection as the basis of modern urbanism.

The exciting atmosphere in Berlin propelled Hegemann's attention in many directions. He was absorbed in practical matters, organizing guided tours and lectures, greeting important visitors, and arranging the expanded exhibition in Düsseldorf. Somehow he also found time for a number of related articles and pamphlets, giving thought to documenting both exhibitions. The result would be two volumes that go substantially beyond an overview of the events.

Hegemann's initial perception of Berlin 1910 was written before it closed, and may have been intended to counterbalance the opinions of others in the press. With an indicative title, "*Die Städtebauausstellung und ihre Lehren*" (The city planning exhibition and its lessons), the account was published in an illustrated weekly and addressed the public at large rather than architects and planners.[45] Reading like a manifesto, it eloquently stated Hegemann's views of the future metropolis. It also reported that in the first twenty days after the show's opening, 40,000 admission tickets were sold and "several" thousand visitors were admitted free of charge just to see the Greater Berlin entries, with another 3,200 attending the lectures. According to Hegemann, these figures confirmed a strong interest that reached well beyond engineers, architects, and other professionals. It was also a significant triumph for his faith in the role of exhibitions as magnetic events for raising the understanding of and support for urban and social issues among a broad spectrum of citizens, as well as stimulating tourism.

Another article by Hegemann gives a historic overview of city planning competitions, which he considered to be of the utmost importance for the development of new theories.[46] He compared them to universities devoted to urbanism, which did not yet exist. In connection with competitions, conferences furthered the discussion of urban problems which required the input of a range of experts. Hegemann commented on competitions that took place in Europe dating back to the early eighteenth century, and became a tradition by the mid-nineteenth century with those in Brussels and Vienna. More recently the competitions for Greater London and that for Greater Berlin were inspiring other cities to follow suit.

From the success in Berlin, Hegemann emerged as a "publicist extraordinaire" and an intellectual educator in a modern sense.[47] He captured what Walter Benjamin perceptively diagnosed when he considered publicity the essence of modernity. In Hegemann's article on Berlin 1910 and others he wrote in connection with his social activism regarding housing and open space, he comes across as an impassioned crusader. For Hegemann the "lessons" derived from the exhibition demonstrated that the problems resulting from the rapid growth and population increase in major cities in recent times called for the adoption of fundamental principles. In his view the population increase was actually the product of the cities themselves, and he described this in vivid terms:

> The powerful agent [*das gewaltige Werkzeug*] which has enabled this population increase is the 'City'! The city, a product of modern traffic and transportation, the city, an expression of modern socialization of humanity, offering the possibility that had never previously existed of working together intellectually and physically with the widest divisions of labor. The city as agent! As an agent for administration, for the interchange of ideas, the exchange of goods and the production of goods. In order to become a modern administrative or cultural center, a city presently must be a traffic center. However, in order to provide food for millions, the city must be fashioned into a first-class instrument.

The lasting importance of Berlin 1910 was stressed many decades later by Miron Mislin, in a tribute to Hegemann's one hundreth birthday. Mislin considered it an example for the 1984 IBA (Internationale Bauausstellung) International Building Exposition in Berlin.[48] He concluded that in its comprehensiveness and its impact on urbanism, the earlier exhibition could not be equaled.

According to Hegemann, another of the manifold teachings conveyed by Berlin 1910 was the importance of housing, preferably the detached, single-family home or *Kleinhaus*, combined with recreational open space. He stressed adequate housing and parks as essential elements of a well-functioning city, referring to examples from abroad. Once economic and social matters were resolved, attention could be devoted to their aesthetic and architectural realization. This third, artistic aspect of city planning had been mistakenly considered its primary task, while in reality the economic, social, and artistic elements all commanded equal importance. Hegemann praised the city as the spiritual symbol of a nation, embodying a shared culture and collective memory. He envisioned that in the future city planning would no longer be the passion of powerful rulers but would become the "proud banner [*Panier*] of the masses."

Should the Städtebau-Ausstellung have succeeded in raising the understanding and commitment regarding these urgencies, the next urgency would lie in achieving the goal of a Greater Berlin. The Propaganda-Ausschuss für Gross-Berlin (Steering Committee for the Promotion of Greater Berlin) was established in 1912 to advance its implementation, especially in the area of housing and parks. Hegemann devoted much of his energy and organizational skills to this movement, which was anticipated by his article-*cum*-manifesto, envisioning social activism "of the masses."

During the remainder of 1910, Hegemann attended to the demands of the Berlin and Düsseldorf exhibitions and took part in the Town Planning Conference in London (October 1910). Guérin's drawings of the Chicago Plan and Burnham's presence enhanced the prestige of the conference. Another aspect contributing to its renown, perhaps even more in retrospect than at the time of the event, was Patrick Geddes's Civic Survey of Edinburgh.[49] It was displayed apart from the general exhibition of historic and contemporary material from various countries, in the smallest room called "The Black and White Room." Adshead described Geddes's innovative exhibition with astonishment and awe:

> Finally, in the little black and white room, Professor Geddes had got together his bewildering but fascinating survey of Edinburgh which we understand to be triply expanded in the Crosby Hall. . . . This exhibit served at once to demonstrate what an acquisition it would be if every town stood possessed of a civic museum. A museum where the history and growth of the city could be graphically related, where its mistakes could be clearly demonstrated, and its tendencies suggested.

Perhaps it was the preparation of this display that kept Geddes from visiting the exhibition in Berlin, an occasion that presumably would have drawn his attention. The events in London offered Hegemann opportunities to become personally acquainted with Patrick Geddes and his work. Considering Hegemann's international network and the proximity of their ideas, it is curious that neither Geddes nor Hegemann mention each other. The Scottish urbanist/sociologist is one of several contemporaries with whom one would expect Hegemann to have had stimulating contacts. The methodology and purpose of Geddes's civic survey of Edinburgh, although more focused, were strikingly comparable to the goals Hegemann had in mind for the German exhibitions.

Similarities between Geddes and Hegemann, incipient in this early period, persisted throughout their careers. Notably, both thought that regional planning ought to be based on surveys that encompassed wide aspects of humanity, the built and natural environment. During his American lecture tour of 1913–15, and in related publications, Hegemann advocated surveys as a step preceding planning, without mentioning Geddes.

Hegemann took part in an engrossing dialogue on impressions and ideas generated by *Berlin 1910* and related events, where a confluence of international urbanists searched for solutions to the problems of the modern metropolis. Visitors from abroad, intent on informing colleagues at home, wrote reviews and articles that expanded on the reactions in Germany. More than *Düsseldorf 1910*, *Berlin 1910* contributed to this interchange and diffusion, resulting in overviews that surpass individual travelogues. The responses by those who came to Berlin were inclined to focus on the totality of the exhibition, rather than on the competition entries or other topics of special interest to German planners. An exception was the report by Raymond Unwin, who was the official delegate of the Royal Institute of British Architects and involved in the impending Town Planning Conference in London, scheduled for October 1910.[50] His prominence in the profession was enhanced by a book published the previous year, *Town Planning in Practice*, which contained a positive as well as critical response to Sitte's *Der Städtebau*, a book Unwin knew from the imperfect French translation.[51] In the Introduction to the second edition (1934) of his book, Unwin comments on the exhibitions in Berlin, Düsseldorf, and London of 1910, elaborating on points he had raised earlier. In another article on Berlin published in 1910, Unwin referred to Sitte's debated influence in that city and on German town planning.[52] From his own position vis-à-vis Sitte's principles, Unwin perceptively observed the problematic doubts they were causing in Berlin, where the journal *Der Städtebau* was published. Critical of the distortion of Sitte's artistic leanings at the hands of some of his followers, which had resulted in excessively irregular streets, Unwin welcomed the recent emphasis on a more formal, classical style derived primarily from architecture. He commented, "The architects of Berlin seem to be settling down to a style which is at once dignified and restrained, and adapts itself to the requirements of modern buildings."

Hegemann and Unwin shared a range of ideas concerning town planning, one being its close relationship to architecture. Both were also concerned with regional planning and the expanding metropolis, Camillo Sitte's contribution—pro and con—housing, and skyscrapers in the modern city. Their first personal contact probably came about in connection with Berlin 1910 and was reinforced at the Town Planning Conference in London. They maintained an admiring friendship throughout their lives, and their families stayed in touch after Hegemann's death. Unwin and Hegemann's positions regarding skyscrapers and their commitment to housing are discussed in later chapters.

Hegemann facilitated the inclusion of material from the Berlin and Düsseldorf exhibitions to be shown in conjunction with the conference in London, notably Burnham's Chicago plan. He attended the conference but was not invited to present a paper, although his comments are cited in the *Transactions*.[53] While in London, Hegemann was still relatively unknown and youthful compared to others at the gathering. Elder statesmen were asked to give papers on topics for which he might have considered himself qualified to speak. Certainly he could not compete with Daniel Burnham, who gave the inaugural lecture on "A city of the future under a democratic government," with Josef Stübben on recent German schemes, nor with Rudolf Eberstadt on "Town planning in Germany: The geater Berlin competition," which dealt primarily with housing, the speaker's specialty.[54] Eberstadt's introductory remarks provided a wider context—"The task of town building is an international one, where every nation has to learn and every nation may contribute to our knowledge"—and praised England as the country "where the modern system of town building has been created." Eberstadt related that English specialists coming to his own country to study town planning were shown impressive wide streets lined by tenement barracks, and as a result they praised "this street-planning—not town-planning—system." He urged his countrymen to devote critical attention to other, more adequate types of housing that existed in Germany, "the only land where you can study closely the inseparable connection between town planning, street planning, and the basis of social life—that is, housing." Eberstadt's *Handbuch des Wohnungswesens* (Handbook of housing) had just appeared in a second edition and was receiving considerable attention.[55]

Hegemann's keen interest in housing as an important element of city planning was undoubtedly reinforced by Eberstadt's eloquent and knowledgeable presentation in London. His own reputation was dramatically enhanced with the 1911 publication of his first volume documenting the German exhibitions. The latter part of Hegemann's second volume on the City Planning Exhibitions and his involvement with the *Für Gross-Berlin* movement reflect a social activism regarding housing that went far beyond his previous intellectual engagement with it, and brought him into meaningful contact with Eberstadt. Hegemann's preoccupation with housing as a determining factor in city planning came into renewed focus during his years in New York, when he worked on three volumes entitled *City Planning: Housing*.[56] His acknowledgment of housing as a component of universal urbanism evolved impressively during his lifetime.

Among the American planners visiting Berlin 1910, George B. Ford represented a progressive rational trend, which formed the basis of a congenial relationship with Hegemann. Ford's review, "City Planning Exhibition in Berlin," emphatically evoked the event's significance and impact.[57] In *The American City*, Ford wrote that taking advantage of previous exhibitions, "the Berlin Exhibition developed into far and away the largest and most far-reaching aggregation of city-planning material that the world has ever seen . . . it was primarily a place for study of the subject and not a place, as the others had been, to arouse interest in the subject." He mentions an attendance of 70,000 people from all walks of life, including members of labor unions, all of whom had paid admission. Guides conducted groups of 25 to 100 through the exhibition and explained important topics. One unique and very successful feature was a display of books on city planning to be studied in conjunction with the exhibition, which were available for purchase. Ford singled out the emphasis of the competition entries on transportation and transit in relation to improved housing for the great mass of people dwelling in the notorious rental barracks in the center of Berlin. The control of density by means of districts or zones was, much to Ford's surprise, generally accepted by property owners. The emphasis on open space and playgrounds caught his attention. Hegemann had made a personal contribution with a selection of his own photographs of American playgrounds, mostly from Chicago, that were greatly admired by the public. Ford commented, "the one thing that most attracted people of all countries were the plans, photographs and models of garden cities, for one and all, the nations of Europe have accepted the English Garden City idea as probably the best solution of their housing difficulties."

Ford came to Berlin after attending the Ninth International Housing Congress in Vienna, which ran from May 30 to June 4, 1910. He had reported on the Vienna conference in the previous issue of *The American City*, writing at length about the English garden city, which was captivating enthusiastic attention in Europe and the Americas.[58] Ford was not alone in recognizing Berlin 1910 as an important diffuser of the English invention as a promising remedy for the housing misery in the older congested cities. He reported on Vienna: "From an American standpoint the most interesting subject for discussion was the question of tenement or single-house, or as it was there called 'Cottage vs. Bloc.' The unanimity with which the delegates from all countries agreed that the tenement should be supplanted by the cottage was most noteworthy." This was a position with which Hegemann certainly concurred. He maintained this position throughout his career, without considering the spatial expansion involved, and even in the face of the "Siedlungen" designed in the 1920s by Bruno Taut, Martin Wagner, Ernst May, and others. Housing was very much on Ford's mind, and he photographed or obtained a set of pictures of German cottage-type housing shown in models at the Berlin Exhibition.[59] These were sent to his brother James Ford, who was organizing a "Housing Exhibit" with an accompanying catalogue at the Social Museum at Harvard University.[60]

Bertel Jung from Helsinki, one of several visitors traveling to Berlin from the Scandinavian countries, concluded his article reviewing Berlin 1910 observing that the "most interesting room in the enormous exhibition space was the reading room comprising nearly all the literature which can be located under the concept of 'Städtebau'."[61] It seems that for Jung and others, including Hegemann, the exhibition represented a seminar or open university, complete with a research library, offering lectures and discussion sessions, and advocating a comprehensive understanding of this challenging new discipline. At a time when urbanists were searching for viable training in the absence of an "Ecole" for planners, the presentations in Berlin, Düsseldorf, London, and the various civic museums provided welcome alternatives.[62]

Other than review articles Berlin 1910 generated a substantial 120-page book published in Barcelona in 1913, *Las Modernas Ciudades y sus Problemas á la luz de la Exposición de Construcción Cívica be Berlin (1910)* by Cebriá Montoliu.[63] Written in Spanish rather than the author's native Catalan, the publication carried the concepts of the exhibition to Spain and Latin America. Montoliu was the secretary of the Sociedad

Cívica, La Ciudad Jardín founded in 1912 and the librarian of the Museo Social in Barcelona.[64] Montoliu's visit to the exhibition in Berlin reinforced his zeal to turn urbanism into a "*ciencia cívica*"—"cívics" in English—a civic science not to be confused with "civic art." This innovative "*ciencia cívica*" he conceived as a comprehensive discipline based on surveys, investigation, and analysis, linking him to the ideas of Hegemann and Geddes. The Berlin exhibition and the two volumes by Hegemann provided the impetus for Montoliu's *Las Modernas Ciudades*. It is not a mere Spanish version of *Der Städtebau nach den Ergebnissen*, but elaborates on it. According to Montoliu, the multiple aspects of contemporary cities convincingly presented in the Berlin exhibition went beyond "*Städtebau*" = "*arquitectura urbana*," justifying the more comprehensive term "*construcción cívica*"(civic building). He suggested that the Berlin Exhibition should have been converted into a permanent museum, a "*museo cívico.*" In his overview of Berlin 1910, Montoliu dwelt on his particular interest—garden cities and the problem of providing affordable housing in modern cities. He considered this to be the most important issue facing urbanists.

Montoliu's book represented a state-of-the-art survey of urbanism that widened the impact of the lessons derived from the Berlin Exhibition, making them available to those unable to visit it or read Hegemann's volumes in German.

Among those affected by the events in Berlin was an individual whose reactions contributed in consequential ways to architecture and planning in the coming decades. Le Corbusier is recognized as probably the most provocative architect of the twentieth century, a position not only deriving from his built and unbuilt projects, but almost equally from his writings. Despite having expressed his ideas eloquently, he remains enigmatic and persistently intriguing. His early years, when he still used the name Charles-Edouard Jeanneret and traveled to Germany and the Far East, have been unraveled. His letters, diaries, and sketchbooks from that period provide a rich source of documentation.[65]

When Jeanneret set out on the first segment of his German tour in the spring of 1910, he was imbued with Camillo Sitte's ideas, which he expressed in the early text and drawings of his manuscript *La Construction des Villes*. Frequently cited in connection with Jeanneret's enthusiasm for Sittesque curved streets is his comment, "the lesson of the donkey is to be retained" (*La leçon de l'âne est à retenir*), a position he later reversed completely.[66] The competition for Greater Berlin and the exhibition represented new trends in city planning, and exposure to these changes contributed to turning Jeanneret away from the medieval and toward the classical/Baroque and away from Sitte as he had perceived him.

Jeanneret's arrival in Berlin in June of 1910 and his visits to the Allgemeine Städtebau-Ausstellung have to be considered in the context of this ambience. His comments do not contribute to our knowledge of the exhibition, but rather clarify how it influenced Jeanneret's incipient and at this time somewhat circumscribed comprehension of urbanism. His encounter with Berlin 1910 was primarily visual, as the reading of the German texts was an effort.

Jeanneret's second sojourn in Berlin, from November 1910 until spring 1911, when he was working for Peter Behrens in Neu-Babelsberg and Hegemann was completing the first volume of *Der Städtebau nach den Ergebnissen*, might have provided possibilities for contacts between them. It is intriguing that Jeanneret was exposed at this time to ideas closely associated with Hegemann, notably the complexity of the modern metropolis demanding a comprehensive urbanism, relying not on form and aesthetics, but city planning as the basis of architecture. These concepts do not figure in the Le Corbusier/Hegemann exchange of letters of the 1920s, which revolves mostly around skyscrapers. Apparently the only time they actually met was in Paris in 1926, although ideologically their paths crossed in Argentina in 1929 and 1930.[67]

Berlin 1910 is mentioned in Jeanneret's letters to his parents from Berlin, to Charles L'Eplattenier and William Ritter in the *Carnets* (Notebooks), and in his book *Etude sur le mouvement d'art décoratif en Allemagne* (Study of the decorative art movement in Germany) of 1912.[68] A section in the latter, under the heading "*Die Allgemeine Städtebau-Ausstellung,*" includes specific comments. Jeanneret observes: "The Berlin exhibition, organized from an admirably broad perspective, has shown the enormous results already obtained here and there, particularly in Germany. I should say that in Germany the efforts were exclusively reformist, by contrast in America these efforts were founded on the tremendous American genius for building. . . ." He considered the Greater Berlin competition projects shown in the "*salle d'honneur*" to be "enormous, gigantic, impressive, and perhaps very beautiful. One senses that over there men are capable of facing any problem. Berlin wanted not only to be practical, clean and pleasant, but also beautiful. . . ." Jeanneret ends with a subtle recognition of his own peripheral position regarding the emerging discipline: "Clearly this exhibition addresses itself to specialists. What did inattentive visitors see in these mysterious graphics? I devoted several days of work to touch upon the subject of urban planning; I was at the time writing a paper on the subject and these hours were well spent."

Conceptual Consequences of the Universal Exhibition

The period from 1904 to 1914 may be considered the most vibrant interlude for the emerging city planning discipline, which subsequently suffered with the beginning of the Great War. It was propitious that Hegemann par-

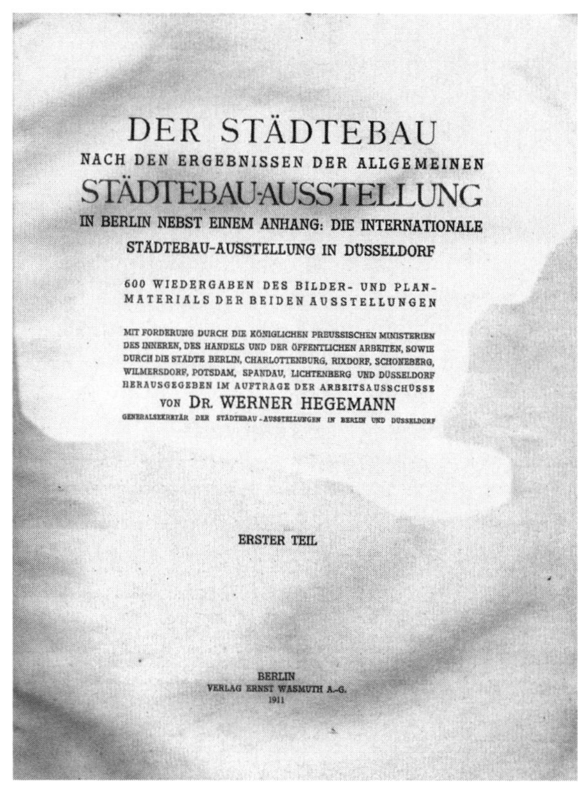

DER STÄDTEBAU
NACH DEN ERGEBNISSEN DER ALLGEMEINEN
STÄDTEBAU-AUSSTELLUNG
IN BERLIN NEBST EINEM ANHANG: DIE INTERNATIONALE
STÄDTEBAU-AUSSTELLUNG IN DÜSSELDORF

600 WIEDERGABEN DES BILDER- UND PLAN-
MATERIALS DER BEIDEN AUSSTELLUNGEN

MIT FORDERUNG DURCH DIE KÖNIGLICHEN PREUSSISCHEN MINISTERIEN
DES INNEREN, DES HANDELS UND DER ÖFFENTLICHEN ARBEITEN, SOWIE
DURCH DIE STÄDTE BERLIN, CHARLOTTENBURG, RIXDORF, SCHONEBERG,
WILMERSDORF, POTSDAM, SPANDAU, LICHTENBERG UND DÜSSELDORF
HERAUSGEGEBEN IM AUFTRAGE DER ARBEITSAUSSCHÜSSE
VON DR. WERNER HEGEMANN
GENERALSEKRETÄR DER STÄDTEBAU-AUSSTELLUNGEN IN BERLIN UND DÜSSELDORF

ERSTER TEIL

BERLIN
VERLAG ERNST WASMUTH A.-G.
1911

Fig. 5. Title page of Werner Hegemann's Der Städtebau, *Volume I, 1911.*
CCCC

ticipated in this phase on both sides of the Atlantic. Historians and urbanists continue to benefit from the legacy of his theoretical contributions and his publications.

In the wake of the exhibitions and conferences of 1910 in Germany and England, he devoted his energy to composing the volumes documenting Berlin 1910 and Düsseldorf 1910. At a preparatory stage of the event in Berlin, the decision was made to produce a catalogue, perhaps only to summarize what was displayed. The task was assigned to Hegemann, who expanded it into a state-of-the-art treatise on city planning-*cum*-urban history, blending two innovative disciplines (Figs. 5, 6).

Der Städtebau nach den Ergebnissen stands apart from the prescriptive textbooks by Reinhard Baumeister and Josef Stübben. Hegemann approached the city in its entirety as an "object of thought" and intellectual inquiry. His socially framed history of architecture and urbanism place his volumes in a unique category.[69] Antecedents to his approach are found in the work of the French scholar Marcel Poëte (1866–1950), whom Donatella Calabi considers "one of the inventors of the morphological approach toward the history of the city."[70] Calabi writes that for Poëte, as

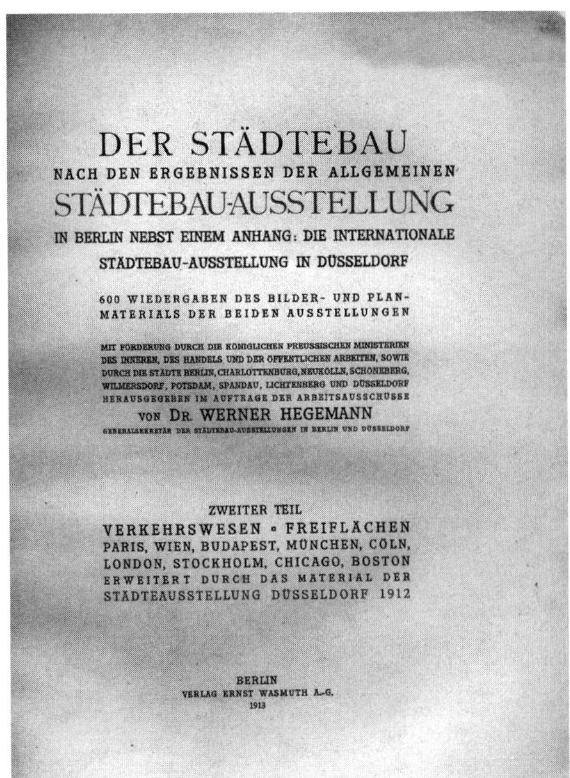

DER STÄDTEBAU
NACH DEN ERGEBNISSEN DER ALLGEMEINEN
STÄDTEBAU-AUSSTELLUNG
IN BERLIN NEBST EINEM ANHANG: DIE INTERNATIONALE
STÄDTEBAU-AUSSTELLUNG IN DÜSSELDORF

600 WIEDERGABEN DES BILDER- UND PLAN-
MATERIALS DER BEIDEN AUSSTELLUNGEN

MIT FÖRDERUNG DURCH DIE KÖNIGLICHEN PREUSSISCHEN MINISTERIEN
DES INNEREN, DES HANDELS UND DER ÖFFENTLICHEN ARBEITEN, SOWIE
DURCH DIE STÄDTE BERLIN, CHARLOTTENBURG, NEUKÖLLN, SCHÖNEBERG,
WILMERSDORF, POTSDAM, SPANDAU, LICHTENBERG UND DÜSSELDORF
HERAUSGEGEBEN IM AUFTRAGE DER ARBEITSAUSSCHÜSSE
VON DR. WERNER HEGEMANN
GENERALSEKRETÄR DER STÄDTEBAU-AUSSTELLUNGEN IN BERLIN UND DÜSSELDORF

ZWEITER TEIL
VERKEHRSWESEN ∘ FREIFLÄCHEN
PARIS, WIEN, BUDAPEST, MÜNCHEN, CÖLN,
LONDON, STOCKHOLM, CHICAGO, BOSTON
ERWEITERT DURCH DAS MATERIAL DER
STÄDTEAUSSTELLUNG DÜSSELDORF 1912

BERLIN
VERLAG ERNST WASMUTH A.-G.
1913

Fig. 6. Title page of Der Städtebau, *Volume II, 1913.* CCCC

for Geddes, with whom he is often compared, "town planning [was] a 'science of observation'." Hegemann certainly avowed surveys and analysis, insisting on visiting the cities in Europe about which he wrote in his volumes *Der Städtebau nach den Ergebnissen.* A far-reaching concern advocated by Geddes, Hegemann, and Poëte was to educate the public at large about the city and its history. Poëte went so far as to consider "the knowledge of the city a civic duty."[71]

Hegemann's *Der Städtebau* endures as salient in the expanding literature on the city.[72] Initially the intention was to produce a third volume, and it is remarkable that even two were completed in a relatively short time. Emphasizing that the scope of his work reached beyond the material displayed in the exhibitions, Hegemann mentioned repeatedly that he traveled to all the European cities discussed. In a curriculum vitae letter to Prof. Ford of January 1916, he wrote:

> The committees of the exhibitions in Berlin and Düsseldorf also appointed me to lay down the results of the two exhibitions in a book and secured subsidies for this publication from thirteen German cities and three departments of the Prussian Government. I accepted this commission under the condition that I

> was permitted to study on the spot everything that I was to describe in the book, i.e., that I was to visit all the municipalities that had exhibited . . . . The subjects dealt with in the volumes are investigated in the field and in the libraries of the respective cities and in continuous exchange of ideas with the men best posted to give the desired information. I paid prolonged visits especially to Berlin, Paris, London, Vienna, Budapest, Munich, and Stockholm; shorter visits to all European capitals, excepting the Balkans. The aim of the publication in question is to help create a scientific basis for the wide city planning discussion, which so far was largely in the hands of men with a training either mainly technical (engineers, architects) or specializing in one single phase (e.g., housing, transportation) of the many phases which in their coordination only make up city planning.[73]

During the four weeks of his journey, Hegemann was accompanied by the American Edward T. Devine (1868–1948). Devine has often been called "the dean of social welfare" and ranked with Jane Addams, battling poverty in America and in Europe while availing himself of his many influential positions and publications.[74] He was the founder and editor of the progressive periodical *Charities*, later *The Commons*, and subsequently *The Survey*, in which Hegemann would publish articles.

Devine was a stimulating travel companion who shared Hegemann's interest in social issues. Hegemann's position is cogently put forward in his landmark volumes, where he argues for a socioeconomic interpretation of the contemporary city within its urban and political history, made visible in the evolving environment composed of planning and architecture. His diachronic study of the city blends methodologies from the humanities with those derived from a scientific and pragmatic foundation akin to Patrick Geddes's surveys.

Reviews of *Der Städtebau* from Germany and abroad appeared soon after the publication of Volume I. Citations from them were gathered by Hegemann in a publicity sheet, apparently prepared for his forthcoming American lecture tour of 1913, and later updated.[75] Among the comments is one by Patrick Geddes from *Cities in Evolution* (1915): "Of foreign manuals Dr. Werner Hegemann's *Der Städtebau* (two volumes published), Berlin 1911 and 1913, may be especially recommended." It is the only mention Geddes ever made of his contemporary. Other reviews were less terse and noted the author's engaged and vivid style of presenting scientific and thoroughly researched subjects.[76]

The Finnish architect and planner Bertel Jung, who had previously written on the Berlin exhibition, wrote an insightful review of Volume I. Uncannily prescient of Hegemann's *Das steinerne Berlin*, to be published in 1931, Jung commented in 1912:

> the author has not limited himself to publishing a know-all report solely based on the exhibition material. . . . The drawings and statistics exhibited are only the skeleton around which he forms his description of the varied life of a con-

> temporary giant city, and even if Berlin here is the central one, the conclusions which he draws contain general value, the German capital therefore appearing to the reader as a particularly successfully chosen international example of the development of a modern urban community.[77]

Jung considered the extensive Introduction to Volume I "the focus of the work" and mentioned that two additional volumes were forthcoming.

Volume I of *Der Städtebau* is almost entirely devoted to Berlin. Its organization is unusual, with the ninety-page "Introduction" subtitled "Retrospective View," comprising more than half of the book. It is followed by Chapter One—the only one—entitled "*Berliner Pläne*," which is divided into two segments: "The Great Brandenburgian-Prussian Town Planners" and "The Monumental City." The section of notes is extensive, and there are more than one hundred illustrations, color plates, and maps. Scattered throughout the volume at the headings of pages are quotations from a range of individuals. The topics of these maxims range widely, including history, literature, and urbanism. They are suggestive of notebook entries testifying to the scope of Hegemann's reading, as are the copious notes. One can rightly wonder how he found time for such demanding, multilingual research while being involved in so many other activities, particularly as there is no indication that he had assistants working for him at this time, except possibly for mounting the exhibitions.

The "Introduction: Retrospective View" is a justification of Hegemann's "long view" of examining the antecedents which led to present conditions. He considered knowledge of antecedents essential to finding solutions for current problems and the future city. The exhibitions contributed to bridging the gap between the historical context and the forces that shaped it, and the evolving future metropolis. At the beginning of his "Introduction" Hegemann states:

> The Universal City Planning Exhibition cannot be comprehended as an event that came about overnight, but rather it should be viewed as a significant phenomenon within a decades-old struggle that is reaching continually wider spheres.
>
> If the exhibition is primarily considered a landmark in the development of metropolitan Berlin, the city of Greater Berlin, the wider meaning is derived from the fact that Berlin's development may be representative of international events. Presently Berlin is becoming the international storm center in the pursuit of the promising creation of a completely new world which we are inhabiting.[78]

Hegemann's retrospective view of Prussian history and its impact on the city holds events and decisions responsible for dashing hopes for improvements. Singled out are Berlin's dismal housing conditions, the housing famine, the notorious *Mietskasernen* (housing barracks), and the lack of open space for children. According to Hegemann, the major cause for the predicament of the urban poor everywhere was land speculation. Making housing a dominant theme of Volume I, he is emphatic: "The first and primary purpose of town planning is the dignified satisfaction of the need for housing in the broadest sense of the term."[79]

Moving between topics, Hegemann interwove a matter-of-fact presentation of grim contemporary predicaments with political and cultural history. He was not always successful in balancing the longer view with a survey of the present reality based on statistics, analyses, and factual documentation. Citations and references to studies by others contribute to, but in some instances obscure, his arguments. *Der Städtebau* is formidable in its density. Those seeking an overview of the exhibitions in Volume I might be disappointed; however, it is contained in the second volume.

Volume II is almost twice the size of Volume I. Pages and illustrations are numbered consecutively, with a total of 397 pages and 423 illustrations.[80] Following the title page is a full page devoted to the author's dedication, which cites the eight members of the recently constituted Propaganda-Ausschuss für Gross-Berlin and the men and women of Greater Berlin, who advanced the aims of that committee with "*Wort und Schrift, Rat und Tat*" (Words and publications, advice and action). The dedication is indicative of Hegemann's intensified political position regarding urban reform and his involvement with the Propaganda-Ausschuss, which was committed to providing open space and alleviating problematic housing conditions. Citations from Gustav von Schmoller and Rudolf Eberstadt, individuals with longstanding concerns for the betterment of the lower classes, substantiate the agenda of this organization.[81] On the following page, almost as an afterthought, Hegemann expresses gratitude to those who had made the exhibitions in Berlin and Düsseldorf possible.

In his preface, Hegemann regrets that a lecture tour abroad would prevent him from proofreading and checking the footnotes in Volume II. Once more he stresses the importance of researching and confirming factual data in the various cities discussed, even referring to the length of his visits to each city during the previous ten years![82]

The major focus of Volume II is the second chapter, "Metropolitan Traffic and Transportation: Paris, Vienna, Budapest, Munich, Cologne, London, Stockholm, American Cities." Hegemann justified giving pride of place to traffic and transportation by noting that its importance was widely recognized for the first time in the Berlin Exhibition. The additional comprehensive plans shown in Düsseldorf provided the theoretical framework for this aspect of city planning, which represented a novelty for Germany. When he contemplated the entries for the Greater Berlin competition, Theodor Goecke was moved to declare, "the greatest surprise regarding the entire competition . . . is perhaps the realization that so far we do not have any comprehensive traffic plan, and yet such a large-scale plan ought to precede the comprehensive master plan."[83]

Hegemann attributed the emergence of transportation as an element of urban planning to the decentralized Anglo-Saxon and American cities, contrasting them with the congested continental towns, some of which were still surrounded by ancient and now obsolete fortifications. No reference was made to Soria y Mata's mid-nineteenth century linear city concept, which made transportation the rationale for an open-ended, evolving town. According to Hegemann, expanding suburbs, open space, and park systems should be combined with transportation networks, resulting in a vital synergy. These ideas were closely studied by urbanists such as Eberstadt, who was well acquainted with English garden cities. Hegemann noted that in 1893 Eberstadt, referring to English examples, was the first to differentiate between a *Verkehrsstrasse* (traffic road) and a *Wohnstrasse* (residential road), emphasizing the cost-saving factors.

To justify the large section of the text devoted to transportation and anticipate Chapter Three on open space in Paris, London, American cities, and Berlin, Hegemann discussed each with great thoroughness. The quantity and quality of the illustrations, many reproduced in color, is impressive, and the captions and noted sources add to their research value. Not all of the illustrations were displayed in the exhibitions, and a few are rarities that can only be studied in Hegemann's publication. One example is the colored plan of Paris on which are drawn the transformations agreed to by Napoleon III and G. E. Haussmann (Figs. 7, 8). Only three examples of this plan were made for the World Exposition of 1867. One was presented on that occasion by Napoleon III to the King of Prussia (later Kaiser Wilhelm I). The other two plans disappeared. The plan in the Royal Collections of Prussia was not shown in the Berlin Exhibition of 1910 but was reproduced in Volume II, whole in color and in detail. It has since vanished.[84]

Hegemann had spent two years studying in Paris, was fluent in French, and had a lifelong predilection for the city. The section on Paris stands apart for its comprehensiveness, and the copious notes testify to Hegemann's knowledge of the city and his numerous personal contacts, whose assistance he gratefully mentions.[85] For Hegemann, Paris with all its problems as well as attractions was the example *par excellence* for the development of a centralized city, which he then compared to others. This methodology was also one of the enlightening aspects of the arrangement in the exhibitions, where material was grouped by topic, rather than by country, city, or chronological sequence. In Volume II, Hegemann combined this approach with separate sections for individual cities.

The theme that runs throughout Volume II is transportation as it relates to housing and open space and expands from an established center. Following the sections on the European mainland, the discussion switches to London, where, according to Hegemann, some of the most successful solutions had been implemented.

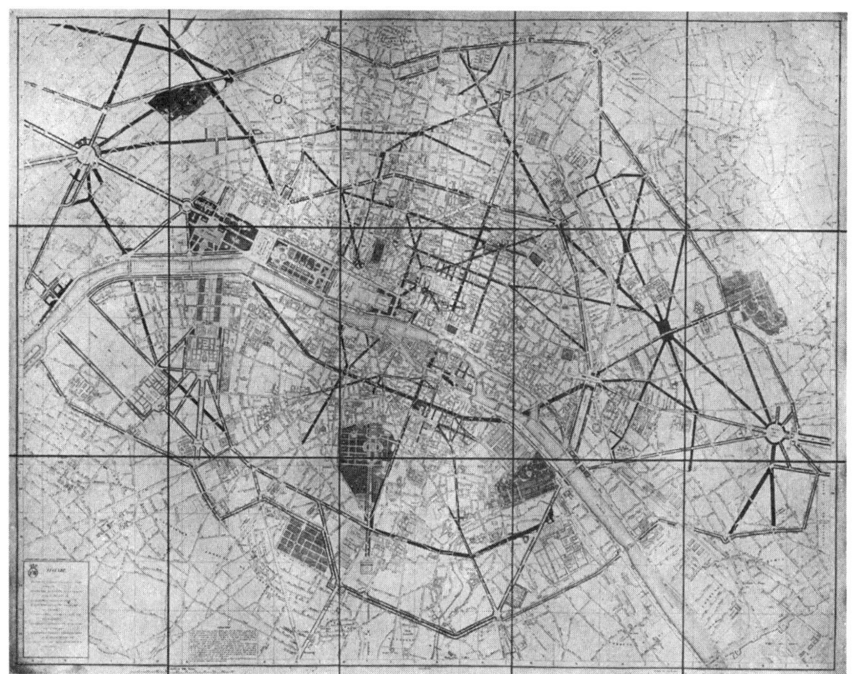

Fig. 7. Plan of Paris, indicating projects proposed by Napoleon III, from Hegemann's Der Städtebau, *Volume II.* CCCC

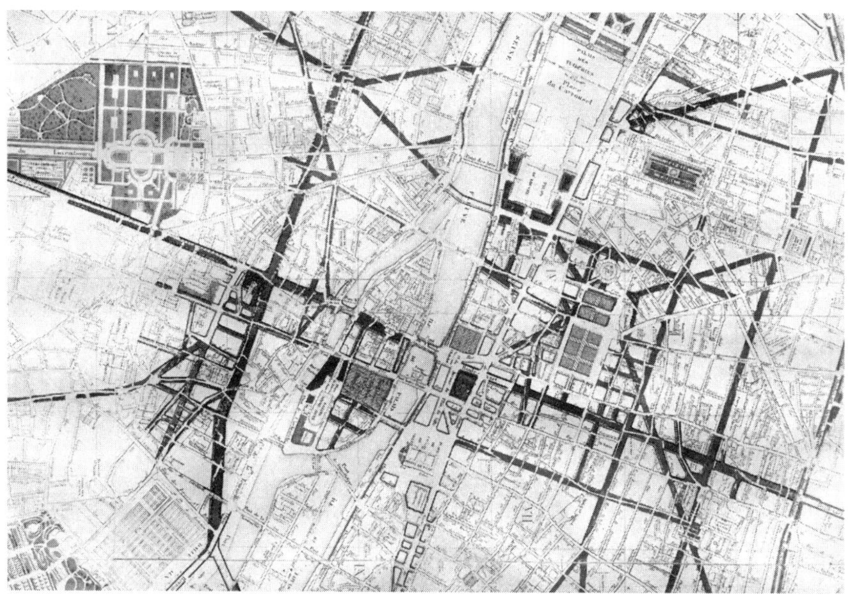

Fig. 8. Detail of the Paris plan, from Hegemann's Der Städtebau, *Volume II.* CCCC

London is discussed in the section "Centralization and Decentralization, Absolutism and Autonomy and Their Repercussions for City Planning." All the above-mentioned sections are part of the extensive Chapter Two. Hegemann analyzed connections between political and urban history and city planning in his 1930 book *Das steinerne Berlin* (The Berlin of stone), publications on Prussian history, and in his historical novels. He believed this correlation to be emblematic for the inherent complexities of the modern metropolis.

Hegemann considered Boston and Chicago in Chapter Three, entitled "Open Space: Paris, London, American Cities, and Berlin." His interest in this topic derived from his American experience, specifically from his acquaintance with Boston's "Emerald Necklace." Hegemann's preoccupation with open space resulted in a cluster of related publications and lectures, among them the pamphlet *Ein Parkbuch*.[86] The *Parkbuch* accompanied a traveling exhibition shown in Bremen, Cologne, Dresden, and Frankfurt. Hegemann was not the first to draw German attention to American open space and park systems, but he was a pioneer in considering them together with transportation and housing as integral elements of comprehensive planning. In this respect his *Parkbuch*, his lecture in Düsseldorf, and Chapter Three in Volume II went further than an article by H. Kayser, "North American Parks" published in 1905, by emphasizing the integral relationship of open space to regional planning.[87] Hegemann referred several times to Kayser's detailed report, which was replete with tabulated statistics and sources, as well as information on practical aspects of park management such as underground watering. In his article, Kayser noted that "all . . . separate parks—and this is characteristic of American city parks—are combined into systems" and connected by "parkways."

In connection with Volume II, Chapter Three, Hegemann's 1910 lecture in Düsseldorf is important for both its content and timing. It was delivered at a conference convened by the President of the Regional Government for the mayors and other higher administrators within the jurisdiction. The meeting was summoned to discuss the possibility of planning and implementing a "*Wiesen und Waldgürtel*" (ring of meadows and forests) in the industrial region, as part of the pioneering regional plan (SVR) by the Ruhr Planning Association.

Hegemann was invited to give the inaugural lecture and spoke primarily on recent American park planning.[88] The lecture is one of the most cogent examples of his ability to weave together theoretical concerns and references to Greater Berlin with the contemporary problem facing Düsseldorf of acquiring forest tracts in its environs. His presentation was based on a firsthand survey he had conducted in the SVR region prior to the conference and gave convincing substance to his pragmatic suggestions. The scope of the presentation is noteworthy: He conceived of an open-space system of forests, farmlands, cemeteries, parks and parkways, interconnected if possible, and protected from development in perpetuity. Emphasis was placed on mass transit and automobile transportation to provide access from residential areas.[89]

Chapter Three of Volume II in *Der Städtebau* also contains an overview of the distinctive aspects of French parks with their axiality and vistas, contrasting them with the picturesque nature parks in England. According to Hegemann, both American and English versions were imitated, often in exaggerated, awkward ways. In Europe the transition from idiosyncratic private parks to those in the public domain allowed for the incorporation of recreational elements. Eventually open space was specifically set aside to relieve urban congestion, and it became a planning consideration.

The development of American urban planning resulting from open space and park systems was recognized with some incredulity in Europe. The names of Frederick Law Olmsted Sr., Charles Eliot, and others became known for their travels on the continent. Their professional status had reached a level not achieved by their German peers until the 1920s. Discussing the Metropolitan Parks District of Greater Boston and the public parks of New York in Volume II, Hegemann called Olmsted Sr. the greatest "Park-Architect" and "Park-Organizer" of modern times.[90]

The creation of neighborhood playgrounds for children and *Volksparks* (public parks), especially those in Chicago with their field houses and organized activities, was considered a particularly innovative component of American policy. Scattered throughout the city, these parks were within easy walking distance for mothers with young children. Photographs of playground activities and various plans were displayed in the exhibitions and in Hegemann's *Parkbuch*, and contrasted with the scarcity of play space for the children of Berlin.

Compared to France and the Anglo-Saxon countries, Hegemann noted in Volume II, Chapter 3, that Germany's achievements in *Parkkultur* were meager. The exceptions were the great parks in Wörlitz, Muskau, Branitz, and Babelsberg by Count Pückler-Muskau, which inspired Charles Eliot, and the public park created (1802–09) in Bremen on land formerly occupied by the ring of fortifications. Hegemann never ceased to point out that the public parks and recreational facilities available to Berlin's citizens, especially those for children, were truly minimal, and he was not alone in this opinion. In 1874, the Countess Adelheid v. Dohna-Poninski, using the pseudonym "Arminius," wrote with bitterness about it in her frequently cited book, *The Housing Shortage in Cities and the Basis for Radical Improvement*.[91] Rudolf Eberstadt later published a devastating critique of the "impotence" of Berlin's bureaucracy responsible for parks, which was capable of wasting funds on ornamental garden strips, but blind to the urgent needs of children.[92]

Another critic of inappropriate park design in Germany was the landscape architect Leberecht Migge (1881–1935). Hegemann admired Migge's political and social ideas regarding urban green spaces and featured some of his designs in his *Parkbuch* and *The American Vitruvius: An Architects' Handbook of Civic Art* of 1922. Migge advocated active recreation and productive vegetable gardens within the congested cities and many of his projects realized ideas that Hegemann proposed in his polemical writings.[93]

Für Gross-Berlin

The latter part of Volume II is devoted to Prussian history and the conditions in Berlin, with scant references to other cities. Hegemann's mode of expression took on a markedly polemical tone and reflected a heightened conviction that city planning was a science and social policy of action which demanded collective intervention. Chapter 3 on open space in Berlin evolves into a discussion of two organizations with similar names and overlapping yet conflicting aims: the Zweckverband Gross-Berlin (Local Administrative Union for Greater Berlin) and the Propaganda-Ausschuss für Gross-Berlin (Steering Committee for the Promotion of Greater Berlin) (Fig. 9).

The Zweckverband für Gross-Berlin was established by law by the Prussian State in April 1911 and went into effect in February 1912. Its purpose was to coordinate and rein in the pursuit of the Greater Berlin regional plan by the city of Berlin, which was intent on enhancing its autonomy and prominence. While the Zweckverband für Gross-Berlin was being debated, Hegemann called attention to the comprehensive plan for Greater Boston as a comparable example.[94] In Boston the unification of thirty-nine independent communities had come about gradually in the late nineteenth century, initially motivated by the need to coordinate the flow of sewage into the harbor. Hegemann considered of major significance the formation of Boston's Metropolitan Park District, which comprised 102,400 hectares (253,000 acres) and 1.6 million citizens and was dedicated to planning an open-space system of parks and parkways. These initiatives led to the establishment of a commission for the study of a regional Greater Boston in 1907.

However, developments in Boston did not have to overcome the predicament generated by Berlin's position as *Reichshauptstadt* (capital city) of the German Empire, which added a poignant rivalry between state and city to the situation. Membership of the Zweckverband was politically conservative, weighted toward state and municipal functionaries and representatives of military and real estate interests. Architects, city planners, and other technical advisers were not included, a fact which caused much dismay and rancor, as they had initiated the movement for Greater Berlin.

In March of 1911, just prior to the enactment of the law, the journal *Der Städtebau* published a communiqué reiterating to the two houses of the Representative Assembly that the undersigned had submitted recommenda-

Fig. 9. Cover of Für Gross-Berlin *brochure, No. 1.* CCCC

tions to be included in the formulation of the Zweckverband für Gross-Berlin.[95] The most important item in their proposal was that the Director of the Administrative Union should have an advisory council of experts in town planning, transportation, social economics, and sanitation who were *not* members of the administration of the various municipalities to be integrated into Greater Berlin. The communiqué proceeded to explain the need for such an advisory council to advance a comprehensive master plan. Among those signing it were Otto March, Rudolf Eberstadt, Theodor Goecke, Hermann Muthesius, and Paul Schultze-Naumburg. The Zweckverband did not accept the proposal. The refusal contributed to the formation of the Propaganda-Ausschuss Für Gross-Berlin, a pressure group intended to act as a critical conscience and whip to the Zweckverband. It focused on housing, transportation, and open space within the comprehensive master plan as it had been envisioned by the competition program. The membership of the Propaganda Ausschuss included civic reformers and professionals involved with progressive social concerns. The two organizations exemplified the perennial conflict between the state and the city, which Hegemann made a dominant theme in many of his publications, especially *Das steinerne Berlin* (1930). It is no surprise that he was a founding member of the Propaganda Ausschuss. Seeing no progress on urban improvements, he considered public social action the logical and expedient choice.

In the wake of these events, he believed citizens ought to set things in motion. He dedicated the final pages of Volume II of *Der Städtebau nach den Ergebnissen* to the promotion of this cause, even including a considerable part of the Propaganda-Ausschuss brochures for which he was responsible.[96] According to Hegemann the objective of the Propaganda Ausschuss was "to convince the public at large by means of a consciousness-raising crusade to constitute an action-ready contingent . . . ," compelling the Zweckverband to promote the building of single-family homes, an affordable transportation network, parks, and playgrounds. Members of the Propaganda-Ausschuss, impressed by the range of new ideas revealed in the exhibitions and discussions of 1910, especially those from abroad converging with those from their own country, were determined to see them carried forward to fruition.

Although Hegemann is not singled out among the impressive supporters listed, his name figures as the business address. He became a vital participant in and zealous publicist for the Propaganda-Ausschuss Für Gross-Berlin. His manner of expressing himself in a scholarly vein had changed toward the latter part of Volume II of *Der Städtebau*, and is evident in an article eliciting support.[97]

His writing style in the two *Für Gross-Berlin* pamphlets and related publications of this period is comparable to that of the American "muckraker" Lincoln Steffens (1866–1936).[98] Steffens's no-holds-barred criticism of municipal mismanagement, deeming it responsible for urban evils, seems to have set the tone for Hegemann. Steffens laid bare not merely the corruption of municipal systems, but the bankruptcy of an entire political ethic. Comparably, Hegemann directed his caustic critique at the Prussian State. The critique reached a high point during the period 1911–13 and emerged later in his historical novels and notably in his book *Das Steinerne Berlin.*

The Propaganda-Ausschuss Für Gross-Berlin became Hegemann's personal crusade with a socialist urban agenda. In addition to handling the publicity, he recruited participants, endeavoring to include a spectrum of people complementing the core of progressive reformers. One instance of his recruiting efforts is described by the art historian Werner Weisbach (1873–1953), author of several scholarly books in his field, and a review of Volume I of Hegemann's *Der Städtebau*, in which he emphasized the housing problems.[99] In the second volume of his memoirs Weisbach relates his first meeting with Hegemann in January 1912.[100] He describes him, "with a short, neatly trimmed, blond, full beard, of moderate height rather than tall, trim and limber, in his conversation very lively and persuasive, but objective, calm and considering every word."[101] According to Weisbach, the Propaganda-Ausschuss was to consist of eight members, among them the architect Hermann Muthesius, the politician Bernhard Dernburg, and the social-democrat Albert Südekum. Weisbach suggested adding the Protestant theologian Edvard Lehmann, a university professor from Denmark who was partial to social gospel convictions. Hegemann presented Weisbach with the plans for his "consciousness-raising crusade." The display of large posters on the advertisement pillars in Berlin were to be a striking element. The idea of the posters and their design most likely derived from Hegemann. They displayed the image of an emaciated young girl carrying her infant sibling, and were based on a lithograph by the artist Käthe Kollwitz (1867–1945), which also appeared with slight variations on the Propaganda-Ausschuss stationery and announcements (Figs. 10, 11).[102] This heart-rending image was accompanied by the text: "In Greater Berlin 600,000 people live in dwellings in which each room is occupied by five or more individuals. 353,000 public school children lack playgrounds." In the background a sign such as those seen in most rental barracks read, "Playing on the stairs and in hallways and courtyards is *forbidden.*"

Weisbach considered the idea of the posters a possibility in America, but not appropriate for Berlin. Hegemann replied that people would have to get used to this novelty. The posters went up and generated strong objections from the Lord Mayor of Berlin, Martin Kirschner, and Dr. Reicke, Mayor of Berlin, who questioned the statistics; from the police, who con-

FÜR GROSS-BERLIN

IN GROSS-BERLIN WOHNEN 600 000 MENSCHEN IN WOHNUNGEN, IN DENEN JEDES ZIMMER MIT 5 UND MEHR PERSONEN BESETZT IST.

WEITRÄUMIGE BEBAUUNGSPLÄNE FÜR GESUNDE KLEINWOHNUNGEN.

AUSBAU DES SCHNELLBAHNNETZES UND BILLIGE TARIFE

LEICHT ERREICHBARE PARKS UND SPIELPLÄTZE. WALD- UND WIESENGÜRTEL.

Propaganda-Ausschuß: Carl Rudolf Bergmann, Schatzmeister; Dr. Bernhard Dernburg; Stadtrat Prof. Dr. E. Francke, Herausgeber der „Sozialen Praxis"; Dr. Werner Hegemann, ehrenamtlicher Geschäftsführer; Dr. R. Kuczynski, Direktor des Statist. Amtes Schöneberg; Dr. Edv. Lehmann, Prof. der Religionsgeschichte, Kgl. Universität Berlin; Geh. Reg.-Rat Dr. Hermann Muthesius, Architekt; Dr. A. Südekum, M. d. R., Herausgeber der „Kommunalen Praxis"; Dr. Werner Weisbach, Privatdozent d. Kunstgeschichte, Kgl. Universität Berlin.

Bankkonto: „Für Groß-Berlin" bei Depositenkasse D der Bank für Handel und Industrie, Grunewald, Hohrechtstraße, welche Beiträge entgegennimmt.

Geschäftsstelle: Grunewald, Trabener Straße 25. Telefon: Pfalzbg. Nr. 790

Spielen auf den Treppenfluren und den Höfen ist verbo…

HUNDERTTAUSENDE VON KINDERN SIND OHNE SPIELPLATZ.

Die vom Propaganda-Ausschuß herausgegebenen Broschüren

FÜR GROSS-BERLIN

sollen die Stimmung freudiger Anteilnahme festhalten, mit der weite Kreise der Groß-Berliner Bevölkerung in bewegten Volksversammlungen zu den bevorstehenden folgenschweren Entscheidungen des Zweckverbandes, des jüngsten der deutschen Parlamente, Stellung genommen haben.

Das Groß-Berliner Verbandsparlament repräsentiert eine Bevölkerung, die etwa den vereinigten Bevölkerungen des Königreichs Württemberg und des Großherzogtums Baden entspricht. Die Tatsache aber, daß in Berlin, als der gleichzeitig größten und als der Hauptstadt deutscher Zunge, alle wirtschaftlichen und ideellen Möglichkeiten und Schwierigkeiten auf die in der deutschen Gegenwart denkbare äußerste Spitze getrieben sind, verleiht der Verbandspolitik, die sich jetzt entwickeln muß, eine so überragende Bedeutung, daß sie von unmittelbarem symptomatischem Interesse weit über die Zweckverbandsgrenzen hinaus erscheinen muß. Wer einmal gewürdigt hat, wie folgenschwer das Beispiel der Reichshauptstadt vielfach auf die Geschicke unseres Volkes wirkt, muß verlangen, daß dieses Beispiel auch segensreich sei, und muß wünschen, daß aus dem Rattenkönig widersprechender Kirchturmsinteressen, der sich heute noch unter dem Namen Groß-Berlin versteckt, eine wirkliche Hauptstadt entstehe. Aus „der Misere von Groß-Berlin, der gegenüber nach den Worten von Oberbürgermeister Kirschner die Verhältnisse des seligen Deutschen Reiches einfach und geregelt waren", muß eine Stadt werden, deren Organisation, deren Wohnungsverhältnisse, deren Spielplatz- und Verkehrsverhältnisse dem deutschen Namen keine Schande machen. „Wir Deutschen", sagt Heinrich von Treitschke, „sind das einzige Kulturvolk, das ohne eine große Stadt sich die Stellung einer Großmacht erobert hat; die Vorzüge und die Schwächen ländlich-kleinstädtischer Bildung liegen uns tief im Blute. Nun unternehmen die aufstrebenden Kräfte einer neuen Zeit vor unseren Augen, dies alte unnatürliche Gebrechen zu heilen, das allein aus den Wirren und dem Unglück einer höchst verwickelten Geschichte sich erklärt. Unsere Hauptstadt wird bald die größte Kommunalverwaltung der Welt besitzen und als „Provinz Berlin" den beengenden Formen der Städteordnung entwachsen."

Diese stolze Kommunalverwaltung nun endlich zu schaffen oder wenigstens tatkräftig vorzubereiten, ist die Aufgabe des jungen Groß-Berliner Parlamentes. Zur Würdigung der Bedeutung dieses Parlamentes sollen die Broschüren „Für Groß-Berlin" beitragen.

INHALT DES 1. HEFTES: **Die Besprechung im Reichstagsgebäude vom 12. Februar 1912:** Dernburg, Muthesius, Südekum, Kuczynski, Hegemann, Waldschmidt, Jäger, Reicke, Kirschner, Nathan, Ewald, Stern, Petersen, Albert Levy, Albert Kohn, v. Posadowsky. **Was erwarten wir vom Zweckverband?** Dernburg, Dominicus, Muthesius, Südekum, Kuczynski, Heidenreich.

INHALT DES 2. HEFTES: Das Tempelhofer Feld vor und nach der Bebauung. Umschlag und S. 33. **Die Versammlung vom 10. März 1912.** Prof. Dr. E. Francke S. 35. Exzellenz Dernburg S. 35. Dr. Friedrich Naumann S. 39. Dr. Albert Südekum S. 41. Oberapotheker Linke S. 44. J. Lubahn, Bund D. Bodenreformer S. 45. H. Kötschke, Gr. B. Mieterbund S. 46. Gartendirektor Lesser S. 46. Magistratsbüroassistent Wege S. 47. **Das Wachsen Groß-Berlins.** S. 48. Von Dr. W. Hegemann mit 23 Bildern. Fortsetzung der Diskussion: Direktor Albert Kohn. S. 59. Direktor Dr. R. Kuczynski (zur Frage über die 600 000) S. 61. Regierungsbaumeister a. D. G. Langen (über „das Ende des Grundstückhandels" S. 63. Reichsbankkalkulator Ladendorff S. 65. Oberingenieur O. Stegemann (zur Groß-Berliner Verkehrsfrage) S. 66. **Keine Mietskasernen mehr außerhalb der Ringbahn.** Dr. Kuczynski S. 72. Regierungsbaumeister a. D. Lehwess S. 74. Baurat Albert Weiß S. 75. Berliner Handelskammer S. 75. **Das verbotene Plakat.** S. 76 (hierzu 3 Bilder auf S. 88). **Interessante und interessierte Statistik.** Ulm S. 77. Die finanzielle Grundlage von „Grundbesitz und Realkredit" S. 78. Hausbesitzerprivileg S. 79. Amerikanisches gegen deutsches Wohnwesen S. 79. Baukosten S. 80. Der Stand des Streites über die 600 000 S. 80. Die Groß-Berliner Mietskaserne von Ausländern beurteilt S. 81. Drastische Angst vor dem Wohnungsgesetz S. 82. **Groß-Berliner Ansiedlungsblätter.** Zweckverband u. Selbstverwaltung v. Dr. K. Keller S. 82. Das angeblich unparteiische Preisgericht der Grundbesitzinteressenten S. 83. Die techn. Aufgaben des Zweckverbandes S. 84.

Verantwortlich für den Inhalt: Dr. Werner Hegemann, Grunewald.

Fig. 10. Title page of Für Gross-Berlin *brochure, No. 2. Drawing by Käte Kollwitz.* CCCC

Fig. 11. Leaflet with drawing by Käte Kollwitz. CCCC

sidered them provocative; and from the association of property owners, who felt threatened. These reactions contributed to the notoriety and effectiveness of Hegemann's publicity. Kollwitz's image and the catchy text are on the cover of pamphlet #1, which summarized two meetings. The first, in February 1912, was by invitation and was called to discuss with the Zweckverband ways to support the implementation of its goals. It took place in the Reichstag building and included a wide range of government functionaries and political figures from Berlin and the municipalities to be integrated into Greater Berlin. Lord Mayor Kirschner considered the "agitation" unnecessary. He and Mayor Reicke insisted on questioning the housing and play-space statistics, which were cited in many speeches. René Kuczynski, director of the Office of Statistics in Schöneberg, vouched for their accuracy. Kirschner and Reicke published their objections in the newspapers, and the opposition, in turn, showed a recent photograph of three children in front of a sign by a fenced-in meadow stating: "Trespassing on the playground by unauthorized individuals will be prosecuted. The City Park Administration" (Fig. 12). This soon resulted in the removal of similar signs, permitting access to playgrounds during certain hours.

The February meeting had sharpened the antagonism between the two sides. The next event was a public gathering scheduled for a Sunday in March, which was announced by the posters that were causing a sensation. The event drew 1,800 people and took place in one of the largest assembly halls in Berlin, called Neue Welt, in the Hasenheide. Principally used as an entertainment venue, it was favored for political gatherings as well, especially by the Social-Democrats.[103] The choice of the Neue Welt was indicative of the increasingly contentious spirit of the Propaganda Ausschuss, which was also reflected in the speeches delivered and later published in pamphlet #1, *Für Gross-Berlin*. The accusations of the Zweckverband, claiming erroneous statistics, were refuted in the citing of unquestionable sources. The speakers vehemently assailed the Zweckverband for rejecting the expert advice of those who gave the initial impetus to the Greater Berlin concept.

Albert Südekum, a member of the Reichstag, went so far as to declare "that [the Zweckverband] was instituted to obstruct what was greater and better, and not to promote progress—at least how I myself and a hundred-thousand in this city understand [progress]." Like most of the other speakers, he concentrated on the problem of affordable housing, referring to the widely recognized expertise of Eberstadt.

Before turning to the topic of housing, the architect Hermann Muthesius reminded the audience, "Among the most important tasks for

Fig. 12. Children under a sign forbidding playing in the park behind them, 1912. Photograph by W. Hegemann, for the campaign Für Gross-Berlin. CCCC

the Zweckverband should be projects in the purview of architects. The most extensive was the establishment of the master plan for Greater Berlin." Extensive preliminary work toward this had been done in connection with assembling the program for the master plan competition at great expense in effort, time, and financial cost. According to Muthesius, the sharpest criticism of the reasonable proposals for healthy and attractive housing and open space came from the Association of Property Owners, who commanded a powerful lobby in the Zweckverband. It was unusual for Muthesius, not a vocal civic reformer, to take an active position in the Propaganda Ausschuss. He was respected as the architect of villas and for his admiring study of English houses and garden cities. Social housing and city planning were not known to be his interests, yet his convincing emphasis on the role of architects added a valuable element to the discussions.

The cover of pamphlet # 2, *Für Gross-Berlin*, features a view of the Tempelhofer Feld before it was built upon, showing crowds of people enjoying the meadow on a Sunday outing (Figs. 13, 14). Also on the cover are the names Dernburg, Naumann, and Südekum, which refer to their comments at two further meetings on March 10 and 15, 1912, and are

Fig. 13. Cover of Für Gross-Berlin *brochure, No. 2.* CCCC

Fig. 14. Construction of Mietskasernen (rental barracks) on the Tempelhofer Feld. CCCC

reported in excerpts. Hegemann's slide talk "*Das Wachsen Gross-Berlins in Bildern*" (The development of Greater Berlin in pictures) was announced in large type for the later date. It is noted that all illustrations in the pamphlet formed part of his presentation; some are presumably photographs taken by him, others derive from *Der Städtebau.* The text repeats arguments which had previously been aired in the press; several Berlin newspapers reported in early May that the police had forbidden the public display of the Propaganda-Ausschuss posters at the instigation of the Association of Property Owners. They were considered "very provocative" and the information questionable. The police based their prohibition on a Prussian law of 1851 directed at newspapers. A short article in pamphlet #2, entitled "*Das verbotene Plakat*" (The forbidden poster), signed by W. Hegemann, protested this censorship law as outdated.

In a move to needle the property owners, the Propaganda Ausschuss launched a revised version of the poster showing an elegant dancing couple with the inscription "Greater Berlin, the world's most beautiful city, hurrah!" (Fig. 15) In the same sarcastic vein, Hegemann composed "An Appeal to the Home and Property Owners of Greater Berlin."[104] It commenced, "Seldom has a year brought so many painful surprises for the property and real estate owners of Berlin as the year 1912, starting with the request for instituting a municipal housing authority." The tongue-in-cheek article refuted every critical point the housing reformers raised against the rental barracks and other policies of the real estate faction. It concludes by condemning the Propaganda Ausschuss as being controlled by demagogues, and was signed, “Hans Biedermann, property owner and real estate speculator.”

At the same time, when the Spandau town council placed the foundation stone of its new town hall, it proclaimed, “May the Emperor protect us from Greater Berlin and the Zweckverband!” Spandau and other towns objected to being annexed by Berlin and were opposed to both the Zweckverband and Für Gross-Berlin.

The associations active in housing reform (Ansiedlungsverein Gross-Berlin), the protection of green spaces (Berliner Waldschutzverein), and those who feared the loss of their town’s autonomy, all entered into the fray. The *Vossische Zeitung* in Berlin and other newspapers published numerous articles representing the different points of view.

A year after the establishment of the Zweckverband, the art and architecture critic Karl Scheffler commented on “The State [Prussia] and the

Fig. 15. Announcement of the next meeting, with ironic take-off on advertisement for a dance, in Für Gross-Berlin *brochure, No. 2.* CCCC

PRO DOMO / Der Propaganda-Ausschuß auf dem Wege zur Besserung!

(Siehe den Artikel: „Das verbotene Plakat“, Seite 76).

Der Propaganda-Ausschuß hat auf Anzeige eines Hausbesitzervereins sich vom Polizeipräsidenten überzeugen lassen, daß sein Plakat in der Tat aufreizend wirkt, und hat, um ein in keiner Weise aufreizendes Plakat zu finden, die Berliner Anschlagsäulen einem eifrigen Studium unterworfen. In der Hoffnung, in obigem

Plakat (rechts) ein jedes aufgereizte Hausbesitzergemüt beruhigendes Motiv entdeckt zu haben, erlaubt sich der Propaganda-Ausschuß als Resultat seiner Bemühungen die zu unterst abgebildete Fassung seines Plakates dem Hausbesitzerverein mit der ergebenen Bitte um Genehmigung zu unterbreiten.

Housing Policy of Berlin."[105] He considered that initially improvements had been expected from the Zweckverband, but it had soon become obvious

> that also the establishment of this Zweckverband is a political action by the State Government, and is directed to a certain extent against Berlin. Instead of expanding city ordinances that are long outdated for our metropolises, and to support our towns in all their endeavors for their own rehabilitation with laws and police ordinances, the State Government created with its Zweckverband only another means to increase its control over the authority of Berlin's self-government at the moment when it felt itself threatened. . . . We are observing . . . a power struggle between State and City, in which the City will certainly be defeated.

Salient topics for the Propaganda Ausschuss Für Gross-Berlin were *Kleinhaus kontra Mietskaserne* (single-family houses versus rental barracks), transportation, and open space. Alleviation of these problems as foremost for urban improvement was a pervasive and somewhat overly optimistic belief. Hegemann's conviction that housing was an integral and important element of city planning weighed heavily in these considerations. With the exception of land speculation, other economic factors such as employment and labor issues were less frequently considered. This is surprising in the case of Hegemann, whose university studies and dissertation had been in economics, and whose interests in housing had been stimulated by Lujo Brentano and by Charles Gide's courses in *économie sociale*.

Two events in Berlin epitomized the concerns of the Propaganda Ausschuss Für Gross-Berlin. One was the construction of rental barracks on the Tempelhofer Feld, which is illustrated in its unspoiled state on the cover of pamphlet #2 (see Fig. 13), and shown on the first page at an early phase of the construction of the barracks. The large area (145 hectares, 716 acres) was owned by the state and had been used as military drill ground. Plans for developing this unique piece of land as a combination of park and housing were proposed by Herman Jansen and Theodor Goecke. Despite opposition from the advocates of low-density residential settlements, the ministry of war, anxious to receive the maximum profit from its choice property, insisted on high-rise rental barracks for the Tempelhofer Feld. It became a much debated instance of land speculation—in this case not by private real estate interests but by the Prussian state, to the detriment of the citizens of Berlin.

Another case involved the destruction of a historic grove of chestnut trees, the *Kastanienwäldchen*, on the campus of the Friedrich Wilhelms-Universität. It was to be sacrificed for an expansion of the university promoted by the emperor and the municipality of Berlin. Two years earlier a book with the captivating title *Die Berliner Waldverwüstung* (The devastation/destruction of Berlin's forests) had alerted the public to the ongoing disappearance of forests.[106] The threat facing the cherished *Kastanienwäldchen* was protested by the Forest Preservation Association and by a group of university alumni who formed the Group of Twelve under the chairmanship of Otto March. Hegemann acted as its secretary and supported the campaign with lectures and publicity. The issue was closely related to his interest in parks and park systems as integral to urban planning. Two of his articles in the journal *Bauwelt* relate to the cause of the grove of chestnut trees, which Hegemann considered in the context of redesigning the entire university complex.[107] His recommendations for a comprehensive plan of the university comprising buildings and open spaces reflected his esteem for the American campus, although he did not refer to it outright. In the article on metropolitan *Parkpolitik*, Hegemann advocated park systems and discussed the international interplay of ideas regarding the design and usage of urban open space. He praised American accomplishments in New York and Boston, commenting on Charles Eliot, who carried the *Parkpolitik* for Boston to its fruition and had been inspired by Goethe's ideas and Count Pückler-Muskau's parks in Germany. Hegemann noted that the inner-city playgrounds of Chicago reflected an international "cross-fertilization" from England and the German *Volksparks*. While progress regarding *Parkpolitik* had taken place in Bremen and Hamburg, Berlin was still lagging far behind. Hegemann urged Berlin to respond to the examples shown in his *Parkbuch* and to heed the American maxim: "The boy without a playground is the father of the unemployed."

Hegemann's publications and drafts of letters inviting support for the Forest Preservation Association and the Group of Twelve in defense of the chestnut grove are emblematic of his commitment to civic causes, which always stressed visual appeal for the general public. One example was his proposed slide lecture on behalf of the campaign on *Moderne Parks und Spielplätze*, of which only the announcement exists.[108]

Berlin was teeming with civic movements to captivate Hegemann's energy and attention. He mentioned with pride his involvement in one of the early cooperative building associations in Britz, Berlin, known as Ideal.[109] As with the park question, it was intimately linked to his wider planning concerns. Hegemann was elected to the managing board of Ideal as one of three members, and although his name does not appear in the seventy-fifth anniversary publication, an article by Paul Westheim refers extensively to Hegemann's connection to "Ideal."[110] Under the provocative title "*Das Viermillionenchaos*" (The four-million chaos), Westheim is highly critical of Berlin's congestion, especially regarding the rental barracks.[111] He comments on the housing built by the Cooperative Building Association Ideal as one of the first to implement Eberstadt's suggestion of differentiating between the widths of streets serving homes and major traffic arteries in order to effect a substantial cost reduction.

Westheim cites cost analyses by René Kuczynski and Walter Lehweiss displayed at Berlin 1910. These were also published by Hegemann with an illustration showing layouts of the "old system" and the "new system," as well as statistics and a caption, "The new system battling with the rental barracks."[112]

From the late nineteenth century onward, housing policy became a paramount preoccupation in all industrialized countries and generated numerous organizations and an extensive body of literature. Concerns regarding congested housing and the "housing famine," or lack of affordable dwellings, were motivated not only by humanitarian considerations but by fears of revolutions and social upheavals. Since the mid-twentieth century, attention to housing, especially by architects, has diminished to a degree that makes it difficult to comprehend the passions seething in Berlin prior to World War I and in the 1920s. To be sure, the housing situation in the city was unusually dismal. The high value of land in the congested center was considered primarily responsible for the notorious *Mietskasernen*. Speculation was rampant, and not only by private individuals, as demonstrated by the case of the Tempelhofer Feld. The Propaganda Ausschuss, the local branch of the German Association for Housing Reform, and other groups were unsuccessful in persuading the Zweckverband to confine the construction of rental barracks to the center of Berlin and forbidding them in the adjacent towns to be annexed. An effort to implement zoning regulations failed to control the density of development as a means to promote the construction of single-family houses.

In Germany the movement for nonprofit housing began in the nineteenth century. Cooperative housing associations or *Baugenossenschaften* evolved as a feasible and flexible alternative. Financial support was provided by municipal loans, pension and insurance funds, banks, and charities.[113] The *Baugenossenschaft* Ideal in Rixdorf (later Neukölln or Britz) was initiated in 1907 by the local *Krankenkasse* (healthcare fund) to improve health in the community. The healthcare fund was not permitted to use its funds for housing nor to obtain low-interest loans from the state, the city, or banks. Against all odds it became possible for 173 members to purchase cooperatively a site for *Kleinwohnungen*, individual dwellings and low-rise apartment buildings. Ideal began to offer housing for ownership and for rent to its members and was immediately successful.[114]

In 1912 the journal *Der Städtebau* reported on the Garden Suburb Ideal. The article noted that Ideal had put into practice the planning concept of Eberstadt-Goecke and Kuczynski-Lehweiss of combining five-story buildings on the periphery with small one-family houses in the interior of the block.[115] Houses and apartments provided standards considered luxurious at the time for affordable rents and purchase costs. Garden areas, shops, communal laundries, central heating, and hot water installations justified the name "Ideal."

Proud of its initial achievement, the cooperative association sent out a questionnaire to specialists of renown regarding the plan for a proposed expansion.[116] The layout, by the architects Deute and Paul, was included with specific questions. All the replies were favorable. Among those responding to the questionnaire whose replies were cited were Theodor Goecke, Hermann Muthesius, Bruno Möhring, Rudolf Eberstadt, Hegemann, and a member of the surveyor's office of Rixdorf. The most extensive reply came from Hegemann, who was a member of the board for this successful housing development.

For Hegemann and others impressed by the results of Ideal, it was obvious that a housing policy had to be considered in conjunction with transportation and open space and be mandated by the Zweckverband as an integral part of the Greater Berlin master plan. Housing reform and urban planning needed to work with, as well as modify, existing conditions. On the other hand, zoning regulations were difficult to impose on built-up areas and were best applied to undeveloped land.

Hegemann did not cease to agitate on behalf of his convictions. Family lore has it that he was threatened with imprisonment for participating in street protests for better housing with the artist Käthe Kollwitz. Her commitment to social and political concerns was as vehement as Hegemann's. He expressed his convictions in publications, exhibitions, and actions, while Kollwitz imbued her artistic creations with her humanitarian and universal beliefs. Among the posters she contributed to these causes was one demonstrating her pacifism—the gripping "Never again war!" of 1924—a sentiment fervently avowed by Hegemann in the wake of World War I.

The concluding months of 1912–13 in Berlin, during which Hegemann was absorbed by dauntless activism, eerily foretold his valiant opposition to the rise of Nazism that led to his exile in 1933. Hegemann's eventful three years in the city came to an end when he accepted an invitation to lecture and consult in America. He departed in early March 1913 and embarked upon a new phase of his life and career. He would not return to Europe until 1921. In retrospect, his pre–World War I sojourn in Berlin had the quality of an interlude, before he was drawn once again across the Atlantic to partake of "the freedom of the great Anglo-Saxon Republicans from Milton to Walt Whitman, from which we can never learn enough."[117]

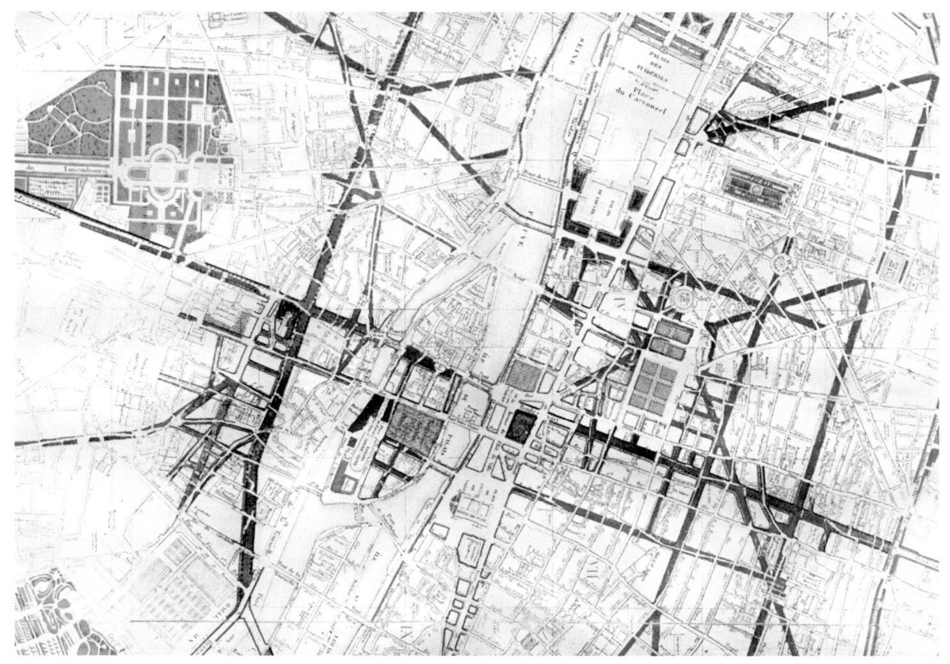

Detail of the Paris plan, from Hegemann's Der Städtebau, *Volume II (see page 65).*
CCCC

Cover of Für Gross-Berlin *brochure, No. 2 (see page 74).*
CCCC

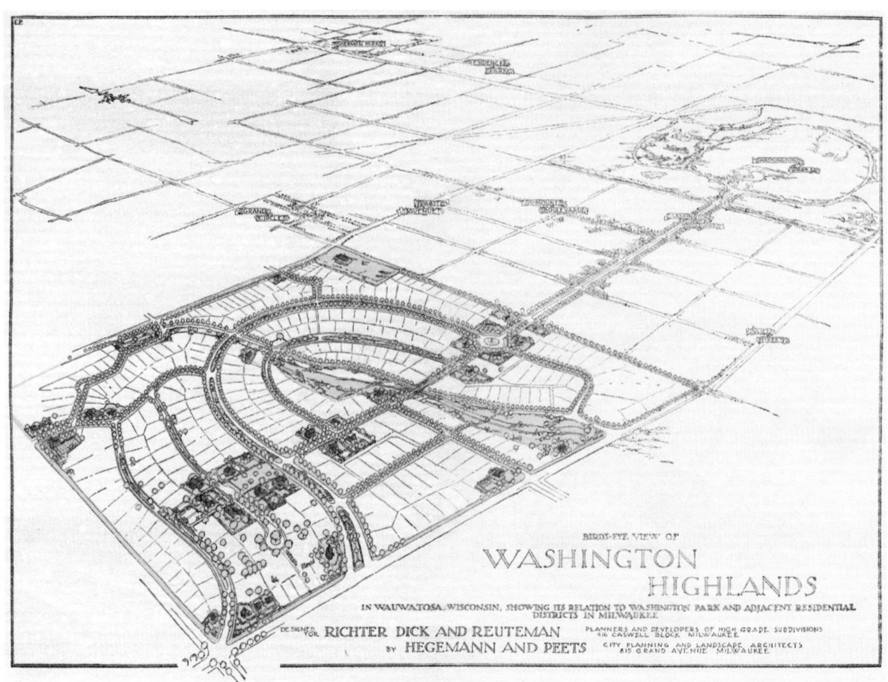

Plan of Washington Highlands and adjacent street grid of Milwaukee (see page 128). CCCC

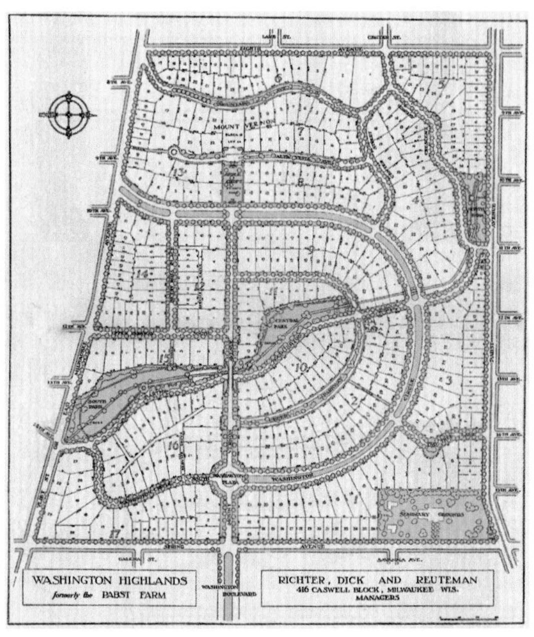

Cover of the promotional brochure for the residential development of Washington Highlands, Wisconsin, by Hegemann & Peets, 1919 (see page 126). CCCC

Plan of Washington Highlands indicating building lots, parks, and parkways (see page 129). CCCC

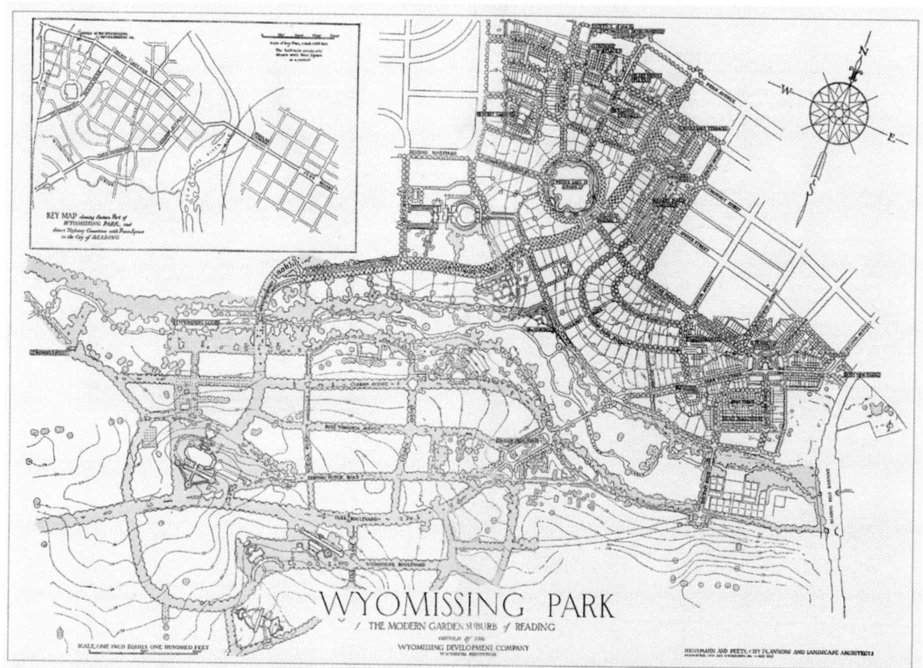

Plan of Wyomissing Park, by Hegemann & Peets (see page 136). CCCC

Business center, Wyomissing Park, 1919 (see page 138). CCCC

Das Brandenburger Thor.

The Brandenburger Gate and Schinkel's Gate houses (see page 282). CCCC

Brochure by the British Labor Party, 1934 (see page 347). CCCC

3. New Worlds

The Lecture Tour of 1913

Hegemann returned to America after a three-year absence and was received as an international authority, having established a reputation from organizing two major city planning exhibitions and fostering international contacts with urbanists. His youth still hampered this recognition in Europe, but in the New World his youthful vitality and innovative outlook were welcomed. America offered him the opportunity and proper environment to refine his ideas and pursue his quest for the pragmatic ideal in city planning. His lecture tour turned into a significant phase of his exploration of urban possibilities adapted to a range of geographic and cultural situations.[1]

The invitation to lecture and consult on city planning in America had undeniable allure, while Hegemann's social actions in Berlin had become strained. The proposition was organized by Frederic C. Howe, managing director of The People's Institute in New York. According to the introduction to Hegemann's posthumous *City Planning: Housing*, Howe asked the mayors of German cities whom they suggested for informing on German planning in the United States.[2] Conceivably Hegemann's American acquaintances, among them Frederick Law Olmsted Jr. and Edward T. Devine, might have also recommended him.

Howe described The People's Institute as "a kind of popular university, which conducted a popular forum at Cooper Union and carried on various educational activities."[3] The institute evolved into a center for lectures and debates on socialism and feminist issues and welcomed speakers from abroad to its platform. Hegemann's commitment to introducing the general public to urban concerns and his social activism made him an ideal lecture candidate. The geographic distance made it impractical to invite

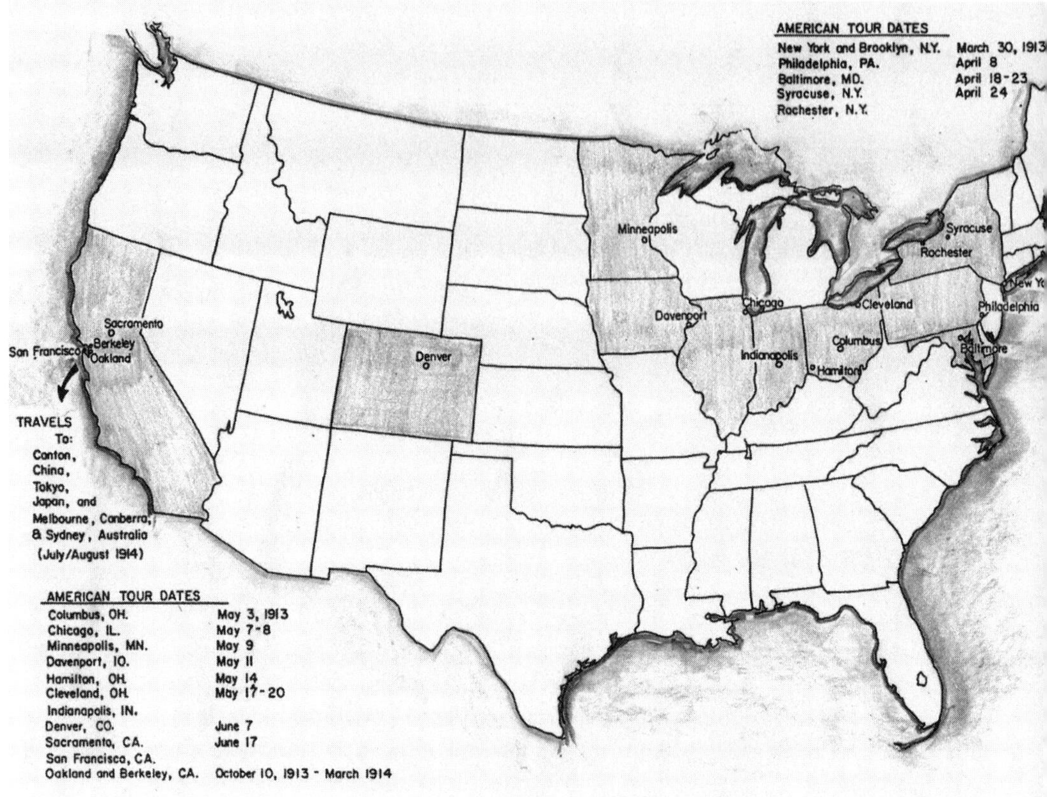

Fig. 16. Map of the United States indicating locations where Hegemann lectured and consulted in 1913. Map by Jeannette Rausch. CCCC

Hegemann for only one or two lectures; instead, Howe arranged an itinerary that included visits to over thirty cities across America.

Publicity was set in motion several months prior to Hegemann's arrival. On its letterhead The People's Institute sent out an "Important Announcement to Cities Engaged in Town Planning Projects, the Laying out of Suburbs or Civic Centers, the Grouping of Public Buildings, the Planning of Docks, Harbors or Other Public Undertakings."[4] The communiqué explained that:

> the motive of the Institute in bringing Dr. Hegemann to America is to offer to our cities the experience of Europe in the solution of big problems of city building that are now actively engaging the attention of most of the larger cities of this country. . . . Dr. Hegemann will be available for expert work or lectures for from three to six months after January 1st, 1913, at the rate of $100 a day, $300 a week and $50 a day thereafter, and local expenses.

One hundred dollars in 1913 was the equivalent of $1,912 in 2004, a substantial fee for a consultant. The fact that over thirty cities requested Hegemann's services attests to a keen interest in urban improvement and an eagerness for obtaining expertise from abroad (Fig. 16).

Throughout his career, Hegemann struggled with the difficulty of reconciling his progressive theoretical approach with his aesthetic interests, sense of history, and cognizance of the symbolic value of civic centers and monuments. He was mindful that this ambivalence was shared by a number of those concerned with the urban environment in the United States, where he was to appear as "the expert." The City Beautiful movement had created a heightened awareness of civic improvement and public art in America, where admiration of European historic ensembles and picturesque townscapes prevailed and was tinged by envy. However, this preoccupation with aesthetics was beginning to wane, and Americans were increasingly turning to Europe, and especially to Germany, to study models for municipal legislation, zoning, and social reform. A young generation of progressive urbanists and political scientists was advancing new approaches. The status of the planning profession was stimulated by the favorable recognition American accomplishments had received in Berlin, Düsseldorf, and London.

In order to prepare his German friend for the situation awaiting him, Howe composed a list of sixteen "Suggestions" regarding "what the various organizations before which you are to speak, . . . want to hear."[5] The list proceeds from the general to the specific, with an initial admonition that "old plans were made by kings and rulers interested in embellishing their cities and without social vision." Howe considered building regulations and zoning to be of special interest in America. The last of the suggested topics was one Hegemann had recently emphasized in Europe: what the two countries could learn from each other. Both Howe and Hegemann concurred in stressing the "experience" rather than the "example" of Europe and the benefits of a dialogue across the Atlantic.

Hegemann apparently prepared a fifteen-page manuscript as his "basic" lecture in anticipation of the trip.[6] This may have triggered Howe's "Suggestions," because Hegemann's outline primarily discusses European urban history and comments only in passing on his host country, bluntly urging it not to repeat the blunders that contemporary planners in Germany had recognized and learned to avoid. He emphasized that the "artistic question" ought to be addressed within the context of a comprehensive plan. He also singled out the mistakes resulting from haphazard development and concluded with three specified principles of modern city planning: "Transportation for goods and persons" connecting outlying residential areas with the central business district; "the distribution and reservation of open spaces"; and a street system that differentiated between major traffic arteries and "cozy little streets and paths" in the suburbs. These three points surfaced in the discussions in every city he visited on his tour.

Hegemann's article, "European City Plans and Their Value to the American City-Planner" responds to Howe's "Suggestions."[7] Published in the journal *Landscape Architecture*, the article was based on Hegemann's observations during his journey across the United States and his interaction with a range of specialists and the general public. A *New York Times* review by James Russell Lowell mentioned Hegemann's extensive study of American cities and noted that the article summarized his observations.[8]

In his essay, Hegemann commented on the admiring attitude of American travelers visiting European cities and called attention to the "inhuman conditions of overcrowding" prevailing in these major "model cities." Such conditions could only be remedied at enormous expense and effort. He considered that from past experience "two fundamental facts . . . for the future development of any modern city can be learned." First is that a lack of planning is "very detrimental to the growth of cities." Second is Hegemann's strong belief in the evolving nature of the city: "Since the needs and ideals of modern city-building differ fundamentally from the ideals of past centuries, even the best plans made for great cities in the past can be adapted to the growth of modern cities only after very material changes." The expense of clearing congested areas in the city center presented acute problems in European cities ringed by obsolete fortifications. However, American cities such as Boston and New York were also at a disadvantage because of the cost of widening streets. Congested housing, a lack of open space, and other "calamities" in cities such as Berlin resulted from the absence of comprehensive planning. This was anticipated by concerned individuals in the nineteenth century, yet advice went unheeded or was applied only to outward appearances devoting "exaggerated importance" to "artistic aspects." Hegemann, elaborating this point, confronted the advocates of the City Beautiful movement, who tended to idealize the historic cities of Europe for their "artistic values . . . holding them up for imitation in modern cities."

Hegemann admired the English and American system of decentralization made possible by improved transportation to residential developments with small houses. He contrasted the benefits of home ownership with the dismal conditions in the tenements, which tended to breed social unrest and "revolutionary attitudes."

Answering the rhetorical question of what the American city looked like to a traveler, Hegemann listed its built components, which, "in comfort, and often in beauty, very favorably compared with similar buildings erected during the last generation in European cities of similar size." Lacking regulations restricting the height of buildings, American business districts had a "disorderly appearance. [However,] the alternating sky-line of two-story and twenty-story buildings, commonly found in American cities, can work out very surprising effects in architectural beauty; but, since practically no thought is given to these effects, they are only accidental. . . ." He was impressed by the "high-class" residential districts, or suburbs, and even more so by the "miles and miles with modest, but sometimes quite charming little houses, surrounded, or half-surrounded with little gardens along cheaply paved [or un-paved] streets. Often playgrounds, and sometimes splendid great parks, can be found in the neighborhood."

According to Hegemann, "the value of European city plans rests mainly on the esthetic inheritance from an older time." Reiterating Camillo Sitte, Hegemann noted that these towns manifested a "marvelous 'feel of the land,' the intimate and sympathetic adjustment of the lines and grades of streets, as well as the character and the quality of buildings, to the beauties of natural contours. . . ." To introduce these qualities in modern cities, particularly those in America, would amount to only one aspect of city planning and "hardly the most important one." For achieving the goal of modern city planning to comprise all practical, technical, and aesthetic elements, it was necessary for civic bodies and local organizations to rise to an informed level for a meaningful discussion of these issues.

Hegemann enumerated all "utilitarian objects" to be considered essential for a new "civic art" and concluded that: "City-planning is the science of investigating and achieving these results. Extraordinary efforts and quite new departures must be made in order to develop a new type of city, free from the old plagues."

Hegemann's lecture circuit began in late March 1913 at the University Club in Brooklyn. The audience included city officials and members of the Brooklyn Committee on City Plan [*sic*].[9] Hegemann spoke on the similarities between Brooklyn and Berlin, drawing on the draft manuscript he had written earlier. He also mentioned that leading city planners in Germany had shown interest in American accomplishments when he had returned to his country in 1909. This was manifested in the attention paid to American examples in the exhibitions, including the traveling show on parks and Hegemann's publications and lectures.

German architects and the general public had focused increasingly on the skyscraper in American cities. Hegemann's presence in the country that had invented this building type enhanced it as a major topic for him. During the three years between his return from Boston and his departure for the lecture tour, Hegemann was drawn into the debate regarding the appropriateness of high-rise "office towers" for Berlin. A survey in the newspaper *Berliner Morgenpost*, addressing the possibility of "*Berlins dritte Dimension*" (Berlin's third dimension), was initiated by Bruno Möhring.[10] Replies, in addition to Möhring's, came from Peter Behrens, Berhard Dernburg, and Hegemann. All four referred to their firsthand impressions of the American "city" and favored a comparable business center with skyscrapers for Berlin. In his letter, Hegemann noted that he had worked in skyscrapers, and deduced certain requirements for high-rise buildings in the center of cities. In particular, these pertained to their location in the urban plan, the width of the surrounding streets, the setbacks of upper floors to allow for light and air, technical and hygienic considerations, and their impact on traffic. Only weeks before his departure for America, Hegemann published a longer response to the *Morgenpost* inquiry, "*Soll Berlin Wolkenkratzer bauen*?" (Should Berlin build skyscrapers?). His article showed a view of New York with the caption, "Skyscrapers as a preventive to the threat of business expansion into quiet residential streets."[11] Disapprovingly he added that in New York this good idea had been spoiled by the haphazard concentration of skyscrapers that obstructed light and air, the iconic aims of modernism. Additional illustrations show other high-rise buildings in New York, including the Woolworth Building, and Madison Square Garden. Hegemann commented on American skyscrapers as "office-towns built into the air" and megastructures that required special building and tax regulations, considerations that should be heeded in the event that such buildings should be realized in Berlin.

During his previous stays in Philadelphia and Boston, Hegemann had paid little attention to the skyscraper as an innovative building type. His awareness of the pros and cons of high-rise towers increased while he became engrossed in the Greater Berlin debates. Cognizant of his American experience, German urbanists and architects expected knowledgeable opinions from him, which he was eager to provide. Hegemann's lecture tour intensified his preoccupation with the skyscraper and its relationship to the city plan. It evolved into a major theme in his talks in the United States, and continued when he eventually returned to Germany in 1922 and became "infected" by the *Hochhausfieber* (skyscraper fever), a mania raging at the time.

Within the context of Hegemann's urban concepts, the skyscraper debate is emblematic of the way he transferred ideas and impressions back and forth across the Atlantic. In Germany where the "tower per se" or singular high-rise building was favored, he saw the advantage of an American "city" center for Berlin, albeit with certain restrictions. On the other side of the Atlantic, he recommended single skyscrapers, providing monumental focal points in the urban fabric.

Arriving in the country that prided itself on having invented the skyscraper, Hegemann did not shy away from commenting on this American icon in Brooklyn, and, a few days later, at the City Club of Manhattan. The New York event was convened by borough president George McAneny, who announced the formation of a Special Legislative Commision on "city planning and the city beautiful," declaring that "New York has not only lagged behind many foreign cities, but even behind American cities as to correct city planning."[12] The commission was to work with the Board of Estimate on a wide range of improvements and on "formulating a code for the regulation of the size and height of buildings." President McAneny made the startling prediction that "there would be no more skyscrapers built in this city."

An audience of over 200 attended the meeting, and the main speaker was Werner Hegemann, identified as "an expert on improving conditions in German cities." According to one newspaper report, Hegemann "shattered several cherished American idols" by illustrating the congested and chaotic conditions of lower Manhattan with "stereopticon views."[13] He criticized "low buildings sandwiched in alongside of huge sky-scrapers, making a weird, higgledy-piggledy effect." Tempering this opinion, Hegemann said he did not consider the skyscraper per se to be undesirable and praised the Metropolitan Life Insurance Building, which fronted on a park. He questioned the placement of Manhattan's major railroad terminals, Pennsylvania and Grand Central stations, located in the center of the city with railroad lines "stopping dead" without connections between the stations.

A few days after the event the *New York Times* published an extensive essay by Edward Marshall on Hegemann's lecture.[14] The long headline reads, "Vaster Skyscrapers Inevitable, Says German Expert; Dr. Werner Hegemann, one of the world's greatest authors on city planning, says our present high buildings mean intolerable congestion and will be succeeded by structures ten times as great but more widely separated—Faults of subways pointed out." The extensive quotations from Hegemann's text are interspersed with Marshall's comments and questions he directed to Hegemann. Dispelling impressions that he disapproved of skyscrapers or high-rise buildings, Hegemann replied to the reporter's questions, saying that "skyscrapers are things of beauty, marvels, startling triumphs of both architects and engineers, but that we [the Americans] crowd them far too closely, to the detriment of both their usefulness and beauty, to the peril of public health, to the benefit of none but land owners." Hegemann's observations of 1913 are uncannily prescient of Le Corbusier's visionary projects of the 1920s.

Marshall's article in the *Times* represents a remarkable summary of Hegemann's major ideas on the city and its buildings, actually surpassing his essay in the journal *Landscape Architecture*. Marshall considered Hegemann's opinions to be especially illuminating because, contrary to other foreign visitors, he was well acquainted with the country from his previous stays. Despite his obvious knowledge, he is described as "a very modest man, supremely anxious not to give offense." Hegemann found many comparable elements in American and European cities: they were seldom planned and their growth rate was similar. American cities had the advantages of being self-governed and located in a young country that offered opportunities to build new cities and welcomed the lessons that could be learned from their European counterparts. Hegemann urged that attention be paid to "workingmen's dwellings," not to be considered "mere incidents in city planning," but a principal element of every urban improvement scheme. He continued on this topic: "It should not be understood that the term 'housing' means merely providing shelter, preferably tight, against the weather. It means much more than that. It means not only the shelter of the population in the right sort of buildings, but the right location of those buildings. . . . 'Housing' includes the open space as well as the built area—the street before the house, the yard or garden at its back . . . and playgrounds for the little ones . . . ." Hegemann noted that inner-city parks were recognized in America as "one of the best weapons to kill the slums" and praised the creation of park systems even if they caused hardships to property owners.

Toward the conclusion of his statements, Hegemann reiterated that he was not a "foe of skyscrapers" and noted that when their introduction to Germany was protested as "an American invention," he had raised his voice in their favor. However, "these enormous . . . incredible towers" should not be "planted thick as grass upon the surface of your island [Manhattan]." As an alternative he recommended, "your suburbs are your only hope, and your suburbs only can be reached through much improved transportation facilities."

In New York Hegemann focused on skyscrapers, and they turned into a prevailing preoccupation for him, accompanying him on his travels in the United States and back to Europe. At the next stops in his journey, Philadelphia and Baltimore, he considered the placement of high-rise buildings in the context of another unique aspect of American cities: the grid plan.

In April 1913 Hegemann spent ten days in Philadelphia, which evoked memories of his previous stays in the city and Simon N. Patten's teachings. He entered debates on current issues on the municipal agenda, including rapid transit, which he emphatically linked to low-cost housing. The *Philadelphia Public Ledger* reported that he sided with elevated trains and against subways, justifying his choice as more economical. Perhaps in jest he commented, "We must break away from the old superstition that a railroad, because it was unknown to the Greeks, is necessarily an ugly thing. Everything that spreads health and happiness can be made beautiful, and everything ought to be beautiful in the country of Walt Whitman."[15] Hegemann's suggestions for the beautification of blocks of small houses were presented in diagrams drawn for the *Public Ledger*. The "old way" showed two wide streets with a rigid alignment of houses. The "new" layout suggested by Hegemann had narrow streets and houses with alternating setbacks. He also urged districting that would protect residential developments from industrial and commercial buildings.

Another concern at the time of Hegemann's visit to Philadelphia was the Fairmont Parkway (now Benjamin Franklin Parkway), which had gone through various proposals. It exemplified the difficulties caused by inserting radial boulevards into grid plans (Fig. 17). Hegemann ruffled feathers by declaring the project an unnecessary beautification undertaken while efforts toward improving housing conditions were more important. He spoke from firsthand experience, because only five years earlier, in 1908, he had worked as housing inspector in Philadelphia. Hegemann's con-

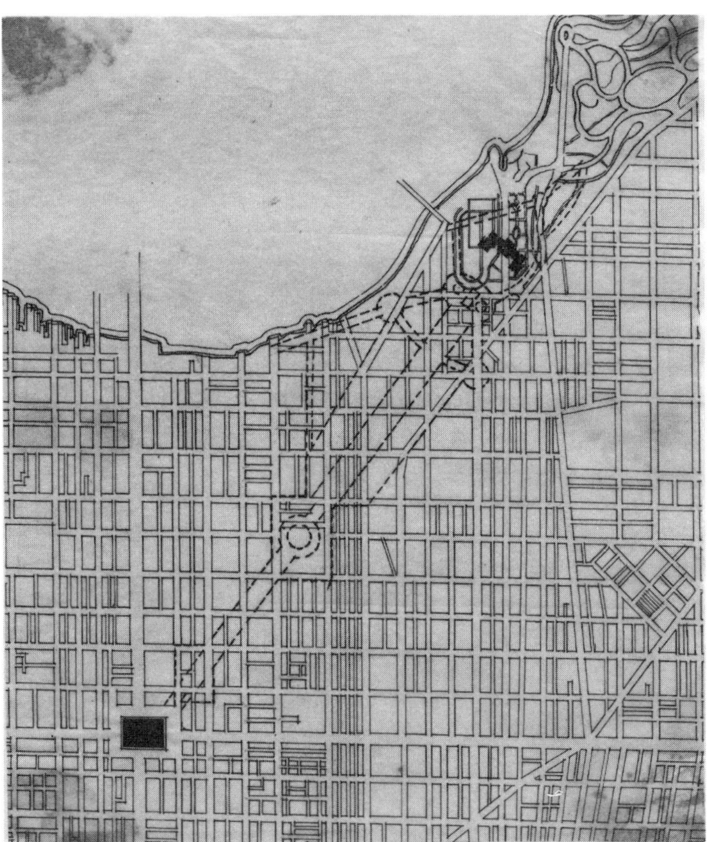

Fig. 17. Plan of Philadelphia, showing projected Fairmount Parkway. CCCC

frontational remarks in lectures and interviews incited stern replies, extensively reported in the newspapers in articles with provocative titles, such as "Opposes Parkway and Broad St. Tube," and "Parkway a 'Useless Luxury' Hegemann tells City Club." A letter by the local planner B. Antrim Haldeman to John Nolen in Cambridge is cautious and not entirely complimentary to the German expert: "his theories [are] perfectly sound, but [they] cannot be worked out in the logical manner he advocates in this country, where we often have to compromise. . . . He places practically every problem of urban improvement subordinate to that of properly providing for the homes and health of the people and is at his best on that subject, which is, of course, one of the vital issues of our modern theories of town planning."[16] Haldeman did, however, praise Hegemann for courageously going after "the root of most of our troubles in this country, the unnecessary inflation of land values."

New York and Philadelphia were familiar to Hegemann. The next leg of his journey took him to new places, the first of which was Baltimore.

Upon arrival he visited Mayor James Harry Preston, saying that he would take a few days to study the city before commenting on the various issues under consideration.[17] His most acceptable (tactful) recommendation addressed the civic center for Baltimore. He is quoted as saying: "The finest city center . . . would be . . . a fine American skyscraper as a City Hall, high up at the top of Light Street, making the fine plaza still more beautiful by a fine tower ruling the whole city, a good American skyscraper and hard-headed business building surrounded by plenty of light and air and forgetting altogether those academic imitations of old European Renaissance." Historic Mount Vernon Place and the residential Roland Park met with Hegemann's unreserved enthusiasm, not only for their aesthetic appeal but also for the regulations that preserved their unique character. He also spent time inspecting more modest residential sections in East Baltimore and Patterson Park.

Hegemann considered the lack of a long-range master plan the cause of Baltimore's present "civic imperfections" (Fig. 18). In a two-page fragment of a draft for public discussion, he asserted that the city would come to regret having spent $2 million to build retaining walls along the Fall River.[18] The city was faced with having to spend an equal amount for a comprehensive improvement of the Fallsway to accommodate railroad lines and subways. Hegemann stated stated that Baltimore was "legally

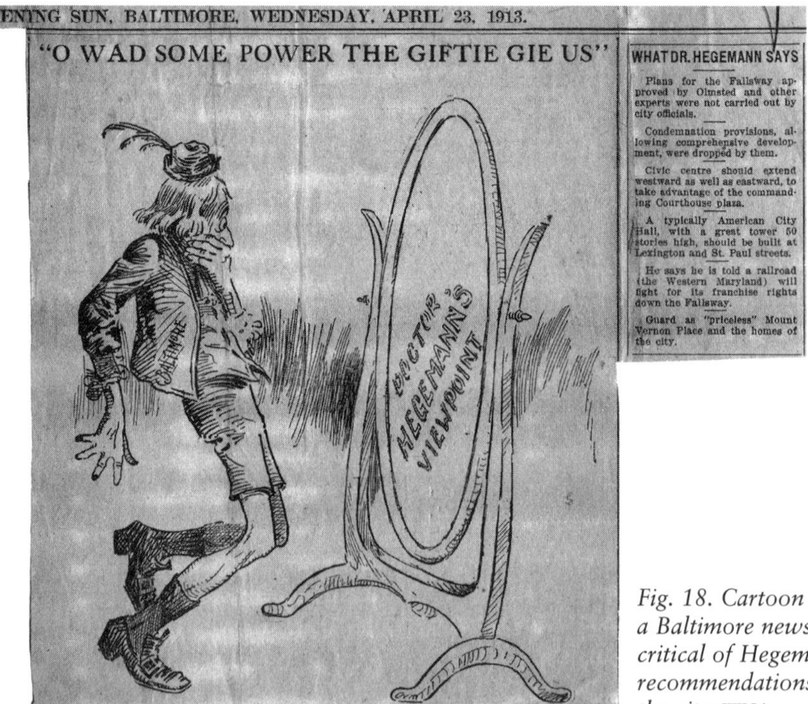
ENING SUN, BALTIMORE, WEDNESDAY, APRIL 23, 1913.

"O WAD SOME POWER THE GIFTIE GIE US"

WHAT DR. HEGEMANN SAYS

Plans for the Fallsway approved by Olmsted and other experts were not carried out by city officials.

Condemnation provisions, allowing comprehensive development, were dropped by them.

Civic centre should extend westward as well as eastward, to take advantage of the commanding Courthouse plaza.

A typically American City Hall, with a great tower 50 stories high, should be built at Lexington and St. Paul streets.

He says he is told a railroad (the Western Maryland) will fight for its franchise rights down the Fallsway.

Guard as "priceless" Mount Vernon Place and the homes of the city.

Fig. 18. Cartoon from a Baltimore newspaper critical of Hegemann's recommendations for the city. WHA ruled by infants," and recommended comprehensive planning for residential developments and carrying out Olmsted's 1904 open-space plan, which projected a park along Jones Falls.

It is no surprise that Hegemann's bluntness was resented by Mayor Preston and Chief Engineer Hendrick, who scolded him in a spirited reply for "presuming to discuss Baltimore's problems with which he was practically unfamiliar." They went on to berate the expert from Berlin, who should have known that the situation of two railroad companies claiming the Fallsway as their turf, combined with the rights of adjacent property owners, was enormously complex and could not be resolved quickly or easily. He was reminded that America was a republic and not an empire.

On the eve of his departure from Baltimore, Hegemann explained his position in a newspaper interview. He asserted that he had been correct in his criticism, which was based on facts. He voiced regret that the comprehensive plan for the Fallsway by the well-known urbanists Olmsted, Carrère, Brunner, and others was not followed in its entirety because the city shied away from the required property condemnations. Hegemann concluded by affirming that he had investigated all matters before voicing his opinions."I did not come here and hurry around the city and then criticize. I pointed out things that you must face." He promised to return to Baltimore, calling it "a beautiful place."

It is notable that his lecture itinerary took him beyond the major American metropolises to medium-sized cities and small towns previously unknown to him, and which rarely attracted European architects. Hegemann's trajectory was unique in providing him with an overview of small-town American life, particularly in the Midwest. With few exceptions the grid plan was prevalent in cities and towns. He deemed the rational and economic advantages of this layout convincing, but found its disadvantages troubling and in need of creative solutions. Especially problematic were the lack of responsiveness to topographical features and the inherent faceless neutrality of the checkerboard layout. Equally troublesome, in Hegemann's opinion, was the grid plan's resistance to interventions in the form of radial traffic arteries and the placement of civic centers, which would provide an urban distinctiveness and sense of place. The projected Fairmont Parkway in Philadelphia, connecting the City Hall with the Art Museum, was a conspicuous example of these difficulties which Hegemann encountered numerous times. His major book, authored with Elbert Peets, *The American Vitruvius: An Architects' Handbook of Civic Art* (1922), reflects these observations and addresses historical and recent solutions to interventions within a grid-plan context.

It might have been expeditious if the consultant Hegemann had evoked European precedents. However, he persisted in exploring local conditions and discussing the issues at hand with municipal authorities and concerned citizens. There are echoes of Patrick Geddes's "survey-before-plan" recommendation in Hegemann's methodology. In his lectures, which he illustrated with slides, some from his own photographs taken locally, he shared his informed enthusiasm for America with a diverse audience. This approach gained in assurance as he left the East Coast and moved further inland.

From Baltimore, Hegemann proceeded by way of Wilmington, Delaware, to Syracuse and Rochester in New York State. The Syracuse newspapers announced a week's visit by one of the "foremost authorities in the world on city planning and city beautification," under the auspices of the local Chamber of Commerce city planning committee. After a "thorough study of all conditions," the German expert was scheduled to report on several occasions, ending with "a mass meeting free to all [with] citizens in general cordially invited to attend."

In response to these expectations, Hegemann summarized his observations in a lengthy and detailed essay, "The City Planning Situation of Syracuse," and in an additional brief report.[19] Although Hegemann refers to situations in Syracuse, drawing comparisons to other cities in America and Europe, these documents provide insights to his basic city planning concepts. At this early stage of his journey in America, ideas he had brought from the other side of the Atlantic were validated and modified in response to distinctive urban features.

According to Hegemann, the growth pattern between major cities and medium-sized towns—such as Syracuse—saved the latter from serious mistakes. In the nineteenth century sudden growth primarily affected the larger cities, producing crowded conditions and haphazard expansion. Smaller cities had time to reflect on these flaws and plan wisely "along decent and efficient lines." Syracuse was an example that showed "an admirable start toward good city planning." Comparison with cities such as Chicago and Philadelphia highlighted the advantages that Syracuse enjoyed. The growth of those big cities was so sudden that it wiped out nearly all the connections between the open country and the city. Philadelphia, which he had recently visited, was now struggling to create a single radial connection between the heart of the city and the surrounding countryside, while Syracuse had been provided by its founders with "a nearly complete system of radial streets," planted with trees, and over time converted them into boulevards. Hegemann recommended that Syracuse should develop its radial arteries for rapid transit in order to relieve the increasing congestion in its business and residential districts. This would require relocating the elegant central residences to peaceful, narrow streets in residential neighborhoods. He warned against the circular boulevards that had replaced the obsolete fortifications of European cities, emphasizing that modern cities required radial arteries leading from the center to suburbs on the periphery.

In the longer document "City Planning Situation of Syracuse," Hegemann explained that the brevity of his stay in the city prevented him from producing a thorough survey, and he gratefully acknowledged the assistance of the City Planning Committee for providing him with information. His report is impressive and thorough, while tactfully balancing positive and critical comments. Hegemann considered the most important problem facing the city to be transportation, "especially the steam railroad and water transportation, and the connections for the industries that depend on them." In Syracuse the railroad tracks ran along the level of the main street, with trains noisily blocking crossings and ringing their warning bells. Others ran next to side streets and along the canal, requiring bridges to be raised. As was the case in many towns, a conflict existed between the demands of the railroad companies, the public interest, and efficient urban planning. Hegemann recognized the difficulties entailed in a comprehensive rearrangement of the railroads that provided links to the barge harbor and future industries on the lake front. He recommended the development of workers' housing and open space in close proximity to the industries. The use of the canal for water transportation, its preservation for pleasure, or its drainage for sunken tracks was another major decision to be considered within a comprehensive transportation network and long-range urban plan. As in Philadelphia, Hegemann favored elevated trains.

The city's business district was already showing some signs of crowding, and the hotel where Hegemann was lodged was "badly lighted." He warned of conditions resembling those in New York. However, he commented that the skyscraper was "more and more recognized as being able to produce architectural effects of the highest value by producing a fascinating skyline. The skyscraper by itself, therefore, if treated properly can be a good thing, provided it is surrounded by plenty of light and air." He mentioned that building regulations addressing this matter were presently considered. It would be desirable and bring "most satisfactory results if real estate owners could more and more be induced to get their plans for new office buildings (or apartment and tenement houses) made in reference not only to the single lot but to the entire city block even if owned by different owners," contributing to a comprehensive plan. Hegemann envisioned tall buildings "securing maximum results of light, air and truly rentable floorspace," prescient of Le Corbusier's "towers in the park."

The subject of housing was also discussed as part of Syracuse's development. It was Hegemann's persistent belief that housing was an integral element of city planning, and that it should never be considered in isolation. On the economic side, Hegemann was certain that real estate speculators were holding back rapid transit in order to increase land values in the central areas. In continental Europe the overcrowding in such areas was hidden behind "spectacular facades," driving costs up even further. Hegemann warned that "it is a serious mistake made in many American cities to believe it desirable to imitate this kind of artistic effect. The modern city has to work out its own city planning art, developing a new artistic way of setting detached houses, and appreciate the value of green and open spaces in the city plan, not only as an ornament, but as a very important factor in every city planning scheme." Smaller towns might become so attractive that the inhabitants of big cities would prefer to move to them.

In towns such as Syracuse, benefits could be achieved by changing the layout of streets and the primary methods of transportation without increasing the cost for property owners. Hegemann recommended different widths for streets; wide streets in residential neighborhoods were wasteful and undesirable, interfering with their attractiveness. On the other hand, major arteries should have the width to accommodate the heavy traffic of automobiles and tramways. Rapid transit by elevated railroads and streetcars would enhance the possibilities for decentralization and relieve congestion. Converting the diagonal boulevards in Syracuse to traffic arteries might jeopardize their scenic beauty and would reinforce the urgency of creating a park system. Hegemann also stressed the need for playgrounds, noting that several schools in Syracuse did not have any.

From Rochester, New York, Hegemann proceeded to Columbus, Ohio, where he suggested that the flood control work should include scenic improvements and parks.[20] The next stop on his itinerary was Chicago for the the Fifth National Conference on City Planning, which ran May 5–7, 1913. "The presence of our distinguished German guest," was noted by one of the speakers.[21] The occasion provided Hegemann the opportunity to renew contacts with leading American urbanists whom he had met previously in 1909, among them Frederick Law Olmsted Jr., John Nolen, and Flavel Shurtleff from Boston, Edward M. Bassett from New York, and George B. Ford. Also present was Walter Burley Griffin, who had recently won the Canberra competition. In the intervening four years Hegemann's professional prestige had increased and he was now received as a "distinguished" city planner among equals. A prior announcement of the conference mentioned that it would be attended by "unquestioned leaders of city planning in America and . . . foreigners as well . . . among the latter . . . will be Edward G. Culpin, editor of 'Garden Cities and Town Planning,' London, and Werner Hegemann, of Germany." The title of Hegemann's talk is given as "German Methods of Paying for Improvements Out of Excess Land Purchases."[22] The event was emblematic of the remarkable and productive interchange that shaped emerging urbanism, soon curtailed by the outbreak of World War I.

Although Hegemann participated in the conference, he is noted to have been prevented by illness from preparing his contribution for publication in the *Proceedings*.[23] Some of his comments were reported in the Chicago newspapers, which gave extensive coverage to the National Conference on City Planning. The accounts of Hegemann's statements do not conform with the title of his announced lecture and were probably based on interviews.[24] In a critical vein, he considered it wrong for

American city planners to admire Berlin and Paris as examples, because both cities had failed to take transportation into account, which had produced crowded conditions in their centers. According to Hegemann, the Chicago Plan had mistakenly emulated Paris, while London would be a more appropriate model for "building outward from the center" to provide the benefits of living in the countryside.

Interviews with Edward M. Bassett speaking on transportation in New York and with Hegemann contain some of the latter's general considerations. He admired the efficient efforts by the Chicago Plan Commission to promote the ideas of good city planning, which had been done in Germany, attempting "to bring a better knowledge of this important matter to our people." He observed, "many times I have been told by Americans that good city planning can be performed more easily in Germany because Germany is supposed to benefit from a paternal form of government. I believe the opposite is true. Every man who has worked in practical city planning knows that no lasting reform can be pushed through without educating people up to it." For following this approach, democratic America was better prepared to obtain results. He praised the open-mindedness of the Chicago Plan Commission, which had confirmed his "belief that the international exchange of ideas is highly desirable," stating that "I am in America in order to learn new ideas for my work." Hegemann considered that new concepts resulting from the Greater Berlin competition, particularly with regard to transportation, might benefit Chicago and other American cities. The competition had shown the importance of routing trains through Berlin from north to south and east to west, rather than having them come to dead ends in the city. If transportation had not previously been a serious concern for German city planners, they came to realize that it was a basic element, and that transportation experts should be consulted from the very beginning of any comprehensive planning project.

Chicago represented a highlight in Hegemann's trajectory above and beyond the City Planning Conference at which he relished the congenial spirit and interchange with American urbanists. He absorbed ideas from the presentations, particularly when they substantiated his own. For example, Frederick Law Olmsted Jr. affirmed in his inaugural address that the method of proceeding on a city plan demanded three steps, notably, "the winning of public support; second, the planning itself; and, third, the translation of plans into facts." The need for public support was a requisite Hegemann had learned from the *Boston 1915* movement and brought to Berlin. Now he heard it singled out by Olmsted and Charles H. Wacker, chairman of the Chicago Plan Commission, in his lecture on "Gaining Public Support for the City Planning Movement."[25] Wacker presented a detailed narrative of the complex steps and deliberations leading to the Chicago Plan of 1909. Drawing on this experience, he considered "three major elements in successful city planning: . . . the conception, the creation and the promotion of the city plan." Wacker recommended the enthusiastic devotion to an ideal but acknowledged that "Chicago cannot provide . . . any formula for stirring the civic impulse of the people of American cities." Hegemann was well acquainted with the Chicago Plan, having obtained photographs and, later, Jules Guérin's original drawings for the exhibitions of 1910 in Berlin and Düsseldorf. Additionally, Hegemann had published a thorough and copiously illustrated study of Burnham & Bennett's plan and its history.[26]

George B. Ford's lecture on "The City Scientific" called for teamwork by specialists in landscape architecture, housing, recreation, and transit to secure comprehensive results. He was well aware that his approach would not be well received in the city that had set the "City Beautiful" movement on the map with the World's Columbian Exposition (1893), and had gained renown as the "White City." To assuage sentiments, Ford reassured his colleagues "that in emphasizing the scientific side of city planning I do not wish to administer a snub to the aesthetic side. Both phases are necessary to the complete city."

Ancillary to Hegemann's participation at the conference were experiences in Chicago that tied into his preexisting interests, particularly parks and playgrounds. He had published on American parks in *Ein Parkbuch*, including a well-informed section on Chicago.[27] He greatly admired the city's unique contribution to urban open space, especially the playgrounds and the water-parks, projected by Burnham and Bennett. He vividly described Burnham and Bennett's design and contribution to the well-being of the people based on his acqaintance with them from a brief visit in 1909. During this visit, he photographed them and stayed at Hull House, a center of progressive reform founded by Jane Addams (1860–1935), who was the leading promoter of the playground movement.[28]

Small playgrounds were established in the inner city of Boston and Chicago as early as 1887, and recognizing the need for related activities during inclement weather, Jane Addams proposed building fieldhouses within playgrounds, which had begun to include recreational elements. Similarly Hegemann promoted "*Nutzparks*" for Berlin, parks for active recreation and sport that were modeled on those in Chicago, and supported efforts along these lines by the landscape architect Leberecht Migge. Hegemann urged that playgrounds be located within *Kinderwagen-Entfernung*, areas reachable while pushing a baby carriage. He was prone to say, "the boy without a playground is the father of a man without work" from his belief that a youth deprived of active play would turn into an unproductive citizen.

The personal contacts between Jane Addams and Hegemann in 1913 are not documented. While it is unlikely that Addams considered herself a city planner, Hegemann was prescient in recognizing women reformers and "housers" as participants in the planning movement. For Hegemann, "women's concerns"—housing, clean air, open space, and playgrounds—represented important elements of comprehensive planning. He commented on precisely this during a visit to Williamsport, Pennsylvania, where prevailing winds carried smoke from the industrial plants into the residential areas of the city, and women were engaged in earnest efforts to eliminate the problem. The local newspaper reported that "Hegemann took the occasion to compliment the ladies by declaring that a great many of the most essential changes in the civic life of cities were brought about by the agitation of women."[29]

In later years Hegemann's commitment to pacifism deepened his respect for Jane Addams and other women activists. During the years he worked as a planner in the American Midwest (1916–21) he visited Hull House on several occasions, and sought out its founder, with whom he shared many convictions. His recognition of the role of women in city planning intensified in America, and he became more vocal on this topic. As an invited speaker at the closing dinner of the Eighth National Conference on City Planning in Cleveland, June 5–7, 1916, he devoted the concluding portion of his lecture to the subject, commenting that "a city plan should be well considered and flexible" and "provide more that the solution of technical questions."[30] He also noted that good administrators and committee men should do justice to a variety of interests: "In order to achieve this highest aim of city planning, the co-operation, not only of all men professionally interested in the planning of the many aspects of the city, but the co-operation of all citizens and especially also of the women is necessary." Hegemann said he had intended to lecture "about the great work done in city planning by the ladies," stating that it was not a "far-fetched idea" because "a number of the greatest measures in city planning have been taken by great women." Among these he mentioned historical figures and his contemporaries, Countess von Dohna Poninski, Dame Henrietta Barnett, Jane Addams, and Theodora Kimball Hubbard. Hegemann concluded that if women actively entered city planning, "we men . . . may look forward to better times."

Hegemann's lecture tour of 1913 reached a climax in Chicago, but did not end there, criss-crossing back and forth through several Midwestern states before he arrived in California. There is scant documentation for some of his stops, but the impression gained is that of a curious, highly motivated wayfarer exploring the heartland of America. Somewhere toward the end of this leg of his journey, he switched from riding trains between stops to driving a car. The *Family Saga* relates that "the money he received for his work he put into his first car and travelled along the Pacific Coast from Canada to Mexico, through Nevada and to the Great Salt Lake." It does not say when or where he acquired his automobile or learned how to drive.

From Chicago Hegemann took the train to Minneapolis, Minnesota. He likened it to his native city, Mannheim, for its inland harbor and waterways in addition to railroads. Newspaper reports mention that he showed slides in his lectures on subjects such as diagonal traffic arteries and the advisability of varying the width of streets.[31] In light of his visit to Chicago, he was asked if he approved of fieldhouses in parks. He assured his audience that he did, especially for holding dances.

Briefly stopping in Davenport, Iowa (May 11) and Hamilton, Ohio (May 14), Hegemann arrived by train in Cleveland, Ohio, amazed at the age of the Union Station built fifty years earlier.[32] He expressed concern that railroads had a strong "grip" on American cities and prevented the "development of civic beauty" (Fig. 19). He toured the city by automobile and admired Euclid Avenue, urging the preservation of its "natural beauty" and the "distinctive architectural style" of its residential buildings, recommending building regulations to prevent business encroachment. He stated that streetcar lines were inapproppriate for Euclid Avenue, which should ideally become part of the park system, and suggested that Cleveland's existing public squares and parks would benefit from additional trees and benches.

Many of the points Hegemann raised in Cleveland repeated observations he made elsewhere. Indeed, many American towns would have profited from similar suggestions. These included addressing transportation, projecting radial arteries through the prevalent grid plans, and expanding park systems. One may wonder why a foreign expert was required to make these recommendations, most of which were self-evident, but presumably an outside opinion was helpful in overcoming political controversies and a certain timidity vis-à-vis city planning questions from the hosting parties. Hegemann's criticism was not always well received, as in Philadelphia, but on the whole the comments in the newspapers were favorable. Cleveland even considered appointing Hegemann as its city planning engineer when he returned to the American Midwest in 1917, but there were objections to hiring a German alien "to plan our city."[33]

One of the smaller towns where Hegemann made a short official appearance was Lima, Ohio.[34] It was emblematic of the dedication to sound civic progress in towns of moderate size. Hegemann was consulted by a committee on several improvements under consideration, among which was the development of low-lying land along the Ottawa River, where the required flood control was intended to be combined with a scenic boulevard. The committee was also anxious to hear Hegemann's opinion regarding Lima's expanding industrial section, which was attracting a population influx.

On his way to Denver, Colorado, Hegemann traveled for a week by train, making stops along the way. In Bismarck, North Dakota, he found it curious and amusing that a small town in the American West had been named for the German "Iron Chancellor," Otto von Bismarck. The intention had been to attract German investments to the town, a major railroad center with a port on the Missouri River. Before Hegemann changed trains in Bismarck, he had enough time to look it over and write about "one of

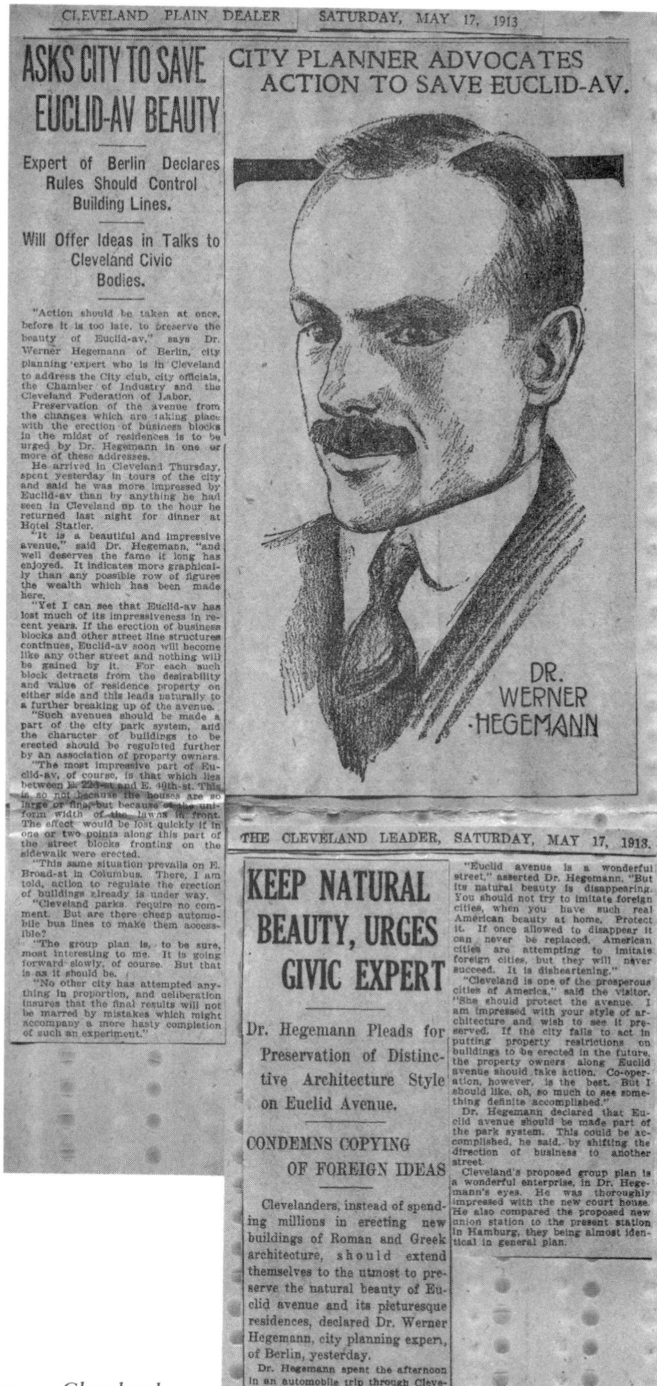

CLEVELAND PLAIN DEALER SATURDAY, MAY 17, 1913

ASKS CITY TO SAVE EUCLID-AV BEAUTY

Expert of Berlin Declares Rules Should Control Building Lines.

Will Offer Ideas in Talks to Cleveland Civic Bodies.

"Action should be taken at once, before it is too late, to preserve the beauty of Euclid-av," says Dr. Werner Hegemann of Berlin, city planning expert who is in Cleveland to address the City club, city officials, the Chamber of Industry and the Cleveland Federation of Labor.

Preservation of the avenue from the changes which are taking place with the erection of business blocks in the midst of residences is to be urged by Dr. Hegemann in one or more of these addresses.

He arrived in Cleveland Thursday, spent yesterday in tours of the city and said he was more impressed by Euclid-av than by anything he had seen in Cleveland up to the hour he returned last night for dinner at Hotel Statler.

"It is a beautiful and impressive avenue," said Dr. Hegemann, "and well deserves the fame it long has enjoyed. It indicates more graphically than any possible row of figures the wealth which has been made here.

"Yet I can see that Euclid-av has lost much of its impressiveness in recent years. If the erection of business blocks and other street line structures continues, Euclid-av soon will become like any other street and nothing will be gained by it. For each such block detracts from the desirability and value of residence property on either side and this leads naturally to a further breaking up of the avenue.

"Such avenues should be made a part of the city park system, and the character of buildings to be erected should be regulated further by an association of property owners.

"The most impressive part of Euclid-av, of course, is that which lies between E. 22d-st and E. 40th-st. This is so not because the houses are so large or fine, but because of the uniform width of the lawns in front. The effect would be lost quickly if in one or two points along this part of the street blocks fronting on the sidewalk were erected.

"This same situation prevails on E. Broad-st in Columbus. There, I am told, action to regulate the erection of buildings already is under way.

"Cleveland parks require no comment. But are there cheap automobile bus lines to make them accessible?

"The group plan is, to be sure, most interesting to me. It is going forward slowly, of course. But that is as it should be.

"No other city has attempted anything in proportion, and deliberation insures that the final results will not be marred by mistakes which might accompany a more hasty completion of such an experiment."

CITY PLANNER ADVOCATES ACTION TO SAVE EUCLID-AV.

THE CLEVELAND LEADER, SATURDAY, MAY 17, 1913.

KEEP NATURAL BEAUTY, URGES GIVIC EXPERT

Dr. Hegemann Pleads for Preservation of Distinctive Architecture Style on Euclid Avenue.

CONDEMNS COPYING OF FOREIGN IDEAS

Clevelanders, instead of spending millions in erecting new buildings of Roman and Greek architecture, should extend themselves to the utmost to preserve the natural beauty of Euclid avenue and its picturesque residences, declared Dr. Werner Hegemann, city planning expen, of Berlin, yesterday.

Dr. Hegemann spent the afternoon in an automobile trip through Cleveland parks and along Euclid avenue, with City Engineer Hoffman.

He seemed displeased at the lack of "patriotism," as he characterized it, of Clevelanders in allowing the natural beauty of Euclid avenue to disappear.

"Euclid avenue is a wonderful street," asserted Dr. Hegemann. "But its natural beauty is disappearing. You should not try to imitate foreign cities, when you have such real American beauty at home. Protect it. If once allowed to disappear it can never be replaced. American cities are attempting to imitate foreign cities, but they will never succeed. It is disheartening."

"Cleveland is one of the prosperous cities of America," said the visitor. "She should protect the avenue. I am impressed with your style of architecture and wish to see it preserved. If the city fails to act in putting property restrictions on buildings to be erected in the future, the property owners along Euclid avenue should take action. Co-operation, however, is the best. But I should like, oh, so much to see something definite accomplished."

Dr. Hegemann declared that Euclid avenue should be made part of the park system. This could be accomplished, he said, by shifting the direction of business to another street.

Cleveland's proposed group plan is a wonderful enterprise, in Dr. Hegemann's eyes. He was thoroughly impressed with the new court house. He also compared the proposed new union station to the present station in Hamburg, they being almost identical in general plan.

Fig. 19. Article from a Cleveland newspaper with a portrait sketch of Hegemann. WHA the ten-thousand small towns of the American West."[35] Leaving town the train crossed the Missouri River leaving behind, according to Hegemann, the farthest corner of Bismarck's empire. On the other side of the river began the "endless, rolling, pale yellow, flecked with brown grassy plains."

If we are to trust Hegemann's narrative, the train also stopped in Ronan, an Indian reservation in western Montana, where he had his first encounter with Native Americans, the icons in German adventure stories by Karl May, who never left his country to write about them.

After a week-long interlude in the northern states, Hegemann's journey turned southward to Denver. As other newspapers had done, the *Denver Times* featured a portrait photograph of him and described him as "dapper in appearance, small of stature, but big of ideas of the city beautiful."[36] Hegemann spoke out against "apartment houses with disappearing beds . . . disappearing children and disappearing gardens." Regarding skyscrapers, he favored tall buildings if they were not crowded together, but rising above surrounding structures. As usual, he promoted thoroughfares radiating from the center, intersecting the checkerboard plan. He predicted that ideally "the cities of the future will resemble a wheel . . . with spokes radiating in all directions and the 'spokes' connected by a network of cross streets." The Denver report mentions that Hegemann's address was illustrated with slides reproduced from photographs taken on his travels.

Hegemann owed the invitation for an entire week (June 10–17) of consultation in Sacramento, California, to the Chamber of Commerce. Extraordinary efforts were made to arrange a dense schedule of lectures and meetings with diverse groups, including the Woman's Council, the Temple Circle at the Synagogue, the Civic League, the Architects' League, the employees of the Southern Pacific Railroad Company, several Catholic organizations, the Housing and Sanitation Committee, labor organizations, and a "large mass meeting" at the Sacramento High School. The Chamber of Commerce and members of a special committee were paying Hegemann $100 a day and requested that "every citizen make an effort to attend the lectures, all of which would deal with different subjects." The response was lively and the events received ample coverage in the press.[37]

His first lecture to the Woman's Council presented an auspicious occasion to expound on his vision of the role of women in urbanism. According to the newspaper report, "The speaker pleaded with the women present to interest themselves more and more in civic work, declaring they would be more successful than men. The true meaning of city planning Dr. Hegemann characterized as the making of a city homelike and convenient." He urged the preservation of trees and the development of playgrounds, considering them "the best example of the influence of women." He also counseled that the city's waterfront along the Sacramento River, presently occupied by the railroad and warehouses, be reclaimed for scenic developments and public parks. The Woman's Council was working in conjunction with the Housing and Sanitation Committee of the Chamber of Commerce and welcomed Hegemann's suggestion of reducing the width of streets to provide more open space around houses. These were proposals he had made on previous occasions in other towns, but this occasion seems to have been the only time he addressed a women's association.

At the other meetings in Sacramento, interspersed with site tours, Hegemann elaborated on the aforementioned themes. He promoted the collaboration of the municipality with business corporations to develop the riverfront to include a modern harbor with facilities for handling freight and passengers, as well as scenic open space and "lodging houses" for seasonal workers. The harbor problem and adjacent industrial zones required the cooperation of the city, the railroad, and shipping and real estate companies. For a comprehensive master plan for Sacramento encompassing the region and considering future growth, Hegemann recommended organizing a competition. He advised that the resulting studies would be beneficial and worth the money, even if they did not produce a definite plan. Referring to the experience in Berlin, he stated that "such competitions always have a direct and tremendous bearing upon the city building which follows. It is also surprising what remarkable changes such competitions are bound to bring about in the prevailing ideas regarding city planning." Public hearings on the results of the competition would provide opportunities for comment and criticism. Hegemann also suggested the establishment of a planning commission as part of the city administration to address these matters.

The thoroughness with which Hegemann responded to the consultations in Sacramento probably derived from his impressive fee and the genuine interest of the city's citizens in matters pertaining to their home. It conveyed to him their realization that urban progress would benefit everyone and could not be left to chance but required the advice and guidance of specialists.

The experience in Sacramento was an auspicious entrée to California and served as a preparation for the final portion of Hegemann's American lecture tour in San Francisco, Berkeley, and Oakland, from late June 1913 until March 1914 (Fig. 20). His presence in the Bay Area was well timed, coinciding with the increasing public interest in planning that preceded the opening of the Panama Canal in October 1913. Moves were made to overcome the competition between San Francisco and the East Bay cities, thereby facilitating plans for a comprehensive harbor development, including the metropolitan area enclosing the entire bay. The harbor complex was envisioned as the major port on the Pacific Coast of the Americas. The rivalry for shipping and commerce had brought important urbanists to the region, including Daniel Burnham, who was invited to San Francisco in 1904–05, but whose City Beautiful plan was rejected. The city of Oakland, which is on the inland side of the bay and had a good harbor and intercontinental railroad connections, was eager to edge out San Francisco in commercial significance. In both cities business leaders understood and

OAKLAND, CALIFORNIA, SUNDAY MORNING, OCTOBER 5, 1913.

Ideal Oakland to Be Reality City-Planning Expert Here

Beautification of Municipality to Receive Careful Study

The Ideal Oakland of the Future, predicted by city officials and civic patriots, is to be. The first work on the building of the future city was done yesterday, when the city council commissioned Dr. Werner Hegemann, the first expert in the world on city building, to render a report showing what shall be done to make the city ideal. This report will be rendered after the famed German authority has gone thoroughly over the ground and made a new plan of the city that is to be. Dr. Hegemann is now at the Hotel Oakland, where he will make his headquarters while in the employ of the city.

Dr. Hegemann is a graduate of the University of Heidelberg and has also taken scholarships in many of the great schools of Europe. He has made reports on city building for the municipalities of New York, Chicago, and Philadelphia, and is the author of many books on parking, city planning, street systems, and other methods of modernizing municipalities. His report on Oakland will deal with facilitating traffic by arrangement of streets, bearing in mind future growth and needed traffic arrangements and facilities; beautifying of the city, and general development of its possibilities.

WOMEN MOST CHARMING.

"Oakland," says the expert, "has, so far as natural resources are concerned, a 100 per cent advantage over any city in the United States that I have ever seen. I admire California generally, especially the women. For the women of the Golden West have a charming frankness and candor never seen in the women of the old world. Compared with the old world, where land is high and five-story houses are crowded on small lots, the beautiful homes of this state, surrounded by lawns and shrubbery, make California to the European a veritable paradise."

Dr. Hegemann, before coming to this country, toured Europe, making extensive observations in the cities he visited. He saw France, England, Belgium, Austria, Russia, Norway, and other countries, viewing them with the analytical eye of an expert and with a view to utilizing what attractions they might offer.

the city-planning exposition of Berlin, and the other great show at Dusseldorf, two of the greatest affairs of their kind in the world's history. He was also associated with similar expositions at Frankfort and Bremen.

The doctor made his last European tour as a representative of the labor committee of Berlin and Dusseldorf, and was backed in his trip by the Prussian state ministry and nine Prussian municipalities. He made a report, in three volumes, of his findings, which are considered the last words on the great subject.

Herr Doctor Hegemann was the secretary of the committee of 12 for the architectural development of Greater Berlin, and one of the judges in the competition for the building plans of Dusseldorf. He is a special writer on city building for the Berlin Tagblass, the Frankfort Zeitung, and the Stadtbeau, official organ of the city building authorities of the world.

The famed expert will address the Oakland Commercial Club Friday, this body having made elaborate plans for his entertainment. Plans are also under way by the local German-American colony to entertain their distinguished visiter during his stay

Oakland 100 Percent Better Than Any City

"Oakland has, so far as natural advantages are concerned, 100 per cent advantage over any other city in the United States.

"I admire your charming California women. Their frankness and candor is most refreshing and far different from the ladies of the old world.

"Compared to the old world, where houses are crowded, five-story buildings being erected on small lots, your California homes, surrounded with lawns and shrubbery, form a veritable paradise."—Dr. Werner Hegemann, expert in city building, who will render a report on Oakland.

STEWART PHOTO

DR. WERNER HEGEMANN, BUILDER OF CITIES, WHO HAS COME TO DESIGN THE IDEAL OAKLAND OF THE FUTURE.

Fig. 20. Headline from an Oakland newspaper, including a portrait of Hegemann, "the builder of cities," and a cartoon of him sitting at his desk studying maps. WHA

supported the social importance of civic improvements, as was the case in Chicago and Boston. Unfortunately, the contentiousness between San Francisco and the East Bay cities continued unabated and blocked progress on regional harbor development.[38]

San Francisco experienced local controversies regarding the placement of the Civic Center and the Panama-Pacific International Exposition projected for 1915. Although it was not carried out, the influence of Burnham and Bennett's plan and City Beautiful aesthetics eventually prevailed and contributed to San Francisco's charm.

Oakland, while unable to match San Francisco's allure, was recognized for the scenic appeal of its waterfront, Lake Merritt in the heart of the city, and its large homes and gardens (Figs. 21, 22). Frederick Law Olmsted Sr. had been there in 1860 and recommended a park system with a green belt along the hills that reached into town along canyons and creeks. In practical advantages the city actually surpassed San Francisco: when the transcontinental railroad was completed in 1869, Oakland profited by becoming the end of the line. The trains brought an influx of immigrants, and the city experienced a boom in commercial and industrial development.[39] Frank Mott, Oakland's energetic mayor from 1905–15, embarked on a range of civic developments and succeeded in easing the controversies regarding the waterfront. Most importantly, Mott convinced the citizens of Oakland about the urgency of civic improvements. In 1906, perhaps to emulate San Francisco, Mott asked Charles Mulford Robinson of City Beautiful renown for advice and a follow-up on some of Olmsted's park system ideas.

Avoiding the debates in San Francisco with their surfeit of participating parties, Hegemann accepted Mayor Mott's invitation to Oakland. He was encouraged and proposed by the architect Charles Henry Cheney, who had participated in some of the recent meetings in Sacramento. Cheney has been called a "crusader for city planning" for his dedication to advancing the profession.[40] In numerous newspaper articles he stressed the importance of planning with an emphasis on the "city practical" rather than the City Beautiful. The well-connected Cheney became Hegemann's link to West Coast urbanists, easing his way into an atmosphere seething with tensions.

Coming from abroad, Hegemann enjoyed an advantage by providing an "outside opinion." His professional experience and convictions equipped him for an ideological match with Oakland's progressive strivings. Upon his arrival he was welcomed by a newspaper article featuring his photograph with a superimposed drawing showing him at a desk, pencil in hand, working on sheets marked "Plans."[41] The article gave extensive, if somewhat inaccurate, information on Hegemann's background. However, it mentioned several times that the City Council had commissioned him to "render a report showing what shall be done to make the city ideal . . . after the famed German authority has gone thoroughly over the ground and made a new plan of the city that is to be." During his stay "in the employ of the city," his headquarters were established in the Hotel Oakland. According to the article, Hegemann endeared himself to his hosts by declaring that Oakland was better than any other city in the United States and that he admired the "charming California women," whose "frankness and candor is most refreshing and far different from the ladies of the old world."

Charles Henry Cheney positioned himself as Hegemann's advocate with a series of articles presenting the ideas of "the apostle and prophet of German city planning."[42] A note to the first article in the series explains that Cheney would later address the imperative for a comprehensive city

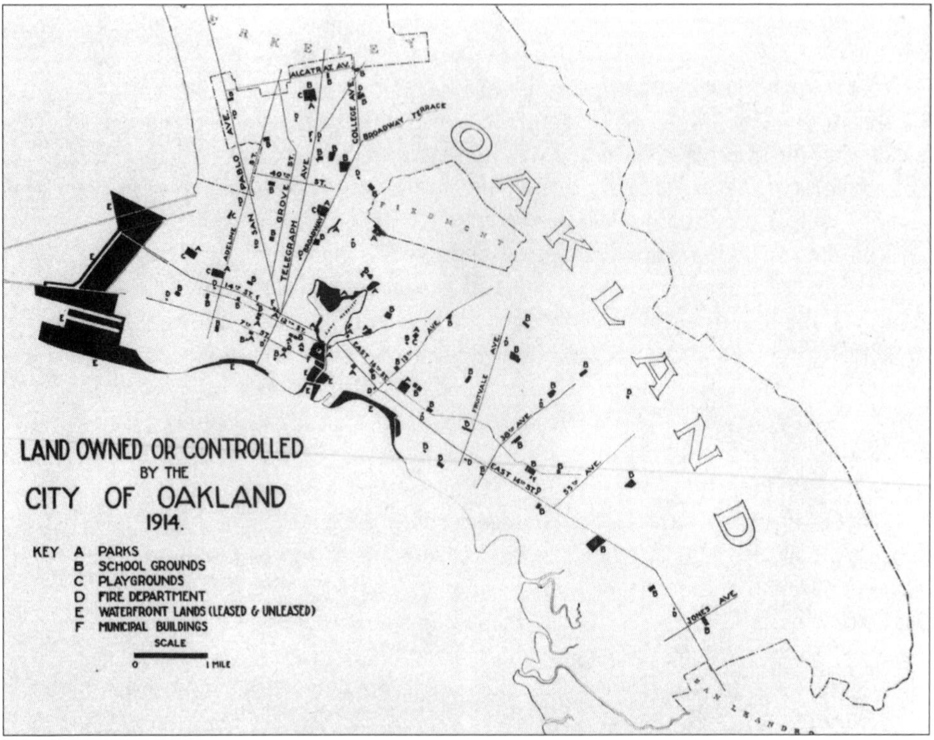

Fig. 21. Map of Oakland indicating land owned by the city, from Hegemann's Report on a City Plan for the Municipalities of Oakland & Berkeley. CCCC

Fig. 22. Residential street in Oakland. Photograph by Hegemann, from his Report on a City Plan for the Municipalities of Oakland & Berkeley. CCCC

plan, certainly one of Hegemann's major principles. Cheney refers to the enthusiasm and civic commitment awakened in the entire community of Sacramento by Hegemann's discussions; a committee of 150 was now engaged in carrying forward his suggestions, especially regarding the improvements of the waterfront and transportation. Cheney portrayed Hegemann as a "practical idealist, who never loses sight of utilities and commercial possibilities in his schemes for making cities attractive," and stressed his approach of survey and analysis. Cheney's articles imply extensive conversations between the two urbanists, benefiting their mutual understanding. Many passages by Cheney read as if composed by Hegemann, and reappear in Hegemann's 1915 *Report on a City Plan for the Municipalities of Oakland & Berkeley*.[43]

While preparing his *Report*, Hegemann was devoted to acquainting himself with Oakland and Berkeley and the individuals that made them function. At the celebration for the completion of the Panama Canal on October 10, he was asked for his advice on housing the expected waves of immigrants. In addition to housing, Hegemann's attention was drawn to the waterfront, parks, transportation, city center, and what was generally grouped under "beautification." He combined his own inquiries and conclusions with the work of others, adhering to his conviction that comprehensive planning demanded teamwork and the input of a range of specialists. Cheney took the opportunity to promote the establishment of a city planning commission for Oakland, a move that had resulted from Hegemann's initiatives in the other cities on his tour.

When the comprehensive plan for Oakland's western waterfront by Thomas H. Rees of the United States Army Corps of Engineers was presented to the Commercial Club Harbor Committee, Rees mentioned Hegemann's suggestions for a park system to be combined with the harbor facilities without interfering with the commercial development on the mainland side.[44] Hegemann envisioned an area of water parks for boating and recreation, comparable to the lagoon parks in Chicago. His proposal called for one or more island parks between the deep navigation channel and the bay, projected by Rees to extend from Oakland to Richmond. Instead of just a dyke protecting the channel from silting up, Hegemann anticipated these "pleasure islands" to benefit the general public, attract tourism, and stimulate the local economy.

When planning parks and open space, Hegemann collaborated with the German-born Oscar Prager, who had arrived in California around 1906, attracted by the region's engagement in urban and park design.[45] Little is known of Prager's career prior to his work as Director of Parks in Oakland, which ended in 1914. Why he was favored above American park specialists with proven knowledge of California's natural and administrative environment may have derived from the esteem German city planning and "*Gartenkultur*" enjoyed in America. Frederick Law Olmsted Sr. and his followers, including Charles Mulford Robinson, had visited Germany in the first decade of the twentieth century and returned with admiration for building regulations, zoning, and picturesque townscapes. This receptiveness favored Hegemann as well, and his presence strengthened Prager's position, particularly as he lacked professional credentials. Their shared interests and ethnic background developed into a friendship, and the scant information on Prager's activities as Director of Parks is recorded in Hegemann's publications, primarily his *Report.*

Hegemann sought out contacts at the University of California in Berkeley. Shortly after his arrival in October 1913, he was asked to give a lecture in the presence of the university president, with a mandolin orchestra providing music. He was also invited to a banquet given by the Chamber of Commerce honoring prominent East Bay citizens, including Mayor Frank Mott. Two months later, Hegemann submitted the initial results of his report, accompanied by slides, to the City Club in Berkeley.[46]

While maintaining connections to Berkeley, Hegemann's main headquarters during this time were in Oakland, and there he produced a remarkable work on comprehensive city planning. Hegemann's *Report* is the least known of his publications, perhaps because of its title, which gives the impression of addressing solely local concerns, and the date of its appearance, which coincided with the conflagrations of World War I. Despite these drawbacks, it was and still is considered a landmark work.[47] The book manifests Hegemann's pragmatic ideal of reconciling a rational, scientific approach with responsiveness to the evolving historical and cultural uniqueness of a given city. Concepts contained in Hegemann's Berlin volumes are synthesized and clarified in response to his physical and intellectual journey in America. Encountering young towns and cities laid out in democratic grid plans, he was intrigued by their dilemma of how to develop a sense of place and a distinct uniqueness amid such uniformity. A previous phase in the United States that sought protection from or ignored the surrounding environment had now given way to a responsiveness to nature and topographical features, and these insights informed Hegemann's *Report.* Although the situations in Oakland and Berkeley were emblematic and constitute the focus of his study, the value and significance of its concepts extend far beyond the Bay Area.

The *Report* opens with Hegemann's credo, placed on the reverse of the title page.

CITY PLANNING IS INSURANCE
AGAINST WASTE OF PUBLIC AND PRIVATE FUNDS

> City-planning means co-ordination of the activities that make for the growth of the city, especially the activities of railroad and harbor engineers, landscape architects, street-building and civil engineers, builders of factories, of offices, of public buildings and dwelling houses. Without this pre-planning co-ordination, clashes between these different activities, unsatisfactory results and most expen-

> sive rearrangements, become unavoidable. City-planning therefore does not mean additional expenditure of money, but it means an INSURANCE AGAINST INEFFICIENT EXPENDITURE [*sic*] of the enormous sums that go—in the regular course of events—into the development of a progressive city.[48]

Frederic C. Howe's Preface gives an overview of Hegemann's activities before and during his travels in American cities. Expanding on Hegemann's maxim, Howe writes that city planning "means building cities for people to live in as well as to work in. It means building a community as an agency of civilization, culture and art."

Following Howe's Preface is a long Introduction by Hegemann on the history of "The Great City on the East Side of the Bay. The Old Issue: West, i.e. Peninsular vs. East, i.e. Continental Side of the Bay." The author notes numerous sources on the history of the region, and the sections on "The two lessons to be learned from the history of city-building and city planning," which warn of repeating the mistakes of old cities in America and Europe. In the latter part of the Introduction, Hegemann draws general conclusions from urban history, contrasting the congested European cities, which increase land values in the center, with the English and American "system of decentralization and clear differentiation between business and residence districts." Writing on "the wilderness of the business district and its glory," a characteristic of American cities often criticized by visitors from abroad, Hegemann detects "surprising effects of architectural beauty." He also admires American suburbs with their "square miles of modest little homes with gardens."

The aim of modern city planning, according to Hegemann, is to balance aesthetic aspirations with the scientific investigation and response to the economic, social, hygienic, and recreational life of the communities. What he referred to is spelled out in the Table of Contents under the heading, "The Structural Rank of the Different Elements in a City Plan," grouped under "The City Economic" and "The City Recreational and Beautiful." Ideally, the different elements would form a comprehensive ensemble of beauty and efficiency, intended to evolve and adapt over time. The hierarchy of these elements would vary according to the circumstances. The topics of the two major sections are blended in the text with factual information and statistical data interwoven with the history of each town and region, and comparisons with other cities in America and abroad.

The proposals for Oakland correlate the natural beauty of the site, historic buildings, and the last remaining stand of oak trees into a comprehensive plan with a transportation network linking the city to the rest of the entire country.

The sequence of the elements considered in the *Report* is indicative of the author's rating of their importance. The first is the harbor, and Hegemann's suggestions adhere to Thomas H. Rees's "plan for the ultimate development of the entire Bay frontage," which was intended to transform Oakland into a major port, reaching out to the world at large. Hegemann called it "an admirable harbor project" and recommended the addition of lagoon parks for recreational and aesthetic pleasures.

The section on the harbor is followed by an equally extensive one on Oakland's railroad link to the North American continent, and which he rated of equal importance to the harbor. Freight, passenger, long distance, and urban transportation are discussed on the basis of detailed maps.

The section on streets distinguishes among traffic arteries, business streets, and residential streets both "expensive and inexpensive," an aspect of urban layouts that Hegemann had recommended wherever he consulted on his travels. He also repeats the need for enforcing regulations limiting the height of buildings in relation to the width of streets in business districts, in order to avoid congestion and allow for air and light in high-rise structures. With great admiration, he discusses the elder Olmsted's plan for the university campus in Berkeley and its surrounding neighborhood. Extracts from Frederick Law Olmsted's report are interspersed with Hegemann's own comments. The harmonious blending of layout, landscape, lush vegetation, and the architectural style of East Bay homes in Berkeley and surrounding Lake Merritt in Oakland captivated him. He deemed it the result of "the genius of American landscape architecture." Breaking away from wide streets in a grid, he considered these residential areas far superior to those in San Francisco. Hegemann did not limit himself to surveying upper-class neighborhoods. For "medium priced and cheaper homes and houses of the working man" he also recommended less monotonous developments, and devoted attention to the economic implications of low-income housing. However, he lamented not being able to analyze these problems in depth in his *Report*. He repeats his conviction that the housing question would be solved only when it became integral to city planning, asking "Will the American West establish new standards? The time when these standards for cheap workingmen's homes in the American West are set will be a period of the very greatest importance in world history."

Related to the above topics are Hegemann's suggestions regarding parks and open space in Oakland, particularly the canyons and creeks around Lake Merritt, which were frequently used for refuse. Hegemann acknowledged the precedents for his considerations in "Parks, Parkways and Playgrounds," citing "the valuable suggestions of the elder Olmsted, Charles Mulford Robinson and Oscar Prager." The older landscape pioneers had stressed the importance of a large park around Lake Merritt and preserving the natural landscape of the canyons. Ideally, the parks were to be connected by parkways, forming a total park system preferably on a larger regional scale. In the *Report* Hegemann mentions cooperating with park director Oscar Prager in formulating these recommendations and composing a map showing "proposed parks for Oakland & Berkeley."

Hegemann had a particular interest in playgrounds for children as components of the park system and near schools, which had become a unique feature in American cities inspired by the example of Chicago.

The concluding chapter in the *Report* addresses "Civic Art and Civic Centers" and ends with Hegemann's closing remarks and acknowledgments. Significantly, he distanced himself from the City Beautiful movement; the title of this section is indicative of his particular aesthetics of city planning. The term "civic art" and its meaning was to become the primary theme of *The American Vitruvius: An Architects' Handbook of Civic Art*, composed at the end of Hegemann's prolonged American experience.[49] It is sequentially related to the introductory passage of the section "Civic Art and Civic Centers," which dispells the assumption of his advocacy of the City Beautiful movement:

> There was a time not long gone by when people thought city-planning could beautify a city by the mere adding of artistic ideas without considering the basic necessities expressed in the systems of transportation, parks and playgrounds, and in the housing of the people. Today everybody knows that a really beautiful city can be created only by considering right from the beginning the proper co-ordination of all the needs and ideals of civic life and its physical expression.

According to Hegemann, several "minor improvements" would enhance the appearance of the "organic scheme," for instance, underground electric cables and harmonious street furnishings. He thought that advertising columns, popular in many European cities, should replace American billboards.

Hegemann expressed admiration for the high standards of home building in the Bay region as a modern, democratic type of civic beauty exemplified in the architecture of Bernard P. Maybeck and Louis Christian Mullgardt. He recognized that individual efforts were enhanced by a well-designed layout, and urged that "ill advised orgies of individualism" should be avoided.

Emphasizing that proper satisfaction of all civic problems should culminate in a community's effort to create a civic center, the major part of Hegemann's chapter is devoted to the grouping of public buildings in Oakland, Berkeley and its university campus, and San Francisco, all shown in successive plans. The illustrations feature alternate proposals for a Berkeley Civic Center by Lewis B. Hobart and Charles H. Cheney, several views of the campus, and the recently completed Civic Auditorium in Oakland. Hegemann praised the latter for its "simple form like a great tent of concrete—a real structural form rejecting classical masquerade or gingerbread," and welcomed the intention of making it the focus of the Civic Center. He also recommended the closure of gaps between buildings and placing an emphasis on vistas.

A number of the illustrations was displayed at an exhibition by the Bay Cities League of Municipalities held in March 1914 in Berkeley and Oakland.[50] Cheney, one of the organizers, was intent on promoting the establishment of city planning commissions in all Bay cities and advocated periodic joint meetings to discuss mutual concerns and coordinate efforts toward a regional plan. The exhibition was inaugurated in Oakland in the presence of the mayors and delegates from the East Bay and San Francisco. Mayor Mott and others delivered talks, and Hegemann gave a lecture. According to the local newspaper, "thousands" attended the event. This was testimony that the exhibition was a catalyst for stimulating general and fiscal interests in urban matters.

Based on his previous experience, Hegemann collaborated with Cheney and his acquaintances in Berkeley and Oakland in organizing the city planning exhibition and related events. The exhibition, which took place exactly a year after Hegemann's arrival in New York for his lecture tour, had for him the aura of a finale. In March 1914, Hegemann decided to use his earnings to cross the Pacific Ocean and complete a trip around the world before returning to Germany. His voyage took him to Honolulu, Yokohama, Tokyo, Hong Kong, Canton, Ceylon, and Australia.[51] The scant documented portion of this trip is the sojourn in Australia, where he visited Sidney and Melbourne. On July 14, 1914, he received a letter from the Acting Secretary of the Minister for Home Affairs regarding the Federal Parliament House Architectural Competition.[52] The letter inquired whether Hegemann would translate into German the "programme" of the competition, of which a copy was enclosed, and have 2,000 copies printed and distributed.

The letter was sent to Hegemann's hotel in Melbourne, but he was unable to respond due to unexpected circumstances. The day he received the letter, Hegemann left Australia on the German ship *Prinzessin Cecilien* with the intention of returning to Germany. However, as the *Family Saga* relates, "When about to enter the Red Sea, news reached the ship that war had been declared between England and Germany. There were several English ships which controlled these waters, but with the help of another German ship, the *Königsberg*, the *Prinzessin Cecilien* was able to escape from the English ships and help in the sinking of the English freighter *City of Westminster*. "This," wrote Hegemann, "I must mention because nothing has astounded me more than the intentional sinking of a useful and sound ship." Witnessing this calamity may well have stimulated his antiwar sentiments. The *Prinzessin Cecilien* took refuge in Delagoa Bay, Portuguese Mozambique, in August 1914. For nine months, the passengers were not permitted to go ashore for fear of tropical diseases. Hegemann read every book in the ship's library and wrote up his observations on the places he had visited since leaving California. Finally, in April 1915 the captain permitted Hegemann to go ashore for just one day. Learning that a Norwegian ship would leave at midnight, he sought out its captain in a local bar and asked to be a passenger. This was not usually permitted, but he was allowed to hide in the cargo hold under a shipment of ropes until the ship reached open waters.

Once the Norwegian vessel was on the high seas, Hegemann was free to go on deck, although the sailors feared that a stowaway on the ship brought bad luck. After rounding the Cape of Good Hope, the ship sailed up the west coast of Africa and to the coast of Brazil. Hegemann heard that the war was continuing in Europe, with no end was in sight. In July 1915, the Norwegian vessel reached the Gulf of Mexico, where it encountered a complete lull in the wind. The sailors suspected that it was caused by the stowaway and there were threats of making Hegemann walk the plank. Eventually, however, a breeze came up and after a three-month voyage, the ship reached Gulfport, Mississippi.

When he left the *Prinzessin Cecilien* Hegemann had abandoned seven trunks containing printed matter, art objects, clothing, and, most important, his notations from his travels. These trunks were unloaded in Lisbon at the end of the war, and when Hegemann inquired about claiming his possessions, he was told his trunks had been declared "abandoned" and destroyed.

Hegemann & Peets, City Planning and Landscape Architects

Unintentionally, Hegemann had returned to the United States. His *Diary* notes his arrival on July 24, 1915. He got in touch with his American contacts, including The People's Institute in New York. Presumably he had sent the newspaper reviews from his lecture tour to the institute before leaving California, thereby saving them from loss during his subsequent adventures. The Institute's Lecture Bureau then composed a brochure announcing "a new arrangement with Dr. Werner Hegemann to lecture and aid in the promotion of city planning projects, to make town planning surveys and to cooperate with municipal authorities."[53] It provided details of his successes of 1913, which culminated in his *Report*. The institute's pamphlet mentioned that Hegemann "undertook a comparative study of city development in the capitals of Australia and the Far East." Listed among the titles of his "popular" lectures were "City Planning and the Architects" and "The Story of Great Women in City Planning." Hegemann's name also appeared among speakers at the institute for the spring of 1916.

Holding off on decisions regarding his future, Hegemann took time to explore the southern regions of the country. Without obligations to lecture and consult, he moved about freely as a tourist, photographing and taking in the scenery. From New Orleans he went by train along the Mississippi

River and visited Houston, Galveston, and San Antonio. The missions surprised him as older than those in California and well-preserved.

On September 10, 1915, Hegemann arrived at the Grand Canyon in Arizona. His *Diary* notes it as a memorable experience, for exactly two years earlier, he had been at the same place. "This is the starting point at which my trip around the world comes full circle. After everything I had seen, I could not imagine a more spectacular point of departure and termination for a voyage around the world." From the spot where he was sitting on the edge of the Grand Canyon, he could catch sight of the Colorado River coursing "deep down in the skyscraping, labyrinthine gorge."

Hegemann might have preferred to return to California's East Bay, where he had established many contacts, had personal friends, and his *Report* had been favorably reviewed. However, since his departure the previous year, the political atmosphere had changed considerably, not only in Europe, but also in Oakland. While Hegemann was marooned in Mozambique, the *Oakland Tribune* suggested that he had studied the Oakland harbor defenses in order to inform the German military.[54] This rumor persisted, despite the fact that Hegemann's *Report* had been issued with the support of the City Council, and the United States did not enter World War I until 1917. Mayor Frank K. Mott, who had welcomed Hegemann and Prager to Oakland, was succeeded in 1915 by John L. Davie, who embraced the city's role in the war effort as a ship-building center. From 1917 on Davie's endeavors included the construction of an airport for civilian and military use.[55]

Hegemann decided to stay in the United States instead of returning to Germany, which still would have been possible in July 1915. Unwelcome in the San Francisco region for political reasons, he settled in Milwaukee, Wisconsin. There is no evidence that he had any previous connections with Milwaukee; however, he may have been aware that the area had attracted a large number of German socialists implicated in the Revolution of 1848, as well as other Germans. The big beer brewing companies, industries, and large farms were signs of their prosperity, which distanced them from their original socialist ideologies. The families continued to be aware of their German heritage and were caught in an ambiguous predicament when America declared war in 1917.

Upon his arrival in Milwaukee, several civic organizations engaged Hegemann to prepare a city planning report. He composed a notable piece headlined, "Thrilling Tale of Wartime Adventure," for a local newspaper, *The Journal*. The narrative dates from 1916 and was obviously written to please a German-American audience. For instance, Hegemann mentions an attempt he made from Australia to contact the commanding officer from his assigned regiment regarding military exercise in Germany, though no records indicate that he was in fact in the military. His adventures are embellished with bravura and given an anti-British slant. It is of special interest that he mentions writing a book on town planning in Japan and China and working on a manuscript on Australian city planning while marooned on the ship in Delagoa Bay, Mozambique. He claims to have completed the book about Australia while on board the Norwegian vessel, although no trace of any manuscript has been located.

Initially Hegemann did not intend to stay in Milwaukee, and he explored other possibilities. In January 1916, he sent a letter with his curriculum vitae to Professor Ford in Cambridge, Massachusetts.[56] He stated that all his publications and activities had the aim of creating "a scientific basis for the wide city planning discussion, which so far was largely in the hands of men with a training either mainly technical (engineers, architects) or specializing in one single phase (e.g. housing, transportation) of the many phases, which only in their coordination make up city planning." Referring to this comprehensive science of city planning, he suggested, "I believe that I could at present serve best if a university with large collections and an atmosphere of intelligent discussion of civic problems could give me an opportunity for research work." Hegemann also mentioned that "city planning not yet being established as an independent science, has to take its place with either one of the following departments: Sociology, Economics, Architecture, Engineering, or Landscape Architecture." He was obviously hoping to do this at Harvard University, but a reply has not been located. Hegemann's proposal for a city planning department reemerged when he was exiled in New York from 1933 to 1936, and Columbia University and Harvard considered his participation.

Concurrent with exploring other options, Hegemann opened an office for consulting and urban planning in Milwaukee, leading to his transition from theory and critical writing to actual implementation. His first task, however, was a report rather than a planning project.[57] *City Planning for Milwaukee* was submitted in February 1916 at the request of a coalition of civic organizations. The coalition called itself "The Metropolitan Park Commission" but later broadened its concerns under the name "The City Planning Commission." In 1911, the commission issued a compendium of *Preliminary Reports*, including one by Frederick Law Olmsted Sr. and John Nolen on a "Modified Civic Center Plan," with radiating parkways.[58] Another report submitted by the Metropolitan Park Commission addresses "neighborhood centers" and playgrounds comparable to those in which "Chicago has taken a lead." It showed several proposals with detailed plans for outdoor facilities and buildings and recommended competent municipal management of these neighborhood centers for their proper functioning. The Commission also presented proposals for the development of river parks, illustrated with the waterfronts in Vienna and Nuremberg, and recommendations for a "parked way system" of avenues.

Hegemann's amply illustrated *City Planning for Milwaukee* is based on the town's considerable dedication and expertise expressed in the commission's earlier efforts. Differing from the *Preliminary Reports*, Hegemann employed his customary methodology, beginning with an explanation of the term "city planning" and a discussion of older congested towns and modern decentralization. A survey of Milwaukee's urban development from an early plan of 1835–36 demonstrated the resulting difficulties of accommodating efficient traffic arteries within a checkerboard grid. A state system of radial highways approaching the city came to forced endings when reaching the grid. Hegemann urged development of rapid transit, inserting diagonal streets, and cooperating with the railroads to provide service to outlying areas. A comprehensive approach required the coordination of urban design features with city services. The situation in Milwaukee was in some respects similar to that of Oakland, where the inland harbor facilities had intruded upon a scenic waterfront. Hegemann supported the previous recommendations for an expanded park system and a compromise between commercial and recreational use of the waterfront. In addition to Lake Michigan, the Milwaukee River, which runs through the center of the city, functioned as part of the port system and required the opening and closing of bridges for the passage of ships, producing awkward delays for both nautical and vehicular traffic. Hegemann envisioned the river as a scenic waterway, like the Grand Canal in Venice, with bridges high enough to permit the passage of rapid transit service and pleasure boats, despite the fact that climate considerations in the Midwest made this improbable. Even today, Hegemann's vision of a pedestrian mall framing both sides of the river remains a viable element of Milwaukee's long-range planning.

The *Preliminary Reports* did not address housing. By contrast, Hegemann recommended treating it as an integral element within the future growth of the city. In the section "Residential Districts and Their Harmony," both the single house with garden—for him the optimum living situation—and apartment houses were discussed. He maintained that good design would benefit both types of housing, and its absence would be harmful. The illustrations juxtaposed good and bad examples from Milwaukee and Germany. Without further comment Hegemann included his own recent study for the subdivision of the Pabst Farm in Wauwatosa, Wisconsin. Another illustration, unrelated to the text, was Leberecht Migge's plan for a public park in Oldenburg, captioned as an example of the "new German park style." An appendix reprinted extracts from Hegemann's *Report on . . . Oakland & Berkeley* selected by W. H. Schuchardt, President of the Wisconsin Chapter of the American Institute of Architects. An additional section provided excerpts from international press reviews of Hegemann's two volumes on the city planning exhibitions in Berlin and Düsseldorf.

While working on the *Milwaukee Report*, Hegemann had set up an office in the city and was asked to plan two residential developments. One request came from Walter J. Kohler, whose company manufactured bathroom fixtures. Kohler was interested in developing a model village for his workers that differed from the existing housing, which was arranged in a grid plan near the factory. He had definite ideas for his "new town," as a result of his visits to Letchworth and Port Sunlight in England, and Krupps's housing in Essen. He was impressed by garden city concepts and desired his single-industry community to be attractive and pleasant to live in. His conviction that good housing and planning would solve urban ills was a position prevalent among American businessmen at that time, especially in Boston, Chicago, and Oakland. Kohler was also interested in the promotional aspect of a uniquely appealing workers' village that could be displayed in the advertising brochures for bathroom fixtures. The single-family, detached houses were to be purchased by the workers, rather than owned and managed by the company, which he considered to be industrial paternalism. Within Kohler's scope were buildings to house single men and women, a school, and other community facilities; in short, a complete village, rather than just housing.[59] Hegemann concurred with these propositions, particularly in their affinity to garden city precepts.[60]

When he approached Hegemann in the winter of 1915, Kohler was already acquainted with the forthcoming *City Planning for Milwaukee*, in particular the section, "How City Planning Can Prevent Housing Problems," which discussed harmonious residential groupings and included relevant illustrations. Impressed with Hegemann's German background and international renown, Kohler was apparently unaware that Hegemann lacked experience as a practicing architect and planner. This is no surprise because experts on urbanism and architecture who were not active practitioners were virtually nonexistent at that time. Aware of his shortcomings and anxious to accept Kohler's proposal, Hegemann followed his client's recommendations and assembled a team that consisted of Milwaukee architects Richard Philipp and Peter Brust, and the Sheboygan civil engineer J. Donahue, who had previously worked for the Kohler company located in that town. Kohler later claimed in a letter that he also suggested the "desirability of having a landscape architect cooperate, and that you [W. H.] stated that you knew of a young man in Boston who might consider coming," referring to Elbert Peets. He also mentions that he paid travel expenses for Peets.[61] The association of Hegemann and Elbert Peets (1886–1968) was of lasting significance for both (Fig. 23). Out of their partnership and collaboration evolved an admiring and congenial friendship, and they corresponded until Hegemann's death.

In 1915, Peets had obtained a Master's in Landscape Architecture at Harvard and was engaged on subdivision projects for the firm of Pray, Hubbard, & White in Cambridge when Hegemann contacted him.[62] Peets's Harvard degree, his landscape expertise, and his exquisite drawing skills were valuable contributions to the partnership of Hegemann & Peets, Architects, Landscape Architects and City Planners. Peets worked with

Hegemann on all the projects in the Midwest and one in Pennsylvania, providing planting plans and design. Notable are Peets's drawings in the promotional brochures for residential developments and in the co-authored *The American Vitruvius: An Architects' Handbook of Civic Art* of 1922.

Hegemann was in charge of overseeing the Kohler Village project in Sheboygan, Wisconsin, on behalf of the partnership of Hegemann & Peets and their supporting associates. Peets was engaged in the landscape and design aspects, Richard Philipp in the architecture, and J. Donahue in surveys and maps. Peter Brust, the other architect, apparently did not participate. Hegemann's responsibility entailed the planning and siting of houses and roads. From all indications it seems that the team worked well together.

Adjacent to the factory, the areas designated West I and South I were designed by Hegemann & Peets. West I included the Ravine Park, and the American Club, a residence for single men, primarily recent immigrants in need of learning English and becoming "Americanized." South I featured the somewhat less scenic Roosevelt Park and the Forest Lodge functioning as a civic club. Both these buildings were designed by Philipp in Austrian Tyrolean style at Kohler's request. The impressive American Club was frequently illustrated in periodicals and later became a tourist attraction and elegant inn.

Two of Hegemann's favored urban design elements characterized the layout of West I and South I. They are tree-lined boulevards and the grouping of houses, preferably homes with gardens. His ideas for Kohler Village are stated in a report presented to Kohler prior to starting the work. The report bears Hegemann's signature and is dated November 21, 1916.[63]

The document is organized in six sections under the headings: "The Factory," "The Residential District," "The Economic Considerations," "The Physical Plan," "The Economic Organization," and "The Social Organization." It begins with comments on the Kohler factory, but the introductory paragraph articulates a social committment expressed in language echoing Hegemann's *Für Gross-Berlin* manifestoes.

> The factory is the economic nucleus of Kohler City and necessarily one of the most dominant features in the life of every man working regularly for Kohler Co. Any improvement of social and esthetic conditions above the average will have to begin with the factory, making it a more ideal place for working, efficiently organized, roomy, healthful, well-lighted, as dust free as possible, and well-equipped with machinery able to save backbreaking and stultifying labor.

Any expansion of the plant should be determined by "efficiency as well as sightliness." Further, Hegemann states, "However splendid an organism such a factory may become, it always will play in the general organism of the community somewhat the role of the stomach in the animal body, essential, but never altogether free from features objectionable to nose and eye." He believed these features should not be considered "shameful," but that

Fig. 23. Elbert Peets.
Courtesy of Cornell University, Department of Manuscripts and University Archives.

they ought to be shielded by trees and landscaping. Turning to specifics, Hegemann recommended widening High Street, the main access to the factory, in order to accommodate two electric streetcar lines for the transport of machinery and workers, who could wait in gatehouses marking the entrance to the industrial precinct. Additionally, the street should be converted into a boulevard lined with trees and landscaped strips.

The section on "The Residential District" addresses organizational and economic aspects of the village. It opens with a general statement that "the building of the residential village should be based on a clear economic and social conception." Steering away from paternalism, the modern worker preferred to receive his income in cash wages and decide for himself how best to use it. Improving his living conditions was, however, often beyond his means. Recognizing the need for adequate housing, the Kohler Company determined to provide its workers a residential community with civic services, social centers, parks, playgrounds, and homes with gardens in addition to cash wages.

Hegemann considered it economically advantageous for the company to build a new town for its workers. The village would promote nationwide interest and would "very clearly establish a precedent of an industrial city with superior conditions where all modern ideas carried out stand financially on their own merits." His understanding and close attention to the economics of housing served him well on the Kohler project. Six pages of the report were devoted to economic detail, taxation, and land acquisition. He proposed the creation of a building-and-loan association, which already existed in nearby Sheboygan and other cities, as well as accident and healthcare benefits, including insurance for the aged.

Ideas regarding the layout of the residential portions were set down in the section on "The Physical Plan." Hegemann was favorably impressed by the surroundings of the Kohler Company, which were "full of delightful gifts of nature, rolling land, fine trees, a most surprising winding stream, high ravines, wide, perfectly framed views; in short, an ideal location for a garden city." The intention was to begin work on West I, where streets ran north-south and east-west, and several older houses already existed. In order to expose the new homes to sunlight, Hegemann proposed placing them so their four corners, and not their walls, would point in the directions of the compass. Even the lot size for the small houses allowed for this manipulation of siting. "The houses should not, by exigencies of economy, be packed together in the streets like dead flowers in a book, but shall be grouped opening up to the sun like living flowers and leaves of a tree in free nature." They should definitely not be placed in a pedantic way, he said, and his sketch showed the placement of a proposed grouping of houses: combinations of three and four homes surround a rectangular playground, and each of two "side courts" are enclosed by three houses. Larger buildings, preferably matched, are placed on the facing corner lots at the street intersections, forming an entrance. He also recommended that on every block buildings should be placed to take account of sun exposure, but also to be treated as a large group. Uniformity in plantings, rooflines, similar materials, and colors should achieve a "satisfying harmony." Each home was to have a distinct character as a member of a distinct group. He mentions out-of-town inspection trips, apparently together with Philipp and Kohler, to prefabricated houses and places such as the factory in Bay City, Michigan, which produced "Aladdin homes."[64] The results were still being discussed when the report was written, but were later rejected as unattractive.

The "Social Organization" envisioned by Hegemann was to take place in the schoolhouse or a civic club and involve activities much like those in the "settlements" in Chicago and New York. He thought an institution for manual training might help the factory develop higher standards in its production.

The concluding paragraph illustrates Hegemann's commitment to the betterment of the working class: "Gradually the deadening monotony and unhealthfulness of industrial life could be overcome by more humane and more promising conditions. If Kohler Garden City strides among the pace setters in this field, its importance will be more than that of a money making concern; it would become an important factor for the civilization of the country."

While some of Hegemann's recommendations can be detected in what was actually built, he may have become impatient with the paucity of progress and the alterations demanded by the client. Although their collaboration lasted only a year and resulted in the completion of a mere fraction of the scheme, the interaction between Hegemann and Kohler produced notable insights regarding the planning of new towns. It poised two "pragmatic idealists" in search of a rational balance of social commitment and humanistic, aesthetic, and economic concerns. Hegemann, claiming city planning to be a science, was actually as visionary in his pursuits as Kohler was in his concept of a utopia that would provide, in addition to housing, a civic center with auditorium, a nature theater, sports facilities, the America House to educate foreign workers, and, eventually, a university, all marked by the Kohler name. Hegemann and Kohler learned from each other through both their shared visions and their disagreements. The ruffled feathers of the two strong personalities led to the termination of their relationship and the erasure of Hegemann's contribution to the village and its underlying concepts.

Hegemann & Peets were contracted for other projects while working at the Kohler Village. This and Hegemann's absences from the Milwaukee area contributed to Kohler's irritation toward him. As a result, the parting of Kohler and Hegemann & Peets was rancorous. It is documented in letters preserved in the Kohler Company archives, where they were discovered after decades of obscurity. The exchange of letters that resulted in Hegemann's termination as planner dates from December 1916 and January 1917.[65] Hegemann was in San Francisco, undergoing throat surgery, when he replied to a letter by Kohler of December 1. His client was dissatisfied with the planting plan for River Front Park, primarily conceived by Peets, which he felt was too elaborate. Hegemann expressed regret that "a large amount of work bestowed upon the subject should go to waste." Another argument concerned plans and specifications for the Lake Front Park, which Kohler claimed was included in their contract, but said that he had received "nothing but a picture." Hegemann assured the client that Peets would provide a more detailed version at no extra cost, although the planners had already contributed out-of-pocket to the work at Kohler. Hegemann mentioned that the Lake Front Park was not intended for the workers, but for wealthy abutters, who might share in the expenses. He delved further into financial matters because Kohler had criticized the houses by the architect Philipp as too expensive. Hegemann reminded his client that he should regard "the role of a tasteful and practical builder of a new city" as valuable as the expense for a painting or sculpture. Hegemann suggested that to save money, perhaps prefabricated houses could be used, although Kohler, Hegemann, and Philipp had visited several firms producing low-cost houses and considered them unsuitable. After holding this frank letter for three weeks, Hegemann sent it with an accompanying apologetic note on January 8, 1917.

Kohler's answer was "equally as frank." He reminded Hegemann that at his request all business transactions were with him (W. H.) and not with

Peets. The Lake Front Park was actually owned by the city and was intended to benefit people of modest means. The money was not available for the current plan, and it had to be revised. He noted, "We should have had a definite contract, but that sort of was overlooked." He was offended by Hegemann's "out-of-pocket payments," stating that "we do not accept charity and do not want you to donate anything to the Kohler family or this community," and said he would reimburse him. Regarding the architect Philipp, Kohler considered him a respected friend to whom he would send a copy of this letter, and he expected Philipp to do all future architectural work for him. Turning to the total cost of planning, which had initially been estimated at $4,000, he noted that it had far exceeded this sum. On the other hand, "is it not natural to assume that any project conceived in some spirit of altruism, as you will agree this was, would not provide for an excessive burden of expense. . . ." Saving money by using Aladdin products would have resulted in "a battery of monotonous rows of houses," and he was fully satisfied with all that was accomplished during the past year to make the Kohler Village "an attractive and desirable place to live," thanks to the work by Hegemann & Peets, the architect Philipp, and the engineer Donahue. Kohler was disappointed that Hegemann & Peets had spent so much time on River Front Park, when the completion of West I and the building of workingmen's homes should have come first. He had hoped that these and the American Club would be available for occupancy in the summer of 1917. However, he felt that much had been learned from all aspects of city planning, landscaping, and the architecture and placement of houses.

Concluding his letter, Kohler wrote that "we should take time to digest the plans already made, . . . develop West I, and to leave the details of the other sections, now tentatively planned, until the time when there is prospect of their being needed. . . ." In a postscript he implied the termination of his arrangement with Hegemann, stating that "the incident is closed." The work on Kohler Village continued following the plans provided by the partnership, until further development was resumed in 1924 by Olmsted Associates.

The Kohler Company and the Kohler Village have generated numerous publications. The longest strikes in American labor history—in 1934, and from 1954 until 1960, and litigations which took another five years—gave the company unwelcome notoriety. Kohler, still primarily a family business, now has international reach with diversified enterprises.[66] In the company's publicity and articles, the Kohler Village, frequently described as a planned garden-industrial community, is proudly singled out. Mentioned as planners and consultants are the Olmsted Brothers Associates in Brookline, Massachusetts, with Frederick Law Olmsted Jr. Hegemann & Peets's initial work was expunged, and its records are hard to come by.

Although the partnership was involved with Kohler Village for barely a year—from 1916 to 1917—the imprint of their concepts persisted in the two sections they completed, West I and South I, and in the River Front Park. Traces can even be detected in the later work of Olmsted Associates, who were engaged by Kohler in 1924, with Henry V. Hubbard assuming the supervision of the development.

The results of the Kohler Village remained truncated as far as Hegemann & Peets were concerned, and they are not noted by Hegemann in his later publications on other American urban projects. Kohler failed to produce visually attractive documentation comparable to the brochures and drawings of their other endeavors. The project's value rests in the fact that Hegemann's ideas were focused on planning a new town rather than a residential development. For Peets the experience served him well for his later career in Franklin D. Roosevelt's Resettlement Administration, under the direction of Rexford Guy Tugwell, in the planning of three "greenbelt" demonstration new towns.[67] Peets' work on these towns relates markedly to the projects by Hegemann & Peets, leaving open to conjecture which one of the partners was primarily responsible for their layouts.

Breaking away from Kohler gave the partners time for unrelated and pending projects. Discussions on the development of Washington Highlands in Wauwatosa, Wisconsin, formerly the vast Pabst Farm, began in 1916. A legal agreement, dated August 1917, specified "Dr. Hagemann's [*sic*]" responsibilities, in addition to providing the general plan for the subdivision. Hegemann showed a plan for Washington Highlands in his 1916 report on Milwaukee. This plan was also reproduced in Hegemann's volume *Amerikanische Architektur* of 1925–26.[68] The accompanying description notes that it was the first design for the subdivision of a very topographically irregular area. This first plan is nearly identical with those of 1917, when the partnership of Hegemann & Peets was in place. The clients for this substantial enterprise were Richter, Dick & Reuteman, Planners and Developers of High Grade Subdivisions of Milwaukee (Figs. 24, 25). The attractive promotional brochure of 1917 shows the influence of the English garden city publications.[69] The large double-page plans and color illustrations of houses are credited to the partners, yet only one small black-and-white sketch is in Peets's distinctive style and signed "EP" (Figs. 26, 27, 28).

The brochure announced Washington Highlands as "a new type of subdivision for Milwaukee." Because of its 133-acre size, it might be called a "super-subdivision," not only for its large area, but also for the amount of capital involved. It also touted a "unique system of a novel type of restrictions" and "home protection" to reinforce and maintain the scenic, park-like character. Washington Highlands was proclaimed in the brochure to be the "largest restricted area in Milwaukee." Only homeowners who were members of a "Privileged Park Association" would be permitted to use the numerous parks and playing fields. Specifications converted

Fig. 24. Cover of the promotional brochure for the residential development of Washington Highlands, Wisconsin, by Hegemann & Peets, 1919. CCCC

Washington Highlands into a contained and "secluded" residential development enclosed by hedges and walls, comparable to contemporary gated communities. The restrictions addressed the preservation of "harmony in architecture and landscape architecture . . . with neighboring structures and topography . . . precluding counter purposes." At the end of the description of the restrictions and to ameliorate its antidemocratic character, the brochure stated, "Washington Highlands is a *Civic Undertaking* founded on a patriotic belief in Milwaukee's present and future greatness."

The *Restrictions and Protections* were also issued as a separate handbook for the homeowners.[70] The 33-page booklet of detailed prescriptions, couched in legal language, transferred from the Washington Heights Company to the Washington Homes Association "the right, power and authority . . . to enforce, by every remedy allowed by law, the observance and performance of each and every of said restrictions, protections, ease-

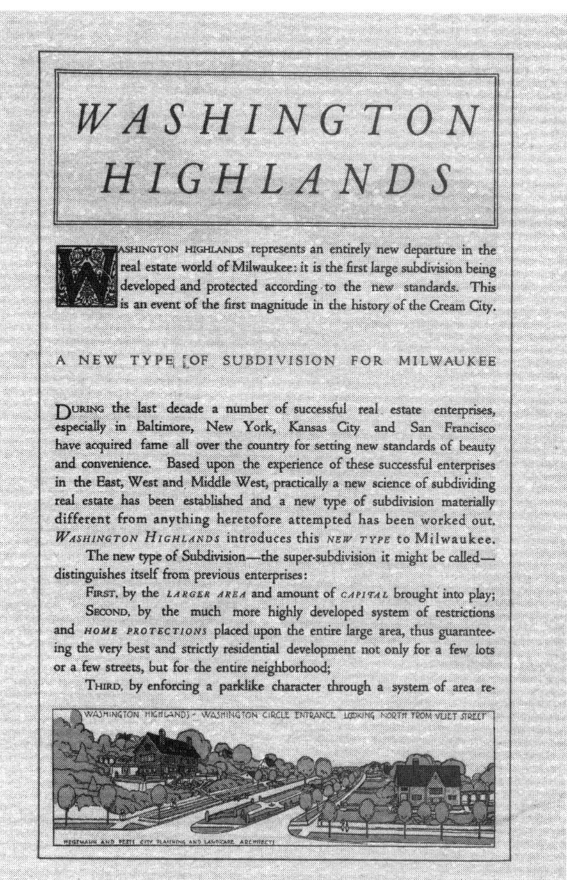

WASHINGTON HIGHLANDS

WASHINGTON HIGHLANDS represents an entirely new departure in the real estate world of Milwaukee: it is the first large subdivision being developed and protected according to the new standards. This is an event of the first magnitude in the history of the Cream City.

A NEW TYPE OF SUBDIVISION FOR MILWAUKEE

DURING the last decade a number of successful real estate enterprises, especially in Baltimore, New York, Kansas City and San Francisco have acquired fame all over the country for setting new standards of beauty and convenience. Based upon the experience of these successful enterprises in the East, West and Middle West, practically a new science of subdividing real estate has been established and a new type of subdivision materially different from anything heretofore attempted has been worked out. *WASHINGTON HIGHLANDS* introduces this *NEW TYPE* to Milwaukee.

The new type of Subdivision—the super-subdivision it might be called—distinguishes itself from previous enterprises:

FIRST, by the *LARGER AREA* and amount of *CAPITAL* brought into play;

SECOND, by the much more highly developed system of restrictions and *HOME PROTECTIONS* placed upon the entire large area, thus guaranteeing the very best and strictly residential development not only for a few lots or a few streets, but for the entire neighborhood;

THIRD, by enforcing a parklike character through a system of area re-

Fig. 25. Title page from the Washington Highlands *promotional brochure.* CCCC

ments, covenants, conditions, charges or provisos. . . ." Consideration was given to physical aspects and uses, for instance excluding any form of business activity, and also "Limitation of Ownership to persons of white race." Nonwhites were permitted only as "domestic servants while employed by the owner or occupant of any land included in the tract"—a racist covenant permitted at the time.

It is surprising that Hegemann did not object to an affiliation with a development espousing this type of social control. The completed Washington Heights became highly successful and remains one of the partnership's most recognized works. In 1988 it was proposed as a Historic District by the State of Wisconsin in a report that praised its lasting uniqueness as a garden suburb.[71]

Other than the *Restrictions*, the program presented to Hegemann & Peets conformed to their most cherished concepts. Paramount was the

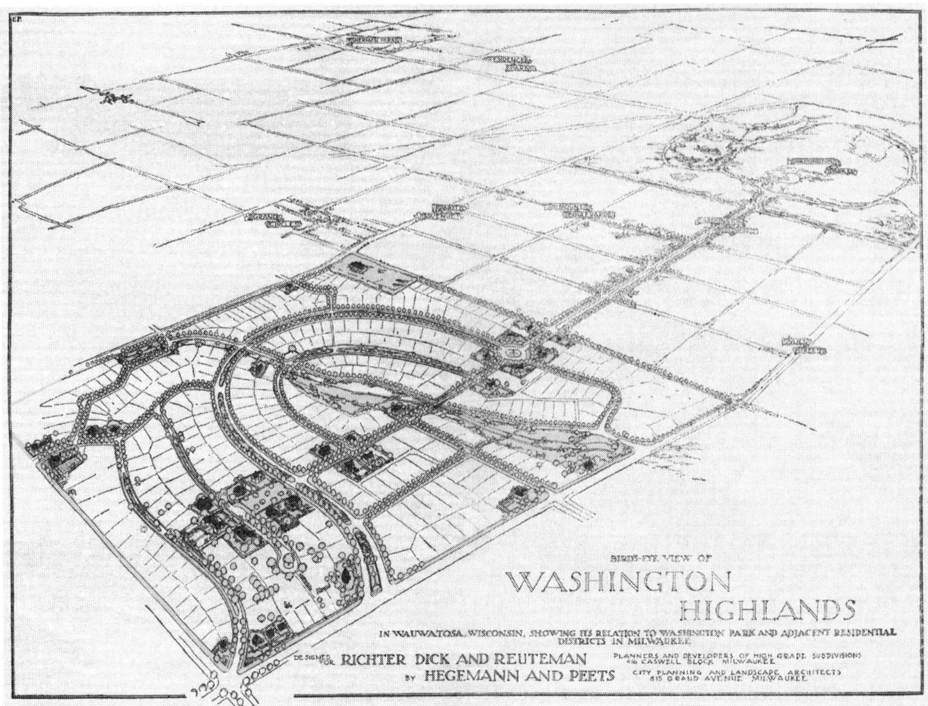

Fig. 26. Plan of Washington Highlands and adjacent street grid of Milwaukee. CCCC

preservation of the topographical and natural features—especially trees—of the former scenic Pabst Farm, still held dear by the family. The plan in the brochure shows substantial park areas along the creek and extensive tree planting along the roads. A split-level circular boulevard adjusts to the hillside, most, but not all, of the roads are gently curved, and there is a particular avoidance of dead-end streets. A linear central avenue functions as the main connection to the street grid surrounding the garden suburb. Some of the buildings are grouped around small parks. The houses in the brochure are not of equal design, but contribute to an overall harmony. The attractive entrances or gateways to the development emphasize its exclusiveness, and the entire area is enclosed by hedges and rows of trees.

Lots in the garden suburb sold well, which led to the nearby subdivision Grand Circle, also designed by Hegemann & Peets for Richter, Dick, and Reuteman, and advertised as the "Realization of a New Idea." A bird's-eye view is reproduced in Hegemann's volume *Amerikanische Architektur*, where he described the site as flat and monotonous.[72] Into the preexisting grid plan, the planners inserted a circular tree-lined boulevard surrounding "a private garage court" that served fourteen choice lots fan-

Fig. 27. Plan of Washington Highlands indicating building lots, parks, and parkways. CCCC

Fig. 28. Plan of the Grand Circle Subdivision designed by Hegemann & Peets, near Washington Highlands. CCCC

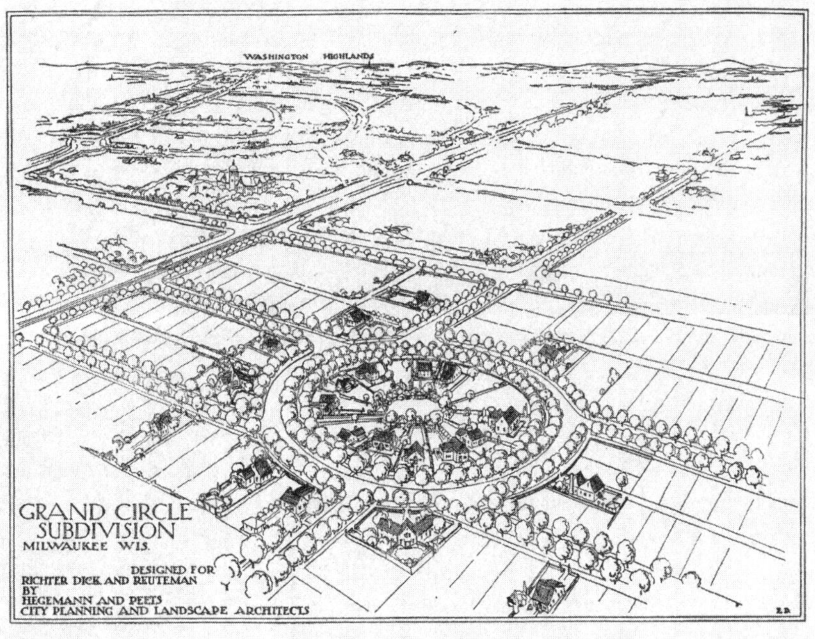

ning out like the spokes of a wheel with wide frontages on the boulevard. Hegemann thought the illustrated plan, drawn for advertising purposes, lacked an additional access road to the boulevard, and he disapproved of the "romanticized" style of the houses. Exceptions to the uniform house-lots were those at the corners of the street intersections. With its regularity, the Grand Circle subdivision differed markedly from Washington Highlands, however, it was equally successful and stands largely as Hegemann & Peets had planned it.

In addition to Washington Highlands and Grand Circle, Hegemann & Peets were involved, off and on from 1916 until 1920, in the development of Lake Forest on the outskirts of Madison, Wisconsin. The scheme by two realtors from Madison, Chandler B. Chapman and Leonard Gay, was for a satellite community to Wisconsin's growing capital city on the southern shore of Lake Wingra. The location of this scenic parcel near the University of Wisconsin campus promised success. The developers anticipated that their engineers could overcome the marshy conditions of the land by installing drainage canals and lagoons; however, this proved unsuccessful and contributed to fiscal problems and the project's eventual failure in 1925. The land was later sold to the University of Wisconsin and converted into an arboretum. Lake Forest acquired the somewhat mysterious designation of "The Lost City."[73]

The earliest verified participation of Hegemann & Peets in the Lake Forest proposition are three "preliminary studies," dated November 25, 1916, and displayed in small plans in *The American Vitruvius* and *Amerikanische Architektur*.[74] Schemes A, B, and C show a "straight shot" at the State Capitol of 1904, by the architect George B. Post. In Scheme A there is an additional direct view line to the dome of Bascom Hall on the University of Wisconsin campus. Of the three studies, Scheme A is the most classic, with broad avenues radiating from the circular civic center that forms the hub for other radial streets as well. Scheme B shows a linear boulevard emerging from a rectangular civic center and a narrow lagoon that encloses short dead-end roads. Scheme C shows the vista axis as an elongated lagoon extending from a circular civic center. All three plans reflect the influence of Washington, D.C., perhaps derived from Peets's study of L'Enfant's plan. Hegemann's penchant for waterfront development and lagoons had prevailed in many of his recommendations for the towns he had visited.

Additional proposals for Lake Forest were likewise classic in design, especially the proposed athletic fields along Lake Wingra on both sides of Capitol Avenue.[75] Provisions were made for track and field sports, and for a large open-air theatre. A wide mall extends from the intersection with Capitol Avenue to the shore of the lake. The flat marshland surrounding the regular middle section was suggested for a nine-hole golf course. Willow trees were proposed for the marshy grounds.

Hegemann considered Wisconsin's unusually tall State Capitol emblematic for the placement of a prominent public building in a grid plan with vista diagonals pointing toward it. He had frequently encountered this problem during his travels across the country, and "Gridirons and Diagonals" was a significant theme in *American Vitruvius*, where it was scrutinized in a wide range of examples. According to Hegemann, the State Capitol in Madison, which tried to combine a monumental dome with four office wings, was a flawed design. Its program called for attractive angles (views) from eight sides, and the resulting problems were enhanced by the radiating diagonals. The effort to improve the building's relation to its site gave the incentive for several proposals by Hegemann & Peets. They are designated as "thumbnail studies bearing on the problem of the large public building located at the center of a star of eight radials," in *The American Vitruvius*, and "Madison: Studies for the Development of Capitol's Plaza" in *Amerikanische Architektur*.[76] These small drawings demonstrate the partners' endeavor to provide various contextual settings for George B. Post's building. In one, the street pattern is altered by the insertion of additional diagonals connecting the others to create an octagon. Another design provides the building with eight entrance courts. The enclosure of the Capitol Square with an arcade or "colonnaded pergola" is utilized for a unifying, pedestrian-friendly effect. In 1920, when the developers resumed activity after a hiatus for fiscal reasons, the partners suggested a similar device for the Civic Center in Lake Forest, surrounding the circular central square with an arcade and trees. Its purpose was to tie together future public buildings to be located around the center.

In addition to major projects, Hegemann & Peets undertook a number of others, including some unrealized "suggestions." These are cited in the two volumes and briefly mentioned in Hegemann's diaries and letters. Examples of these proposals are the "formal treatments of street-ends overlooking Lake Front Park," in Sheboygan, Wisconsin, part of a complete park plan that is not shown. The six sketches were intended for streets terminating abruptly upon reaching the shore. By means of landscaping the designs opened up scenic views, facilitating access down the slope to the lake.[77] There are more formal designs for the cemetery "Wanderers Rest" in Milwaukee and for a park-like setting for the Detroit Art Museum.[78] Hegemann & Peets were also consulted with regard to private estates, although they were recognized as city planners and landscape architects, rather than architects.

Hegemann had an interest in loghouses that found expression in building a summer retreat in Oconomowoc, Wisconsin, for the parents of the American composer Otto Luening.[79] Luening's father, Eugene, had studied music in his native Germany and later became the director of the Milwaukee Musical Society. When he received an appointment at the University of Wisconsin, the family moved to Madison. Hegemann was introduced to the Luenings by the Pabst family and was attracted to their immersion in music, and their socialist/anarchist inclinations, which meshed with his own. This personal acquaintance led to his 1921 design of a small loghouse appropriate for an elderly couple. Hegemann often joined the Luenings for musical gatherings, and as remuneration for the house-plans, Eugene Luening played Beethoven sonatas for him.

One project for a private client that brought considerable satisfaction for Hegemann & Peets was laying out Myron T. Maclaren's estate in Milwaukee on the shore of Lake Michigan in 1919–21. A few years later it became the subject of an article in *Wasmuths Monatshefte für Baukunst* (1926). Among the many illustrations were photographs sent by Maclaren showing developments in the gardens and some changes from the partners' original plans, all of which gave Hegemann the incentive to write an article with the nostalgic title, "Recollections of an American Garden."[80] Hegemann commented on his mixed feelings upon receiving the pictures showing deviations from the original plans. He noted that he had gladly accepted the project in 1918, when the anti-German atmosphere made it difficult for him to obtain work. He explainined that nearly all architecture of private homes in America was "garden city building," merging the activities of the town planner with that of the landscape architect, and the partnership had been successfully engaged in the development of garden suburbs. According to Hegemann the conditions of working for the Maclarens were ideal and without financial limits. The partners were responsible for the layout of the grounds and the siting of the future villa, but not its architecture, which Mrs. Maclaren wanted in Tudor style. Hegemann welcomed the clients' wish to place the house as close to Lake Michigan as possible. He persuaded them to accept a driveway approach from the side, rather than a circular rotary on the front, which would disrupt the relationship of the villa to the garden. Views of the Palace Zichy in Hungary are shown in the article to demonstrate this division. The partners' admiration for the gardens and well-sited villas by the American Charles A. Platt was reflected in their Maclaren plans and was emphasized in the text.[81] Hegemann was unable to persuade his clients to build their house to resemble those by Platt. In the same article the house designed by Hegemann in 1922 for his own family in Nikolassee, Berlin, echoes Platt's classical simplicity in its avoidance of extraneous elements and its integration into the garden.

Hegemann & Peets's garden for the Maclaren estate is exemplary in its landscape style, which seeks a balance between the formal and the natural. While responding to the scenic qualities of the site, they tended to avoid Olmsted's picturesque approach. Comparable to Platt's gardens and Leberecht Migge's parks, they created axially aligned, defined spaces with and within nature. In their scheme for the Maclaren estate the walls and architectural features, pergola, fountain, stairs, the mall, tennis court, and swimming pool are all integrated into a well-conceived total design. It is easy to understand Hegemann's disappointment when this totality was dismissed by later changes to the plan, particularly the Tudor-style mansion.

Before the United States entered World War I in 1917, Hegemann was at liberty to travel, and he took advantage of renewing old contacts and establishing new ones. Such an occasion was the Tercentennial [*sic*] Pilgrim City Association celebration in Boston in March 1916. Hegemann was one of the invited speakers; also included on the extensive guest list were John Nolen and the architect Ralph Adams Cram.[82] The attendees gathered around a model of Plymouth Rock to discuss a monument to be displayed at an 1920–21 exhibition. Hegemann is noted for recommending something more permanent than a "passing show." Perhaps under the influence of the Kohler Village project, he envisioned an entire model city "comprising its economic fabric, its residences, . . . factories and parks, terminals and playgrounds." Whatever the name, "New Plymouth," "New Boston," or "Pilgrim City," it would benefit the business interests of Boston and more. Some of those present preferred a civic center on an island in the Charles River, but Nolen supported Hegemann's idea of a new model city as a memorial.

Despite the anti-German antagonism caused by the conflagration in Europe, the Hegemann & Peets partnership was remarkably active from 1916 to 1918. The end of the war allowed Hegemann once more to travel freely and expand his activities beyond Wisconsin. Elbert Peets was absent from the office from January 1917 until December 1918, while working with the U.S. Army Camp Planning Section of the Construction Division.[83] Peets's travels in Europe, which aided their work on *The American Vitruvius*, took him away from Milwaukee as well.

In order to cover for his partner, supervise the expansion of their office, and assume work on a residential development near Reading, Pennsylvania, Hegemann engaged Joseph F. Hudnut (1884–1968) as his assistant. His diary notes Hudnut's arrival in Milwaukee on February 14, 1918. Hudnut had met Hegemann the previous summer upon completion of his studies at the School of Architecture at Columbia University.[84] The association of Hegemann and Hudnut had a profound impact on their professional lives, which extended into the 1930s. Arguably Hudnut, later dean of Harvard's Graduate School of Design from 1935–52, may be considered Hegemann's most genuine follower.

The year 1918 was eventful for Hegemann. The end of the war in November enabled him to discard the ambiguous nature of his position as an enemy alien and pacifist. The association with Hudnut and the development of the garden suburb of Wyomissing Park in Pennsylvania led to the establishment of a branch office in New York. Of greatest and lasting import, however, was the meeting of Hegemann and his future wife, Ida Belle Guthe, in Ann Arbor, Michigan, on December 18, 1918. He marked the day with an asterisk in his diary.

The ensuing relationship and marriage in June 1920 had an invigorating effect on Hegemann and induced him to consider his private and professional future. From the start the couple exchanged daily letters, written in English, although Guthe, whose father was originally from Germany, was fluent in German. Their letters are a valuable resource for researchers and are the basis of the *Family Saga* later composed by Ida Belle Hegemann.

Concomitant with the developments in his private life, Hegemann, Peets, and Hudnut became absorbed with the design of Wyomissing Park, which was their last cooperative project, and a major one. The New York office served as a base for Hudnut and increasingly for Hegemann and his research in the city's libraries for Hegemann & Peets's treatise *The American Vitruvius: An Architects' Handbook of Civic Art.* Previous endeavors also demanded occasional attention, and clients continued to present new requests.

In December 1916, Hegemann was approached to consider the planning of an unspecified industrial town for 5,000 people in Pennsylvania.[85] He noted on the letter that he was willing to accept, with a fee of $1,200 for two months to cover all expenses for himself and his assistant. This may have been an initial inquiry regarding Wyomissing Park, to be designated "The Modern Garden Suburb of Reading, Pennsylvania." Hegemann had multiple connections to Philadelphia and a high professional regard for John Nolen, whose friendship and expertise had played a role in the Madison propositions. Nolen had written a report in 1910 on Greater Reading for its Civic Association, and the 1919 promotional booklet for the subdivision stated that the Wyomissing Development Company engaged Hegemann & Peets to follow Nolen's inspiring precedent.[86] The company promised to spare no effort "towards the creation of a truly modern residential park in harmony with the best city planning thought."

Reading's growing textile and other industries created an acute housing shortage that affected all income levels and propelled the city's westward expansion. According to the brochure, Wyomissing Park proposed providing affordable housing for the working class, and residences for the affluent (Fig. 29). The social ethics of this enterprise were more in accordance with Hegemann's inclinations than those of Washington Highlands. His text in the brochure reflects this frame of mind, and it is shown in the title of the introductory section, "Democracy of the Garden City in Wyomissing Park."[87] One can assume that Hegemann's passages were approved by the developers: "The creation of Wyomissing Park deserves special interest and commendation because it is not guided by the ordinary desire to profit by providing an exclusive residence park for the wealthy few." The aim was to achieve "the happy blending of homes of various cost, tied together by harmony of design, [that] breathes the true spirit of democracy," as had been realized in Hampstead Garden Suburb in

Fig. 29. Cover of the promotional brochure for Wyomissing Park, a garden suburb of Reading, Pennsylvania, designed by Hegemann & Peets. CCCC

London. The plan envisioned for Wyomissing Park would not have the monotony of upper-class subdivisions with their "residences dotted over the ground in fairly even intervals" suggesting a "country house cemetery." Nor should modest houses be packed together in tedious rows, as was customary in Philadelphia and Reading. Instead, Hegemann saw a democratic ideology reflected in the comprehensive plan for this residential community. The message established Wyomissing Park's uniqueness and urban significance. Hegemann is listed as the author of the text, and Elbert Peets and Joseph Hudnut as authors of the drawings, excepting one by Armin Frunk. A considerable number of the drawings and plans is reproduced with explanatory captions by Hegemann, but without the attractive coloring in the *American Vitruvius* and *Amerikanische Architektur.*[88]

Comparable to his approach in the *Report on Oakland and Berkeley*, Hegemann availed himself, with the publication of the marketing brochure for Wyomissing Park, to go beyond describing the development and to lay down planning principles for residential settlements of general validity. These are convincingly demonstrated in the attractive illustrations and the design of the pamphlet.

Although the contract was signed in 1919 and the report bears that date, it was based on a two-year study. Some of the drawings are dated

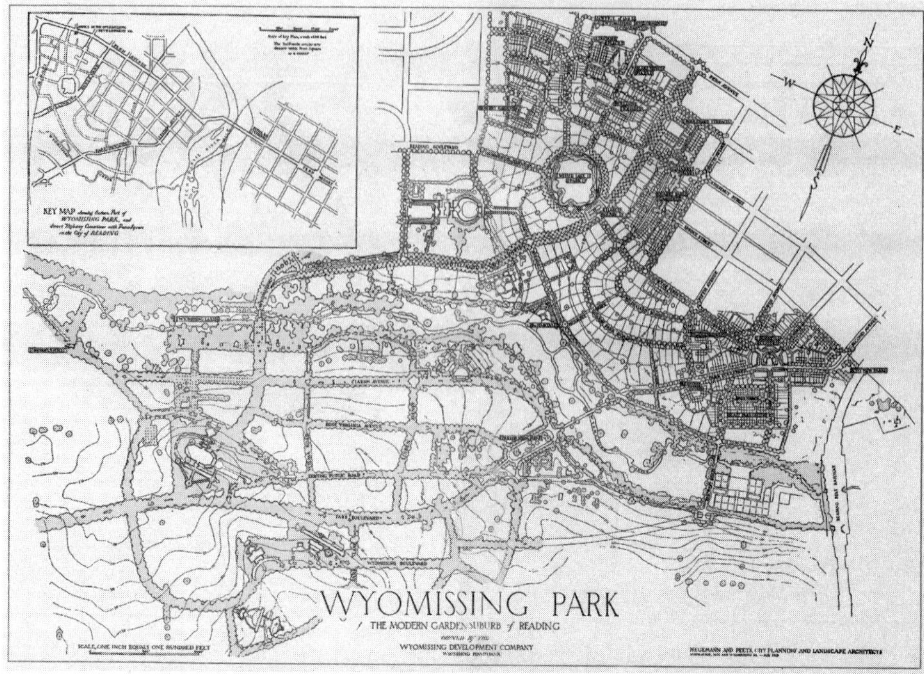

Fig. 30. Plan of Wyomissing Park. CCCC

1917, and according to Hegemann's diary the arrival of Hudnut in February 1918 intensified the work. They spent considerable time together on the site, which comprised 500 acres within walking distance of the business center of Reading. "The Modern Garden Suburb" called for affordable housing and larger residences, as well as a business center, two boulevards, twelve plazas, courts and squares, parks and playgrounds. Hegemann & Peets's plan refrained from proposing a rigid layout "drawn with a T-square." They foresaw a regional scope and "a living organism reflecting in prismatic variety the surrounding topographical conditions . . . accentuating certain features of the topography" (Fig. 30). The harmony and conjunction between architecture and landscape design was an important characteristics for which the partners considered themselves singularly well prepared.

The use of local building materials and the adaptation of the traditional Dutch-colonial style were recommended for the architecture of the row houses as well as the large residences. Two villas, including one for E. Richard Meinig, are shown, but the majority of the illustrations display a wide variety of groupings enclosing courts and squares for attached affordable houses (Figs. 31, 32). The option for attached rather than small detached houses on individual lots, as was customary in the Midwest, was readily accepted in Pennsylvania. Alleys along the backyards of the rows provided access to garages, anticipating that the industrial workers would own cars. Located near the more densely placed housing is the horseshoe-shaped, two-story business center (Figs. 33, 34). In the middle, a park with benches serves as an inviting yet contained civic gathering place. The resemblance in shape and color of Hegemann & Peets's business center in Wyomissing, to the Gross-Siedlung Britz, the Hufeisen-Siedlung in Berlin, designed by Bruno Taut and Martin Wagner in 1925–26, is notable.

The scenic beauty of the large tract in the Wyomissing Creek valley favored the preservation of the landscape and an emphasis on parks. Three types are specified: neighborhood parks, small parks, and landscape parks, forming a contiguous open-space network. Seven acres, formerly a "farm dump," were set aside for active sports, including twelve tennis courts, a baseball and football field, a croquet ground, and a swimming pool. The section in the brochure entitled, "The Re-Democratization of American Country Life" describes possibilities for a nine-hole golf course in the valley of the creek, responding to the growing popularity of golf for all social classes. The sport facilities and the landscape park bordering the creek were available to the general public, not only to the property owners of the garden suburb.

Figs. 31 and 32. Groupings of buildings around small parks or courts. CCCC

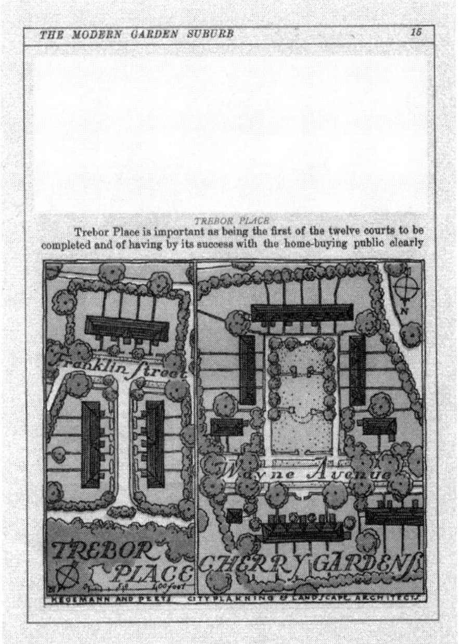

THE MODERN GARDEN SUBURB 15

TREBOR PLACE

Trebor Place is important as being the first of the twelve courts to be completed and of having by its success with the home-buying public clearly

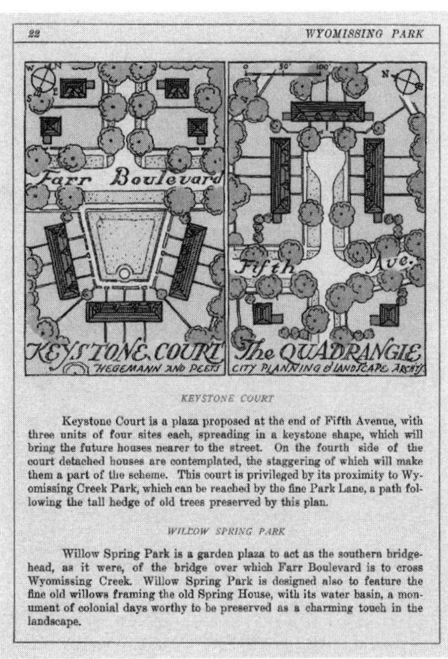

22 WYOMISSING PARK

KEYSTONE COURT

Keystone Court is a plaza proposed at the end of Fifth Avenue, with three units of four sites each, spreading in a keystone shape, which will bring the future houses nearer to the street. On the fourth side of the court detached houses are contemplated, the staggering of which will make them a part of the scheme. This court is privileged by its proximity to Wyomissing Creek Park, which can be reached by the fine Park Lane, a path following the tall hedge of old trees preserved by this plan.

WILLOW SPRING PARK

Willow Spring Park is a garden plaza to act as the southern bridgehead, as it were, of the bridge over which Farr Boulevard is to cross Wyomissing Creek. Willow Spring Park is designed also to feature the fine old willows framing the old Spring House, with its water basin, a monument of colonial days worthy to be preserved as a charming touch in the landscape.

Fig. 33. Business Center, Wyomissing Park, 1919. CCCC

Fig. 34. Bruno Taut and Martin Wagner's Siedlung Britz, Neukölln, Berlin. Built between 1925-26, it resembles Wyomissing Park's Business Center in shape and the use of color on the buildings. CCCC

The avoidance of monotony and the variety offered in Hegemann & Peets's proposal for Wyomissing Park are remarkably harmonious and balanced. Contextual cohesion is achieved by the landscaping and the similarity of style and materials of the buildings. The architecture was inspired by Pennsylvania's Dutch-colonial building traditions, which were easily adaptable to modern requirements. In the illustrations, this homogeneity does not appear forced because of the diversity in the layout of the streets, courts, and squares. Anxious to maintain this judiciously calibrated equilibrium, the promotional brochure lists restrictions placed on future building sites, reserving for the management of the subdivision the right of approval for all building and gardening. According to Hegemann, even thoughtfully drawn up restrictions could lead to stereotypical results and disagreements among individual property owners, although he agreed that certain rules offered protection against the invasive development of factories and excessive density and would maintain uniform set-backs and spaces between houses.

What Hegemann aspired to in Wyomissing Park was a community "combining individuality with a general feeling of harmony." He continued to express this tenet in his publications and critical writing.

The American Vitruvius: An Architects' Handbook of Civic Art

Following the end of the war Hegemann renewed contacts with his European colleagues, many of whom had no idea what had happened to him after he had left California. As an enemy alien he had only been permitted to move about in connection with his work within Wisconsin, and via New York to Reading, Pennsylvania. Now he was once more at liberty to travel about the country.

The partnership with Elbert Peets and collaboration with Joseph Hudnut was successful and personal relations were positive, yet there are indications of Hegemann's restlessness and a yearning for concerns beyond actual planning projects. Primarily he was preoccupied with the dilemma of finding his place in the world and a longing to return to Europe. However, two eventful years elapsed before Hegemann and his wife would leave America in the fall of 1921.

Despite the progress of the Wyomissing Park development, Hegemann was casting about for a professional change. In September 1918 he sought out Fiske Kimball (1881–1955), a pioneer in the emerging field of American architectural history.[89] Kimball was on the faculty of the University of Michigan at Ann Arbor, where Hegemann had lectured in 1913. Now, five years later, he wrote to "Professor Kimball" asking to enroll in his lectures as a graduate student.[90] The correspondence reveals that in addition to Kimball's course in "Methods of Research," Hegemann intended to take "Architectural Design," taught by Emil Lorch, and to devote "several hours a day to drawing." The partnership with Peets, who possessed exceptional drawing skills, had reinforced Hegemann's awareness that he lacked this ability. In his letter to Kimball, he mentioned Goethe's advice regarding drawing "as the means to enter the spirit of works of art." Kimball cautioned him about the time this ambitious program would require. Responding to Hegemann's inquiry about lodging, Kimball offered a spare room and bath in his own home for rent "as a strict business arrangement." Hegemann gave up his apartment and office in Milwaukee, stored his possessions, and moved to Ann Arbor. He stayed at the Kimballs' house over the winter, while they were in Massachusetts, and commuted to Wyomissing from his new location.

The relationship with Kimball and his wife Marie Goebel, both fluent in German, developed into a lasting friendship. The couple arranged a blind date for Hegemann with Ida Belle Guthe on December 14, 1918, and their courtship progressed from that day on. Her late father, originally from Germany, had been a professor of physics and dean of the graduate school at Ann Arbor.[91] According to Guthe, her widowed mother and brothers were initially opposed to her marriage to Hegemann, who was fifteen years her senior and divorced. In the course of their friendship, Hegemann inquired via Switzerland about his marital status. Much to his relief a divorce had taken place during his absence in 1916. His first wife, Alice Hesse, had remarried and was raising their daughter Ellis, who was born in 1906. Considering that it was just after the Armistice of World War I, the Guthe family was understandably concerned about Hegemann's German citizenship. He made it clear that he did not wish to give it up, and expressed his intention of returning to Germany to live and rebuild the devastated country. Despite these misgivings, they planned to marry but decided to wait until Ida Belle's graduation from college in June 1919.

Hegemann left his studies at the university in Ann Arbor after one semester, and in January 1919 he reestablished an office/studio in Milwaukee. The letterhead of his business stationary changed to "Hegemann and Peets–Hudnut and Montgomery, Associated Architects and Landscape Architects, New York, Milwaukee."

Interspersed between visits with the Guthe family in Ann Arbor and trips to Wyomissing and New York, Hegemann traveled to Chicago, Cleveland, Detroit, and San Francisco. His frequent letters to Ida Belle record what and whom he saw, and what he thought. He always wrote in English, occasionally slipping in a phrase in German or French. Their correspondence is testament to their immediate and lasting rapport and their shared interests in literature, the theatre, art, and music.

Hegemann's letters contain some descriptive passages, comparable to the writings of the renowned flaneur Walter Benjamin. In 1919 he wrote to Ida Belle from Chicago:

> I had quite a restful night in the train, and walked into the foggy atmosphere of Chicago, with a brisk and refreshed mind and body. The fog seemed at the same time curiously high and dense, and one walked like in the tallest of laundry yards: could not see very far ahead looking into the white sheets of waving cloth of fog, everywhere, but a high sky over one's head. Arriving in Chicago and seeing Michigan Avenue and the Lake is always a sensation for me. My first arrival here was ten years ago. . . . Again I enjoyed the majestic purity of some of the skyscrapers facing the lake, fine documents of the best perhaps in modern building, and curiously wondered again at the strange contrast between them and the adjoining buildings of the more conservative school of architects, with their classic apparatus. The whole long bitter struggle since the preparations for the Chicago World's Fair to this day passed my eyes in documentary evidence: the huge mass of the new gigantic Marshall Field Museum rising immediately east of the railroad station spelled victory for the conservatives. The big city began to team [*sic*] around me. . . .[92]

In the same letter Hegemann mentions staying at Hull House, where he had lodged ten years earlier. He expressed regret that "Miss Jane Addams, the great Mistress of Hull House . . . is in the south, [was] beginning to become a mythical figure." He also noted a meeting with the architects George G. Elmslie, "a very charming and most able modern architect," and "the 'great Sullivan,'" with whom he had a good chat.

In February 1920 Hegemann journeyed by train and stagecoach to Oregon and California. He wrote to Ida Belle that he was "travelling in the stage on the same roads along the coast I have driven up and down in 1913 and 1916/17."[93] From San Francisco he reported, "I am drinking the captivating sweet wine of the climate, blossoms and sunshine, and the even greater joy of meeting many dear, good old friends, all of whom seem to be glad to see me again, and to all of whom I feel tied by old bonds." Among his "old" friends was Duncan McDuffie, agent for the garden suburb St. Francis Wood, planned by the Olmsted brothers. In a newspaper interview Hegemann commended St. Francis Wood as comparable to Roland Park in Baltimore and Forest Hills Gardens in New York and remarked on the protection of its attractiveness by means of restrictive covenants. He provided McDuffie with an extensive transcript of the interview.[94] Photographs of St. Francis Wood, perhaps by Hegemann, are reproduced in *The American Vitruvius* and *Amerikanische Architektur*.[95]

Upon his return to Milwaukee, Hegemann sent out cards announcing the resumption of the partnership's practice after spending his vacation studying recent architectural developments and landscape gardening in California. He also mentioned Peets's Charles Eliot traveling fellowship from Harvard University and his study of Washington, D.C. The result was to be published in book form, conceivably referring to their forthcoming co-authored volume that would "clear up many misconceptions about . . . American town planning and landscape architecture."[96]

When exactly Hegemann and Peets embarked on their magnum opus, *The American Vitruvius: An Architects' Handbook of Civic Art*, is not certain. Peets's departure for Europe in the spring of 1920 is mentioned by Hegemann in a letter to Ida Belle written two weeks after his return from California. He referred to Peets's studies of Washington as "brilliant" and his partner's leaving in a few weeks. With a touch of envy, Hegemann expressed a need to "extract" himself from his professional obligations, which were interfering with "more important work along the lines of my private studies that appear most pressing to me at present."[97] From then on he frequently commented on his "immersion" in books, signaling a transition to a new phase dedicated to scholarly work, and turning away from his successful planning practice.

While pondering this decision, a personal benchmark was his marriage to Ida Belle Guthe. Following her graduation and summer with her family, she taught school in a small town in Montana. In his letters and during visits with her, Hegemann urged her to hasten the wedding. At the end of her teaching assignment in June 1920, they were married in a small ceremony surrounded by her family and their friends.

During the next year they lived in Milwaukee and spent time in New York, where Hegemann did library research and continued to work at Wyomissing with Hudnut. Upon Hegemann's completion of the manuscript for *The American Vitruvius* in the fall of 1921, the couple left the United States. This time frame implies that the co-authors concluded the text and the selection of 1,203 illustrations in less than two years.

The American Vitruvius: An Architects' Handbook of Civic Art, by Werner Hegemann and Elbert Peets, was published in 1922, when Hegemann had returned to Berlin and Peets had established himself as an independent landscape planner.[98] It is frequently referred to by its subtitle, *Civic Art*. Although by no means Hegemann's only publication in English, it is his best known work in the United States. It has received scant recognition in Germany, conceivably due to a title that implies an exclusively American focus.

The authors' interpretation of "civic art" is stated in the Foreword and substantiated by choosing a synopsis of Camillo Sitte's teachings for the first chapter. The following passage, in which Hegemann updated and broadened Sitte's principles, serves as a precept for his position regarding the city and the primary message of *The American Vitruvius*:

> One of the foremost aims of this book on civic art is to bring out the necessity of extending the architect's sphere of influence, to emphasize the essential relation between a building and its setting, the necessity of protecting the aspect

> of the approaches, the desirability of grouping buildings into harmonious ensembles, of securing dominance of some buildings over others, so that by the willing submission of the less to the greater there may be created a larger, more monumental unity; a unity comprising at least a group of buildings with their surroundings, if possible entire districts and finally even, it may be hoped, entire cities.[99]

The inclusion of Sitte's "principles" under the heading "The Modern Revival of Civic Art," emhasizing his attention to Renaissance, Baroque, and medieval precedents, served to acquaint the English-speaking public with his ideas. Raymond Unwin singled this out in his detailed review of *The American Vitruvius*, which also praised the book's international scope.[100] The concept favored by Hegemann, which links the book to Sitte's *Der Städtebau*, considers the city as an evolving process within which architectural monuments and civic complexes provide points of quiescence and symbolic continuity. Another similarity between both landmark books ascribes equal importance to the space between buildings—the plaza, its shape, and relationship of the mass of buildings that frames it—volume and void forming an intrinsic synthesis. These points weighed prominently for the co-authors and were reinforced for Peets by his year-long study tour in Europe.

Peets's contribution to *The American Vitruvius* included a notable number of drawings that visually realizes the salient concepts. His engaging on-site sketches analyze the placement of monumental buildings in relation to open space. Peets tended to employ a slanted bird's-eye view, prescient of his later interest in aerial photography.[101]

Hegemann's extensive picture research and use of illustrations from existing sources are complemented by Peets's original drawings, and those by Franz Herding of the architectural firm of Herding & Boyd in St. Louis. Many of these were also done on-site in Europe. Examples from the pamphlets by the Hegemann & Peets partnership, including some of Hudnut's drawings for Wyomissing Park, were also included.

Comparable to the methodology Hegemann had evolved for the Berlin 1910 Exhibition, he orchestrated the over 1,203 examples from a range of historical epochs and geographic regions, creating meaningful page layouts. Items are grouped by subject and juxtaposed without consideration of time or place of origin. Notably, American examples are fully integrated with those from Europe, both in terms of prominence and for visual effectiveness. Hegemann admired "America's valuable contributions . . . her university groups, world's fairs, civic centers, and garden cities . . . promising even greater ones through the development of the skyscraper, of the zoned city, and of the park system."[102] On the American continent his consideration of skyscrapers within the modern cityscape had changed considerably since the earlier "Turmhaus" debate in Germany. He came to favor the placement of skyscrapers in American civic centers and featured New York's Municipal Building as frontispiece in *The American Vitruvius*. He affirmed emphatically that, "The intelligent use of the skyscraper in civic design will be America's most valuable contribution to civic art." Plans and bird's-eye views of "Civic Center Suggestions" by Hegemann & Peets were rendered by Herding and later also reproduced in *Amerikanische Architektur*.[103] Regardless of the few slanted roofs, the designs are strikingly modern, presenting ensembles of high-rise buildings enclosing inner-city plazas, some featuring central towers and multilevel traffic arteries. A caption states: "These studies by the authors illustrate the adaptation of various Renaissance motives to modern conditions and gridiron street plans." They are shown in the section "Groupings of Buildings in America."

The interpretation of "Civic Art" and how it differed from City Beautiful aesthetics provided the framework for the seven chapters and the range of visual material. However, one searches in vain for a succinct definition of the term. Hegemann approximates the concept from all angles, but challenges others to unravel its complexity.

The American Vitruvius seldom refers to the interaction of city planning and urban history, yet for Hegemann "Civic Art" bears civic connotations, comparable to those reflected in the Spanish term "*arte cívico*." The meaning of "Civic Art" is certainly broader and more sympathetic to modern urbanism than the "City Beautiful" movement with which it should be neither confused nor pigeonholed. Aspects of "Civic Art" are comparable to Hegemann's interpretation of Classicism, which evolved into a key premise of his architectural criticism in Berlin.

A definition of "Civic Art" might read: "For the authors of *The American Vitruvius*, 'Civic Art' is a valiant, if problematic, attempt to reconcile a rational city plan based on social scientific theory with a three-dimensional, artistic arrangement of buildings and spaces. Only this interpretation would explain and justify the inclusion of American garden cities (really garden suburbs), park systems, and skyscrapers as manifestations of 'Civic Art.'"[104]

In their Foreword the authors' purpose is described as the compilation of a "thesaurus" to be perused and not be taken as a prescriptive manual. Early reviewers were puzzled by this intention, and some questioned Hegemann's objections to "informal planning" as pertaining to park and garden design. On the whole, however, *The American Vitruvius* was received with awe and assigned the status of a landmark in architecture and planning literature.[105]

Favorable initial reviews in the United States, England, and Australia were followed by decades during which the work was either ignored or deemed reactionary by architects and scholars. Like its primary author, the book became a victim of the selective narrowness of the prevailing approach to Modernism, until a more inclusive and balanced view gradually reversed this trend. The recent rediscovery of *The American Vitruvius* and a recognition of its relevance for contemporary architecture and urban design have been fostered by the search for a cultural context and sense of place, and by proponents of residential developments following the tendencies of the New Urbanism.

Knowledge of the authors, particularly Hegemann, and the circumstances of the genesis of the volume remained sparse. A reprint edition in 1988 aided the incipient interest in *The American Vitruvius* and shed light on Hegemann and Peets. Contributions by A. J. Plattus and L. Krier address the significance of the book for modern city building, and C. Crasemann Collins's essay provides an overview of the authors' intellectual trajectories and the circumstances of the realization of their volume.[106] The European theorist and the pragmatic Midwestern landscape planner converged as collaborating authors. Hegemann's Foreword claimed his primary responsibility for the text, excepting the section on the plan of Washington, D.C., and asserted that "form and content are expression of their common judgment."

With regard to Hegemann, the concepts presented in *The American Vitruvius*, as well as the book itself, form part of a sequence of major works. Preceding its publication in 1922 were the seminal volumes *Der Städtebau* (1911, 1913), the *Report on a City Plan for Oakland & Berkeley* (1915), and a series of smaller pamphlets and brochures on American topics. Following *The American Vitruvius* were Hegemann's books on political history and its effect on urban developments, presented comprehensively in *Das steinerne Berlin* (1930). Toward the end of his life the three volumes of *City Planning: Housing* (1932–37) were intended to complement his earlier American publication. The assemblage of these works constitutes a synthesis of his concepts regarding the present and future metropolis. The significance of *The American Vitruvius* is enhanced when considered in this context, rather than as an astonishing, isolated phenomenon.

4. Theory and Criticism

Back to a Broken Continent

Having completed *The American Vitruvius*, Hegemann accompanied his wife to Italy in the fall of 1921. They traveled through Italy and Greece before settling in Villa Martinelli in Posillipo, near Naples, to await the birth of their first child, Eva Maria, in January 1922.

Hegemann had been considering a return to Europe for some time and chose to make a cautious reentry via Italy. Opting for Posillipo indicates a choice informed by his interest in antiquity and Classicism. Naples was and still is rich in remnants of its early history. An ancient Greek colony, it was conquered by the Romans in the fourth century B.C. The scenic Campanian coast gained favor among wealthy Romans for respite and relaxation, turning it into "a center of fashion and cultivated leisure."[1] Posillipo, or Pausilypom—Greek for "pause from pain"—on the headland extending into the bay of Naples, became the site of sumptuous Roman villas and developed into a sophisticated cultural and intellectual resort alive with theaters and music. Evidence survives in the remains of the villas along the coast and is described in ancient inscriptions and by historians. Hegemann's interest in Posillipo probably derived from contact with Dr. Gerald F. Else, Chairman of the Department of Classical Studies at the University of Michigan at Ann Arbor. He also may have read the description of Posillipo by the scholar Günther: "No spot on the Italian littoral, extensive as that littoral is, lends itself to the development of the peculiar style of marine architecture (employed by wealthy Romans in their villas) . . . so well as this short strip of Campania that lies between Misenum and Pausilypon. The requisites are: an almost tideless sea, comparative shelter, a relative narrow foreshore backed by the cliffs of a soft volcanic rock, easy to quarry, hardening in use. . . ."[2]

For the expatriate Hegemann, the serene atmosphere on the Bay of Naples provided an interlude of several weeks to contemplate the complexity of his convictions on how to center his future life in the defeated Vaterland. The duality of his loyalty vacillating between America and Europe was akin to Goethe's "two souls, alas, dwell in my breast." An additional preoccupation was the conflict between his pacifist convictions and the war that had torn apart an admired and cherished world. As had always been his inclination, he turned to composing his thoughts on paper. After his long immersion in the English language, writing in his mother tongue provided Hegemann a home of sorts at a time of ambiguity. The resulting book synthesized ideas evolved during his prolonged stay in America and formed a transition to his deliberate choice for a new phase in his life.

Hegemann's initial works of fiction, *Deutsche Schriften: Iphigenie* and *Sieben Gespräche über das Königsopfer*, list the pseudonym Manfred Maria Ellis as author and Werner Hegemann as editor and compiler. The volume was published in Berlin in 1924. The eleven illustrations for Iphigenie were by the Greek artist Markos Zavitzianos, who became a close friend, often staying with the family in Nikolassee, Berlin.

The atmosphere of the Hegemanns' rented Villa Martinelli was recalled in a sequence of later publications also following the themes initiated in *Deutsche Schriften*. In this work fictionalized events unfold at the Villa Boccanera, patterned on the Villa Martinelli.[3] Of all his fictional works *Deutsche Schriften* is the most site specific and contains arresting descriptions of the place as Hegemann actually experienced it. These passages are prescient of his literary ambitions as a *flaneur*, which ran parallel to his critical and scholarly activities. For instance, he captures the unique atmosphere of a late afternoon on the terrace of the Villa: "Far below the sea washes ashore against the foundation pillars of the building. Above the gulf the solemn play of light and shadows between the sinking sun and the softly smoking Visuvius repeated itself. The bay lay nearly calm in the greyness of the descending evening. From the hell of the fiery eruption arose golden and glowing a column of steam into the sunny sky, golden like the eternal shafts of the Parthenon."[4]

Themes of this first of Hegemann's literary fictions were incorporated into nearly all his subsequent works; at times entire sections are repeated with minor variations. Thus, with some justification, Hegemann's historical fiction has been considered repetitious. However, it is also admired for its elegant style and literary content.[5] *Deutsche Schriften* was recast into the books on Frederick II, "The Great" and *Der gerettete Christus*, which generated heated controversies for their contentious ideas, and to a lesser extent, into *Napoleon*.

Turning from notable publications on city planning and related subjects in German and English, Hegemann made his entrée into literary endeavors under a pseudonym in the guise of an upper-class American intellectual. The critic Karl Scheffler sharply opposed Hegemann on various issues. Regarding his attack on *Deutsche Schriften*, Hegemann replied in an open letter in *WMB* that Scheffler "called it 'funny' that I used the occasion of a small breathing-time (space) between my American and German activities to write a historical-political satire. In this case it is a transparent mystification."[6]

The subterfuge of the pseudonym was not immediately discovered when *Deutsche Schriften* was privately published in 1924. A review in the *Frankfurter Zeitung* in October of that year, apparently by Scheffler, failed to notice the deception and was berated for its ignorance in the *Weltbühne* by an acquaintance of the book's publisher. Hegemann, defending the *Frankfurter Zeitung* for not uncovering the *Verschleierung* (concealment), stated that only the value of the content mattered.[7] Comments regarding the mysterious author added a piquant note to discussions in the press.

The choice of the three names for the pseudonym is unusual. From early on Hegemann had selected Manfred as the name for a future son. Maria became the second name for his daughter born in Naples. His daughter from his first marriage was Ellis.[8] The fictional Manfred Maria Ellis is described by Hegemann in his Introduction as a wealthy Boston Brahmin, whom he met in connection with his activities for the Boston 1915 Exhibition of 1910. Manfred Maria Ellis's mother, an Austrian aristocrat, had encouraged a European education and refinement for her only son. After spending considerable time overseas, the multilingual Ellis returned to Boston to oversee his late father's vast enterprises. Hegemann recounted time spent as Ellis's houseguest enjoying the company of the sophisticated American cultural elite, thus intentionally blurring the lines between reality and fiction. He continued to embellish his own Boston experiences, and throughout *Deutsche Schriften*, actual events and acquaintances, frequently veiled or distorted, are interwoven with the fictional.

The model for Manfred, as he is usually referred to in the book, could have been Edward Albert Filene, the philanthropist, social reformer, and promoter of the *Boston 1915* movement, whom Hegemann knew well. However, Filene was not a Brahmin but a self-made businessman. A possible model from the Boston elite was Philip Cabot, whom he had indeed met in that city. Many years later he wrote to Fiske Kimball: "In Boston I had a very good friend in Mr. Philip Cabot, who once offered money to Harvard to have me lecture there. Unfortunately, his relation to me has been dangerously interfered with by the war. . . . In my first book about Frederick II (Introductory Chapter), I tried to erect something like a monument to Mr. Philip Cabot and to his views."[9] Cabot and his wife are among those participating in the *Gespräche* (conversations).[10] Most significantly Manfred is an alter-ego for Hegemann with respect to bridging the cultures and *Weltanschauung* of America and Europe and exemplifying this complexity without an attempt to achieve unity.

In *Iphigenie* and in the first set of the *Gespräche*, Hegemann evoked the cultural memory of antiquity after his absence in America, and recalled the sophisticated cultural life in the Roman villas of Posillipo. His travels in Italy and especially in Greece and visits to museums and monuments within the vicinity of Naples coalesced with the preparations for *The American Vitruvius*, which included Camillo Sitte's descriptions of classic sites. Also present in Hegemann's mind may have been Goethe's *Italienische Reise*. A lifelong admirer of Goethe, he is said to have always carried with him a volume of the poet's work.[11] Goethe's *Iphigenie* inspired his own version, and Johann Peter Eckermann's *Gespräche mit Goethe* (Conversations with Goethe) may have prompted the format and title of the second part of *Deutsche Schriften*, "*Das Königsopfer: Sieben Gespräche über Goethe, Voltaire, Friedrich II & Christus. . . .*"

Constructing the text as dialogues or forums lent a certain cloak of immunity to Hegemann's controversial themes in several of his historical works. As a literary device, the dialogue, favored by Hegemann, derived from his penchant for the theater. On his travels and during his years in Berlin, he zealously attended performances and actually aspired to become a playwright. Hermann Kesten, himself an author and editor, wrote perceptively on Hegemann the "stylist," singling out his choice for the dialogue format:

> The dialogue format of Hegemann's book is also an artifice, a fabrication. It offers the pamphletist, who is embued with the ardent wish to be right, to provide the propagandistic demands of his sense of justice with the appearance of broad objectivity, of impartiality. It solicits trust. A trust which the author indirectly needs and pursues even more urgently, on account of having chosen such a difficult route. Because he does not offer, like other historical writers, the results of his research but rather opts for presenting to his reader the material in a contradictory manner turned this and that way.[12]

Hegemann adopted from the theater the icon of the mask and all its derivatives, primarily in his endeavor to unmask historic personages. Using pseudonyms, he concealed himself behind a mask and masked the separation between reality and fiction, blurring the boundaries in perplexing manner, and craftily creating a lie. Particularly in *Deutsche Schriften* the link between the author's biographical narrative and the experiences of the fictional personages remains intentionally veiled.

This is evident in the postscript to the seven *Gespräche über das Königsopfer* (Conversations regarding royal sacrifice) in which Hegemann relates that at the conclusion of his stay in Naples, he left for America to pursue urban projects. On board ship he sorted through the notations he had made during the discussions at the Villa Boccanera at his friend's request. Manfred, having joined the German-American Red Cross, perished in 1916, when the ship *Alsatia*, on which he was traveling to Europe, vanished on the high sea.[13] The fictional incident is similar to the actual loss of Patrick Geddes's city planning exhibition in transit to India, when a German battleship sank the English *Clan Grant*. The choice of the ship's name, *Alsatia*, for Elsass-Lothringen was probably a reference to the Versailles peace treaty of 1919, which ceded the territory to France. By Hegemann's account, after Manfred's death his friends asked him to edit the notations on the conversations and publish them together with *Iphigenie*. Inexplicably, Manfred is resurrected in Hegemann's later *Napoleon*.

Why the title *Deutsche Schriften* was chosen is not explained. Analyzing in depth the multitude of ideas discussed in the salon at the Villa Boccanera presents a formidable task. It would require separating out the input of Manfred, Hegemann, and others based on citations from a range of characters, both real and imagined. Within the scope of the real Hegemann's intellectual framework, the one salient theme of the *Deutsche Schriften* is pacifism. His unmasking of Frederick II and the deconstruction of hero worship are also important themes, and their wellspring is contained in Hegemann's first fictional work.

Pivotal in *Deutsche Schriften* are pacifism and the concept of a unified pan-Europe beyond nationalist strife. When Hegemann wrote the book, the illusions of a transnational Europe had been shattered by the Great War. He had been preoccupied with these utopian aspirations while he remained in the United States and did not return to Germany to take part in the conflagration. *Iphigenie* is emblematic for the objectionable sacrifice of youth. In Ellis's play she was not butchered but sent to Tauris. Nevertheless, her fate impelled a discussion of all aspects of the sacrifice of youths, especially in war, vindicated by hero worship. How these evils could be circumvented by the elimination of fanatic nationalism that stirred up hatred and war brought up the possibility of an international organization to supplant national sovereignties. In view of the tensions brewing in the Balkans in 1913, the concept of a pan-Europe was a hopeful possibility which Hegemann presented in retrospect a decade later.

These themes prevail throughout the nearly 650 pages of the three parts of the *Deutsche Schriften*, and the sixth *Gespräch: Tod fürs Vaterland und der Adel* (Death for the fatherland and nobility), is particularly meaningful.[14] The characters involved in this dialogue are Manfred, Pierre Liévre, Zavitzianos, later Pastor Dietrich, and to a minor extent, Hegemann. Manfred's American voice represents Hegemann arguing against Pastor Dietrich's German nationalism. To give topicality to the discussion, it begins with expressions of concern about the nearby war, which Manfred feared would escalate into a world war.

> Manfred/Hegemann's ideas regarding the meaning of *Vaterland* and the need to defend it are stated emphatically, and pose the quandaries that preoccupied him when he remained abroad during the war: The 'Vaterland' has to be defended; that is a duty; to doubt this I consider impossible. But here is a ques-

tion which comes up repeatedly when one researches European and especially German history: What can be called 'Vaterland' in Europe? What is for instance 'Vaterland' for a German? What is at this time the 'Vaterland' for a person who strives for a 'Bildung' (culture) as promised by Goethe? and what is truly one's duty toward this 'Vaterland'?

Hegemann cites a passage from the venerated Goethe: "There exists a level where national hatred vanishes altogether, where one stands as it were above nations and perceives the fortune and the grief of a neighboring country as if it were happening to one's own. This cultural level agreed with me and I was firmly settled in it long before I reached my sixtieth year."[15] This sentiment manifested and validated Hegemann's beliefs. The concept is referred to several times in *Deutsche Schriften* as the idea of a pan-Europe, entertained by Bismarck in the form of a *Gesamtnationalität* (national synthesis) and by Napoleon in his ambition for a unified empire. Manfred/Hegemann suggests a "Greater Switzerland," incorporating France, Austria, Italy, and Germany into a nation where statesmen would be dedicated to govern peacefully. Knowledge of several languages would be an essential requirement for this utopia.

For Hegemann the concept of a pan-Europe was closely related to, and just one step beyond, regional planning. After Greater Boston, Greater Berlin, and the Ruhr Verband, it was a logical development. His interest in advancing an auxiliary, internationally understood language has been discussed in relation to Berlin 1910 and affiliated events. In the future, he would also consider it an attribute of Classicism as a style comparable to a universally understood auxiliary language.

Remaining at a distance, Hegemann had not experienced the carnage of World War I, which he perceived as a futile and meaningless conflict. His Wisconsin community of German descent was equally horrified by the events and torn by loyalties. In this context Hegemann's pacifist convictions may have been both nurtured and questioned. They were emphatically expressed in the *Deutsche Schriften* and did not diminish in the ensuing years. Pacifism surfaced, for instance, in his 1929 conversations with the English author H. G. Wells, primarily known for his science fiction, but also yearning for a world without strife.[16] Hegemann related a conversation with Arnold Zweig, Fiske Kimball, and others discussing with Wells, "the prophet of peace," how worldwide capitalism might lead to the realization that war was unprofitable and should be abolished. In the 1920s and ensuing years Hegemann found congenial support for his convictions among the left-wing intellectuals gathered around the journal *Die Weltbühne*, some of whom had taken an antiwar position during World War I. A major figure in this group was Carl von Ossietzky, who was nominated for the Nobel Peace Prize and persecuted and jailed by the Nazis for his convictions. While in exile, Hegemann energetically tried to raise support to obtain Ossietzky's release from prison. Pacifism in Germany, in the Friedensbewegung and other organizations, and the plight of those opposing Nazism captivated Hegemann's attention and drew his vigorous involvement in the years before he left the country in 1933, and with increasing urgency after he reached a safe haven on the other side of the Atlantic.

The decade between Hegemann's interlude in Posillipo and his departure from Europe in 1933 might be considered the most significant phase of his professional life, bringing resolution and structure to the complexity of ideas with which he returned to Europe to face a conflictive and explosive world.

Wasmuth Verlag

Hegemann's awareness of the postwar urban scene in Berlin while still in Milwaukee is demonstrated in the selection of illustrations from recent publications for *The American Vitruvius*. They included plans of residential groupings from Hermann Muthesius's book *Kleinhaus und Kleinsiedlung* (1918) and reproductions credited to the journals *Der Städtebau* and *Wasmuths Monatshefte für Baukunst* of 1920–21.

Correspondence for obtaining permission from the publishers or subscriptions to the journals does not exist. However, the connection to these periodicals is of interest. The architect and critic Heinrich de Fries (1887–1938) became the editor of *Der Städtebau* in 1919 after the death of its co-founder, Theodor Goecke. De Fries held this position until 1923, when the journal was suspended for economic reasons. He was also the editor for *Wasmuths Monatshefte für Baukunst* from 1919 until 1924. Within the architectural scene of that time, de Fries was often described as a publicist. He and Hegemann shared comparable interests, convictions, and even temperaments.[17] De Fries's books, *Vom sparsamen Bauen* (Economical building, 1918) and *Wohnstädte der Zukunft* (Homes of the future, 1919), addressed postwar housing conditions and advocated small family dwellings within the center of the city to replace rental barracks. The topic of housing called his attention to Hegemann's publications and activities in Berlin prior to his 1913 departure for America. Both Hegemann and de Fries deemed housing a basic element of city planning. De Fries considered the "fundamental renovation of minimal housing" a prerequisite for every metropolis. By virtue of the similarity to Hegemann's principles regarding housing, de Fries strongly recommended him for the position of *Städtebaudirektor* (Director of City Planning) of Berlin.[18] In 1920 the city had at last achieved the goal of a unified Greater Berlin proposed more than a decade earlier. In reply to an unsigned article in the *Berliner Tageblatt* (December 19, 1920), de Fries wrote in *Der Städtebau*:

> The article clamours for a housing director for Greater Berlin, because the city magistrate Lange, the principal chairman of the house of representatives is too

> overtaxed to accomplish anything positive. The public is demanding a strong hand, but does not reveal who is meant . . . . The man not identified in the *Berliner Tageblatt*, that housing director, who is an expert in the subject of city planning, and housing, and is capable of assuming the magnitude and social responsibility of the task, is in fact presently not in Berlin . . . one of the most recognized professional experts in city planning . . . Werner Hegemann. . . .

He continued with a description of Hegemann's accomplishments in Berlin from 1909 to 1913, emphasizing that he was not a candidate of any political party or association, and at this time, not even a candidate for the position for which he was so highly qualified. He also mentioned that Hegemann would undoubtedly welcome a return to Berlin.

The unification of Greater Berlin brought into focus once more the urban debates of the years before World War I, with which Hegemann had been so intimately involved. Walter Lehweiss wrote in *Stadtbaukunst alter und neuer Zeit* about the activities of the Zweckverband Gross-Berlin (local administrative union)—not to be confused with the Propaganda-Ausschuss für Gross-Berlin—that had terminated (October 1, 1920) after eight years as a result of the unification.[19] The Zweckverband published an administrative report used by Lehweiss to review its accomplishments, noting that the open-space strategy had been by far the most successful.

A few months later, the city planner Bruno Möhring commented in the same periodical on the enormous difficulties the new *Städtebaudirektor* could anticipate.[20] He suggested teamwork and a pyramidal administrative structure to manage the nine districts now encompassing Greater Berlin. After a year-long debate, the city planner Karl Elkart was named *Generaldirektor für Städtebau, Wohn-und Siedlungswesen* (General Director for City Planning, Housing, and Development).[21] Although Hegemann was not appointed to the position, de Fries's suggestion may have contributed to his resolve to return to Germany.[22]

Prior to leaving Milwaukee, and probably due to the renewed attention to the unification of Greater Berlin and Hegemann's earlier activities in the city, he received a letter from Bruno Möhring, who, together with Rudolf Eberstadt, had presented a winning entry in the Greater Berlin Competition.[23] Möhring asked Hegemann to become a contributor to *Die Stadtbaukunst in alter und neuer Zeit*, publication of which had recommenced despite the dire economic conditions in Germany. Cornelius Gurlitt and Walter Lehweiss, both known to Hegemann, were also working with Möhring in this endeavor. The architect Bruno Taut was to be responsible for the *Führung der jungen Bewegung* (Leadership of the new movement) with the inclusion of the avant-garde section, *Das Frühlicht*. Möhring's letter to Hegemann referred to "modern youth, whose aims, despite their eccentricities, one cannot ignore, because they are inspired by lofty idealism." It is not clear if

Hegemann gave consideration to Möhring's suggestion or preferred to wait out other leads, such as the position proposed by de Fries.

Ida Belle Hegemann reported that in April 1922, while she remained in Naples, her husband "went to Berlin to see what changes had taken place since he had left the city, nearly 10 years ago."[24] In Berlin he stayed with his Tante Ria, the widow of Otto March, visited old acquaintances and architects, and attended concerts and the theater. Among those he visited was Bernhard Dernburg, a political figure with liberal social convictions, who had participated with Hegemann in the Für Gross-Berlin movement of 1912. Hegemann observed that despite the mounting economic crisis, Dernburg was less pessimistic than others about Germany's plight.

On May 8, 1922, Hegemann wrote, "this afternoon I visited another prominent editor [of the *Bauwelt*, an architectural paper with a large circulation]. I feel like a prince to whom many people of some importance explain their experience and ideals, and I listen with interest and ask occasional questions sometimes succeeding in appearing intelligent."

Beginning on May 13 Hegemann had meetings with Günther Wasmuth and Heinrich de Fries regarding a position at the Wasmuth Verlag, renowned for publications on art and architecture. In a May 17 letter to Ida Belle, he reported that "the dealings with Wasmuth are concluded to my satisfaction. They have signed the contract granting me a salary much higher than the last publication [*Bauwelt*] would have given, and leaving one half of my time free for my own use. There are other features in this contract which make it especially attractive and I am seriously contemplating signing this document." The next day he wrote of his search for a place to live and his hope of finding one with a view. He commented: "The expectation of combining in one town a decent job, a decent home, magnificent collections, excellent music and drama, the finest minds in all subjects, a number of good friends, etc., all that fascinates me. The contract which I may sign also provides for liberal travelling and for two months vacation. I have almost decided to accept *unless* Vienna should talk even better. . . ." There is no clarification as to what the position in Vienna might have been. Hegemann's hesitation in accepting Wasmuth's proposal is difficult to comprehend, unless he was overwhelmed by the circumstances of his return to Germany and the esteem he was receiving. It is also possible that he was daunted by the prospect that the position at *Wasmuths Monatshefte für Baukunst* would involve not only city planning but also contemporary architecture, a subject with which he was less familiar.

On his way back to Italy, Hegemann traveled throughout Germany and to Vienna. With some apprehension he sought out his former wife, Alice Hesse, in Munich. She had remarried, and his daughter Ellis, now in her teens, lived with her mother. He also went to Heidelberg and his native city, Mannheim. He wrote to his wife, "I had the strangest feeling in Mannheim and in Heidelberg, the feeling of finally being back where I belong, and I again and again felt that I could not quite understand how it should be necessary that I had to leave again instead of simply staying. . . ."

On June 3, 1922, the contract with Ernst Wasmuth Architekturverlag, Architekturbuchhandlung und Kunstanstalten A.-G., was signed by all parties. The Hegemanns gave up their intention of spending a year in Rome or Vienna and instead looked for an appropriate building site in Berlin. Mounting inflation made quick decisions advisable, and on July 2, 1922, ground was broken for a house of Hegemann's own design in Nikolassee. It was to be the only design by Hegemann built in Germany.[25] In December the family settled into their spacious home surrounded by an attractive property with trees and shrubs. Nikolassee had developed into a suburb of villas by well-known architects such as Hermann Muthesius and Walter Lehweiss and attracted others active in the cultural scene of Berlin in the Weimar years.

Somewhat sooner than anticipated, Hegemann began at Wasmuth, which provided his primary income. This was supplemented by his earnings from lectures and consultantships in various cities, articles, and books on architecture and history. With the improvement of the German economy in 1924, the Hegemanns enjoyed a comfortable lifestyle.

Although Hegemann had begun working at the publisher, *Wasmuths Monatshefte für Baukunst* continued to list only Günther Wasmuth as editor. Hegemann was apparently introduced gradually to his responsibilities. This makes it almost impossible to fix the exact beginning date of his editorship. It was not until 1925 that Hegemann's name appeared on the masthead. It may have been agreed that he would not devote himself fully to the periodical until 1924, allowing him time to gather insights. Wasmuth may also have been reluctant to trust Hegemann's circumscribed acquaintance with the architectural developments in Europe. Indeed, he had returned to Berlin at a singularly exciting and charged time for architecture and the arts. After an absence of nearly a decade, he entered the scene as an outsider, a role fraught with hazards, but also promising fresh perspectives.

During the summer of 1923, Hegemann spent two months in Gothenburg, Sweden, following an invitation to edit the English catalogue for The International Cities and Town Planning Exhibition initiated by Albert Lilienberg.[26] His wife joined him for some of the time while her mother watched over their infant daughter and the house in Nikolassee.

Among the organizers of the exhibition, Lawrence Veiler was listed for the United States, but Hegemann was asked to expand the American section and he obtained large photographs of "California-style" houses and additionals plans. At his suggestion Fiske Kimball was invited to send examples of his urban projects, but the invitation arrived too late. The section in the catalogue devoted to the United States is signed by Hegemann and draws on *The American Vitruvius* for some of its text and illustrations. He also wrote the text for the French section, and the representatives of the other countries provided their own reports, which were translated and edited by Hegemann. The organizer of the German section was Gustav Langen, who showed his Traveling Museum and some newer housing schemes by Bruno Taut, Adolf Rading, and Rudolf Salvisberg. The regional plan for the *Ruhr* district received special exposure. It is not clear if Hegemann contributed in other ways to the exhibition or participated in the conference.

During his stay in Gothenburg, Hegemann renewed previous acquaintances with the urbanists Bertel Jung from Finland, Albert Lilienberg from Sweden, Sverre Pedersen from Norway, and Raymond Unwin from England. This proved consequential for Hegemann, who in 1925 became the editor for the journal *Der Städtebau* in addition to *Wasmuths Monatshefte für Baukunst*. In both publications he gave ample exposure to architecture and city planning in the Scandinavian countries and Finland, where a strong interest in German accomplishment and in garden cities persisted.[27]

In the aftermath of the Gothenburg 1923 catalogue, Hegemann embarked on a major volume announced by Wasmuth Verlag for the fall of 1924 but not published until 1925. A second edition followed in 1927. The book is usually cited as *Amerikanische Architektur & Stadtbaukunst* (American architecture & urban planning, Fig. 35). The first edition included a second title page bearing the imprint *Der Städtebau nach den Ergebnissen der Internationalen Staedtebau-Ausstellung Gothenburg* (City planning according to the Gothenburg International City Planning Exposition).The first edition, *Amerikanische Architektur & Stadtbaukunst*, portrayed the work as an expanded catalogue of that event, and harked back to Hegemann's volumes on the Berlin and Düsseldorf exhibitions of 1910. The 1927 edition of *Amerikanische Architektur* did not include the additional title page.[28] In his Introduction Hegemann mentioned that Wasmuth, which also published the journal *Der Städtebau*, intended to devote special issues to other sections of the Gothenburg Exhibition, eventually reporting on the entire event. Actually, the first edition of the book in 1925 was also considered by Wasmuth to be a resumption of the monthly *Der Städtebau*, which had been dormant since 1923.

The content and format of *Amerikanische Architektur* resemble *The American Vitruvius* and the third volume of Hegemann's posthumous publication, *City Planning: Housing* (1937). The prelude to this sequence was *Der Städtebau nach den Ergebnissen*. With its deliberately recurring and evolving themes and variations, the series of books can be likened to an orchestrated rendition of Hegemann's concepts. The themes are presented in the texts and in the choice and placement of the illustrations, and the overall leitmotif is stated in the Introduction to *Amerikanische Architektur*: "In the entire publication the author wishes to express his conviction that all architecture must be understood as town planning and that the consideration of architecture from the point of view of city planning is the most significant and productive."[29]

Fig. 35. Announcement of Werner Hegemann's Amerikanische Architektur & Stadtbaukunst, *1924.* CCCC

Walter Lehweiss, the editor of *Stadtbaukunst alter und neuer Zeit*, expressed similar ideas in his introductory remarks celebrating the third anniversary of his journal. These ideas had persisted as the philosophy of *Stadtbaukunst* since its inception (in 1920): "we want to nourish and emphasize architecture in the sense of the term '*Stadtbaukunst*': not to consider each building as an individual entity, but as a building element within the city, as a component within the vast organism of the economic and intellectual life of the nation."[30]

Hegemann's conviction regarding architecture as an integral part of an evolving urban synthesis motivated his criticism of Modernism in the pages of *Wasmuths Monatshefte für Baukunst*. However, it fails to explain his exclusion of Frank Lloyd Wright and Louis Sullivan from *Amerikanische Architektur* and his emphasis on McKim, Mead & White, Carrère & Hastings, and Bertram Goodhue.

Amerikanismus and the Frank Lloyd Wright Debate

Hegemann took over his responsibilities at Wasmuth Verlag gradually. Günther Wasmuth continued as *Schriftleiter* (editor) through 1924, while

Hegemann contributed articles to the journal under his name. The following year, both G. Wasmuth and Hegemann figured as *verantwortliche Schriftleiter* or "responsible editors." When precisely Hegemann made the transition to become the sole editor is not clear.

Considering the length of Hegemann's stay in the American Midwest, one could surmise that *Amerikanische Architektur* would include Frank Lloyd Wright and Louis Sullivan. Before Hegemann had returned to Europe in 1922, Wright and Sullivan were already recognized on the continent as innovative, unique, and controversial American architects. In the 1920s the Frank Lloyd Wright debate in Europe gained momentum in connection with the deliberations of where the New Building was going. Attention was focused on two trends, the functional and the organic. Wright was pivotal within this discourse.

Wright's influence on European architecture, and the impact of Europe and the world at large on the architect, have been explored in depth by Anthony Alofsin.[31] Early awareness of Wright's work on the other side of the Atlantic has generally been attributed to the Wasmuth publications of 1910 and 1911.[32] Alofsin disqualifies this attribution as rudimentary. Even if it is debatable, the Wasmuth involvement has implications for Hegemann's position vis-à-vis Wright because of Hegemann's pre–World War I link to the publisher. Hegemann was actively involved with the city planning exhibitions in Berlin and his own books at the same time Wright's volumes were in production at Wasmuth. Wright was in Europe during this period and frequently visited Berlin to oversee the publication of his work. Bruno Möhring also gave a lecture showing Wright's drawings, but despite these coincidences, Hegemann did not acknowledge these events or apparently met Wright.[33]

Among German publications to recognize Wright's originality was a 1920 article by Ludwig Hilberseimer and Udo Rukser. Hegemann no doubt knew that Hilberseimer's main interest was city planning and was probably aware of the article.[34] The authors stated that American architecture had to find new solutions to problems for which precedents did not exist, and that "in this sense American architecture derived from technology, and owed the majestic monumentality of its silos, warehouses and skyscrapers to a '*formgewordenen Sachlichkeit*' [Functionalism converted into form]."[35] They singled out John W. Root's Monadnock building in Chicago as a pioneering example that separated the country's architecture from "Europeanism." However, they considered that Wright went beyond Root's "elemental monumentality" and achieved a universal synthesis. The authors saw an expression of Wright's genius in the relationship of the exterior to the interior and to the surrounding landscape as unique to his buildings. This assessment of Wright is comparable to Hegemann's view of American architecture. Hegemann, however, valued the responsiveness to the urban rather than the natural environment, and considered Wright anti-urban. This interpretation is reflected in Hegemann's omission of Wright from *Amerikanische Architektur* and his subsequent articles.

The focus of this study precludes situating Hegemann's book among the numerous publications on American architecture by German travelers.[36] His opinions were the result of prolonged stays and professional experience in the United States, while others gathered primarily visual impressions during brief visits to a few cities and national parks. Hegemann had absorbed the premises of American Progressivism and civic commitment during his formative years. His perceptions of architecture and the city on both sides of the Atlantic manifest an *Amerikanismus* different from what has been generally grouped in this category. Without being aware of his nonconformist position, and responding to an insatiable interest in descriptions from across the Atlantic, Wasmuth opted for enlisting Hegemann's participation.[37] As the leading publisher of architecture and city planning, Wasmuth provided considerable prominence to Hegemann's book, and the publishers's link to Frank Lloyd Wright raised expectations for a promulgation of American accomplishments.

Though Wasmuth may have expected a responsible critic, Hegemann launched himself into the role of an aggressive crusader. It is remarkable that the offer for the position was not withdrawn when Hegemann's snub of Frank Lloyd Wright in *Amerikanische Architektur* became notorious, considering that Wasmuth had published a two-folio monograph, *Executed Buildings and Designs by Frank Lloyd Wright,* in 1910–11, as well as a smaller picture book of the same title.[38] European architects became aware of Wright in significant measure through these publications, and many of them crossed the Atlantic expressly to see his work, hoping to meet the master himself. Wright's impact on the Dutch modernists was particularly notable and, in turn, permeated the New Building in Germany. Wright's influence in Europe extended beyond architctural form to the discourse on the true meaning of Modernism.

Hegemann's disparagement of Wright was unexpected and remains difficult to comprehend. It caused dismay among those admiring the architect's work, and contributed to Hegemann's reputation as antagonistic to Modernism. This stigma has persisted into the present. Nevertheless it is simplistic to consider Hegemann anti-modern and his penchant for "other" architecture reactionary. His adherence to an alternative point of view merits scrutiny and enhances the understanding of the complex debates taking place at the time.

Hegemann's main title, *Amerikanische Architektur*, was deceptive. The subtitle, *Ein Überblick über den heutigen Stand der amerikanischen Baukunst in ihrer Beziehung zum Städtebau* (A survey of contemporary American architecture and its relation to town planning), alerted the reader to an emphasis on buildings within the urban context. Of all building types, the skyscraper intersected most prominently with modern city plan-

Fig. 36. Adolf Loos's design for the Tribune Tower competition, Chicago, 1922. Drawing by an unidentified artist for Hegemann's City Planning: Housing, *vol. 2, 137, p. 365.* CCCC

ning. It was also emblematic of American technical ingenuity, economic drive, and "the sky is the limit" philosophy. In Germany the "*Turmhaus*"—an isolated tower—already hotly debated before World War I, later meshed with the visionary schemes of Expressionism. From 1919 on a virtual skyscraper fever gripped the country.[39] Debates agitated pro and con in architectural periodicals and newspapers read by the general public. Hegemann addressed the latter in the *Berliner Illustrirte Zeitung* on the "dangers" of the high-rise building.[40] Illustrations show visionary underground traffic arteries in New York City and a skyscraper with a Gothic-style church on top. Gothicizing modern skyscrapers was reserved for Hegemann's special anathema.

Interest in skyscrapers was stimulated by Le Corbusier's schemes and the *Chicago Tribune* Tower Competition of 1922, in which several German architects participated. Closer to home, the 1921 competition for a skyscraper at the Friedrichstrasse in Berlin brought forth numerous entries by well-known architects, including Mies van der Rohe's noteworthy triangular glass structure. Neither of these competitions produced a truly modern first-place entry.

Two sections in Hegemann's *Amerikanische Architektur*—"Die Stadt-Mitte," the city center or "heart of the city," and "*Das Hochhaus als Quelle von Verkehrsschwierigkeiten*" (The skyscraper as the source of traffic problems)—were devoted to the topic of the skyscraper. Hegemann favored the placement of towers/skyscrapers within American civic centers, where they served a symbolic and monumental rather than a business function. His choice of illustrations showed civic centers with significant tower buildings accommodated in a grid plan. He recalled that Karl Friedrich Schinkel had devoted much attention to the design of a "tower per se" at the end of the Leipziger Strasse in Berlin.[41] In Hegemann's volume the entries for the *Tribune* Tower Competition were reproduced on a double-page spread. Only a few show faint suggestions of their surroundings, and no plan of Chicago indicated their intended location (Fig. 36).

The notoriety of the chaos and traffic congestion in New York caused by skyscrapers contributed to the aversion toward tall buildings in German cities. Similar to the article mentioned above, Hegemann's chapter on this topic referred to Raymond Unwin's article, "Higher Building in Relation to Town Planning," which was read before the Royal Institute of British Architects.[42] It contained technical data and illustrations showing the "chaos" on the streets of New York and Chicago. In his book Hegemann allotted several pages to possible solutions and to the New York zoning ordinance of 1916. His earlier articles on the Congestion Show of 1909 in New York lamented the absence of a master plan for the city that would specify regulations for various areas, building heights, and setbacks. Appropriately he entitled the chapter in *Amerikanische Architektur*, "*Zonenbebauung*" (zoning architecture), commenting on the aesthetic repercussions of the zoning ordinance. Initially considered a purely utilitarian measure to regulate the height and bulk of buildings, it gave impetus to a zoning-inspired setback style for skyscrapers that was uniquely American.[43] This was illustrated in drawings by Hugh Ferris in the journal *Der Städtebau* with the caption, "Synthetic study of building masses developed under the New York regulations of 1916."[44] A significant result of the New York zoning regulations, soon adopted by other American cities, was that skyscrapers, formerly considered isolated towers, were now acknowledged as integral elements of the modern metropolis. The setback regulations unexpectedly motivated visionary futuristic urban schemes, such as the multilevel traffic proposals of Harvey W. Corbett that Hegemann selected for his book.

The section on garden suburbs demonstrated Hegemann's partiality toward layouts and a certain reluctance to comment on architecture. Included as precedents were Roland Park in Baltimore; Lake Forest, Illinois; less-known developments of single-family housing in Bridgeport, Connecticut; and projects by Fiske Kimball in Scottswood, Michigan. Several designs by Hegemann & Peets were shown as well. Although they had been published in *The American Vitruvius*, they were unknown in Germany and continued to be ignored. One searches in vain for Wright's Prairie-style houses among the examples from the American Midwest.

Anticipating criticism, Hegemann's concluding remarks to *Amerikanische Architektur* defended his preference for an architecture that "embued old forms with a new spirit . . . achieving convincing solutions to unprecedented problems."[45] He was convinced that this interpretation would mediate a promising transition toward functional Modernism.

The severe negative reactions to the book were not only directed at his partiality toward American versus European endeavors; Adolf Rading vehemently accused Hegemann of ignoring "the reality of truly modern architecture in the U.S.A." He concluded his review, "books such as this should be publicly burned because of their bias"—eerily forecasting the fiery fate of Hegemann's works at the hands of the Nazis in May 1933.[46] Rading's attack focused primarily on Hegemann's exclusion of Frank Lloyd Wright and Heinrich de Fries, the editor of the periodical *Baugilde*, who had declared Wright "un-American" by commenting on his empathy with Chinese building forms.[47] Hegemann's reply to Rading took the form of an article in *Wasmuths Monatshefte für Baukunst*.[48] It followed an unsigned article by Hegemann on the Amsterdam School, which was strongly influenced by Wright, and adjacent to one by Richard Konwiarz on the "new" architecture in Breslau, where Rading was professor at the Staatliche Kunstakademie.[49] Hegemann took issue with Rading's personal attack and accused him of "ignorance, unwillingness to work, unworldliness, paltriness, and godlessnes [*sic*]." On the subject that had caused Rading's outburst, Hegemann explained that he agreed with de Fries's assessment of Wright's work as "un-American" and therefore unsuitable for *Amerikanische Baukunst*. According to de Fries, "Wright's work has its roots in the Far East, in the ancient building and landscape culture of China, which evolved in harmony with geomancy and astronomy out of the 'Weltanschauung' of the Far East (Orient), embued with religion and philosophy."[50]

In the polemics surrounding Wright, his preoccupation with Japan tended to be erroneously ascribed to China. Wright's love of the prints and traditional architecture of Japan was stimulated by his sojourns there beginning in 1905. However, he vigorously defended his originality against those seeing foreign influences in his work and stated, "As for the Incas, the Mayans, even the Japanese—all were to me but splendid confirmation."[51] Although Chinese architecture had influenced that of Japan, the frequent references to China in German articles on Wright are misleading. De Fries's comment on geomancy possibly derived from an article by the architect on geometry.[52] Geomancy has been defined as "the science of putting human habitats and activities into harmony with the visible and invisible world around us." Vestiges of its practice can be found worldwide, and it is not unique to the Orient.[53] Wright's sensitivity to nature and the landscape demonstrated in the siting of his buildings is imbued with the spirit of geomancy, but the term was not used except by de Fries. In his Introduction to *Frank Lloyd Wright: Aus dem Lebenswerke eines Architekten*, de Fries speaks of the architect's aiming at the "unpretentiousness and deep bonds to nature, which he cherished in the culture of East-Asia.[54] He comments on Wright's interpretation of a building as a "living, breathing, . . . even flourishing element of nature, of organic life," as probably the most important and unique characteristic of his work.

De Fries's labeling of Wright as "un-American" was actually highly laudatory. He contrasted Wright's "external form as secondary to the evolving organic sense of a building," regardless of whether these were factories or villas. He concluded this significant passage by stating that it confirmed "the realization that the American architect Wright seems to us as un-American as possible. Surely he cannot be considered as representative of any 'American' architecture." Elsewhere in his essay de Fries made this point even clearer: "The nationality of this architect is completely unimportant; considering the present attitude in America, his reverberations in Holland and Germany should be valued even more highly than those in the U.S.A. His achievements are in no way of a national character, but rather the creative result of a unique humanism."[55]

Hegemann and Rading both misinterpreted these comments, taking them out of context and manipulating the intended meaning to serve their own objectives. It is particularly perplexing that Hegemann, a well-traveled citizen of the world, would have adhered to such a narrow interpretation of "national," failing to honor the "universal" in Wright. There is no indication that Hegemann applied similar criteria regarding national versus universal to German or French architects.

Hegemann's reactions to Rading's review were published in *Die Baugilde* together with a somewhat conciliatory response by Rading, in which he acknowledged the inappropriateness of his personal attacks and vehement reaction. He also agreed with Hegemann that American eclecticism was superior to that practiced by European architects.[56] The moniker "plagiarism" for the borrowing of forms was frequently used by Hegemann, but not in connection with Wright. The architect was barely known in his native country, although he possibly could have been recognized as an exceptionally gifted eclectic. Hegemann reported that when he embarked on his lecture tour in 1913, he wanted to publicize Wright's work, which he admired at that time. He was astonished by Wright's limited success among the "superbly trained eclectic American architects."[57]

In the conclusion to *Amerikanische Architektur* Hegemann reaffirmed his ranking of American architects as ahead of those in Europe, with the exception of "the secessionists of Chicago such as Sullivan and Wright, [who are] better known in Germany and Holland than in their own country." He praised the "masters" McKim, Mead & White, who were, on the other hand, ignored on the "haughty"continent. He deemed Pennsylvania Station in New York their highest achievement and its vast entrance hall exemplary for the utilization of the new materials, steel and glass. It was emblematic of the *Nachahmung und Neugeburt* (Reproduction and recreation/rebirth), which Hegemann judged to be incipient Modernism.

After the *Amerikanische Architektur* episode Hegemann never missed an opportunity to make disparaging remarks about Frank Lloyd Wright in his articles. The rationale for his antipathy remains obscure. It may be related to his dislike of heroic figures, whom he endeavored to unmask. Indeed, many years later Frank Lloyd Wright was described by others as a "man of many masks." There is only a single indication that Hegemann had read any of the architect's publications. It occurred in one of his last published comments on Wright, Hegemann's brief "Baumeister: Frank Lloyd Wright" of 1929, written on the occasion of the architect's sixtieth birthday. He wrote: "Theory and praxis are as distant from one another in Wright as in many other artists. However, it demonstrates Wright's intelligence that he decidedly rejects another great German [*sic*] architect, the French(man) [*sic*] Le Corbusier, frequently celebrated by youthful Germany. Also our Erich Mendelsohn wishes to recognize in Le Corbusier only a literary figure, and what could be a more damaging designation for an architect! Unfortunately, there is also much 'literature' contained in Frank Lloyd Wright."[58]

The stress of Hegemann's last years in Berlin and his subsequent exile and death in 1936 limited his acquaintance with Wright's work to the architect's early period, rather than his productive 1940s. Hegemann's remarks on the Prairie-style houses were unfortunate, even inane. Referring to Wright and Sullivan as "secessionists" without explaining a connection to Austria was as cursory as his use of the term *romantisch*. Hegemann gave this term consistently derogatory connotations, applying it to all that was not *klassisch* and functional. When applied to Sullivan and Wright, stylistic meanings for these terms are avoided and their implications are vague. In a passage on *Anlehnung an überlieferte Formen* (emulation of traditional forms), Hegemann noted that Wright's work was replete with "romantic recollections" from his travels in China—although he had never visited that country—and Japan, "truly pathologically romantic" and presented by the architect as "native/authentic vernacular" and American *Präriestil*. Hegemann continued, "the romantic trivialities by F. L. Wright have within American architecture the effect of foreign bodies."[59] In his critical editorial notes to an article on Belgian architecture, Hegemann referred to "the gothicizing romanticism . . . the protruding pillars . . . which F. L. Wright brought to us from China," and the influence of these *chinesische Pylonen*.[60] Sadly missing in Hegemann's assessment of Wright is a recognition of his uniqueness, which eludes classification. Neither did he see the spontaneity of Wright's organicism and the vernacular as an antidote to historicism.

WMB published an appraisal of Sullivan, and tangentially of Wright, differing from Hegemann's, with Fiske Kimball's essay, *Alte und neue Baukunst in Amerika: Der Sieg des jungen Klassizismus über den Funktionalismus der neunziger Jahre* (Old and new architecture in America: the triumph of new Classicism over the functionalism of the nineties).[61] An introductory note to the article by Hegemann calls his friend "one of the most esteemed architectural writers in America." Kimball was an architect and an art historian with degrees from Harvard who had numerous scholarly publications to his name.[62] His interest in the history of American and European architecture contributed to his professional work in preservation and restoration. Subsequent to a teaching career, he was named director of the Pennsylvania Museum of Art in Philadelphia in 1925. Hegemann had lodged in the Kimballs' home during his brief stay at the University of Michigan in Ann Arbor, and in ensuing years Kimball and Hegemann frequently corresponded.

Initially two articles by Kimball were proposed, one on Louis Sullivan and another on McKim, Mead & White, and others.[63] Lack of time prevented Kimball from following through, and Hegemann blended the two segments, writing a continuation as a separate article under his own name.[64] Kimball's views, especially regarding Louis Sullivan, differed markedly from those of his colleague. Hegemann's remarks were limited to calling Sullivan a "secessionist," although in a letter to Kimball of 1919, he wrote that "in Chicago I had interesting visits with Mr. Sullivan and Mr. Elmslie, the latter one having been Mr. Sullivan's first designer for 15 years."

Kimball's opening paragraph introduced his insights on organic architecture:

> In Louis Sullivan American architecture had a great master of Realism. He belongs to a small group of thinkers and artists, the leaders of the scientific school of the nineteenth century, Ruskin, Viollet-le-Duc, Semper, Otto Wagner. More than anyone of these, it was Sullivan's destiny to convert their organic theory into vibrant, innovative creations. Since the genesis of Gothic construction nothing had evolved that could be compared to the steel skeleton construction of the skyscraper. Sullivan was the first to give artistic form to this new development.

Kimball associated the tenets of Modernism regarding rationality and truth in architecture to the "ancient" laws of nature, citing from the thinkers named above, who had influenced Midwestern architects in their search for a "modern" and "American" style. He considered Chicago the fountainhead of these developments, which included the skyscraper, and Sullivan its "poet." Kimball's description of Sullivan's buildings, illustrated in the text, is followed by excerpts from Sullivan's writings.[65]

Comparable to Hegemann, Kimball deemed that the progression of American architecture toward Modernism was spurred on by the technological innovations leading to the development of the skyscraper, and that American building had preceded European developments. "Modern," according to Kimball, was a relative concept changing from generation to generation, perpetually in flux. In his essay the extensive section on Sullivan was followed by one on other architects and their buildings, demonstrating this progression. He considered McKim, Mead & White influential for their use of the "monumental and classical for public buildings." This trend provided a balance for the striving for truth, expression of function, and structure, which had led functionalism to lose all sense of form. In a letter to Hegemann, Kimball expressed this more emphatically: "The important thing to my mind is the reversion to a realization that the cardinal point for architecture is not the expression of structure but the abstract composition of form. . . . I have greatly admired the article by Oud where he suggests that the importance of the new works lay 'not so much in their truthfulness as in their transparency.'"[66]

With the publication of *Amerikanische Architektur* Hegemann entered into the *Amerikanismus* debate in Germany, which pitted those admiring America for its technological and economic acumen, seeing it as emblematic of progress, against those who saw a lack of culture and an absence of historical awareness. Both sides of the debate included a mixture of modernists and traditionalists. It has been noted by Detlef Peukert that "the public debate about 'America' was really a debate about German society itself and the challenge that modernity posed to it. What was at issue was the value to be placed on a 'rationalized' form of life emptied of all the ballast of tradition."[67] Hegemann placed himself between the two factions, claiming that during nearly ten years as an observer in the North American continent he had gained insight into its true essence. He questioned the presumed absence of tradition in architecture and introduced the German audience to the American Classic Revival as a rebirth of tradition that simultaneously advanced Modernism. It was this Neoclassicism that had stripped skyscrapers and other monumental buildings of historicist decoration and had massed their pure forms within the urban grid of American cities. Hegemann remained partial to the grid plan as democratic, enabling expansion, and accommodating the placement of civic centers. General interest in American urban planning, prevalent in the previous two decades, diminished in the 1920s, despite American skyscrapers garnering renewed attention.

It might be assumed that Hegemann's adversarial position vis-à-vis the New Building commenced with his return to Berlin and his editorial position at Wasmuth. The move provided him the opportunity to acquaint himself with the tendencies that had evolved while he was overseas. In reality he returned to Berlin with a distinct point of view shaped by his American experience, which affected his position regarding Wright and influenced his reactions to the New Building and its proponents in Europe.

The Weimar years, fraught with political and economic tensions, were a stimulating period for architecture and the arts, with new ideas stirring in the immediate postwar years. In retrospect this period has not lost its fascination and lustre and continues to hold the attention of cultural historians. For students of architecture and the city it is one of the most captivating decades, generating a literature now being analyzed for its own sake. Scholars are seeking to unravel the reduction of the complexities of the modern movement that prevailed in earlier interpretations. The resulting revisions view Modernism as multifaceted and in flux, rather than dominated by a canon of absolutes progressing toward the International Style.

Consideration of Hegemann's critical output has benefited from recent tendencies in historiography which are reluctant to marginalize or ignore alternatives as deviant. Historians are also beginning to differentiate between modernity and a more radical avant-garde.[68] This interpretation would position Hegemann with cultural modernity, allowing for his wariness of New Building to be understood as exclusively stylistic. A careful reading of *Amerikanische Architektur* suggests that his position evolved from his assessment and interpretation of American accomplishments, casting light into the recesses of his mind.

Mendelsohn, "One of the Most Inventive among Modern Architects"

While Hegemann's judgment of Frank Lloyd Wright stands apart from those involving European architects, it affected his relationship to others, among them Erich Mendelsohn. Frequently considered the most prominent German architect of the 1920s, he is arguably one of the most interesting and diverse.[69] Within the range of his ideas and experiences, there are several that correspond to those of Hegemann, for whom he held a particular fascination.

Volume VIII, 1924, of *Wasmuths Monatshefte für Baukunst (WMB)*, the first on which Hegemann collaborated, although he was not yet listed as editor, devoted its entire first issue to *Erich Mendelsohn: Bauten und Skizzen*.[70] On sixty-six pages, including three double-page spreads, his drawings, sketches, photographs, plans and sections of his works, from the expressionistic Einstein Tower to the Mosse Haus and more, were shown, accompanied by Mendelsohn's explanatory texts. Also illustrated were his projects for Haifa, Palestine. Excerpts from his writings on architecture were featured as the introduction.[71] Although it is unlikely that Hegemann had any input to this, his first issue, the remainder of volume VIII of the journal included numerous pieces by him, and the table of contents noted that unsigned articles were written by Hegemann. Not counting book reviews, this made him responsible for ten articles, possibly meant as a test by Günther Wasmuth, who still had editorial oversight.

The literary style of Hegemann's first signed essay seems misplaced in the journal. The long title gave the content away: *Weimarer Bauhaus und Ägyptische Baukunst. Tut-Ench-Amun. Betrachtungen eines am Nil reisenden deutschen Baumeisters über die Trefflichkeit des Weimarer Bauhauses, der Spengler'schen Architekturphilosophie und der Ägyptischen Baukunst* (Reflections by a German architect traveling along the Nile on the excellence of the Weimar Bauhaus, Spengler's architectural philosophy and Egyptian architecture).[72] The German "*Baumeister*" was Hegemann, who was not an architect, and had not visited Egypt. The subterfuge of the author assuming the role of commentator is one he used in the *Deutsche Schriften*, and would rely on in his later historical fiction.

The point of departure for this lengthy and involved essay was the publication by the Weimar Bauhaus (1919–23) featuring Walter Gropius's manifesto-like *Idee und Aufbau des Staatlichen Bauhauses*.[73] Hegemann was captivated by the guiding principle for the Bauhaus to "strive for the unification of all arts-and-crafts within a new architecture as inseparable elements."[74] In the idea of a new universalism, as well as in the layout and format of this "astonishing" book, Hegemann found much comparable to ancient Egyptian art, which he analyzed on the basis of recent publications. An Egyptologist had pointed out the connections to Spengler's ideas, and Hegemann's actual encounter with the philosopher is the link to the fictional travel along the Nile. Two years earlier Hegemann wrote to his wife from Munich: "In the late afternoon I spent two hours with Oswald Spengler who had invited me for tea, and has given me the second volume of his book which is not yet out."[75] In his article, Hegemann disagrees with Spengler's disdain for works of the XVIII Dynasty, which he valued from the photographs. His long passages on Egyptian art and architecture are similar to the descriptions he sent to his wife from his journeys in that country in 1927–28.

Searching for a convincing relevance of the ancient Near East to the present, Hegemann turned to city planning, in particular workers' housing, comparing ancient and contemporary efforts. In the old city of Thebes he detected antecedents to the garden cities suggested by Friedrich Paulsen and Leberecht Migge. He agreed with Spengler that the axiality in Egyptian architecture and the experience of space evolved from the path as a symbolic form. Even the Nile partook of this idea as a symbol of life's path and trajectory. Hegemann believed architecture could not depend only on logic or function, as demonstrated by Gropius's buildings and Frank Lloyd Wright's Prairie-style houses.

The concluding passages of this essay are devoted to Hegemann's architectural and urban ideas, substantiated by the achievements of the past, Spengler's contemporary philosophy, and an innovative architect/

builder and teacher, namely Gropius. Hegemann maintained that the development of historical form responded to new building materials and techniques, which creative architects ought to acknowledge. He stated: "This principle is the most important one among the 'indivisible elements' of our architecture, the most important of the disciplines of artistic handicrafts, in their renewed unity advocated meritoriously by Walter Gropius in the establishment of the Weimar Bauhaus." The coherent townscape mattered for cities, with buildings as elements within a larger whole. This was designated a "demand for '*Dauerkunst*' [Long-lasting art]" by Hermann Muthesius, contrasting it with ambitious individual achievements. Hegemann thought the metropolis should be an *Einheitskunstwerk* (a total work of art) as proclaimed by Gropius—a synthesis and totality beyond a mere sum of separate parts.

At the outset of his career at *WMB*, Hegemann used this essay to disclose and validate his position as theorist and critic for the next decade: "Whoever contributes in this manner to the development of our architecture, recognizing and evolving what possesses vitality, appropriating new building materials, honored by intelligently modified ancient forms, and finding solutions for the multiple new tasks of the present without smacking worthy building customs in the face or destroying the harmony of the townscape, that individual will accomplish a task equally difficult as what confronts the most superior statesman." Hegemann's articles in the remainder of the 1924 volume were less philosophical and their literary style more in line with the journal's intentions. Some dealt with transformations and additions to existing office buildings in the center of Berlin, while others drew on his familiarity with English garden cities exhibited the previous year in Gothenburg.

Hegemann traveled extensively during 1924, including visits to Austria and Switzerland. In daily postcards and letters to his wife, who was homebound with their second child, Idolene (born in January 1924), he described the towns, visits to museums, concerts, and the theater. His correspondence with her was always in English and seldom referred to contacts with architects or urbanists. However, these journeys and meetings were linked to his work for Wasmuth, and he mentioned correcting proofs and writing captions.[76]

From Vienna he reported briefly on walks through the city with Siegfried Sitte, an architect and urban planner, like his father Camillo Sitte. Hegemann's primary purpose in visiting Vienna was literary and personal. He wrote eloquently to Ida Belle about seeing Arthur Schnitzler and Hermann Bahr, whom he had contacted in Munich, and his disappointment at being unable to meet with Hugo von Hofmannsthal. He had sent copies of his *Deutsche Schriften* and *Iphigenie* to these well-known authors, asking for their opinions. On his meeting with Arthur Schnitzler he commented, "He, like Hermann Bahr who ranks with him for really fine comedy . . . was absolutely charming, interesting and most flattering. I have no right whatsoever to doubt that my book is just as good as I could and did hope for, since such fine men read it and speak of it as fascinating." Regarding the fictitious conversations in his book, Hegemann wrote: "Curiously Hermann Bahr (who is the nearest we have to B. Shaw) said to me he was sure that I knew Shaw well, since I had pictured him so vividly and convincingly."

Discourse with these prominent authors was important for Hegemann, who was considering devoting himself to writing fiction, plays, and works on history, rather than essays on urban planning. This quandary is expressed in another letter to his wife : "I am tortured by the idea that all the big guns who were really nice to me believed firmly in the existence of Ellis [pseudonym for Hegemann and/or Philip Cabot in *Deutsche Schriften*]; while all those who could not be but irritated (the supposed partners of the bluff) treated me with polite indifference. If nothing new develops to destroy this fatal idea in my mind, I miss the main object of this entire trip, namely to elucidate myself as to the validity of my claim of being a writer. This is mortifying: having to rely on one's own judgment in such a matter. . . ."[77] Hegemann resolved to combine literary pursuits with his career as a critic of architecture and urbanism. In his active life he managed to achieve a balance between these two pursuits, which often overlapped. His creative work as a literary author may have compensated for his not being a practicing architect, which he recognized as a painful deficiency.

In July 1924 Hegemann attended the International City Planning Congress in Amsterdam and later accompanied Raymond Unwin to England, where he stayed with his family. In brief notes in *WMB* he reported on a proposal initiated by Robert Schmidt, Regional Planner of the Ruhrgebiet, for a general city regulation that was favorably received by the international urbanists gathered in Amsterdam. In an article on regional planning published in *Der Städtebau* two years later, Schmidt explained this concept, which so far had not been clarified theoretically or legally.[78]

In Amsterdam, Hegemann visited Dutch workers' housing and subsequently commented on the minimal size of the dwellings in his introductory note to Ernst May's article on the advantages of space-saving built-in furniture. At the Amsterdam congress Hegemann established valuable contacts with Dutch architects, especially Cornelis van Eesteren and J. J. P. Oud. Visits to Michel de Klerk's buildings contributed to a sequence of controversies that began with a disparaging article on de Klerk and culminated with a boycott by leading modern architects against Hegemann as editor of *WMB*.[79]

For additional contributions to the journal, Hegemann reworked sections from *Amerikanische Architektur* into longer essays of current interest: *Das Hochhaus als Verkehrsstörer und der Wettbewerb der Chicago Tribune:*

Mittelalterliche Enge und Neuzeitliche Gothik (The skyscraper interfering with traffic and the Tribune Tower Competition), and *Wirkungen der New Yorker Bau-Ordnung von 1916* (The effects of New York's building ordinance of 1916).[80] The illustrations shown in the book were supplemented by some full-page presentations of Hugh Ferris's drawings.

The major portion of the last issue of *WMB* for November/December 1924 was taken up by several articles on housing developments and *Siedlungen,*[81] starting out with Hegemann's essay *Die Rettung des Tempelhofer Feldes* (The rescue of Tempelhofer Field).[82] The fate of this large centrally located open space had been a key issue for Für Gross-Berlin twelve years earlier. Against strong protests the city, trying to maximize the value of the site, had proceeded with the erection of five-story rental barracks densely placed in an obtuse street layout. Luckily the war had put a halt to the development. In his article Hegemann reported on a nonprofit organization, Tempelhofer Feld, A.G., which had been established to rescue the unbuilt portion of the disputed site. Eventually the architect Fritz Bräuning designed a garden city with one- and two-family middle-income houses surrounded by green areas. Martin Wagner, soon to become the *Stadtbaurat* (town planning councilor) of Berlin, praised the project and even the traditional look of the houses. Hegemann, who was well acquainted with the earlier Tempelhofer Feld struggles, used urban history to address political disputes and to provide an overview of the contemporary results. Compared to other *Siedlungen* of the 1920s, the Gartenvorstadt Tempelhofer Feld was unique in that it was centrally located, offering a strikung contrast to the nearby *Mietskasernen.*

The Tempelhofer Feld organization was forced to make concessions for a multistory development with residential buildings and stores at the edge of the site, including a tower building for Junkers Luftverkehr, A.G., whose airport was in the area. A competition for the multistory structure, called by Tempelhofer Feld with a jury of its choice, was open to architects from Berlin and a selected few from elsewhere. Hegemann reported that the tower with a roof deck to observe the air traffic generated the widest range of solutions among the 91 competition entries.[83] He noted that Bonatz, invited from Stuttgart, received one of the three awards with a design that showed the influence of the *Fischerschule,* reflecting its preference for shifting the prominent tower away from an axial placement. According to Hegemann the tower building ought to be positioned as a focal point within the classic Berlin plan. Obviously the debate over the Tempelhofer Feld had not ended. It also involved the height of the residential buildings, which was increased from four to five stories, comparable to the abhorred rental barracks.

After his first year at *WMB* and not yet formally in charge as editor in 1924, Hegemann was testing the waters and feeling his way into the architectural scene churning in Berlin and elsewhere in Europe. Initially he kept a cautious distance from the proponents of the New Building, and from Erich Mendelsohn, whose work and ideas were so prominently displayed in the January/February issue of *WMB* of that year. It was only Frank Lloyd Wright at whom he launched frequently out-of-context barbs.

With *WMB* volume IX, in 1925, the name *Werner Hegemann* appeared as editor responsible for the content of the journal. Readers were informed that the journal *Der Städtebau*, which had interrupted its publication in 1923 and resumed in 1924, would henceforth appear in six double-issues per year. A subtitle was added, indicating an expansion of subject matter—*Monatshefte für Stadtbaukunst, Städtisches Verkehrs- Park-und Siedlungswesen*. Both *WMB* and *STB* were considered interrelated. The fact that Hegemann was the editor of both was not mentioned in the announcement, but the last paragraph declared his intention:

> Our building art, according to the most eminent interpretation of the term as well as our present perception of it, will only be able to achieve a vigorous future if it is perceived within the greater urban context. For this reason, an attempt will be made to structure both periodicals, *Städtebau* and *Wasmuths Monatshefte für Baukunst*, in closest concert and mutually complementing each other. Combined they will render as thorough an overview as possible of the most important developments in architecture.[84]

The publishers soon announced that subscriptions to *WMB* and *STB* had increased substantially, making it possible for monthly publication to be resumed. Both journals began to be printed on costlier semi-gloss stock, enhancing the quality of the illustrations. These changes reflected the influence of Hegemann's penchant for visual presentation. His book *Amerikanische Architektur* (1925/1927) had been overshadowed by Mendelsohn's *Amerika: Bilderbuch eines Architekten* (1926/1928), resulting from the architect's three months in the United States in 1924.[85] The featured photographs by Fritz Lang and Karl Lönberg-Holm were undeniably more captivating than the reproductions that Hegemann gathered for his own volume from the Gothenburg Exhibition and *The American Vitruvius*. A comparison of the publications, which had dissimilar objectives, is unfair to both. Architect Mendelsohn conveyed his enchantment with the glamorous spectacle of America: the light, the tempo, and the chaos. Hegemann, an intellectual ambassador between the continents, intended to acquaint the German public with an America that valued its national history and traditions as expressed in the built environment. His purpose was to present another side of an America that was known and criticized in Europe for a primary interest in technology and economic progress. Within the discourse on city planning in conjunction with Berlin 1910, criticism had centered on the American grid plan. Hegemann was not alone in defending it, and now he confronted another erroneous interpretation of America, a country he admired. The pages of *WMB* provided a widely available forum for his intentions. One occasion was an article on the large building for the German *Funkindustrie* (radio industry), recently completed in Berlin/Charlottenburg by the architect Heinrich Straumer. Notably the structure used only wood to avoid interference with radio transmission. Straumer commented:

> Mechanization to meet the technical demands of modern life must not necessarily mean an "Americanization." If this were the case, then, according to everything one hears these days from "abroad," one could assume that the contemporary functional building would no longer require the input of an artistic architect in the European sense. Vital beauty without romantic recollections is incomprehensible for me.[86]

Hegemann's response to Straumer elaborated on this issue:

> The equalization of "Americanization" with "outright mechanization" as is done by Professor Straumer, although not uncritically, by borrowing European linguistic usage, is indeed, somewhat of a slogan. It certainly has in no way the same meaning in American architecture that is often ascribed to it in Germany. On the contrary, "outright mechanization" is as much or even more decisively rejected by successful American architects as by Professor Straumer, for whom "alive beauty without some romantic recollections is incomprehensible." The majority of distinguished American architects goes even further. . . . They consider the response to traditional examples not as "romantic recollections," but rather as the natural, the inevitable, the sound, the practical, and—the most genuine.[87]

Not only did their widely different books connect Hegemann and Mendelsohn, but so did the architect's journey, which took him to many places Hegemann knew well. For instance, Mendelsohn visited Ann Arbor, Michigan, and lectured at the university. Fiske Kimball, whose article "*Alte und neue Baukunst in Amerika*" appeared in *WMB*, had already moved on to New York and the University of Virginia in Charlottesville.[88] In response to Kimball's essay and a "*Diskussion*" Mendelsohn had with him and Hegemann, Mendelsohn wrote a response that was published in *WMB* and in *The Life-Work of Frank Lloyd Wright*.[89] In it, Mendelsohn expressed the wish to find a way that would lead those opposed to Wright's work and those who "loved" it to a common goal.[90] By publishing a reply to Mendelsohn's piece in *WMB*, Hegemann broke a promise he had made to Mendelsohn that he would not add editorial comments to it. The reply appeared under the name of Leo Adler, his colleague at Wasmuth, but the words were undoubtedly Hegemann's.[91] Mendelsohn's annoyance over Hegemann's deceitfulness contributed to the decision by the members of the Ring, the association of modern architects, to boycott *WMB* as long as Hegemann was editor.

Mendelsohn and Hegemann converged and contrasted regarding the modern metropolis, and this became the essence of their interaction. The

Fig. 37. Erich Mendelsohn's Herpich Store renovation, Berlin, 1925–26. CCCC

architect's view evolved from one colored by the cautious hostility toward the city espoused by the Expressionists and by his fascination with its vibrant rhythm, motion, and light.[92] Mendelsohn derived a certain kinship with Camillo Sitte's esteem for townscape from his mentor Theodor Fischer and from his own appreciation of imagery. Impatience with Sitte's persisting influence on city planning had already stirred the profession during the years of the Greater Berlin competition and the events that followed in its wake. The emphasis on the picturesque by Sitte's followers was based on a misinterpretation of his teachings and damaged his reputation for decades. Hegemann counteracted these misunderstandings in an article on the competition for the Münsterplatz in Ulm, which pitted advocates of the *Fischerschule* against its opponents.[93] Awareness of the need for comprehensive, regional planning fostered a rift between architects and urbanists that carried over into the 1920s. Differing from Wright, both Mendelsohn and Hegemann were enthralled by the modern metropolis. They shared a strong commitment to the city, but represented divergent points of view. The Berlin architect designed singular buildings which enhanced the townscape, but was seemingly indifferent to the totality of the planned city.

Hegemann's interpretation drew him into a controversy with Mendelsohn that was much discussed and contributed to his reputation as anti-modern. Although he explained his position in the press, the repercussions lingered. In 1924 Mendelsohn received the commission to expand and renovate the existing C. A. Herpich Sons store near Alfred Messel's eminent Wertheim Department Store. Mendelsohn's innovative design emphazised the horizontal, contrasting with the admired landmark (Fig. 37). City officials, spurred on by Ludwig Hoffmann, the conservative city architect, refused the required building permit for over a year.[94] In 1925, when numerous complaints and the support of fellow architects and critics had failed to resolve the logjam, twenty-three of them organized a meeting for the signing of a statement in favor of Mendelsohn's design as currently presented. Among those at the gathering, Hegemann was the only one who refused to sign. His vindicating letter to Mendelsohn was published in *Der Städtebau.*[95] In it he referred to his complimentary comments on the Herpich-House in a recent article on the competition organized by Wasmuth.

In the section "*Die Strasse als Einheit*" (The street as a harmonious unity), Hegemann recommended an orchestration of the facades along Unter den Linden responding to the rhythm of the trees.[96] He criticized Messel's Wertheim building for introducing an inappropriate Gothic verticality and steep roof, thereby establishing a historicizing model which had to be considered in future developments on this important avenue. The passage on the Wertheim store was followed by complimentary remarks on Mendelsohn's Herpich House, at that time partially under construction. The scaffolding gave it the appearance of a vertical sweep, with colonnades in front of the store windows on the street level. Hegemann praised the solution by "one of the most inventive among modern architects, Erich Mendelsohn . . . ," for using setbacks to add stories while maintaining a cornice line in harmony with that of nearby buildings. These stepped setbacks may have been suggested to the architect by New York skyscrapers built after 1916, when zoning regulations began to influence the design of high-rise buildings. In both statements on the Herpich House dispute Hegemann repeated his support of Mendelsohn regarding the difficulties and the needless delays caused by the Berlin authorities. In his letter to Mendelsohn, Hegemann gave as the reason for his refusal to sign the testimony of support the use of the bay windows on both sides of the modern facade. He considered them leftovers from a time when the street was lined by tasteless residential buildings, alien to modern commercial structures. Apparently he was unaware that they were requested by the client.

The Herpich House affair contributed to the founding of the Ring in 1924 by architects representing the New Building.[97] Because of Hegemann's ill-considered refusal to support Mendelsohn's design, his reputation was tarnished early on in his career at Wasmuth. He revisited the Herpich House controversy several times in future years. His position was consistent with his belief in the primacy of the urban context vis-à-vis individual buildings. It was a position which the advocates of Modernism found difficult to tolerate.

Mendelsohn figured conspicuously in Hegemann's book *Facades of Buildings*, published by Wasmuth in English and German in 1929.[98] The 501 illustrations were probably drawn from the vast reservoir of photographs at the publishers. They show examples ranging from the historic to the modern and from all over Europe. Mendelsohn's buildings outnumbered all others among the well-represented modern architecture. The brief text of thirty-one pages included two sections on the difficulties of "infill" and "the architecture of additions" within an existing urban fabric. In "Harmony or Discord in Rows of Facades" and "Special References to Two Specific Examples," Hegemann's point of view was supported by a repertoire of examples. *Facades of Buildings* may not be one of Hegemann's most significant publications, but it is noteworthy in addressing the perennial difficulties faced by architects working within a built continuum. He did not advocate absolute homogeneity, but rather a harmonious collage, acknowledging the effectiveness of an occasional "discordant" building: "It is not only people of romantic temperament who can take pleasure in the confused competition between skyscrapers in an American city."[99] He noted that in some cases it was the client who desired that the renovation of his property should generate publicity, "regardless of the architectural standards prevailing in the neighborhood." An example, according to Hegemann, was the case of Mendelsohn's expansion of the Berliner Tageblatt building for Robert Mosse, shown in three illustrations in *Facades of Buildings*.

The section "Special References to Two Specific Examples" centers on the Wertheim Department Store and the Herpich House, within the context of the Leipziger Platz and the Unter den Linden. Hegemann was not alone in promoting a dignified ensemble for the area to enhance Berlin's status as a capital city and metropolis, rescuing it from being a "colonial"—hence "American"—town, as Karl Scheffler had lamented. The Unter den Linden competition was part of this endeavor. The architects of the two most prominent buildings—Mendelsohn and Messel—had followed their own intuition and remained aloof to the overall assemblage. Messel's introduction of Gothic elements, the pitched roof and especially the pillars—which, according to Adolf Loos, belonged to the interior of a medieval building rather than on the facade—were judged an affront to Schinkel's classic Gate Houses. Hegemann considered Messel's later additions to his building particularly awkward, whereas arcades might have provided for a continuity of shops on the street level of the Leipziger Platz. Opportunities lost prior to Mendelsohn's Herpich House modified the criticism of its horizontality, which was the primary issue of contention for the building authorities of Berlin. Hegemann, who had earlier disapproved of the bay windows as carryovers from the old structure that had stood on the site, now thought favorably of them, stating that, "On the contrary, it probably helps the effect of the new building that its strong horizontal rows of windows are balanced by the strong verticals of the projecting bays at each side of the facade, thus producing something like the visual equilibrium which historians of architecture like to call 'classical.' In fact, the new Herpich

House appears at present as the finest building on the long Leipziger Strasse and one of the most interesting buildings of our period."[100] Hegemann's about-face regarding this significant example of the New Building was noteworthy for supporting his view of modernity and urban planning as aspects to be reckoned with in the evolving city.

Haunted by the Herpich House debacle, he revisited it in 1930-31, emphasizing the arduous path to obtain a building permit in Berlin. In *Das steinerne Berlin* Hegemann showed a diagram by Mendelsohn of the *Instanzen-Weg* the architect had to pursue to secure the permission to build. In the text Hegemann contrasted the verticality of the department store cathedrals by Messel and his followers with the buildings by the partners Luckhardt and Anker that stressed the horizontal. He added, "Even better than either is the impression of a building like Mendelsohn's Herpich-Haus in the Leipziger Strasse, which successfully achieved an equilibrium between the horizontal and the vertical."[101]

One of the most admiring and perceptive essays by Hegemann on Mendelsohn discusses the Schocken Department Store in Chemnitz.[102] Appended are brief comments by Charles du Vinage on Mendelsohn's sketches and Le Corbusier's drawings; illustrations made available from recent books on the architects' work. The photographs, several full-page, of the Schocken Store with night illumination are striking. In his review of the building, Hegemann atoned for his earlier occasional rebukes and misunderstandings. He considered that with the Schocken Department Store Mendelsohn had achieved a new creative summit, surpassing the Herpich Haus in Berlin. He praised the functional use of glass, enabling a fairytale night illumination, and how the steel construction allowed for "elastic lightness and structional clarity." Emphasizing functional design at its most successful, Hegemann finished with a flourish, "The Chemnitz Department Store is a triumph for Erich Mendelsohn, hardly to be surpassed."

Hegemann admired Mendelsohn above other German architects, yet his admiration was not uncritical. From his perspective this was justified, and he was defensive of his role as architectural critic. In an untitled and undated draft of a response regarding a legal process against him initiated by Mendelsohn, Hegemann voiced his dismay over the loss of a valued friendship.[103] According to Hegemann a prerequisite for the architectural critic was sacrificing professional practice in order to remain impartial and not compete for commissions. The critic had to maintain impartiality, and should not be expected to act as an advertising promoter. For these reasons Hegemann welcomed Mendelsohn's conciliatory greetings for his fiftieth birthday in 1931: "I wish you well, but above all keep your sharp tongue. We will provide the whetstone."

Regarding the disagreement that prompted Hegemann's unpublished clarification, one may assume that Mendelsohn had reacted to two articles by Hegemann. One took issue with the architect's own Haus am

Rupenhorn (1929–30) and another with Mendelsohn's lecture "*Der schöpferische Sinn der Krise*" (The creative spirit/sense of the crisis), delivered in Zürich in May 1932 and published in Berlin. In both instances Hegemann disputed Mendelsohn's beliefs rather than his architectural work.[104] Although he sharply attacked the design of his private "*Palais*," sarcastically comparing it with Goethe's early eighteenth-century house, he primarily criticized Mendelsohn's convictions and his lack of social sensitivity. Hegemann's review concluded with a chastising statement: "Until the salvation of our country from threatening economic collapse has been achieved, and once more healthy economic conditions for the great masses of the population and its intellectual champions are a reality, until that time such luxurious capitalist private mansions as the Mendelsohn House will impress as a clean and very smart, but also a very dangerous 'Wilhelminismus.'"

The housing question that had preoccupied Hegemann with such intensity during his earlier Berlin years (1909–13) was surfacing again as a reaction to the widespread economic crisis. A year prior to the above essays, the *Kölnische Zeitung* published on January 1, 1931, a New Year's supplement dedicated to the coming decade. Hegemann contributed a piece on housing, town, and regional planning. The title, "*Baut euer eigen Heim sehr schlicht . . .*" cited the beginning of an old saying that continues, "*und nur im Dienste des öffentlichen Wohls verschwendet euer Gut und eure Kraft*" (Build your home unpretentiously, and devote your wealth and energy to the public good).[105] According to Hegemann, Raymond Unwin had used the adage years earlier in a New Year's greeting card, which showed a sketch of the unassuming houses of an English garden city. Recently Hegemann had welcomed his English friend in Berlin, where people still dwelt in crowded rental barracks. With permission from the owner/architect he showed his visitor the latest place of interest—Mendelsohn's own villa. Unwin mentioned this occasion in a letter to Christy Booth: "We had Sat. and Sun. in Berlin. . . . Went to see Dr. Hegemann and in the evening to see the latest thing in new houses built by Mendelsohn, a famous German architect who works in the very modern style."[106] In a similar vein Hegemann commented: "A first-rate accomplishment . . . realizing all the most advanced ideas." Mendelsohn had incorporated remarkable technology into his design, creating the "dreamworld of a better future." However, Hegemann expressed unease at viewing this *Wunderhaus*. He considered its great cost, comparing it to the unpretentious home where the Unwin family lived "in refined simplicity." The housing conditions of the lower and middle classes in Berlin had not improved since before World War I. In his newspaper article Hegemann reprimanded the government for spending funds for unnecessary urban improvements, instead of providing affordable single-family homes with gardens. He never wavered from the ideal of the garden city as the solution to affordable housing.

Hegemann's critical remarks on "*Der schöpferische Sinn der Krise*" were severe. They were appended to a favorable essay on the Columbus House on Potsdamer Platz, defending its modernity against those who described the facade as resembling one bent out of cardboard. Hegemann feared that the economic predicament would make this *Hochhaus* unrentable, like so many others in Berlin. From these comments he turned abruptly to Mendelsohn's "*Schöpferische Sinn der Krise*," interlacing his own remarks with those by others and out-of-context citations from the architect's text. Mendelsohn's position was labeled antiquated, and errors were pointed out in his references to architectural innovations. The derogatory term *Kauderwelsch* (gibberish) was used to characterize his rambling literary style. Mendelsohn's euphoric essay recalled Expressionist Utopian manifestoes, but times had changed and people were less receptive and hopeful.

In 1932 Hegemann was not alone in reacting to the looming threats, which would soon propel him and Mendelsohn into exile. The reaction by an unidentified respondent to Mendelsohn's lecture at the Zurich conference is cited by Hegemann: "An end to these 'Weltanschauung' fantasies. They amount to nothing. We do not want to hear anymore about the universe and instead concern ourselves with the demands of today and tomorrow."

The economic crisis and the political threat were increasingly casting shadows on perceptions of the modern movement. Its critics could no longer be categorized as reactionary traditionalists. Socialist and left-wing intellectuals, who had sided with the avant-garde, were becoming impatient with the fading of its social commitment and with a functionalism that was turning into no more than another stylistic "ism." Was Modernism evolving into an exclusive taste celebrating architects as heroes? Hegemann's criticism of a functionalism compromised by aesthetics prevailed in his editorial policies and was prescient of this trend. In the later 1920s his position gained urgency and affected all aspects of his writing and actions.

Conflicting Visions of the Modern City

Tracing Hegemann's involvement with Mendelsohn's architecture over several years, the shift in his position concerning urban planning underscores the multiple interconnections to his architectural criticism. From his earliest encounters with urbanism, Hegemann perceived architecture and city planning as interrelated. Rather than discrete, immutable objects, he viewed buildings as integral to the context of the evolving city, "cells within the urban organism," as his contemporary G. A. Platz said.[107] According to Hegemann buildings were integral elements of the city, which he considered the ultimate cultural achievement and a synthesis of historical, economic, and humanistic factors in perpetually evolving flux. These dynamics were chaotic and difficult to comprehend in their totality, but could be studied from various perspectives that magnified particular aspects. Hegemann's approach was city planning-*cum*-urban history, and he was a pioneer in recognizing the latter as paramount to a comprehensive reading of the city. Hegemann's position illuminates his understanding of Camillo Sitte's contextual town planning and "artistic principles," which figured in the debates of the 1920s as they had previously at the time of Berlin 1910.

The unification of Gross-Berlin had become a reality in 1920, which was also the year Heinrich de Fries proposed Hegemann for the position of *Stadtbaurat* for Berlin. A related event was the founding of the journal *Stadtbaukunst alter und neuer Zeit* by Cornelius Gurlitt and Bruno Möhring, with Walter Lehweiss as editor. Initially appearing bimonthly, it was published monthly beginning in 1922. Hegemann was asked to contribute to this publication before returning to Berlin. Instead, he assumed the position of editor for two prominent journals published by Wasmuth. His decision, and especially the revival of *Der Städtebau*, may have aroused competitive feelings between him and the urbanists at *Stadtbaukunst*, who knew each other from the days of their shared engagement for Greater Berlin.

At Wasmuth Hegemann had a free hand to cover a range of tendencies in city planning and its relation to urban form. These trends were less contentious than those in contemporary architecture, more flexible, and even overlapped. From its emergence in the first decade of the twentieth century, urbanism was an international movement energized by exhibitions and conferences. The Great War had dampened this spirit, but it did not disappear altogether. Under Hegemann's guidance *Städtebau* became a vehicle for reviving it. *Stadtbaukunst* also covered topics from abroad, but its primary focus was the restoration of German towns devastated by the war and economic hardship. Within the discourse of the pros and cons of the Sittesque *Fischerschule*, *Stadtbaukunst* leaned toward the picturesque and the preservation of historic townscapes. The journal *Städtebau*, although founded by Camillo Sitte, shunned the misinterpretation of his "artistic principles" by his followers.[108] Sitte's analyses of urban spaces and streets were accepted by his followers as prescriptions to be imitated, which was actually contrary to his intention. His message became muddled for generations, with many of his mistaken followers laying out curvilinear streets without regard for the natural site, arbitrarily introducing irregularities. Sitte considered towns to be perpetually evolving and manifesting the pulse of time. He was well aware of the dilemma inherent to contemporary interventions intent on avoiding the cloning of the historic past.

Prominent among those who distorted Sitte's ideas were Theodore Fischer, Karl Henrici, and other members of the *Fischerschule*. Hegemann became acquainted with the opposing factions regarding Sitte in connection with the exhibitions and discussions of 1910. Years later, working with

Elbert Peets on *The American Vitruvius: Civic Art*, he included the first and most accurate English synopsis of Sitte's principles as the opening chapter, "The Modern Revival of Civic Art," illustrated with images from Sitte's 1889 work, *Der Städtebau nach seinen künstlerischen Grundsätzen* (City planning according to artistic principles, 1889). In relation to contemporary German planning, Hegemann mentioned that Sitte's love of the Renaissance was "strengthened by a healthful distaste for medieval picturesqueness" and had "produced plans . . . not only formal in detail but . . . pulled together into large formal schemes."[109]

In the journal *Städtebau*, founded by Sitte, Hegemann shunned the tenets of the *Fischerschule* and steered a more inclusive course (Fig. 38). He was particularly outspoken in his commentaries on the competition for the Münsterplatz in Ulm (1925–26), for which the jury was dominated by representatives of the *Fischerschule*.[110] The contentious Ulmer Münsterplatz debate between the faction sympathizing with the *Fischerschule* and its opponents was carried out vigorously by the Swiss critic Peter Meyer (1894-1984) in the *Schweizerische Bauzeitung* and by Hegemann in *Städtebau* and *WMB*.[111] Both critics excelled in polemical repartee. Meyer, a student of Theodor Fischer, took the side of his mentor in a series of articles on axiality and symmetry, "*Über Axe und Symmetrie: Ein Beitrag zu der neuen Polemik der 'Ostendorferschule' gegen die* 'Fischerschule'" (Regarding axis and symmetry: A contribution to the recent polemic by the

STÄDTEBAU
MONATSHEFTE FÜR STADTBAUKUNST
STÄDTISCHES VERKEHRS= PARK= UND
SIEDLUNGSWESEN
DIE ERWEITERUNG DER HAMBURGER CITY
UND DER MESSEHAUS-WETTBEWERB / LONDONER
VERKEHRS- UND FREIFLÄCHENFRAGEN / CASSEL
ANGORA—ZÜRICH / KÖLNER HOCHHAUS-STREIT
STRASSBURG / MENDELSOHNS HERPICH-NEUBAU
ULMER MÜNSTERPLATZ: *HORROR VACUI*
DIESES HEFT ENTHÄLT 75 ABBILDUNGEN
EINZELPREIS 2.50 MARK
HERAUSGEBER: WERNER HEGEMANN
VERLAG ERNST WASMUTH A=G BERLIN
JAHRGANG 1925 HEFT 9-10 SEPT.-OKT.

Fig. 38. Cover of the September-October 1925 issue of Der Städtebau, *noting content including the Ulmer Platz controversy and Mendelsohn's Herpich Store renovation.* WHA

"Ostendorf-School" against the "Fischer-School").[112] P. M., as he always signed, distinguished between the concepts of line of sight, center line, axis, and symmetry. All were relevant to the problem of how to design the space around the monumental Ulmer Münster, one of the tallest cathedrals in Germany, where the adjacent structures had been removed in the previous century. Sitte had warned against the freeing up of Gothic churches, recommending that only the front should be exposed to a plaza. The symmetrical facade ought to be visible from a distance with streets leading toward the main portal.[113]

The *Fischerschule* accused its adversaries of historicist "Classicism" for recommending an axial approach to the facade of the cathedral. The opponents rebuked the *Fischerschule* for misunderstanding Sitte by ignoring medieval examples. Both sides claimed a modern point of view. Camillo Sitte was rarely mentioned in the numerous articles published on the Ulmerplatz controversy in 1925 and 1926, except those by Hegemann. The rationale of the controversy certainly pertained to his ideas and could be summed up as Sitte's misunderstood "artistic principles," contrary to Friedrich Schinkel's and Ostendorf's Classicism. In his influential book of 1927, G. A. Platz devoted a section of his chapter "*Die Gesetze der Architektonischen Komposition*" (The laws of architectural composition) to symmetry.[114] Responding to the Ulm debate regarding this concept, Platz referred to Sitte, who had called attention to the different meaning given to symmetry by "the Ancients," for whom it signified proportional harmony, rather than a mirror-image likeness of right to left.[115] Sitte cited Vitruvius: "Symmetria is a proper agreement between members of the work itself, and relation between the different parts and the whole general scheme." He traced the modern concern with symmetrical axes and the notion of right and left to the development of architectural drawing by Gothic masters. However, Sitte warned against prescriptive axiality in town planning. The Ulm competition jury, chaired by Theodor Fischer, was weighted toward the picturesque and asymmetrical. In Platz's discussion, he recommended a synthesis that combined an axial frontal plaza with diagonal sight lines from the angles.

In the numerous articles by Hegemann and the others selected by him for *STB* and *WMB*, he illustrated historic examples, many from Sitte's treatise and *The American Vitruvius*, to demonstrate the mistakes made in choices made by the Ulm jury (Fig. 39). Hegemann conspicuously cited Goethe, who recommended that vis-à-vis important personages (such as the Ulm Münster), one should not act in an unrestrained manner.[116] Hegemann noted that the members of the competition jury had conveyed to the participants that "it was regrettable that there reigned great confusion as to when and where the methods of strict axiality would be in place." The proposals had therefore been adversely affected to the extent of encumbering the monumental Münster. According to Hegemann, the rejected proposals showed a superior understanding of

Fig. 39. Elbert Peets' design cover for an issue of Der Städtebau. CCCC

medieval precedents and Sitte's principles, and he devoted ample space to them in his articles.

The polemical duel between Meyer and Hegemann incited by the Ulmerplatz controversy motivated Hegemann's ironic response to the editor of the *Schweizerische Bauzeitung*. P.M.'s "sharp attacks" had also been taken up in the *Baugilde*. Hegemann claimed to be amused by them and refuted them in his own publications. P.M. continued his aggravation, now shared by the editor of the newspaper. Hegemann politely asked de Fries to renew his friendship, but his irritation with Hegemann lingered, and Meyer was joined by his colleague Karl Scheffler writing for *Baugilde*.[117]

In connection with these events, the matter of naming a new *Stadtbaumeister* (town planner) for Berlin acquired greater significance for Hegemann. De Fries, who had recommended him for the position in 1920, had been his predecessor at Wasmuth, and was now the editor of *Baugilde*. The relationship between the two had cooled and become adverserial. In January 1926, de Fries made a surprisingly hostile move by writing to the municipality of Berlin and vehemently opposing Hegemann as a candidate for *Stadtbaurat*.[118] In reality Hegemann had not applied for the position; rather he had been proposed by several organizations advocating housing and land reform. As he explained in *WMB*, he would only consider a candidacy if the most appropiate candidate, Dr. Robert Schmidt from Essen, or the former *Stadtbaurat*, Elkart, could not be persuaded to accept the position.[119] De Fries's action was sharply rebuked in the *Bauwarte*, especially for his accusation that Hegemann showed "insufficient commitment toward contemporary sociopolitical concerns."[120] De Fries's recommendation of Hegemann in 1920, published in *STB*, and listing his numerous qualifications, was now reprinted in its entirety by *Bauwarte*. The *Stadtbaurat* incident was injurious to de Fries and served to renew Hegemann's reputation as an urbanist after his long stay abroad.

Throughout his career Hegemann was aware of his limited practical involvement with planning and his lack of drawing skills. Other than his collaborative projects with Elbert Peets and Joseph Hudnut in America, there are very few documented plans by Hegemann. Those for Berlin are shown in *Das steinerne Berlin*, and one was published in *STB* in 1925, called "A proposal by Werner Hegemann adapted by Oskar Lange, Halle" (Fig. 40). The full caption reads, "Conceptual sketch for the development of the Potsdamer Platz with pedestrian connections between the railroad stations and the Leipziger Platz on the level of the train tracks, according

Fig. 40. Redesign proposal for Potsdamer and Leipziger Platz, by Hegemann, with the aid of Oskar Lange. Der Städtebau, *November-December, 1925.* WHA

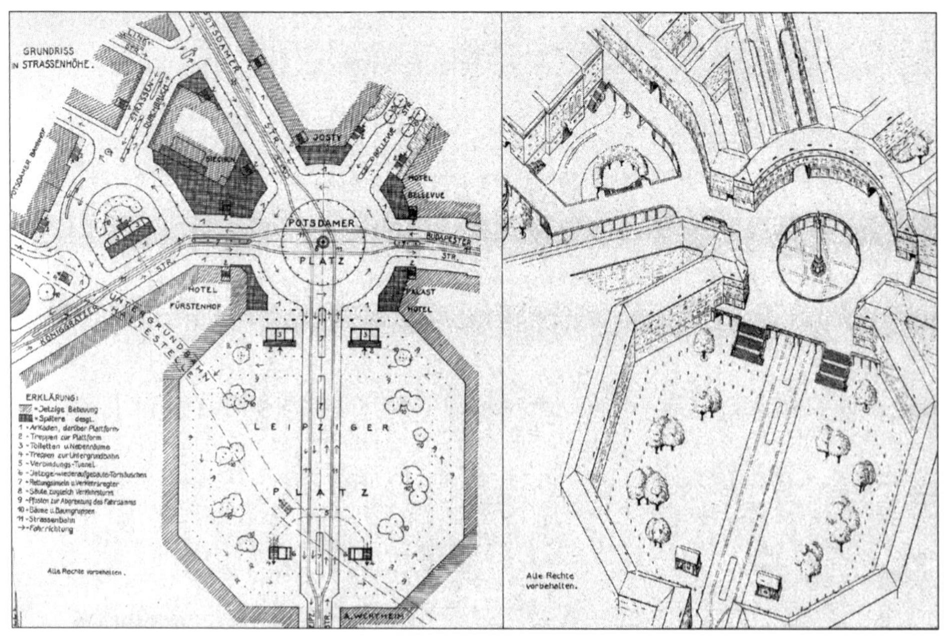

to a proposal by Werner Hegemann, adapted by Oskar Lange, Halle."[121] Two illustrations of this design occupy a full page and are marked "copyrighted." One is a plan of the lower level, the other a perspective rendering of the upper, elevated level of the multilevel solution to the traffic problems. They show existing and proposed buildings in an attempt to solve the traffic problems, and the connections between the Potsdamer and the Leipziger Platz. The opposite page shows a detail of the Potsdamer Platz and two proposals by Oskar Lange. Hegemann's text is critical of Lange's versions as more "fantastic" than practical. His own multilevel proposal was based on what he had seen in Sydney, Australia, and what was being considered for San Francisco. He mentioned that the elevated Potsdamer Platz would resemble a stage with the Leipziger Platz as an auditorium.

Hegemann's return to Berlin brought his experience abroad to bear on his earlier activities in Germany. By 1925 a transition in his concepts was taking place. It affected his work for *Städtebau*, the Ulmerplatz debate, and the Unter den Linden competition. It was also reflected in his relationship with other urbanists in Berlin, including those associated with the journal *Stadtbaukunst.*

In 1922 Walter Lehweiss founded the Freie Deutsche Akademie des Städtebaues (Free German Academy of Town Planning, or FDAST) under the umbrella of the journal *Stadtbaukunst*, which published its reports.[122] It became an active association, holding general and regional meetings. The membership included many prominent architects and planners, among them Robert Schmidt from Essen and Karl H. Brunner from Vienna. Both were well known and admired by Hegemann, who also became a member. He did not always attend the meetings of the local chapter in Berlin, Märkische Arbeitsgemeinschaft. Nor was he listed as present at the major International Congress for Town Planning and Housing in Vienna in September of 1926. It is not clear if his lack of participation in the FDAST was due to his travels, or because he preferred to distance himself from its leadership while promoting his own agenda. During his controversies regarding the Weissenhof Siedlung, Stuttgart in 1927, and with Martin Wagner in 1928, Hegemann revived his connection with the FDAST, seeking its support.

The two competitions for Berlin, which he initiated in conjunction with Wasmuth, were significant for Hegemann's renewed involvement with city planning. They attest to his penchant for staging urban events to arouse public awareness. The January/February 1925 issue of *Städtebau* announced an extension of the deadline for the first of the competitions for concepts, asking for an essay on "Which architectural project is most important and most popular for Greater Berlin?" The objective was to gather opinions from professionals and the general public to inform architects and planners. It was a conspicuous move by Hegemann to utilize the journals *Städtebau* and *WMB* to address contemporary and future urban issues. Although the proposal and the prizes were modest, ninety-seven entries were received. They came primarily from architects and addressed every conceivable aspect pertaining to Greater Berlin, including one suggesting the use of durable colors to enhance the townscape.[123] The jury agreed that the most important problem was the establishment of connections between the four major railroad stations: the Lehrter and Stettiner stations receiving trains from the north, and the Anhalter and Potsdamer stations receiving trains from the south. This task, however, was deemed too extensive and technical, and therefore beyond the intent of the competition. In consideration of the request for an aesthetic approach, the first three prizes were given to entries suggesting the architectural development of Unter den Linden. The first prize went to Erich Karweik, who recommended in his entry, "*Westachse*," that a "detailed planning of the Lindenachse" should precede work on the re-routing of train connections.[124] The outcome of the "Baukünstlerische Aufgabe" survey resulted in the selection of the theme for the second and more important international competition, "How should Berlin's main thoroughfare 'Unter den Linden' be developed in the twentieth century?" (Fig. 41) It is usually referred to as the Unter den Linden Competition, and the prizes offered were consider-

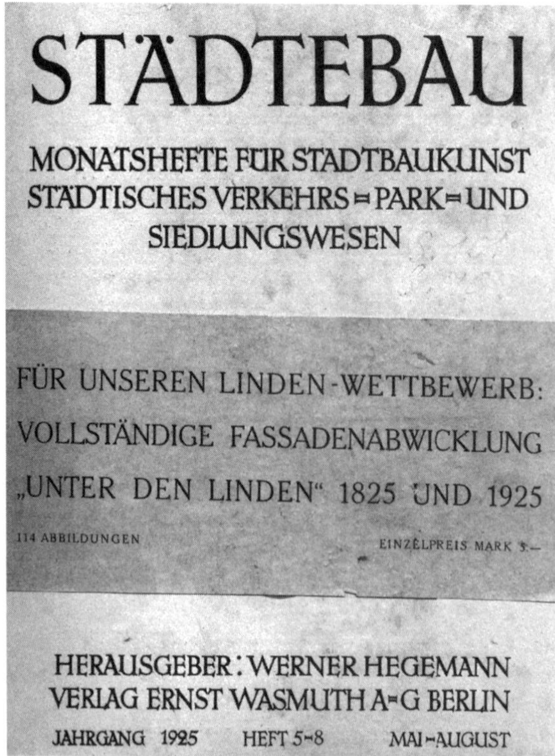
STÄDTEBAU

MONATSHEFTE FÜR STADTBAUKUNST
STÄDTISCHES VERKEHRS= PARK= UND SIEDLUNGSWESEN

FÜR UNSEREN LINDEN-WETTBEWERB:
VOLLSTÄNDIGE FASSADENABWICKLUNG
„UNTER DEN LINDEN" 1825 UND 1925

114 ABBILDUNGEN EINZELPREIS MARK 5.—

HERAUSGEBER: WERNER HEGEMANN
VERLAG ERNST WASMUTH A=G BERLIN
JAHRGANG 1925 HEFT 5=8 MAI=AUGUST

Fig. 41. Cover of Der Städtebau *with wraparound text announcing the illustration insert of Unter den Linden's facades from 1825. May–August, 1925.* WHA ably larger than in the first competition.[125] The jurors were the same: *Stadtbaudirektor* Elkart; architects Poelzig, Fahrenkamp, and Dernburg; Günther Wasmuth; and Hegemann. The specifications requested ideas for the stretch between the Brandenburg Gate and the Friedrich's Forum in the form of sketches suitable for publication and exhibition. A band wrapped around the cover of *Städtebau* announced, *Für unseren Linden-Wettbewerb: Vollständige Fassadenabwicklung "Unter den Linden" 1825 und 1925.* The entire trajectory and history of Unter den Linden from 1680 to 1925 was illustrated in double-page spreads, primarily showing the facades. Hegemann often used the term *Schauseite* (display side) instead of *Fassade.* In detailed captions he documented the urban history of this important avenue. The pages were intended to be removed from the magazine, glued together and pinned to the wall, providing a cinematic overview of an evolving cityscape over nearly four hundred years. The message for the participants was that their task involved an intervention in an ongoing historic process, generating ideas beyond Unter den Linden.

For Hegemann, the second international competition became a turning point in his views on urbanism, comparable to the watershed of Berlin 1910. This repositioning was brought into focus by the debate surrounding Mendelsohn's Herpich-House, and was reflected in Hegemann's article addressing the difficulties of additions to major buildings and infill architecture.[126] It has remained a topic of continuing pertinence for dense urban centers pressured by changing demands.[127] With a new perspective Hegemann considered the heart of the evolving city an episode of the present and the unpredictable future, requiring adjustments within a process of continuous renewal. He began to focus on the city as a complex system arising out of constituents interacting in variable ways. Comprehensive planning for an entire metropolis might be an idealistic goal, but incremental interventions in the center could bring about immediate positive results affecting wider areas. Foresight was obligatory, and Hegemann urged architects to represent their own present time rather than the past.

In his article on the "re-conquest" of Berlin's architecture, Hegemann showed examples of the modernization of late-nineteenth-century ornate buildings. They had been stripped of excessive decoration and adapted to the requirements of contemporary commercial use at a time when economic conditions made the construction of new offices prohibitive. Adaptive reuse frequently required *Aufstockung*, the addition of floors, which could have unfortunate results for the neighboring buildings. According to Hegemann, historic landmarks and ensembles required special vigilance within an overall plan. Building regulations could have prevented blunders like Messel's Wertheim Department Store from "gothicizing" the baroque Leipziger Platz.[128]

The theme Hegemann confronted in the Unter den Linden competition was how to achieve a balance between a significant historic context and contemporary and future requirements. In this case it involved the major boulevard of Berlin, laden with collective memory and extending between landmark buildings and plazas. An unusual parameter was the four rows of majestic linden trees, which predated the structures on both sides. The trees had suffered from environmental stress, and their lushness had diminished to the extent that they no longer diverted attention from the buildings. One of the questions posed in the competition program concerned the fate of the trees: whether they should be replaced or eliminated altogether. The linden trees were one of the numerous components to be considered for a vital public space. Awareness had shifted to an orchestration of the edifices and the design of commercial buildings responsive to contemporary needs. Hegemann wrote, but did not sign, several brief illustrated texts relating to Unter den Linden that were interspersed with the facade-sequence (*Fassadenabwicklung*). Particularly relevant is the essay on the street as a harmonious entity, "*Die Strasse als Einheit*."[129] The author stated that it resulted from the discussions preceding the formulation of the competition program. Agreement had been reached on aiming for a phased transformation based on a long-term artistic plan. The danger that gradual, phased development would cause further disharmony, aptly called by Goethe a combination of "Form und Unform," could not possibly be worse than the existing conditions.

On the basis of the illustrations Hegemann demonstrated that Unter den Linden had never achieved architectural significance. What had contributed beauty and grandeur to the boulevard were the four rows of trees, and no cohesive plan for the buildings had ever existed. Opposition to building regulations for "systematic order" was voiced by "romantic free spirits." In an aside to the Ulmerplatz debate, Hegemann noted that these same individuals had objected to symmetry and axiality, considering these acceptable only in the Baroque period. His reply to this resistance was posed as an urban design question: "How can an important street in a growing metropolis be satisfactorily designed?" If everyone were to do as he pleased regarding built form, the results would be intolerable. Aesthetics were not the only consideration for the development. For instance, arcades featured prominently in many historic examples and were valued by the author, but could hamper the access to light from the windows unless properly designed. He repeated his approval of the Herpich House by "one of the most ingenious modern architects," Mendelsohn, for his solution to this problem by designing large display windows unobscured by arcades. He also called attention to the set-back of the two top floors designed by the architect. This expedient avoided a conflict with the established cornice line on Leipziger Strasse by moving the added height to the interior of the block and out of sight from viewers across the street. Praising these innovations for adding new dimensions to the old buildings nearby, Hegemann expressed hope that the competition would encourage others to seek original solutions for an auspicious street development.

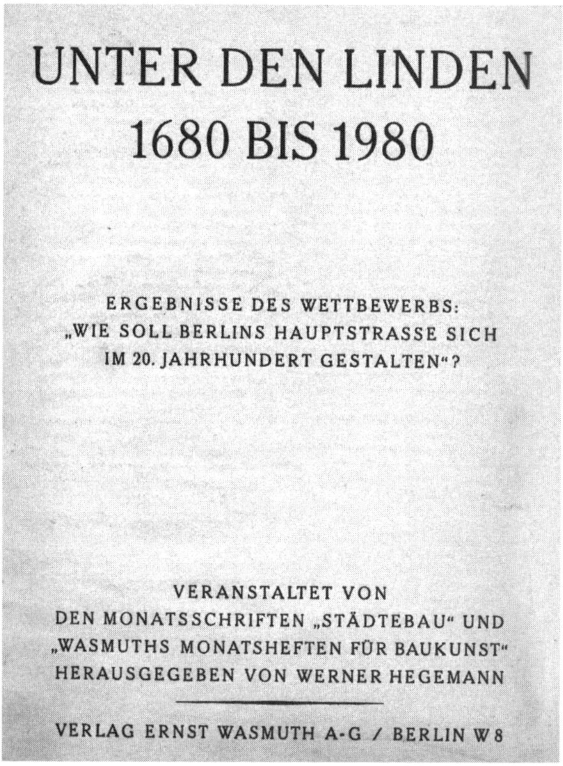

UNTER DEN LINDEN
1680 BIS 1980

ERGEBNISSE DES WETTBEWERBS:
„WIE SOLL BERLINS HAUPTSTRASSE SICH
IM 20. JAHRHUNDERT GESTALTEN"?

VERANSTALTET VON
DEN MONATSSCHRIFTEN „STÄDTEBAU" UND
„WASMUTHS MONATSHEFTEN FÜR BAUKUNST"
HERAUSGEGEBEN VON WERNER HEGEMANN

VERLAG ERNST WASMUTH A-G / BERLIN W 8

Fig. 42. Cover of the special edition of the Wasmuth periodical, which described the results of the Unter den Linden competition, 1925. WHA

Thirty-three proposals were received, answering many expectations.[130] The full jury, consisting of Hermann Dernburg, Karl Elkart, Emil Fahrenkamp, Hegemann, Hans Poelzig, and Ewald Wasmuth met on October 20 and 21, 1925, and selected seven entries for further consideration (Fig. 42). All of them contained useful suggestions. The first prize of 1,500 *Reichsmarks* was awarded to the Dutch architect Cornelis van Eesteren (1897–1988) for his entry "*Gleichgewicht*" (equilibrium).[131] It was generally acknowledged that Hegemann's opinion was decisive in the selection of the most farsighted and modern among the seven winning entries. All were publicly exhibited from October 26 to November 7, 1925, at the Ernst Wasmuth Verlag.[132]

Van Eesteren's concise explanation enhanced his proposal and demonstrated a superb grasp of the program.[133] His analysis of the problems addressed by the Unter den Linden competition had validity for other metropolitan centers envisioning balance and unity by combining the demands of an avenue as a historic monument and tourist attraction, and a thriving commercial center serving as an economic stimulus. These insights were presented convincingly and with elegant economy in van Eesteren's entry. It received first prize, even though it proposed the demolition and rebuilding of the entire stretch of Unter den Linden from Brandenburg Gate to Friedrich's Forum. Additionally, the proposal included a tower building at a time when skyscrapers were suspect in Germany.

Hegemann's comments on van Eesteren's prizewinning entry verified that he defended it during the jury's deliberation.[134] He noted the skill with which the architect differentiated between the four-floor height of the commercial buildings along the avenue, equal to Brandenburg Gate, and the higher set-back elevations in the interior of the blocks. As Hegemann had noted on several occasions, this feature derived from the New York zoning regulations of 1916. From America their effect had spread to Europe, and they were now generally utilized for practical as well as aesthetic reasons. Van Eesteren's rhythmic placement of higher buildings demonstrated how the scale of four stories did not have to be adhered to slavishly. The only fault singled out by Hegemann was a lack of attention to traffic concerns.

According to Vincent van Rossem, van Eesteren's "Equilibrium" plan represented "a high point but at the same time a breaking point in his urbanistic thinking . . . the epilogue of a tradition: a final ingenious attempt to reconcile the traditional street facade with the problems of tall buildings and the irresistible pressure to centralize business functions at the expense of residential ones, within the physical constraints of the historic city."[135] These ideas had preoccupied Hegemann even before his departure from Europe in 1913, and were reinforced by his American experience. The presence of historic districts was less important in the New World, yet within the European context a break with historic continuity was problematic. However, Hegemann was becoming increasingly aware of the distinction to be made between new architecture and architectural history. Undoubtedly he was pleased to receive a letter from van Eesteren, stating: "I repeat, I am not a modernist who wants to make something else [just] for a change. The so-called Modern leaves me cold."[136] Hegemann encountered in van Eesteren an architect/planner with whom he shared fundamental insights, and who could present them graphically in realizable form—an ability he himself regretfully lacked. Their admiring regard for each other is documented in their correspondence and in van Eesteren's diaries and interviews.[137]

The two urbanists concurred in their consideration of the city as a continuous collage and their regard for urban history as it was reflected in the teachings of Marcel Poëte, whom both admired. At different times they had partaken of "*urbanisme*" in Paris, and of Charles Gide's "*économie sociale.*" For van Eesteren many ideas crystallized during his time at the Bauhaus in Weimar from 1927–30. In 1923, he used the term "urban elements" for the components of the functional city: railroad stations, dwellings, factories, etc. According to van Eesteren the "task of the urban planner [is] to establish their proportion and functional relationship to one another. . . ."[138] Several years earlier, on the West Coast of America,

Hegemann had expressed a similar view on "the structural rank of the different elements in a city-plan" in a prefatory statement to his *Report on a City Plan for the Municipalities of Oakland & Berkeley* (1915).[139] This paragraph may stand as Hegemann's enduring urban credo:

> City-planning is the co-ordination of the different activities that make for the physical growth of the city. . . . The different factors that together make up a city and are essential in organizing and developing the tremendous areas covered by a modern metropolis are all objects of city-planning, i.e., of logical and comprehensive consideration and forethought. Consideration must be given to these different *elements* of the city-plan according to their structural rank . . . .

Among the elements listed by Hegemann, and later discussed in the *Report*, are harbors, railroads, streets, parks and playgrounds, and civic centers. For each metropolis the ranking of these elements would differ in response to the circumstances. Hegemann also envisioned an equilibrium between the City Economic and the City Recreational and Beautiful. Hegemann's *Report* never reached a European audience, probably because it was published shortly before the United States entered the war, or because it was thought to address only local conditions in California. The similarities between Hegemann's concept of a city composed of elements anticipating van Eesteren's plan a decade later are remarkable. Exposure to the innovative regional plans for Greater Boston, Greater Berlin, and the Ruhr-Gebiet scheme had previously galvanized Hegemann's thinking at the expense of giving serious attention to the design components of urban centers. Upon his return to Berlin his focus shifted to three-dimensional components within a larger context, and he began to see the city as a synergy of elements. This vast conglomerate within a larger whole gave the city the flexibility to adapt to constant change and renewal in response to wide-ranging demands. Van Eesteren shared this view of the city, considering it "a-classical" and ultimately modern. The affinity with Hegemann's ideas deserves recognition because it links him to the modern and postmodern urbanism of the subsequent decades. Van Eesteren became prominent in CIAM (Congrès Internationaux d'Architecture Moderne, or International Congresses of Modern Architecture), founded in 1928, but Hegemann did not participate and would have questioned the functional city planning advocated by the Athens Charter in 1933.

A less theoretical accord between van Eesteren and Hegemann was their use of slides in lectures and their interest in film. Hegemann had shown slides as early as 1910, many made from his own photographs. In the 1920s van Eesteren projected numerous slides in his lectures while keeping his spoken comments brief. A reviewer of one of these lectures compared the approach to "a movie." Van Eesteren was actually considering the possibility of replacing lectures with films.[140] The grouping of visual images by subject to clarify theoretical topics was comparable to

Hegemann's orchestration of the Berlin 1910 Exhibition, and the illustrations in *The American Vitruvius* were arranged similarly. For his lectures in Argentina in 1931, Hegemann showed a film on city planning on several occasions.

Pitfalls of Criticism

Efforts to further the understanding of the ambiguities of the Modern Movement have turned historians' attention to the role of architectural critics and others who might be called "readers of the city." Books, articles, and correspondence of individuals who were not themselves builders, but responded to the architectural achievements of the 1920s, are increasingly perceived as offering valuable insights. Those who shaped opinions are gaining recognition, and their contributions enhance our comprehension of a complex period receding into historical time.[141]

The emergence of the architectural critic, as distinct from historians and writers of manuals, was related to the proliferation of professional journals clamoring for articles. Illustrations and essays captivated the attention of a wider audience and stimulated awareness of the urban environment. While architects were creating an innovative formal language, critics augmented the vocabulary with new terminology. As built structures and concepts changed, terms acquired new meanings, presenting difficulties for interpretation and translation. Among scholars venturing into this area of inquiry are Adrian Forty, in *Words and Buildings: A Vocabulary of Modern Architecture*, and Rosemarie Haag Bletter, writing on "The Terms of the Debate" in Adolf Behne's *The Modern Functional Building*.[142] Terminology is becoming a concern in connection with the publication of monographs on critics and their writings. Recently published books on contemporaries of Hegemann include those on Adolf Behne, Heinrich de Fries, Peter Meyer, Lewis Mumford, and Gustav Adolf Platz.[143]

Haila Ochs characterizes the art and architecture critic as a mediator or intermediary between the architect or artist and the public, and one who adds to understanding by providing an informed point of view. According to Ochs, critics should be clear regarding their particular position, while encouraging others to arrive at their own conclusions. Among those Ochs refers to is Hegemann. She is one of a select few to recognize his status as comparable to that of Behne, de Fries, or Scheffler; his voice has generally been disregarded or dismissed entirely. Ochs's portrayal of the role of the critic is more appropriate regarding Hegemann than his label as "*Publizist*" prevalent in German-language publications. He often expressed himself regarding his role as a critic and his editorial policy at Wasmuth. Especially apt are his comments in an unpublished reply to Mendelsohn, where he noted: "For the architectural critic, who sacrificed his own architectural praxis for the sake of exercising his critical role, it is a satisfaction when his colleagues recognize his impartiality. . . . It is painful for the critic when he must fear that he is welcomed only as a praising publicist (propagandist), who is not permitted a derogatory opinion."[144]

The term *Publizist* does not do justice to Hegemann as an architectural critic, although it could be applied to his position of calling public attention to urban issues by means of exhibitions and publications. For Hegemann the orchestration of exhibitions was an expression of criticism. Both with the exhibition work and in his writings on architecture, he sought insights from contradictions. Comparable to his attitude regarding historical heroes, he harbored no complacency vis-à-vis the salient figures of Modernism assuming heroic stances. He repudiated the idea of heroes as "absolutes" not to be questioned, and equally rejected iconic stylistic categories. Hegemann's inclination toward "unmasking" the moderns made it convenient to brand him as "anti-modern" and reactionary, although socially and politically he was more progressive than the majority of those who felt victimized by his criticism. His position was far more informed and balanced than the either/or of pro- and anti-Modernism.

Hegemann's written output during his Berlin years (1922–33) was impressive and controversial. As the editor of two prominent journals, *WMB* and *STB*, he was the subject of high expectations and was vulnerable to censure. His editorial intentions and polemical style were demonstrated on the pages of these publications, which provided the stage for the *Federkriege* (wars of the pen) he fought with verve.

The respectful, congenial relations between Hegemann and van Eesteren were similar to those he had with J. J. P. Oud (Jacobus Johannes Pieter Oud, 1890–1963), as revealed in their correspondence and in letters Oud exchanged with others.[145] Therefore it was with reluctance that Oud became the node of intersection for the displeasure addressed to Hegemann by his adversaries. Among these were Behne, Hugo Häring, Mendelsohn, and Adolf Rading. They were provoked by Hegemann's polemical criticism of the Dutch architects Michel de Klerk, who was no longer alive, and Hendrik Petrus Berlage, the Belgian Henry van de Velde, Frank Lloyd Wright, and others.

Hegemann's initial contacts with Dutch architects and urbanists occurred at the 1924 International Town Planning Congress in Amsterdam. He reported in *WMB* that these meetings stressed the importance of regional planning and open space, topics emphasized by Robert Schmidt, director of the Siedlungsverband Ruhrkohlenbezirk, and Fritz Schumacher from Hamburg and Cologne.[146] Professionals attending the congress were impressed by the Dutch government's postwar achievements in housing, viewed on arranged tours. Hegemann's article commented on the Amsterdam group of architects, singling out Michel de Klerk (1884–1923), and describing his work as "fantastic . . . quixotic witty film sets."

According to Hegemann, the Amsterdam architects declared their buildings "modern," based on practical considerations. He contrasted them with the "serious" work by J. J. P. Oud and Granpré Molière in Rotterdam, and he returned to this topic on later occasions.

Oud and Hegemann began their correspondence following the Amsterdam conference. Hegemann sent copies of *WMB* to Oud, asking for his opinion and apologizing for the first issue of 1925, not yet fully under his oversight. He promised to make the journal at least as "progressive" as *Die Baugilde*, edited by de Fries.[147] A few weeks later *WMB* published Oud's "*Ja und Nein: Bekenntnisse eines Architekten*"(Yes and no: an architect's convictions) with illustrations of his recent buildings.[148] Hegemann's introductory note described Oud as the "leader of new Dutch building," who had liberated himself from the "mannerism" prevailing mainly in Amsterdam. Shown were his public housing complexes Tusschendijken in Spangen and Oud-Mathenesse in Rotterdam. Oud's terse and clear affirmation of his beliefs was substantiated by the photographs of his buildings. Hegemann respected Oud's opinions and valued him as a pioneer of functional Modernism. Asserting the contrast to the tendencies in Amsterdam, Oud's article was followed in the same issue of the periodical by one of Hegemann's most notorious pieces, "*Aus der Amsterdamer Schreckenskammer*" (From Amsterdam's chamber of horrors).[149] An introductory note explained that the review was based on a report written by an anonymous envoy, who was sent by *WMB* to the International Town Planning Congress. It was actually Hegemann hiding coyly under the guise of an unidentified reporter. He once again used subterfuge as he had in writing *Deutsche Schriften/Iphigenie* under a pseudonym, which was published the same year as the Town Planning Congress. In an editorial note to the "*Schreckenskammer*" article, and under his own name, he begged forgiveness for excessive emotional fervor. The "highly respected old-master Berlage" was asked to disregard his youthful outpourings. Despite these attempts to ameliorate the stinging criticism of the Amsterdam School and especially of the work of the revered Hendrik Petrus Berlage (1856–1934), it was considered disgraceful. For months to come reactions to "*Aus der Amsterdamer Schreckenskammer*" were published in *WMB*, other periodicals, and personal letters. Hegemann wrote Oud a letter to coincide with the appearance of the April issue of *WMB*, hoping that Oud would be pleased with the complimentary editorial comments to his article, and explaining that Hegemann was the *Sonderberichterstatter* reporting on the Amsterdam School. Oud replied at some length, disapproving of the discrepancy between the editorial note to the "*Schreckenskammer*" that praised Berlage and the derogatory remarks in the article. Oud contrasted this with his "Convictions" in which he established tension between various points of view to stimulate creative energy and affirmed: "While life out of its innermost core ought to be full of an inner nature, so that it is capable of accepting everything organic—in every form and nature—in order to transform it into objects, which [must] impress us as obvious without imposing on us too emphatically this 'self-evidence' (certainty?)." He elaborated on the concept of "tension" between the machine and art, reiterating: "this was the meaning of the 'Convictions', that life ought to be accepted in its full measure in every aspect, neither onesidedly, nor as a 'pseudo-morphology,' but as crystallized form of everything organic."[150]

Oud's thought-provoking letter differed from other, accusatory reactions to Hegemann's "*Amsterdamer Schreckenskammer.*" The numerous responses attested to the publication's wide readership, thus complying with Hegemann's editorial policy intent on making *WMB* "a forum for the exposition of conflicting opinions."[151] For Hegemann, the periodical constituted a forum for impassioned discourse, which complemented his literary ambitions. His articles and reviews provided ample substance for interchange in the "arena" of *WMB*. His policy was to foster continuity by linking the various issues of the journal by means of his editorial comments, in which he established sequences and stirred up expectations in the manner of the installments of adventure films. The editorial notes he attached to articles written by others were considered irritating and insidious; likewise his stratagem of asking contributors to express *his own* opinions under the cover of *their* names. Another ploy resented by Hegemann's adversaries was the frequent out-of-context or incorrect citations from articles or letters to the editor. Several architects expressed their displeasure on these peculiarities in their letters to J. J. P. Oud.

It is difficult to ascertain Hegemann's intentions beyond giving breadth to the debate surrounding the Modern Movement. His keen dislike of the German penchant for hero worship, the main theme of his historical novels, came into play in his criticism of architects assuming heroic postures. The controversies with which he became embroiled prompted the formation of the Ring, the affiliation bonding architects of the New Building together against those holding other points of view. For Hegemann, cliquish associations indicated bigotry, and as an ingrained individualist, he was disinclined to join associations or groups even when he sympathized with their premises. The complex discords of the 1920s certainly involved a range of architects and critics besides Hegemann, but his position as an editor made him fair game for rebuke. It is possible that he relished the role of muckraker, as did Lincoln Steffens, and considered it stimulating.

"*Aus der Amsterdamer Schreckenskammer*" was notable for its muckraking polemics, which set Hegemann's contemporaries on edge. He proclaimed his disdain for an architecture derived from nineteenth-century eclecticism and resembling German Expressionism, branding this style *romantisch*, a term which for him had only derogatory connotations. It was a style he thought was exemplified in the work of Berlage, de Klerk and the Amsterdam School, van de Velde, and Frank Lloyd Wright.

Hegemann considered Berlage's early work, the Insurance Buildings in Amsterdam (1892–94 and 1894–95), with their turrets and pinnacles, to be "worse" than the "restless" facades by Richardson and Sullivan, whom he also categorized as *romantisch*. He confessed to be "unable" to share Dutch enthusiasm for Berlage's mature Beurs (1897–1903) and the Diamond Workers Union Building (1899–1901). It is astonishing that he did not acknowledge Berlage's use of large simple masses and planar textured surfaces or his distaste for nineteenth-century applied ornamentation. These characteristics and Berlage's dramatic use of internal space inspired younger architects in Holland and elsewhere. Hegemann's article fails to mention Berlage's urban planning and his two-month sojourn in America in 1911, comparable to Hegemann's own experience. Berlage's first-hand acquaintance with the American grid plan had convinced him of its positive qualities, especially regarding the placement of skyscrapers.[152] These impressions led to Berlage's reconsideration of Camillo Sitte's legacy, a change of heart similar to Hegemann's.

A semi-complimentary response to the *Schreckenskammer* article by Wilhelm Kreis appeared in *WMB* in the form of a letter with an added note by the editor.[153] Although agreeing with the criticism of de Klerk, Kreis expressed his high regard for Berlage, who would later be considered a *Klassiker* of Dutch architecture. Kreis contrasted the wild "romanticism" of the Amsterdam School with the *sachgemäss* (functional) style of a new generation of *Klassiker* in Germany represented by Mendelsohn, Luckhardt, Korn, and Mies. Hegemann was not altogether in accord with Kreis, but his note affirmed his commitment to editorial impartiality and representing all sides on controversial topics.

As anticipated, there were negative reactions, especially from Mendelsohn, Behne, and Bruno Taut. Indeed, Hegemann's position had been observed with suspicion by the avant-garde for some time, and the "*Amsterdamer Schreckenskammer*" was the last straw. Because this article dealt with Dutch architects, Oud, who was well-known in Germany, received much correspondence on the "Hegemann case."[154] A sequence of letters from Behne to Oud began in December 1925, when Behne sent Oud his book *Der moderne Zweckbau* (The modern functional building).[155] He wrote that he would welcome an exchange of views on Hegemann's recent attack on van de Velde and would like to organize a protest. He mentioned that Hegemann had published an altered version of his complaint regarding the attack on Berlage. A few days later Behne asked if Oud would participate in a protest, which might be joined by Gropius, Mendelsohn, and Taut. Behne enclosed a copy of a letter he wrote to Hegemann, expressing his anger at the way Hegemann had changed the meaning of his (Behne's) texts. Behne also objected to Hegemann's method of pitting people against each other instead of addressing architectural topics.[156] Becoming more heated, Behne questioned the use of "gibes, citations, alibis, quotations from X and Y . . . ," which resulted in Hegemann contradicting himself. In January 1926 Behne mentioned that Mendelsohn suggested a boycott or refusal of contributions to *WMB* by like-minded architects, a group which included Mendelsohn, Behne, Gropius, Scharoun, Häring, and Rading. The protest was directed at Hegemann's critical mannerisms rather than against criticism per se.

The case of Behne was poignant because he and Hegemann had much in common. Both were primarily critics and authors who shared socialist leanings and a dedication to adult education. After an early involvement with Expressionism, Behne came to reject its "understandable utopianism." Hegemann's impassioned publicity for Für Gross-Berlin was actually comparable to the Expressionist manifestos. One could speculate that Hegemann might have joined this movement had he been present in Germany at the time. In retrospect he disdained Expressionism as a style and disregarded its social message and literature. Behne's *Der moderne Zweckbau* of 1923 was not published until 1926. Rosemarie Haag Bletter considers that "it presciently unmasked many of the ideologies of functionalism, rationalism, and European Modernism of the 1920s."[157] It was this book that Behne sent to Oud with regard to the Hegemann affair that in its ramifications intended to unmask many of the contradictions besetting a movement of veiled complexities.

In February 1926 Mendelsohn insisted in a letter to Hegemann that he would only permit the publication of his article on Frank Lloyd Wright, meant for *Wendingen* and reacting to an essay by Fiske Kimball, if he could be absolutely assured that it would not be altered, and that there would be no editorial note.[158] Hegemann agreed to this but published a response by Leo Adler that expressed his own opinions. In June 1926 Mendelsohn informed Oud of the formation of the Ring, hoping that it would expand into an international organization. The Ring, established in 1926, had evolved from the earlier, smaller Zehnerring of 1923-1924, which was an outcome of the dissolution of the "Arbeitsrat für Kunst."[159] Hugo Häring, secretary of the Ring, explained in a June letter to Oud that the group was reacting to Hegemann's "objectionable fight against modern architecture, by ridiculing and mocking it in every possible way. . . ."[160] Häring reported that the members of the Ring had decided to refuse contributions to *WMB* and *STB*. Oud was asked to join in this boycott and replied to Mendelsohn in two letters dated only three days apart.[161] He wrote that he differed from most of his colleagues in the Angelegenheit [case] Hegemann, whose output he considered intelligent, even as he objected to much of it. "I am not partial to a press saying "yes and Amen" to everything that goes under the designation of 'modern.' A genuine criticism is for modern formalism now and then very, very necessary, and I have sometimes found Hegemann's comments just after my own heart. On the other hand many of his comments have often irritated me enormously." Oud considered the modern movement sufficiently strong and vigorous that other opinions could be laughed off, explaining, "it is our work and not the suppression of an opinion that gives it strength." Should Hegemann actually damage Oud's German colleagues, he would join their protest, but he did not condone their boycott. Oud was respected as a leading modern architect and his opinion regarding the Hegemann affair carried weight. Indicative of this was an immediate reply from Mendelsohn, who agreed with some of the points raised by Oud and suggested a meeting of both with Hegemann in Berlin. He was hoping that a frank discussion might render a boycott unnecessary; however, the meeting failed to take place. A letter by Häring to Oud informed him that the Ring went ahead, deciding on a boycott that would also go against de Fries. Victimizing de Fries was certainly unacceptable to Oud, and he answered Häring:

> I must tell you that I am a passionate admirer of a free exchange of opinion and that I am unable to join this boycott. I am willing to promote modern art in every possible way, but I believe that it is precisely in its strength that it needs not fear anything: neither worthy nor unworthy opposition. I believe that the decision of the "Ring" will damage the movement; one cannot defend the spirit with other than intellectual (spiritual) means, it is even better to let it speak for itself.

In a similar vein Oud wrote to Mendelsohn, who had informed him of another incident. Hegemann had agreed, in writing, to publish Mendelsohn's article on Frank Lloyd Wright, intended for *Wendingen*, without alterations or comments, but then printed a nasty reply by Leo Adler.[162] Oud also wrote for *Wendingen* on "The Influence of Frank Lloyd Wright on the Architecture of Europe," concluding with a warning that the imitation of modern masters was more damaging than "academics honestly exposing their front to the attack."[163] Hegemann would have been in agreement on this point.

Prior to the Mendelsohn/Wright incident and anticipating the threat of the boycott, Hegemann had published an article by Theo van Doesburg, followed by his own on van de Velde, in the last issue of *WMB* for 1925.[164] Behne referred to these articles in his letters initiating the protest. In January 1926, Hegemann took the occasion of the van Doesburg article to express his satisfaction that Oud was not intending to adhere to the action against him.[165] He was also replying to a letter by Oud (November 15, 1925). Aware of Oud's rift with van Doesburg and withdrawal from De Stijl in 1921, Hegemann commented on their being of one mind on what constituted "genuine/authentic modernity." He explained that he disagreed with van de Velde's opinion that it was necessary to break with tradition, yet he thought it important to oppose the thoughtless use of it by the "pseudo-traditionalists." In his letter he referred to van Doesburg's

Programme (manifesto) "*Die Neue Architektur und ihre Folgen*" (The new architecture and its consequences) and its illustrations. Cautious not to offend van Eesteren, who had joined van Doesburg in Paris, Hegemann avoided his customary editorial comments, choosing to express his point of view visually by contrasting images selected by the author of the article with those representing the work by architects he considered "genuinely modern." Examples in this compare-and-contrast endeavor included buildings by Oud, Auguste and Gustave Perret, Adolf Loos, Otto Wagner's Postsparkasse, as well as Le Corbusier and P. Jeanneret's Maison Ozenfant. Also featured was a large illustration of Mies van der Rohe's 1922 model for the curvilinear skyscraper entry for the Friedrichstrasse competition in Berlin. Hegemann's caption stated that although the extensive use of glass was impractical for climatic reasons, Mies's model had a "grand quality and demonstrated that the serene and regular repetition of a possibly questionable idea, if manifested in a formative and artistic manner, would be much more effective than the chaotic confusion of . . . the forced 'dissolutions of form' shown . . . by van Doesburg." Featured were works by van Doesburg, van Eesteren, and Mallet-Stevens.

Of the seventeen points in van Doesburg's *Programme*, Hegemann considered the concept of *Formlosigkeit* (dissolution or absence of form) the least acceptable. In his letter he sought Oud's consensus. Replying to Oud's question as to what he truly wanted with his stance, Hegemann repeated the Dutchman's own characterization of him, that he was "more passionate than the academics." With a certain contriteness he added by hand to his typed letter: "Probably I do not want anything, and will try to change for the better."

Oud's answer to Hegemann came several months later in a personal vein hoping to find some closure to the dire affair, at least for himself.[166] He mentioned that nervous strain had kept him from his work and from replying to Hegemann's letter. Now Oud was feeling better and was trying to complete his design for the competition for the Bourse in Rotterdam. He gave assurance that the drawings, promised for publication in *WMB*, would soon be ready. Oud reiterated much of what he had expressed to his colleagues and restated that he would not join the boycott because of his passionate devotion to a free exchange of views. On the other hand, he considered that to a certain extent Hegemann's polemical approach deserved the boycott. Oud explained that while he admired Hegemann's intelligence and style, he seldom agreed with his point of view, and thought it hopeless to oppose a development in architecture that was so absolutely necessary. He was unable to forgive Hegemann's manner of conducting his battle, which he considered "unclassical," "unmonumental," and unworthy of the author of the *Fredericus*, presented to him by Hegemann. Oud offered to mediate between Hegemann and his "enemies," attempting to resolve the discord, and suggested that Hegemann moderate his contentious approach. As proof of his esteem for Hegemann's knowledge and ability, Oud allowed that he would continue collaborating with him, even if this jeopardized his relations with the other architects.

Several years later, and after the Weissenhof episode (1927), Oud signed a testimonial document honoring Hegemann's fiftieth birthday (June 1931), expressing his regards. He wrote: "You know this: what is significant for me in your great talent is that I seldom agree with your opinion and almost always learn from you. *From my whole heart* I am sending congratulations for your 50th birthday!"[167] Hegemann thanked Oud, hoping to renew their contact.[168] He called his attention to the fact that *WMB* had recently resumed publishing the work of Mendelsohn, Luckhardt, Martin Wagner, and others close to Oud, and suggested that he might also provide him with something for the journal.

The boycott curtailed Hegemann's editorial intention of creating a "forum for airing contradictory opinions." However reproachable his editorial style and twists, they unmasked the disparities prevailing within an architectural movement that is generally presented as homogeneous and progressing along a single track. His criticism unveils the tangled relationships and conflicting convictions, opening up new perspectives for examining the Modern Movement.

The Ring members' decision to discontinue contributions to *WMB* was not entirely advantageous for them. Oud's suggestion to seek a common ground by means of a dialogue might have led to a stronger position for the avant-garde in confronting the imminent ideological and political threats. The Nazis excelled at nurturing divisiveness within the ranks of those interfering with their aims. Undoubtedly they welcomed the feud between the prominent architects of the Ring and the well-known critic. Although Hegemann was an early opponent of Nazi ideology, he wrote approvingly on Schmitthenner and Schultze-Naumburg, two architects with ties to emerging Nazism. Soon, however, he disavowed these partisan architects and devoted himself to battling Nazism and all its sinister ramifications. Ironically, several architects who had sided against Hegemann would experience a common fate with him—going into exile, either voluntarily or by force.

The boycott backfired for its participants in that they were deprived of international exposure for their work. Since assuming the position at *WMB*, Hegemann had expanded the journal's worldwide scope. This direction was reinforced by his reaction to the attitude within Germany. The yearly "Table of Contents" was structured as an index and in 1925 Hegemann added to the title and author categories those for buildings by towns and by architects. Beginning in 1926 the section "Buildings, Projects and Plans by Country" recorded architects by nation, listing over twenty, including China, Japan, Turkey, and others beyond Europe and America. Presumably subscriptions to *WMB* reached these countries, in response to the journal's content and fostered by Hegemann's personal global network. Where the German language presented a problem, some 1,500 illustrations per year brought news to distant regions.

Only part of Hegemann's copious correspondence in connection with *WMB* exists in the archives of some recipients, notably Le Corbusier, J. J. P. Oud, Steen Eiler Rasmussen, Fiske Kimball, and Hegemann's acquaintances in Argentina. The publisher's archives in Berlin, which included Hegemann's professional correspondence, were destroyed during World War II, effecting a considerable gap in the documentation of the Modern Movement.

In the aftermath of the boycott, Hegemann looked beyond the Ring and Germany to keep the journals vital. He made a wise choice in selecting Le Corbusier, whose prominence and far-reaching influence on Modernism generated a vast literature, making it redundant to dwell on his work and ideas other than in their convergence with Hegemann. Although during Hegemann's lifetime their renown was comparable, the intersections between the two have received scant attention. Regrettably, the two men never established a meaningful rapport, which might have bridged Le Corbusier's visually oriented modernity and Hegemann's theoretical approach to city planning.

A decade after their intellectual paths crossed in Berlin in 1910–11, Le Corbusier sent Hegemann his project for *La Ville Contemporaine* in 1923. It had been exhibited at the 1922 Salon d'Automne in Paris, the same year that Hegemann & Peets's *The American Vitruvius* was published in New York. Hegemann had not yet assumed his position at Wasmuth, where he could have promoted Le Corbusier's work, but the architect's motive for sending his project was to initiate a dialogue with an expert on city planning. Le Corbusier's interest in skyscrapers, considered an American invention, prompted him to seek out Hegemann because of his prolonged stay in the United States.

From June 1923 until September 1926 they exchanged some eighteen letters.[169] Le Corbusier had to wait until October 1923 for Hegemann's reactions to *La Ville Contemporaine*. Writing in French, Hegemann apologized for the delay and explained with some complacency that he had been in Gothenburg for the city planning exhibition. He commented critically on Le Corbusier's project: "I do not favor the grouping of the skyscrapers, either from an economic or an aesthetic point of view. . . . Or, to be less vague: economically, I believe these buildings to be dangerous from many points of view, and aesthetically, I believe that you placed them in a very monotonous arrangement; as you see, I am frank."[170]

These remarks demonstrate that Hegemann failed to recognize the affinity between Le Corbusier's emphasis on a geometric plan and skyscrapers placed as monuments with his own ideas on monumentality in the city. His letter mentioned personal observations made in New York, where the grid plan did not permit exceeding the size of the rectangular plot. *La Ville Contemporaine* was intended as a model for any congested contemporary city, and with its reliance on the gridiron pattern of straight lines and skyscrapers, it was akin to American examples. Despite Hegemann's critical response, the architect's reply was remarkably conciliatory. He referred to the street layout in New York as "in complete opposition to the system of high construction," and expressed the wish to obtain a copy of *The American Vitruvius* to acquaint himself with the city, which he would not visit until 1935.[171] The remainder of their correspondence did not pursue the matter of skyscrapers, but turned to the possibility of publishing Le Corbusier's work in *WMB*, which led to their meeting in Paris in July 1926.

Their encounter was preceded by Le Corbusier's *Plan Voisin*, exhibited at the Pavillon de l'Esprit Nouveau in 1925. The project specifically addressed the reorganization of the center of Paris, requiring massive clearance and rebuilding. More than other schemes by the architect it generated wide and lasting response and objections to its scale and "inhumanity." Le Corbusier did not consider his proposals futuristic or visionary, but rational and technologically feasible. This contributed to the irritation they elicited. Hegemann joined the numerous reviewers of the *Plan Voisin* with his article "*Kritik des Gross-Sanierungs-Planes Le Corbusiers*" (Critique of Le Corbusier's plan for metropolitan clearance) in 1927.[172] He was not dazzled by the architect's daring proposal of replacing the historic center of the major tourist city of the world with skyscrapers, arguing that the project would not achieve the promised rational urban improvements. Hegemann considered it "theatrical, romantic, unreasonable and generally detrimental." Comparing Le Corbusier's scheme with Haussmann's "overrated interventions," which became outdated with the arrival of railroads, Hegemann commented: "I would like to reproach Le Corbusier's plan for the same reasons, namely that it is only *vieux jeu*, and that the grand intention of introducing the American skyscraper idea may impress as sufficiently powerful, but it is far removed from a bold realization of truly modern concepts in city planning."[173] These were harsh words addressed to the famous avant-garde architect. Hegemann also faulted specific features of the skyscrapers of the *Plan Voisin*. Regarding the "*Lichtradiatoren*" (radiators of light or light shafts) he recalled his experience of living and working in skyscrapers, which had demonstrated to him that the amount of natural light did not depend on the level of the floor, but on the distance to the neighboring wall blocking the sunlight. He cited statistics on traffic congestion predicted for the "skyscraper city" in Paris in comparison to the Equitable and Woolworth Buildings in New York City. He concluded: "In view of these considerations and statistics, Le Corbusier's proposal may be regarded as a jest, but not as a practical endeavor for the renewal of our metropolises, so urgently in need of improvement. The lack of critical discrimination with which supposedly 'modern architects' take such jests seriously demands energetic opposition."

Hegemann's incisive critique was published a year after his visit with the architect in Paris and four years before he encountered the impressions left by Le Corbusier in Buenos Aires. The interchange generated by the two urbanists in the Southern Cone reverberated for years to come. Although Hegemann must have known of the *Plan Voisin* when he met Le Corbusier in Paris in 1926, it was not brought up in their cordial conversations.

In March 1926 Hegemann traveled to Rome via Switzerland. A few weeks after his journey to Italy, he traveled to Leipzig and Düsseldorf with the Danish architect and town planner Steen Eiler Rasmussen (1898–1990) and then on to Paris in July 1926. This trip was specifically planned to see Le Corbusier's work and meet the architect, and to visit Hegemann's long-time friend Pierre Lievre. Their acquaintance dated from Hegemann's student years in Paris, 1903–06, and continued when both were threatened by the Nazis.[174]

It is somewhat surprising that Hegemann asked Rasmussen to accompany him on this important occasion to meet Le Corbusier, especially since Rasmussen was not fluent enough in French to follow the conversations with the architect. On the other hand he had read Le Corbusier's publications and commented on them in his article, "*Le Corbusier; Die kommende Baukunst?*"[175]

Rasmussen, whom Hegemann had met in Gothenburg, provided him with a vital liaison to Scandinavian Neoclassicism and its representatives. Scandinavian work was frequently shown in *WMB* and *STB*, and Rasmussen regularly contributed articles on other topics as well. For several years he was the co-editor of the journal *Architekten* in Copenhagen, with which *WMB* collaborated. Rasmussen's international career took off in the late 1930s. He taught in England and the United States, and wrote many publications in Danish, English, and German.[176] When Hegemann failed to convince Wasmuth to publish a book on China based on Rasmussen's travels in that country, excerpts and sketches from his diary were included in *Städtebau*.[177] His frequent visits with the Hegemanns in Nikolassee and their copious correspondence testify to their cooperation and friendship.[178] This friendship did not, however, preclude differences of opinion. Rasmussen was quite candid on these in the paragraph he wrote for the testimonial volume honoring Hegemann's fiftieth birthday: "You know that from the beginning I disagreed with you, when you held up the works of Classicism as models for the present. . . . I hope that we will also in the future find topics on which to disagree, because it is your intellectual independence which I value so much in you. . . ."[179]

Hegemann recognized the kinship between Danish Classicism, Modernism, and Le Corbusier's "architecture of tomorrow" responding to the challenges of the Classicism of antiquity. Affirmations of Le Corbusier's delight in discovering Classicism are his sketches and photographs from his travels to the Orient, and it is reflected in his villas.[180] Hegemann admired the architecture of Friedrich Schinkel and was drawn to Le Corbusier's exploration of Classicism, transposing it into an architecture for the present and future. For Hegemann there was an affinity among Le Corbusier, Adolf Loos, and Oud in their striving for an alternative to Modernism as a formal style. The importance Le Corbusier gave to criticism and theoretical writing in his effectively illustrated and designed publications resonated with Hegemann. Mindful of these affinities and aware of the architect's prestige, Hegemann restrained his arrogance when they met in Paris.

In a postcard to his wife dated July 14, 1926, Hegemann noted briefly: "This morning we had a long trip to Perret's new church and R. [Rasmussen] and L. [Lievre] are waiting for me to go and see Le Corbusier. . . ." Rasmussen's article for *WMB*, based on their visit, is more revealing. He cited conversations with Le Corbusier, who accompanied them to view the "house in Auteuil" (Villa La Roche, 1923–24) and the residential community at Pessac (1923–26). Rasmussen began his article with a discussion of the difference between the contemporary so-called classicists and the modernists, using the example of columns, which the former used as details that had a value per se, transferred or glued onto a building, thus connecting it to historic antiquity. The modernist would endeavor to design using "forms appropriate for our time." Architects who shunned forms with associations—for example, Wright or Oud—had other spatial and plastic means available. Yet now there existed an architecture that did not use *Plastik und Raum*, a truly "new architecture."[181] With this, Rasmussen turned to a discussion of the entrance hall of Le Corbusier and Jeanneret's Villa La Roche in Auteuil, which was not conceived as "spatial and even less plastic." The illustrations of the Villa La Roche in the article were provided by the architects and are those shown in the *Almanach d'Architecture Moderne*. Rasmussen commented on the elongated window, which merged with the surface of the wall. Le Corbusier had explained to Rasmussen that the window signified for him the most important element of the building. For Rasmussen this aspect removed it from the traditional Raum-Plastik-Architektur and moved it toward two-dimensional modern painting, such as a still life by Amédée Ozenfant. The result was an architecture of lines and flat surfaces. Rasmussen believed that Le Corbusier's architecture found the most lucid expression in his recent housing scheme at Pessac, sponsored by Henri Frugés. The majority of the numerous photographs of Pessac and others shown in the article were taken by Hegemann, and others by Rasmussen, who regretted that they were in black-and-white, "giving only a faint impression of this elegant world." Rasmussen was entranced by the colors, which changed at the corners from one side of the house to the other, creating a "strange and fantastic, but not chaotic" impression.[182] The architectural design, employing standardized modular elements for a low-rise garden city community for the working class, fascinated both visitors, who shared a longstanding interest in housing. They saw Pessac before it was inhabited, and Rasmussen envisioned the flat roofs covered with flourishing gardens, the courtyards with laundry drying in the sun, and children playing. He asked rhetorically if this was the architecture of tomorrow, referring to Le Corbusier's book *Vers une Architecture* (1923) that had just been published in Germany as *Kommende Baukunst.*

Rasmussen thought that the houses in Pessac and those shown in *Vers une Architecture* demonstrated few of the functional aspects that one might expect from a pioneer of functionalism. Rather they conveyed the impression of an "artistically determined creation." In a conversation with Hegemann, who was taking pictures of Pessac, the architect confirmed this impression, declaring that it was his intention to create something poetic. Enumerating the disadvantages of the Pessac houses for working-class people, Rasmussen assumed that they should be considered experimental. He concluded his article by noting that while many contemporary architects produced "heavy, even grotesque results, [Le Corbusier] employs a light and elegant hand with his personal expressive means, of which he is becoming increasingly conscious and which he applies ever more logically; he enriches our imagination and our vision, showing us wonderful new possibilities."

Hegemann refrained from adding editorial comments to Rasmussen's article, perhaps in reaction to the boycott. Brief passages in his letters to Rasmussen affirm that their collaboration extended beyond the conversations with Le Corbusier and the photographs, into the content of the essay as well, and that he was pleased with it. Shortly after returning from France, and having received the latest issue of *Architekten* from Copenhagen, which was almost entirely devoted to Le Corbusier, Hegemann expressed the urgent wish to publish an article by Rasmussen on the architect. He mentioned that "our" publication would appear soon, making the sacrifice in time and money for Bordeaux (France) worthwhile, because it would give to the article the advantage of journalistic topicality.[183]

Rasmussen's article met Le Corbusier's approval; he sent only three brief factual corrections, stating that flat roofs were less expensive than sloped roofs, which changed the figures for the cost of the various house types, the roof gardens being cost-free. He also explained that the walls were not of concrete but of *Schlackensteine* (slag-stone), which provided better insulation. The architect noted that the houses were not intended as workers' houses but were available for general purchase.[184] Le Corbusier provided photographs of his work for an exhibition in the gallery space at Wasmuth's office building, thus indicating his satisfaction with the journal. The exhibition was announced in *Städtebau* for October 1926.[185]

A long response, "Away from Architecture?," intended for publication in *WMB,* arrived from Elbert Peets.[186] Hegemann passed it on to Rasmussen, asking for his opinion and indicating that he would like to publish it.[187] Peets's commentary was never published because he assumed that Le Corbusier's houses in Pessac were built of "ferro-concrete," a fact that Le Corbusier denied in his note published in *WMB*. In his letter to Rasmussen, Hegemann cited in French the architect's corrections, concerned that he might not have used the proper term in his German translation. Le Corbusier's passage reads, "*Les murs ne sont pas en béton, mais en machefer creux, parfaitement isolant (meme murs que Auteuil, Bologne etc.).*" Hegemann added that he did not remember precisely from his visit to Pessac what "*machefer creux*" was, and wondered if it could be *Hohlziegelbau* (air-brick), but finally settled on the term *Eisenschlacke*. Le Corbusier's explanation negated Peets's main argument, and his commentary remained unpublished.

Rasmussen's piece on Le Corbusier prompted an exchange with Hegemann on the meaning of "*klassisch*" and "*klassizistisch.*" Hegemann explained to his Danish colleague that in Germany there existed a great lack of clarity regarding these concepts. "*Klassisch*" was generally used only for something considered perfect, though Hegemann himself considered "*klassizistisch*" the "striving to create '*klassisch*' works." He was concerned that Rasmussen employed the terms "*klassizistisch*" and "*fetischistisch*" interchangeably in his essay.[188]

In another response to the essay, from Günter Hirschel-Protsch, Rasmussen was placed in the camp of "*klassizistisches Dänemark.*"[189] The author of this letter located himself in the farthest left category of the *Baurevolutionäre*. He faulted Le Corbusier's lack of social concern and true functionalism, which disqualified him from being an active participant in the *kommende Baukunst*. He did stress, however, that Le Corbusier occupied an important position regarding modern architecture as an *Anreger* (stimulator).

Le Corbusier certainly motivated Hegemann and Rasmussen to examine the concepts of "*klassizistisch*" and "*klassisch*" as they applied to modern architecture. Hegemann viewed architecture of any period in relation to what he could justify as "*klassisch.*" Hegemann's definition of "*Klassizismus*" will be discussed in the context of the ideosyncratic interpretation he attributed to terms and concepts.

The article by Rasmussen and the ensuing exchange with Hegemann are significant within the post-boycott periodicals. How much of the change in editorial viewpoint was a consequence of the Ring's decision is uncertain, but it seems to have contributed to Hegemann's approach becoming more circumspect and less polemical.

WMB's volume XI for 1927 lists Hegemann as *Herausgeber* (publisher) and Leo Adler as *Schriftleiter* (editor) and contained almost as many articles by Adler as by Hegemann. Reviews of the work by non-German architects increased, representing an international spread and modern tendencies. Included, among others, were Le Corbusier, Auguste and Gustave

Perret, Oud and other Dutch and Belgian architects, Albert Chase McArthur (a follower of Wright), Moisei Ginsburg, and Giuseppe Terragni. Also included in the journal were several overviews of developments in Scandinavia and Russia.

Notable was a sequence of articles showing numerous plans and illustrations reporting on the 1927 global competition for the League of Nations Building in Geneva. The majority of the reviews were by Adler, there was a brief commentary by Hegemann, and others were contributed by Konrad Hippenmeier from Zürich, and W. Vetter, a student of A. Perret's.[190] The importance of this competition for architecture has been compared to that of the 1922 Tribune Tower competition in Chicago. The Modern Movement had gained ground in the intervening years, but when the jury in Geneva made its decision, it once again voted against the truly modern designs.

Considering Hegemann's advocacy of a peaceful, united Europe, it is surprising that he distanced himself from personally reviewing the League of Nations competition. Time constraints may have contributed, and he turned the task over to Adler. At this point Hegemann was finalizing his manuscript of *Napoleon, oder "Kniefall vor dem Heros"* (Genuflection before the hero), which included an Introduction dated August 1927.[191] There is a surprising similarity between the setting of the book and the site of the League of Nations.

Selecting finalists of the 367 competition entries did not imply that any of them would actually be built. That decision was made by a later jury, even more conservative than the first. The fact that Le Corbusier's design did not win has been considered a major defeat for Modernism, and the League of Nations competition drew keen international attention from the architectural professions. Several articles in *WMB* were timely, such as the "preliminary report" by Adler.

Adler's second report quoted from the architects' texts that accompanied their proposals. Of interest is the statement by Meyer & Wittwer: "Our League of Nations building symbolizes nothing, nothing at all. . . . It wants to be judged as a structural invention." This declaration points to the Modern Movement's difficulties regarding monumentality with symbolic connotations.[192] Skyscrapers of monumental size avoided this problem. The competition for the League of Nations headquarters brought this dilemma into focus; the conservative architects still leaned toward historic precedents for inspiration and assurance.

The third report was by the Zürich architect Hippenmeier. An introductory note by Hegemann concentrated on Le Corbusier's entry and his house at the Weissenhof Siedlung in Stuttgart.[193] He mentioned that a jury of five, none an architect, was charged with selecting the winning entries and that Giuseppe Vago and Le Corbusier were among the finalists. Of Vago's design Hegemann wrote that it showed so much *abgestandene*

Architektur-Romantik (stale architectural romanticism) that it failed to display anything noteworthy. In contrast, he wrote, Le Corbusier's project offered a remarkable study in acoustics and "a daring advance into the territory of the new engineering romanticism, and its realization promised surprising results. These results could contribute to the importance for our architectural developments because in the new capital city of Europe they would be experienced and discussed by representatives of all nations." Hegemann compared the section for the president of the League to Le Corbusier's house at the Weissenhof Siedlung, citing Hans Bernoulli, who celebrated the Weissenhof Siedlung house's creative design, despite its lack of functionality. As was his habit, Hegemann veiled his own critique by citing the opinions by others.

Hippenmeier commented that Le Corbusier's design was among a "small group advocating absolute simplification at the absolute abandonment of any extraneous frill . . . a group that could almost be called a fountain of youth." He compared Le Corbusier and Jeanneret's design, which stressed the horizontal, with Meyer & Wittwer's vertical sweep, considering it difficult to relate the latter to the park setting. Hippenmeier ended his review noting the dismay of modern architects in response to the jury's decision, wavering between Giuseppe Vago and Le Corbusier.

The years 1927–28 were climactic for modern architecture in defining itself while confronting the opposition. The League of Nations competition and the Weissenhof Siedlung in Stuttgart were landmark events, soon followed by the founding of CIAM, which also addressed town planning and housing. Hegemann was situated at once on the periphery and in the center of the debates. Chastened by the boycott and recent developments, he was searching for a discerning understanding of Modernism, prescient of the questioning prevalent in later decades.

In 1927, *WMB* featured two articles and an editorial note by Hegemann indicating his position.[194] A copiously illustrated essay about new buildings on venerable squares reiterated his criticism of interventions that failed to take into account the existing context, even if this context was not truly noteworthy. Modern architecture had a uniquely difficult time within urban centers, and Hegemann singled out the recent expansion of Messel's Neo-Gothic Wertheim Department Store, which conflicted with Schinkel's classic Gate Houses, as an example. A new addition to the building worsened this aesthetic clash. Ludwig Hoffmann, the recently retired conservative *Stadtbaurat*, faced rebukes for his responsibility regarding these errors. Recalling Mendelsohn's difficulties in obtaining Hoffmann's approval for his Herpich House, Hegemann commented that in the end it was more successful than the Wertheim addition, but that blaming Hoffmann for all such mistakes was unjust in view of the accumulation of unfortunate results over several years.

Hegemann's editorial note to an extensive response by Börries von

Münchhausen, an author of ballads, emphasized the need for contemporary architecture to be respectful of the historic precedents while considering contemporary demands. He sympathized with von Münchhausen, who lived in a fifteenth-century castle and wished for modern conveniences and a balcony.[195] Hegemann ignored a section in which von Münchhausen asserted his view of Jews as culturally superior to "us," but incapable of creating great works and only able to celebrate their own worth. This insinuated anti-Semitism was undoubtedly repugnant to Hegemann, who remained free from this prevalent attitude throughout his life. Hegemann preferred to argue the paradox of modern architecture vis-à-vis the traditional. His opponents believed that the discovery of new building materials could do away with the past, declaring it unworthy of preservation. On the other hand, his friends would sacrifice the old selectively and only if it was deemed to be without value and unable to coexist or adapt to progress. Hegemann concluded his editorial note: "If we believe in an organic development in art, then the conscientious affiliation of the New to the best of the Old will protect us from the playful dissonances, which delight certain 'modernists' today. This would grant us the artistic merit required to deliver without mercy the finishing blow to the bad Old and enable us to vanquish it with a better New."[196]

In his extensive essay "*Künstlerische Tagesfragen beim Bau von Einfamilienhäusern*" (Contemporary artistic problems regarding single-family houses), Hegemann homed in on key topics in the architectural debate.[197] Patrons for family homes and villas had provided major commissions for the advocates of both traditional and New Building. The architects' income and renown depended on these projects. In his article Hegemann compared Schultze-Naumburg and Ernst May, choosing two prime representatives of the opposing sides. The debate, taking on political shrillness, leaned toward an emphasis on style or form, while functional and economic considerations lost ground. In his discussion comparing a large villa by Schultze-Naumburg with Ernst May's own house, Hegemann focused on aspects of siting, layout, and exterior, aiming to convince the reader that the mansion was more functional than May's house. Many of his points demonstrate his familiarity with sharing space from his own experience living with four children. For instance, he noted as awkward May's design for access to the servants' rooms. He did not comment on the different lifestyles represented by Schultze-Naumburg's villa and May's home, a difference of philosophy as well as economic status. Although certainly not an *Existenzminimum* (subsistence level) example, the May house was modest compared to the villa. Spaces flowed together in an aesthetic statement that could accommodate an unpretentious lifestyle. The villa exuded upper-class privilege and social position. Hegemann mentioned having known and esteemed both architects since 1910 and hoped that they would not react adversely to his criticism as others had done. He referred to the boycott, which had induced one participant to refuse to buy books at the Wasmuth Bookstore.

The second part of Hegemann's article, "Schräges oder flaches Dach" (Pitched versus flat roof), dealt with a topic that evolved from functional and economic considerations into an icon of the stylistic and political architectural debate.[198] It has never truly subsided. Regardless of climate or local building traditions, the sloped roof remains emblematic of a conservative mindset.

Hegemann's discussion was touched off by the replies to an international inquiry launched by Walter Gropius addressing the technical feasibilities of flat roofs. The replies were published in *Bauwelt* in 1926, in an article by Schultze-Naumburg, and in other expositions in the press.[199] Gropius posed five questions, hoping to allay the arguments by the opponents of the flat roof who doubted its practicality. He cited answers "from the past" and from living architects partial to the flat roof. Most of the replies stuck to the purely technical concerns of construction, materials, and cost, based on the architects' own experiences. A more philosophical answer came from Oud, who disagreed with Gropius's premise that the "horizontal roof had resulted from 'advances in technology.'" In Oud's opinion it was primarily a matter of function and secondarily one of aesthetics for which a technical solution was sought. "In building . . . technology turns out to be completely behind the times to carry out our intentions. However, I am convinced, that the flat roof will prevail—without much dispute—because its practical usefulness makes it obligatory for everyone."

Hegemann opened his remarks with a sharp attack on Schultze-Naumburg, a prime defender of the pitched roof, accusing him of lack of objectivity. He explained that, although he had previously praised or criticized him as an architect in the pages of *WMB*, he considered the architect's newly adopted posture of *Rassentheoriker* (racial theorist) highly regrettable. Especially "unfortunate, unproductive and '*unsachlich*,'" according to Hegemann, was Schultze-Naumburg's rejection of the flat roof on the basis of *rassenpolitische* (racist/political) arguments. Schultze-Naumburg claimed that the flat roof was *kleinasiatisch* (from Asia Minor) and not *nordisch-germanisch* (nordic-Germanic). Hegemann referred to a statement by Nietzsche that recommended that all people should avoid *verlogenen Rassenschwindel* (deceitful racial swindle).

Turning to Oud's reply to Gropius's inquiry as to whether technology had kept up with creative ideas, Hegemann pointed out that not all defenders of the flat roof were in agreement regarding its practicality, particularly the difficulties of drainage and unsightly gutters. Hegemann proudly related that in his own house in Nikolassee, with a moderately inclined roof, he had installed drainage conduits through the interior. He had accomplished this several years prior to Le Corbusier's recommendation of the system. Hegemann mentioned with amusement that Schultze-Naumburg had called

Le Corbusier a dilettante for this solution to the drainage problem.

Hegemann took a generally pragmatic and impartial position in the roof debate, except to recommend the pitched roof for small houses for practical reasons. Shown in conjunction with his article was a page of photographs taken by Hegemann on a walk in the "Wild West" of Berlin. They depicted a lighter side of the controversy, bearing the title "*Die Überwindung des Daches*" (The conquest of the roof) and including whimsical illustrations and captions.[200] The photographs showed that the choice between the flat and pitched roof carried over into everyday life and modest buildings not necessarily designed by elite architects. For the general public, especially in Germany, the roof remained an easily grasped symbol, representing *Heimat* (home place) and security.

The racial and political connotations brought up by Schultze-Naumburg soon dominated the controversy, dubbed by the press the "War of the Roofs" for the much discussed case of flat and pitched roofs across the street from each other in the Berlin-Britz Siedlung. Practical considerations receded in the heated political and racial arguments, which culminated regarding the Weissenhof Siedlung in Stuttgart in 1927.

Modernism: Style or Function

Even prior to its opening in July 1927, the Weissenhof Exhibition in the outskirts of Stuttgart was mired in controversy. Organized by the Deutscher Werkbund to demonstrate modern housing, it was paid for by the city. Mies van der Rohe was chosen to design the site plan and select the participants. Every step was heatedly questioned by the fractured architectural profession, especially Mies's selection of the sixteen architects, a group of members of the avant-garde that included several non-Germans. Members of the prominent Stuttgarter Schule were initially invited, but later withdrew. These included Paul Schmitthenner, Paul Schultze-Naumburg, and Paul Bonatz, representing what has been called the *traditionalistische Moderne*. Mies insisted that he was not aiming at a unified style; however, he did require flat roofs. This was a commendable response to the hillside site, with views that would be obstructed by pitched roofs and an insensitive placement of buildings.

The Weissenhof Exhibition closed in November. Following its mandate it has been preserved as a residential development, drawing international attention and differing opinions in response to its status as a landmark of modern architecture. The vast literature it generated placed it at the vortex of the politicized architectural culture of its time.[201] Historical evaluation is gradually moving away from euphoric toward more discerning interpretations of a stirring moment in twentieth-century architecture.

Hegemann's reactions to the Weissenhof Siedlung are complex.

Comparable to many of his positions, his appraisal of Weissenhof was both unique and ambiguous. It falls outside the accepted canon, but cannot be placed in either the camp of the Ring or with the recently constituted opposition "Block." In retrospect the line between the pro and con camps in the debate appears less sharply drawn than when the impressions of Weissenhof were fresh.

Studies of the event have singled out Hegemann's article "*Stuttgarter Schildbürgerstreiche und Berliner Bauausstellung 1930*," in *WMB*, as a prime example of his anti-modernist polemics.[202] Several commentaries on Weissenhof were published in *WMB* beginning in 1927, and those not under Hegemann's name were frequently followed by his editorial notes or by replies selected by him as the "engaged" editor. Presumably he assigned key articles to those sympathic to his own ideas, however, it would be unjust to suspect him of exercising total control over points of view expressed in the pages of *WMB*. In Leo Adler, a contributing author since 1925 and *Schriftleiter* from 1927 on, Hegemann had a like-minded colleague who wrote an increasing number of articles for the journal. Among the reactions to the Weissenhof Siedlung, those published in *WMB* and expressed in the correspondence by Oud are most relevant to Hegemann's position.

Hegemann welcomed the exhibition's aim to present experimental housing employing the latest technology, materials, and construction methods, and to establish prototypes. His keen interest in housing was developed during his student years in Europe and America, as well as during his early Berlin and later American periods. It persisted throughout his life, and he remained committed to housing issues upon his return to Berlin in 1922. Always partial to low-cost cottages surrounded by garden plots, he had difficulty accepting the advantages of the Zeilenbau Siedlungen of the 1920s compared to the *Mietskasernen*. On the other hand, his incisive review of the multistory social housing in Vienna published the previous year recognized its advantages.[203]

The Weissenhof Siedlung was unlike the Siedlungen surrounding Berlin and Frankfurt, or the housing in Vienna. The majority of the buildings were single houses, and did not exude social commitment. Mies's site plan and the placement of the buildings had certain affinities with the English garden city admired by Hegemann. It was the rational Zeilenbau that was generally favored by avant-garde architects, who considered a layout with "Kleinhäuser" to be bourgeois, reactionary, and Sittesque. While this caused a split within the Modern Movement, it was not an argument specifically raised in the Weissenhof debate. However, for Hegemann the Zeilenbau Siedlungen-versus-garden-city-type housing presented a dilemma because it also confronted him with the Sittesque-versus-classical planning controversy raised in connection with the Ulmer Münsterplatz competition. Within the Weissenhof debate that posited the avant-garde against the Stuttgarter Schule, the fact that Mies van der Rohe's layout was site-specific and avoided a "rational" Zeilenbau did not become an issue. Weissenhof resembled Le Corbusier's residential scheme for twenty houses designed for a property on the outskirts of Buenos Aires the following year (1929).[204] Both designs provided garden city, even Sittesque settings for strikingly modern houses.

The quandary pertaining to housing concerns, central to Hegemann's commitment to the social implications of urban planning, may have contributed to his reluctance to debate as vigorously upon his return to Berlin as he had previously. In the eyes of the members of the Ring Hegemann's criticism of the supposedly *sachlich* (functional) buildings of Weissenhof and the Zeilenbau developments placed him in the reactionary camp, which is perplexing considering his advocacy of pragmatic functionalism.[205]

In response to the widespread discord and his personal ambiguity, Hegemann turned to literary trope and irony in his article "*Stuttgarter Schildbürgerstreiche*." With its distinctive title it is analogous to the earlier "*Aus der Amsterdamer Schreckenskammer*," veiling criticism in comical allusions.[206] For their conspicuous titles and polemical content both gained notoriety and overshadowed the seriousness of his other articles.

The title "*Stuttgarter Schildbürgerstreiche*" requires a translation-*cum*-explanation. A *Schildbürgerstreich* is a silly action performed by a simpleton. By attributing such undertakings to the mayor and the administration of Stuttgart, Hegemann blamed them for provincial shortsightedness in ignoring a prominent architectural institution, the local Stuttgarter Bauschule, in their search for big names to attract tourism to the Werkbund Exhibition. The responsibility of Mies van der Rohe in the choice of architects was not mentioned. Hegemann's attack on the city leaders of Stuttgart caused a public uproar and was repudiated by two well-known members of the Bauschule, Bonatz and Schmitthenner, in a letter published in *WMB*.[207]

In his article Hegemann targeted the failure to present "practical, economical, feasible" housing prototypes, and the squandering of taxpayers' money on "romantic, impulsive, artistic" creations. In particular he found fault in the houses by Oud, whose work he had admiringly discussed many times in the pages of *WMB*. His sharp rebukes were echoed by Alexander Klein and Leo Adler.[208] Klein applied graphic analysis for a functional evaluation of dwellings, and compared those by Oud at Weissenhof with some of his own. Employing criteria such as usable space, circulation paths, and ceiling heights, among others, Klein pointed out numerous defects in Oud's row houses.

These two articles and one by Edgar Wedepohl, which preceded Hegemann's "*Schildbürgerstreiche*," humiliated Oud and may have contributed to his fragile health. A sequence of letters between Oud, Hegemann, and Wedepohl testifies to Oud's disappointment, especially in the light of his renown as a designer of housing.[209] The exchange began with a letter by Oud to Hegemann (August 25, 1927) in which he referred to the review by Klein, hoping that it would not harm their friendship. Hegemann replied (October 1, 1927), apparently dictating the letter and addressing him very formally "*Sehr geehrter Herr* Oud!" Hegemann mentioned sending him "*mit schwerem Herzen unsere Besprechung der Stuttgarter Ausstellung*" (With a heavy heart our review of . . .), presumably the article by Wedepohl. Hegemann continued: "Because for some time now I have the impression that you are not progressing in the most direct way toward the lofty ideal of clarity, simplicity and functionalism, which we both strive for wholeheartedly." Disturbed by these comments, Oud wrote a long reply the next day addressing it to "*Lieber* Dr. Hegemann," as they had done previously, wondering if the new formality was a sign of their relationship unravelling. Apparently he had not yet received the journal but suspected that it would contain Hegemann's disparagement of his work. Oud's letter contained an impassioned exposition of his architectural philosophy, and acknowledged his regard for Hegemann's friendship and judgment. He was concerned that Hegemann's remarks were not aimed at single buildings, which he could accept, but rather at the totality of his work. Referring presumably to the Ring and the boycott episode, he reminded his colleague that he never hankered after groups or slogans. Hegemann replied rather curtly to "*Lieber Herr* Oud," assuring him that the author, Edgar Wedepohl, was not a pseudonym for Hegemann, as Oud had suspected. He said that he intended to visit Weissenhof and would follow the visit with a review that would give careful attention to the content of Oud's letter. This exchange preceded both Wedepohl's and Hegemann's Weissenhof articles, yet Oud had already anticipated the negative reaction from his esteemed critic.

Wedepohl, an architect active in Cologne, published an extensive article in *WMB* shortly after the Weissenhof Exhibition opened, when some of the houses were still unfinished.[210] He stressed the exhibition's experimental nature and, referring to many photographs and plans, gave a detailed overview of each of the buildings, including materials and methods of construction. He appended brief sections of general assessment: "*Negative und productive Kritik*"(Negative and productive criticism), "*Aufgeklärter Traditionalismus*" (Enlightened traditionalism), "*Was ist neu?*" (What is new?), "*Das Problem der Form*" (The problem of form), "*Klassik und Romantik*" (Classicism and Romanticism), and "*Gestaltung als Aufgabe*" (Design as obligation). Wedepohl referred to Goethe in defining "productive" criticism as one that questioned whether a clearly stated purpose had been achieved. He also explained that in commenting on the unusual aspects of Weissenhof, he was not comparing them with historicist "disasters" but with examples of an enlightened traditionalism as represented by the architects of the Stuttgarter Schule. In retrospect this movement tends to be designated "traditional Modernism" or "critical traditionalism." Wedepohl called attention to Mies van der Rohe's opposition to *die Form als Ziel* (form as aim/goal), questioned the discrepancy between *Zweckform* (functional form) and *Kunstform* (artistic form), and the apparently intentional avoidance of harmonious design in the exhibition while striving for technical perfection. He lamented that at Weissenhof the "new house" lacked "form" and a coherent spatial design, thereby not answering the tenet of the New Building as stated by Adolf Behne: *das Ganze zu fassen und einfach zu sein* (To design the totality with simplicity).

Wedepohl wrote favorably of Oud's row houses as "the most functional and best conceived buildings of the exhibition," fulfilling their expectations by providing "the typology for a decent, comfortable, practical, small dwelling with optimum spatial utilization, appropriate for mass-production." Wedepohl's comments on shortcomings were minimal, giving little weight to Klein's analysis. His conclusion lauded Oud for surpassing all others in answering the mandate of Weissenhof. Hegemann had apparently conveyed Oud's apprehensions to Wedepohl, who wrote to Oud when the article had reached him in Rotterdam. Wedepohl emphasized once more his esteem for Oud's work and posed questions regarding the size of windows, balustrades on balconies, color on the exterior, and flat roofs. He mentioned that these points or details were only of importance if one appreciated the intention of the building and the status of the architect. In a concluding paragraph Wedepohl mentioned his great hesitation in accepting the assignment to write an article on Weissenhof at Hegemann's urging and said he had always been disinclined to attack colleagues, preferring to talk about issues, and acknowledging Goethe's guidance on matters of criticism.

Oud replied to Wedepohl by return mail expressing his delight at knowing that Wedepohl really existed and was not a cover for Hegemann. He went on to say that Wedepohl should, however, not be offended by being confused with Hegemann. On the contrary, Oud considered "Dr. Hegemann to be one of the best authors and critics of our time, although [he] rarely agreed with his point of view." Oud was glad to read the *WMB* review, not having expected to receive much attention for his attempt to build a "real home" or proper dwelling, calling it "*un-architektonisch.*" Turning to Wedepohl's questions, he answered all of them at length in his eight-page letter. It is as revealing for an understanding of Oud's work as his more philosophical exposé to Hegemann dated October 2. The briefest summary of Oud's remarks suggests his eloquence. He favored color only in the city, not for buildings surrounded by nature, and advocated bands of windows to provide the ample light required by modernity and by clients. Regarding oversized windows he stated, "for me the rational is only the *point of departure*—quite seriously (very scrupulously), but only a *point of departure*—function and form are in continuous reciprocal interplay and so the building evolves. Why should I deny that I consider *this* window in *this* room beautiful? I don't care the slightest for pure functionalism without form, even regarding the machine for living!" Oud agreed with Wedepohl that balustrades on balconies were dangerous for children; on the other hand, it was hardly possible to safeguard them except by constant supervision. His longest reply was to the question of flat versus slanted roofs, declaring that both pro and con were equally dogmatic. For aesthetic and other reasons he was partial to the flat roof, but not as a rigid doctrine. When circumstances required it, a pitched roof was preferable. On the hillside of Weissenhof, the flat roof was more "beautiful," because the inclined roof "related badly to the slope of the mountain." He illustrated this point with a small sketch that justified the uniformly flat roofs at Weissenhof. Oud hoped that Wedepohl would find his answers satisfactory and looked forward to further contacts with him.

Immediately following the publication of Hegemann's "*Stuttgarter Schildbürgerstreiche*," Wedepohl wrote a carefully worded rebuttal of Hegemann's unwarranted criticism of Oud's building (January 9, 1928). Wedepohl called it "one of the saddest chapters of your *Stuttgarter Schildburgerstreiche*," a reference to Hegemann's characterization of Oud's building as "one of the saddest chapters of the exhibition." Wedepohl refuted point by point the defects listed by Hegemann, all of which addressed minor practical matters. Hegemann described Oud as the "most capable, practical and most *sachlich* among architects striving for a new 'form,'" but by contrast his contribution to Weissenhof was the most disappointing component of the exhibition. Hegemann's review of Oud's buildings at Weissenhof stands out for its unwarranted pettiness, even as compared to his commentary on the works of other architects. In literary style, content, and coherence this article is an example of Hegemann at his least commendable. It is incomprehensible that he should have risked impairing their friendship and injuring Oud when he was unwell. Hegemann substantiated his own opinions by echoing the rebukes by Alexander Klein and Leo Adler, and inserted a long passage by "one of the most experienced practitioners in the building profession," not revealing Paul Bonatz's name and excerpting only a section critical of the exhibition.[211] "*Schildbürgerstreiche*" also included excerpts from a report by Marie-Elisabeth Lüders, a well-known sociologist. In October 1927, Lüders had published an article entitled "*Baukörper ohne Wohnung*" (Building without living space), analyzing houses from the standpoint of performing daily household tasks and caring for children, pointing out numerous inadequacies. Although Oud is not mentioned in the passages cited in "*Schildbürgerstreiche*," some of the references implicated his houses.

Adler sent Oud the January 1928 issue of *WMB* with Hegemann's article on Weissenhof while Hegemann was vacationing in Egypt. Oud's disappointment and bitterness were aired in a letter addressed to "*Lieber* Dr. Hegemann" (February 4, 1928) which mentioned "admiration for your critical insight," but said that the seriousness of his own work demanded a more "magnanimous" berating: "as an enemy, based on this criticism, I do not assess you highly." Oud thought that some of the minor defects listed by Hegemann warranted changes, but that the overall value of Oud's building rested on improving what had been previously neglected by the architectural profession. Considering that one ought to be selective in one's choice of enemies, he would not welcome Hegemann's enmity if he persisted in this vein. Oud recommended modification and a higher level for Hegemann's criticism, which he did not fear, but wondered why Hegemann had singled him out in this manner. Everyone else was dealt with sharply but magnanimously. Although Oud was hurt and disenchanted, he ended on a conciliatory note: "Be true to yourself once more with a new animosity. Gladly I will respond to the challenge. In loyal affection for the brilliant Hegemann, yours. . . ." Hegemann replied from Cairo, mentioned another letter by Oud, and confessed that he had anticipated the architect's dissatisfaction. He hoped to meet Oud upon his return to Berlin in March to talk further about these matters.

The Hegemann–Oud relationship is noteworthy for revealing aspects of the critic's mindset and the remarkably independent, impartial attitude of the architect. They were comparable in their pragmatic idealism and faith in a functionalism devoid of stylistic rigidity. Their letters provide valuable insights into the complexities of the Modern Movement encountered by Hegemann during his peak years at Wasmuth.

The sequence of articles on the Weissenhof Siedlung in *WMB* began in 1927 with those by Alexander Klein, Edgar Wedepohl, Leo Adler, and Konrad Nonn. Hegemann's "*Schildbürgerstreiche*" was published later, in the first issue of 1928, while he was abroad. The interchange generated by the closely paced reviews was exactly what Hegemann had sought to achieve as editor and critic—a questioning debate rather than bland uniformity. However, similar to the reactions to the "*Aus der Amsterdamer Schreckenskammer*," which resulted in the boycott, the repercussions of the Weissenhof reviews were far-reaching and grave.

Hegemann was at this time in a state of utter exhaustion, "almost at a breaking point," from overwork, finishing the book *Napoleon* and other commitments. In mid-December 1927 he departed for a vacation in Egypt, and he may have written the article on Weissenhof before he left Berlin. In a letter to his wife he observed that a friend had notified him that he had made many enemies with the article, but mentioned that Paul Bonatz had complimented him on it.[212] He was probably referring to a letter signed by P. Bonatz and P. Schmitthenner published at their request in *WMB*.[213] They justified their frank rebuttal of Hegemann's attacks on the administration of Stuttgart, mentioning that "*Schildbürgerstreiche*" was published between two favorable articles on their own work.[214] The signers of the letter stated that the exhibition had originated with the Werkbund, which had full control over all aspects, including the selection of the participating architects.

Bonatz and Schmitthenner affirmed that they voluntarily withdrew from the Werkbund in response to initial discussions. The letter emphasized that Hegemann was therefore incorrect in accusing the Stuttgart City Administration of ignoring the Stuttgart School of Architecture. Its members were in fact working on several projects for the city. Obviously they did not wish to damage their relationship with a major client.

Hegemann's respite in Egypt extended far longer than expected. An intestinal illness and high fevers weakened him for several weeks and delayed his return to Berlin until the spring of 1928. When he was not laid up with his illness, he visited the sights. He and his wife wrote to each other daily and his letters include descriptions of walks though the old section of Cairo, excursions to Luxor, the Giza pyramids, Minieh, and the Sphinx. After three months in Egypt, he set out in mid-February on a return trip via Jerusalem, Haifa, Damascus, Baalbeck, Constantinople, Athens, Belgrade, and Budapest. In a letter of February 11, 1928, he wrote to his wife, who was anxiously awaiting his return: "Please do not be angry with my staying away so long. My value as a critic and the balance of my mind depend vitally upon the amount of first hand information I can gather. I am not loafing, but attending to my business to the best of my ability." Mindful of this, he wrote a travelogue in the form of his letters home, composed while riding in trains or sitting in restaurants, often on a sequence of postcards. His wife in turn reported on the family, contacts with Wasmuth, their friends, and professional associates. Even far from Berlin, Hegemann could not ignore the contentious situation awaiting him upon his return in March.

The negative response by the members of the Ring toward anything having to do with Hegemann and the prevailing boycott was heightened by the bad feelings stirred up by the Weissenhof debacle. The animosity not only affected the "traditionalists," who were excluded from participating. Mies van der Rohe had chosen primarily architects, rather than urbanists, with the possible exception of Le Corbusier, Hilberseimer, and Oud. Hegemann, a theoretician but not a practicing planner, was predictably not involved, but neither were Ernst May and Martin Wagner, both of whom had ample experience in urban planning and housing. Surprisingly they were not even consulted.

Reacting to the ramifications of Stuttgart/Weissenhof the idea of organizing a *Bau-Ausstellung* on the *Messe Gelände* (fairgrounds) in Berlin gained momentum. Since the Greater Berlin competition and the 1910 exhibition, the city had cherished its renown as a metropolis at the forefront of architecture and urbanism. Hegemann's article of 1928, "*Stuttgarter Schildbürgerstreiche und Berliner Bau-Ausstellung 1930*," pointed toward this connection, even suggesting a date for an event in Berlin. Discussions for such an undertaking had begun in 1925 with the first of two competitions for the *Messe-und Ausstellungsgelände*. The following year *WMB/STB* published the results and followed up on further developments.[215] The disagreements surrounding the first competition prompted Robert Schmidt, director of the Ruhrsiedlungs-Verband, to comment that in "Berlin everyone works against one another." In July 1928, the *Oberbürgermeister* (lord mayor) of Berlin launched a revised competition and instituted the *Verein Bau-Ausstellung* to take charge of carrying forward a permanent building exhibition planned to last ten years.[216] These steps renewed hope for the event's realization, but also led to a heated debate on how to finance the project. Martin Wagner, the *Stadtbaurat*, was an energetic participant in these debates promoting the architectural aspects of the exhibition. Concerns were expressed that the Werkbund and the Ring would dominate, as was the case at Weissenhof, and this might affect the outcome and attraction for tourists. The press quoted Martin Wagner reassuring the public that he would not think of "excluding or boycotting any association." A steering committee of six was organized to bring clarity to a chaotic situation, with Wagner its most vocal member.

Hegemann's involvement with the *Bau-Ausstellung* 1930 began in 1927. He perceived in it the possibility for a permanent civic museum or "open university" as he had envisioned for the Berlin 1910 Exhibition.[217] He commented on the agreement between the city of Berlin and the *Verein Bau-Ausstellung,* emphasizing the importance of a permanent exhibition as a mega-event attracting an audience from beyond Berlin.[218] The entire setup should demonstrate contemporary town planning with every building representing an element within a metropolitan totality. Hegemann envisioned lecture halls in the various buildings and a future congress hall in which technical demonstrations would be integral to the exhibitions. Presumably the comprehensive program included in Hegemann's article was issued by the *Verein Bau-Ausstellung*. A section of his article "*Stuttgarter Schildbürgerstreiche*," entitled "*Die wissenschaftliche Bedeutung der Dauer-Bauausstellung* Berlin 1930" (The scientific significance of the permanent . . .), quoted at length from a report by Professor Siedler of the Technische Hochschule, Charlottenburg, on its anticipated value as an educational and research institution.[219]

Although Hegemann was neither an architect nor a city planner, he had been immersed in Berlin as a theorist, historian, and critic for over two decades and had no intention of staying on the periphery, especially considering the recent success of the Unter den Linden competition. His ultimate goal was that the sequence of the Greater Berlin and Unter den Linden competitions and the *Bau-Ausstellung* 1930 would transform Berlin into a *Weltstadt* and genuine metropolis of global renown and political importance. The objective Hegemann had in mind was to use the exhibition as a catalyst for furthering urban interests among the city's bureaucracy, the business leadership, international architects, planners, and a wider general public. The worldwide significance of the *Bau-Ausstellung* was also stressed by its business executive, Dr. Coerper.[220]

The proclamation "*Aufruf zur fruchtbaren Kritik*" (Appeal for productive criticism), published in April 1928, was initiated by the journal *Städtebau*.[221] It emphasized that the *Bau-Ausstellung* would become an event of major economic importance, lastingly enhancing the global reputation of Berlin and Germany, particularly by the manner in which artistic aspects were either resolved or ignored. Wagner was an important member in the steering committee and had persuaded the city to invite architectural participation. With the *Aufruf* an additional voice was injected into an already tense situation. It developed into a full-blown confrontation, pitting against each other two prominent urbanists, Martin Wagner and Hegemann, who in reality were more in agreement than in disagreement on architecture, planning, and housing. Their dispute gained notoriety in the media, with opposing factions reflecting the brewing political tensions. Proponents of the boycott and the Ring sided against Hegemann, who used the eminent periodicals *WMB* and *STB* as his mouthpieces. Friedrich Paulsen, editor of *Bauwelt*, backed Wagner.

The *Aufruf* in *STB* considered that the competition was invalidated, because Wagner, together with Hans Poelzig, had completed a design—an oval-shaped "egg"—for the central section of the fairgrounds and had publicized it before the deadline. This meant that other participants either had only a fragmented site available or would have to ignore the Wagner/Poelzig project. Because Wagner was a member of the jury, it was highly unlikely that his entry would not be selected as the winner. The *Aufruf* suggested that Wagner should resign from the jury, and perhaps even withdraw the "egg." It was also proposed that comprehensive designs for the entire site should be evaluated by a new jury put together by *STB*. The members, presumably selected by Hegemann, included Paul Bonatz, Max Osborn, J. J. P. Oud, and Günther Wasmuth, with Paul Schmitthenner as an alternate. As expected, the composition of the jury raised protests, although Osborn had published favorably on the Wagner/Poelzig "egg" in the *Vossische Zeitung*. The intended balance of positions was affected by the resignations of Oud and, later, Schmitthenner. In a lengthy letter to Poelzig, primarily regarding the forthcoming exhibition in London, Hegemann explained that he had contacted Mies van der Rohe to replace Oud.[222] He was unable to get a positive response from van der Rohe, who apparently considered his abstention a favor to Poelzig. Hegemann had tried to have Poelzig intervene, noting "I was particularly keen on having a second supporter of your inclination on the jury." When his attempts to get van der Rohe on the jury failed, Schmitthenner was asked, but later resigned. With his letter Hegemann tried to repair his relations with Poelzig and to persuade him to intervene with the angry Wagner. A meeting by the Freie Deutsche Akademie on the *Bau-Ausstellung* had been scheduled and, according to Hegemann, Bruno Taut had suggested that he should speak, but he was not listed on the agenda. Hegemann wondered if Poelzig would arrange for his presentation, but this did not occur.

Oud, who was now the *Stadtbaumeister* of Rotterdam and ailing, had been in a similar predicament during the boycott debate. He was pressured by members of the Ring to refuse acceptance to the jury, and urged by Bruno Taut not to let Hegemann take advantage of him.[223] Taut explained that Wagner had not considered his plan to be an *absolut*, but merely a means by which to convince the building industry, with its rigid business interests, of other points of view. The letter also commented on the political difficulties Wagner faced in his position as *Stadtbaurat*.

Oud received several letters from Hegemann. One written immediately after his return from Egypt expressed his joy over the tone of a card from Oud that implied their relations were improving after the "*Schildbürgerstreiche*" annoyance. Only two days later, having sent him a copy of the *Aufruf*, Hegemann thanked him for accepting a position on the jury. Hegemann regretted Wagner's anger and anticipated that he might try to persuade Oud to resign. Although it was explained in the *Aufruf*, Hegemann emphasized that the main purpose was to make the entire fairgrounds available to all participants in the competition for a comprehensive plan, rather than merely fragments left over from the Poelzig/Wagner design. He also mailed Oud a copy of his letter to Poelzig. From the opposing side Oud received a copy of Wagner's letter, which appeared in *Städtebau* and *Bauwelt*. Oud's withdrawal from the jury was communicated to Hegemann by Mrs. Oud, who noted that the situation with the competition was far more complex than Hegemann had explained. She wrote that her husband was not taking an either/or position, and, on orders from his physician that he was to avoid tension, he did not wish to get involved in the quarrel. She also mentioned that Oud considered his possible replacement of him by Schmitthenner "unpleasant."[224]

The exchange of letters regarding Oud took place over the course of barely a week and only ten days after Hegemann's return from Egypt. The polemics of the Martin Wagner/Werner Hegemann case and its repercussions extended far longer and were ventilated primarily in the press.

An addendum to the *Aufruf* published reactions to it, including Wagner's letter and Hegemann's response. The Bund Deutscher Architekten, Rheinland u. Westfalen, supported a comprehensive plan for the entire *Bau-Ausstellung* as proposed by the *Aufruf*. The Deutsche Bauzeitung took a similar position for economic reasons and design considerations. A comprehensive, "organic" layout for the fairgrounds would be hampered, it argued, by the oval shape of the Poelzig/Wagner "egg" because its enclosed form prevented spatial connections to the surrounding area.

The editorial notes by Hegemann added to Wagner's letter directed to "*Sehr geehrte Schriftleitung*" of *STB* mentioned that the Poelzig/Wagner project was given out for publication while the competition was still in progress, and Wagner was on its jury. The *Aufruf* received support and so did Wagner. The text of Wagner's letter of March 23, 1928, as published in *STB*, was edited and shortened, and the complete version appeared in *Bauwelt*.[225] It was a detailed attack on the position taken by the "*Aufruf zur fruchtbaren* [productive] *Kritik*," which Wagner called "*unfruchtbar*" (unproductive). He considered that the new competition called by Hegemann and company lacked the necessary groundwork for authoritative proceedings and should therefore be dismissed as "merely literary dust." Hegemann's position was that while Wagner was a member of the jury, he presented his own project, and there was confusion over when it was displayed and by whom. This he considered the crux of the controversy. In his letter Wagner called Hegemann's *STB* statements "slanderous insults" and threatened legal action. Friedrich Paulsen, editor of *Bauwelt*, added a cautious note in support of Wagner, but did not agree to making the periodical available as a battleground by accepting a reply from Hegemann. Referring to the freedom of the press law in a letter to Paulsen, Hegemann succeeded in having his reply to Wagner published in *Bauwelt*.[226] It is brief and only refuted the gist of Wagner's arguments as to when and by whom the Poelzig/Wagner project was shown, and why there was a delay in withdrawing Oud's name from the list of *Aufruf* jurors. Published on the same page as Hegemann's letter was another reply by Wagner. It referred to the confusion between an earlier comprehensive plan by Poelzig and Wagner and the limited "egg" model. According to Wagner this confusion could have been clarified if Hegemann had personally approached him or Poelzig. He would have been informed that this general plan predated the existence of the *Verein Bau-Ausstellung* and the competition. On the matter of Oud's refusal to be a juror and when it was announced, a topic given exaggerated importance by both Wagner and Hegemann, no agreement was reached.

Aspects of the Hegemann/Wagner dispute verged on the ridiculous. When Hegemann brought legal action for personal slander against *Bauwelt*, because the periodical had published Wagner's personal insults, *Bauwelt* editor Paulsen stepped in as mediator and Hegemann withdrew his accusation.[227] On December 6 and 17, 1928, the case of *Hegemann v. Wagner* was heard in court and settled. Each party had to declare that it was not his intention to insult the other. They signed the compromise, agreed to share the legal expenses and refrain from disclosing the details of the settlement. The document was, however, published with a summary of the whole affair by Hegemann in *STB*, apparently without further repercussions from Wagner.[228]

The altercation was exceedingly painful for both Hegemann and Wagner. The rationale, blurred in the agitation, can be interpreted as a reaction to the Weissenhof Siedlung in Stuttgart and disappointment with its failure to achieve the expectations harbored by some members of the

Ring and by the so-called opponents such as Hegemann. The high hopes that the *Bau-Ausstellung* Berlin 1930 would surpass Weissenhof's "international" ambitions in worldwide significance were shared by a spectrum of architects, planners, businessmen, and the administration of Berlin. Wagner and Hegemann, both idealists, ultimately cherished the same goal. They undoubtedly were aware of this, which adds particular poignancy to the "Fall Wagner/Hegemann."

Historians writing on the Bau-Ausstellung Berlin 1930 have brushed aside this preamble as a mere squabble and concentrated on the event itself. In fact the discourse generated by the Hegemann/Wagner case affected the resulting exhibition, which took place in 1931 after being postponed for a year due to the economic crisis. There was time to arrive at a final design, which incorporated suggestions from the *Aufruf* competition with the Wagner/Poelzig original project.[229]

Having reconciled their differences, both Wagner and Hegemann published articles in *WMB* on the resulting plans for the Bau-Ausstellung exhibition grounds.[230] Wagner described the comprehensive proposal by him, Poelzig, and other collaborators and included plans and photographs of models. The focal building of their proposal was the large conference center connected by arcades to the existing exhibition halls surrounding the Funkturm and a restaurant. The ambitious proposal included outdoor amenities in the form of a rock garden designed by Leberecht Migge and an outdoor swimming pool to be converted into a skating rink in the winter. According to Wagner, some of these elements were destined for a later phase: "For these proposals to be realized in their present configuration will depend entirely on future developments. In any case they do show the results of studies, which will form a basis upon which a successful exhibition enterprise in the city of Berlin can expand with an exemplary lay-out."

The conciliatory tone of Hegemann's review markedly contrasted with the *Aufruf* and the letters of 1928. He noted that the new design responded to many of the suggestions derived from the *WMB* competition, notably the much-debated "egg," had been transformed into a mere shell. He voiced sympathy for the difficulties Wagner faced in his position as *Stadtbaurat* and the political chaos in Berlin's municipal administration that stood in the way of any large-scale urban intervention.

When the Bau-Ausstellung opened in May 1931, it was primarily a trade show for the German building industry. Some sections, however, presented an international overview of city planning, housing, and residential developments. "*Die Wohnung unserer Zeit*" (Today's home) displayed furnished rooms and parts of buildings. An unsigned article, presumably by Hegemann, showed views of the "Ausschuss für Gross-Berlin" activities of 1912–13 contrasting with modern examples by Marcel Breuer, Otto Haesler, and Hugo Häring, an instigator of the boycott. The article also provided a double-page spread of Mies van der Rohe's well-known house in the Bau-Ausstellung.[231]

Some aspects of the event gratified Hegemann's expectations for an encore of Berlin/Düsseldorf 1910. The International Federation for Housing and Town Planning held its XIII Congress in conjunction with the exhibition, combining lectures and discussions with tours of Berlin and its surroundings. On this occasion the Ciudad Lineal de Madrid presented a bilingual exposé of its theory and accomplishments to a gathering of town planning experts favoring the English garden city model.[232] In contrast the Spanish model was an open-ended plan that combined housing, open space, minor industry, and agriculture, arranged along a transportation trunk that could be extended indefinitely. Hegemann, who was about to leave for South America, traveled via Spain and visited Madrid, perhaps enticed by the Ciudad Lineal presentation.

Hegemann had always considered city planning an effective tool for promoting peace and preventing war. Channeling political discontent into urban progress was his ultimate, albeit idealistic, goal for global peace and understanding. In the notations for a radio interview about the Bau-Ausstellung with Lutz Weltmann ("Citizen of the world," possibly a pseudonym or fictional character), he elaborated on this conviction. The point of departure was an article by Jean Giraudoux—(1882–1944), a playwright, journalist, and diplomat—comparing Berlin and Paris.[233] According to Giraudoux, a German general had enthused about well-built barracks for his army, while today a German statesman would declare "the Nation is a matter of '*Städtebau*.'" Giraudoux noted that in this respect Berlin had achieved a prominent position in Germany. Hegemann enumerated in the interview the benefits of sound urbanism, especially adequate housing. An interest in city planning shared by all nations would lead to " communal work uniting people." This spirit could be stimulated by conferences and exhibitions and, hopefully, lead to world peace.

Hegemann expanded on this theme in an article for a Swiss journal.[234] He stressed the importance of the Bau-Ausstellung as the culmination of a sequence of city planning exhibitions since 1909, noting that he had been associated with them all. World War I had dashed the hopes that the vast expenditures needed for urban improvements would not once more be squandered on "bloody wars." Presently the Deutsche Bau-Ausstellung in Berlin held great promise for the recognition that city planning implied planning whole regions as already implemented in the Ruhr region. Regional planning, which would evolve into *Landes-Planung*, was followed by *Reichs-Planung*. This was demonstrated in the current exhibition of Sörgel's visionary scheme for Europe and Africa. Hegemann ended his essay on a euphoric note, echoing the Expressionist manifestos clamoring for a utopian brotherhood of mankind: "The sums that can be productively applied to rational city and regional planning are actually so enormous, that their fantastic power [*phantasiebeflügende Kraft*] will gradually even match the temptations of the smell of blood and cannon thunder, which up to now intoxicate people. . . . Whoever considers this hope childish will be convinced by the inspirational impulse of a worldwide buildable future as shown in the exhibition halls of the Funkturm."

Hegemann's pacifist convictions, intertwined with his dedication to urban planning on a global scale, had kept him from returning to Germany to participate in the Great War. In the late 1920s his contact with the intellectuals associated with the journal *Die Weltbühne* energized his hopes for world peace and a pan-Europe, which was by this time closely tied to opposing Nazism.

After Hegemann's stay in Egypt and voyage home to confront the Wagner dispute in 1928, a less contentious occasion presented itself. He was asked by the Architectural Association in London to organize an exhibition of modern German architecture of the previous twenty-five years and to give a lecture. Eager for some time with her husband after his long absence, his wife had made arrangements for the care of their three children so that she could join him in London, where they enjoyed the theater and excursions to Cambridge and Oxford.

The exhibition was scheduled for April 30 to May 19, 1928, and the announcement noted: "The selection of subjects has been influenced by lack of time and other circumstances beyond the control of Dr. Hegemann, and in some cases it was not possible to select the most notable and characteristic work."[235] The material was largely drawn from illustrations published in *WMB*, which for the preceding four years had been consistently boycotted by the members of the Ring. In a letter to Hans Poelzig, Hegemann wrote that he had called attention to the architect's work in his lecture, but regretted that Häring had persuaded Poelzig to refuse his contribution of examples for the exhibition.[236] "Mr. Häring not only refused me your works, but also revoked Mr. Mendelsohn's contributions to the exhibition of which I had been assured. The result of Mr. Häring's negative attitude, was that, much to my regret, a reduced number of modern rather than older buildings was displayed." A review in the London *Times*, cited in the *Vossische Zeitung*, mentioned only conservative architects. It was also reprinted with minor changes in *WMB*.[237]

In his London lecture Hegemann gave equal exposure to traditional and modern architects. He wrote to Poelzig that the head of the Architectural Association had asked him where he stood, because he had given such a balanced overview of both tendencies. By adhering to Häring's insistence on the boycott, members of the Ring missed the opportunity of making their recent architectural accomplishments known in England, but they achieved their purpose of upholding Hegemann's reputation of being averse to Modernism. Reverberations of the animosity by the Ring persisted throughout Hegemann's lifetime and may have contributed to his consignment to oblivion after his death, when historians accepted the

Ring's position on face value. Efforts by Hegemann to break through the rigidity of the Ring and establish a dialogue were to little avail, and he had no choice but to circumvent the obstacles.

Hegemann summarized his London impressions in an article and reported a conversation with an unidentified English architect, who remarked on the "indestructible 'beauty of the metropolis,'" which could not be damaged permanently by the "incompetence or meanness" of the architects. He also referred to a comment by Hermann Bahr, who compared riding on the upper level of a bus along the entire stretch of the Friedrichstrasse in Berlin or Oxford Street in London to listening to Beethoven's Ninth Symphony. Hegemann's English acquaintance expressed doubt that this could, indeed, be said about London's Kingsway or Regent Street, because recent additions by members of the Royal Institute of British Architects and the Architectural Association had damaged its beauty. According to Hegemann the controversies of modern architecture and buildings responding to proven traditions were comparable in Germany and England.

The director of the School of the Architectural Association, Howard Robertson, also published on this topic in *WMB*, describing the school's program as favoring as well as seeking new and modern solutions to contemporary problems. He also mentioned the difficulties he encountered defending this approach against more conservative colleagues.[238] Hegemann was impressed by the Architectural Association, even a bit envious of its handsome quarters serving as a meeting place for architects, a venue for lectures, journal offices, and particularly as a school for training young architects. In his well-attended lecture Hegemann had been somewhat critical of Edwin Lutyens, and he tried to correct this in his article. As on other occasions, he defended his role as an impartial critic positioned outside the constraints of any particular contingent or faction:

> The fact that in my London lecture I compared without inhibitions the efforts of academic and modernistic architects had the result that after the lecture I was asked by several people: "Do you stand on the side of the young or the old?" Should it be impossible to fight for good architecture, regardless where it is to be found and without belonging to a clique or by surpressing uninhibited criticism? Is the editor of a professional journal to be respected only when he debases himself to become a publicity agent?[239]

Race and Culture

Anticipating the vexations awaiting him in Berlin may have influenced Hegemann's extended journey returning from Egypt. The Nazis were waging a successful campaign to co-opt cultural tendencies and exploit conflicts to their advantage. Paramount for Hegemann in this situation was his position regarding the traditionalist architects, represented by Paul Schmitthenner and Paul Schultze-Naumburg, and the Ring with its rancor against him. He found himself between factions, not truly adhering to either, seeking insights from contradictions where others perceived irreconcilable opposites. To him such rigid categorizing was akin to fascist ideology. In the course of his remaining years in Germany he became increasingly conspicuous as a nonconformist.

Within the architectural profession the lines were drawn sharply. The Block was founded in May 1928 in opposition to the Ring, reacting to the Weissenhof episode and Walter Curt Behrendt's triumphant *Der Sieg des Neuen Baustils* (The victory of the new building style) (1927). As expected the Block endeavored to gain Hegemann's membership, which he refused.

Two 1928 letters by Hegemann hint at efforts by the Block group to persuade him to join. He mentioned lunching with Schultze-Naumburg, Adler, and Münter Frohwein "to talk about 'Kunst u. Rasse'" and wrote that he was "invited to a meeting of the Block at the home of Professor Gessner in Gatow just on the other side of the Wannsee. I was driven out with Prof. Seeck, it was a fine ride." He described the Gessner home as "charming," and continued "about 11 PM we were driven back; again a lovely ride in the open car. I like that. I won't forget that day in spite of rather little coming out of our discussions." On the back of this handwritten letter is a typed fragment of a communique or agenda, perhaps handed to Hegemann at the meeting. It reads: "-2- . . . needing some directions for his work and business management. Members of the Block at present are: Bestelmeyer, München; Bonats [*sic*], Stuttgart; Schmitthenner, Stuttgart; Schultze-Naumburg, Saaleck; Blunck, Gessner, Seeck, Berlin; [under these names are three lines scratched out by pencil]. . . . Once membership has been increased to about 30, the Block will make its first public pronouncement, which will also be published at this place."[240] The Block manifesto was published in *Baukunst* in 1928 with only one additional signer, Stoffregen.[241] It is important to note that Hegemann may have agreed with some of their tenets, for instance "rejecting an overly hasty propaganda for modish creations, which endangers healthy progress." Hegemann's name appears briefly on the title page of the Block's journal *Bankultur* from 1929 until the spring of 1931.[242]

During 1928, Hegemann continued to support the architecture of Bonatz, Schmitthenner, and Schultze-Naumburg. *WMB* published numerous articles showing their work, including a special issue dedicated entirely to the Stuttgarter Schule where these architects taught. An introductory note by Hegemann identified Schmitthenner as the guest editor of issue number 11, 1928.[243] The occasion was an exhibition dedicated to the school's work at the Royal Academy in Copenhagen, and the *Sonderheft* can be considered its catalog. Reprinted were the inaugural comments by the dean of the academy and a lecture by Paul Bonatz. The comprehensive overview of the Stuttgarter Schule included work by the faculty, students, and alumni, and was shown in a country known for the adaptation of classical architecture and timeless principles in contemporary conditions. Hegemann had been responsible for drawing attention to Scandinavian neoclassical architecture by publishing articles, organizing exhibitions in Berlin, and welcoming contributions by Rasmussen. Numerous illustrations and notes on the program of the Stuttgarter Schule overshadowed Hegemann's brief commentaries in the special issue of *WMB*. In his Introduction he gave as the reason for this *Sonderheft* (special issue) the criticism by the modernist camp, which was achieving success by means of "clever political maneuvers and propaganda." Salient among the latter was the book by Walter Curt Behrendt, *Der Sieg des neuen Baustils*, displaying Weissenhof under triumphant flags on the cover.[244] According to Hegemann, "*Modernismus*" considered itself a "*Stilbewegung*"—a stylistic movement—yet it had produced few examples of practical and artistic building except the Herpich House by Mendelsohn in Berlin. Even the advocates of Modernism had occasionally expressed recognition of the Stuttgarter Schule. Without revealing the name of the author, Hegemann cited at length from the *Zentralblatt der Bauverwaltung* of October 10, 1928. Continuing on the topic of "*Stilbewegung*" in a short piece with that title further on in *WMB*, he referred once more to the comment by the unnamed member of the opposition who lamented that an understanding between the factions was difficult, primarily because the followers of the modernist *Stilbewegung* saw the other "not as the beginning of a development, but as an end." According to Hegemann the break with historical precedents and continuity was equally harmful in the theater and in painting. He emphasized that he was by no means an unconditional admirer of Bonatz and Schmitthenner, but preferred their work to the "'stylistically imbued' formless creations—such as Bruno Taut's own house—or . . . 'stylistically stirring' unpractical engineer's romanticism, such as the masters' houses in Dessau by Gropius, who had designed better things."

On the other hand, in a previous article Hegemann had been sharply critical of the railroad station in Stuttgart by Paul Bonatz and F. E. Scholer for its "pseudogothic modernizing knight-castle and cathedral-architecture," similar to their skyscraper in Düsseldorf.[245] Ever partial to a non-historicist Classicism, Hegemann argued against the *Germanen-Schwärmer* (fanatic Germanophiles) who failed to acknowledge the classic heritage in the so-called German building forms. The Stuttgarter Bahnhof compared unfavorably to Pennsylvania Station in New York. In these comments published in the prominent *WMB*, which was by now considered Hegemann's mouthpiece, one detects an edginess to his position regarding Bonatz, Schultze-Naumburg, and Schmitthenner, especially the latter.

Paul Schmitthenner was one of the earliest and most prominent architects captivated by Nazi ideology. His trajectory has been documented by historians and is frequently called "*Der Fall Schmitthenner*."[246] This could be translated "The Schmitthenner Case," but *Fall* also means "downfall," which in this context is equally appropriate. Schmitthenner not only fell low in the eyes of many for his adherence to Nazism, but Nazis pushed him aside.

Schultze-Naumburg was a founding member of the Heimatschutz in 1904 and the German Werkbund in 1907. Widely known and respected in pre–World War I conservative reform circles, his multivolume *Kulturarbeiten* was influential for calling attention to the culture of the environment and the German "*Heimat*."[247] This early part of Schultze-Naumburg's career pales in comparison to his propagation of racial theories, which benefited from the renown of his previous work. In 1928, the year the Block was launched, he published *Kunst und Rasse*, declaring modern art and architecture the result of *rassischer Entartung* (racial aberration). The connection between culture and race had infused German thinking since the mid-nineteenth century, and in the early decades of the twentieth century it nourished and eventually poisoned movements such as Heimatschutz and historic preservation that had started out innocently. It was just one more step to declare architectural style an expression of race and to declare the buildings at Weissenhof "oriental," "foreign," and "degenerate." For Nazism the culture–race link provided a major ingredient in its ideological witches' brew of anti-Semitism and the promotion of a pure Aryan German race. An examination of Hegemann's relationship with Schmitthenner and Schultze-Naumburg plainly reveals that his initial admiration of their work turned to a revulsion against their support of Nazism and their architecture with its cultural and political implications.

Kunst und Rasse was discussed at the Block meeting attempting to persuade Hegemann to join, probably providing a strong reason for his refusal. Two years earlier Hegemann had sharply attacked Schultze-Naumburg as a *Rassentheoretiker* (race theorist) for views he expressed in his article on the pitched and flat roof debate.[248] In a particularly strong rebuke, Hegemann blamed Schultze-Naumburg for his lack of functionalism and for confusion in labeling the flat roof *undeutsch* (un-German), and of an "even more villainous origin," pronouncements Hegemann perceived as anti-Semitic. He mentioned an answer to Gropius's inquiry on roofs, sent from Israel, to the effect that in that country flat roofs were judged impractical. According to Hegemann, even the zealous advocate of "*nordischer Rassenpolitik*" (Nordic racial politics), Sesselberg, declared in his book *Das flache Dach im Heimatbilde* that the whole question had nothing to do with racial notions. Hegemann backed up his berating of Schultze-Naumburg with a quotation from Nietzsche that recommended "avoid[ing] relations with anyone who takes part in mendacious racial fraud."

For some time Hegemann continued to distinguish between "classic" and "classicistic" architecture and those advocating the former in conjunction with embracing Nazism and confronting Modernism. Favorable articles on Schultze-Naumburg and Schmitthenner's architecture continued to appear in *WMB* in 1929 and 1930. On the occasion of Schultze-Naumburg and Poelzig's sixtieth birthdays, when they were awarded honorary doctorates from the Technische Hochschule Stuttgart, Hegemann referred kindly to the *Kulturarbeiten.*[249] He commented on Schultze-Naumburg's "*Kampf gegen Kitsch und Kulturlosigkeit*" (Fight against kitsch and lack of culture), which had been influential since its publication thirty years before. Contrasting Schultze-Naumburg, from the Block, with Poelzig and Tessenow, who were leading figures in an "extremist architects' group," Hegemann mentioned that opinions of Poelzig's work, even from those close to him, were not always favorable. Poelzig had achieved his status by building "distant from functional objectivity" in a manner which several of the "extremists" had overcome. As an example, Mendelsohn, formerly a *Romantik*, had recently praised Poelzig's I. G. Farben building in Frankfurt as being "simple, mature, classic." Hegemann wondered what the concept "*klassisch*" might mean for Mendelsohn. Should it be interpreted as "*einfach, ausgereift, klassisch*" (simple, mature, classic) in the sense of qualities defended in the pages of *WMB*, but for which the periodical had been attacked? He cited Schinkel, with whom Poelzig was occasionally compared: "The highest representation of the ideal of functionality determines the artistic value of a building."

Hegemann also quoted at length from a birthday article (*Frankfurter Zeitung*, April 30, 1929) by W. C. Behrendt, the champion of the "extremist" architects.[250] Poelzig's "romantic excesses" were described as a balancing act on the highwire of his fantasy between art and kitsch. Hegemann wished to shield Poelzig from his friends and to bridge the sharp divide separating the older masters from the younger generation who, according to Behrendt, demonstrated a determined commitment to reality.

There is no hint in this essay of the polemic surrounding Schultze-Naumburg's *Kunst und Rasse* (1928). Hegemann vented his anger regarding this book and anti-Semitism and racism in general in a series of typewritten drafts, which were not published in their entirety. A summary entitled "*Kunst versöhnt die Rassen: Auseinandersetzung mit Schultze-Naumburg*" (Art reconciles the races: a debate with Sch.-N.) appeared in the newspaper *Vorwärts* in 1932.[251]

Schultze-Naumburg had become a member of the Kampfbund für Deutsche Kultur (Association for the defense of German culture) and was named minister of culture for the Third Reich. In that position he was held responsible for the demise of the Bauhaus. Surprisingly he was attacked for this deed by the ultra-right *DAZ* (*Deutsche Allgemeine Zeitung?*) for having smothered creativity in the new Germany. In the *Vorwärts* article Hegemann ironically predicted that Hitler might declare *Geistesfreiheit* (intellectual freedom) and ask Mies van der Rohe to design his presidential palace.[252] Hegemann wrote for the *Weltbühne* and the *Generalanzeiger Dortmund* on the Bauhaus topic, noting this only briefly in "*Kunst versöhnt die Rassen.*" In the latter, based on the extensive drafts, Hegemann cleverly mocked Schultze-Naumburg's book, in which he favored the slim "nordic" women represented by Italian and French painters, contrasting them to the "heavy and voluminous" women of Rubens and Rembrandt and labeling the latter as typical of an "*ostische Rasse.*" Schultze-Naumburg concluded: "The art that surrounds us today shows brazenly the desire of the subhuman individual, who seems to be content in his sordid world of grimaces and twisted bodies. Should the task of building the future world be delegated to him, it will resemble his pictures." Hegemann asked rhetorically how a woman whom a patriotic German would be permitted to love and marry should look. He referred to the contrary advice given around 1890 by the father of "national/socialist *Heimatkunst* and racist passions," Julius Langbehn, in his book *Rembrandt als Erzieher.*[253] Langbehn praised Rembrandt as a true "*Nibelunge*" and exemplary Germanic type, yet, as Hegemann pointed out, he painted the "Jewish brides" of Amsterdam and "*ostische*" women, thus promoting "*Rassenverschmelzung und Völkerversöhnung*" (The merging of the races and reconciliation of the nations).

Hegemann's fragments, all on the same theme, passed judgment on the new edition of Langbehn's *Rembrandt als Erzieher* (1928), which had been altered and expanded by H. Kellermann to include some violently anti-Semitic passages. Hegemann considered that Langbehn's original 1890 text was of "great and ominous influence." Now supposedly "enhanced" in the revised edition, with the addition of a long chapter on "*Jugend und Juden*" (Youth and Jews), the new edition also pertained to Bismarck's statements regarding Jews in his speech given at the Landstag in 1847, and on eliminating the role of several prominent Jews in his government. Citations from the Jewish poet Heinrich Heine did not make it into the new edition of Langbehn's book. Hegemann maintained that Langbehn had transformed Nietzsche into the "re-interpreted 'fateful' Nietzsche of the National Socialists," and had brought the philosopher to Hitler's attention. Hegemann concurred with K. A. Bernoulli that Germans saw their savior in Nietzsche and that his prominence was not based on rational convictions but was comparable to a "hysterical epidemic."

Based on his fragmented outpourings of despair, possibly intended for publication, Hegemann composed an essay in dialogue format, "Hitler *plaudert mit Nietzsche über die Juden*" (Hitler talks with Nietzsche about the Jews.)[254] It was published in various languages in 1933, the same year his *Entlarvte Geschichte* (see note 272) appeared and was burned by the Nazis, and the year the Hegemanns went into exile.

Although there is a lapse of five years between Schultze-Naumburg's

Kunst und Rasse, the revised edition of Langbehn's *Rembrandt als Erzieher*, and Hegemann's essay on Hitler, Hegemann perceived Nietzsche and anti-Semitism to be closely linked. He came to the realization that his own literary and polemical skills ought to be applied to combat the most dangerous and threatening aspects of Nazism. Hegemann zealously dedicated himself to this objective during his remaining years in Germany and from abroad.

In "Hitler *plaudert mit Nietzsche über die Juden*," Hegemann counterposed two figures worshipped as heroes in Germany: Nietzsche, the venerated philosopher who provided inspiration and justification for Nazi ideology, and Hitler, the leader of the *Volk* and the implementer of the Third Reich. Hegemann chose his favored dialogue format, with the speakers uttering their own opinions, providing immediacy and credibility. The conversation was described as in a stage setting with the actual bust of the philosopher confronting Hitler, who had asked to be photographed next to the sculpture. The picture was intended to be included in Hegemann's unpublished book, *Hitler, wie ihn keiner kennt* (The unknown Hitler). According to Hegemann's introductory note Hitler had set in motion his great persecution of Jews when he assumed the position as *Reichskanzler*. As a result the spirit of Nietzsche took notice of him and this led to the subsequent fictitious conversation. Hegemann assured the reader that every word and passage in quotation marks was cited verbatim from Nietzsche's works. Some of Hitler's replies were direct quotes as well. The remainder of the text was cleverly, and with noticeable relish, composed by Hegemann. Nietzsche opened the discussion by accusing Hitler of falsely claiming to be his disciple, although Hitler always did the opposite of what Nietzsche taught. Hitler countered that Nietzsche had presaged the concept of the "*Über-und Führermensch*" (superman and leader) as well as his *Rassenpolitik* (racial politics), facts that were then proven to be misinterpretations of Nietzsche's text. A quote from the program of the N.S.D.A.P. (*Nationalsozialistische Arbeiterpartei*, or Nazi Party) followed: "Anti-Semitism is, one might say, the emotional basis of our movement. . . . Every national socialist is anti-Semitic." Nietzsche was prompted to state his "*Maxime*" "To avoid relations with anybody taking part in the mendacious racial fraud" and he curtly reprimanded Hitler once more for claiming to be his follower. The exchange ended with Nietzsche repeating his recommendation to grant Jews a permanent and worthy place in society, expelling instead the anti-Semitic *Schreihälse* (screamers). Hitler is counseled regarding his political posturing to reflect on Nietzsche's message: "Shame to those who now officiously present themselves to the masses as their savior!"

Hegemann's active opposition to anti-Semitism did not derive from Jewish ancestry: his family included several protestant clergymen. His father, Ottmar Hegemann, had published several controversial books on religious topics, which were confiscated. Werner qualified as what Hitler considered "pure" Aryan. Hegemann had no tolerance for anti-Semitism and had many Jewish friends and colleagues. His lifelong friendship with Pierre Lievre dated from his student years in Paris and was resumed by the families after World War II. The German occupation had brought great hardship to the Lievres and, reluctantly, they disposed of some of Hegemann's papers which they had sheltered. An early letter by Hegemann to the editor of *The Milwaukee Herald* in 1920 suggested that the newspaper should publish a passage from the book *Our America*, by Waldo Frank, for the interest of its many readers of Jewish and German background. The passage praised Jewish ensembles and performances of classic and modern plays presented in Milwaukee and other American cities at that time.[255]

In Europe, and particularly in Berlin, Hegemann sought out the Jewish intellectuals and architects on whom he published, including Erich Mendelsohn and Hans and Oskar Gerson. Hegemann left no trace of distinguishing between his Jewish and non-Jewish acquaintances. For a "citizen of the world" all people were equal. He made no declaration regarding his position, rather reaffirming it in various ways through writings and actions. His association with the periodicals *Die Weltbühne* and *Das Tagebuch* in Berlin, and with the New School for Social Research in New York provided him contacts with like-minded individuals.

The culture–race debate and the growing threat of Nazism motivated Hegemann to shift his attention increasingly from architecture and urban planning to political concerns. His brazen stand vis-à-vis Nazism affected the rest of his life and his exile years. To later generations confronting the unimaginable events of the Holocaust, Hegemann's prescient opposition provides insight to early Nazi motivations. He deserves recognition for enabling efforts to render approachable the inexplicable.

How Hegemann's convictions affected his views on architecture, especially regarding Schultze-Naumburg and Schmitthenner, is not easily clarified. As it pertained to Hegemann the "*Fall* Schmitthenner" impinged on architecture more directly than the case of Schultze-Naumburg, although the latter had published *Das Gesicht des deutschen Hauses* in 1929. This book was intended to counteract the "machine for living" demonstrated at Weissenhof, and almost all its illustrations depicted houses designed by Schultze-Naumburg. His claim that these houses represented the German "face" may seem ridiculous today. However, when the book was published, the assumption dovetailed with the prevailing theories of Ernst Kretschmer and others, who related personality characteristics to body and racial types. In that same year Kretschmer's *Körperbau und Charakter* was published in its eighth edition.[256] These morphological interpretations carried over into the arts and architecture, supporting Nazi racial policies.

Emphasis on the "face" of the houses typifying German culture branded Modernism as foreign *Kulturbolschewismus* (cultural Bolshevism).[257] From 1928–31 the Swiss author Alexander von Senger wrote several articles identifying avant-garde architecture as an international communist conspiracy. In Germany the concept took hold with alacrity and merged with Schultze-Naumburg's racial suppositions. The New Building, of which Le Corbusier was considered the main proponent, was accused of destroying the German *Heimat*. A slender publication entitled "*Kulturbolschewismus?*" by Paul Renner defended the "*Neues Bauen*."[258] A review by the Swiss critic Peter Meyer supported the arguments expressed in Renner's chapters on "*Individualismus oder Kollektivismus*" (Individualism or collectivism), "*Die antisemitische Hetze gegen die moderne Kunst*" (The anti-Semitic campaign against modern art) and "*Die politische Hetze gegen das Neue Bauen*" (The political campaign against the New Building).

Hegemann addressed the "*Kulturbolschewismus*" charge from a different angle in an article published in *Die Weltbühne*, responding to the author Tretjakow's proclamation on "the new type of author."[259] The Russian declared that the "bolshevist thesis" no longer accepted works of art created by individuals contemplating their navels. Instead "*Kollektiv-Kunstwerke*" would result not from single ingenious minds, but from forty or one hundred workers. The cult of the individual was to disappear and the anonymity of minds would awake. Hegemann gave a historical overview of accomplishments resulting from cooperative efforts that did not disregard individual creative input, including cathedrals, Schinkel, American skyscrapers, and contemporary projects by Martin Wagner and others. He also commented on the theater and newspapers, all examples of "*Kollektivleistungen*" (collective achievements) developing out of the accomplishments of predecessors. Hegemann's essay was one more version of his belief that the city, and even more so the modern metropolis, was continuously evolving from a multitude of efforts over time.

The primary battlefield of the architectural controversies was the printed page in periodicals, newspapers, and books. It was a *Federkrieg*, a pen-and-ink war, whose vehemence detracted attention from shared underlying principles. Peter Meyer expressed concern that "sensationalist and exaggerated propaganda" tragically obscured the leading ideas of modern architecture.[260] Hegemann often singled out "classic" aspects in the work of both unquestionably modern and traditional architects. On the other hand he called the builders of the Weissenhof Siedlung "*Stuttgarter Literatur-Architekten*," although he himself was a man of the pen with literary ambitions.[261] The war of words gave exceptional prominence to critics and authors, who now demanded attention equal to that devoted to the architects cognizant of their voices. The language in which thoughts about building, style, and cultural politics were expressed deserves scrutiny. Terminology and concepts went through frequent changes and were invented and reinvented to meet new requirements. Nazism also used language in novel ways and excelled in burdening existing German expressions with connotations to suit its ideological program.

The early twentieth century produced a constellation of books that had a great impact on urbanism and architecture. Some have been mentioned in relation to the Weissenhof controversy, the Stuttgarter Schule, and the race/culture dispute. Two earlier publications are tangential to this group for their influence on the debates that peaked in the 1920s. Paul Mebes's *Um 1800* went through a third edition in 1920, with an introduction by Walter Curt Behrendt which bridged the pre– and post–World War I generations.[262] The fate of Friedrich Ostendorf's *Sechs Bücher vom Bauen, 1913–19* (Six books on architecture), was affected by the author's early death in World War I. Both Mebes and Ostendorf had considerable influence on the Heimatschutz movement, Schultze-Naumburg's *Kulturarbeiten, Das Gesicht des deutschen Hauses*, and on the ideas advocated by the Block.

In the years after the Weissenhof Exhibition, a time of heated discourse, Paul Schmitthenner received foremost attention in architectural and political circles. His adherence to Nazism and his book *Das Deutsche Wohnhaus* (1932) were pivotal in redirecting and severing Hegemann's allegiance to a person and an architecture he had previously admired.[263] Under the influence of the new ideology, the only things that counted regarding an individual were race and being German; all other attributes of a person evaporated, and Schmitthenner's architecture could no longer be separated from his espousal of Nazism.

Schmitthenner's career and political involvement are the subject of well-documented studies advancing different perceptions of these vexing topics.[264] The controversy involving Hegemann and Schmitthenner's *Das Deutsche Wohnhaus* transpired during the short period between the publication of the book in the fall of 1932 and Hegemann's departure from Germany in May 1933. It is recorded in three letters, two by Hegemann and one by Schmitthenner, published in *WMB*, and in the correspondence between Hegemann and the authors René Schickele and Annette Kolb.[265] Schickele and Kolb were clients of Schmitthenner. Their houses were shown in *WMB* in 1929 with comments by Hegemann and Kolb, while Schickele wrote about Schmitthenner's own house as "*Die Arche über Stuttgart*" (The ark above Stuttgart). The meanings for "ark" are various and can be grouped under sacred and ritualistic artifacts. Both Schickele and Schmitthenner came from the Alsace region and had strong ties to it and to each other. The vernacular building traditions of Alsace markedly influenced their houses and others by Schmitthenner, especially Schickele's house, with its low-pitched roof nestling into the garden and landscape, which resembled the home of an affluent peasant in his native area.[266] The long article with its numerous illustrations was complimentary of Schmitthenner's work, praising what Hegemann would later condemn in his book review.

In a letter of November 1932 Hegemann asked Schickele to read his review of *Das Deutsche Wohnhaus*, because it mentioned him several times. He also asked Schickele, who was Jewish and, like Hegemann, a pacifist, where he stood regarding the Schmitthenner affair. Hegemann confessed that hardly anything in his circle of friends had hurt him more deeply than Schmitthenner's voicing support for Hitler. He concluded, "suddenly everything regarding Schmitthenner became questionable for me . . . ," and mentioned that in composing the essay, he had attempted to ignore the architect's "political aberration." Schickele's letter, which is not available, pleased Hegemann, who did not agree that Alsace should be considered German, at least not in the sense Schmitthenner gave to that designation. Hegemann awaited Schickele's permission to bring the author's letter to Schmitthenner's attention.

Hegemann's review took the form of a letter addressed to "*Lieber Herr* Schmitthenner," and responded to the architect's invitation to write an "in-depth review" of his book. Hegemann reminded the architect that he had never reacted angrily to his criticism, and called attention to the numerous occasions he had pointed out his refined sense of form and masterful command of construction methods. However, he noted that the book delivered weapons into the hands of Schmitthenner's opponents. Assuming an adversarial role, Hegemann proceeded to demonstrate, point by point, the architect's lack of rationality and his *Unsachlichkeit* in the text and illustrations of *Das Deutsche Wohnhaus*. As he had mentioned to Schickele, he disagreed with the architect's considering Alsace and its traditions German instead of *alemannisch*, as Schickele would do. Hegemann ridiculed and proved Schmitthenner's cherished tradition to be *alemannish* and provincial rather than *deutsch*. The emphasis on "*deutsch*" in the title of the book, throughout the text, and in the dedication to "Theodor Fischer *dem deutschen Baumeister gewidmet*" (Theodore Fischer the German architect) was for Hegemann an indication of the architect's "political aberration." In the short section "*Von deutscher Baukunst und von der Tradition*" (On German architecture and on tradition) following Schmitthenner's Introduction, the word "*deutsch*" was repeated five times on the first half page.[267] Further on, Schmitthenner commented on "*fremde Art*" (foreign customs) as the "*Zerstörer der Tradition*" (destroyers of tradition) and summarized this in a manifesto-like declaration:

> And therefore German builders should start out from what is our own native character, if they want to serve German architecture, and thereby want to contribute toward the development of a new German culture. And therefore also all striving toward an international architecture will lead to the absence of culture, and we have to reject it as in the deepest sense foreign.

While Hegemann refrained from using political arguments in his letter,

Peter Meyer directed barbs against Schmitthenner for building only for the affluent class and using the *Völkisch, Deutschtümlich* (vernacular for "Germanic") as a political weapon against the international functionalism.[268] In most aspects the two reviews were comparable and complemented each other.

It was painful for Schmitthenner to be told by Hegemann that he was not traditional in the sense of Karl Friedrich Schinkel. Hegemann agreed with a range of others in admiring Schinkel as a precursor of the best and most valid contemporary "*Formtradition.*" The comment about Schmitthenner's misunderstood Classicism was supported in the sharp criticism of specific aspects of his work, many of which Hegemann had formerly praised. For instance, he now objected to the pitched roof and small windows, placed to conform to the appearance of the facade or "face" of the building. When Schmitthenner pointed out Hegemann's inconsistencies, the latter countered that in eight years as a critic and practicing architect he had the right to acquire additional insight. In Hegemann's copy of the book his notations, some unfortunately barely legible, reveal him to be a reader with a keen eye for discrepancies. Marked in the book and singled out in the review are Schmitthenner's contradictory statements on "*Technik*," all in short sequence:

> The meaning of technology and industry replaced the standard of quality with that of quantity, and this was the reason for its turning alien to culture. (p. 5)
>
> The victory march of technology threatens to totally trample the land of humanity. (p. 8)
>
> Our machines are the best examples for rational thinking expressed in form. Here design has achieved the ultimate, simplest form, combined with the highest quality and obvious beauty. (p. 10)

Referring to the illustrations showing works exclusively by Schmitthenner, Hegemann penciled the ironic line, "My 18 houses are 'the German house.'" The notations in the book are more spontaneous and revealing than the fifteen-page typewritten draft for the letter-review, which contains only a few grammatical and editorial corrections in Hegemann's writing and was published in its entirety in *WMB*. Assuming that it was his first and only version for this important letter, its cogent argument and style are impressive and demonstrate his exceptional command of language.

Despite Hegemann's assurances at the end of the letter that he admired Schmitthenner's buildings and hoped for better work by him in the future, the architect was offended. He requested that his reply should be published in *WMB*. As an architect, he wrote, he considered himself a poor match for the "master of the pen." For this reason, Schmitthenner relied heavily on citing from Hegemann's earlier, favorable comments on his architecture that contrasted strikingly with those in the recent review. Even so, Schmitthenner lost out. Hegemann appended a lengthy postscript to the architect's letter, repeating his previous rebukes which declared the placement of windows *Fassadensklaverei* (enslavement by facades), noted the lack of natural illumination for interiors due to small windows, criticized the room layouts as awkward, and questioned the avoidance of the flat roof, as it was favored by Schinkel in many buildings.

Schmitthenner perceptively noted that it mattered far less to Hegemann to compose a serious review of the book than to write "one of his clever essays on '*bauliche Dinge*' [Matters of architecture]." Although this remark was not entirely correct, the "*Fall* Schmitthenner" represented an occasion for Hegemann to clarify his position regarding modern architecture and its future. *Das Deutsche Wohnhaus* signified a watershed and the pretext for recording and substantiating his ideas with obvious examples.

In the last paragraph of the postscript Hegemann mentioned a crucial experience that influenced his appraisal and change of heart regarding Schmitthenner. It was the subject of his essay "*Schinkelscher Geist in Südamerika*" (Schinkel's spirit in South America).[269] He summarized it briefly for its relevance:

> In South America it was an impressive experience for me to observe that traditional architecture, when it is not confined to old channels by romanticizing architects, develops quite freely with the use of new building materials for the manifestation of those new forms, which we call pretentiously 'Modernism.'"[270]

Hegemann's stay in Argentina in the fall of 1931 enhanced his awareness of those qualities in Schinkel's work which were most valuable for international Modernism. Upon his return, Schmitthenner's "German" houses impressed him not only as provincial, but also as anti-urban. While Hegemann was partial to single-family houses in a garden-city setting, he kept a cautious distance from the Heimatschutz Bund and its tenets, rejecting them as nationalist and anti-urban. Cultural and political developments reinforced his apprehension regarding the fanaticism emerging from the Heimatschutz. Nationalism represented a major threat to a united Europe and global brotherhood. Hegemann had always adhered to these convictions and was ready to defend them regardless of personal consequences.

Schinkel's Classicism was international and timeless and facilitated Hegemann's long-held ideas. At Wasmuth he consistently advocated an all-embracing approach toward coverage, a mandate supported by the publishers when they chose him as editor on the basis of his experience and outlook. In the aftermath of the Weissenhof Siedlung, he wrote about an "*Internationale Architektur*" that demonstrated an affinity beyond the obvious use of building materials such as steel, glass, and reinforced concrete, to include intellectual elements, preparing the way toward "*eine Art Internationale in der Architektur.*" The wording imparted a socialist connotation.[271]

Hegemann's alertness to worldwide concerns was reinforced by his journey to South America via Spain, which provided contacts with professionals in regions he had not previously visited. Another motivation came to him in corresponding with the French-born historian Albert Léon Guérard, a professor at Stanford University. Guérard's interests ranged from history and literature to city planning. In the spring of 1931, he wrote to Hegemann about his own books on Napoleon and his more recent *L'avenir de Paris: Urbanisme francais et urbanisme américain.*[272] Hegemann replied that he had received Guérard's initial letter upon his return from a brief visit to Paris, where he gathered material for a "*Steinerne* Paris," never completed. None of the many experts he had consulted there had mentioned Guérard's book to him. *L'avenir de Paris* proposed a "Greater Paris" comparable to the regional plans for other metropolises that had captured Hegemann's attention. City planning and French history were not the only interests they shared. Guérard's son, Albert J., wrote that his father spoke of Hegemann as "a kindred spirit, someone with whom he felt a close affinity." He described his father as "a socialist in principle, a free thinker, a believer in United Europe and a real world order, . . . a lover of city planning," and noted that he contributed to the Committee to Frame a World Constitution.

A. L. Guérard was also the foremost authority on and promoter of an "auxiliary language," a universal language to be understood internationally, which was a vital interest of Hegemann as well. In an obituary Guérard was praised as a true citizen of the world who respected the "infinite variety of unique individuals and the fundamental unity of the human race," preaching with eloquence that "no fraternity of nations can exist except in liberty and equality." Guérard and Hegemann never met personally and their correspondence was scant, yet for Hegemann the contact with a proponent of his most cherished ideals was encouraging. It occurred at a critical time in his life and at a juncture that foretold the end of his career as an architectural critic in Europe.

5. Life in Ideological Times

Alemannenstrasse 21

As Hegemann took up his post at Wasmuth in July 1922, ground was broken for the family house at Alemannenstrasse 21, in Nikolassee. In a letter written to her mother at the end of the month, Ida Belle Hegemann reported: "The cellar walls are already finished, and this week we hope to get part of the ground floor finished. . . . As Werner says: We are building on land that is not ours, building without a police permit, building without materials, without plans, without money!"[1] They did actually own the land but were still awaiting the final papers. Her tone reflected the economic conditions and rampant inflation prevailing in Germany at the time, a situation requiring quick decisions amidst continually rising prices. According to Ida Belle, their property was "a heavenly piece of land with many trees of all sorts, many shrubs, . . . within a five-minute walk from a chain of lakes (the Wannsee)."

While the workers were still painting and hammering downstairs, the family moved into the top two floors of their partially finished house. Hegemann's wife reported that her husband had begun to spend the greater part of his time at Wasmuth but soon embarked on lecture tours and consultations in various cities, which boosted their financial resources. His main income derived from his position at Wasmuth, and was supplemented by writing books and articles for other publications.[2]

Hegemann designed the Nikolassee house and was very proud of his only built work other than the residential developments in America. During their years in Berlin the Hegemann house, which is no longer standing, was a cherished refuge. Several exterior and interior views as well as floor plans are illustrated in *Moderne Villen and Landhäuser* (Modern villas and cottages, by H. de Fries (Figs. 43–46). The floor plans were also shown and discussed in Hegemann's article, "*Sklaven eines falsch verstandenen*

Klassizismus?"[3] De Fries described Hegemann's "country house" or "cottage" as "thriftily and functionally executed." It was built of stucco with a red tile roof and green shutters. Some aspects of it recalled American houses, such as the entrance porch with windows and built-in benches on each side. The low-pitched roof allowed for an attic, which was eventually used as Hegemann's work area and a guest room. On the ground floor a large "garden room" functioned as a music and dining room. It opened to the terrace and back yard. Next to this multipurpose family room were a library, a study, and the kitchen. Upstairs were three bedrooms, a maid's room, and one and a half bathrooms. In his article Hegemann defended his design from A. Klein's criticism regarding *Fassadensklaverei* (slavish dependence on the the design of the facade), implying that the symmetry of the facade did not correspond to the interior layout. Hegemann, however, admired the symmetry that existed in colonial-style houses in America. Klein objected to the circulation pattern of the ground floor in the house, particularly the somewhat awkward entrance to the garden room from the entrance hall. Countering Klein's criticism, Hegemann explained that the economic conditions of 1922 compelled him to make maximum use of limited space. Klein also disapproved of the long hall on the upper floor, and Hegemann explained that it was intended to shield the bedrooms from the noisy railroad adjacent to their property. The stairs and built-in closets acted as sound buffers as well. He commented that these explanations substantiated the need to appraise every house within the parameters of its time and place.

In order to accommodate the family that soon included four young children—Eva Maria, born in 1922, Idolene in 1924, Manfred in 1926, and Elinor in 1929—plus Hegemann's daughter, Ellis, during her school vacations, and frequent houseguests, the attic floor was built out and central heating installed. Houseguests often stayed for several weeks. Ida Belle's mother and other relatives came from America, as did Fiske and Marie Kimball. Raymond Unwin and his wife and Steen Eiler Rasmussen are also known to have visited. The Greek artist Markos Zavitzianos lived with the Hegemanns for some time, and in the late 1920s Hegemann's secretary, Günther Baum, resided upstairs.

The Hegemanns enjoyed offering hospitality to their friends. Ida Belle brought an open, casual lifestyle from America and liked having company and socializing with friends and neighbors, who frequently dropped by with their children. Compensating for the absence of warmth in his own childhood, Hegemann was a dedicated, fun-loving father and a devoted husband. His letters and postcards to his wife and children are affectionate, often filled with nostalgia and inquiring about the predicament on the home front. This side of Hegemann's character is obscured by his professional persona, which could be seen as arrogant. His private life in Nikolassee provides another aspect of Hegemann's personality.[4] Ida Belle

Fig. 43. Streetfront view of Hegemann's house in Nikolassee, designed by Hegemann, from H. de Fries, Moderne Villen und Landhäuser, *1924.*

Fig. 44. Hegemann's house, garden side.

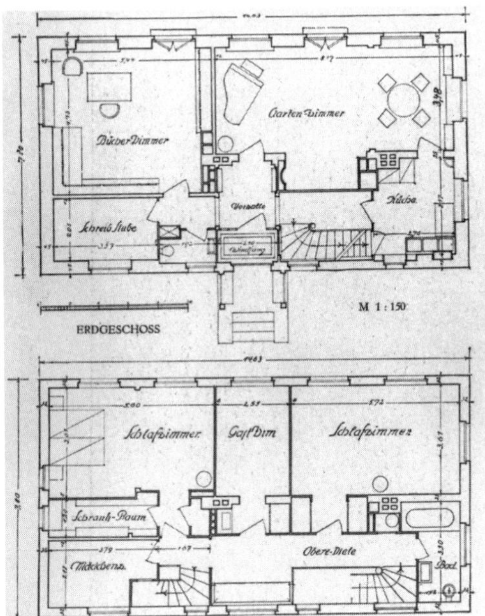

Fig. 45. Hegemann's house, layout of rooms and stair landing.

Fig. 46. Hegemann's house, view into the dining room.

shared with her husband a love of music and the theater, and they regularly attended concerts and plays. The family spoke English at home, partly to maintain privacy in front of their maid. Eva Maria Hegemann Ladd recalled that her mother had help from servants and that the family lived comfortably, and frequently entertained at home.

Ellis Hesse, Hegemann's daughter from his first marriage, was in her late teens when she became reacquainted with her father, whom she hardly knew, and his young family. She commented that Ida Belle was "warm and kind," but that her father "did not know how to handle an obstreperous teenager," and she never felt close to him. On the other hand, she wrote, "I always was fond of Ida Belle and the step-siblings."[5]

The social gatherings or informal salons at their house in Nikolassee included personal friends and people with intellectual and cultural interests. Among the visitors from abroad was the American historian and scholarly diplomat George F. Kennan, whose family knew Ida Belle Hegemann's family, the Guthes. In 1928, when he decided on a diplomatic career that would take him to Germany, his family facilitated a connection to the Hegemanns. Kennan described the social gatherings in Nikolassee in the years 1929–30 as lively and intellectually stimulating, and Hegemann as "charismatic."[6]

Another participant was Fritz H. Landshoff, whose career in publishing began in 1924, as co-owner of the Gustav Kiepenheuer Verlag in Potsdam, which brought out many well-known authors whose works, like Hegemann's, were burned in May 1933. Threatened because he was Jewish and considered a *Kulturbolschewist* (cultural Bolshevist) by the Nazis, Landshoff left Berlin in January 1933. In Amsterdam he headed the "*Exilverlag Querido*" and founded the periodical *Die Sammlung*. In 1941 he fled to the United States, where he later joined Harry N. Abrams, Inc. In an interview at the age of eighty-one, Landshoff referred to Hegemann as "*der leider heute kaum noch bekannte Werner Hegemann*" (W. H. who today, unfortunately, is barely known). He remembered little of their contact, other than having discussed with Ida Belle the possibility of hiding some of his papers in their house before leaving for Amsterdam, but they had decided that it was too dangerous. He regretted that after they left Berlin in 1933, he lost touch with Hegemann, while "in the last few years before our emigration I did have regular contact with him and published an important book of his, *Das steinerne Berlin*."[7]

The author Arnold Zweig and his wife Beatrice were friends and neighbors of the Hegemanns in Nikolassee. The friendship continued by letter after the Zweigs left Germany in January 1933 and settled in Haifa, and the Hegemanns reached New York in the fall of that year. Both authors had published with Kiepenheuer Verlag and contributed to *Die Weltbühne*, the venue for left-wing intellectuals opposing Nazism. The strong mutual bonds and esteem between Arnold Zweig and Hegemann are eloquently expressed by Zweig in letters, a commemorative essay in the *Neue Weltbühne*, and in the section "*Meine Nachbarn*" in his book *Über Schriftsteller, 1936*.[8] Hegemann was among many neighbors who were authors, and Zweig, in describing frequent meetings with him and visits to his home, evoked him as "this city planner, who knew the world better than any one of us, was, regarding interior politics, the most sagacious supporter of German culture, perceived by him as a citizen of the world, and expressed with utmost urbanity. He was the best citizen among all of us." Zweig's commemorative essay in the *Neue Weltbüihne*, "*Auch* Werner Hegemann . . . ," of June 1936, has been reprinted variously with justification, and is featured as the introduction to a reprint edition of Hegemann's *Entlarvte Geschichte*.[9] It was a moving tribute to Hegemann the person and the intellectual representing the best of European culture, and as a perceptive historian "who lived wholeheartedly in the present, working for the future." Zweig esteemed him as a *Baumeister und Städteplaner*, who excelled as an author and enriched literature as an "important and productive outsider." Zweig's elegy is also a lament for a vanishing culture and those who represented it, now dead or scattered to the far corners of the world, "while the howling and the misrepresentations of mind-destructing madness pours down day after day on the ears of the easily confused people of central Europe."

Many of the Hegemanns' acquaintances left Germany after 1933, and some have provided rare insights into times long past. Lene Shulof, living in London, wrote regarding Hegemann, "I mostly remember his strong personality which so often led to spirited conversations; I remember his biting wit, his graceful gallantries—in short (as Ida Belle has told you)—I remember him as '*den letzten Ritter*' [the last knight]."[10]

Enlightening comments regarding the manner in which Hegemann conducted his work with his colleagues at his Wasmuth office are revealed in letters by his longtime assistant Margret Ohlischlaeger von Bismarck. Ostensibly employed as a secretary although she had a doctorate in "*Germanistik*," she was soon asked by Hegemann to edit and translate English articles. One of two informative letters was written in 1936 to Ida Belle upon the death of her husband.[11] Fearing repercussions in Nazi Germany if she addressed a letter to Hegemann in America, Ohlischlaeger took advantage of a vacation in Italy to write. She mentioned that she had learned "crucial things" while working for Hegemann at Wasmuth. What she admired foremost was his "intellectual swordplay" and his "incorruptible critical judgment." She had appreciated "a comradeship between a boss and his staff, so unusual in Germany." She described Hegemann as a "most strenuously engaged and un-slacking worker at his task, often requiring one hour to arrive at the proper wording of a passage." She mentioned that Hegemann's colleague Hans Josef Zechlin did not dare to write from Berlin, because he was suspected by the Nazis for his collaboration with Hegemann.

Years later, at the age of eighty-three, Margret Ohlischlaeger von Bismarck wrote that her memories were now affected by her age.[12] But her recollections complemented what she had written to Ida Belle. Hegemann had selected her to assist him at Wasmuth at the beginning of organizing his editorial office, and she was the last to bid him farewell when he said goodbye to his staff in February 1933, looking "very thin and pale." He developed a staff of colleagues with a team spirit that was considered "*amerikanisch*." She recalled being given an article on vernacular buildings on the Greek island of Santorini, showing cubic forms and flat roofs, which "Hegemann defended pugnaciously as a principle of modern design against the furious protests of the conservative architects." Her assessment of Hegemann's position regarding the contemporary discord differs from what was commonly attributed to him; she added, "At this time of opposing movements of modernity and of conservative nationalism, W. H. was a troublesome witness." He certainly did not lack "polemic sharpness" and had "adversaries even at the publisher. . . . He had robbed the homey little German house of its lustre. . . . In short, he was controversial, but we young colleagues, who despised the national dirt, were proud of him."

These evocations supplement the impressions of Hegemann derived from letters and diaries, the *Family Saga*, and correspondence with and from others. In addition, the occasion of his fiftieth birthday in 1931 generated numerous statements of friendship and esteem. A private celebration took place at Alemannenstrasse 21. According to his wife, "Twenty-five people came to help celebrate Werner's 50th birthday, on Sunday, June 14." She describes flower arrangements and gifts, and continues, "The architects presented him with a large book, bound in parchment, a wonderful praise of him as to personality, work, influence, etc. After a few hours some went home, but 16 stayed for an impromptu supper. After supper the Grammaphone was turned on in the *Gartenzimmer* and people danced there or on the terrace. But the real birthday was Monday. There was a huge cake with 50 candles on it. . . ." More gifts arrived, " . . . and all day telegrams from all over the world. . . . Mr. Wynand brought the bust he had made of W. H. in bronze."[13]

The official celebration was planned by a steering committee of twenty, which included Paul Bonatz, Hermann Dernburg, the brothers Gerson, Alexander Klein, Paul Schmitthenner, Hans Josef Zechlin, and Paul Zucker. Zechlin was at that time the editor of *WMB/STB*, and Hegemann and Günther Wasmuth were listed as publishers. The steering committee issued its letter announcing the celebration for Hegemann on stationery with the Wasmuth address, but without the name. On May 21, 1931, one hundred invitations were sent out with copies of the dedication, asking the recipients for their signatures and comments. The committee hoped the recipients were in agreement with the content of the dedication. Ninety replies were received from within the country and from abroad.[14]

On his birthday, Hegemann was presented with the large leather-bound volume, a *Festschrift* in his honor, containing the dedication written in elegant calligraphy. The summary of his career contained a few errors, which were corrected in *WMB/STB* (see below). The dedication concludes:

> Not only with your scholarly work you have influenced the development in architecture and city planning, but also as editor of the periodicals "WMB" and "STB", independent of all partisanship in daily struggle you have served with unwavering courage the great concerns of architecture. The belief that is basic to your critical work seems to us best expressed in Alberti's proud words:
>
> *Praeterea quae scribimus, ea nos non sed humanitati scribimus.*
>
> (Moreover, those things which we write, we write not for ourselves but for humanity.)

The dedication proceeded to connect Alberti's maxim to Hegemann's admiration of classic works, declaring that he never tired of holding them up as models for the present. This statement did not accurately represent Hegemann's convictions, and it elicited objections from some of his colleagues, including Steen Eiler Rasmussen and the brothers Luckhardt. Other comments in the dedication emphasized Hegemann's role in promulgating architecture from abroad in Germany and disseminating German works internationally.

The album contained loose sheets signed by a worldwide coterie of friends and acquaintances. Some of the signatures were accompanied by personal tributes, although even just the signatures of individuals such as Peter Behrens or Martin Wagner were an honor for Hegemann, with whom they had formerly disagreed.

A number of those who endorsed the dedication wrote commentaries that convey a great deal in a succinct phrase. Among the latter is Adolf Loos's brief, "To the thinker [*Denker*] among the architects! With gratitude and regards Adolf Loos." Paul Westheim used his calling card to make a play of words on Hegemann's book *Das steinerne Berlin*, "Heartfelt congratulations in the name of non-petrified Berliners, if I had a mandate." A reference to the *fruchtbare Kritik* debacle in connection with the Bau-Ausstellung came from Paul Zucker: "With sincere gratitude for your productive criticism with heartfelt esteem." Fritz Höger recognized Hegemann as "The great promoter of architecture to whom Germany and foreign nations owe so much." A brief and fitting comment arrived from Sverre Pedersen, "No one else in our time has such great personal knowledge of all town planning as W. H. His intellect shines clear and bright in a tumultuous time."

J. J. P. Oud's astute observation, "I seldom share your point of view and nearly always learn from you" was cited in the review of the birthday honors in *WMB/STB*. Hegemann's reply, enclosed in a carbon copy in the album, expressed "great joy," at Oud's greeting, coming after their relationship had cooled with the Bau-Ausstellung debacle. He hoped that the architect's health had improved. Asking for new work to publish in *WMB*, Hegemann mentioned that works by several architects close to Oud had recently been shown in the periodical. Among them were Mendelsohn, the Luckhardts, and Martin Wagner, previously alienated and adhering to the boycott.

Preserved in the album is Erich Mendelsohn's frequently cited telegram, "I wish you well, but above all keep your sharp tongue. We will provide the whetstone." Hegemann's thank-you letter elaborated on Mendelsohn's theme: "Your comparison with the whetstone is very witty. It could be vastly expanded. Because one would have to discover who is the sharp polished one and who is the blunt one and who is the polisher, or if it might be a knife-grinder. . . . I suggest that we do not continue to spin this comparison along, but rather continue to live in harmony, also in the future, as we have done previously."[15] Hegemann's play on words loses something in translation. The reference to their harmonious relationship is perhaps optimistic as it had experienced many ups-and-downs, and the following year would bring further disagreement over Mendelsohn's villa and his "*Der Schöpferische Sinn der Krise*."

There are other compelling commentaries. Karl Heinrich Brunner, the Viennese city planner and editor of *Baupolitik*, which was published with *WMB/STB* four times yearly, wrote from Santiago, Chile, where he was active as a consultant at the invitation of the government: "As one who appreciates your impressions based on your engagement in the cultural leadership in Germany in a young welcoming nation in a distant region, I add my good wishes to those of your colleagues, your sincerely devoted KHB." Also from the Southern Cone came greetings to the "distinguished intellectual" from Angel Guido in Rosario, Argentina, whom Hegemann would soon meet in person during his stay in that country.

Iván Kotsis, professor at the University of Budapest, recognized the great value that Hegemann's publications had for Hungarian professionals because of the similarity of their search for an appropriate solution for contemporary problems in architecture and city planning within their own country and in Germany. A comparable recognition came from Ivan Vurnik at Ljubljana University: "Your work '*Der Städtebau*' 1911/13 is truly a treasure trove for the study of town planning. I consider it an honor to be permitted to sign for the architects of Yugoslavia." Other greetings from abroad included those from John Nolen and Elbert Peets from the United States, Raymond and Ethel Unwin, F. R. Yerbury, Robert Mallet-Stevens, Auguste Perret, and several architects and urbanists from the Scandinavian countries, Finland, and Czechoslovakia.

The architects Hans, Oskar, and Ernst Gerson, "the Brothers Gerson," wrote a separate letter in addition to signing the declaration, which they believed insufficient to express their "admiration for [Hegemann's] ruthless courage" with which he defended "reason," "clarity," and "functionalism" in architecture, and they equally expressed admiration for the courage with which he was conducting the battle for reason in matters of ideology and history. "This battle is aimed at the gigantic shadows of warring 'heroes'; . . . and no battle requires more courage than the battle for the ideas of peace."

Steen Eiler Rasmussen objected to the passage in the dedication stating that Hegemann always held up Classicism as a model for the present. In his birthday greetings Rasmussen was full of admiration: "Your town planning, and also your political-historical publications, have been a major revelation for me. They have influenced my work and my belief so profoundly that I would like to celebrate you at any time—especially when it can be done in a way that does not inhibit you as the intelligent, stimulating and independent Hegemann."

The architects Luckhardt provided an explanation of the album's passage on Classicism that came closer to Hegemann's own point of view. "You see the past free of trite Romanticism. As you single out clearly and courageously what is true and false in tradition, we are convinced that, nourished by your intrinsic youthfulness, you will continue to contribute to the re-creation of our time and its exemplary architecture."

Alexander Klein signed the dedication expressing his heartfelt gratitude for Hegemann's fundamental support, noting that he had been the first in Germany to show interest in his work. In a letter accompanied by a flower, Klein hoped that Hegemann would not object to this gift, because it was neither *statisch* nor *dynamisch*. If it delighted him, it would assure Klein that, "in spite of his custom," he would occasionally have "romantic" feelings. Hegemann's reply emphasized his feelings of kinship with Klein, who was in empathy with his own exceptional and painful predicament as an outsider. He confessed this with unusual candor: "Because of your emigration from Russia, where you had a leading appointment, to Berlin where you had to start everything all over again, you find yourself in a predicament very similar to my own. Before the war I had considerable success in Berlin, then was forced by the war to build up a new practice in America, and upon returning home, I stood there as a foreigner."

Among Hegemann's literary friends, Hermann Kesten, editor at Kiepenheuer Verlag, signed the declaration noting: "Your literary-critical knowledge represents an endeavor of enlightenment for which the practicing architects cannot be sufficiently grateful." Kesten also sent a telegram: "In admiration and esteem for your varied and extensive knowledge and your exceptional personality, I wish you heartfelt congratulations on your fiftieth birthday." Hegemann also received a long telegram from Kiepenheuer Verlag that praised him for a range of accomplishments, and as an "exemplary author, . . . stylist, . . . and champion for truth, justice and public well-being, and a kind *Mensch*." In his reply to Hermann

Kesten, Hegemann apologized for the delay in finishing his manuscript for the publisher. He reported that his wife was going on a seven-week vacation to the seaside with their four children, who were recovering from the measles. In their absence he was planning to closet himself in the attic to work, and the lower floors would be rented out for the duration.[16]

Berthold Jacob, contributor to the *Weltbühne*, and only recently released from a prison sentence, informed Hegemann of the latest Nazi attacks on Jews in addition to conveying good wishes to his friend. He considered that Hegemann's work was not receiving enough recognition, adding, "I am convinced that if, as I assume, your own plans and goals lie in the political arena, you will encounter welcome possibilities in the coming years."

Both Ewald and Günther Wasmuth wrote long letters to their effective, although occasionally troublesome, editor. G. Wasmuth was at this time listed together with Hegemann as *Herausgeber* of the combined periodicals that were experiencing financial difficulties. In his long personal letter Wasmuth expressed his hope that Hegemann would find a teaching position: "Particularly I would welcome it, if a teaching position might give you the possibility of making your valuable knowledge and experience available to a young generation, and this would provide to you in addition to intellectual also material benefits for a life free of worries." During his decade in Berlin Hegemann apparently did not entertain possibilities for an academic career. As Wasmuth pointed out, a teaching position would have fostered disciples among the younger generation, who would have carried his concepts forward and might have prevented the obscurity that engulfed him after his death. In the course of his search for income when he arrived in New York in 1933, he taught with considerable success at the New School for Social Research and at the School of Architecture at Columbia University. Previously, while "stranded" in the American Midwest, he had explored establishing a department of city planning at Harvard University.

An interesting factor mentioned by G. Wasmuth is that they had met in the United States almost ten years earlier without anticipating the future outcome of their encounter. Eventually Hegemann became editor of the journals and developed considerable influence in Germany. Wasmuth noted that despite certain disagreements, they agreed on basic points and shared a strong desire to advance the periodicals. He was hoping that the economic climate would improve and that they would continue to work together. Wasmuth's comment regarding their meeting in America is the only mention of it, and there is no hint in the descriptions of his interviews with publishers upon his return to Berlin.

Ewald Wasmuth had left the publishing house in 1929 and was living in southern Germany near the Bodensee when he wrote to Hegemann. He admired Hegemann's aggressive stand and criticism, even if he was not always in conformity with him. Hegemann's long, friendly response welcomed E. Wasmuth's hope for a rapprochement between critics and those criticized, and he reported his surprise upon receiving congratulations from all camps of the architectural debate. An exception was Poelzig, who had not forgiven Hegemann's remarks on his sixtieth birthday. Hegemann wished to obtain a copy of a new book by E. Wasmuth and promised to read it. In this connection he mentioned lectures by Veidt Valentin and Husserl at the Berlin University, which signaled a change in the political education of the students. Margret Ohlischlaeger's regard for the collaborative atmosphere at the publisher is substantiated in Hegemann's acknowledgment to the clerks and employees of Wasmuth. He expressed his gratitude and joy over the fact that they considered him "one of them" and could not wish for anything more in the future.

The birthday volume also comprised greetings in the form of letters, cards, and telegrams as well as carbon copies of some of Hegemann's letters of appreciation. Some of his letters expressed his wish for contributions to the periodicals and his hopes of renewing contacts after misunderstandings such as those with Bruno and Max Taut and Bernhard Dernburg.

Among Hegemann's replies is one directed to Dr. Giedion, Internationaler Kongress für neues Bauen, Zürich, Dolderyal 7. He thanked him for his note, which is not included in the album, and asked him to clarify a contradiction. Giedion had asked to have a certain news item published, but then added that the matter was not really intended for the public. This brief communication represents the only trace of contact between Hegemann and the Congrès Internationaux d'Architecture Moderne (CIAM). However, a newspaper report on the third CIAM, held in Brussels in 1930, and probably written by Giedion, stated that their position was that "the city must more or less lose its stony character," while retaining some of its density. The reference was to Hegemann's *Das steinerne Berlin*.[17]

Hegemann's birthday celebration was a welcome event at a time when his career was fraught with stress. Mounting political and economic tensions contributed to a low point in his life. Recognition and esteem were voiced by many people who represented the gamut of his interests in architecture, city planning, literature, politics, and social commitment. The tributes resemble a compendium of obituaries, eerily anticipating a "death foretold." The acknowledgments advance our understanding of Hegemann's complex intellectual and professional career, especially considering the disappearance of the correspondence from the Wasmuth offices, and close a gap in the records of a pivotal decade in Hegemann's life.

The occasion was written up in *WMB/STB*, once again published jointly for economic reasons.[18] The dedication was reprinted with a footnote correcting factual errors in the description of Hegemann's early career.

It explained that he had not been the secretary of the Zweckverband für Gross-Berlin, but rather the honorary business manager for several community organizations, including the Propaganda-Ausschuss für Gross-Berlin.[19] The list of signers is reprinted with excerpts from some of their comments, such as those by Rasmussen and the Luckhardts. Two illustrations accompany the account; one shows Hegemann in the Luckhardts' studio with one of the architects contemplating the model of the revised version of the Haus Berlin for the Potsdamer Platz.[20] The other illustration is of the bronze portrait bust by Paul Wynand.

Included in the *WMB/STB* write-up is Hegemann's speech upon receiving the album. He addressed in particular some of the remarks regarding his role as a critic, a topic of persistent concern for him. On this festive occasion, his touch was light, and he told the audience that it was a rare privilege to receive recognition for his "conscientious endeavor." In jest he said that upon reviewing the friendly remarks by the well-wishers, his critical work might come to an end, as now he would be able to express only favorable opinions. "In the future I will have to be quiet!" As he uttered this, Paul Mebes interrupted, shouting, "At last, we have succeeded!" Hegemann continued that after further consideration of the declaration, he should perhaps engage in renewed, ruthless action, because so many architects from within and outside the country, whom he had sharply confronted, had nonetheless signed. He was impressed by the equanimity of his colleagues, but he would restrain himself from assuming that everything was permitted. Wilhelm Kreis noted, "If he says yes or no, W. H.'s opinion is for us a matter of conscience, never damaging, because it is honest and informed, and therefore always valuable." Hegemann replied, "On the contrary, because of the indulgence shown to me, I will be obliged from now on to adhere to greater accuracy, so that the generous opinion of Professor Kreis, to be 'never damaging,' will also be true in the future. The times are becoming increasingly serious, and therefore criticism must also become more serious!"

Hegemann may have had a premonition that his fiftieth birthday was not only a chronological landmark but also a turning point in his active life. He anticipated that his position at Wasmuth would end. It was opportune that in mid-July he had been approached to lecture and consult in Argentina. He accepted the offer and departed the following month.

Urban Interchange in the Southern Cone

The multiple tensions impinging on Hegemann in the spring of 1931 rendered the suggestion to lecture and consult in Argentina most welcome. The invitation provided the possibility of loosening the increasingly strained bonds with Wasmuth. The publisher was experiencing economic difficulties

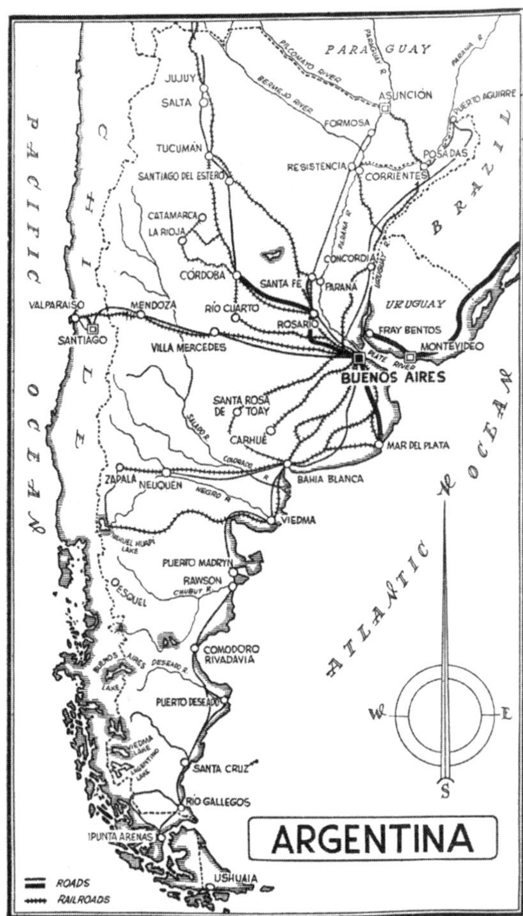

Fig. 47. Plan of the Southern Cone of South America. CCCC

and feared repercussions from the anti-Nazi stance of its well-known editor, whose attention was shifting from architecture and city planning to political concerns. Extricating himself from this among other troublesome situations, Hegemann departed from Berlin shortly after his birthday in August 1931. He was eager to familiarize himself with a part of the world he had not previously visited. It is unlikely that he anticipated the impact the urban interchange in the Southern Cone would have on his ideas (Fig. 47). Hegemann's three-month sojourn and immersion in Latin American subjects central to his knowledge have been overshadowed by the circumstances preceding his exile, and have not received merited attention.

The rapid development of South American cities in the late nineteenth century and a growing awareness that city planning required specialized knowledge created a climate that welcomed experts from abroad. Among those arriving in the Southern Cone during the first decades of the twentieth century were Joseph Antoine Bouvard, Jean Claude Nicolas Forestier, Léon Jaussely, and Alfred Agache from France, and Karl Heinrich Brunner from Austria. Le Corbusier's presence in Buenos Aires, Montevideo, and Brazil in 1929 is considered to have led to the overtures extended to Hegemann.[21] Both urbanists were aware of their predecessors, some of whom continued to be active in the region. Le Corbusier and Hegemann made their entry on the scene at a time when the international modern movement and national identities were contending for new ground, creating an ambient that presented them with unexpected challenges. Their responses and influence were notably different. However, both were affected by the South American exposure in a reverse transfer of ideas regarding the built environment. The effects on Le Corbusier's architecture and urbanism are reflected in his work and writings. Hegemann expressed himself in the lectures he gave in Argentina and Uruguay, reported in the local press, the pamphlets published during his visit, and a series of articles in *WMB/STB* and the *Berliner Tageblatt*. These articles and the drafts of his lectures reveal the influences, including dialogues with local planners and architects. The result was a distillation of Hegemann's planning concepts and, notably, of his views regarding modern architecture.

Hegemann's eagerness to travel contributed to the circuitous route he took to reach Buenos Aires. He journeyed from Berlin to Hamburg for discussions with Fritz Schumacher, and then by airplane to Cologne and Essen for a meeting with Robert Schmidt regarding the Ruhrsiedlungsverband. Both visits were used to gather additional material for an exhibition loaned to him by the Bund Deutscher Architekten to be shown in Argentina. Considering the exhibition somewhat conservative and lacking in city planning, Hegemann added photographs of work by Mendelsohn and the Luckhardt brothers, as well as views of open space systems. His voyage also included a stop in Paris and Marseilles, he then flew over the Pyrenees to Barcelona, where he had his first look at Antonio Gaudí's buildings. In Madrid he acquainted himself with the Ciudad Lineal and established contacts with Spanish architectural journals, to which he later contributed.[22] After a few days in Lisbon he boarded the *Antonio Delfino* on August 8, crossing the Atlantic with a stop at Tenerife in the Canary Islands.

In daily letters Hegemann reported to his wife on his travels and later his experiences in the Southern Cone.[23] Several of the letters—some in German, others in English—were written while he was onboard the *Antonio Delfino*, and were mailed from Tenerife, Rio de Janeiro, and Montevideo. In one letter, Hegemann wrote:

> Lissabon is the most beautiful city one can imagine. Similar to Paris and Madrid, she has the advantage of a topography of various heights as well as the ocean, reminiscent of Naples, fantastic, wonderful! Every new trip by tram, automobile, elevator (lift), or by trains ascending the mountains reveals new unexpected and astonishing views. For instance, one train took me to an

> aqueduct of the most impressive Roman beauty. An elevator lifted me over the *Rocío*—meaning "dew"—a beautiful plaza [shown in Hegemann & Peets, *Vitruvius*]. Located on the summit is a Gothic church in ruins, apparently damaged by the major earthquake which caused the young Goethe to have his first doubts regarding God's wisdom. The Plaza del Comercio on the shore of the mighty Tejo River with steps leading down to the salty water [flowing in from the estuary of the ocean]—which I tasted—is of unequalled beauty.

While enjoying the tranquility on the ocean Hegemann recalled "streetscapes of phantastic audacity" perceived on the Iberian Peninsula. He took Spanish lessons, reading only in that language, and sought out Spanish-speaking passengers for conversation, fretting in his letters that he relied on Italian words. When he arrived in Buenos Aires three weeks later, he managed fairly well in the language and gave his lectures in Spanish from the texts translated for him. Among his acquaintances on the ship was an architect from Buenos Aires with whom he could discuss the city's plan. A group of South American passengers organized a tour of Rio de Janeiro in an open automobile, motivating Hegemann to observe that the city was "unsurpassable as a stage-setting, incredible and tropically phantastic."

The *Antonio Delfino* docked in Montevideo, Uruguay, on August 26, 1931, and arrived in Buenos Aires the following day. The interlude of the sea voyage prepared Hegemann for the challenges awaiting him in an unknown country, where his arrival was anticipated with high expectations, enhanced by the rumor that he had been invited to counteract the visit of Le Corbusier in 1929. Comments regarding the latter were still circulating, referring in particular to the architect having brought his proposal for the complete urban reorganization of Buenos Aires in his suitcase, based on plans he had envisioned for the French capital. Presented with this assessment, Hegemann tactfully mentioned that Le Corbusier had assumed similarities between Paris and Buenos Aires. Indeed, Argentina's capital proudly claimed her status as "The Paris of South America," and aspired to French sophistication.

Members of the social elite of Buenos Aires, owners of vast *estancias* in the *pampas* (plains), emulated France with virtual obsession. They dreamed of converting the capital of their country into a replica of Paris, where many of them spent considerable time. The well-known author Victoria Ocampo belonged to this coterie and associated with the Amigos del Arte, who were dedicated to stimulating local artists and writers and bringing visitors from abroad. Encouraged by Ocampo, who knew Le Corbusier from her extended stays in France, the Amigos de Arte had sponsored his visit. The architect was welcomed by an audience anxious for an infusion of French culture. Le Corbusier's proposal for Buenos Aires resembled his "Plan for a Contemporary City of Three Million" (1922) and the "Plan Voisin" of 1925. Speaking in French, he presented it to his audience soon after gaining initial impressions of the city on the La Plata river. He had not pursued contacts with local urbanists regarding their ideas for improving the congested city with its tight grid plan and a notorious lack of open space.[24]

Hegemann's sojourn, on the other hand, was sponsored by the Amigos de la Ciudad, composed primarily of professionals and city officials exploring solutions for the shortcomings that were preventing Buenos Aires from functioning as a modern metropolis. They turned to Hegemann based on his reputation as an international expert with a theoretical and historical grasp of city planning in the broadest sense. He was suggested to the Amigos de la Ciudad by the American planner George B. Ford, and, most significantly, by Carlos María della Paolera, a pioneer urbanist in Argentina. Della Paolera had studied at the Institut d'Urbanisme in Paris and although he had not met Hegemann previously, their shared methodology combining a scientific approach with an affinity for the culture and historical evolution of cities became the basis for a cordial friendship. The mutual recognition of their expertise facilitated Hegemann's activities in Argentina, which consisted of consultations with local urbanists and authorities, lectures, the exhibitions, the screening of a film, and two reports. The articles published upon his return to Germany in 1932 furthered international awareness of South American accomplishments. Hegemann's visit evolved into an effective catalyst for moving urbanism and architecture in Argentina and the Southern Cone region toward self-assured independence from Europe.

He encountered this region of the "new" world with an open mind and without preconceptions. Following his earlier practice in the United States, he surveyed the city and its surroundings, as well as the built, natural, and cultural environments, prior to composing his lectures and offering recommendations. In his diary, Hegemann noted his hesitancy to do so: "The greatest danger of city planning [is] the misunderstandings, the misapplication of outdated concepts to new situations. It is almost impossible to make oneself understood by/to a public, which one does not know well." Nevertheless his hosts were impressed and supported his interests with a crowded program of tours by automobile and airplane, social gatherings, and discussions. Included were visits to slaughterhouses and refrigeration plants essential to Argentina's economy, which relied on exporting meat to Europe. Hegemann preferred Argentinian contacts and sought to avoid members of the German community, who were beginning to embrace Nazism. Information about Hegemann's political leanings had not preceded him across the Atlantic, and there was no hesitation to celebrate the expert from Berlin.

In his letters to his wife, Hegemann related his activities and concerns. Among his activities was a twenty-minute airplane survey of Buenos Aires, during which he made a film. He commented: "I am enthusing myself here

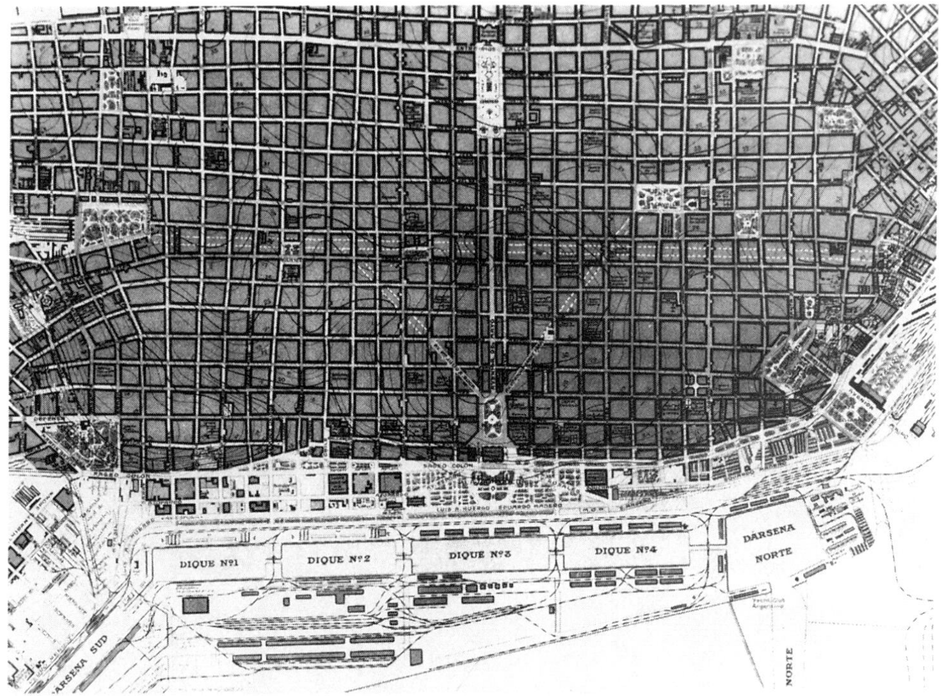

Fig. 48. Plan of the center of Buenos Aires showing projected streets intersecting the historic grid, ca. 1930. CCCC

about the possibilities of this fantastic city, and then again, I feel sick at heart because after all, what can I do?" Struggling to prepare the first of his lectures in Spanish, he reported, "I am working with all my might to produce lectures adapted to local conditions and to have them translated into decent Spanish."[25] The translator was J. B. Jaimes Répide, the secretary of the Amigos de la Ciudad, and he was assisted by Della Paolera, which generated lively discussions with Hegemann. Presumably they relied on French as a common language. The official "Report" by the Amigos notes that the success of Hegemann's presentations was due to Jaimes Répide's effort to render the lectures into Spanish under considerable time pressure.[26]

Hegemann's lectures were open to the public and accompanied by slides, many from photographs taken locally. The drafts of seven lectures in Spanish are preserved, though the plan to publish them in their entirety in Buenos Aires was not carried out.[27] Among the topics he addressed were the congestion and lack of open space in the center of Buenos Aires, which he called a *Häuserwüste* (wasteland of houses), drawing comparisons to European and North American cities. It was commonly assumed that these problems, which had preoccupied local urbanists and citizens, resulted from the tight grid plan of the colonial Spanish city (Fig. 48). According to

Fig. 49. Jorge Kalnay's model of a building block following the building ordinances of 1928, from WMB/STB, *February, 1933.* WHA

Hegemann, the density of the historic plan had actually been worsened by the building regulations intended to bring about improvements. In particular, a 1928 ordinance limited the building height at the street frontage but permitted unlimited height in the interior of the block. According to Hegemann this absurdity was a contributing factor that would allow the population in central Buenos Aires to increase to 160 million in the foreseeable future. The architect Jorge Kalnay built a model of one of these superblocks, which took advantage of the ordinance (Fig. 49). The model was displayed at the exhibitions, generating lively discussions. Kalnay, from a Hungarian family, had studied in Germany and acted as Hegemann's able interpreter and assistant in Buenos Aires.

In his lectures, Hegemann defended the open-ended "*dámero*" grid of the historic city core and disapproved of the insertion of diagonals à la Haussmann. Following the recommendations of the French planner J. A. Bouvard, diagonals approaching and intersecting the Plaza de Mayo had been implemented, resulting in chamfered building lots and awkward intersections. Hegemann was prone to compare situations in Argentina with those he had observed in Europe and America. To represent diagonals inflicted upon grid plans, he referred to Philadelphia. Bad examples from abroad were introduced to lift local self-esteem. Hegemann suggested that the problems of congestion and absence of open space ought to be addressed by converting central Buenos Aires into the geographic nodal point of a vast metropolitan region interconnected by a radial transportation network with arteries fanning out to the periphery (Fig. 50). Schemes along these lines had been proposed previously, but without the ambitious scope of a comprehensive master plan. Hegemann called attention to the *Ruhr-Siedlungsverband*, which encompassed industrial development, transportation, housing, and designated vast open spaces for a park system. The attractive results of large-scale planning were featured in the 1930 film *Die Stadt von Morgen* (The city of tomorrow), by Sven Nolden, M. V.Goldbeck, and Erich Kojter. Hegemann accompanied the film with commentaries translated into Spanish by Jaimes Répide. The film's message was euphoric, promoting a future city that could be a true home for mankind, allowing for a healthy life in touch with nature. Industrial zones, satellite towns, rapid transportation, and areas reserved for agriculture were advocated as part of this regional plan. Achieving this ideal "city of tomorrow" required the energetic support and committment of the government.

Hegemann was well aware that implementing the territorial expansion of a "Grand Buenos Aires" depended on political intervention, and he was certainly cognizant of the difficulties the local urbanists were facing in this respect. He presented his recommendations to political figures, city officials, and influential individuals, as well as architects, planners, and the

Fig. 50. Buenos Aires as the hub of a transportation network. CCCC

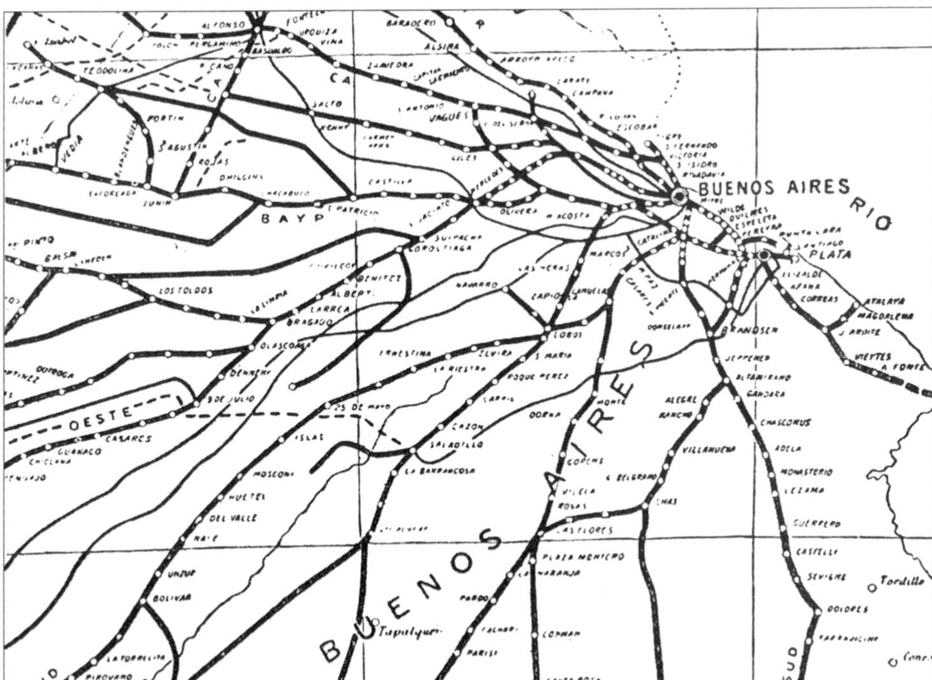

general public. The association with Greater Boston and his participation in the struggles for Gross Berlin had provided Hegemann with insights and tactical expertise for confronting the predicament in Buenos Aires, which he had diligently studied in the short time available to him. He also profited from contacts with the knowledgeable Della Paolera, Kalnay, and others associated with the Amigos de la Ciudad. Hegemann urged the entities in power to embark on a Grand Buenos Aires regional plan before the unregulated build-up in the periphery began to impede the development of a cohesive transportation and open-space system of parks and parkways.[28]

Hegemann refrained from proposing the unqualified transfer of foreign models; instead he favored the diffusion of ideas and their application, from which much could be derived—both from the successful accomplishments and the mistakes. Fostered by decades of worldwide comparative observation, this point of view had developed into an essential tenet of Hegemann's mature urbanism. His exposure to the Southern Cone of America, its environment, people, and culture, clarified and synthesized his preexisting convictions, which are expressed in the articles he published upon returning to Berlin. A sequence of six articles in *WMB/STB*, addressed urban planning as an international profession, and three in the *Berliner Tageblatt* were composed on similar topics and destined for the general public.[29] The corpus of these essays, and two reports based on Hegemann's lectures in Mar del Plata and Rosario—including summaries of his presentations in Buenos Aires—provides insight into the emerging urbanism in South America and the scope of Hegemann's ideas after decades of dedication to the subject.[30]

In addition to the publications mentioned, Hegemann's ideas were brought to the public through commentaries published in the local newspapers. Arguably important are three articles published in Buenos Aires in German language newspapers. The *Argentinisches Tageblatt* reported on Hegemann's first lecture, and *La Prensa* addressed a lecture that accompanied the exhibition.[31] Two articles in the *Deutsche La Plata Zeitung* (which was still printed in *fraktur* type), written by Hegemann, discuss town planning in Buenos Aires and other major cities in the world.[32] Summaries and excerpts from these extensive exposés appear in other publications and lectures, but these essays seem to be the original versions. They represent the complete text Hegemann intended to deliver as his inaugural lecture, and are composed in a format that addresses an audience. Considering that he had arrived barely three weeks previously, the accuracy with which he refers to specific aspects of Buenos Aires and compares them to those in other metropolises is notable. Illustrations and plans of the city are shown together with those of Europe and America which he brought with him as slides and photographs. As was his practice for arranging exhibitions, Hegemann used images, captions, and text to elucidate his concepts for both professionals and the general public. His overview touched on themes he later elaborated, but in these two articles they are blended into the concept of a regional master plan. Hegemann was a persuasive advocate of regional planning for Buenos Aires, demonstrating the benefits it had achieved for other major cities, especially London and Berlin. He considered it futile to improve congested inner cities without directing efforts to the surrounding districts. The official Ciudad Federal of Buenos Aires, dating from 1887, formed a relatively small congested core, presently surrounded by vast built-up areas. According to Hegemann, this totality represented the "real" Greater Buenos Aires.

The first article in the *La Plata Zeitung* concludes with comments on Le Corbusier's proposal of transferring his plan for Paris to Buenos Aires, entailing the demolition of great parts of the city. Hegemann did not consider this feasible, but neither did he favor the unconditional preservation of older buildings. While saddened that the colonial Cabildo was being torn down, he affirmed that he knew contemporary architects were confronted with tasks unheard of in historic times that required modern solutions.

In the second segment of the essays in the *La Plata Zeitung* Hegemann discusses the urgency of educating "the masses" on matters pertaining to urban planning. Citing José Ortega y Gasset's *The Revolt of the Masses* (1929), Hegemann uses the term "masses"as the Spanish author did in his book. Drawn to Ortega y Gasset's style and social commitment, Hegemann interpreted "*rebelión de las masas*" as the "enlightenment of the public."

Hegemann had the opportunity to apply his suggestions to a specific example when he was asked for consultations in Rosario, Argentina's second city, which had ambitions to supersede the capital. The municipality invited him to review a proposal by Adolfo P. Farengo, pending since 1924. Rosario, advantageously located on the Paraná River, was considering a major renovation involving the reorganization of all its railroad lines, linking them to one centrally located station. The plan involved placing the tracks in open trenches crossed by bridges so traffic interruptions could be avoided and the inner-city transportation could be tied into the regional railroad network. The removal of the switching yards from the shore of the Paraná River would make this area available for development, parks, and a scenic boulevard. In his report, Hegemann supported the Farengo plan enthusiastically, commenting that it represented "urban planning ideas that I have advocated with great conviction in all my works and books."[33] He recalled his *Report on a City Plan for Oakland & Berkeley*, which similarly combined commercial and recreational uses for inland harbor facilities on a scenic waterfront. He suggested an island park in the Paraná River comparable to one proposed for Oakland. Della Paolera accompanied Hegemann to Rosario, and in 1935 he collaborated with Farengo and Angel Guido on the *Plan regulador y de extensión* for Rosario, which acknowledged Hegemann's recommendations and others derived from his report for Oakland and Berkeley.[34]

Hegemann's visit to Mar del Plata, on the Atlantic coast south of Buenos Aires, preceded his consultation in Rosario, from which it differed considerably. His host was the Comisión Pro-Mar del Plata, which sought advice on how to regulate the surge in construction threatening the attractive resort. Under the title "Mar del Plata *y el urbanismo moderno*," Hegemann's lecture primarily addressed architecture rather than planning, and sharply criticized the eclectic styles of the resort's seasonal villas. Hegemann characterized the chaotic mixture by citing a visiting Mexican dignitary who had called it a "detestable salad of architectures and decorations of the worst taste," demonstrating an objectionable "lack of culture." Hegemann attributed the pretentious imitations of imported styles to vulgar upstarts and praised the traditional, indigenous building forms. These could still be observed, though they were now nearly smothered by pseudo-castles. He spoke of the "*estilo indígena y moderno*," which should guide future building in the resort, and showed recent recreational and sports facilities in Europe and the United States.

Hegemann's emphasis on the "urban defects" of Mar del Plata stirred up angry resentment. Reactions to his lecture were published in the *Mar del Plata* pamphlet, which also included a summary of his lectures in Buenos Aires. In his Foreword to *Problemas urbanos de Rosario* Della Paolera defended his colleague's candor as "criticism replete with lessons." He cited from Hegemann's remarks, noting the existence of "two ways to protect oneself against ridiculous architecture. One consisted in pursuing . . . a tradition still alive in one's own country. The other approach consisted of building only with the greatest simplicity and the strictest rationality aiming at something truly functional." The controversy generated by Hegemann was also considered beneficial because it called attention to a problem prevalent everywhere and emphasized the advisability of pursuing functional Modernism.

Hegemann's lifelong interest in housing as an integral element of city planning turned his attention from the superblocks in central Buenos Aires to the "*barrios*" in the outlying areas. The majority of these unregulated, low-rise settlements were chaotic in appearance and lacked essential utilities and proper roads. Hegemann, however, was intrigued by the makeshift dwellings because of their gardens and patios, replete with flowers, vegetables, and domestic animals. He documented them in numerous photographs for his lectures and publications (Fig. 51). They came close to his ideal of a small house with garden, and he compared them to the provisional shacks in the *Schrebergärten* (allotment gardens) in Germany, which suffered from municipal interference. Working on his *Housing* volumes in 1935–36, and focusing on self-built and prefabricated units, he wrote admiringly of those he had discovered in South America. The ironic titles of some of his articles compare Berlin's rental barracks with the minimal dwellings built out of discarded materials in the *barrios*. He commented on

Fig. 51. Self-built houses on the periphery of Buenos Aires, photographed by Hegemann, from WMB/STB, *May, 1932.* WHA

the "victory" of the settlements in the periphery of the city over the high-rise tenements, wondering if one lived more pleasantly in Buenos Aires than in Berlin. The mayor of Buenos Aires favored small houses with gardens, while the mayor of Montevideo enthused over the municipal housing blocks (*Gemeindebauten*) in Vienna.

Hegemann's sojourn in Argentina and Montevideo added new perspectives to his perceptions of architectural Modernism. He detected signs of it in the modest houses and the classic sobriety of the Palladian style buildings in the central city. Endeavors by Hegemann to define his own tenets of Modernism singled out the attributes of a purified Classicism—not a "*klassisistisch*" style—invariably leading to Karl Friedrich Schinkel. Connecting the renowned architect—on whom he frequently published—to his observations in Argentina and Paraguay is noteworthy for relating high art to innate local building. Even today Hegemann's revelations about South America continue to evoke pride by providing a prescient link between the New World and the celebrated Modernism in Europe. Hegemann affirmed that there was no need to introduce Modernism to the countries he visited, because they had arrived independently at their own distinctive building forms from which they could move forward.

The title of Hegemann's article, "*Schinkelscher Geist in Südamerika*" (Schinkel's spirit in South America), in *WMB/STB* is emblematic of these ideas as it refers to *Geist* (spirit or meaning) instead of objectified examples. It follows his brief piece on "Schinkel *als Fassadenkünstler*" discussing Schinkel's design for a department store that "hides" four floors behind a two-story facade. Also mentioned is his essay honoring Schinkel's 150th birthday. Both provide a context for extending the architect's international sphere to America. Hegemann's foremost attention is dedicated to Schinkel's *klassisistische Nüchternheit*, or sobriety, and its source in English Palladianism, rather than Palladio's buildings in Italy. The flat roof preferred by the architect prevailed as a traditional form in southern countries on both sides of the Atlantic. In Argentina and Uruguay simple, classic buildings devoid of mannerist decoration were preserved and continued to be constructed, resisting the influence of eclectic styles. In his illustrations Hegemann contrasts the conflicting tendencies. Particularly striking are two pompous skyscrapers by the Italian architect Palanti, one in Rosario and the other on the classic main plaza in Montevideo. For Hegemann, the mixture of foreign architectural influences from a range of countries, including the United States, had resulted in an "international salad." He cited Anatole France's question of whether this could be called an "international architecture." Hegemann vigorously supported architectural regionalism in the Southern Cone, publicized it in his own articles, and selected articles by other authors for the Wasmuths' journal. As editor he had always endeavored to include South and North American topics, and during his stay abroad, discussions of a recent sport stadium in Montevideo and Alfred Agache's plan for Rio de Janeiro were published.

Hegemann stayed in Argentina longer than expected. In a letter of December 2–3, he informed his wife, who hoped he would return for Christmas, that he had not concluded his work on Rosario. Another reason for his lengthy visit was his treatment for recurrent stomach problems by a Dr. Solomon, whose "sanatorium" he entered for five days to rest and undergo a series of tests. He reported to his wife that nothing important was diagnosed and that he managed to gain some weight. He mentioned his intention to visit Paris on his return trip and explore the possibility of relocating there. "I do not like the idea of being caught in Germany by political opponents that may be in power by that time, and may never let me get out." This letter crossed one by Ida Belle from the same date in which she expressed her disappointment that he would not be with the family at Christmas.[35] She described the economic and political conditions in Berlin as "like a nightmare," with the newspapers filled with accounts of murders and suicides, and "the Nazis doing no end of queer and impossible things." Important news for her husband was that Ossietzky had been condemned to a year and a half in prison. Wasmuths *Monatshefte* had declared bankruptcy and was bought by the publisher Ullstein. The new owner initially dismissed Hegemann, his associate editor Zechlin, and his assistant Fr. Ohlischlaeger, but later changed his mind and rehired all three. Now Wasmuth was ordered to clear the premises by January 1. Hegemann's wife understood her husband's urgency to explore professional possibilities outside of Germany in Argentina or France, although both were reluctant to leave their comfortable home in Nikolassee.

During his stay in Montevideo, before embarking on the *Cap Arcona* on December 15, Hegemann gave a lecture and opened the exhibition brought from Europe. More than in Argentina, he was embraced by the German community and the ambassador. He managed to do some sightseeing and contacted local architects. From the ship Hegemann replied to his wife's alarming news from Berlin, assuring her that to save their financial resources they should desist from meeting in Paris at this time.[36] He feared eventually suffering the same fate as Ossietzky, and stated that they should carefully deliberate how and when to leave the country. He posted the letter upon his arrival in Paris.

After an absence of four months Hegemann returned to Berlin on January 1, 1932. Upon his arrival in Buenos Aires in late August he had written with foresight to Ida Belle, "I will come back in somewhat better health. I think the change in social atmosphere will do me well. It is a crime the way I am treated in Berlin, while here everybody welcomes me. This feeling of being welcomed instead of having to fight for every inch of life was necessary for my recuperation and for new fight."[37] With eerie foresight of what the remaining years of his life held in store, Hegemann was bracing himself for a courageous fight.

Romanticism, Classicism, Style, or Virtue

Hegemann's unique facility for writing resulted in a number of books and publications. He continues to be recognized as a consummate and sophisticated stylist for content, a meticulous choice of words, and avoidance of jargon. The author and editor at Kiepenheuer Verlag, Hermann Kesten, wrote a perceptive tribute to Hegemann's literary skill: "His style is capable of everything, his language is a perfect instrument." He also noted that Hegemann embraced the classic vocabulary of the mature Goethe and the rational Romantics.[38]

Hegemann's fluency in English, French, and Italian, in addition to German, enhanced his distinct use of language. His gymnasium education had included Latin, and later he acquired a fair knowledge of Spanish. He wrote with ease in English and French. With rare exceptions, he abstained from using foreign words or their "germanized" versions.

Mastery in formulating concepts and giving them permanence in written form preserved Hegemann's legacy as a theorist and critic. His skill with the pen contributed to the family's economic well-being and supplemented his salary from the Wasmuth Verlag. There are indications that payments from other publishers or journals were eagerly awaited. Hegemann's freelance activities involved lectures as well but his main focus was on articles and books. Other than Wasmuth, his publishers were Gustav Kiepenheuer, Jakob Hegner, and Friedrich Ernst Hübsch.[39] Next to Wasmuth, Hübsch was the most prominent publisher for architecture. Hübsch brought out an architectural monograph series, *Neue Werkkunst*, with exceptionally designed covers, layout, and typography. Hegemann wrote the introductions for several of these slender volumes, presumably for financial reasons.[40] In his thank-you letter answering the birthday greetings from Hübsch, Hegemann expressed the wish that in the future they would "collaborate not less frequently" than in the past. Drafts of the introductions for the series are typed on Hegemann's personal stationery with his home address, an indication that he kept this work separate from his activities at Wasmuth. The sources given for the illustrations show that they were provided by the architects, rather than by the Wasmuth photo archives.

Hegemann's introductions complied with his own mandate to single out positive aspects in the architects' work, and these texts avoided the polemical tone of his critical reviews in the journals. The majority of the architects in the *Neue Werkkunst* series were not associated with the *Neues Bauen*. Some are barely known today, while others are gaining renewed attention. Hegemann's commentaries stress modern, functional, and formal aspects of the architects' work and demonstrate his grasp of Modernism. From the more than ten books in the series for which he wrote, a few are particularly indicative of Hegemann's position.

His cordial relations with the architects Ernst, Hans, and Oskar Gerson, whose work and articles were published in *WMB/STB* from 1925 on, may have prompted the special attention Hegemann devoted to the volume on the architecture of the "Brothers Gerson" (1928).[41]

He admired the "Hamburg spirit," which adhered to proud traditions while striving judiciously toward new goals. The Gersons's office buildings, especially the Ballin-Haus (1923–24), he characterized as typical of the "Americanization" of German business enterprises and the kind of architecture they favored. The Ballin-Haus was truly functional and avoided the *Ingenieur-Romantik* that characterized many other recent office buildings. "*Ingenieur-Romantik*" was a derogatory term frequently used by Hegemann, and in this context it referred to the neo-Gothic aspects in American skyscrapers.[42] Hegemann empathized with the international, enterprising spirit of the Hanseatic city represented in its architecture, particularly the Chilehaus (1923) by Fritz Höger, with whom the Gerson brothers collaborated on another large office building, the Sprinkenhof (1926). An aerial view in *WMB* shows the Sprinkenhof in relation to the Chilehaus, and Hegemann included these impressive buildings in his London exhibition and lecture.[43]

Ernst Gerson wrote on his trip to the United States in *WMB* (1929) and *STB* (1930).[44] The main purpose of his travels were skyscrapers and this took him from New York to Chicago and Detroit. Presumably he had discussed his itinerary with Hegemann and was acquainted with his book *Amerikanische Architektur*, because he visited Hegemann & Peets's Wyomissing Park. Gerson's trip to America reinforced his earlier interest in an office complex for Greater Hamburg. It was reflected in the Gerson brothers' competition entry for the *Messehaus* (exhibition center), conceived within a vast business center, or "city," as it was called. Hegemann published the Gersons' unbuilt project in *STB* in 1925, signaling the beginning of his interest in their work.[45] While their buildings for Hamburg's forward-looking commercial enterprises represented the modern functionalism Hegemann favored, he had less to say about the villas they built for members of the upper class on the estates facing the Elbe River. Although respecting their clients' traditional tastes, the architects' designs reflect a modern interpretation of interior spaces and natural settings.[46]

In another book of the *Neue Werkkunst* series Hegemann highlighted the American influence on the design and management of department stores, commenting on those built for the Karstadt chain by Philipp Schaefer.[47] The clients had studied American examples and collaborated closely with the architect. According to Hegemann, the resulting buildings surpassed those in the United States, although some overemphasized the verticality of American and other German precedents. The innovation of placing the Karstadt stores on the city's periphery, as in Berlin, rather than in the centers, added to their attraction and accessibility. It also contributed to "a healthy decentralization of the metropolis." Hegemann described the new department store in Rixdorf (Berlin) as an innovative, colorful "Arabian bazaar." Enchanted, he claimed that even this comparison did not do it justice: "When at nightfall on the Hermannplatz in Berlin, the towering, vertical bands of light structure the gigantic volume of the department store in ways quite different from its daytime appearance, more surprising and powerful, and when above the entrance hall columns of light dart into the dark sky, then it appears that one of the utopian worlds of technology, imagined in the novels of Jules Verne or Wells, has become a reality." Three photographs of the Karstadt department store on the Hermannplatz in Berlin appear in the book, two of them illuminated night views (Fig. 52).

Another Hamburg firm, Klophaus, Schoch, zu Putlitz, impressed Hegemann with its response to contemporary requirements by the establishment of an architectural office that incorporated architects as well as structural and mechanical engineers in order to provide aesthetic, technical, and economic expertise to their clients.[48] The firm's large commercial and industrial projects combined elegant design with modern functionalism. The partners participated in major international competitions, such as

Fig. 52. Karstadt department store at night, by Philipp Schaefer. Neure Warenhausbanten der Rudolph Karsdadt, A.-G. 1929.

the League of Nations in Geneva in 1927 and the Columbus Memorial in Santo Domingo. Their project for the latter involved input from the German industries Zeiss and Siemens-Schuckert. Hegemann was particularly impressed by the technical innovations, such as the projections planned for the interior of the cupola, nighttime lighting effects, and powerful movable light beams to aid air and sea navigation.

Previously eclipsed by the heroic figures of the International Style, German Bestelmeyer and Otto Kohtz have recently been rediscovered.[49] Hegemann perceived modern Classicism in their work; in the interiors of Bestelmeyer's additions to the Technische Hochschule in Munich, he noted a "wonderful, innovative starkness, which in many ways surpasses the traditional forms of rigorous Classicism, a truly modern Classicism, that achieves within the spirit of our own time an artistically realized functionalism."

Otto Kohtz has regained attention for his contributions to the development of the skyscraper in Germany. Hegemann called attention to Kohtz's response to the urban setting of skyscrapers as singular architectural features, comparing him in this respect to Schinkel. Contrary to placing skyscrapers into a tight grid, as was frequently the case in American cities, Kohtz "fought for the realization of the idea to which Schinkel had devoted numerous designs, that important locations within the city plan—as for instance in Berlin at the terminus of the Leipziger Strasse, the Friedrichstrasse (by the Hallesche Gate), the end of the Siegesallee, the Alexanderplatz, etc.—demanded a major architectonic emphasis in order to provide sight and reference points within the chaos of the streets." Another characteristic of Kohtz's skyscrapers noted by Hegemann was his emphasis on light and air by means of set-backs, as required by New York's zoning regulation of 1916. Hegemann valued the architect's awareness of the relationship between architecture and city planning, mentioning Kohtz's proposal for assembling all official buildings of Germany and the State of Prussia at the Platz der Republik, to create a government forum similar to that in Washington, D.C. This proposal, deemed too "fantastic" in 1921, was welcomed in 1929.

Neumann notes that Hegemann was the first to call attention to Schinkel's project for the *Denkmalsdom* of 1814—celebrating the wars against Napoleon—and to urban considerations pertaining to the skyscraper debates in Germany.[50] In his 1924 article, "*Das Hochhaus als Verkehrsstörer und der Wettbewerb der Chicago Tribune*" (The Skyscraper as traffic disturbance, and the Chicago Tribune competition), published just prior to his *Amerikanische Architektur und Stadtbaukunst*, Hegemann commented on Schinkel's predilection for the "tower per se" as an effective feature within the townscape.[51] On the other hand Hegemann objected to Schinkel's viewing the tower building as a "mere decorative object." He also faulted the gothicizing elements of contemporary skyscrapers and department stores.

Remarks in "*Das Hochhaus als Verkehrsstörer . . .*" and in the introductions in the *Neue Werkkunst* monographs provide a sampling of Hegemann's numerous references to Schinkel's work and ideas considered in relation to classic modernity in architecture and urbanism. Other than a cluster of articles dedicated specifically to Schinkel around 1931, the anniversary of his 150th birthday, Hegemann referred to him in many instances as emblematic for his own concept of Classicism.

Hegemann's interpretation of *Klassizismus* was one of essence rather than of a historic style of formal elements. The latter could be imitated, although he never advocated it. The dedication in Hegemann's fiftieth birthday *Festschrift* stated erroneously that he proposed classic works as models for the present. This misinterpretation of Hegemann's affirmation of Classicism persisted and, to his detriment, has prevailed and is frequently associated with his consideration of "civic art."

The complexity of the modern movement is inextricably related to the various terms, their multiple interpretations, and the ways in which they were wielded, manipulated, and devised in the debates. Controversies often hinged on the various meanings given to the same term. Revisions of

Modernism have directed attention to the terminology of the discourse, and it is clear that Hegemann's case was neither unique nor isolated. The terms and concepts recurring in his critical output command scrutiny, notably *Klassizismus*, *Romantik*, and their adjectives and variations.

Hegemann's preoccupation with the literature, myths, and sites of the ancient world is reflected in his evaluation of Classicism, which is more philosophical than the customary eclectic Neoclassicism. For him Classicism was not a style and therefore surpassed imitation. He endeavored to clarify this cardinal point of his approach to architecture and planning, as much for himself as for others.

In letters to Steen Eiler Rasmussen, with whom he visited Le Corbusier in 1926, Hegemann commented on the meanings of *klassisch* and *klasizistisch*. Rasmussen's article on Le Corbusier had compared the borrowing of stylistic details by classicist and modern architects, intending to give their buildings the aura of a desired style, and had assumed *Klassizismus* and *Fetischismus* to be equivalents in this respect.[52] The meaning of *Fetischismus* in this context was eclecticism and akin to what Hegemann frequently labeled *Plagiarismus*. Hegemann corrected Rasmussen on this point: "On the concepts '*klassisch*' and '*klassizistisch*,' we (in the German language) experience a great lack of clarity. Many believe that '*klassisch*' implies perfection. . . . Until now I have designated as '*klassizistisch*' the effort to create '*klassisch*' works. You want to equate '*klassizistisch*' with '*fetischistisch*,' and I am certain that Mr. Taut and Mr. Mendelsohn would agree with you completely."

Hegemann's disdain for eclecticism was forcefully stated in an article he wrote with Leo Adler, "*Warnung vor Akademismus und Klassizismus*," published as an editorial in the first issue of *WMB* in 1927.[53] The authors defended the journal against complaints that its advocacy of "simplicity, strict functionalism, architectural harmony, serenity, and lucidity" represented a dangerous promotion of *Akademismus* and *Klassizismus*. These accusations attributed erroneous meanings to the terms. The editors stated that *WMB* opposed eclecticism or a "salad of details borrowed from historic styles [and] dished over buildings." This justified their rejection of Bruno Schmitz's national monuments, which certainly represented the very worst *Akademismus*. Bad *Klassizismus* attached columns to contemporary buildings, resulting in "unpleasant exoticism" and falling into that same category. These points were illustrated with convincing examples. The article repeated the principles of functionalism and composure (harmony, serenity), lucidity, and restraint promoted by the journal (i.e, Hegemann). Many of these qualities had been achieved in classic works, though Hegemann contended that historic accomplishments should be no hindrance to striving for even greater perfection in response to present demands and contemporary building technology. His interpretation of Classicism can be read as complying with a definition of Modernism, which he brought to bear on his appraisal of modern architecture, singling out representative works by Adolf Loos, Le Corbusier, and J. J. P. Oud.

While Hegemann clarified his interpretation of Classicism, the meaning he attributed to Romanticism remains elusive and even ambiguous. It would be convenient to consider his interpretation of *romantisch* as merely the antithesis of all that did not qualify as classic. However, Hegemann used it as a label with a variety of derogatory connotations. *Romantisch* was an expedient tag for any architecture that transformed modernity and functionalism into a formalistic style. In an essay on Schinkel, Hegemann referred to his own "most important principle of all building" as affirmed in the old adage: "Necessity is the primary rule of all architecture." He continued: "Intentional digression from functionalism (the demands of necessity) is called Romanticism, and such Romanticism is an offense against the foremost rule of architecture."[54] *Romantik* was also a comprehensive designation for architectural aberrations that indiscriminately borrowed motifs from historic or exotic styles, exemplified by the eclecticism of the late nineteenth century, even though it was a manifestation of the search for a new style.

His scorn was directed against the architecture and urban designs that suffused the Ulmerplatz controversy. Commenting on the negative review of A. E. Brinckmann's new books by Joseph Gantner, Hegemann took the occasion to vindicate Sitte.[55] It should be remembered, he urged, that Sitte had been misunderstood so regretfully by his admirers that he was cited as the source of the most objectionable contemporary Romanticism. Disapproving of Gantner's opinion of Brinckmann, Hegemann acknowledged Brinckmann's contribution toward setting in motion the "great cleansing of Sitte's town planning ideas" that began around 1910.

German literature of the Romantic period, and certainly the admired Goethe, were exempt from Hegemann's vendetta. On the other hand he branded as prime examples of *romantisch* the architecture of the Jugendstil, Expressionism, and the Dutch Amsterdam School. Neither did Frank Lloyd Wright escape this categorization. Hegemann assessed certain buildings by Le Corbusier and Gropius as *Ingenieur-Romantik*, because they incorporated technological motifs as stylistic elements under functional pretexts. He elaborated on this topic in the article, "*Romanticismo y realismo en la arquitectura moderna*" for the Spanish periodical *Obras*.[56] Functionalist architects, he noted, had succumbed to highly romantic conceits, believing that a building should resemble a machine or a ship for it to be considered modern. Similarly, even offices and industries imitated medieval cathedrals in the name of "modern style."

His contemporary, the critic Gustav Adolf Platz, interpreted "*Klassisch und Romantisch*" in a section of his 1927 landmark book *Die Baukunst der neuesten Zeit*.[57] Platz's passage on *Romantik* is comparable to what Hegemann alluded to in his essays. Platz stated: "Romanticism in architecture is the built expression of religious reveries and historicist rapture. . . . Only half of architecture is art, the other half is technical achievement. Under those circumstances Romanticism turning toward the past becomes a sham." Further on Platz backs away from Hegemann's categorical rejection of *Romantik*: "If the concepts classic and romantic should have any meaning for modern architecture, the purist architectural intention with its end goal of mathematical, symmetrical perfection would be the classical, while the eurhythmic, frequently fantastic, free inclination should be considered the romantic. In this time of infinite variety there should be room for both, and the future ideal might be a synthesis."

How to accommodate "romantic" elements in modern architecture was the theme of a dicussion on sculpture in functional buildings—whether it was to be considered decoration or enhancement. Participating in the dialogue were Hegemann, the sculptor Rudolf Belling, and the Luckhardt brothers, in whose studio the gathering took place. The discussion was written up in *WMB/STB,* preceded by a statement signed by Georg Kolbe and accompanied by a photograph of Mies van der Rohe's Barcelona Pavilion, which prominently displayed Kolbe's sculpture.[58] Kolbe clearly stated his position vis-à-vis functional architecture: "Sculpture is not a decorative element of architecture, but rather an independent work of art." He did not object to the absence of sculpture complementing blank walls: "not every white sheet requires writing"; however, "New Building and sculpture get along splendidly. Mies van der Rohe repeatedly included one of my sculptures in the spaces of his remarkably functional buildings. The result is greatest fulfillment—mutual enhancement. I do not require from the architect a wall surface—but space." In the discussion with Belling, Hegemann steered the conversation away from historical examples of sculpture in architecture, instead commenting on "the fate of sculpture in the architecture of today and tomorrow. Sculpture as exorcism, which is romanticism, is no longer of concern for us." Belling, whom he had considered a *Klassiker*, now claimed to be a *Romantiker* because he liked comfortable interiors. Hegemann replied that "comfort is highly modern. On the other hand, a 'Romantiker' is a person who clings to obsolete, impractical, misunderstood ideals." The architect Luckhardt urged caution regarding *Romantik*. Perhaps responding to this warning, the conversation turned to instances of sculpture in contemporary buildings. Hegemann's comments on the possibility of "romantic" elements in the form of sculpture being acceptable in modern buildings are comparable to his search for a reconciliation of Schinkel's Romanticism with his Classicism.

The Heimatschutz (protection of the homeland) movement is generally associated with Romanticism, traditionalism, historic preservation, and the surge of nationalism leading to disastrous consequences in the twentieth century. Hegemann kept a wary distance from the movement, which was associated with the mythical notions of *Volk*, racism, and culture, often grouped together as Romantic Nationalism. Hegemann favored selected aspects of *Heimatschutz* tenets, for instance, the emphasis on low-rise cottages in small-scale developments. He admired the work of Muthesius and Tessenow reflecting these ideas. However, he probably agreed with Peter Meyer, who declared that "*Heimatschutz* topics were a particularly tricky border region between architecture and tradition," and condemned the imitation of historic examples to preserve context.[59]

Hegemann rejected the *Heimatschutz* infatuation with village life and the picturesque as anti-urban Romanticism and its defensive origins in regional culture as provincial. Nazism feasted on the *Blut und Boden* (blood and soil) aura of these notions. By contrast, Classicism for Hegemann represented a timeless metropolitan and international spirit with universal appeal, comparable to an "auxiliary" language facilitating brotherhood and understanding among nations. Hegemann's advocacy of the transnationalism of a pan-European culture was an affirmation of his pacifist convictions.

Strikingly comparable to Hegemann, Walter Curt Behrendt attributed the renewed appeal of Classicism to its cosmopolitan character in his Introduction to the 1920 edition of Paul Mebes's *Um 1800*. Behrendt noted that in 1914, he had commented on Classicism as a "world-style," and that "through its international diffusion [it had] acquired something of a universally understood world-language, a quality that rendered it, especially today, . . . once more a preferred means of artistic expression."[60]

Hegemann's perceptions contributed to his change of heart regarding Schmitthenner and Schultze-Naumburg, whose architectural Classicism was a style devoid of the meaning he ascribed to it. Rather, it was imbued with nationalistic and anti-international implications, which for Hegemann represented a contradiction with his own idealistic beliefs.

Friedrich Ostendorf (1871–1915), author of the series *Sechs Bücher vom Bauen*, was a pre–World War I figure dedicated to the regeneration of German architecture.[61] His career was cut short by his death in battle on the Western Front. In conjunction with an exhibition celebrating the hundredth anniversary of the Technische Hochschule Karlsruhe in 1926, his ideas re-entered the debate. The Hochschule was founded by Friedrich Weinbrenner (1766–1826), whose work Ostendorf had studied, and he had taught there from 1907–14. The exhibition honored both Weinbrenner and Ostendorf with an overview of their work. The *Sechs Bücher vom Bauen* were reissued, heavily edited and expanded by Walther Sackur. Sackur had studied with Ostendorf and had also taught at the Hochschule. This combination of circumstances drew attention to Ostendorf's books, which he had composed to clarify his own ideas and act as guidebooks for his architectural principles. His struggle to free himself from Weinbrenner's preference for historical precedents in architecture and town planning are demonstrated in his own buildings and books.

Werner Oechslin's thoroughly documented article summarized Ostendorf's theses, which might be considered "modern." They are: "a reference to a universally valid tradition, a design process striving for the 'simplest formal representation,' as well as the endeavor to create spaces in architecture." By "tradition," according to Oechslin, Ostendorf did not mean historical style, but preferred the term *Baukultur*, or building culture, with its more inclusive range of accepted values.

These premises were akin to Hegemann's convictions, and under his editorial guidance *WMB* dedicated twenty pages to Ostendorf, although none of the articles was written by Hegemann. In 1926 the journal published a commemorative essay in honor of Ostendorf with numerous illustrations. A note indicated that the accompanying drawings were by Hans Detlef Rösiger, the author of the article, the photographs and some of the critical captions by Edgar Wedepohl, and other captions by Hegemann. Rösiger's article was followed by one by Wedepohl on the tasks and limits of architectural theory, and with an unsigned review of the town plans by Karl Gruber, a student of Ostendorf's.[62] This latter piece was by Hegemann, and the pages in *WMB* reveal that he valued Ostendorf.

For an understanding of how he assessed Ostendorf's principles, a genuine source exists. Hegemann owned the first three volumes—and perhaps others—of the *Sechs Bücher vom Bauen*.[63] Volume 1 is especially valuable for the extensive annotations in Hegemann's hand. In the margin, he marked with "S" the passages that Sackur had added without indicating them. It appears that Hegemann was comparing the fourth edition, which he owned, with Ostendorf's original version. He also made editorial corrections in Sackur's wording, especially his use of non-German monikers, and suggested the translation of French and Latin quotations.

Beyond these minutiae, Hegemann's comments reveal a thorough reading of the book. Full pages of carefully written notations, cross-references singling out contradictions or comparisons, and clarifications of the connection between statements and illustrations amount to an in-depth analysis of Ostendorf's Volume 1 by a knowledgeable critic. Hegemann also examined the drawings and plans, penciling in axes, designating names when not indicated, and identifying as *neu* (new) the illustrations supplied by Sackur. Fastidious regarding terminology, Hegemann singled out the term *situation* throughout the text, replacing it with *Lageplan* (site plan). He was hypercritical of Sackur changing Ostendorf's key words: *Einfachheit* (simplicity, clarity) to *Simplizität*, and *Reichtum* (abundance) to *Kompliziertheit*. In general, Hegemann found fault with Sackur's contributions because of his misinterpretations and the distortions of Ostendorf's concepts from their intended version.

Ostendorf opened the first chapter with his leading principle, fundamental to all others, that it was the primary goal of architecture to create spaces. Hegemann penciled in the margin, "to create spaces and volumes."

In relation to the lingering Ulmerplatz controversies, Hegemann was particularly interested in Ostendorf's amply illustrated excursuses on axiality as the organizing dictum and, akin to it, symmetry. Ostendorf differentiated between strictly geometric axiality, a *Spiegelachse* (mirror-image axiality), and one in which minor deviations did not disrupt an overall harmonious relationship. He also distinguished between a *Zielachse*, an axis with a focus or viewpoint, and a *Symmetrieachse* or *Spiegelachse*. In a long commentary, Hegemann interpreted these concepts:

> The need to differentiate clearly between symmetry and axiality, that is "mirror image identity" and "axiality," is demonstrated by the comments to illus. 147. "S" [Sackur] has not fully comprehended these important conceptual and functional distinctions, which explains his numerous misunderstandings. The axis, which determines the axial identity or mirror image likeness, could be designated a mirror-axis; the axis which determines an axial trajectory leading toward a goal, a directional axis. The first one is applicable to planes and volumes, seldom for spaces; they are both essentially different.[64]

The referenced drawing 147 is a view of Karlsruhe that bears Hegemann's notation: "The creation of an axis trajectory by means of a directional axis, not by a symmetrical axis . . . the walls of the path of the axis do not have to be identical mirror images, no more than in a room. . . . The axis toward a goal or vista is less demanding of axial similarity than of the target itself; it is satisfied with a clear directional guidance toward the vista." These notations are written in pencil by Hegemann and are unknown to scholars.

Based on these premises, Hegemann analyzed the plans and facades illustrated in Volume 1. He drew axes on the plans and wrote comments, pointing with arrows to details in the illustrations. In some cases he indicated on the plans that axial symmetry pertained to the layout but not to the spatial relationships. Ostendorf stressed the importance of a conceptual continuity between the interior and the exterior "situation," thus creating a sequence of rooms or spaces, even at the expense of maintaining precise axiality. According to Hegemann, Ostendorf and Sackur disagreed on this point. The former preferred harmoniously designed rooms and considered strict symmetry a requirement only within the room sequence.[65]

Hegemann was perhaps drawn most keenly to Ostendorf's Chapter VL, "*Raumgruppen. Bedeuting der Symmetrie für Raum und Körper. Romantische und Klassische Kunst*" (Spatial groupings: the meaning of symmetry for space and volume. Romantic and classic art). The chapter did not provide a clear definition of what Ostendorf considered romantic and classic, although his principles of clarity and symmetry were similar to Hegemann's interpretations. Ostendorf's ideas also applied to spatial groupings, and he reminded his readers that "lack of clarity was the root of all aesthetic distress, preventing our desire for visual understanding from achieving peacefulness." A few pages later he referred to Blondel, who declared the regularity of the room plan to be the prerequisite for a room to qualify as a work of art.

The sections on town planning in Volume 1 were added by Sackur. They contain few notations by Hegemann, yet he singled out Sackur's comments on Schinkel's lack of interest in matters of town planning as detrimental for Berlin. Sackur noted that in nineteenth-century Germany town planning disappeared from the architects' horizon, only to be rediscovered by Camillo Sitte. Oddly, this is the only reference to Sitte in the volume, although his *Der Städtebau nach seinen künstlerischen Grundsätzen* resembles Ostendorf's treatise in content and in the illustrations and plans. When Ostendorf began to publish his *Sechs Bücher vom Bauen* in 1913, Sitte, who had died ten years earlier, was revered for his *Der Städtebau nach seinen künstlerischen Grundsätzen*, and was not yet affected by the later distortions of his principles. In fact, what happened to Sitte's landmark publication and its altered French version is comparable to Ostendorf's *Sechs Bücher vom Bauen* at the hands of Sackur.

The Stones of Berlin

During Hegemann's last three years in Berlin, and particularly the time after his return from South America in January 1932 until he went into exile, his professional and political circumstances converged with foreboding density. This pivotal period of his life benefits from consideration of representative and overlapping episodes rather than a chronologcal account. This approach allows for *Das steinerne Berlin* (1930) and the "Berliner" architect Schinkel, actually predating Hegemann's fiftieth birthday, to be followed by a discussion of his other literary activities. However, it was the publication of his Berlin book that contributed to the renown bestowed upon him in June 1931.

Das steinerne Berlin: Geschichte der grössten Mietskasernenstadt der Welt was published in January of 1930 by the Gustav Kiepenheuer Verlag in an elegant edition of 505 pages, bound in linen and emblazoned with the crest of the imperial eagle protected by the bears of Berlin.[66] The dustcover showed a wraparound aerial photograph of the city. The book immediately generated reviews from architects, urbanists, and other notable individuals, among them the *Staatssekretär* (parliamentary secretary) Wilhelm Abegg, and the authors Joseph Roth and Walter Benjamin. Benjamin's "*Ein Jakobiner von heute: Zu* Werner Hegemann's '*Das steinerne Berlin*'" was reprinted as the Preface in a later, abridged edition of the book.[67]

Das steinerne Berlin has become the best known of Hegemann's publications in the German language, and it has been reissued several times. It is frequently referred to in connection with the recent surge of interest in

Fig. 53. Aerial view of the Berliner Schloss and the Dom, ca. 1930. CCCC

the "new" capital of Germany.[68] However, the book has remained an isolated interest, particularly in Hegemann's native country, failing to bring attention to his role as a critic and his other works, even those from which *Das steinerne Berlin* drew extensively.

Hegemann dedicated *Das steinerne Berlin* to "Hugo Preuss, who shaped the idea of Berlin's development into a new metropolis." He expressed his gratitude to Preuss for alerting him, after reading *Der Städtebau nach den Ergebnissen . . .*, Volume 1 (1911), that the political damage to the city of Berlin predated the nineteenth century. Hegemann took up this suggestion in Volume 2, and it motivated his preoccupation with Frederick II, "the Great," and earlier Prussian rulers (Fig. 53). In the Introduction to his book on Berlin Hegemann proceeded to explain that its essence was a summation of his previous studies. In the spirit of his admired mentor, Hugo Preuss, he hoped that this work would overcome the dangerous German illusion "that an ideal metropolis could be possible, while the so-called intellectuals were almost bragging of understanding hardly anything about urban matters." Hegemann chose Berlin to demonstrate a conviction he had pursued since his early American years, that an informed public was essential for urban progress and well-being. *Das steinerne Berlin* is integral to his ongoing crusade to disseminate information on urbanism by means of exhibitions and publications addressing a general audience with the aim of stimulating civic awareness and pride.[69]

Another theme promoted by Hegemann and affirmed in this book was the government's duty to devote economic resources to urban progress rather than waging war. He never tired of pointing out the human and financial waste incurred by warfare, establishing a pragmatic link between pacifism and city planning. His campaign for the improvement of housing and employment possibilities was integral to his pacifist convictions. This was eloquently expressed in the last chapter of *Das steinerne Berlin*, "The Free and Capital City of the Future." The page after this section bore Berlin's crest of 1448, before the city succumbed to the domination of the Prussian state. According to Hegemann, Prussia's misguided attitude toward Berlin caused a multitude of urban blunders, exemplified by the notorious *Mietskasernen*, and had prevented the city from becoming a world-class metropolis. The litany of these evils composes the main portion of the book. It is a synoptic reworking of *Der Städtebau nach den Ergebnissen* . . . and his books on Frederick II and Prussian history, with a focus on Berlin.

Two decades earlier, in the two volumes of *Der Städtebau nach den Ergebnissen* . . . , Hegemann had considered the totality of the evolving city as a cultural phenomenon and object of critical inquiry.[70] He applied to the history of the city a morphological approach comparable to the innovative work by the French scholar Marcel Pöete. In his treatise Hegemann blended city planning with political history in the firm belief that mastering contemporary problems required an understanding of their origin. By taking a long retrospective view to analyze present predicaments, his methodology became a precursor of the innovative discipline of urban history.

More effectively than its antecedents published in 1911 and 1913, *Das steinerne Berlin* won attention as a history of Berlin's built form and for demonstrating the complexity of the political forces that shaped it and other cities. The book gained prominence as a biography of Berlin and as a chronicle of the city victimized by the thoughtless rulers of Prussia, whose personalities and intentions were unmasked by the author with scholarship and cunning.

The subtitle, "History of the Greatest City of Rental Barracks in the World," identified what Hegemann considered the major flaw, adequate housing being the prime requisite for a livable city. He traced the reasons for the *Mietskasernen* of Berlin using detailed documentation, primarily Frederick the Great's mortgage regulations of 1748. Hegemann outlined the ensuing rampant real estate and land speculation in the chapter "*Friedrich der 'Grosse' begründet den Berliner Bodenwucher*" (Frederick the Great establishes land speculation in Berlin). Heartrending descriptions and statistical data on the conditions in the unhealthy dwellings, especially for women and children, echo those publicized by Hegemann in 1911–13 that led to the *Für Gross-Berlin* movement for improvements in housing and open space.

A solution Hegemann persistently advanced was the development of cottages in settlements in outlying districts. Decentralized low-rise housing, requiring the costly development of infrastructure, was a much debated proposition, and he was aware of the disadvantages. In 1926, after several visits to Vienna, he published an article in *WMB* favoring the multistory *Gemeindebauten* in that city, followed by his own evaluation of Vienna's social housing program.[71] He considered that the choice between *Hochhaus oder Siedlung* (high-rise or low-rise developments) depended on the cost of land, infrastructure, and other parameters that differed among cities. The housing debate suffuses all chapters of his active life, and comes full circle in the posthumous three-volume *City Planning: Housing*.

In his generally favorable review of *Das steinerne Berlin*, *Staatssekretär* Wilhelm Abegg disagreed with Hegemann's advocacy of small cottages as an antidote for the rental barracks.[72] Abegg feared a spread, truly a sprawl, on the periphery of the city that would be costly and difficult to administrate. He considered that Hegemann's comparison of Berlin's situation to examples of decentralization abroad, especially in America, had led him into a *Sackgasse* (blind alley). Abegg hoped that the author's "one-sided excessive polemics" would not turn people against *Das steinerne Berlin*, because there was a great urgency for reforming Berlin's bureaucracy and dedicating it to urban planning, seeking solutions for the housing crisis, and propelling it toward becoming a representative capital city.

Berlin as a *Weltstadt* (cosmopolitan city) and metropolis was a pervasive desire. In the extensive literature on the theme of city versus country, Berlin commanded an emblematic role.[73] It was the main topic of Karl Scheffler's *Berlin, ein Stadtschicksal*, and Döblin's fiction, *Berlin Alexanderplatz*, to name just a salient few.[74] Obviously it figured as a subject in works on the political history of Prussia, foremost for Hegemann.

Within the literature preoccupied with city life, *Das steinerne Berlin* represented a new category by entering the borderland of urban history. It attracted a considerable number of literary rather than architectural reviews. The most notable was by Walter Benjamin, who wrote a recollection of his childhood in Berlin (ca. 1900). In the early 1930s he embarked on *The Arcades Project*, primarily focused on Paris, which remained unfinished.[75] In "*Ein Jakobiner von heute: Zu* Werner Hegemanns '*Das steinerne* Berlin'" Benjamin referred to the extensive *Spezialliteratur* on Berlin and other cities, much of it non-interpretive and appealing only to local interests. By contrast, Hegemann's book presented a *Weltstadt* of European scope in a monumental history of the building of Berlin. Benjamin praised the precision and imagination with which Hegemann approached all his topics. Citing Chesterton, he calls *Das steinerne Berlin* a *rebellische Phantasie* (rebellious fantasy) with which the author, a rational historian, wrote a *Skandal-Geschichte* (scandalous history), accusing Berlin. Benjamin described how all those who had suffered in the rental barracks finally would have a voice on Judgment Day. He compared the style of this work on Berlin favorably with the dialogue format Hegemann employed in his books on Frederick II, Napoleon, and Christus. Benjamin considered that Hegemann's fanatic negativism was not representative of leftist radicalism, but of a democratic credo as advocated by the Jacobins in 1792. Benjamin valued the book; however, he wished for greater objectivity and "ventilation," asking for a balance of the positive and the negative. Although stating that "negativist appraisal of history was an absurdity," Benjamin ended his essay by recognizing the "power, passion and talent" that had enabled Hegemann to achieve a work of richness and worth.

The author Joseph Roth, identifying himself as a "reader," not a historian, waxed enthusiastic on *Das steinerne Berlin*, reviewing it in *Das Tagebuch*.[76] His opening sentence addressed the city as if it were an ailing person: "Berlin is a young, unhappy and future city." He praised Hegemann's passionate engagement, biting wit and knowledge, ably combined with an admirable literary style. Roth relished the muckraking approach, which offended others, and did not question the historical veracity of Hegemann's disclosures.

A promotional pamphlet for the book quoted from the positive opinions of Abegg, Benjamin, Roth, and from Friedrich Paulsen's statement in *Die Bauwelt*: "Hegemann's objective criticism of the tragedy of this town plan is certainly justified and very notable. . . ." Hegemann also wrote his own *Selbstanzeige* (self-promotional announcement) of *Das steinerne Berlin*, summarizing its content.[77] He described himself as "a man who in 1909 directed the first international city planning exhibition, and since had been active within the country and abroad as an architect and historic author, engaged in matters of city planning and the impact of political history on it." Hegemann's unfounded claim of being an architect, which he continued throughout the book, misled some of his biographers.

Differing from the favorable reviews, and not mentioned by Hegemann, was a long essay by the historian Ernst Kaeber. Kaeber was a liberal democrat and the director of the City Archive of Berlin; he had published extensively on the city's history and made his career based on his interest in urban history. This background gave him an indisputable position from which to judge *Das steinerne Berlin*. Kaeber's essay was published in the *Mitteilungen des Vereins für die Geschichte Berlins* and carried considerable weight.[78] He was acquainted with Hegemann's early activities on behalf of *Gross-Berlin*, his volumes on the 1910 exhibitions, his American experience, and his recent position as editor for the Wasmuth periodicals, all accomplishments Kaeber respected and which prompted him to write an essay on *Das steinerne Berlin*, rather than a short review. He admired the "old" Hegemann, represented in Volume 1 of *Der Städtebau nach den Ergebnissen . . .* , and detected an abrupt, unexplained change in the author's assessment of the Hohenzollern rulers in Volume 2. In Volume 1 some of their decisions regarding Berlin were not seen as directly responsible for all the deplorable social conditions in the city, particularly the rental barracks that were described so vividly by Hegemann, who had also acknowledged the voices of individuals seeking improvements. In Volume 2, Hegemann had turned from the social to the political, addressing Prussian absolutism with a relentless attack. *Das steinerne Berlin* was based extensively on the later Volume 2, and it was this "new" and present Hegemann whom Kaeber challenged in his essay: "To be sure, the content of the new book is based primarily on the results of the author's pre-war research, adopting it literally, or condensing or expanding it, adding to it or carrying it forward into recent times. Its tenor, however, has changed. There is seldom some recognition, and light and shade are not distributed as done previously. It is truly a 'new' Hegemann who speaks to us, despite all accord between the content of the older and the recent work."

Kaeber doubted that this change of heart was provoked by Hugo Preuss, whose comments are referred to by Hegemann, and considered by Kaeber to be "constructive criticism," misinterpreted by the author of *Das steinerne Berlin*. This is one of the countless errors in the book singled out and documented by Kaeber, who cited historical sources and recent publications. He refuted Hegemann's negative interpretations throughout the book. It would take a specialist in Prussian, and certainly in Berlin history, to verify or dispute Kaeber's assertions. If Hegemann succeeded in "unmasking" Frederick the Great as "hero," Kaeber, in turn, endeavored to unmask his unmasking. He considered it regrettable that Hegemann's tendentious distortions created a caricature of Berlin's urban history and detracted from his worthy political aim of orienting the public against absolutism and toward democracy. According to Kaeber, these political distinctions mattered less than the difference between "social and unsocial" (*sozial und unsozial*) partisanship.

The sections in *Das steinerne Berlin* in which the author stayed within his own expertise were deemed valuable by Kaeber. He considered the chapter on Schinkel brilliant and agreed with Hegemann that Schinkel "was not only the greatest architect of Berlin, but one of the greatest architects of all times."

Hegemann's attention was drawn to the architect in connection with his work on *Das steinerne Berlin*; Schinkel's 150th birthday in 1931 coincided with his own fiftieth birthday, and the trip to Argentina where he noticed "Schinkel's spirit" in the vernacular houses. The history of Berlin became a subterfuge for confronting Schinkel's impact on the city (Fig. 54).

Hegemann's previous publications had referred to Schinkel in relation to work by others, weaving comments through the assessment of contemporary architects by providing a measure for comparison. While his appraisal of Schinkel was not entirely favorable, his criticism was invari-

Fig. 54. The Brandenburger Gate and Schinkel's Gate houses. CCCC

ably restrained and qualified. The vast and growing literature on Schinkel has ignored Hegemann's comments. They provide notable insights to Hegemann's frame of mind toward the end of his tenure at Wasmuth, when he viewed Schinkel with admiring awe and this sentiment permeated the cluster of writings published around 1930. The most important were *Das steinerne Berlin* and the article "*Zu Schinkels* 150. *Geburtstag*" in *WMB/STB*.[79] The latter is similar to Chapter 19 in the book, "Schinkel's *Romantik und unsere Neueste Baukunst*," extracting what pertained to his architectural work from all but the essence of the historical circumstances.

Hegemann's writings on Schinkel are worth considering for what they reveal about the architect's work and the ideas that influenced Hegemann, rather than what they might add to an understanding of Schinkel. In view of the vast literature on Schinkel, Hegemann's views might otherwise seem redundant, but within the context of his intellectual journey and coming toward the end of his dedication to architectural criticism, his focus on Schinkel provides a closure to his involvement with Berlin.

Hegemann's essay honoring Schinkel's birthday is a summation of what appeared scattered throughout other publications. In view of the anniversary, Hegemann related the beginnings of Schinkel's career and his dependence on King Friedrich Wilhelm II and especially his wife Queen Luise, both clients with definite tastes. It is well known how the king steered the architect from the Gothic—according to Schinkel "the impressive style of old-German architecture"—toward Classicism. Schinkel shared a prevailing assumption by ignoring the French origin of the Gothic style. Interestingly, Hegemann was only mildly critical of Schinkel's romantic yearning to produce a Gothic building. The *romantische* Schinkel later succeeded in the Palace Babelsberg near Potsdam, but at the same time he began to experiment with combining gothic and classic forms, searching for the creation of a new style. Hegemann cited the architect's description of his endeavor, "to preserve among us unadulterated and alive what is valuable from former times and discover a measure of its application to the present." Hegemann explained Schinkel's unusual "back-and-forth" between classic and gothic forms as a result of his *romantisch* interpretation that "the style of a building should be determined by its '*Zweck*' (function), and this '*Zweck*' demanded once gothic and another time classic forms." In several instances Friedrich Wilhelm II ordered the architect to use one style or the other, and he obeyed his client. This inconsistency continues to challenge the assessment of Schinkel's buildings. For Hegemann the architect's romantic interpretation of Classicism was confounding, yet he valued Schinkel as the harbinger of a contemporary classic and functional style, in contrast to its opposite, romantic, *unsachlich*.

Referring to the illustrations in his article, Hegemann pointed to the stylistic discrepancies in Schinkel's buildings for Berlin, some of which existed only on paper. Hegemann noted that the Schauspielhaus drew international attention, and the Altes Museum achieved a prominent status. "Schinkel's Altes Museum was not, like all prior building in Berlin, merely the achievement of a German province, but the first museum building on the main land . . . certainly equal to the British Museum being built at the same time in London." Schinkel had transformed provincial Berlin into a metropolis, even a *Weltstadt* of architecture, comparable to what Goethe had achieved for "little" Weimar. Euphorically, Hegemann claimed that Schinkel led the European Classicism begun by Palladio to an acme of perfection, and that he was not only the greatest architect of Berlin, but the greatest architect of all time.

Hegemann's recognition of Schinkel's significance for the Modern Movement is discernible in his early commentaries in the Wasmuth journals. The architect's work and his ideas regarding style and structure exemplified what Hegemann considered most valuable for present and future New Building to emulate. After Hegemann's immersion in the debates on Modernism, his involvement with Schinkel gained particular resonance in his publications of 1930–32. From his later perspective he singled out the prescient Modernism in Schinkel's unbuilt designs for a department store, a library, *Schloss Tegel*, and the *Kavalierhaus*. He considered the department store "100 years ahead of its time" in its functionalism and design, devoting a short article to this unbuilt project for *Unter den Linden*.[80] The title called Schinkel an "artist of facades," and in discussing sections and floor plans, Hegemann demonstrated how Schinkel skillfully accommodated four floors of useful space behind a facade of two stories with large windows. The lightweight roof over the arcade protected pedestrians without obscuring the windows for the lower level of the building.

In "*Zu Schinkels 150. Geburtstag*" and *Das steinerne Berlin*, Hegemann praised the restrained cubic forms and the flat roof of the *Kavalierhaus*, noting that "reactionary racist theorists" battled these as Semitic, probably referring to Schultze-Naumburg and like-minded others. He recommended that they study Schinkel's buildings. For those favoring Modernism, Schinkel's statements were as inspiring as his buildings, and Hegemann frequently quoted them in support of his own ideas. One he favored declared that the new style in architecture should not stand out or be conspicuous emphasizing its novelty when it emerged from "all that exists from the past." On the other hand, while relying on proven accomplishments, "everywhere one is only truly alive, where one creates the new." Hegemann chose these pronouncements in support of his recurrent reprimands of contemporary architects who, wishing to be conspicuous, applied non-functional *industrie-romantisch* elements to their buildings. He lamented that "unfortunately not only the friends of the New Building but also architectural reactionaries could refer to Schinkel."

Hegemann judged that "in the important subject of town planning Schinkel failed almost totally." This was an important shortcoming in view of his regarding architecture and the urban context as interdependent. Within the skyscraper debate Schinkel's "tower per se" placed as a marker and focus in a vista was commendable, which actually concurred with his main principle: "Every edifice should be discrete and self-contained. If connected to another edifice of a different nature, that one should also be self-contained, and it should only find the most comfortable place, position and angle to join the former." Hegemann considered this principle a "declaration of bankruptcy for town planning." He feared that it would result in a "romantic degeneration," with everyone building as he pleased without responding to the neighboring context. Hegemann had devoted much thought to the insertion of buildings into the urban fabric and their problems for contemporary architects. The latter had frequently turned their attention away from the central city toward the sparsely built-up periphery, a move considerd anti-urban. Lack of interest in creative town planning prevailed in Berlin during Schinkel's time, only to be rediscovered in the nineteenth century. Explaining this, Hegemann was perhaps looking for an excuse for the flaw in Schinkel's perception and the absence of significant urban contributions by him in the center of Berlin.

The above passages refer to Hegemann's essay "*Zu Schinkels 150. Geburtstag*," which is notably similar to a chapter in *Das steinerne Berlin*.[81] Throughout the book Schinkel's career is linked to the Hohenzollern rulers. The *WMB/STB* article derived from the chapter "*Schinkels Romantik. . . ,*" which pertained to his architecture and ideas, rather than the political apparatus. Whole parts were extracted verbatim from the more expansive version and synthesized in the article. While the essay is valuable, the representation in *Das steinerne Berlin* is primary, particularly on Schinkel's failure to overcome Berlin's weakness in town planning. Hegemann attributed the city's predicament to the backwardness of Frederick II in matters of art and architecture. He regretted that Schinkel did not create a single harmonious "*Platz*" or site his buildings to optimum advantage. According to Hegemann, he could not be compared to Friedrich Weinbrenner (1766–1826), who abandoned the "Berliner *Romantik*" for *Karlsruhe*, where he accomplished what Schinkel failed to do for Berlin *Mitte* (center).

If Schinkel's bequest to the city did not include a fully realized urban space, he certainly assumed a commanding presence with his individual buildings and monuments. Hegemann's intense dislike for the pompous commemorative statuary of the nineteenth century was shared by many. It affected the reception of the *Reichsehrenmal* competition of 1931–32 and became an occasion for seeking out Schinkel's legacy. It was suggested that his classically severe Neue Wache should undergo interior alterations to convert it into an impressive center for honoring the fallen soldiers. This proposition was supported by the union of the country's veteran associations. Hegemann was an enthusiastic proponent and published three articles on the *Reichsehrenmal* debate. A draft of his personal thoughts on memorializing the "known" war dead remained unpublished.[82]

Hegemann's essay in the *Neue Rundschau* praised the selection of Schinkel's Neue Wache, rescuing it from becoming a dead *Museumsstück* and enhancing its meaning. In this building of 1813, he saw Schinkel's achievement of a creative blend of the spirit of Weimar with the cruder and more military spirit of Prussian Potsdam, and turned briefly to a review of war memorials in Germany and abroad. In response to his pacifist convictions, he wished for a memorial dedicated to all the ten million victims who lost their lives on both sides in World War I as a gesture of *Völkerversöhnung* (reconciliation of nations).

With the *Reichsehrenmal* discussions having drawn attention to Schinkel, Hegemann's article related his career and noted that the architect had volunteered in 1813 to defend the *Vaterland* in the 1813–15 War of Liberation. While others perished, Schinkel was soon relieved from military duty and embarked on building the Neue Wache for the Prussian army in Berlin. Hegemann described the combination of a Roman castrum behind a hall of Doric columns as "a literary folly," which did not, however, encumber the formal integrity and artistic worth of the building. The proposed alterations, under the architect Hermann Tessenow, would leave the exterior of the Neue Wache untouched, so that the objections to its conversion were unjustified. Hegemann compared Schinkel's striving for an architecture of simplicity and severity with the even more urgent demands for these qualities in contemporary architecture. Although frequently the new functionalism would convert into a mere "pose," one ought to recognize that today's determination and vigor devoted to functionalism by comparison rendered Schinkel's architecture "literary and nonfunctional."

Hegemann's other articles on the *Reichsehrenmal* repeated some of these points, but are primarily devoted to the political wrangling surrounding the competition, which involved Nazi ideology and factions. The *Reichsehrenmal* debate is emblematic of the difficulties presented by monuments and monumentality for modern architecture.[83]

Schinkel's enduring presence in Berlin was noted in various projects for the Potsdamer Platz. His Gate Houses (1822–1825) at the entrance to the adjacent Leipziger Platz were untouchable icons, and his designs for a focal point at the end of the Leipziger Strasse in the form of a tower inspired a later attempt to formally integrate these two significant open spaces. One proposal for the Potsdamer Platz involved buildings by Mendelsohn and the firm of the brothers Luckhardt and Anker, contemporaneous with the *Reichsehrenmal* and Neue Wache discussions that had turned attention to Schinkel's buildings and unbuilt projects (Figs. 55–58). Hegemann's article, "Luckhardt's *und* Erich Mendelsohn's *Neubauten am Potsdamer Platz*," revisited these earlier schemes in relation to the contemporary.[84] He linked the Luckhardts' design for the Berlin Haus to Schinkel's for the focal point tower by establishing a *Blickpunkt* (focus). He described how Schinkel's search for an appropriate style for the "tower per se" had led him to make numerous drawings, and ended with his eventual decision that Classicism was unsuitable for a tall building. From medieval examples, Schinkel chose what was advantageous for the construction of a tall edifice, excluding the superfluous. As cited by Hegemann, he required that a new style should "apply everything that had evolved and proven to be of advantage for building, as a not formerly known, but now discovered as a perennially beneficial addition not lacking in aesthetic effectiveness." According to Hegemann, the Luckhardts' design for their skyscraper fulfilled these requirements and was a worthy substitute for Schinkel's unbuilt scheme. Unfortunately, the first and better version of the Berlin Haus had to be modified at the request of the client, the Wohlfahrtsministerium, who thought it resembled a gas tank.

The addition of two distinctive buildings contributed greatly to the Potsdamer Platz. As Mendelsohn pointed out, the Potsdamer Platz was not truly a "*Platz*," but rather an intersection of radial streets, and only by combining it with the Leipziger Platz could an improvement be achieved. As he had done previously, Hegemann wrote admiringly of Mendelsohn's ability to create functional and aesthetically innovative buildings that responded to their urban context.

Several years earlier, attention had focused on the Ulmer Münsterplatz controversy and Hegemann was re-entering city planning debates by initiating the Unter den Linden competition. As mentioned, he presented his own solution for the Potsdamer/Leipziger Platz traffic prob-

Fig. 55. Hegemann in the atelier of architects Hans and Wassili Luckhardt. CCCC

Fig. 56. Hegemann in the Luckhardts' atelier discussing their revised design for the "Haus Berlin" on the Potsdamer Platz. CCCC

lems, one of his few urban designs (see Fig. 39). Hegemann's two plans were published in *STB* in 1925 and in *Das steinerne Berlin* with the caption "*Vorschlag zur Neugestaltung des Potsdamer Platzes*" (Proposal for a reorganization of the Potsdamer Platz) by the architects Werner Hegemann and Oskar Lange.[85] The reproductions in the book and the explanatory notes are the same as those in the article. On the opposite page of the Hegemann/Lange proposal is a contemporary aerial photograph showing the awkward relationship of the two plazas and Schinkel's Gate Houses dwarfed by the surrounding large buildings. By contrast, a drawing by Schinkel presents the Gate Houses against a leafy wall of trees, and in the background the church steeple he had intended for a view point at the end of the Leipziger Strasse.

Another proposal signed by "Architekt: Werner Hegemann, Berlin" and reproduced in *Das steinerne Berlin* is for a harmonious unification of the *Gendarmenmarkt* (Fig. 59). After a fire had devastated the theatre on the square, Schinkel replaced it with his large Schauspielhaus (1819–21), which gained attention beyond Berlin and Germany. In his proposal Hegemann sought to link himself to the renowned architect. The drawing is likely by S. E. Rasmussen, whose design is shown on the same page. A photograph of the square provides the background for Hegemann's suggestions, which involved eliminating whatever marred the formal unity of the three major buildings, including the centrally located Schauspielhaus. Hegemann enclosed the rectangular plaza with a dense row of trees, shielding the open space from the buildings on the periphery. This feature was akin to the trees forming the unifying element along the Unter den Linden. Hegemann's proposition, more classical than Rasmussen's design, has the disadvantage of isolating the *Gendarmenmarkt* from its urban context. The only gap in the wall of trees was opposite the Schauspielhaus.

A third proposal included in *Das steinerne Berlin*, also crediting Hegemann as architect, was signed jointly with Leo Adler. Previously published in *STB*, it addressed an attempt to salvage the Opera House by Georg W. von Knobelsdorff.[86] A strongly worded critique of the proposals to enlarge the Opera House accompanied the suggestions by Hegemann and Adler for more moderate alterations. Responses generated a polarized debate in professional journals and Hegemann reported on the affair with polemical savvy in *WMB*, using expressions such as *schamlose Verschandelung des Opernhauses* (shameless defacement of the opera) and *der bürokratische Hexenssabbat auf dem Berliner Opernplatz* (the bureaucratic witches' sabbath on the Opernplatz of Berlin).[87]

References to Hegemann's personal involvement with urban issues in Berlin and his vigorous crusade for improvements permeate *Das steinerne Berlin*. Interspersed with his history of the city are recollections from his brief early years in Berlin, which compressed an astonishing amount of civic action. He was rightfully proud of these accomplishments, which were

Fig. 57. Model of a redesigned Potsdamer and Leipziger Platz with the Haus Berlin by Luckhardt and Anker. On the far right is the site for Mendelsohn's Columbus-Haus. WMB/STB, *May, 1931.* WHA

Fig. 58. Model of the second version of the Berlin Haus by Luckhardt and Anker, with details of cars and figures. WMB/STB, *May, 1931.* WHA

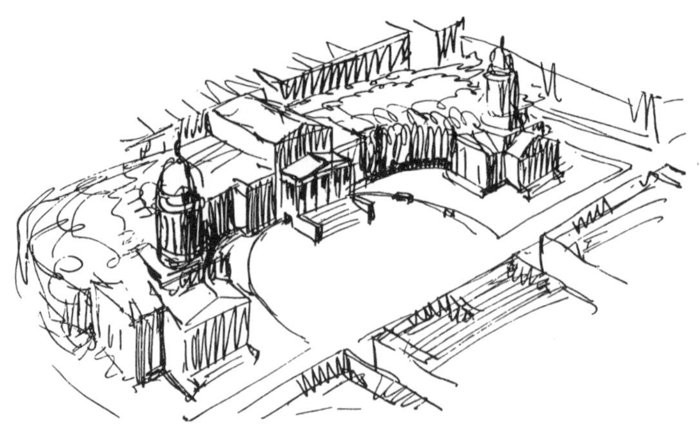

Fig. 59. Hegemann's proposal for redesigning the Gendarmenmarkt. *Drawing by Georg Münter and Rasmussen's* STB, *1928, No. 10 and* Das steinerne Berlin. WHA

later mostly forgotten as a result of his long stay in America and the passage of time that included the Great War and social upheaval. On the other hand, reproducing his plans and signing himself as "architect" verged on gratuitous promotion of his reputation.

In line with this tendency was a biographical curriculum vitae in the form of a lengthy footnote to "*Berlins Freiflächen, Bodenwucher und Bodenpolitik*," the last chapter in *Das steinerne Berlin*.[88] Although chapters in the book address distinct topics, the politics of land use and housing, especially low-income housing, was invariably brought up. Hegemann relentlessly called attention to the urgency of providing adequate shelter. His biographical note makes clear that this was the salient theme of his formative years and his career. This is also substantiated in this chapter, which interconnects the issues of open space, land speculation, politics, and transportation, bringing them into the present. Hegemann had grappled with these issues decades earlier, and their urgency had not diminished. While the scope of this chapter and the "*Schluss*" was confined to Berlin and Germany, Hegemann's ultimate study of the housing question, written in New York in 1935, comprised both America and Europe.

Das steinerne Berlin, the preoccupation regarding housing, and the reconsideration of Friedrich Schinkel brought Hegemann full circle on themes that had dominated his attention and activities. Prescient of the impending political crisis, he turned with fearless ability and energy to opposing Nazism.

Despite some negative reactions, since its publication *Das steinerne Berlin* is rated a landmark work, and for many it is the only work associated with Hegemann's name, linking him to the city where he spent several significant years.

Hegemann, Belletrist

Returning to Europe in 1921 after his prolonged stay in America, Hegemann crossed the Atlantic and the threshold into writing historical fiction. This pursuit developed into a serious avocation that lasted until his exile in 1933. In a little over a decade he became the author of five extensively researched volumes and countless articles on topics outside of architecture and city planning. He also oversaw the translations of several of these books into English and French.

Das steinerne Berlin represents a borderline case of this category. *Deutsche Schriften, Iphigenie*, published in 1924 under the pseudonym Manfred Maria Ellis, was the first of Hegemann's historical novels. With only the most tenuous precedents, it emerged from and is intricately connected to Hegemann's interlude in Naples. *Deutsche Schriften, Iphigenie*, and the ensuing conversations have been discussed in connection with Hegemann's return to Europe. In some respects *Deutsche Schriften, Iphigenie* was a tentative work, part narrative and part stage play with a philosophical dialogue. Its significance was heightened by transmutations into subsequent works linked in a variety of ways to this initial imaginative fruit of his pen. The later works also employ the dialogue format involving contemporary, historical, and fictional figures, weaving fictitious and real events with creative license. This distinctive literary device echoes Hegemann's latent ambition to write for the theater, which may have been stimulated by his reading of classic dramas.

These works of fiction by Hegemann are of a literary genre labeled *Historische Belletristik* in Germany, a genre which received a negative connotation from the historical establishment. The subtitle of Gradmann's study of this literary category defines *Historische Belletristik* as "popular historical literature interposing politics, scholarship and society in the Weimar Republic."[89] The controversy between the "legitimate," academic, and predominantly conservative historians, and the liberal authors of the *Historische Belletristik*, including Hegemann, is aptly described by Gradmann. Hegemann's belletristic was attacked by the academic establishment, which refrained from criticizing his writings on architecture and city planning.

His historical publications followed one another in quick succession, considering that he had recently returned to Berlin, begun his editorial employment at Wasmuth, designed and built a house for his growing family, and traveled frequently. Günther Baum, a young Austrian, stayed with the family and at times acted as Hegemann's secretary, making the profusion of his literary output possible. The third-floor attic of the house contained Hegemann's "atelier" and a small apartment with a kitchenette and bath for an in-house assistant.

Deutsche Schriften, initially published privately in a limited edition, came out in three volumes as a second edition in 1924.[90] *Fridericus oder das Königsopfer*, based almost entirely on *Deutsche Schriften*, was published 1925, and again, slightly expanded, in 1926. That same year he published a related but different endeavor, a German version of Paul Claudel's play *Proteus. Napoleon oder "Kniefall vor dem Heros"* followed in 1927, and *Der gerettete Christus, oder Iphigenies Flucht vor dem Ritualopfer* in 1928. *Das Jugendbuch vom grossen König, oder Kronprinz Friederichs Kampf um die Freiheit* appeared in 1930, the same year as *Das steinerne Berlin.*[91] The latter can be considered a biography of the city, but it is not an example of *Historische Belletristik*. Nor was the last book in this sequence, *Entlarvte Geschichte*, published in the spring of 1933. It was the culmination of Hegemann's scathing attacks against Hitler, and resulted in his exile.

It lies beyond the focus of this study to engage thoroughly with Hegemann's historical works as literature and explore connections to other authors, notably to Goethe, Nietzsche, Thomas Mann, H. G. Wells, and Bernard Shaw. Neither will the arguments regarding the interpretation of historical events be addressed in depth. Attention will focus on the importance of the themes and intentions of these works for an assessment of Hegemann's life and accomplishments. The dominant strands of his intellectual trajectory were urban history, its effect on the built environment, and his commitment to social progress linked to pacifism. These pursuits intersected, but also developed independently along parallel courses.

Indicative of the attraction literary authors held for Hegemann are his dedications. The one for *Deutsche Schriften* read, "Dedicated by the author to his friends Bernard Shaw, Hugo von Hofmannsthal, Anatole France with admiration and gratitude." He cherished contacts with men and women of letters, gathering them in the imagined "salons" of his historical fiction.

Comparable to his writings on architecture and city planning, Hegemann's historical and political output represents writing as protest, using words as weapons in his resolute battle for a world of peace and righteousness. There is a quixotic and tragic aspect to his crusade and in this respect his historical writings and political publications coincide with his aim as an urbanist and architectural critic.

Hegemann's historical biographies generated a profusion of reviews both positive and negative.[92] Those in favor praised his style and wit, while others accused him of distorting facts, although his thorough research was recognized. Criticism was expectedly severe regarding *Fridericus*, and the author devoted a lengthy *Nachwort* in the 1926 edition, refuting the "*Feldzug des geistigen Leibregimentes*" (the campaign of the intellectual bodyguard) against his *Fridericus*.[93]

In these works, Hegemann reserved his sharpest attacks not for the Prussian kings or Napoleon I but for the entrenched academics who distorted history and transformed dangerous, power hungry individuals into mythical heroes. Especially singled out among this breed of historians were Preuss, Ranke, Treitschke, Schmoller, and Delbrück, all members of the so-called *geistiges Leibregiment* (intellectual bodyguard) defending the Prussian rulers. Following their lead, a gullible public acclaimed these heroic figures with religious fervor. In Germany Frederick the Great was considered an untouchable national icon, although this was a fabrication by the scholarly establishment. Hegemann was prescient in recognizing the dangers of the German hero cult, which would lead to the blind faith in a leader or *Führer*.

In 1927 the controversies surrounding Hegemann's *Fridericus* generated a veritable battle for Frederick the Great. In the pages of the *Frankfurter Zeitung*, the intellectually well-matched "Professor" Veit Valentin and Hegemann duelled in a sequence of articles.[94] Some of the copies, preserved in the Hegemann Papers, are heavily underlined and contain comments by Hegemann in pencil and red ink. Other individuals entered into this "war of the pen" as well, considering Hegemann's position *amerikanisch* and unpatriotic. However, his critics failed to detect in his approach the American muckraking journalism practiced by Lincoln Steffens who exposed the "shame of the cities" in his articles and books. Hegemann's alter ego, the supposedly American Manfred Maria Ellis, expressed himself with greater stylistic sophistication than Steffens.

The notoriety haunting Hegemann's belletristic works and his articles on Frederick II responded to the groundwork for welcoming Hitler as the successor of the legendary "Great" king. Hegemann called attention to it in his exposé, "*Die 'geheimen Testamente' des ersten 'Nationalsozialisten,'*

Friedrich des Grossen." Frederick II's testaments were written in French and deemed so damaging by Bismarck that they were not made public until after World War I. Yet surprisingly, at an event in Berlin's Lustgarten in 1932, a leader of the National Socialists officially declared Frederick the Great the "first National Socialist." In the eight sections of his article Hegemann documented the similarity between Frederick II's declarations and Hitler's "Program" and statements in *Mein Kampf.* Hegemann's article was published in newspapers in Berlin, Dortmund, Vienna, and Zürich.[95]

It is doubtful if Hegemann anticipated these connections to Hitler and Nazi ideology when he embarked on the dismantling of the Frederick II hero myths in 1922. His agenda, beginning with *Deutsche Schriften*, was the unmasking of heroes by exposing repressed historical truths. Walter Benjamin called Hegemann the *Heldenschläger* or "killer of heroes," like Saint George, a killer of dragons. Benjamin recommended the book *Fridericus* to his friend Gerhard Scholem in a letter of July 1925, calling it "the most radical attempt imaginable to vanquish the 'Greatness' of this monarch. Besides it is superbly written and gives an impression of reliability." Benjamin's comment is cited in an essay by Lothar Müller on the various assessments of Frederick II in the twentieth century, on the occasion of the hundredth anniversary of his coronation as King of Prussia in January 2001.[96]

The explanation Hegemann gives for launching his campaign against the perpetrators of the hero cult is the topic of his Preface to *Das Jugendbuch vom grossen König* (1930).[97] Writing at the beginning of Hitler's rise to power, Hegemann referred to Manfred Maria Ellis's "American criticism" voiced in the earlier *Fridericus oder das Königs Opfer* (1925–26), which expanded on the prior *Deutsche Schriften.* Ellis "left not a good hair on Frederick the Great or his historians," and one reviewer noted that "the history of Frederick the Great had not yet been written."[98] According to Hegemann this remark prompted him to write an additional book on the Prussian king, resulting in the *Jugendbuch.* He dedicated it with admiration to "The significance of Frederick the Great and Napoleon I for the present time." The intention of Hegemann's "new," revisionist historical writing was to search for sources other than the official documentation, which was invariably laudatory and lacked impartiality. In his Introduction of 1930, Hegemann compared the idealized image of Frederick II with the cult of Hitler. He cited a Nazi admirer: "The appearance of a Hitler . . . is completely irrational and almost mythical in its effect."

The "new historiography" advocated by Hegemann attempted to unmask the idealized Frederick II by lancing the myth-makers and exposing previously ignored sources that substantiated the reprehensible realities of his life and reign. He achieved a ruthless deconstruction of the "greatness" myth of Frederick II and, uncannily, of Hitler as well. Similarly he contended with the "hero" Napoleon.

Hegemann's historical books are linked together in a series that explored and elaborated these themes, evolving from the fictitious discussions initially published as *Deutsche Schriften*. Conversations are structured between individuals representing different points of view, with the narrator (Hegemann or his alter ego) acting as catalyst. The author explained the interrelationship of his publications in the Foreword to *Der gerettete Christus*: "The notorious discussions engaged in by the German/American Manfred Maria Ellis and his guests in the Villa Boccanera in Naples before and after the World War have already been published in excerpts in the book *Iphigenie, ein Lustspiel, nebst den sieben Gesprächen über das Königsopfer*. This book appeared in 1924 in two small private editions by the Sanssouci-Verlag. Only a selection from it—with some additions dealing, like the excerpts, with Frederick the Great—was published in 1925 and again in 1926, with the title *Fridericus, oder das Königsopfer*, by Jacob Hegner, Hellerau."[99] According to Hegemann, the book on Christus, who was saved from becoming the victim of misguided religious fervor and mythic hero worship and was, rather, a contradictory human being, was an expansion of the discussions of "bloody human sacrifices" in ancient and recent times. A study of Napoleon beyond the scope of *Fridericus* would be forthcoming.

Woven into the book's extensive discussions of Frederick II's questionable decisions and actions in the political arena are topics concerning Hegemann's city planning and cultural concerns. Apparently many of the Prussian ruler's deeds intentionally prevented Berlin from becoming a *Weltstadt*, a metropolis of cultural status. He wrote of Frederick II as "an enemy of architecture," who violated von Knobelsdorff's plans for Sanssouci so that its southern side "emerged like a temple of the pharaohs out of the mudd [*sic*] of the Nile." The king ruined the classic design for the Opernplatz in Berlin, also by von Knobelsdorff, with the construction of a tall baroque library. While insisting on his own architectural "caprices," Frederick II expressed himself crudely against the contemporary architects von Knobelsdorff and Winckelmann, who favored a "pure" Classicism.

Even during his lifetime Frederick was notorious for his infatuation with France and his disdain for the achievements of his own country. French was his primary language; his use of German was minimal. His admiration for his confidant Voltaire contrasted sharply with his open contempt for German authors and artists, including his contemporary, Goethe. Comments on this subject are expressed by various individuals in the *Deutsche Schriften*, notably Goethe and Thomas Mann, and are absorbed into *Fridericus*. Hegemann may have chosen the title *Deutsche Schriften* for his book as emblematic of German literature contradicting Frederick II's ill-informed attitude. Hegemann's fluency in several languages and his awareness of their role in advancing pacifism was integral to his advocacy of a transnational European culture. Referring also to Goethe's *Gesamtnationalität*, this conviction emerged again in *Napoleon*.

The volumes deriving from *Deutsche Schriften* included a number of personalities from an international intellectual elite. The author as narrator commanded pride of place as facilitator, and he was careful to cite from the participants' publications, rather than inventing their contributions to the conversation. Occasionally the quotations were taken out of context, rendering them problematic within the controversies engulfing the books on Frederick II and *Der gerettete Christus* of 1928.[100]

Napoleon oder "Kniefall vor dem Heros" (Napoleon or prostration before the hero) elaborated many of the themes of *Fridericus*, primarily the lure of a charismatic "great" strong- or super-man revered and followed blindly as a leader and savior.[101] Hegemann commented in the Foreword to the English translation of 1929 that Frederick the Great was "one of the most obnoxious figures in the history of the world, . . . [who] does not only affect German politics. . . . [This] is a question of international and of high moral significance. If my thesis that he was obnoxious is right, then the fact that he could be held up for a hundred and fifty years as the model for kings, seems to me a world tragedy."[102]

Napoleon starts out with Hegemann's extraordinary invention. As related in *Deutsche Schriften* the fictitious American Manfred Maria Ellis, host of the gatherings at the Villa Boccanera, supposedly vanished crossing the Atlantic in 1916, but he now re-emerged, seven years later to the delight of his family and friends.[103] As the host at the Villa in Posiollipo and at the sessions concerning Napoleon, Ellis linked these two events. Reacting to the criticism of his "American" comments on Frederick II, the real Ellis begged the author not to publicize his fate or mention his name in the forthcoming book on Napoleon. In response to his friend's wish, the fictional Ellis was referred to as *Der Hausherr* or "the host." Once again he contrived to be a pivotal participant in a multinational symposium that included personages both alive and dead, real and imaginary. Among them were Anatole France, Berthold Vallentin, H. G. Wells, George Bernard Shaw, Oswald Spengler, Benito Mussolini, and a few unidentified women.[104]

Hegemann provided the forum with a grand setting in the form of an "enchanted castle" located at the summit of Mont Blanc. Referred to as the *Zauberschloss*, it evokes Thomas Mann's novel *The Magic Mountain*. Mann also figures among Hegemann's fictional participants at Mont Blanc. In his description of the "enchanted castle" Hegemann combined aspects of Expressionist visionary architectural schemes with those of popular science fiction. The passages also reflect his interest in the theater, scenography, stage sets, and contemporary film, such as *Metropolis* (1927).

The design of the "enchanted castle" was dictated by the purpose of holding international symposia. The unusual architectural features of this mediation [*sic*] center play a provocative, even major role in the discussions. In order to stimulate communication between the participants from diverse cultural and intellectual backgrounds and to further a fruitful dialogue, the host did not shy away from employing unique devices. They bear an uncanny resemblance to Hans Scharoun's and Bruno Taut's *Volkshaus* (community center) designs and Taut's superstructures of glass for mountaintops shown in his *Alpine Architecture*.[105] The interior of the "enchanted castle" was prescient of Norman Bel Geddes's 1930s project for a revolving restaurant in the air. Hegemann described revolving discs of rock crystal in the floor of the "hall of peace" and the dining hall of translucent glacial ice, enabling guests to meet each other as if in an "international carousel."[106]

The emphasis on the site-specific location, architectural design, and grandiose setting nearly drowns out the debate on Napoleon. Within this framework, or stage setting, Napoleon is presented as an ambiguous figure—on the one hand, the conquering hero of brutal military campaigns, and on the other, the enlightened savior and planner of a multinational empire. Rather than a biographical narrative, *Napoleon* serves as a subterfuge for analyzing the pros and cons of war and the possibilities for promoting a peaceful pan-Europe.

The fictional forum in the "enchanted castle" was initiated by the *Hausherr*, i.e., Hegemann, alias Manfred Maria Ellis. The *Hausherr* welcomed a gathering of politicians, historians, and authors, who arrived in transit to and from Geneva, where international conferences were taking place. The League of Nations is not actually mentioned in the novel, although in 1927, when Hegemann was working on the *Napoleon* volume, the pages of *WMB* covered the competition for the League of Nations building in Geneva. Hegemann was engaged in these proceedings as an architectural critic and an advocate of pacifism and worldwide understanding. The edifice of the "enchanted castle" and the dialogue in the "hall of peace" represented his personal visions of a "world center" or *Mundaneum* as a symbol of universal brotherhood and communication. Not being an architect, he exposed his ideas for a League of Nations headquarters in a fictional format. As a result Hegemann's urban, architectural, and political considerations intersected more decisively in his *Napoleon* than in his previous books on Frederick II.

In a lengthy welcoming address, the host playfully called attention to some positive aspects of war.[107] For instance, war moved people around and promoted new alliances, comparable to the rotating discs and tables in the palace which activated a less bloody world motion. A geopolitical carousel would provide a worldwide planning scope to this concept. To accomplish this, the earth had to be cut into a thousand slices, like a hard-boiled egg, with every second slice rotating around the axis, which would force the inhabitants to get to know each other. No blood would be spilled in this global merry-go-round and it would likely cost less than Napoleon's far-reaching campaigns.

Continuing on a regional scale, the conversation turned to climate control made feasible by futuristic technology, that would provide more lasting benefits than the vast capital outlays for war. Some of the schemes brought up were also suggested in the earlier Expressionist utopias and in popular science fiction. The host observed that skyscrapers, which rendered Manhattan into a "crazy mountain range," could be put to good use. From their towering height tubes could suction water from the *Wolkenfeger* (cloud-sweepers) and balloons, and conduct it via energy-producing turbines to ground level. Another possibility would be to capture clouds and drag them to arid regions to provide humidity. The bad climate of Europe had probably incited Napoleon to yearn for warmer regions like Egypt.

The real Hegemann repeated these passages on American skyscrapers and the weather in his reply to an inquiry by the journal *Die Literarische Welt*, under the title "*Das Land in dem ich wohnen möchte: Umzugsgedanken*" (The country where I would like to live; thoughts on moving).[108] The journal addressed poets and authors of renown posing the question of "When, where, and how would you prefer to live rather than here now presently?" In 1932 this question had political implications, which Hegemann avoided, opting for humorous comments on the weather and how to improve it.

Turning to concerns of daily life after putting the finishing touches on *Napoleon*, Hegemann departed on a journey to Egypt. He claimed that the bad European climate had contributed to the congested, unsanitary housing in Paris and Berlin. Instead of devoting economic resources to improve urban conditions, citizens approved wasting funds by celebrating the warmongering *Menschenschlächter* (butchers of mankind).

The lengthy and witty introduction to *Napoleon* by the host concludes with an invitation to the assembled guests to be "whirled around on the rotating stage of the castle to simulate a world-war and migration of nations."[109]

A subsequent chapter, "Napoleon and Frederick the Great ["*die*," plural], and Painting, Architecture and Music," distills insights of Hegemann's ideas on architecture, conveyed by the host in conversation with Berthold Vallentin.[110] Their discussion reveals Hegemann's hope for a statesman and enlightened rational planner to guide the built environment. Napoleon certainly came closer to this ideal than the doctrinaire Frederick II. Throughout the discourse the host is the ultimate arbiter on matters of architecture and planning.

Hegemann deemed Napoleon's position regarding building and planning worthier than Frederick II's. Vallentin considered that while art was a mere diversion for Napoleon, building and urbanism commanded his attention as "historical document, political expression, [and] objects of usefulness and beautification for the state, . . . but certainly not true art." These convictions, rather than any aesthetic criteria, determined Napoleon's preference for Classicism and monumentality. In spite of these limitations, the host rated Napoleon's legacy superior to that of Frederick the Great. The latter clung to the "baroque aberrations of his youth" at a time when leading contemporary architects in France and Germany were nurturing a second revival of Classicism. The Prussian king's reactionary attitude was exceedingly painful for the architects Winckelmann and von Knobelsdorff, as well as for the poet Lessing. Vallentin disputes his host's assumption that Napoleon's reticence from becoming directly involved with architecture actually contributed to the commendable results. On the contrary, Napoleon showed keen interest and demanded that "his own architecture" express "simplicity" and "originality in meaning and forms." The host respects Napoleon's acknowledgment that "an in-depth understanding of classical examples certainly did not hinder the originality and modernity of art, but, on the contrary, contributed to it." Napoleon's statement, "what is genuine, is always beautiful," was applicable to contemporary Modernism. However, this did not apply to all buildings in the Empire style, which harbored discrepancies between the exterior and interior. According to the host, these could be excused, because "architecture, like language, is as much a matter of custom and tradition as of practical requirements." For example, Napoleon urged the use of iron as construction material, inappropriate for classical buildings, but farsighted for nineteenth-century architecture. The host disapproved of the use of iron for the dome of the Capitol in Washington, D.C., a building akin to the Pantheon. Equally farsighted for his time was Napoleon's idea to develop Versailles into a garden suburb of Paris, when the rest of Europe did not become interested in garden cities until the late nineteenth century.

In his dialogue, Vallentin, described by the author as "peculiar," is introduced as a Napoleon enthusiast who changes sides with the host, turning into a critic of the Corsican. Vallentin points out that Napoleon and the Prussian kings shared strong suspicions that architects took financial advantage of their clients. For Napoleon this distrust reinforced his conviction that architecture was an art following its own regulations and goals, using the support of the state without accepting its oversight and control. He favored engineers working within a state-controlled system, and his corps of engineers carried out his admirable plan for a network of streets and boulevards in Paris.

The discourse on Napoleon and his times occupies the first twenty-four chapters of Hegemann's book. It is followed by a section entitled "*Die Geisterbeschwörung: Hebbel, Nietzsche, Spengler*" (The exorcism . . .) comprising another twenty chapters. The first, "Life of the Heroes after

Death," introduces a surrealistic, phantasmagoric ambience into the intellectual forum.

In the forty-first chapter, "Hope for a 'Greater-Switzerland' and the War of the Future," the "well-known German-American M. M. E. . . . came to speak once more on his favorite idea." Now mentioning Ellis by name, Hegemann linked the subsequent passages directly to *Deutsche Schriften*, expanding on his personal vision of a peaceful, multi- and transnational pan-Europe under the umbrella of a Greater Switzerland. The goal was a cleansing of Europe from national hatreds, arriving at the supranational level described by Goethe. The end comes as a violent natural disaster destroys the "enchanted castle." Only Ellis, an Englishman, a Frenchman, and a Russian escape, by descending the mountain.

Hegemann concluded *Napoleon* in Berlin in August 1927. Exactly a year later he completed another book based on the conversations held in the Villa Boccanera. He signed the Foreword to *Der gerettete Christus oder Iphigenies Flucht vor dem Ritualopfer* in August 1928. It is dedicated "in gratitude" to two Protestant clergymen and close relatives: his grandfather Friedrich Hegemann and his brother Otmar Johannes Hegemann.[111]

In the Foreword Hegemann established a close link to his previous books on Frederick II and Napoleon, referring to their dominant themes and suggesting that these heroes had been sacrificial victims or had committed self-sacrifice. Thomas Mann interpreted Frederick II's renunciation of his avocation to philosophy, bowing to the demands of his ensuing role as king, as an act of self-sacrifice. In the debates on Napoleon, the historian Elie Faure maintained that the Corsican and Christ were comparable martyrs sacrificing themselves to realize the kingdom of their dreams. Ellis refutes this interpretation. Throughout the debates, he defends the position that sacrifice and self-sacrifice were never meritorious or praiseworthy heroic acts.

Hegemann's alter ego Ellis advocates mercy and compassion, citing Jesus: "I desire mercy not sacrifice" (Matthew 9, 13). This and other passages from the Bible form the basis for the unveiling of the true Christ as a *Mensch*, a person who did not die on the cross. This is the main tenet of the book *Der gerettete Christus*, illustrated with images from Albrecht Dürer's "*Kleine Passion.*" Divesting and purifying the mythical figure of Christ from popular beliefs—an unmasking of the real historical "*Mensch mit seinem Widerspruch*" (man with all his contradictions)—the narrative included descriptions of comparable expiatory sacrifices of human victims from ancient and historic times and "barbaric" tribes.

Reactions to the publication of *Der gerettete Christus* were, as the author had anticipated, comparably vehement as those greeting *Fridericus*. Denying Christ's death on the cross and considering the venerable imagery of the bleeding Jesus idolatry were denounced as blasphemy. Legal action against Hegemann and the publisher Kiepenheuer was threatened, yet ultimately withdrawn. The case was similar to the persecution of the artist George Grosz in 1929 for his satirical image of Christ on the cross wearing a gas mask and military boots, bearing the inscription, "Shut up and obey!" Grosz was acquitted and left Germany shortly afterwards.

Not all comments on Hegemann's *Der gerette Christus* were hostile, and some even regarded his approach not sufficiently "free-thinking." Reviewers were puzzled by the author's connection to his Protestant clergy relatives, his knowledge of the Bible, and his opposition to accepted Christian doctrine. The author used his alter ego, the resurrected American Manfred Maria Ellis, to elucidate these ideas. By now it was generally assumed that Ellis spoke for Hegemann and his beliefs could be attributed to modern American interpretations of the New Testament. The perception of Jesus as a historical figure rather than a deity and icon has become widespread since Hegemann published his book. Today it would not be received as unusual, but even then not all reactions were negative.

An insightful review came from the theologian Günther Dehn, writing in the periodical *Eckart–Blätter für evangelische Geisteskultur*.[112] Dehn was associated with the Protestant movement for social justice, whose prime advocate was the Swiss philosopher Karl Barth.[113] Both vigorously opposed National Socialism not only in their church, but as political radicals. It is probable that Hegemann sympathized with the theology of ethics and social justice promoted by Barth and his friend, although he does not refer to them by name. In 1928, Dehn, the pastor in a working-class district in Berlin, gave a lecture entitled "The Church and the Reconciliation of Nations," in which he spoke against the glorification of militarism and war on Biblical grounds. He was hounded by right-wing theologians and the press, and his efforts to obtain an academic position ran into difficulties. Dehn's predicament may explain the somewhat guarded tone of his review of *Der gerettete Christus*. Dehn perceived obvious connections between Hegemann's latest book and the previous *Fridericus* and *Napoleon* and he admired the author as one of the most cultivated and learned contemporary minds, who also had exceptional knowledge of a wide range of both historical and current subjects. According to Dehn, these qualities were combined with a passionate dedication to the destruction of false heroic myths and a quest to discover the hidden truth about historical figures. Recognizing the spiritual damage done by gods and idols, their removal made room for the discovery of the true God. Dehn put the challenge to Hegemann: "You have overthrown the gods, now show us God!" He doubted that the book presented an alternative concept of God by demonstrating that Jesus did not suffer an expiatory death for the salvation of mankind. The theologian saw the meaning of God for the twentieth century as charitable and forgiving, akin to the beliefs of American Unitarianism, and wondered if Hegemann had absorbed these ideas during his stays in America. In 1909, Hegemann had established close ties to the cultural elite in Boston, many of whom were imbued with the social commitment emanating from the Unitarian view of God's concerned presence in the real world. During his stay in Boston, Hegemann became acquainted with the prominent Unitarian Francis Greenwood Peabody, founder of the Department of Social Ethics at Harvard University and the Social Museum providing guidance to the academic study of social progress.[114] Hegemann was influenced by Peabody's activities, which demonstrated social ethics as basic to Christian religion. In *Der gerettete Christus*, the fictional Ellis portrays himself as a Unitarian while discussing religion with two German theologians, announcing that he is an "American Unitarian favoring controversy," a perfect characterization of Hegemann himself.[115] How the misinterpretation of Jesus's death has left a legacy of violence, and the view of Jesus as a person persist as important themes for Unitarianism and are very similar to Hegemann's beliefs.[116]

In several articles from this period, and notably in his late volumes on housing, Hegemann connected social planning with a radical Christian ethic and the potential goodness of divine law. The international gospel movement motivating the settlement houses in England and America and related progressivist urban endeavors were facets of an enlightened approach to religion that appealed to Hegemann's pragmatic idealism. The myth of the sacrificial Christ was unacceptable, ceding to the reality of a historic *Mensch*.

The effects of religious concepts on Hegemann's ideas about planning are apparent in several pieces written in the late twenties, as well as his works on housing dating from his last years in exile. Advocating functional planning on a global scale, and addressing God's role in worldwide events are concepts stated in an unpublished draft, "*Entwurf zu einer Einleitung*" (Draft of an Introduction).[117] He introduced the topic as one of current relevance, apparently written in 1933: "Recently much discussion dealt with 'matters of planning.' In connection with this the old wisdom came to mind, that also God did not manage chaotically and planlessly, but instead organized the universe according to his wise plan, which, however, presently cannot as yet be perceived." According to Hegemann the present miserable, unstructured conditions were a stratagem for a contrast to the admirable divine world plan to be revealed in the future. In the meantime human beings would proceed according to their free will, and the idea that "*der Teufel ist los*" (there is the devil to pay). Mentioning the devil as instrumental in derailing God's universal wise plan presumably refers to Hitler, who was frequently designated "*der Teufel.*"

Hegemann's article, "*Christentum, Landwirtschaft und Wohnungsnot*" (Christianity, agriculture and housing shortage), established a direct relationship between religion and city planning. It also demonstrated a curious combination of his convictions as a rational, progressive urbanist with that of a religious mystic. Conceivably the essay was requested by the two journals, both devoted to relgious topics, in which it appeared soon after the publication of *Der gerettete Christus*.[118] The author commented on a revival of religious thought taking place in Denmark, which had begun in the previous century under the leadership of "the prophet of the north," N. F. S. Grundtvig (1783–1872). Hegemann described him as a mystic, a realist, and a nationalist who championed mass education by founding schools for peasants. Instead of directing religious mysticism toward building cathedrals and burning witches, Grundtvig engaged his "joyous Christianity" to elevate the living standards and the political freedom of the small landowners and peasants.

As was his custom, Hegemann published as articles excerpts from *Der gerettete Christus*, which had previously appeared in *Deutsche Schriften* and *Fridericus*. One of these is "*Der Christliche Schülertragödie*," which relates the gruesome sacrificial death of a young boy at the hands of his peers, instigated by the teacher in charge.[119] The introductory vignette to *Der gerettete Christus*, "*Osterlamm und Festmahl*," was republished as "*Die Festfreude der Kinder*."[120] In poetic passages the flaneur Hegemann strolled through the streets of Naples during Holy Week. He observed children playing affectionately with white lambs. The day before Easter, these were slaughtered, often in the presence of the children, and the next day were consumed as the festive meal of the Osterlamm. These observations led Hegemann to reminisce about a childhood experience, when he became attached to a drake in the village pond where he played with his sailboats. Upon the approach of Ascension Day, the seven-year-old watched with horror as the drake was decapitated by the servants. That evening the family gathered for a festive meal of roast duck. Young Werner ate the dinner but forever remembered the incident as one approaching cannibalism.

The connection of *Der gerettete Christus* to *Deutsche Schriften* is notable for the role Bernard Shaw played in the discussions in the Villa Boccanera.[121] Shaw was not aware of it until the English translation was published as *Christ Rescued* almost a decade later.[122] Critical reactions to *Christ Rescued* surpassed those in Germany, probably because Bernard Shaw figured so prominently in the book.

In the spring of 1933 the controversy over *Christ Rescued* generated extensive correspondence between Hegemann, the publishers Skeffington & Son, and the translator Gerald Griffin, and continued after his abrupt departure to Switzerland and France. Bernard Shaw wrote to Hegemann protesting the inclusion of his remarks in *Christ Rescued* without having obtained his permission and without citing the sources. Hegemann replied from Geneva, begging Shaw to allow the book's publication.[123] Shaw relented and *Christ Rescued* was published in London in the fall of 1933.

Hegemann's Preface to the English translation defended the "exhaustive inquiry into the religious significance of human blood-sacrifices in ancient and modern times," which began with the dialogues held in the Villa Boccanera between the American Ellis and his guests and led to an examination of the crucifixion of Christ.[124] He repeated his tenet that the inconsistency of Christ's statements was proof of his having been a genuine person, because posterity did not perceive mythical, fictitious personages as homogeneous characters. According to Hegemann the contemporary relevance of Christ's teachings could be found in his "economic theory" that proposed a sharing of wealth, and a better, more equitable wage for daily work. Regarding war, Ellis thought Christ ambiguous, and as the founder of a worldwide religion, his teachings left room for various interpretations.

In conclusion, Hegemann absolved himself from the claims by those participating, stating that "the dialogues in this book, while representing the views of the speakers, are mainly imaginary." The Preface in *Christ Rescued* is signed Geneva, October 1933, shortly before the Hegemanns left Europe for America.

Berlin 1933

Political relevance permeated Hegemann's thinking, writing, and activities throughout his life, becoming all-consuming in the years just preceding and during his exile. His preoccupation with history was infused with political purpose and the conviction that an understanding of the past could guide and shape the future. During his last years in Berlin his political concerns overshadowed all others, although he kept up his work at Wasmuth and his involvement with architecture and urbanism. Nonetheless, from about 1929 on, his energy centered chiefly on confronting the Nazi menace with his aptitude as a writer and by forging relationships with like-minded persons defending freedom of expression and pacifism. Hegemann developed close ties with the left-wing intellectuals associated with the periodicals-*cum*-institutions *Die Weltbühne* and *Das Tagebuch*. He did not participate in professional politics but was driven by the urgency to enter the political debate as an individual battling for human values. The political and economic climate rendered literary ambitions as art ludicrous. Thomas Mann affirmed this in his "*Deutsche Ansprache: Ein Appell an die Vernunft*" (German address: An appeal to reason) delivered in Berlin on October 17, 1930.[125]

Hegemann's socialist leanings have been recognized, and Ida Belle Hegemann confirmed that her husband was a member of the Social Democratic Party (Sozialdemokratische Partei Deutschlands, or SPD). Party membership was also substantiated by his nephew Dietfried Müller-Hegemann (Essen).[126] Dr. Müller-Hegemann admired his uncle and maintained contacts with the family. He attended the Sunday afternoon anti-Nazi gatherings at the Hegemanns' home and described them as left-leaning. He declared himself to have been a member of the German Communist Party (KPD), while his uncle was a Social Democrat. Hegemann's voter registration of February 1933 does not list a party affiliation.

The discord between the KPD and the SPD and the latter's internal quarrels greatly impaired any organized opposition to the Nazi rise to power. Presumably Moscow's control of the KPD prevented the creation of a united front with the Socialists, considering them bourgeois. When the directive from Stalin to the KPD was reversed in December 1934, proposing a joint confrontation of fascism, it was too late. A newspaper clipping regarding this change was sent to Hegemann in New York by Berthold Jacob from Strasbourg.[127]

The crescendo of Hegemann's anti-Nazi activism was interrupted only by his three-month sojourn in South America in 1931. The Hegemanns' frequent letters from this time are particularly valuable, not only for providing information on his experiences in Argentina and Uruguay, but for his wife's reports on events in Berlin and their effect on the family's daily life.[128] Political tension was compounded by the worldwide economic crisis, which was worse than what the Hegemanns had encountered upon their return to Germany in 1923. Prior to his departure for Buenos Aires, Hegemann had premonitions that his days at Wasmuth were about to end. In October his wife wrote to her husband: "Conditions here are dreadful! Wasmuth has gone entirely bankrupt! Publishing house and bookstore! Fräulein Ohlischlaeger called me this morning and said that although everyone knew it was getting bad, no one expected such a complete washout." In mid-December she reported that the major newspaper publisher Ullstein had bought Wasmuth for a "ridiculous sum." "They have bought your name and have agreed to pay the 100 as your contract called for, but they do not want that nuisance of a W. H." Having first dismissed Hegemann and his assistants, Ullstein later revoked this, and Hegemann and his staff continued to work for the periodical now called *Monatshefte für Baukunst und Städtebau*. Wasmuth had to promise not to open a publishing enterprise or start a journal for the next five years. Worried about the family's finances while her husband was abroad, Ida Belle kept after the various publishers and periodicals to send what they owed him. She was also in touch with friends and acquaintances, sharing concerns and news about daily "fighting and troubles between Nazis and others." Those members of the Hegemanns' circle who could afford it were leaving the country and urged them to do the same.

On his way to Lisbon, Hegemann passed through Paris and investigated possibilities of establishing the family there, in a city he loved and where he had many connections. The news that reached him in Argentina substantiated the threat that he would be unable to find publishers in Germany that dared to print his writings. On the other hand, leaving their home in Nikolassee and relocating with four children to Paris, even temporarily, filled them with apprehension. Thus he replied cautiously to a questionnaire in the *Literarische Welt* concerning the country in which he would prefer to live.

Ida Belle investigated renting out their house, but there was an abundance of houses available whose owners had already left. Weighing these concerns, and "in spite of the great unrest, horrifying rumors and untoward happenings in Germany," they stayed in Nikolassee for another year. The decision reflected Hegemann's resolve that he was more effective combatting Nazism on the homefront than from abroad, even though it became increasingly difficult to place his articles.

In the Introduction to the *Jugendbuch vom grossen König* (1930), Hegemann went beyond an alert concerning the German penchant for hero worship to a forewarning about the dangers of regarding Adolf Hitler as the heroic *Führertyp*. He asked, "How should it be possible, also in the future, for our people to recognize great leaders, when their imagination is misguided by the romantic descriptions by our historians?"[129] As mentioned, he published several articles comparing Frederick II and Hitler, emphasizing a claim that was made by the Nazis as well. The controversies surrounding the earlier *Fridericus* in the pages of the *Frankfurter Zeitung* were revived, now addressing the *Jugendbuch* on Frederick II, with Hegemann replying.[130] The comparison to Hitler was highlighted in a review by a writer with the pseudonym of Celsus in the *Weltbühne*.[131] He referred to Hegemann's "duel" with Fridericus in previous publications and commented on the *Jugendbuch*. Rhetorically the reviewer asked why it was that what had been known previously and was here repeated impressed the reader as novel. The answer, according to Celsus, was inherent in the author's establishing a clear relevance for contemporary events. Celsus perceived a continuation in the present of the *Gamaschenideologie* (Prussian ideology), the erroneous doctrine of the omnipotence of the state and the power of arms as a universal remedy. An example was Hegemann's ironic citation of a poem, which could pass for a hymn on Fredrick II, but was actually written in "praise" of the *Führer*.

Celebrating Frederick II as the "first Nazi"and pairing him with Hitler was promoted by followers eager to link the lower-class Austrian from Linz to the Prussian king and German hero. Hegemann's pursuit of the ideological kinship between them persisted throughout this period and into the notorious *Entlarvte Geschichte* of 1933.[132]

Considering Hegemann's numerous other activities in the late twenties, the number of his political articles in newspapers, documented by those preserved in the Hegemann Papers, is awesome, and he probably produced others that escaped the notice of his clipping service.[133] From August 1932 until he left Berlin in May 1933 Hegemann's political articles appeared primarily in eight newspapers: *Der Abend: Spätausgabe des Vorwärts*, *8 Uhr-Abendblatt der National-Zeitung*, *Arbeiter-Zeitung*, *General-Anzeiger für Dortmund und das gesamte rheinisch-westfälische Industriegebiet*, *Vorwärts*, *Neue Zürcher Zeitung*, and *Prager Tagblatt*. Many, although certainly not all of his almost weekly contributions were not entirely original, but were based on his books on Frederick the Great or other publications. There is no indication that his publishers raised objections. Perhaps it was even thought to contribute to his reputation and the demand for his books. The newspaper articles contributed to his income at a time of economic uncertainty.

A series of commentaries on current events differs from those mentioned. They appeared between August and October of 1932 in the *Berliner Montagspost* published by Ullstein, Europe's foremost newspaper company, which had bought Wasmuth. In his role as journalist/reporter for these articles, Hegemann used the pseudonym Einhart Vorster.[134] Vorster was his mother's maiden name and that of his aunt Maria Vorster March, to whom he was greatly attached. "Einhart" was possibly derived from Einhard, an early biographer of Charlemagne (ca. 817–30). Drafts of several of these articles and the newspaper clippings are preserved, leaving no doubt that they were written by Hegemann. It is possible that his new employer, Ullstein, asked him to write under a nom de plume. In any case, the content was as anti-Nazi as his other writings. Disengaging himself from historical precedents, he reported on the step-by-step destruction of democratic institutions in the last days of the Weimar Republic. As Einhart Vorster he chose to write as a witness, believing that his first-hand reportage had an immediate appeal, and his pseudonym gave him a certain freedom to speak out.

Other articles on current events carried his own name. "*Volkstümliches aus Hitlers Sportpalast*" described a Nazi rally at the Sportpalast in Berlin in March of 1932, which he attended with his wife.[135] While waiting for the address by Goebbels, the jubilant crowd sang Nazi hymns and greeted the uniformed stormtroopers with the Nazi salute. The Hegemanns had difficulty avoiding participation, and, narrowly escaping; they were shaken by the experience.

With the exception of his first article in *WMB* and brief remarks within other architectural reviews, Hegemann avoided writing on the Bauhaus and those associated with it.[136] The topic is notably absent from his critical writings. The piece on the "*Nazisturm aufs Dessauer Bauhaus*" (Nazi attack on the Dessau Bauhaus) of September 1932 and a variation of it, "*Nazi-Reue über Dessau*" (Nazi regrets regarding Dessau) in the *Weltbühne*, are therefore unique.[137] Hegemann barely mentioned the significance of this renowned institution, instead addressing the stupidity of its dismantling by the Dessau City Council under pressure from the Kampfbund für deutsche Kultur in which Schultze-Naumburg had become the spokesman for artistic questions. Hegemann dissected with glee the controversies within the Nazi hierarchy regarding its cultural policy. Some factions, including Goebbels, favored Modernism, and others, such as Schultze-Naumburg and the Kampfbund, led the attack on it as an un-German, international, and Jewish conspiracy. In the Nazi Party there were those who considered the closure of the Bauhaus inappropriate in view of their ambitions for a pioneering New Germany. Also questioned was the extent to which the government should exert control over culture. Ironically Hegemann repeated the circulating blame that Schultze-Naumburg was responsible for the downfall of the Bauhaus, accusing him of *scheussliche Kulturmufferei* (atrocious cultural muzzling), at that time still disavowed by some factions of the National Socialist Party of Germany (NSDAP). Soon, however, purging and censorship became a central policy, culminating in an assault on all cultural manifestations. Combined with the pursuit of racial purity it brought a vibrant and significant interlude in Germany to an end.

Hegemann expressed himself most forcefully on literary censorship and freedom of the press. Possibly self-conscious of his reputation as an anti-modernist, he was cautious about entering into the debate regarding art and architecture. In the majority of his political writings, his voice is that of an author and his allegiance with the literati. Not shunning disapproval, he reported on a speech by Gerhart Hauptmann at the event "*Die Nation greift an!*" (The nation attacks!), in the former Herrenhaus (Prussian Upper House). It was organized by the Gesellschaft für deutsches Schrifttum (Association for German Literature).[138] Hegemann expressed dismay that not only Hauptmann but other authors present encouraged the "intellectual army" to model itself after the Prussian military aristocracy in their defense of German culture. As was evident in his writings on Frederick II, Hegemann considered this a grave error. He also objected strongly to the aggressive Nazi stance adopted by this association, which advocated a policy of international expansion and even contemplated another world war.

He experienced censorship personally in 1929 when the Berliner Rundfunk (Berlin Radio Station) purged sections from the manuscript of his proposed lecture on "*Grossstadtelend und Gartenstadt*" (Metropolitan misery and garden city).[139] The Rundfunk's action received notoriety in the press, which opposed censorship and supported Hegemann. He had criticized the city's excessive investment in wide roads for residential neighborhoods that did not require major traffic arteries, advocating the differentiation between *Verkehrsstrassen* and *Wohnstrassen*, as he had since 1910. He singled out Stadtbaurat Martin Wagner as a progressive expert who understood this difference and acted accordingly. These passages, and others referring by name to the developer of a garden suburb east of Berlin, were altered by the radio station. When at the end of the talk Hegemann referred to the purged passages, he was fined by the Rundfunk and his future lectures were canceled. He discussed the case with the attorney for the Schutzverband deutscher Schriftsteller (Association for the Protection of Authors), who supported his position. The *Kölnische Zeitung* emphasized the importance of the incident and quoted Hegemann:

"Where will we end up when an expert of recognized renown in his profession is obliged to adhere to directives from a radio program regarding his opinion on long-established matters in his specialty?"

Hegemann had joined the international PEN Club and attended some of its meetings in Prague. His report on two evenings of discussion organized in February 1931 in Berlin by its German chapter are indicative of the disagreements which tended to weaken associations opposing Nazism.[140] In this instance Arthur Holitscher praised the role of writers in Russia, only to be confronted by someone who had recently spent time there in prison. Another recommended joining a demonstration by French intellectuals for the preservation of peace in Europe, which Hegemann questioned, wondering, "What will be the use of it?"

A few weeks later a similar situation presented itself at the sixtieth birthday celebration honoring Heinrich Mann. Hegemann reported on it with biting sarcasm in the *Tagebuch* under the title "Heinrich Mann? Hitler? Gottfried Benn? *oder* Goethe?" The incident is also referred to in an article on Benn, which quotes passages from Hegemann.[141] Benn had been asked to deliver the major speach at the banquet by the Schutzverband deutscher Schriftsteller honoring Heinrich Mann. Not only did Benn repeatedly refer to the celebrated author by the name of his more famous brother, Thomas Mann, but he used the occasion to provoke leftist authors. In his article Hegemann ridiculed Benn's bombastic talk; the latter maintained that "poets" could never improve social conditions and sided with Hitler's view of authors as political threats. Hegemann wrote that he had the honor of being asked to form part of the committee to prepare a tribute to Heinrich Mann, including Alfred Döblin, Wilhelm Herzog, Erich Kästner, and Hermann Kesten. It was not an isolated event within the discourse of whether literature should be engaged with social and political concerns. Hegemann's position was notorious and he characterized himself in this article as the "town planner and enemy of tyrants . . . who considers social commitment the obvious and only satisfying aesthetic." He referred to a statement by Anatole France, conveyed to him by Heinrich Mann, that literature hardly mattered when it came to the renown of authors. This opinion was shared in his conversations with Alfred Döblin, Arnold Zweig, and Bertolt Brecht, who admired Heinrich Mann primarily for his political activism rather than as a "poet." Hegemann drew compelling similarities between Benn and Hitler, who accused politically active authors of "Jewish insolence." In conclusion Hegemann wrote that modern artists and authors who conceived of aesthetics as separate from prosperity, health, and justice, not only failed to belong to the "*Schutzverband*" of German authors, but to humanity.

The Kongress Das Freie Wort (Freedom of Speech Congress) was initiated in February 1933 by Albert Einstein, Heinrich Mann, and Rudolf Olden. An impressive committee under their leadership also included

Hegemann. They organized in defense of the freedom of expression guaranteed by the Weimar Republic but recently curtailed by a *Notverordnung* (emergency decree). Freedom of scholarship and art and the independence of universities and art academies were threatened, and the *Rundfunk* (radio) had become a political tool. The demand was for "*freies Wort im freien Land*" (freedom of speech in a free country). Most vocal in the protest and signing the invitation to attend the first meeting of the Kongress on February 19, 1933, were Einstein, Mann, and Olden. In a 1932 letter to Sigmund Freud on intelligentsia and mass suggestion, Einstein wrote, "In my experience, it is much more the so-called intelligentsia who succumbs most readily to mass suggestion because they are not used to drawing immediately from experience but encounter life in its most easily and completely understood form—the printed page."[142] This opinion seemed to render the purpose of Das freie Wort somewhat problematic.

Hegemann's name frequently appeared among the "notable individuals from Germany and beyond" who signed the proclamations. The Hegemann Papers include several announcements and clippings on Das freie Wort. Included are lists of participating individuals and organizations that are testimony to widespread opposition to the Nazis. Hegemann, however, was not among the thirty-six members of the *Präsidium* (Executive Committee) of the Kongress, which included only three architects: Adolf Behne, Walter Gropius, and Martin Wagner. An announcement citing 208 Communist daily newspapers suppressed since 1931 is also in the Hegemann Papers. Several dated reports carry various initials, but not Hegemann's. The "Draft for a Manifesto" and an "Action Outline" are dated March 19 and 20, respectively. "The Jews in Germany" describes two "pogrom waves" that took place in Chemnitz in March and others in Berlin.

Attacks on Das freie Wort were not lacking. The *Berliner Börsenzeitung* questioned whether total freedom of the press had existed under the democratic and socialist parties and whether the organization was truly struggling for the freedom of all people or only for the intellectual elite.

Will Vesper commented in the *Völkischer Beobachter* on a questionnaire circulated by the periodical *Literarische Welt* and published as "*Die Gemeinschaft der geistig schaffenden Deutschlands*" (The intellectually creative community of Germany).[143] The invitation to fill out the "Questionnaire on the Occasion of 'Book Day'" read in part: "Despite all their differences, German poets and authors are a community. Honesty, seriousness, and talent and pure will to act for the German people are the only justification for belonging to this community." From the numerous statements, Hegemann's is eerily prescient of his own fate:

> Probably more than anything else in the politically devided [*sic*] Germany, literature is the most important upholder of national thought. For a long time,

especially those "unpolitical citizens of the world" have been scolded, and like Lessing and Goethe, have become—as champions of German literature—the true saviors of our German beliefs. Perhaps posterity will humbly apologize to some authors, who are reprimanded today.

In Vesper's attack on the piece in the *Literarische Welt*, published in the *Völkischer Beobachter*, Hegemann was described as "one of the most dangerous poisoners and persecutors of *Germandom* [German character]." Another sharply critical response to the questionnaire and periodicals, such as *Tagebuch* and *Weltbühne*, came from Hellmuth Langenbucher. In his article "*Die 'Literarische Welt' derer von gestern*," he takes issue with Hegemann's essay "*Rückkehr zu Novalis*" and accuses him of "besmirching" Hitler and Hindenburg.[144] These were additional barbs within the plethora of adverse criticism Hegemann endured in Berlin during the rising Nazi fervor.

Ida Belle Hegemann's letters to her husband traveling in South America relate an active social life with neighbors and friends, and guests staying at their house in Nikolassee. This continued when Hegemann rejoined the family in January 1932. In May they began a series of Sunday afternoon open houses for tea and conversation, sometimes lasting through improvised suppers. On these occasions politics and alarming events were discussed without fear of consequences. Wives were included in the gatherings, which became so popular that twenty to forty people would arrive, some barely known to the hosts. The open houses were discontinued in August. American scholar and diplomat George F. Kennan remembered them as a stimulating introduction to the intellectual and political climate in Berlin when he arrived from the American Midwest as a young man on his way to Russia. Fritz H. Landshoff, at that time co-owner of the Gustav Kiepenheuer Verlag, also participated in the Sunday salons. The following year he left for Amsterdam and published exile literature in his Querido Verlag and the periodical *Die Sammlung*.[145]

Notably missing from Hegemann's circle of friends were architects. He seemed to be most comfortable with writers, those connected with publishing, and a few politicians, including Wilhelm Abegg. He developed a close rapport with the authors and editors of *Die Weltbühne*. In addition to becoming a frequent contributor to the periodical in the late twenties, he "joined the club" as a valued colleague. Although he also published in the periodicals *Das Tagebuch*, *Die Horen*, *Die Neue Rundschau*, *Die Literarische Welt*, and in various German and international newspapers, *Die Weltbühne* held significance for Hegemann beyond providing a venue for his articles. Its writers and audience have been characterized as "left-wing intellectuals," who may not have formally adhered to the political parties representing leftist ideologies. They were journalists with reputations as literary authors, and as intellectuals they actively supported social causes and reform. Disengaged from German nationalism, they considered themselves Europeans and advocates of a transnational pan-Europe and world peace. A substantial portion of the *Weltbühne* circle came from Jewish backgrounds but did not practice their religion and considered themselves assimilated. Their gentile colleagues repudiated anti-Semitism and demonstrated an unfailing solidarity with them when they were threatened. Not surprisingly, Hegemann valued his rapport with this group.

The founding editor of the original journal *Die Schaubühne* (*The Stage*), Siegfried Jacobsohn, expanded its content, changing the name to *Die Weltbühne* (*World Stage*) in 1918. After Jacobsohn's sudden death in December 1926, Carl von Ossietzky succeeded him as editor-in-chief in October 1927. Istvan Deak has chronicled the "political history of the *Weltbühne* and its circle" with a special focus on Ossietzky's role.[146] Despite the "von" in his name, he came from a middle-class, Protestant Polish family that had settled in Hamburg. Ossietzky was a man of great courage and strong convictions, modest in manner, yet charismatic. Under his guidance, the journal evolved into an internationally recognized forum for pacifism and opposition to Nazism.

Campaigning for the causes of peace and justice, anti-militarism, and freedom of expression resulted in two prison sentences for Ossietzky—in 1927 for ostensibly publishing military secrets, and in 1929 on similar charges including treason. His two-year jail term began in May 1932, and he was photographed in front of the prison gates surrounded by his supporters. In March 1933 the editorial offices of *Weltbühne* were closed by the Prussian police. Following the triumph of the National Socialists, Ossietzky was transferred to the notorious Spandau citadel and the following year to the Moorlager concentration camp.

Accepting the Nobel Peace Prize fifty years later, Elie Wiesel recalled Ossietzky as the German pacifist who had enraged Hitler and the Nazis with his apocalyptic warnings about their developing evil. Leading figures in politics and the press of the Nazi era expressed the opinion that Ossietzky was too extreme in his warnings and revelations, and that his testimony was his doom. In his own acceptance speech Wiesel vowed to "conquer our murderers by attempting to reconstruct what they destroyed."[147]

Hegemann, the *Heldenschläger*, destroyer of heroes, revered Ossietzky as an exemplar for his crusade for pacifism and world brotherhood. Under Ossietzky's editorship, the *Weltbühne* attracted pacifists from Germany and abroad, attempting to bring anti-militarism to the attention of a wide public.[148] Ossietzky walked a tightrope between political factions on both the right and the left, comparable to Hegemann's stand as an architectural critic.

Hegemann's literary endeavors were in line with the tendency of the *Weltbühne* contributors to be journalists as well as authors. He came to their attention with his *Fridericus*, which *Weltbühne* reviewed in 1925, stressing the relevance of Hegemann's book to contemporary events.[149] Readers were alerted to the fact that the author's polemic was not directed at Frederick II, but against the "thousand-year-old German madness of yearning for a nation and unity, while at the same time negating this with federalism." The first article by Hegemann published in the *Weltbühne* retold the story of the torture-death of a schoolboy that had appeared in *Deutsche Schriften* and later in *Der gerettete Christus*.[150]

Although a shade less radical, the *Tage-Buch*, another left-wing weekly, resembled *Weltbühne* in its position. It often published the same authors, Hegemann among them. He had a cordial relationship with the editor, Leopold Schwarzschild, and their friendship continued when the latter fled to Paris in 1933. There he published *Das Neue Tagebuch*, which Hegemann received in New York.

Nazi control of freedom of expression and the transformation of art and the media into the delivery system of political propaganda affected the left-wing liberal press. This was compounded by the fact that many people connected with these journals and newspapers were, according to the Nürnberg Laws, Jewish and therefore in double jeopardy. These conditions eventually convinced Hegemann that he would not be able to publish and survive financially in Germany. His world was coming to an end in every conceivable way. This predicament is reflected in his articles from 1932, which convey an edgy desperation on nearly every topic, but in his desperation he became ever more daring.

The best known of Hegemann's political writings, *Entlarvte Geschichte* (History unmasked) was published by Jakob Hegner in Leipzig in February 1933.[151] The book's reputation was enhanced when it became a victim of the infamous book burning of May 11, 1933. It has been widely considered an iconic achievement and the culmination of the author's opposition to Nazism. However, Hegemann's long campaign against fascist ideology and its contributory ideas preceded *Entlarvte Geschichte* by several years. His convictions issued forth when he crossed the Atlantic and returned to Europe after an absence of almost ten years, merging with socialist leanings held prior to his long sojourn in America. Between *Deutsche Schriften* and *Entlarvte Geschichte* was a voyage during which he manifested his beliefs in the light of evolving events.

According to his wife's recollections, Hegemann began to work on *Entlarvte Geschichte* in September 1932. It was widely assumed that Hitler would seize power, and Hegemann wanted the book to be published before that event. On January 30, 1933, Hitler was declared *Reichskanzler* of Germany and Hegemann became increasingly anxious for the book to appear. Several assistants and Jacob Hegner succeeded in speeding things up. In February the publisher handed an unbound copy to Hegemann and urged him to leave the country immediately. Indeed, some of his friends, attempting to go abroad, were unable to obtain passports. His own passport had almost run out and he decided to leave for Switzerland, "convinced that he could do more for his country from outside than from a concentration camp inside."[152]

Hegemann's departure on February 22, 1933 was arranged in secret because the family's newly hired maid turned out to be an ardent Nazi and they suspected she was spying on them. Ostensibly, he took the train to Ulm for a lecture and consultations. Along the way he changed trains for Basel and went on to Ascona. He did not recognize the trip as the beginning of his final exile. This realization only took hold when he and his family embarked for New York from Le Havre at the end of October 1933.

Within a few days of Hegemann's departure, preliminary bound copies of *Entlarvte Geschichte* were delivered to his wife, who sent them to a list of people he had left with her. Their responses were immediate, and she forwarded them to her husband in Switzerland.

Prior to the publication of the book, the *8-Uhr-Abendblatt der National-Zeitung* printed six numbered articles by Hegemann under the title "*Entlarvte Geschichte*," followed by subtitles.[153] They appeared weekly throughout December 1932 and two followed in January 1933. Without referring to the forthcoming book, the newspaper introduced the series: "We have asked the eminent historical critic Dr. Werner Hegemann to present in the *8-Uhr-Abendblatt*, under the maxim 'History Unmasked,' several significant examples of how great historical figures really look when they are stripped of their textbook glorification." The unmasked individuals were General Blücher, General Wellington, Martin Luther, Bernhard of Clairvaux, and Arminius. The articles were modified versions of the actual chapters and alerted the public to the forthcoming book.

Entlarvte Geschichte reached the bookstores at the end of February. Ida Belle reported to her husband in Geneva that the *braun* (Nazi) bookstores featured the volumes piled in pyramidal fashion in their display windows. Authorities were fooled by the dedication on the book jacket to Paul von Hindenburg and Adolf Hitler, in hopeful anticipation that they would carry out their plans for a better Germany "from darkness to light." This wording was also on the publisher's announcement recommending it to all "thinking Germans." Inside the book Hegemann's ironic dedication read: "Dedicated with expectant admiration to the leaders of the Germans P. v. H. and A. H."

It took the Nazis almost three weeks to discover the scathing criticism of Hitler and former German heroes in Hegemann's book. They were likely distracted by the burning of the Reichstag on February 27th. This event, suspected of being instigated by the Nazis, was exploited by the government, which enacted severe restrictions, including the prohibition of KPD and SPD newspapers. In his postscript to the second, expanded edition of *Entlarvte Geschichte* Hegemann mentions that the first printing sold out in two weeks. Only in mid-March did articles appear in the *Völkischer Beobachter* expressing vehement anger at the author's true intentions. Under the title "*Entlarvter Geschichtsklitterer*" (Manipulator of historical facts unmasked) Hellmuth Langenbucher wrote that the author had reached the "apex of his effrontery" with his effort to incite the public in momentous political times.[154] In response to the dedication, which was meant to deceive innocent readers, Langenbucher considered it his duty to "unmask" Hegemann and demand action from the authorities. He cited numerous passages from the book to substantiate his vitriolics, which demonstrates that he had, indeed, read it. He affirmed that Hegemann characterized Hitler as "an 'unscrupulous hero' and a 'frivolous chap', who intended to send millions of Germans into 'new slaughterhouses'!!!" The reviewer noted that by tearing apart the unity between the swastika- and black-white-red German flags fluttering on all public buildings, the author placed himself outside the German *Volksgemeinschaft*.

Hegemann wrote in the postscript that certain conclusions were added to the 1934 edition responding to recent political developments. Also included is a review of the first edition by L. H. van Elhorst published in Amsterdam on May 6, 1933, just a week before the book burning.[155] Obviously it would have been extremely hazardous to write favorably about *Entlarvte Geschichte* within Germany. Elhorst's piece is an exceptional reaction coming from abroad. His opening paragraph sets the tone: "If the Nazis were really intelligent, they would not repeatedly rant against the 'Jewish bums,' but they would turn their attention toward the greatest and most dangerous opponent, the architect and historian Werner Hegemann." He called Hegemann "the only great pamphletist in modern German literature, [whose] personal courage borders on bravery." Van Elhorst concluded by citing lines from Goethe that Hegemann had frequently quoted and used as an ending to his *Schlusswort*: "It is still day, when man can take action! Night is descending, and no one will be able to act!"

Elhorst added that "'night' was already descending in Germany, and in recent months the country had turned into a penitentiary, hermetically sealed from the outside world," and commented that Hegemann's "grand pamphlet is one of the last documents which has reached us before the onset of this German 'night.'"

The demystification and debunking of German historical heros was actually considered beneficial by some devoted Nazis, and Hegemann referred to them in his *Nachwort* to the second edition. But in fact he attributed to Hitler the Machiavellian acceptance and exploitation of these heros and their deeds. The close link he established in *Entlarvte Geschichte* between historical precedents and Hitler's ideology is noteworthy. It is not clear if the Nazis fully recognized this and whether it contributed to their condemnation of the author. The book represented the last of a multitude of stabs by a skilled, well-known contender, and it was the one that sealed his fate.

The date of the book burning is usually given as May 11, 1933, which is the date on the sheet printed by the Berlin *Telegraphen-Union*, listing the nine *Feuersprüche* condemning the books by sixteen authors to the flames. A report from Berlin dated May 10 was published in the *Prager Presse* on May 12.[156] The banner headline read "*Die Verbannten der Preussischen Dichter-Akademie*" (The expelled by the Prussian Academy of Literature) and beneath it were photographs of four authors, including Alfred Döblin. Below these images were two reports, including one from Berlin. "*Das Deutsche Autodafé*" (The German burning of heretics at the stake) described the gathering of students, many in brown (Nazi) shirts, on the Hegelplatz at the university. Brandishing torches and accompanied by music, their procession was joined by crowds of people, who escorted the wagons piled high with the condemned books. The throng proceeded to the Brandenburg Gate and along Unter den Linden, reaching the Opernplatz at 11:00 PM. The students ignited a pyre and formed a line passing the examples of the *Undeutsches Schriftmaterial* (un-German writings) from hand to hand before throwing them into the bonfire. By 11:20 PM the first of twenty thousand books had been committed to the flames. The symbolic act included the chanting of the "*Feuersprüche*"(incantation) denouncing the authors. The verdict for Hegemann was: "*Against* the falsification of our history and the defamation of our great spirits. *For* respecting our past! I commit the works by Emil Ludwig and Werner Hegemann to the flames!" Among the books burned were works by such well-known intellectuals as Freud, Heinrich Mann, Erich Maria Remarque, Ossietzky, and Kurt Tucholsky. Many of the incantations were anti-Semitic, as evidenced by Reich Propaganda Minister Goebbels when he addressed the gathering and declared that it signaled the end of an "excessive Jewish intellectualism." A similar "cultural action" took place in Frankfurt am Main, where the books were loaded onto a manure wagon drawn by oxen to the sound of funeral marches.

According to the *Prager Presse* the German newspapers were either silent or wrote favorably on the burning of *undeutscher* books. The Prague paper also featured an account from Paris, "*Entsetzen im Ausland*" (Dismay abroad), based on information sent by a journalist in Berlin who described the book burning as "one of the saddest expressions of the new German spirit."

From London Hegemann wrote two items for the "Letters to the Editors" page of the *Manchester Guardian* explaining that there was no official list of books banned by the Nazis, and that the "judgment by fire" was instigated by Goebbels, who probably also wrote the incantations.[157] According to Hegemann, it was suspected that the German booksellers, desperate to improve their standing with Hitler's government, may have conspired in the burning. He emphasized that among the authors, only Ernst Glaeser and Karl Marx were Communists, and that the authors represented a range of opinions, but all opposed Nazi ideology. He alerted English readers that Ossietzky, whose books were burned, had been sent to a concentration camp.

After Hegemann's departure from Berlin, his wife and children remained in the Nikolassee house. They were joined at times by Ida Belle's mother, Mrs. Guthe, who had an American passport. Articles attacking Hegemann appeared in the newspapers, now controlled by the Nazis, but the family felt moderately safe, although the name Hegemann was near the top of the Nazi blacklist. To prevent retribution against his family and friends, Hegemann used the name Monsieur Alfred Lancy for communications to him from Germany. Some of the letters sent to Monsieur Lancy were unsigned or only initialed. One typewritten letter, which ended "With many friendly regards, XYZ," was a three-page detailed report dated April 4, 1933, describing the situation at the Bauwelt-Verlag, Ullstein A.G., Berlin, which had taken over Wasmuth.[158] Most likely the writer was Hans Josef Zechlin, perhaps together with M. Ohlischläeger. Hegemann had asked about his pending payment, and the letter suggests writing to "H. U.," possibly Hermann or Heinz Ullstein. It warned against using the name Hegemann in any correspondence. The leading individual in the *Laden* (business, formerly Wasmuth) was now a "Mr. P." (Friedrich Paulsen), who "misses no opportunity to utter malicious comments regarding your management style and you as a person." The tale of woe continues, "business is deathly still, also after the boycott."

Indicative of the speed and thoroughnesss with which the Nazi government established its total control, all newspapers reported the same things. It was only possible to conceal forbidden information by altering the placement of the news and the type size. At this point the *Deutsche Arbeiter Zeitung* (*D.A.Z.*) was the only leftist paper with a semblance of freedom. Ullstein's *Vossische Zeitung* was censored before it appeared and in the Jewish or partly Jewish publishing houses top executives were demoted. Those who wrote letters to Hegemann devised a means of weaving factual news and information with expressions of despair, such as "With time we will all get it by the scruff of our necks. All is dark and one is deeply shaken by so much brutality. . . . One becomes aware of how one gradually becomes indifferent."

The correspondence between Ida Belle and her husband from this period describes a tense situation, with many friends and acquaintances leaving Germany. Several of the recipients of copies from the initial batch of *Entlarvte Geschichte* wrote enthusiastic letters to Nikolassee and urged the family to "take a vacation." Accordingly, Ida Belle prepared to join her husband, attended to financial matters, correspondence, and the packing of Hegemann's books and papers, which he desperately needed to carry out his professional work. As it was impossible to ship his entire library and all of his papers abroad, several trunks of books were shipped to Hegemann's close friend Pierre Liévre in Paris. Fearing the house would be searched, Ida Belle packed the most important and sensitive papers into a locked box and large duffle bag. After dark, with the help of a friend, she loaded the box and duffle bag into their baby carriage and wheeled it through the streets to a trusted acquaintance for safekeeping. Along the way they were confronted by a Nazi leader who lived nearby. They managed to persuade him that the carriage contained household linens on loan to a friend. The acquaintance then refused to store the bundles because of their size, but Fritz Landsberger eventually agreed to store them in his attic. Shortly after Ida Belle had left Landsberger's house, a Nazi official, who must have witnessed the transfer, ransacked the house, leaving it in complete disarray. The next morning the shaken Landsberger begged her to take back whatever belonged to Hegemann.

It was now incumbent upon Ida Belle to find a tenant for the house and obtain travel permits. She held a German passport, having relinquished her American citizenship at the time of her marriage, and she anxiously sought to renew her passport and obtain papers for the four children. When at last she had the documents, the family departed for a "vacation in Switzerland" on March 24, leaving her mother behind with the task of putting the house in order for rental or sale. Mrs. Guthe had a valid American passport and to protect the Hegemanns' property from seizure, the title was transferred to her. She shipped several boxes of books and papers to Monsieur Lancy, but eventually found herself forced to incinerate the remaining Hegemann papers in the cellar furnace, possibly including those Ida Belle had tried to store with friends in Nikolassee. It was impossible to retrieve the correspondence from Hegemann's Wasmuth office.

So as not to arouse suspicion Ida Belle and the children carried minimal luggage on their trip to Switzerland. Hegemann received them in Geneva, where they stayed at his pension for a few days, and then moved to a small but charming country house in Mornex, Haute Savoie, France. It was perfect for the family, and a welcome respite after the oppressive atmosphere of Berlin. Once settled in Mornex, Ida Belle wrote a four-page letter to her brother Carl in Ann Arbor, Michigan.[159] She described for her American family the events leading up to the exile and the present situation with Hegemann in Geneva and the rest of the family in their pleasant house. Safe from censorship, her report on the far-reaching impact of the Nazi regime on every aspect of private and public life in Germany represents a valuable documentation by an observant contemporary witness.

From the moment he reached Switzerland and established himself in Geneva, Hegemann energetically pursued the prospect of providing for his family as a journalist. Desperate for income, he tried to publish new and previously published articles under different titles in Swiss and Czech periodicals. He interviewed Czech President Thomas G. Masaryk at the Burg in Prague in December 1932, and wrote two long articles for the *Vossische*

Zeitung in January 1933.[160] From Geneva Hegemann tried to arrange for an expanded publication in Prague to coincide with Masaryk's birthday in March. Hegemann was exceptionally skillful in this literary journalism and conveyed a captivating immediacy to his readers. He sent an autographed copy of *Entlarvte Geschichte* to President Masaryk, whom he esteemed as a wise statesman and pacifist. Manuscript copies of two long articles destined for the Prague newspaper are preserved in the Hegemann Papers. One bears the penciled note, "*Bearbeitet von P. M.*" (Edited by P. M.), presumably President Masaryk. Hegemann's astute questions and their ensuing discussions concerned the central European countries of the former Austrian Empire. The articles represent the best of Hegemann's journalism.

With Hitler's sudden rise to power in mind, Masaryk declared in the interviews that in a sense Germany had won the Great War, and hopefully would now exercise a calming influence internationally. At the 1933 Geneva Disarmament Conference, Masaryk facilitated Hegemann's contacts with several leading political figures. Hegemann wrote up his audiences for the *Basler Nachrichten* under the title "*Der verkannte* Hitler" (The misunderstood Hitler).[161] He reported on the French suspicions of British Prime Minister Ramsay MacDonald and the widespread apprehension about Mussolini and Hitler. According to Hegemann, Hitler presented the greatest danger because the economic situation and political chaos in Germany could propel him into a world war in order to divert attention. Other articles resulting from his stay in Geneva also dealt with the threat of Hitler, and some documented conversations with Guglielmo Ferrero comparing the dictatorships of Napoleon, Hitler, and Mussolini.[162]

Hegemann's interview with Margery Corbett-Ashby, an internationally recognized suffragist and politician, and the British delegate to the Geneva Disarmament Conference, is documented in nine handwritten pages in the Hegemann Papers, and was apparently not published.[163] It bears the title, "Adolf Hitler *und die Frauen. Ein Gespräch mit der Delegierten Englands in Genf*" (A. H. and women: a conversation with England's delegate in Geneva), and is noteworthy for what it reveals about the author's position regarding women. Hegemann's interest in the political role of women grew out of his pacifist and social convictions and from his contacts with the social reformers Jane Addams, Mary Kingsbury Simkhowitz, and other activists struggling for housing and urban reform. The Nazi restrictions placed on women had reinforced his attention on the emerging women's movement.

Hegemann asked Corbett-Ashby if she considered men, especially soldiers and jurists, more appropriate participants at the Disarmament Conference. Her reply dovetailed with his own long-held convictions: "Men think exclusively of protecting inert property. Women think instead of the protection of the living and future generations. Men revert too easily to their old delusion, that each nation can shape its own good fortune.

I believe that women comprehend much better that today the well-being of the world depends irrevocably on the success of international treaties and that war under any circumstances is madness."

Hegemann's dedication to journalism was reinforced by his interest in politics and history. In addition he possessed a background in economics, exceptional writing skills, and fluency in the major European languages. Geneva provided a perfect milieu with the headquarters of the League of Nations, frequent conferences, and many diplomats. Frequently it was President Masaryk who facilitated valuable introductions for Hegemann. In the initial weeks after settling in Geneva, Hegemann made brief trips to Paris, Amsterdam, and London to explore professional possibilities and keep abreast of the pending publication of *Christ Rescued*. In London he attended the World Economic Conference and was invited to an official luncheon by Ramsay MacDonald. He was persistently pursuing newspaper reportage.

His conversations with Raymond Unwin, colleagues at the Architectural Association, Steen Eiler Rasmussen, H. G. Wells, and Wickham Steed were important for his future. Contacts with these colleagues in the architectural and planning professions may have shifted his attention away from journalism, and in letters to his wife he mentioned the possibility of moving to England. He also wrote to acquaintances in America asking for advice regarding a position that would provide for his family. The economic depression gripping the country had put many American scholars out of work and compounded the difficulties facing emigrés. Among the sympathetic responses was a reply from Fiske Kimball.[164] A colleague and friend since 1920, Kimball was well acquainted with Hegemann's career. Kimball was himself a distinguished scholar and since 1925 director of the Pennsylvania Museum of Art in Philadelphia. His background and position provided him with an informed overview of possibilities. He noted Hegemann's advantages of having previously lived and worked in America and his language proficiency. He indicated, however, that financial assistance for refugees was primarily funneled to academic institutions and came from Jewish contributors eager to help their own people. Hegemann was at a disadvantage because he was not Jewish and had never held a position at a university. He was certainly aware that having no academic connections was a handicap. To be excluded from funding sources because he was not Jewish may have been somewhat bewildering, considering his long opposition to anti-Semitism and his recent articles in the newspapers on Nazi terror against Jewish individuals, businesses, and institutions.

Kimball mentioned that foundations would offer assistance in response to specific requests by universities and that an exception for circumventing difficulties in Hegemann's case might be "the effort of Alvin Johnson and his New School for Social Research." The New School was shunned as too radical by some organizations, however, it received support from leftist circles. Kimball added, "I will of course write to him [Alvin Johnson] commending you."

Kimball considered Hegemann's expertise in city planning more promising than his literary and political pursuits. It was Kimball's impression that America was indifferent to Nazism, except for its anti-Semitic campaign. On the other hand, lectures on slum clearance and housing by a European authority would be of topical interest, and Kimball mentioned former contacts to be approached along these lines. He suggested that Hegemann might get in touch with E. A. Filene and Philip Cabot, who had figured admiringly in the conversations in *Deutsche Schriften*. According to Hegemann their mutual regard, dating to his sojourn in Boston, had deteriorated since that time as a result of their political differences.

Possibly in response to Kimball, Alvin Johnson wrote on August 6, offering Hegemann an appointment at the New School for Social Research. Hegemann accepted in a letter of August 29, followed by subsequent discussions of details.[165] There was difficulty in obtaining American visas without having to approach a German consulate. This was fortunately resolved when Alvin Johnson increased the guarantee for Hegemann. Through Hegemann's contacts at the League of Nations, the Comité International pour le Placement des Intellectuels Emigrés agreed to provide funding for the family's passage to New York.

They left Monnetier-Mornex on October 26. After a day in Paris—a sad goodbye to a beloved European city—the Hegemanns boarded the *S. S. Manhattan* in Le Havre on October 28 and arrived in New York on November 4, 1933. They were met by a reporter who asked Hegemann how long Hitler would stay in power. The answer he gave has been variously cited as either six months or two years.

After a few days in a hotel, the Hegemanns found a house in Manhasset, Long Island. Hegemann could commute by train to the New School for Social Research, where he began his appointment as lecturer on urban planning on November 14.

6. Exile

New York and the New School for Social Research

During his years in exile Hegemann was under the stress of providing a livelihood for his family and worrying about the fate of friends and acquaintances still under the threat of the Nazi regime. The majority of those leaving fascist Europe to seek safety in the Americas shared this predicament. Hegemann was fortunate to have linguistic skills and expertise in a range of subjects. His contacts from previous stays in the United States assisted in his search for employment, which was difficult because of the economic crisis.

Hegemann's appointment at the New School for Social Research and the informed advice from Alvin Johnson and Fiske Kimball steered him toward academia rather than journalism or consulting, although he had not previously pursued university teaching. Crossing the Atlantic, Hegemann relinquished architectural criticism and the concomitant controversies and focused instead on city planning and housing. His engagement in the political situation in Europe continued in articles and through his extensive correspondence. These letters, and those of condolence later written to Ida Belle, give evidence of a wide circle of acquaintances and the remarkable esteem Hegemann had gained among Americans following his arrival in the fall of 1933.

Alvin Johnson helped Hegemann in practical matters and with supportive understanding of his commitment to city planning, as well as through friendship with him and his family. The call to join the faculty at the New School for Social Research enabled the Hegemanns to come to the United States shortly before the Emergency Committee in Aid of Displaced German (later Foreign) Scholars embarked on its rescue mission. Hegemann arrived in an early wave of anti-Nazi intellectuals. Historians have frequently differentiated between "refugees," who left fascist Europe for political reasons, and "émigrés," whose lives were endangered, foremost by Hitler's anti-Semitic policies. The reasons for leaving, however, often overlapped and the differentiation becomes blurred. In this narrative, "exile" and "émigré" are used interchangeably, while Hegemann would actually belong in the category of politically motivated exile. The cultural contribution of those reaching the United States and other American countries has been documented in numerous publications, and warrants the ironic heading "Thank you, Hitler!"[1]

While many universities were hesitant or encountered difficulties in accepting foreign, predominantly Jewish scholars to their faculty, the largest single group were welcomed by Alvin Johnson at the New School for Social Research, where they constituted the "University in Exile."[2] This remarkable deed tends to overshadow the uniqueness of the New School for Social Research as a progressive educational endeavor since its inception in 1917. The school was the brainchild of two historians, Charles A. Beard and James Harvey Robinson, who resigned from the faculty of Columbia University in protest over the dismissal of a colleague for his avowal of pacifism. The intention of establishing a program devoted to adult education and research in the social sciences, free of the constraints of traditional universities, gained enthusiastic support from a number of intellectuals, including John Dewey, Horace Kallen, and Thorstein Veblen. Classes began in February 1919, and in the coming decades a coterie of leading figures in culture and the arts, such as Patrick Geddes, Lewis Mumford, and John Cage, offered courses at the New School.

From the beginning the evening program for adults was unexpectedly successful, but the commitment to research lagged. In 1922 Alvin Johnson was asked to take on the administration of the New School with the mandate to organize and smooth out relations between members of the faculty and the board and strengthen the research component. After some debate it was agreed to continue the school's adult education, while ameliorating the shortcomings in social science research. Johnson's mission was invigorated in 1927 when he was asked by the Social Science Research Council to become the associate editor of the *Encyclopedia of the Social Sciences*. His travels to Europe to procure contributors for the publication brought him in contact with leading scholars, several of whom were later invited to join his faculty. They formed the graduate division at the New School, a self-governing entity under the title "University in Exile," which began functioning in the fall of 1933. Comparable in spirit to the circle around the *Weltbühne* in Berlin, they were a close-knit, politically liberal and cosmopolitan group, although defensively restrictive as well.

By accepting a position at the innovative New School, Hegemann joined an open university, as he had envisioned with the Berlin 1910 Exhibition, dedicating it to the study of city planning in the service of civic improvements. To Hegemann's surprise and disappointment, and despite Johnson's efforts, the members of the University in Exile, graduate school, voted against accepting Hegemann to their faculty, a position that would have increased his salary and made his position at the New School more secure. The reasons for the attitude of the members of the group are not entirely clear. Their position reflected the political divisions and discords within the left-wing movements of the countries they had left. One possible factor was that Hegemann had not previously taught at a university. However, a more likely motivation, if only whispered, was that his political activism and socialist leanings might endanger the reputation of the other refugees hoping to return to their previous acdemic positions and pensions in Germany. In the meantime, they wanted to protect their safe perch in New York. Hegemann mentioned this in a letter of June 1934 to Rudolf Olden:

> My economic situation is very difficult and made more difficult (this in confidence) because the majority of the German members of the so-called "University in Exile" refused my becoming a member of their faculty. The reason they give is that City Planning and Housing concerns architecture and not social science. This I consider to be fantastic nonesense. The real reason, I am told, is that I pass as politically too exposed and therefore dangerous to the reputation of the "University in Exile." . . . My being politically too exposed was also the reason given to me by the Social Democratic Kultus Minister in Berlin for not appointing me to a professorship. German history repeats itself even in foreign countries.[3]

The argument that Hegemann's specialty, city planning, was not a social science, is not convincing in view of the fact that he had obtained his Ph.D. in economics. In March 1935, the University in Exile added nine people to their faculty, but Hegemann was not among them. In the eyes of posterity his status was diminished by not gaining entrée to this renowned group, which may have contributed to the obscurity assigned him after his death.

In 1931 the New School had moved into its own building on West Twelfth Street in lower Manhattan. It was designed by the Austrian-born Joseph Urban and was strikingly modern compared to its surroundings. An impressive auditorium for cultural functions and a garden courtyard provided a campus-like atmosphere. Johnson's efforts to create an intellectual community and bring the faculty together were aided by the sense of place of this distinctive building. He also initiated an interdisciplinary general seminar to meet weekly on a single theme, such as "America and Europe," "Political and Economic Democracy," and "Power in the United States." The talks were to be published in the journal *Social Research*. Despite the snub by the University in Exile, Hegemann benefited from Johnson's endeavors to bring the émigrés together with American scholars and the public.[4]

Hegemann was the first to be invited to present a paper in the general seminar on "America and Europe" in December 1934.[5] The Dean of the

Graduate Faculties, Emil Lederer (formerly of the University of Berlin), asked Hegemann to limit his talk on city planning to forty minutes, leaving time for discussion. Judging from Hegemann's prepared outline, he intended to address the audience of renowned economists (who had denied him admittance to their faculty) in a serious vein, stressing the economic aspects of his subject. In the third section of the outline Hegemann referred to this imminent situation, stating that:

> So far our academic institutions of learning have made little effort to grasp the significance of city planning. It may, for quite a while at least, be impossible to plan all the pursuits of society. I approve of Professor [Eduard] Heimann's definition separating capitalistic and extra-capitalistic fields of activities. But I believe that in the field of city planning the various possibilities are so closely limited by reason of space, technique and economy that planning for a certain minimum which is to be guaranteed to everyone, is not only possible but necessary. The study of the possible and necessary outlines of this planning and of its legal, economic, social, technical and esthetic limitations deserves the best scientific effort.

In the actual text of his lecture Hegemann recalled meeting Alvin Johnson at a gathering of economists and bankers at the home of the economist Moritz Bonn in Berlin, where a lively discussion interrupted the host's prepared talk after barely five minutes. According to Hegemann, it was presumptuous to condense into forty minutes the "comprehensive and time-honored subject, city planning," that was his specialty, but he was prepared to present his thesis on "the comprehensiveness and timely implications of city planning science," citing a few historical examples, and to "defend" it. The text of Hegemann's lecture, presumably intended to grant him a position in the University in Exile, deviated considerably from this outline. Excursive sections on historical precedents intended to substantiate the interrelationship of "civilization, civic culture, civic art, and city planning," dwelt on the example of Paris, Haussmann, and Napoleon. The urban history of Berlin was characterized by Hegemann as "an ever-repeated tragedy of prophetic and constructive vision crushed by the stolid stupidity of men in power." He affirmed that the "badness" of cities was the result of ignorance and greed above all other factors. The text is laced with citations from Karl Marx and Friedrich Engels, and the tone tends to verge on the defamatory. Arguably this approach detracted from Hegemann's premise of city planning as a social science rather than an activist political agenda, and it may have hindered the desired welcome to the University in Exile.

On the other hand the outline represents an overview of Hegemann's ideas on city planning and the basis of his courses at the New School, which are summarized in the school's catalogues.[6] The cost of Hegemann's classes was ten to fifteen dollars for the term (twelve to fifteen lectures) and one dollar for single lectures, comparable to the fees for other courses in the adult division. Hegemann's offerings included: "Social and Economic Problems in Town Planning," "The Replanning of Old Cities"—on the transition from pre-railroad times to the introduction of the automobile, telephone and radio—and "City, Regional and State Planning and the Problems of Human Settlements." Notes to the latter relate that "it will be based in part upon a critical analysis of the eleven volumes and the succeeding *Information Bulletins* published by the Regional Plan Association of New York, and upon a comparison of its work with that of similar efforts in Berlin, Buenos Aires, San Francisco and other communities, in which the lecturer participated."

The New School also published a brief curriculum vitae for Hegemann. Considering his publications and professional involvement prior to his arrival in New York, as well as the descriptions of his lecture courses, it is unfortunate that the opportunity for establishing a graduate-level program in city planning, based on Hegemann's presence and the innovative thinkers gathered around the Regional Plan Association of New York, was not realized. Alvin Johnson was keenly aware of the significance that such an academic department would represent for the New School. On several occasions he expressed his disappointment at being unable to secure the necessary funding and the support of the University in Exile to carry this idea to fruition. He did so most cogently in a personal letter to Hegemann just before his death.[7] In the letter Johnson expressed his deep admiration for "one of the small and gallant contingent of persons with real contributions to make," and was troubled that he could not ease the financial uncertainties that kept Hegemann from dedicating himself wholly to his work. Johnson anticipated getting together with Hegemann when he was well again to discuss "building up a permanent interest. It would be a service of increasing importance to bring together the various elements of architecture, town planning, finance, and sociology that must operate together if ever we are to get out of our present chaos."

Hegemann's courses at the New School, which were publicized in the newspapers, promised slides and the film, *The City of the Future*, which he had shown in Buenos Aires. He complemented these courses with other lectures, primarily on housing, leading up to his projected volumes on that topic. On one of these occasions he was joined by Carol Aronovici of Columbia University to discuss recent trends in housing. Another time he spoke on "Ideal Housing as a Public Utility" at a meeting of the New York Society of Architects.[8]

Refugee without Refuge

Hegemann's political concerns were intertwined with his preoccupation with the family's economic survival and his search for a secure employment. Central to his political engagement were pacifism and censorship. He had presciently recognized in Hitler's *Mein Kampf* (1925) the threat to world peace and resolve for war. These forebodings had become obvious and seemingly inevitable with Hitler's assumption of power in January 1933. This marked the beginning of a ruthless and indiscriminate elimination of individuals suspected of opposing National Socialism, and of *Gleichschaltung*, or imposition of totalitarian homogeneity in all aspects of political and cultural life. Hegemann grouped together the curtailment of freedom of expression and the persecution of its advocates under the heading of censorship. He saw the latest events with a long view in historical perspective, evoking the repression of intellectual freedom in Germany, especially in Prussia under the Frederick the Great, when many outstanding figures were sent into exile.

At the time of his stay in Geneva, Hegemann wrote two letters to the editor of the *Manchester Guardian* on the plight of the authors whose books were burned or prohibited by the Nazis.[9] He mentioned Carl von Ossietzky, who was imprisoned at that time for his pacifism and editorship of *Die Weltbühne*. The persecution of Ossietzky was an attack on pacifism and freedom of expression, and he became a symbol of Hegemann's opposition to Nazism. When voicing his outrage over Ossietzky's treatment, Hegemann stressed that he was neither a Communist nor a Jew. This latter designation was based on Hegemann's lifelong opposition to anti-Semitism, and the statement should be considered in the context of seeing in Nazism a universal catastrophe for civilization, rather than one directed exclusively against the Jewish people.[10] Hegemann did not live to become aware of the "final solution" and the Holocaust, which would have provided him with an additional perspective without altering his view of Nazism as anything but an isolated historical event.

Hegemann's position was shared by Americans, some of whom contributed to the book *Nazism: An Assault on Civilization*, which also included his article "The Debasement of the Professions."[11] Hegemann's overview of the past and present plight of the intelligentsia in Europe, foremost in Germany, is summarized in this passage: "The utter debasement of the German professions, as it was recently achieved by Nazism, can be understood only by looking at its historical background with its never-ending precedent of intellectuals abused, tortured, killed, exiled, or driven to suicide. 'A German writer—a German martyr! You won't find it otherwise,' said Goethe shortly before he died." According to Hegemann the "highly meritorious Emergency Committee in Aid of Displaced German Scholars" had been able to place only 275 out of more than 1,200 German scholars in new positions. He repeatedly pointed out that Hitler was using the anti-Semitism prevailing in Germany as a smokescreen for his program of universally eliminating freedom of expression and his goal of world conquest. Hegemann insinuated that other nations, including the United States, were not safe from comparable threats to civil liberty.

Other contributors to the book expressed this apprehension, as did Charles A. Beard in an address given at the New School of Social Research.[12] The talk, entitled "Hitlerism and Our Liberties," warned of violating "certain rules of policy deemed essential to the conduct of a civilized society." He called attention to the infiltration of "Hitlerism" as "a menace to the peace and security of America" and its cherished freedoms. He thought that the New School, founded "in protest against the spirit of tyranny and suppression" imposed by fellow Americans, should at this time redouble its efforts and vigilance, and welcome émigrés as "leaders in a common cause." Beard's talk implies the discord among exiles and among those connected with the New School. Hegemann found himself in the middle of what has been described by Lewis J. Edinger as the "centrifugal forces among the exiles," citing Lenin, "God preserve us from the exile colonies and the exile conflicts."[13]

After leaving Berlin, Hegemann stayed in contact with the Social Democratic Party (S.P.D.) of which he was a member who "never had been active."[14] He was aware of the discords and splits in its ranks, opposition to the Communist Party, and its move to Prague when it was outlawed by the Nazis. A determined and united campaign against the Nazi regime was envisioned by many, but never became a reality. "*Organisation des Kampfes gegen den deutschen Nationalismus*" (Organization of the battle against German nationalism) is a typewritten draft, possibly by Hegemann. It bears the typed initials "A. B." and the date April 25, 1933, as well as the handwritten note "*Neue Redaktion*" (revised edition).[15] Its concepts, political approach, and literary style resemble Hegemann's, but the authorship remains uncertain. However, he would have agreed with the premise of the proposed "*Aktion*" on an international scale. The reason for it is expressed in the opening paragraph: "The present system ruling in Germany signifies without doubt an enormous danger for the whole world. The calming assurances by Hitler are too transparent to be believed anywhere, except by the very naïve. In fact, public opinion almost worldwide acknowledges that Hitler's triumph would be a threat to world peace and the entire civilization."

Seven points of a united international "*Aktion*" are outlined, because "only a comprehensive plan promises success." The proposal recommended a differentiation between German émigrés only deserving humanitarian attention and those who could serve as active participants. The statement warns against "dangerous elements," such as Communists, visionaries, swindlers, and the like. Other emigrants, based on their knowledge of German conditions, could contribute positively to an international propaganda effort that could also infiltrate Germany. The creation of a central publishing enterprise located in Prague with branches elsewhere was recommended.

Once in America, Hegemann continued to receive the clandestine S.P.D. newsletters from Prague and later from France. He refrained from overt political activities and devoted his efforts to freeing Ossietzky, who had been transferred to the Sonnenburg concentration camp, also called "*Moorlager*" (Marsh detention camp) in East Friesland.

In 1934, a worldwide movement proposing Ossietzky for the 1935 Nobel Peace Prize gathered momentum, and Hegemann became the major advocate of this cause. He made use of his international network of contacts in his letter-writing campaign, a network expanded by more recent American additions, with remarkable response. His correspondence on behalf of Ossietzky is impressive.[16] Many of those Hegemann approached were themselves in exile and were asked to write to the Nobel Prize Committee in Oslo. Among those voicing support for the cause were Albert Einstein, Heinrich Mann, Thomas Mann, H. G. Wells, Wickham Steed, Rudolf Olden, and Arnold Zweig. Presumably Jane Addams, herself a recipient of the prize in 1931, lent her name and support. Like Hegemann, she made the connection between pacifism and social improvement. The publicity for the Ossietzky cause carried long lists of advocates, including Alvin Johnson, Werner Hegemann, and others from the faculties of the New School and Columbia University. Articles in the *Neue Volkszeitung* of New York were reprinted in the *Neue Weltbühne*, formerly edited by Ossietzky and now issued in Prague.[17] One of Hegemann's numerous initiatives was a cable sent on November 8, 1935, to Thomas G. Masaryk, President of the Czechoslovakian Republic, known for his promotion of peace. Among the signers were Albert Einstein, John Dewey, Alvin Johnson, and, of course, Werner Hegemann.[18]

Hegemann encouraged the organization Der Wendekreis für Aufklärung und freiheitliche Weltanschauung (Circle of Change for Clarification and Liberation of Cultural Life and Human Relations) to found "The Carl von Ossietzky Nobel Peace Prize Committee, U.S.A." John Dewey of Columbia University was honorary chairman of the committee, which consisted of Franz Boas, also of Columbia, Henry MacCracken of Vassar College, and Hegemann. In June 1935 a public meeting sponsored by the group was held in the auditorium of the New School. It was advertised with the slogan, "Into the concentration camp with the Nobel Peace Prize." A few weeks later the C.v.O. Nobel Prize Committee and the Wendekreis sponsored "Art Pays Homage to Carl von Ossietzky," a benefit evening of musical and dance performances at the New York's Hotel Delano.[19]

Due to the deterioration of Ossietzky's health, the international campaign for the Nobel Peace Prize and visits from foreign journalists persuaded the Nazi government to move Ossietzky from the concentration camp to the Police Hospital, and later to a hospital of his choice. Ossietzky was awarded the Nobel Peace Prize in November 1936, but was prevented from accepting it in person. He died in Berlin in May 1938, two years after Hegemann's death.

Academic Prospects

Hegemann was dedicated to energizing his career, and his wife and children were adjusting to life in America. Ida Belle's mother was still in Berlin trying to sell the Nikolassee home, but in April 1934 the house was confiscated by the Nazis, and she watched with horror as the furnishings were carted off. Ida Belle's letters to her mother reveal that the Hegemanns were contemplating a prolonged stay in America. Ida Belle, who had lost her American citizenship by marrying a German, now renewed it. She learned to drive, even venturing into Manhattan, where she joined her husband for social gatherings and lectures. In the beginning of the summer season they were obliged to move from Manhasset to a cottage in Lost Lake, near Patterson, N.Y. Hegemann took a room in New York City and joined them for weekends, taking the train to nearby Brewster. In September 1934, at the beginning of the school year, the Hegemanns settled in New Rochelle, which offered a reasonable commute to Manhattan.

Toward the end of July and early August (1934) Hegemann gave a series of five lectures in Siasconset on Nantucket. Addressing a general public, his talks touched upon city planning, Nazism in Germany, Frederick the Great, and Napoleon.[20] The talks were organized by Joseph Hudnut, who had been named dean of the School of Architecture at Columbia University in 1933. Above and beyond providing valuable assistance in Hegemann's search for a place in academia, Hudnut played a significant role in perpetuating the concepts of his admired mentor and may be considered his most prominent follower. On many occasions he noted Hegemann's influence on his philosophy, which shaped his academic decisions. During Hudnut's tenure as dean of Columbia's School of Architecture, and in the course of his tenure as dean of the Graduate School of Design at Harvard from 1936 to 1953, he referenced Hegemann's ideas on city planning in its modern and postmodern phases. Until recently Hudnut's role in the advancement of American Modernism, and concomitantly, Hegemann's contributions toward urbanism and the future metropolis, was obscured by Walter Gropius's renown.[21] Hudnut's innovative emphasis on a multidisciplinary approach to urban planning and civic space later continued under José Luís Sert at Harvard's Graduate School of Design.[22]

The Hegemann family's enjoyable summer vacation in Lost Lake did not dispel their financial worries. The *Family Saga* states that because Hegemann was not in the University in Exile, his salary was only $1,500 dollars per year. Finding another position or support from a foundation to augment his income turned into an intense and desperate endeavor involving the help of a wide circle of acquaintances.

Universities were hard pressed to take on additional faculty members, as were the organizations dedicated to aiding the increasing number of refugees. Aside from economic considerations, political concerns impinged on the selection of the beneficiaries. In response to these factors the campaign to procure a situation for Hegemann was two-pronged: to find a place in an academic institution and to obtain financial support from foundations or private individuals to subsidize such a position, or to provide him with an outright grant.

Hegemann's American contacts primarily recognized his reputation as an international expert on city planning and housing. His role as an architectural critic and political journalist was rarely mentioned. Hegemann's knowledge and approach to urbanism, however, was considered unique and unequaled by anyone in the United States or among other refugees arriving from Europe. The subject of city planning had not received much attention at universities. Encouraged by these particulars and by the urging of his acquaintances, particularly Joseph Hudnut, Alvin Johnson, Charles A. Beard, and Fiske Kimball, Hegemann embarked in the spring of 1934 on a major work that would result in the multivolume publication, *City Planning: Housing.*[23]

Letters of recommendation comment on Hegemann's distinctive and innovative interpretation of the complexities of the modern city. The historian Charles A. Beard wrote to Hegemann, "I am glad to hear that you are seeking a place where you can develop the social economic aspects of city planning. The work that you have done and the writing you have published in this field attracted my attention long ago, before I had the pleasure of meeting you personally. You are the only working city planner who combines technology, social economy, and a large historical view, and you could shed light on the darkness of the present confusion if you had a chance to develop and apply your powers."[24] Beard's letter was in response to Hegemann's appeal for a recommendation, and suggested that Hegemann should use the letter as an introduction to Abraham Flexner at the Institute for Advanced Study in Princeton, New Jersey. According to Beard, the institute was preparing to "enlarge its program," possibly to include city planning. Hegemann had alerted Beard to the difficulties he faced and wrote, "my research does not show that close specialization is customarily accepted as a guarantee of harmlessness," and stressed his wide geographic approach to "the complexity of our new world."[25] He also informed Beard about the refusal of the "economically independent colleagues" at the University in Exile to appoint him to their faculty because of his active anti-fascism. This was a poignant comment directed at Beard, one of the founders of the New School, who had recently warned his audience regarding the threat of "Hitlerism and our Liberties."

A grant from the Institute for Advanced Study, which did not materialize, would have allowed Hegemann to work on his book without the distraction of additional obligations. Others who wrote to Abraham Flexner on Hegemann's behalf were Sverre Pedersen from the Technical University of Norway, who provided an overview of Hegemann's accomplishments, and Albert Guérard from Stanford University.[26] Guerard proposed "city planning as a possible field of study for the Institute [and] a subject of commanding importance." He noted that at universities it was primarily dealt with as a technical matter, "but rightly understood, City Planning demands a combination of art, history, sociology and engineering, which is extremely rare . . . not obviously 'scholarly,'" yet requiring "knowledge, accuracy, imagination and taste." Guérard considered Hegemann singularly qualified and a "historian with a searching unconventional mind, a sociologist who wants to build a better City in its widest sense," and an authority of "exceptional worth."

Hegemann's longtime friend Fiske Kimball approached the University of Virginia, which showed an interest in accepting Hegemann on the faculty. When Kimball was asked by the university to procure funding toward Hegemann's salary of $5,000, he elicited letters of recommendation.[27] The Carl Schurz Foundation promised to help, but withdrew when Hegemann wrote scathingly after attending its annual dinner. One of the speakers, having recently returned from a trip to Germany, had highly praised "*Herr* Hitler" for having "united the Germans for the first time." Hegemann thought that Carl Schurz, having fled Germany after the revolution of 1848, would have been appalled to have the oppressive Nazi regime that persecuted Jews extolled by a foundation carrying his name. In his letter Hegemann pointed out that Jews, now victimized by Hitler, had made up the greater part of the educated classes in Germany. Although he was not Jewish, he considered it his duty to speak out against the anti-Semitism that he had perceived at the meeting of the Carl Schurz Foundation. Upon receiving a copy of Hegemann's letter, Kimball wrote to him, "I can't ask you to violate your convictions, but if you can moderate your expressions, I think you will find all your friends, of whatever shade of opinion, will rally to your support!"

Kimball continued to aid his friend and suggested the Rockefeller Foundation as a source for funding the position at the University of Virginia, and possibilities at the University of Pennsylvania, where Hegemann had given talks and renewed earlier contacts. The University of Pennsylvania proposed lectures in the Department of Architecture, but according to Hegemann, city planning and housing were to be viewed from the social and economic perspective and preferably placed at the Wharton School of Economics. The Hegemann/Kimball correspondence reveals that the difficulties in finding an academic position for Hegemann were not always merely circumstantial, but also resulted from his personal convictions and beliefs.

While exploring these various leads in the summer of 1934, Hegemann was hoping for something more advantageous to turn up at Columbia University. In a letter to Kimball he wrote, "I might overcome the time until

Columbia secures some money for its Urban Institute, for which our friend Hudnut seems to be desirous to secure my services." It was a few weeks later that Hegemann met with Hudnut in Nantucket, where they contemplated the idea of setting up a department of city planning at Columbia's School of Architecture. Of all the possibilities, this was by far the most auspicious for Hegemann, and, indeed, for the discipline of city planning in an academic setting.

The files of the Emergency Committee in Aid of Foreign Displaced Scholars contain over thirty items of correspondence between its assistant secretary, Edward R. Murrow, and various individuals concerning Hegemann's situation and possibilities for employment. Many were urged to write by Alvin Johnson and Joseph Hudnut.[28] A major portion of the correspondence pertains to the prospects at Columbia's School of Architecture to which Hudnut had been appointed dean. His explicit mission was to bring about a change from the Ecole des Beaux-Arts methods to more modern approaches in the curriculum.[29] This reorganization fortuitously coincided with Hegemann's arrival in New York and led to his discussions with Hudnut, as well as with other American architects and planners. The move toward Modernism at Columbia was not as dramatic and far-reaching as at Harvard's Graduate School of Design (GSD) and has drawn less attention from historians. The particular fact that one of Hudnut's most significant decisions within the restructuring of the School of Architecture at Columbia was most likely influenced by Hegemann has not been previously recognized.

In February 1934 Hudnut sent Frank D. Fackenthal, Secretary of Columbia University, his proposal for an Institute of Urbanism modeled on the Institut d'Urbanisme in Paris.[30] Hegemann may have provided a copy of the summary published in *STB*, based on the brochure by the Institut d'Urbanisme.[31] Hudnut's memorandum states that the institute at Columbia was "to carry on researches relating to the immediate problems of the City of New York," referring to the university's proudly calling itself "in the City of New York." The four areas of investigation to be addressed are strikingly similar to those mentioned in the *STB* article, which emphasizes the "inclusiveness of the subjects" taught at the Institut d'Urbanisme. Topics proposed by Hudnut for his institute were the administrative, economic, and social organization of cities, and urban art. These fields were being researched at Columbia, but in the future they would be coordinated at the institute. The curriculum intended to stress the investigation of real problems, rather than adhering to the Beaux-Arts design focus. Fackenthal was soon informed that the Committee on Housing Research at the School of Architecture would take on the preparatory organization of the Institute of Urbanism, adding new members, including Lewis Mumford.

Over the summer of 1934, the plans for the program firmed up under the name Town Planning Studio, and Hudnut submitted it to the Carnegie

Corporation requesting funding in the amount of $6,000.[32] The detailed proposal mentions the physical space, requirements for the bachelor's and master's degrees and non-degree students, and predicted an enrollment of thirty-five. Hope was expressed that Henry Wright (1878–1936) would be in charge of the Town Planning Studio as "Master" with a professorial rank and three assistants. Wright's "Notes Relating to the Teaching of Town Planning in a University" were appended. The proposal does not mention Hegemann by name but refers to attracting a "qualified scholar" to conduct research. Henry Wright was a well-traveled, prominent architect and planner, as well as the author of numerous publications. Among the projects he designed were Sunnyside Gardens in Queens, New York; Radburn, New Jersey; and Chatham Village in Pittsburgh. He was one of the founders of the Regional Plan Association and an active member of numerous organizations, attending national and international conferences. Wright's primary interests in housing and site planning coincided with those of Hegemann.

Hudnut was anxious for Hegemann's expertise in comprehensive planning to complement Wright's. However, the School of Architecture was unable to procure the $3,000 for Hegemann's part-time position. In his appeal to Edward R. Murrow of the Committee for the Relief of Dispersed German Scholars, Hudnut stated, "Dr. Hegemann's service will be of greatest value to us in connection with our program for an expansion of our Town Planning, and we have already made considerable use of Dr. H.'s services." In a subsequent letter, Hudnut commented that the success of the program depended on the participation of Hegemann.[33] In February 1934, the Relief Committee provided $1,500 for two consecutive years, and the remaining half of Hegemann's salary came in as gifts from friends and acquaintances, with the intention of helping him and furthering Columbia's innovative town planning endeavor. Twenty-nine contributors are noted on a list dated February 27, 1935, with amounts ranging from $25 to $300. With the funding for his salary in hand, Hudnut appointed Hegemann as "associate" for the academic year 1935–36 with the same academic standing as Henry Wright.[34]

With Wright and Hegemann in charge, the Town Planning Studio had a propitious beginning, representing manifold aspects that promised to develop along the line of its Parisian model. Hegemann concurred with Wright's commitment to housing in its relation to city planning, on which Wright had lectured and recently published an important book, *Rehousing Urban America*.[35] In the Preface Wright states, "The idea of this book has been to provide a general and comprehensive digest of the elements of good community planning and housing technique related to a hypothesis of future large-scale city rehabilitation which calls for a fairly compact and carefully related community organization rather than the loosely organized sprawling suburban expansion of the last few decades." Wright's analysis of "housing techniques" in America and Europe, presented as a treatise, was possibly intended for the curriculum at Columbia. Hegemann encountered in Wright a colleague with whom he shared other interests as well. With their enthusiasm and personal charisma, they provided a stimulating environment at the Town Planning Studio.

Wright's approach is expressed in his "Notes Relating to the Teaching of Town Planning in a University," in which he proposed training students in "site engineering" and studying the principles of community organization, and emphasized on-site observation. Contrary to the Beaux-Arts dogma, which focused on presentation drawings and models, the students, according to Wright, needed to expand their own point of view. He regarded the formulation of the problems, study, and discussion of social and economic factors of primary importance prior to concentration on practical solutions. In the absence of a suitable textbook, he suggested that such an aid might result from the research and course work undertaken by the studio.

Although Hegemann had not previously taught in an academic setting, he had devoted considerable thought to the effective propagation of the various elements of city planning in the effort of raising public awareness. The vehicles he chose in this endeavor were exhibitions, slide lectures, illustrated publications, and films. Tied into these pursuits were his interest in exhibition techniques and the possibilities of converting temporary exhibitions into permanent social museums-*cum*-research centers or "open universities."[36] It has been mentioned that in 1916 Hegemann sent his curriculum vitae to James Ford at Harvard University with suggestions for a study and research center devoted to city planning. According to Hegemann, the "science of city planning" should be understood as "the interrelation" between various aspects, including "landscape and civic architecture," and that it should "take its place with either one of the following departments: Sociology, Economics, Architecture, Engineering, or Landscape Architecture."[37] Hegemann composed these thoughts on comprehensive, large-scale planning not long after presenting his *Report on a City Plan for the Municipalities of Oakland & Berkeley* (1915), which demonstrated this tenet with an actual example. Presumably Hegemann envisioned his ideas for a university-based teaching and research center that combined all facets of city planning coming to fruition at Columbia University as a result of Hudnut's determination. Hegemann's expectations were truly fulfilled in his first and only year as a member of the Town Planning Studio.

In the announcements of the School of Architecture for 1935-36 Hegemann was listed as "Associate in Architecture" for four courses; two courses on architectural design were taught by a group of instructors.[38] Hegemann was in charge of the courses on the architecture of New York City and its sequel on the plan of New York City that included field trips and seminars, and were required of all first-year students. A note to this announcement stated, "An analysis of the plan of New York City and of the proposals made for the development of this plan with special reference to the studies made by the Regional Plan Association" and is comparable to a course Hegemann gave at the New School. In the outline for both winter and spring sessions Hegemann expressed his philosophy, which deviated markedly from the Beaux-Arts approach. "The first aim of education (other than moral aims) is to encourage on the part of each student the formation of a clear and objective view of their own world; in architectural education our methods are to be judged successful in proportion as they give the young architect an undistorted view of society and of the relation of society to its environment and a clear true understanding of the architect's place in the social scheme."[39] With the aim of wanting "our students first of all to belong to their own time," the study of classic architecture should be postponed, and the beginning should be "an ordered observation and analysis of contemporary civic life and of civic architecture." Hegemann considered the city of New York "a vast laboratory for this experiment," to be explored on Saturday field trips and in twice weekly, two-hour seminars focused on the "development of the historical sense: of the city as a continuing organism."

In his numerous travels Hegemann had relished wandering through cities to gain an understanding of their built environment and the culture that gave it form. To some extent Hegemann followed Patrick Geddes's methodology of firsthand surveys and observation. It is certain that Hegemann brought a memorable and "unique personal touch" to the student field trips.[40]

Another feature of Hegemann's involvement at the Town Planning Studio presented itself in the form of a proposal for "A Small Residential Park for Inexpensive Houses," carried out under his direction as a project by fourth-year students in the course on architectural design (Fig. 60). Additional faculty members, including Hudnut and Henry Wright, assisted and others gave advice. An illustrated article with Hegemann's text was published in the *Architectural Forum,* and the Greyrock on Sound Development Corporation issued a booklet on the residential park on Long Island Sound between Rye and Port Chester, New York, "offering modern small estates to families of moderate means."[41] Presumably the developers retained only the general outlines of the plan designed by the Columbia group, abandoning the proposed community facilities and increasing the number of more expensive houses.[42]

According to Hegemann's text, some of "the finest modern developments of residential real estate" could be found in American cities, and he named several, including Radburn by the "ingenious planner" Henry Wright. The challenge lay in providing housing for low-income families. The task of the present study was to plan a residential development that

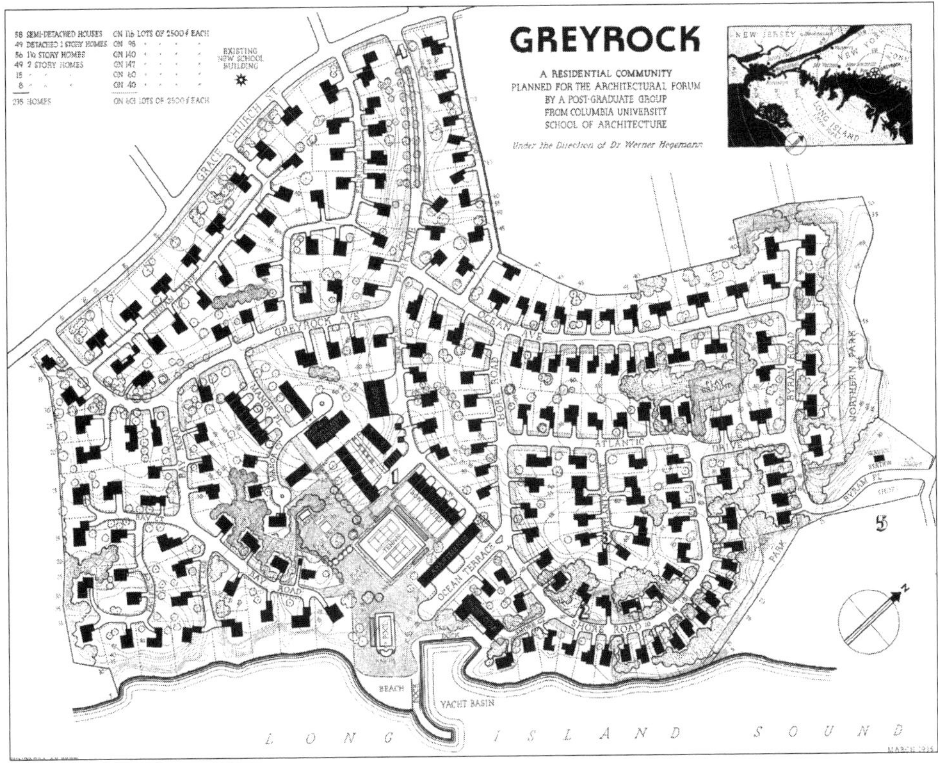

Fig. 60. Greyrock, "a small residential park for inexpensive houses" planned by graduate students from Columbia University School of Architecture under Hegemann's direction. From Architectural Forum, *May 1935. (CCCC)*

included a significant portion of houses selling for $6,000 or less, in addition to properties for wealthier clients. The article on Greyrock preceded others in the *Architectural Forum*, which in 1936 devoted much attention to small houses designed by architects costing $5,000, and published them with illustrations, plans, and technical specifications.[43]

The fifty-three acres of Greyrock were the former Gould Estate that bordered Long Island Sound with rolling hills, picturesque rock formations, and magnificent trees. Greyrock, as Hegemann described it, adjoined two socially dissimilar villages: Rye was a neighborhood of upper-class summer homes and country clubs, and Port Chester was settled by factory workers from nearby industries. The latter was blighted by a five-acre village dump. The New York Regional Plan Association had proposed turning the entire Gould Estate into a public park and preserving its scenic landscape, a suggestion that was abandoned as too costly. The proposal by the Columbia students recommended the transformation of the dump into a park, and the placement of affordable houses in the adjacent northern section. The more desirable southern section would provide large lots for upscale homes. Hegemann noted that "in English garden suburbs, such as Hampstead, inexpensive but well-designed houses blend with more expensive ones."

It was proposed that the old mansion, prominently situated on a hill, be transformed into a community center with a playground, tennis courts, a swimming pool, garages, and a yacht club on the shore. The upper floors of the original dwelling could be converted into apartments with additional units in two extended wings. Thus row houses were introduced into the development, despite being unpopular. According to Hegemann row houses were the most rational house type on narrow lots, and were preferable to the closely spaced single houses in Radburn.

Hegemann's article contains a detailed cost analysis for Greyrock Park, which entailed 212 building lots for small houses costing $6,000 or even less, and 23 lots along the shore for more expensive houses. The foldout plan demonstrates a sensitivity to topographical and natural features, such as the rock formations and the preservation of the existing tree-lined roads. The clustering of houses around courts and the cul-de-sacs resembled Hegemann & Peets's earlier designs for Washington Highlands and Wyomissing Park.

Hegemann's description is followed by a piece by William L. Drewry that presents the plans, elevations, and photographs or drawings of a variety of proposed low-cost house types with specifications on their construction and design. Drewry stated that the criteria followed in designing these small, mostly one-story houses were attention to the circulation between the interior and exterior and within the house, elimination of wasted space, and partitions only where absolutely essential. Care was given to the orientation of the dwellings for maximum sunlight. Types with basements had flat roofs; those built on solid rock that prevented excavating for basements were designed with sloping roofs allowing for attic space. The cost of the sloping and flat roof styles was about the same, but the latter "gave greater freedom in plan arrangement and fenestration." The use of traditional materials and construction methods proved to be more economical. Comparison of costs with prefabricated units showed no savings but that could change when production increased.

Hegemann had a longstanding interest in prefabricated low-cost dwellings. Discussing the plans for the Kohler Village with his client in 1916, the prefabricated houses by "Alladin" were considered as cost-saving but were rejected for aesthetic reasons. For the Greyrock proposition the firms American Houses and General Houses, Inc., in Chicago, were considered. Both companies were pioneers in the manufacture of prefabricated, reasonably priced, and attractive modern homes.[44] Unfortunately the cost proved higher than standard construction.

For personal and professional reasons the link to General Houses was auspicious for Hegemann. It brought him in contact with Robert C. Weinberg, who was at that time working with Howard T. Fischer and Phillip Wills Jr. The relationship between Weinberg and Hegemann evolved into a friendship that continued with the family beyond the latter's death. It encompassed a range of mutual interests and commitments regarding architecture and city planning. Even before making Hegemann's acquaintance, Weinberg had revered his intellectual accomplishments and his unswerving political convictions. Weinberg's loyalty and generous support were of lasting significance for Hegemann's widow and children.

Weinberg (1902–74) came from an affluent German-Jewish background. Because he and his wife had no children, he established the Vinmont Foundation (a translation of his German name) to channel his wealth to the funding of educational and community causes. He also made generous personal gifts and anonymously supplemented Hegemann's salary at Columbia University.

Weinberg had studied architecture and city planning at Harvard and spent most of his professional career in New York City, where he also lectured and published articles. His special concerns were housing and technical innovations, and he envisioned a solution to the housing crisis by means of mass-produced, low-cost, prefabricated homes. Weinberg joined General Houses, Inc., to design the models for the Chicago World's Fair: Century of Progress Exhibition of 1933.

In a memorandum of 1934 introducing Hegemann to his partner Howard T. Fischer, Weinberg wrote: "My own acquaintance with [Hegemann] is due to the fact that I have joined a small group of a half dozen architects who have been meeting with him for discussion at the New School of Social Research every Thursday afternoon." The memo also explains that Weinberg was withdrawing from General Houses because prefabricated houses were by then generally accepted. Indeed, journals were addressing construction with factory-fabricated units of wood and steel.[45] Weinberg recommended that General Houses concentrate on developing its business deals rather than furthering additional research.[46]

An exchange of letters between Weinberg and Fischer concerns an article on prefabricated houses, commissioned from Hegemann by General Houses. The purpose for the article was to demonstrate how well-designed modern homes could result from prefabricated units, singling out examples from the General Houses, Inc. Fischer requested numerous changes in Hegemann's initial draft, which emphasized European precedents and failed to stress modern design. Weinberg encountered difficulty mediating between Fischer and the unobliging Hegemann. A four-page manuscript, "The Progress of the Modern House Abroad," with numbers for illustrations noted in the margin, apparently incorporated the changes requested by Fischer.[47] It was included in a promotional brochure, *Our Homes*, published by General Houses, Inc., describing Hegemann as "An international authority [who] writes of the latest architectural developments in Europe."[48] Numerous illustrations show modern houses by Mies van der Rohe, the Luckhardts, and others, but none except the example from Japan employed prefabricated components. Hegemann began with a discussion of "the refined dwelling houses of Japan . . . light structures of wood and paper." These houses were built out of "highly standardized and semi-fabricated units" that could be "arranged according to the requirements and taste of the inhabitants." He continued, "this imaginative and infinitely variable use of the same unit is not only highly economical, but it produces also that fine rhythm which is an essential feature of great building art." One of the main points raised in the Weinberg/Fischer correspondence was the use of prefabricated units in these traditional houses. Hegemann addressed the possibility that progressive industries utilizing light-weight, adaptable materials could produce prefabricated sections for houses of distinctly modern design. Simpler methods of construction with standardized units were making great strides in Europe and Latin America. One of Fischer's suggestions that he wanted incorporated into Hegemann's article was his observation that America was ahead of Europe in developing techniques for industrial mass production, while Europe had developed Modernism as a style. To placate his client as well as gratify his own predilection for well-designed cars, Hegemann concluded: "It is only natural that the perfection of the prefabricated house idea should find its greatest field in America. In the United States the constructive designers of popular motor cars have shown what superior qualities of elegance and all-around comfort can be achieved by dropping any attempt to fake bygone ideals." He compared the replacement of the traditional dwelling by the "modern machine-made prefabricated house" to the supplanting of the horse-drawn carriage by the automobile.

Despite the brevity of Hegemann's academic involvements at the New School and Columbia's School of Architecture, they were noteworthy within the context of his professional life and might have led to consequential developments. However, three events delivered fateful blows, changing personal lives and altering the landscape of urban studies. Hegemann and Henry Wright died unexpectedly within weeks of each other in the spring of 1936, and Hudnut accepted the call to become dean of the School of Architecture at Harvard.[49] Significantly, he merged the three separate schools of architecture, landscape architecture, and city planning and created the comprehensive Graduate School of Design (GSD), revolutionizing the curriculum. He is credited with the appointment of Walter Gropius and Martin Wagner, who represented Bauhaus and New Building concepts as the introduction of Modernism to America. It is likely that Hudnut would have asked his esteemed friend Hegemann, had he lived, to join the faculty at Harvard's GSD, a vision reflecting one

Hegemann had expressed to James Ford in 1916. As one of those intriguing conjectures or "what ifs," Hegemann's presence would have given modern and post-modern urbanism in America a distinctive turn.

"Housing": Full Circle

Hegemann's preoccupation with housing and its parameters found practical application during his years in the American Midwest when he designed residential developments with Elbert Peets. Upon his return to Europe Hegemann assumed the role of an engaged observer of the efforts to solve the postwar housing crisis, appraising them within the larger context of cultural and economic developments.

The Gothenburg Exhibition of 1923 displayed variations of cottage and garden suburbs, and *Siedlungen* (settlements) were being built in the outskirts of many cities. Among Hegemann's frequent travels were visits to Dutch housing communities and the apartment blocks built by the socialist government of Vienna. In every region and city his attention focused on the need for shelter. Hegemann's commentaries are recorded in his articles and referred to in his books, chiefly *Das steinerne Berlin*. Work on *City Planning: Housing*, and his contacts with American urbanists engrossed in the housing problem intensified by the Depression, converged and brought Hegemann full circle to a topic that had preoccupied him since his early studies in Paris and Munich.

Among Hegemann's discussions of housing prior to his departure from Europe in 1933, some are noteworthy for addressing persistent issues in the housing debate, which subsequently reemerged in the American context. One of these was generated by the international Städtebaukongress in Vienna (1926), which dedicated an entire day to "the rational distribution of single- and multi-family houses," coming to the conclusion that the latter was appropriate for the city center and the other for peripheral areas. In the wake of the conference, Hegemann's article "*Kritisches zu den Wohnbauten der Stadt Wien*" (Critical observations on housing in the city of Vienna) was published together with the copiously illustrated essay, "*Die Gemeindebauten* [Public housing] *der Stadt Wien*," by Günter Hirschel-Protsch.[50]

Hegemann's "critical" analysis dwells on the economic advantages that enabled the Social Democratic government of Vienna to acquire substantial parcels of land within the city for the purpose of constructing public housing. The multistory buildings around a central courtyard provided communal facilities, including laundries, libraries, child-care centers, public baths, clinics, lecture halls, and workshops, and this compensated for the reduced size of the apartments. Opting for centrally located *Höfe* rather than low-rise *Siedlungen* in the periphery avoided the costly development of streets and other infrastructure. In addition to these economic factors, the buildings conformed to Viennese preference and cultural traditions. The few existing *Siedlungen* around Vienna had not been favorably received. The public considered their uniform typology demeaning, and favored the monumentality of the *Gemeindebauten*, which gave a palatial appearance to low-income housing. Although Hegemann recognized the obvious economic and political advantages and impressive accomplishments of Vienna's city government, he persevered in his preference for decentralized low-rise developments and disputed the notion that they were costlier. He emphasized that such settlements required integration into a regional plan that provided transportation and the proximity of industrial employment.

Hegemann's principle of housing as an element of city planning is a central thesis in all his considerations. He did not pay heed to architectural style or form, except for the matter of the flat or pitched roof when it related to functionality. In accord with Alexander Klein's leitmotif of the desirability of a "functional house for frictionless living," Hegemann stressed the importance of circulation routes, patterns of usage, and occupation. His ideal was a cottage with a subsistence garden for enjoyment as well as for fruit trees and vegetables. Prior to his return to the United States in 1933 Hegemann seldom expressed misgivings regarding the expansion of land consumed by decentralized settlements. The feared "sprawl" of later times had not yet entered urban debate.

Several aspects of architecture and town planning in the Scandinavian countries were valued by Hegemann, which led to his cordial and mutually respectful relations with urbanists from those regions. The Dane, Steen Eiler Rasmussen, was one of his closest friends, and facilitated a liaison that resulted in numerous articles on Scandinavian topics by Rasmussen and others from the region published in the Wasmuth journals. Hegemann discerned an incipient modernity in Nordic neoclassic architecture that respected vernacular building materials and customs. Above all Hegemann admired the cottage-and-garden suburbs, which updated and blended ideas derived from Camillo Sitte and those of the English garden city. These trends merged with local traditions and were received not as alien, but rather as enrichment and confirmation of what had evolved over time.[51]

Under Hegemann's editorship Wasmuth's periodicals, in particular *STB*, gave prominence to articles on low-income housing and the debate over the advantages of single houses, row houses, and apartment blocks, how to finance construction and where the developments should be placed. Economic considerations directed attention to typologies and the utilization of prefabricated units. Articles on urban planning and housing note this aspect as a factor of Stockholm's remarkable housing initiatives as early as 1904.[52] They entailed the acquisition of vast areas of unbuilt land on the periphery of the city and dedicated these lands to the development

Fig. 61. Prefabricated Kleinhäuser *being built by families in the outskirts of Stockholm, from* STB, *1928, No. 10.* WHA

of garden suburbs. The city carried the cost for installing the infrastructure and made individual house lots available by means of sixty-year leases with a purchase option. The prospective renters/owners were encouraged to build their own *Kleinhaus* with prefabricated units ordered in bulk by the city (Fig. 61). Professional help was available on the site for consultation, and illustrations in the articles and Volume 3 of *City Planning: Housing* show families with children participating in the task.

Hegemann considered Stockholm's property policies and the goal of providing as many people as possible with their own home and garden an exemplary model to be followed elsewhere. In his 1931 article he noted that Sweden had learned much pertaining to the siting of the garden suburbs and the design and placement of the houses since embarking on its vast undertaking. For instance, the initial plan for the suburb of Enskede showed primarily row houses but was later completed with single houses. Another improvement in subsequent developments was the situating of houses closer to the street, creating a harmonious frontage and allowing for larger backyards.

There is a notable affinity between the Scandinavian garden suburbs and those designed by Hegemann & Peets in the United States in their community-oriented philosophy. This is also due to their shared link to Sitte's revelations and their mutual response to the pervasive influence of the English garden city. Hegemann was not involved with the actual planning of residential developments while he was in Europe, but his vital interest in housing recommended him when he arrived in New York, where *The American Vitruvius: Civic Art* was well known. While still in Germany he published an article, "The Shelter Famine," in the journal *Survey Graphic*, which devoted a special issue to the "New Germany" since the Armistice (Fig. 62).[53] An editorial note describes *Survey Graphic* as "a shuttle of understanding." Conforming to this intent, Hegemann focused on economic factors and stressed the plight of the *Mietskasernen* (rental barracks), land speculation, and political mismanagement. These conditions were contrasted with recent endeavors to bring about improvements such as the developments in Frankfurt under the enlightened mayor Franz Adickes. Housing in Frankfurt was modern in design with flat roofs, constructed with standardized, prefabricated sections. Hegemann was convinced that with government support of industries producing such standardized units, their use would also become increasingly profitable in the United States.

Survey Graphic was widely read by American urbanists and progressives, and Hegemann subscribed to it while in Berlin. Among those associated with the journal were several prominent social reformers and "housers," including Jane Addams, Florence Kelley, Florence Loeb Kellogg, Robert W. deForest, and Edward T. Devine. These dedicated individuals provided encouragement and understanding to Hegemann's efforts to

The Shelter Famine

By DR. WERNER HEGEMANN

Editor of the City-Planning Review, Städtebau; director of the first City-Planning Exhibition, which was held in Boston in 1909

600000

204000 200000

178930

106502

1924 1925 1928 Additional yearly supply of dwellings | Additional yearly demand | Remaining old demand (unsatisfied)

Fig. 1. Demand and supply of dwellings in Germany

THE yearly surplus of births over deaths in Germany dropped in 1927 to 7.8 per thousand. Just before the War it was 12.4. One of the main causes of this sharp depression in the nation's vitality has been the lack of dwellings, profoundly inimical to family health and morale. And the $600,000,000 and more which Germany is supposed to pay from now on over a period as yet undetermined, would just about build the 200,000 small dwellings required even at the present slackening rate of increase of German households.

The figure of 200,000 does not include that even more urgent, because older, need of at least 600,000 dwellings (which would cost some $1,800,000,000) still unbuilt owing to the complete cessation of construction during the War (see Fig. 1). This lack appears vividly in the accompanying chart (Fig. 2) of the German housing famine.[1] Observe that in Berlin, for example, for every 1,000 families with homes, there are 93 sharing quarters with other families.

These figures but feebly represent the actual calamity. Housing conditions were bad, even before the War. During the campaign in 1912 for better housing (of which I was general secretary) our slogan was:

"In Greater Berlin, 600,000 people live in tenements where from 5 to 15 people sleep in a room. Hundreds of thousands of children have no playgrounds."

At the International Housing and Town Planning Congress at Paris this year (1928), the official report of Germany emphasized the unsatisfactory condition of housing conditions and continued:

> If for every household a sufficiently large dwelling were to be built, about 1,700,000 new dwellings would be required. If also the families that, as a result of insufficient dwelling space, have no or not a normal number of children, were considered, a further requirement of about 800,000 dwellings may be estimated. If, therefore, a nation with natural development could be taken as a basis of estimate, all in all 3,300,000 dwellings would be necessary.

Ten billion dollars would have to be spent before Germany's housing could be lifted from the condition into which the incapacity of her pre-war rulers and the immeasurable destruction of capital have thrown the country.

HOW does German building and housing fare under the prevailing conditions?

After having made, during the War, unprecedented but futile efforts of will-power and self-sacrifice, the German people grew very ready to follow suggestions from abroad. Right after the War, Germany threw herself into an orgy of "voluntary Americanization." Even today there exists no strong German resistance to the vigorous advertising campaigns carried on by American business for the introduction of American luxuries into a world badly in need of very different things. Even today one finds eagerness to copy American skyscrapers, subways, palatial cinema theaters, monumental stadia, great fairs, automobile roads and other costly American suggestions which can be financed in the capitals of concentrated American wealth, but are less appropriate for nations struggling for bare economic existence. Although many German experts agree with their English and American colleagues that the skyscraper is a

[1] These graphs are from the printed document No. 3777, published December 14, 1927, by the federal minister of works.

Fig. 2. Map of the home shortage in Germany. In the key (left, under the caption), "über" means over; "bis," under

600

Fig. 62. Hegemann's "The Shelter Famine," from Survey Graphic, *February 1929.* CCCC establish himself when he arrived in New York. The ambience of this circle furthered Hegemann's regard for the role of the women "housers" as active urbanists. He had met several of them on previous stays in America, and now he sought out others, making contact with Edith Elmer Wood, Mary Kingsbury Simkhovitch, and Catherine Bauer, who impressed him with their commitment and publications on the housing question.[54] Women in architecture and planning have since gained warranted attention.[55] Hegemann's respect for women's contributions in a field dominated by men evolved out of his admiration for them as pacifists. During his last years in Europe this thinking was enhanced by his idealistic belief in universal urbanism as a basis of world peace.

In Geneva Hegemann had conversations with Margery Corbett-Ashby on "Adolf Hitler and Women." He was impressed by Corbett-Ashby, the British delegate to the Disarmament Conference, President of the International Alliance of Women and an internationally known pacifist. In their interview, Corbett-Ashby emphasized the connection between Hitler's rush to war and Nazism's attitude toward women. At the New School Hegemann encountered a comrade in exile who shared this view. Frieda Wunderlich was a political scientist from Berlin, where she had held important positions and actively advanced the status of women.[56] She was the only woman on the faculty of the University in Exile. In her numerous publications, Wunderlich asserted that Nazism was a "counter-revolution" in opposing the emancipation achieved by the German women's movement in the previous decades. Nazism reverted women's status to their traditional position in charge of *Kinder, Kirche, Küche* (children, church, kitchen) and the production of children as "cannon fodder."

In an undated draft for a talk on freedom of speech and censorship under the Nazi regime, Hegemann called attention to the independent women's organizations that had been eliminated.[57] Perhaps inspired by conversations with Wunderlich, he related that women, except for those who were older and unmarried, were now discouraged from higher education and ousted from professional work. Younger women were enjoined to get married and bear children, even though the war had caused a scarcity of available men. According to Hegemann, the Nazis were "very honest in their statement" that "Germany wants to conquer other countries, for this it needs an able-bodied population [of] boys and men who will make strong soldiers," supplied by "healthy and strong girls." Regretfully this attitude was welcomed by certain segments of the German population.

During his exile years in New York, Hegemann's focus on shelter as an elemental need was interrelated with his respect for women as urbanists and social reformers. In addition to being an ideological preoccupation, housing took on the character of lifesaver for Hegemann's own family's desperate economic predicament. Hegemann's letters and diaries exude the hope that his major work, *City Planning: Housing*, together with articles and lectures would enhance his prestige and recommend him for a secure academic position. In particular his public lectures gave him welcome exposure. At one such event he joined Carol Aronovici, Director of the Housing Research Bureau of New York City and lecturer on housing and town planning at Columbia University, in a discussion of housing trends at an open meeting of the Welfare Council of the city. Hegemann is also listed among the speakers at the National Public Housing Conference in November 1934. Among the distinguished participants were Mayor Fiorello H. LaGuardia, Raymond Unwin, and Mary K. Simkhovitch.

Aronovici edited a publication for the Committee on Housing to accompany its exhibition at the Museum of Modern Art. The title, "America Can't Have Housing," apparently refers to Aronovici's essay on "The Outlook for Low-cost Housing in America."[58] Hegemann was a contributor to the publication among a coterie of American and international authorities that included Raymond Unwin, Lewis Mumford, Catherine

Fig. 63. Brochure by the British Labor Party, 1934. CCCC

Bauer, Edith Elmer Wood, Walter Curt Behrendt, Walter Gropius, and Henry Wright. Hegemann's article in the anthology, "Political Economy in German Housing Today," was highly critical of the policies of "the two outstanding leaders of the 'Third German Reich,'" the late President Hindenburg and Adolf Hitler. The conclusion was applicable to America as well, stating that "real improvement of housing is possible only in times of a general rise in employment and in wages."

Another event in 1934 was a radio address entitled "Are the United States ahead of the Soviet Union in Planning for Low-Cost Housing?" in which Hegemann raved about the accomplishments of his host country. Considering that he had arrived in the United States barely four months before the broadcast, he demonstrated an impressive knowledge of recent developments. Of the recent "voluminous" New York Regional Plan publication, he commented that it was "the biggest of all planning studies in the world," a design that would house 20 million people around the center of Manhattan.[59]

Hegemann's article, "With Hammer and Trowel," appeared in *Survey Graphic* in November 1934. A letter from the editors shows that he was working on it in the summer while also working on his book and disentangling the difficulties concerning the piece requested by General Houses, Inc.[60] Despite these pressures, "With Hammer and Trowel" is a cogent comparative analysis of the economic and political factors pertaining to housing in Vienna, Paris, Germany, Sweden, and the United States. Hegemann expressed concern that "Uncle Sam" would follow the erroneous "footsteps of Europe," particularly in pursuing slum clearance with the intention of building more tenements in the center of cities, rather than houses (Fig. 63). When the Social Democrats in Vienna lost power in 1934, the *Gemeindebauten* that were the pride of Red Vienna were declared politically dangerous "hotbeds of revolutionary agitation" by the reactionary forces. Other observers praised them for fostering moral standards and community spirit.

According to Hegemann, the debate between high-rise tenements and low-rise housing should be based not on political, but rather on economic considerations. He cited numerous statistics and the international authority Eberstadt, substantiating his own belief that two-story housing was the most cost-effective. He recommended that "Uncle Sam" should desist from slum clearance as a means for building tenements in their place, and instead follow the example of France, Germany, and Sweden by opting for decentralized low-rise settlements. In 1934, slum clearance to make way for the huge Joan of Arc tenement block in Paris led to a series of violent protests. The incident persuaded the city to expand on the periphery following the suggestions of Henri Sellier, the socialist administrator of the public housing office in the Seine Department. Sellier promoted satellite communities, "Cités-Jardins du Grand Paris," envisioning a green belt of socialist-inspired garden cities around the capital. Hegemann corresponded with Sellier to obtain technical information and illustrations of these vast garden cities for his article.[61] The photographs were also shown in Volume 3 of *City Planning: Housing.*

Cooperative building associations subsidized by the government, which had existed in Germany before Hitler's seizure of power, were a valid option for financing low-income housing. The most commendable European model for America was Stockholm's urban policy of decentralized settlements, which Hegemann had described on other occasions. Cost-saving and social benefits accruing from people who built their own one- or two-story prefabricated houses under the supervision of government professionals were impressive. The title of the article, "With Hammer and Trowel," refers to those families who constructed their own shelters with simple tools.

Addressing the situation in the United States, Hegemann emphasized that large-scale comprehensive housing schemes by the government would have a stabilizing effect on the economy and were vastly preferable to piecemeal rehabilitation of existing stock. He was undoubtedly aware of the intense efforts by the National Public Housing Conference under the leadership of Simkhovitch, Wood, and Bauer to persuade the government to enact a comprehensive federal housing policy.[62]

Hegemann's advocacy of prefabrication is notable and was furthered by his contact with Weinberg and H. T. Fischer of General Houses, Inc. Hegemann concluded, "With Hammer and Trowel," with a promotion of this new technology that could also involve sweat-equity building by owners:

> Public authorities who desire to advance the cause of rehousing the nation and of stimulating building industries paralyzed by the depression might offer awards for the best new types of prefabricated houses and might encourage building and loan associations to finance the sale of these truly modern commodities. Cities might collaborate in encouraging competitive private industries by guaranteeing large orders for such new houses. . . . Equally important would be the preparation of beautiful new garden cities—well planned developments to accommodate the new type of prefabricated housing. At present building regulations like those of New York City make such an advance into new fields impossible.

Part Two of *Housing America*, by the editors of *Fortune*, bears the title, "The Future: Housing as It Will Be." The first chapter discusses "Industries' answer, perhaps the greatest single commercial opportunity of the age."[63] Hegemann would have concurred with this publication's assessment of the architects of the International Style, who, although proclaiming functionalism, devoted themselves to stylistic solutions, rather than designing truly innovative houses, and merely provided "new envelopes." Aligned with this opinion, Hegemann was intrigued by the possibilities prefabrication held for low-cost housing in garden communities.

Weinberg owned a copy of *Housing America*, which devoted an entire chapter to General Houses, Inc., "The General Motors of the New Industry of Shelter," and presumably loaned it to Hegemann. Advertisements for General Houses, Inc. compared its products to automobiles, which could be bought at showrooms and taken home. The prefabricated wood or steel houses designed by Fischer were modern, attractive, and livable. Their well-thought-out floor plans featured cost-saving aspects, such as placing the plumbing for bathrooms and kitchens in common walls. What distinguished them from other prefabricated houses and those built by traditional methods was the absence of a distinction between frame and wall because the walls were load-bearing. Under "A New Way of Thinking," the book also featured Buckminster Fuller's Dynaxion House.

Keeping abreast of this effervescent phase in American city planning, which is frequently recognized as one of the most creative, was a demanding challenge for Hegemann. Combined with his own time-consuming activities, it explains his missed opportunities for becoming involved with important contemporary organizations and individuals. Among these were the Regional Planning Association of America (RPAA) and the Committee on the Regional Plan of New York, which galvanized the thinking of a group from a range of backgrounds and talents. These are barely mentioned in the documentation pertaining to Hegemann, who apparently was not personally acquainted with Lewis Mumford or Clarence Stein, with whom he would have shared many interests.

When the exiled Hegemann entered the United States, several significant publications appeared that had a direct impact on his lectures and the book on housing. Among them was Henry Wright's *Rehousing Urban America*, which was described in the Preface as "a manual of good housing practice."[64] He compiled the results of many years of study and numerous previous articles, expanding and organizing them into three parts. Wright analyzed all aspects of his specialty, site planning as related to housing, citing examples from America and Europe. The chapter entitled "Evolution of Modern German Housing and Community Planning" was based on his visit to Germany in the winter of 1932–33. His emphasis on creative siting of residential developments to prevent wasting space and "sprawling suburban expansion" marks an early usage of the term "sprawl."[65] Slum clearance for Wright was not a solution unless it was replaced by adequate low-cost housing. His suggestion of a type of "hybrid" dwelling, combining the qualities of flat, apartment, and row house while avoiding their defects was the primary focus of his book.

Introducing a series of articles published in 1934 by *The New Republic* that had been preserved in Hegemann's files, the editors stated,"At present the notion of slum clearance dominates the housing policy of the nation. What is the validity and what are the possibilities of immediate slum clearance?"[66] The dominant theme of the articles was that the housing crisis could not be solved by slum clearance and piecemeal efforts, but required a comprehensive "gigantic program of urban reconstruction and community planning and building" by the federal government. Among the points raised was one strongly reflecting Wright's and Hegemann's position: "The house is not an isolated unit: it is part of a neighborhood, and the neighborhood in turn is part of a larger regional community, with factories, markets, parks and rural recreational facilities to which it must be related." Developments should provide adequate social and physical environments, playgrounds and schools. These were aspects Hegemann had advocated and actualized in the residential developments in partnership with Elbert Peets.

Sampling this modest selection from the deluge of publications on housing that made their appearance when Hegemann embarked on his own book, *City Planning: Housing*, attests to his courage and determination to proceed with the project. He was convinced that he could make a unique contribution to a theme nurtured by his observations in Europe, the Americas, Asia, and Australia.

Ida Belle and the children spent the summer vacation of 1935 in Lost Lake as they had the previous year, while Hegemann stayed at their house in New Rochelle working on the book project and preparing his fall classes for Columbia University and the New School. In his letters to his wife he complained about the heat and headaches.

The family returned to New Rochelle in the fall for the beginning of the school year. Hegemann's commute for his classes was a considerable strain on him, and he insisted on curtailing their social life to devote all his free time and energy to the book. Despite these less than optimum circumstances, Hegemann made progress during the summer of 1935 on *City Planning: Housing*, Volume 1, *Historical and Sociological*, and on the outlines for Volume 2, *Political Economy and Civic Art*, and Volume 3, *A Graphic Review of Civic Art, 1922–1937*. On the last page of Volume 1 the Architectural Book Publishing Company stated that these books were a continuation of *The American Vitruvius: Civic Art*. According to Hegemann's introduction, the intention was to complement the aesthetic aspects emphasized in *Civic Art* with "the adequate solution of problems of social and political economy as preconditions of artistic possibilities and civic beauty."[67]

Replying to a harshly critical review of *City Planning: Housing* in 1939 by Alan Mather in *Pencil Points*, W. M. McRortie, president of the Architectural Book Publishing Company, devoted a letter published in the journal to "the 'inside story' of the circumstances attending the preparation and publication" of Hegemann's books.[68] In addition to what had been known about Hegemann's stress and declining health, this letter clarified some particulars and enhanced an understanding of the difficulties surrounding the production of the books. Mather had rebuked the publishers for the faulty coordination of the three volumes, although he considered their content valuable but "baffling." McRortie explained that Hegemann "originally proposed to us a single book of illustrations and text to continue the subject matter of Hegemann and Peets's *The American Vitruvius: Civic Art* from 1922 to 1937," and the publishers had agreed. Subsequently Hegemann realized that a single volume would be too unwieldy. Reluctantly, the publishers consented to two volumes of text and an "atlas" of illustrations in the format of *Civic Art*. When Hegemann had finished the manuscript for Volume 1, "he was a very sick man," and he is quoted as saying, "When this book is finished, I am finished." After Hegemann's death, his wife and friends decided that work on the remaining two volumes had progressed sufficiently to allow them to be completed by collaborators. According to McRortie, these "brilliant and devoted people" who assumed the obligation as editors were Ruth Nanda Anshen, William W. Forster, Elbert Peets, and Robert C. Weinberg. The publishers were pleased by the sales.

Regardless of the devotion with which the editors brought Hegemann's work to fruition, it is Volume I that best represents his ideas on city planning and its place in the world. He dedicated the book to his "esteemed friends, Alvin Johnson and Joseph Hudnut," and followed with a long list of those to whom he was "greatly indebted," with expressions of gratitude for suggestions and reading of the manuscript. Hegemann commented in the Introduction that in view of the large number of valuable books and articles on city planning and housing recently published, he would refrain from repeating what others had already said. However, the political background of "urbanism"—a novel term—had hardly received attention, and he intended to fill this gap.

In line with this resolve, Volume 1 was primarily aimed at countering the prevailing American suspicion of comprehensive planning as a dangerous trend toward Socialism or even Communism if embraced by the government. While this apprehension addressed all forms of planning, Hegemann's salient concern was how it affected decisions related to city planning and the current housing crisis. Federal intervention, especially regarding slum clearance, was anathema to real estate developers and private property owners. Responding to this edgy confrontation that pitted planners against anti-planners, Hegemann astutely dispelled the fear of the curtailing traditional laissez-faire by demonstrating that major figures in American history had vigorously supported planning and public works. He singled out events from the country's past in every chapter, demonstrating his customary grasp of the interrelationship of history and evolving urbanism. He noted that a glance at the map of the United States rendered obvious that it was the most planned country in the world, affirming that "from its beginning, [it] was a creation of reasoning and of planfully acting men rather than a growth of purely 'natural' forces."[69] The Declaration of

Independence guaranteed "the pursuit of happiness" within this planned world, rather than through the haphazard acquisition of property. Thomas Jefferson was a master builder and planner, and so was George Washington. With this formidable background the United States achieved an early leadership in city planning. Hegemann attributed a variety of meanings to city planning. Most importantly it meant the laying out of an individual city, and "the planning of a group of cities and subsidiary settlements . . . correlating them by well-conceived public works . . . and locating them in such suitable areas as to make them organizing centers of economic 'regions' and states."

Hegemann's historical perspective reviews the unfolding of America, persistently establishing connections to the contemporary debate regarding the federal position vis-à-vis the housing crisis. He adhered to his methodology of recording the historical background of current problems, in the hope that such problems might be prevented in the future. As was his custom in earlier publications, he made effective use of documentation and the citation of sources. Charles A. Beard, the eminent historian and his colleague at the New School, was a major source for Hegemann. Beard noted in the margin of an early review of Volume 1 that "the book shines and sparkles with the richness of his thought and makes me marvel at the width of his knowledge. It throws new light on our history and unites the thoughts of the two worlds in a common exposition, Chas. A. Beard."[70]

Hegemann refuted the reputation of Abraham Lincoln as an advocate of non-interference by the government as was propagated by the opponents of New Deal policies. He called Lincoln "the least fitting patron saint of laissez-faire," who thought in terms of human lives instead of "dollars and cents."[71] Comparing the financial value Lincoln ascribed to slaves as property to the "tainted" property value of slums, Hegemann suggested that it might take another revolution to eliminate American slums. On the basis of statements by Lincoln, he declared the president "more radical" than Karl Marx. Along these lines the chapter on "Christianity and Housing," opens provocatively:

> There may be, even in America, critics to whom the humanitarian demands made by Abraham Lincoln and his contemporary Karl Marx appear extravagant. Such criticism is more likely to issue from defenders of the accepted religious and cultural tradition. They are apt to oppose any revolutionary changes in the established rights of holding either slaves or real estate. This very kind of criticism has inspired vaunted minds to staunchly defend the cause of slavery and similarly dubious causes.[72]

One of the instances of "dubious" criticism mentioned by Hegemann is the misquotation of Matthew 6:6, by the German historian Heinrich von Treitschke, justifying the congestion in the rental barracks of Berlin that only a small chamber sufficed to pray to God. Hegemann noted with surprise that the United States, a powerful, wealthy Christian nation, was not cognizant of "Christ's clear and simple precept in so fundamental a matter as housing and common decency." As he had done many times previously, Hegemann cited the correct version from the Gospel, which refers to the privacy of one's own dwelling. According to Hegemann, because it supports "one of the most essential demands in modern housing—privacy and approximately one room per person—upon the rock of Christian teaching we may safely return to the two contemporaries, Lincoln and Marx, who, in the nineteenth century, were probably the most outstanding fighters for the realization of practical Christianity, although they did not care to exploit the devine name."[73] Hegemann even hints at the threat that a vengeful God of justice would enact retribution on those who "sinned" by tolerating human misery without taking action.

The linkage between a progressive planning agenda and a religious imperative is somewhat disconcerting when viewed at a moment steeped in the rhetorical abuses of the Christian Right in the United States. However, Hegemann's summons for planning as if people mattered was and is a more authorative voice than can be imagined.

Two American authors and poets who figure prominently in Hegemann's thoughts on Christian ethics and urban planning were Ralph Waldo Emerson and Walt Whitman. Excerpts from Whitman's poetry were included in Hegemann's books on the great exhibitions of 1910 and later publications. Emerson, who is recognized as one of the guiding thinkers of Unitarianism, was a vital inspiration to the Social Ethics movement in Boston. Hegemann was influenced by the emphasis on the belief in religion as social activism, echoing Emerson's concept of goodness to be accomplished by actual work. In the dialogues in *Deutsche Schriften* and other instances, Hegemann acknowledged his own "American" Unitarian Universalist beliefs.

In the chapter "Homebuilders of the Nineteenth Century," Lincoln, Emerson, and Marx are grouped together in a combination of possibly odd bedfellows. All three are quoted in the heading. Hegemann begins with a synopsis of the influence of America's "progressive days of 1776 and 1862" on Great Britain, which gave a political victory to "the people who live in small houses," rather than those in its celebrated "great houses." This brought an impetus to England's housing and city planning policies, which eventually surpassed those of the United States. Referring to Emerson, who praised change and reform for preserving a nation's strength, Hegemann considered it superfluous for America to "seek help from Marx or Moscow as long as Jefferson, Lincoln, Emerson and Walt Whitman—the 'permanent rebel'—remain a living font of political and other regenerative life."[74] Emerson, Lincoln, and Marx, inspired by humanistic and socialist ideals, had fought for social justice. As Lincoln put it, America offered "the homes of a free and happy people." In great detail

Hegemann relates how American events and ideas influenced Marx, and how Lincoln's revolutionary thoughts preceded and were more radical than those in the *Communist Manifesto*. Neither recommended a revolutionary upheaval for America or England. Hegemann leaned heavily on Lincoln to solve the problem of slum clearance. He recommended applying Lincoln's proposal that the government should indemnify slave owners for their loss in property value to the owners of razed tenements.

When Hegemann wrote Volume 1, Communism and the influence of Moscow were heated topics of the day. Presumably it was this discourse that overwhelmed Hegemann's pursuit of his main theme, housing, in the major portion of his book. In the later chapters he shrewdly weighed housing and city planning policies abroad, including those in Russia, maintaining his position that, with a few exceptions, none of them was *in toto* adaptable to American conditions.

The last two chapters discussed the Viennese *Gemeindebauten* and the "Stockholm example," and were based on Hegemann's prior publications on these topics. He recommended Stockholm's housing policy as a model, although it would require land ownership by the city and/or subsidies from the federal government.

Volume 1 is certainly not a treatise on housing in the technical sense. As Robert Weinberg noted, it is rather "a historical inquiry into the 'superstition' that the benefits of real estate speculation must go to private persons, and the equally false assumption that comprehensive planning for better living is a principle at variance with established American custom."[75]

Other reviewers of Volume 1 voiced comparable opinions. One commented that "Dr. Hegemann very shrewdly sidestepped the 'Red' accusation by finding precedent for his recommendations in action and words of none less than Washington, Lincoln, Jefferson, and similarly reputable Americans." Frederick Ackerman pointed out in his review, "City Planning: Yesterday, Today and Tomorrow," that Hegemann's study was "set within an uncommonly wide perspective." Explaining that rather than listing problems and solutions like other works devoted to city planning, Hegemann was concerned with "how it came about that the current problems developed out of a past in which the avowed social and economic aims appeared to be that of preventing the development of just such problems by forethought and action—that is to say, by planning."[76]

Carol Aronovici wrote in *The Survey* barely a month after Hegemann's death and the appearance of the book, noting that the author carried the investigation of the past into the "present struggle to develop and make permanent a national program of housing—city, regional and national planning." A review in the *Architectural Forum* stated that Hegemann's book was "a unique addition" to the vast amount of housing literature. The title was considered misleading, because it was "no objective review . . . , no dry summary of facts and dates: it is straight propaganda, and very good propaganda at that." Comments on the polemical tone of Volume 1 evoke the relationship to Hegemann's writings in *Für Gross-Berlin* of 1911–12, and the muckraking publications of Lincoln Steffens.[77]

Volume 2, *Political Economy and Civic Art*, was edited by Ruth Nanda Anshen, based on the notations left by Hegemann. Her Introduction indicated that she started the task shortly after his death in April 1936. The Preface by Joseph Hudnut was abbreviated from a more personal, earlier version.[78] It dwelt on the importance of his association with Hegemann for his own philosophy and professional life. Their acquaintance began in 1917 when Hudnut joined the office of Hegemann & Peets in Milwaukee. Hudnut's comments offer valuable insights on the meaning of Hegemann's legacy. Beyond giving Hudnut direction, Hegemann influenced concepts Hudnut later brought to Harvard University as dean of the Graduate School of Design. Among the noteworthy remarks by Hudnut in the earlier version of his Preface are these:

> The principle which most surprised me in Hegemann's art was the conception of city planning as the basis of architecture. The city was conceived by him not as an arrangement of streets which afford building sites to an architect, nor yet as an arrangement of spaces and structure which might assure the architect opportunities for the exploitation of his formal principles of pattern: for the imposition of a grandiloquent geometry of plan. . . . To Hegemann a city was a living and growing organism which could by no means be compressed into a mould either geometric or picturesque. The physical pattern of the city . . . must grow out of that idea-pattern, good or evil, which determined and directed the lives of the citizens. Architecture is an art condition[ed] upon the social sciences.

In the Preface published in Volume 2, Hudnut addressed the connection Hegemann established between the provision of shelter, frequently considered a technical matter, and civic art. Hudnut expressed his own hope that housing forming an integral part of city planning would "lead to a redemption of this [civic] art from its present futilities."

Hudnut's Preface and Ruth Nanda Anshen's "Introduction: A Biographical Note," dated July 1936, are attempts to clarify the intentions of Hegemann's treatise. In Volume I Hegemann thanked Anshen for "critical collaboration," and she provided an explanatory summary of the earlier volume in her own Introduction, which is an obituary-like biography of Hegemann. It may be faulted for its emotional tone and some factual errors, which were subsequently copied by others. Anshen did, however, succeed in capturing Hegemann's idealism and lifelong pursuit of reason and planning as requisites for a peaceful world.

Volume 2 would have gained from indications as to which parts were actually written by Hegemann and which were contributed by the editor.

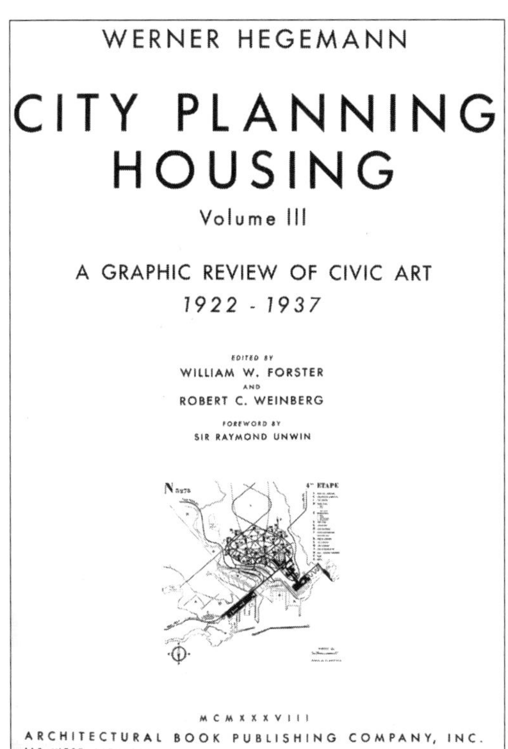

WERNER HEGEMANN

CITY PLANNING
HOUSING

Volume III

A GRAPHIC REVIEW OF CIVIC ART
1922 - 1937

EDITED BY
WILLIAM W. FORSTER
AND
ROBERT C. WEINBERG

FOREWORD BY
SIR RAYMOND UNWIN

MCMXXXVIII
ARCHITECTURAL BOOK PUBLISHING COMPANY, INC.
112 WEST 46TH STREET NEW YORK, N. Y.

Fig. 64. Title page of Hegemann's last book. CCCC

It is helpful to know that the last chapter, "Washington, Williamsburg, the Century of Progress, and Greendale," was written by Elbert Peets, who also assisted with other chapters. Robert Weinberg had considerable input as well, particularly in arranging for the illustrations based on sketches by various individuals. The resulting book combines material from Hegemann's articles and his notations about recent developments in American housing and related events. The latter rely on publications by Catherine Bauer, Lewis Mumford, Elbert Peets, Edith Elmer Wood, Henry Wright, and others whose works are extensively cited. Missing is the theoretical structure that Hegemann would have given this rich melange.

Volume 3, *City Planning: Housing. A Graphic Review of Civic Art 1922–1937*, also referred to as the "Atlas," was edited by William W. Forster and Robert C. Weinberg and published in 1938 with a Foreword by Raymond Unwin (Fig. 64). In 1936 Unwin, still vigorous at the age of seventy-three, was named visiting professor at Columbia University's School of Architecture to provide continuation and prestige to the Town Planning Studio following the deaths of Hegemann and Henry Wright, and the departure of Hudnut. Unwin's longtime friendship with

Hegemann, who was eighteen years younger, suffuses the Foreword to Volume 3. He described his younger colleague as a "remarkable man," recognizing his "penetrating intellect and originality in conception [that were] united with an independence of judgment and fearlessness." According to Unwin, Hegemann was unique as a "firm believer in planning, while remaining a most ardent lover of liberty who highly valued individuality," and was always striving for cooperation between powerful conflicting interests. Unwin sought out the concepts on which he concurred with Hegemann and which had bonded them for over two decades. Their rapport is revealed in Unwin's concluding statement on the value of cooperation: "This is indeed the characteristic of all planning and design, whether of human life or of its environment; that it creates new values from the association in right relations and appropiate proportions of persons, forms, colors or sounds, as the case may be, values which could not otherwise be attained."

The Preface by Forster and Weinberg defines the scope of Volume 3, *A Graphic Review of Civic Art 1922–1937*, as well as its objective of forming a sequel to the earlier *The American Vitruvius: Civic Art*. This new volume presented the conceptual and actual results in worldwide city planning—a scheme proposal so ambitious and broad that it precluded completeness. Therefore a focus was selected to discuss topics of communication, recreation, and public housing by addressing "questions of design and the technical and esthetic solution of the city-planning problems considered."

The images previously assembled by Hegemann were combined with new material, resulting in over one thousand illustrations, roughly half of them photographs and the rest plans and diagrams. The editors thanked many individuals for providing examples and permitting their reproduction. Weinberg conducted extensive correspondence to obtain the additional illustrations.[79] Hegemann is said to have prepared the layout of some sections, and he may have left indications for dividing the content of the "Atlas" into two parts, one on city planning and the other on housing, and subdividing each part into three sections. The page layout and the arrangement of topics is comparable to that of *The American Vitruvius: Civic Art*. Beginning with the exhibitions of 1910 in Germany, Hegemann arranged urban subjects by topic, rather than chronologically or geographically. He transferred this approach to the large-scale pages of *The American Vitruvius: Civic Art*. It was particularly striking in that volume, because examples from diverse regions of the world and historic periods were placed together. *A Graphic Review of Civic Art 1922–1937* covered a limited time frame of fifteen years of urban developments, but they were grouped with a worldwide scope. This was a true reflection of Hegemann as citizen of the world, a status sustained by his extensive travels. The universality of the third volume was furthered by Weinberg's admirable commitment to obtain illustrations which entailed literally hundreds of letters.

The international character of the selections in Volume 3 was favorably singled out by reviewers from regions seldom featured in city planning or architectural publications. Pedro Martínez Inclán from Havana, Cuba, commented on the "didactic" value of the three volumes, especially the first and third, and concluded: "Finally, this third volume is particularly interesting to Spanish speaking professionals because it describes graphically, several works carried out in Spain and South America. Spanish-American countries are frequently forgotten by other similar publications." A review in the *South African Architectural Record* noted that town planning was just commencing in South Africa and knowledge could not be derived from local precedents. "*City Planning: Housing*, Vol. III by Werner Hegemann endeavours to fulfil the above need. It presents detailed information about the most recent Town Planning schemes carried out in all parts of the world . . . . It shows how irresistibly the modern conception of architecture and town planning is slowly sweeping across the world."[80]

Reviewers were not only impressed by the geographic scope, but also by "the outstanding characteristic [of the book's] catholicity of taste and its impartiality." This unnamed author continued, "There has been no pandering to individual dogmas, theories or practices. . . . Good design, according to to-day's standards, has been the only common denominator, the sole arbiter as to what material should be included or excluded."[81]

The reception of Hegemann's last works in America was colored by the lingering shock of his death, as well as the edgy controversy between planners and anti-planners. Some professionals found his rejection of slum clearance for the construction of multilevel housing problematic. In addition, Hegemann's position regarding Marxism in Volume 1 caused uneasiness, although he clearly stated that he considered a totalitarian government inappropiate for the United States.

A Graphic Review of Civic Art 1922–1937 never achieved the renown of its predecessor, *Civic Art*. Yet only for the quantity, richness, and variety of the illustration it is certainly a landmark of fifteen years of urbanism, juxtaposing on the opening pages an aerial view of Washington's mall as it appeared in 1937 with Le Corbusier's plan for Nemours in Algeria. Throughout the volume the captions are cross-referenced to others in the Atlas and to descriptions in the text of Volumes 1 and 2, as well as the earlier *The American Vitruvius: Civic Art*.

Part One of Volume 3, "City Planning," includes regional planning and "New Cities." Among the international assortment are New Delhi, Tel Aviv, Canberra, Goiania (Brazil), and a model of Nemours. Hegemann had prepared much of the extensive section on "New Communities." It is particularly rich in greenbelt towns annotated by Elbert Peets, settlements in Palestine, and variations of the garden city concept in England, France, the United States, and Canada. American developments are particularly well represented, and include some that are not well known.

Correspondence by Hegemann starting in 1934 testifies to his personal interest in the Jersey Homesteads in Hightstown, New Jersey, built in 1935 for the needleworkers union, "a town organized with cooperative agriculture and industry, the workers in control of the tools of production with which to make a living on the basis of union standards."[82] John Nolen designed the layout, and the architect of the flat-roofed modern, one-story houses and the cooperative clothing factory was Alfred Kastner. The idea for this unique cooperative community was conceived in 1933 by a group representing widely divergent interests. It included Albert Einstein, Rabbi Jonah B. Wise, and David Dubinsky, President of the International Union of Ladies' Garment Workers, who secured the financial support of the Resettlement Administration headed by Rexford G. Tugwell, the zealous promoter of the "greenbelt" model towns and experimental cooperative settlements. Einstein's trip from his home in Princeton to Hightstown during construction was reported in the *Architectural Forum*, which showed portraits of Einstein and Kastner, as well as views of the models of the houses and floor plans.[83] A similar residential development for the Hosiery Workers Union in Philadelphia, the Carl Mackley Houses designed by Oskar Stonorov and Alfred Kastner, is featured in the section on public housing in Volume 3, preselected by Hegemann.[84] The section on "extension of existing cities" represents fifteen countries with recent proposals.

Greater New York dominates the pages devoted to slum clearance and prevention and the rebuilding of central areas. These topics were hotly debated at the time and are discussed in Volumes 1 and 2. Efforts in England, France, and the U.S.S.R. are among several others considered. The selection of civic centers and public squares differs strikingly from those in the earlier *Civic Art*, indicating the profound changes taking hold in urbanism. Contrasts are highlighted with pictures of caravans of camels and mules along primitive roads in Kirghiz and Mexico, respectively, and highway construction in progress in many distant areas of the world. Parking garages and airports signaled the importance of new modes of transportation as critical elements in city planning, competing with recreation and waterfront development. Recent urban parks accommodated playgrounds and sport facilities and were moving away from the picturesque landscape design of the Olmsted era.

The second part of Volume 3, "Housing," deserves special attention as a manifestation of one of Hegemann's abiding commitments. In line with his interests, the first chapter is devoted to public housing, opening with sixteen photographs and nine plans of the *Gemeindebauten* in Vienna, on which he had previously published. Equally extensive is the spread on Denmark showing multistory apartment blocks and row houses. Seven pages are dedicated to public housing in Great Britain, favored by Hegemann for the efforts to decentralize and the garden city concepts taking hold. The illustrations are not exclusively of garden developments, and include recently built residential flats in Liverpool and Manchester.

France is represented with a high-rise urban complex near Lyons and several of the Cités-Jardins du Grand Paris. In 1934 Hegemann exchanged several letters with the prominent socialist administrator of the public housing office in the Seine Département.[85] Sellier promoted satellite communities outside Paris based on the garden city and Unwin's influence. Hegemann had obtained the illustrations and financial data directly from Sellier.

From early workers' housing to the most recent *Siedlungen*, the section on German housing spreads over nine pages, including many aerial views and plans. The Weissenhof *Siedlung* in Stuttgart is placed in a later chapter with groups of multiple dwellings. Italy, Mexico, Finland, Poland, and the Netherlands are represented with public housing, with the majority of the Dutch examples coming from J. J. P. Oud.

Weinberg's correspondence file demonstrates his determination to obtain examples from Soviet Russia. A caption notes the influence of the German *Zeilenbau* layout on housing built during the First Five Year Plan, 1928–32. The developments in Spain were dense and dreary and contrasted sharply with those of Sweden on the following pages. Even low-rent apartment buildings, some with balconies, are surrounded by landscaped spaces and access to playgrounds. There was a notable variety of housing types in Sweden combined with the options for financing. Two full pages are devoted to Stockholm's "Small Housing Scheme," utilizing prefabricated sections for self-building. Hegemann had published on this innovative approach for providing low-income families with shelter, and this volume provides a large number of photographs of owners actively constructing as well as the finished products. An aerial view of the recently completed Enskede shows a public park and playing field prior to the planting of gardens and trees. Slum clearance in Zürich made way for a cooperative development of one-story houses surrounded by small lush gardens.

F. L. Ackerman, technical adviser to the New York Housing Authority, introduced the section on the United States, noting that public housing had begun as an emergency measure during the war to accommodate industrial and shipyard workers. The Great Depression of 1933 recognized housing as a stimulus to the economy, but Ackerman considered it curious that it took a major war and a depression to draw attention to a basic need. Weinberg worked closely with Ackerman, Clarence Stein, and other housing experts in compiling illustrations and plans of representative American examples from the entire country. Included were before-and-after photographs of low-income housing.

"Planning for Modern Living: Planned Row Houses" emphasizes the layouts of residential groups by private developers in several countries. Greyrock in Port Chester, New York, designed by students from Columbia University under Hegemann's guidance, is included in this section.

An appendix to Volume 3 consists of tables of technical data and requirements, as well as information on symbols used on urban plans. This was a useful aid for professionals from outside the English-speaking area.

Hegemann envisioned city planning as a universal language advancing mutual concerns within a brotherhood striving for peace. Housing was a prime element in this endeavor, manifesting a universal need. Even though Hegemann did not personally complete the entire *City Planning: Housing*, it represents a worthy testament of his convictions.

An Untimely Death

During the fall and winter of 1935–1936 Hegemann's declining health was masked by his intense work. Communication between Rasmussen and Hegemann had continued after the family had arrived in New York. The last of Hegemann's letters is addressed to "*Lieber* Steen Eiler," rather than more formally, and is dated December 13, 1935.[86] It was written while he was suffering from a "fierce grippe, and filled with sadness." He despaired of his difficulties to find time for working on the *Housing* books, spending ten hours a week on classes without even counting the time for preparation and travel. Recent health concerns included his and Ida Belle's "painful operations" and his tooth extraction. Medical expenses related to these meant that regretfully he was able to repay only a small portion of Rasmussen's loan of $200.

Hegemann's resolve to overcome the difficulties inherent in the ramifications of a new beginning was giving way to a despondency shared by the majority of refugees. His physical decline paralleled that of a world torn asunder by evil forces. It was a world with which he had closely identified and which he had bravely defended from adversity.

Ida Belle reported to her mother in early January that her husband was in bed on doctor's orders with a "severe case of sciatica all along his right side."[87] She added that he was "very much worried about having to stay home from his lectures." After a fortnight he went into town for the first time since before the Christmas holidays. In December he had an infected tooth extracted, and it was assumed that "his trouble was caused by the poison circulating through his body." The pain in his leg intensified so that he could barely walk and he developed a high fever. By mid-February Hegemann remained at home for ten days with a continuous fever, which the doctor could not explain. A stay in a New York hospital for tests was suggested. Hegemann postponed this move until February 21, when the manuscript of Volume 1 of *City Planning: Housing* was "finally all set up and only needed to be proof-read."

On February 25, Ida Belle wrote to her mother that Hegemann was in the hospital "gravely ill with pneumonia" and begged her to come to stay with the children in New Rochelle. She came immediately, enabling Ida Belle to spend all her time with her husband, who was transferred to the care of lung specialists at Doctor's Hospital. From his bedside Hegemann proceeded with proofreading the book and dictating letters to his wife, which she typed at home for him to sign.

The doctors thought that Hegemann suffered from "some form of tuberculosis and recommend[ed] that he be moved to Saratoga Springs." Having spent all day Saturday, April 11, with her husband, Ida Belle drove home to New Rochelle. At 2 AM she was informed by the hospital that Hegemann's condition had taken a turn for the worse. She rushed back, but "was too late to see him still alive. This was April 12, Easter Sunday."

She decided against an autopsy, considering it pointless and too costly in addition to the medical expenses.[88] A memorial service was held at the Ferncliff Crematory in Hartsdale, where the casket was covered with rosebuds, and many people attended the service. Alvin Johnson paid tribute to his admired colleague and friend.

The children had been taken to the cottage in Lost Lake by their grandmother. Days later, when Ida Belle drove to pick them up, she collected her husband's ashes at the crematorium. She relates that somewhere on the way out to Lost Lake she "climbed a fairly high hill with the ashes, opened the box and let the wind carry the ashes away."

On behalf of a number of Hegemann's friends and colleagues, Alvin Johnson asked for her permission to hold a memorial for him at the New School.[89] "The object of such a meeting would be not only to do honor to a man whom we loved and admired but also to give expression to the continuous influence of Dr. Hegemann's work." He assured Ida Belle that she should not feel pressured to attend if it was too painful for her, however he would like to have her consent to go ahead. In fact she did attend.

At the New School on May 14, Alvin Johnson repeated the words he had spoken at the earlier memorial service.[90] Joseph Hudnut, now at Harvard, the architect Albert Mayer, and his colleague Henry Wright from Columbia University were among those who eulogized Hegemann's wide range of work and his influence on city planning. Johnson's "In Memoriam" is notable for its recognition of Hegemann's unique attributes, paying "homage to a brave and knightly man, a soldier in the cause of a humane and rational civilization." He noted that Hegemann had refrained from seeking "shelter within narrowly specialized professional activities from the political storms afflicting the world." Convinced that "the city might rise to unexampled greatness, in a material sense, and yet crush out the lives of those destined to live in it," Hegemann had turned to the study of political and social philosophy and the economics of the modern state. Working while subjected to the shadow of the Nazi menace, Johnson perceived his friend to be "a prophet of a better day . . . when men will learn to apply their immense technical resources to the creation of conditions under which the mass of mankind may live in health and dignity . . . and the disguised slavery in which a vast fraction of mankind now lives will be abolished."

In late May Ida Belle set down the details leading to her husband's death in a long letter to her aunt and uncle in Ann Arbor, Michigan, and told them that she did not wish to move back to her hometown.[91] She mentioned that in the last phase the illness had reached Hegemann's brain, causing "meningitis," and during the final days he was heavily sedated and suffered no pain. She did not think that he had been aware of the seriousness of his condition until the last week, when he became greatly concerned for his family. According to his wife, the children, except for the oldest, Eva Maria, did not comprehend their father's absence, and she did not want them to "feel badly about death."

Before leaving for the summer at Lost Lake, Ida Belle packed up the family's possessions at their house in New Rochelle and gave up the lease. In the fall they found a more reasonable rental and the children continued at their previous schools.[92] Throughout the family's many moves in the following years, Hegemann's papers and publications were included in the transport of their posessions.

Hegemann died not quite three years after the family's arrival in the United States, yet they had made a remarkable number of personal friends in addition to his professional contacts. The outpouring of helpful concern and assistance in practical matters eased the family's transition. Besides undertaking the completion of the pending two volumes of *City Planning: Housing*, Robert C. Weinberg assisted Ida Belle with the sale of Hegemann's books in order to generate urgently needed funds and to supplement the salary that Columbia University had agreed to pay for the remainder of the academic year. Weinberg approached the Avery Architectural Library at Columbia and the libraries at Harvard University, and purchased a number of the books himself, as well as photographs and slides from Ida Belle. He counseled her to preserve Hegemann's notes and papers. Weinberg continued to provide financial assistance to the family, and during the following years he and his wife Marion remained loyal friends.[93]

The number of obituaries in New York newspapers and both American and international periodicals is notable, as is the collection of condolence letters. Writing to her aunt and uncle, Ida Belle mentions answering over two hundred letters and having more than fifty to go. The majority of their German friends were scattered in exile, and the news of Hegemann's death only gradually made its way through the refugee network.

Obituaries in the local newspapers appeared quickly and summarized Hegemann's career, which had been abruptly cut short when it was entering a promising new phase.[94] The detailed information was presumably provided by the academic institutions with which he was affiliated. Professional journals stressed Hegemann's contributions to city planning. Two obituaries, in particular, demonstrate an American perspective: One was published in *The Survey*, where the unidentified author refers to Volume 1 of *City Planning: Housing*, published just days before Hegemann's death, and emphasizes what "a great loss the constructive forces of this country suffer in his passing." It continues with the statement that while America had "plenty of technicians of ability in the field . . . Dr. Hegemann's contribution was unique; he was among the few who understood that city planning isn't merely technical proficiency, that it is a fight against vested interests." Hegemann is lauded for grasping the "fact that any real accomplishment in housing or city planning involves a bitter struggle . . . and that city planning is not only desirable, but is an indispensable part of life and of civilization." The tribute concludes by calling Hegemann "a clear-sighted man who realized the necessity of courage and struggle, and who never hesitated to act on this realization."[95]

Flavel Shurtleff, who was, together with F. L. Olmsted, a founder of the American City Planning Institute in 1917 (later The American Institute of Planners), challenged the younger generation of American planners to make up for the loss of a significant group of urbanists who had recently died. The staggering list included several who had been close to Hegemann, in particular Henry Wright (1936), George B. Ford (1932), and Theodora Kimball Hubbard (1935). Shurtleff knew Hegemann from his activities in Boston in 1909 and noted that, "Among the distinguished citizens of other countries whose works and writings have contributed to the advance of planning . . . was Werner Hegemann, whose most considerable volume, 'City Planning and Housing,' was interrupted by his recent death." In a short span the American planning movement had been diminished by an amazing number of its leaders, and it was hoped that others would respond to the challenge of the moment and aim for new achievements.[96]

The tributes by Shurtleff and those in *The Survey* are indicative of the esteem Hegemann had attained in the United States for his ideas on urbanism, something that had eluded him in his native country. On the far side of the Atlantic this recognition was enhanced by his vigorous opposition to fascism. As his longtime friend and colleague Elbert Peets noted, "Werner Hegemann was a man of extraordinary bravery, learning, charm, energy, and versatility. . . . By clarifying purposes and by stimulating to action he added strength to the movements that seek to better the world's cities."[97]

Hegemann's death had poignant resonance for his fellow exiles, who assumed that escaping from certain annihilation at the hands of the Nazis meant safety. These feelings were expressed in letters of condolence and the obituaries. The friendship between Hegemann and Arnold Zweig and his wife, for example, had begun soon after the Hegemanns returned to Berlin in 1922. It was based on mutual interests including city planning and convictions which they shared in discussions at each others' homes in Nikolassee. Arnold Zweig referred to these occasions in his essay "*Meine Nachbarn*" (My neighbors) and described Hegemann as "the most exceptional outsider in German literature." Zweig portrayed his friend as a "city builder, who knew the world better than anyone of us, [and] regarding national politics was the most astute proponent of German culture, perceived from the perspective of a citizen of the world and expressed with utmost civility. He was the best citizen of us all."[98] In addition to being neighbors, Hegemann and Zweig were both published in *Die Weltbühne* by Kiepenheuer Verlag and were active in the Schutzverband Deutscher Schriftsteller. Zweig cherished his friendship and admiration for Hegemann, often referring to him in his fiction.[99]

Beatrice Zweig wrote to Ida Belle from their exile in Haifa regarding the death of "their dear friend and their best neighbor," who was "irreplaceable."[100] For the Zweigs, Hegemann represented a Germany which they could love as their *Heimat*, and that Hitler was destroying. Grieving their loss, Beatrice wrote that "the world is becoming empty and one becomes ever lonelier." Arnold Zweig conveyed similar emotions in his obituary "*Auch* Werner Hegemann . . . " published in the *Neue Weltbühne*.[101] He mourned Hegemann as a friend and for representing the worthiest attributes of their country. When during those trying times thoughts turned to the future, they always focused on Hegemann, who was a man of the present seeking the future. Only from this point of view had he studied past history. The gigantic task of rebuilding Germany and its citizens after the cultural destruction carried out by the Third Reich would not benefit from Hegemann's presence. Appropriately, Zweig's eulogy was reprinted as an Introduction to a new edition of Hegemann's *Entlarvte Geschichte*. In a diary entry dated March 1933, when Zweig was leaving Germany, he recorded reading the book which had just been published and considered it "the exemplar of cultural and political irony."[102]

Another member of the *Weltbühne* circle in exile was the pacifist Rudolf Olden, who published "Werner Hegemann: *Dem Freund und dem Kämpfer!*" (W.H.: the friend and combatant) in the *Pariser Tageblatt*.[103] He lamented the grave loss that Hegemann's death signified not only for those in exile, but for the German *Geistesleben* (intellectual ambience), the true and eternal Germany which might reemerge on the country's soil—the "Germany of the mind, the European and universal Germany, that is part of the world and which embraces the world." Olden considered Hegemann a fellow combatant, a *Kämpfer*, opposing the hero worship leading to the "total militarization" of Germany. He mentioned that had Hegemann remained in Germany he would have joined the pacifist Ossietzky in a concentration camp. On a profoundly sad note, Olden concluded the eulogy: "Now he is dead. The rows are diminishing rapidly, the air around us is getting thinner. Only three years have passed, but, like war years, they count double. Already the group of men fleeing German lands to represent a better Germany seems diminished. With apprehension we look around: who will continue the task?" Olden wrote to Ida Belle to express his sadness over the loss of a true friend, who was a part of the world which he loved and which was now impoverished, affirming that Hegemann was "an important, irreplaceable part of a Germany . . . which is now disappearing."

An anonymous obituary in *Das Neue-Tagebuch*, which after 1933 was published in Paris, was likely written by its editor Leopold Schwarzschild. It lamented: "In Werner Hegemann the world has in fact lost one of its most versatile intellects, particularly one of the most sagacious and disillusioned among the contemporary writers on history. In addition, we are personally mourning the death of a close collaborator and comrade-in-arms."[104] He extolled Hegemann for deconstructing the heroes created by German academics through distortion of historical reality, thereby presenting a grave contemporary danger. Hegemann was not only forceful in his historical writings, but presciently and actively opposed Hitler before he became the *Führer*.

The great number of condolence letters received and preserved by his widow present a compendium comparable to the congratulatory album honoring Hegemann's fiftieth birthday in Berlin. The six intervening years had brought drastic political upheavals in Germany that profoundly affected Hegemann's career and personal life. For many of his friends and acquaintances his death increased the awareness of the worldwide changes and their inescapable impact.

The publisher had rushed Volume 1 of Hegemann's work to him while he was in the hospital. Ida Belle sent copies of the book to friends and colleagues with brief notes announcing his death and mentioning that he had intended to write a dedication. Response to her gesture and comments on the book were included in several replies. She also sent out copies of Alvin Johnson's tribute to those unable to attend the memorial service. Appreciation was expressed by Albert Guérard, who regretted never having met his "brother in spirit" with whom he had "vital interests in common."[105]

Of the American women planners whom Hegemann had championed, Mary Simkhovitch wrote twice. At the memorial meeting she had seen Ida Belle "looking so beautiful and so composed," and a few days later she wrote upon receiving Hegemann's book, which touched on many aspects of their shared interests. Edith Elmer Wood reproached herself for not having responded to earlier news of his illness and belatedly expressed her sympathy to his wife. Of Hegemann's book, Wood, the foremost expert on housing, wrote, "This new book is destined, I feel sure, to play a big part in the future of American planning and housing." She acknowledged that "Dr. Hegemann knows his America so well, and yet has the great advantage of perspective in viewing from the outside." Frieda Wunderlich,

Hegemann's colleague at the New School, wrote that she had hoped for closer contact with him and his family.[106] Acknowledgments of Hegemann's participation in the Welfare Council of New York City and the City Club of New York were not merely formal, but testified to an appreciation for his thoughtful contributions and understanding of the problems facing New York City.[107]

In addition to hearing from East Coast acquaintances, Ida Belle received letters from Hegemann's distant contacts who predated their marriage. Among them was a letter from Henry and Cora Cheney in California. The Pabst family, whose vast farm Hegemann had designed as the Washington Highlands residential development, wrote of his frequent visits to their home during the war years, where he had enjoyed the "admiration and regard of the entire family."[108]

Albert Lilienberg and Sverre Pedersen wrote from Stockholm and Trondheim, respectively, recalling Hegemann's collaboration at the Gothenburg exposition, where Ida Belle had met them.[109] Their acquaintance with Hegemann actually dated from the *Berlin 1910* events, and as editor at Wasmuth Hegemann had published extensively on planning in the Scandinavian countries. This was also a component of his longstanding friendship with Steen Eiler Rasmussen, which had been sustained by many visits and a lively correspondence.

Hegemann shared the fate of the Jewish authors termed by Joseph Roth "soldiers of the intellect who were defeated by the Third Reich!"[110] Although an Aryan, Hegemann believed Jewish intellectuals represented what was most valuable of German and, indeed, European civilization.

The recognition and prestige honoring him at the time of his death proved ephemeral. The obscurity which submerged his life and work can be partly explained by the political events that riveted world attention in the next decade. Hegemann, however, continued to be denied the acclaim which, during his lifetime, was comparable to that of Le Corbusier, Raymond Unwin, and Lewis Mumford.

An outsider par excellence, Hegemann abetted controversial causes and fell between the cracks of various vocations and interest groups. Intellectual compartmentalizing contributed to denying Hegemann a niche for his warranted renown, and posterity persists in finding it difficult to assign him a place. His efforts on behalf of conciliation and the global transfer of ideas in search of a universal common ground have been viewed as suspect or naively visionary. With his untimely death Hegemann's life remained suspended between elusive aspirations and the darkening threat of irrational horror. The present generation, however, is challenged by his pragmatic idealism to resume and carry forward his search for a better world.

Notes

1: A Transatlantic Education

1. George R. and Christiane Crasemann Collins, *Camillo Sitte: The Birth of Modern City Planning*. (New York: Rizzoli, 1986).
   Christiane Crasemann Collins, "Werner Hegemann (1881–1936): Formative Years in America." *Planning Perspectives* 11 (1996): 1–21.
   ———. "A Visionary Discipline: Werner Hegemann and the Quest for the Pragmatic Ideal." *Center, Journal for American Architecture in America: Modernist Visions and the Contemporary American City* 5 (1989): 74–85.
2. Walter Benjamin, "Die Wiederkehr des Flaneur; Zu Franz Hessels 'Spazieren in Berlin'." *Die literarische Welt* (Oct. 4, 1929).
3. André Gueslin, *L'invention de l'économie sociale: Le XIXe siècle francais.* (Paris: Editions Economica, 1987), 4 and passim.
4. Simon N. Patten, *Essays in Economic Theory*, ed. Rexford G. Tugwell. (New York: Knopf, 1924), xvii.
5. Werner Hegemann, *Mexikos Übergang zur Goldwährung; Ein Beitrag zur Geschichte des mexikanischen Geldwesens (1867–1906)*. Series: *Münchener Volkswirtschaftliche Studien*, eds. Lujo Brentano and Walther Lotz. (Stuttgart/Berlin: Cotta, 1908).
6. Collins, "Formative Years" (see note 1).
7. Cornelius P. Hanlon, Biographical Preface in Sylvester Baxter, *The Ring and the Tree.* (Boston: Bruce Humphries, 1938), 7–8.
   Baxter, "The German Way of Making Better Cities." *Atlantic Monthly* 104 (July 1909): 72–85.
   Cornelius Gurlitt, "City Planning in Germany (1903)," trans. S. Baxter. *Architectural Record* (1908): 135–48, 350–63.
8. Frederic C. Howe, *Confessions of a Reformer*. (New York: Scribner's, 1925).
9. Ibid., 113–14.
10. Frederick C. Howe, *The City: The Hope of Democracy*. (New York: Scribner's, 1905, 1913, and later editions).
    ———."City Building in Germany." *Scribner's Magazine* (1905). Also published as Bulletin 14, Social Service Series. (Boston: American Unitarian Association, 1910).
11. *Program of the First National Conference on City Planning*, Washington, D.C., May 21–22, 1909. Issued as U.S. Senate Document no. 422.
12. B. C. Marsh, *An Introduction to City Planning: Democracy's Challenge & The American City*. (Privately printed, 1909).
    Harvey A. Kantor, "Benjamin C. Marsh and the Fight Over Population Congestion." *American Institute of Planners Journal* (Nov. 1974): 422–29.

13. Program of the First National Congress. . . (note 11), pp. 52–53.
14. Mel Scott, *American City Planning Since 1890*. (Berkeley, CA: Publisher, 1969). Sections 1–3 provide particularly pertinent background to Hegemann's encounter with American urbanism. In this chapter the scope of American trends is treated only summarily as it intersects with his career and the developments surrounding "Greater Berlin." The beginning of the city planning movement in America produced a substantial literature, which is not cited here.
15. Charles, Mulford Robinson, "The City Plan Exhibition." *The Survey* (July 22, 1909): 313–18.
Hegemann, "Die Ausstellung für Städtebau und städtische Kunst in New York." *STB* (1909): 127–30, 146–48.
16. Robinson, p. 316.
17. J. Carroll Moody and Gilbert C. Fite, *The Credit Union Movement: Origins and Development 1850–1970*. (Lincoln: University of Nebraska Press, 1971), 26–102, and passim.
The National Cyclopedia of American Biography (New York: James T. Unite Co., 1930).
18. *Program*, 105 (note 11).
19. Hegemann, "Plans for City Planning Exhibitions." *HP*.
20. Jon A. Peterson, "Frederick Law Olmsted Jr.: The Visionary and the Professional." In *Planning the Twentieth-Century American City*, ed. Mary Corbin Sies and Christopher Silver. (Baltimore: Johns Hopkins University Press, 1996), 37–54.
———. "The City Beautiful Movement: Forgotten Origins and Lost Meanings." *Journal of Urban History* (Aug. 1976): 415–34.
The author expresses her gratitude to Jon Peterson for generously sharing his knowledge of American planning and providing copies of correspondence between Olmsted and Hegemann.
21. Hegemann to Olmsted, Boston, Nov. 2, 1909. Olmsted to Hegemann, Brookline, Feb. 28, 1911. Box 268. Olmsted to Thomas Adams (London), Brookline, June 11, 1911. Library of Congress, Olmsted Associates, Box 263. Hegemann to Olmsted, Berlin, Dec. 9, 1912. Library of Congress, Olmsted Associates, City Planning. General Subjects, Box 268.
22. James Sturgis Pray, "The Department of Landscape Architecture in Harvard University." *Landscape Architecture* 1, no. 2 (January 1911): 53–70.
Anthony Alofsin, *The Struggle for Modernism: Architecture, Landscape Architecture, and City Planning at Harvard*. (New York: W. W. Norton, 2002). I am most grateful to A. Alofsin for sharing his research.
23. John A. Garraty, *Henry Cabot Lodge: A Biography*. (New York: A. Knopf, 1953).
Senator Henry Cabot Lodge's bitter rivalry with the democratic President Woodrow Wilson extended from debating his pro-neutrality during World War I to his bitter opposition to the League of Nations, which he thought would compromise American sovereignty. These positions were contrary to Hegemann's. During the summer of 1909, Lodge was away from Boston and in seclusion at his summer residence after the death of a son.
24. *Boston-1915*. Bulletin No.1, No. 2, Boston 1909.
Paul U. Kellogg, "Boston's Level Best: The '1915 Movement' and the Work of Civic Organization for Which It Stands." Reprinted from *The Survey Magazine* (June 5, 1909). Bulletin No. 2: 3–34.
25. *The "1915" Year Book: A Directory of Information Concerning Boston and the Metropolitan District*. Boston-1915 [1910].
26. *New Boston, A Monthly Record of Progress in Developing a Greater and Finer City*. 1, no. 1. (Boston: Directorate of Boston-1915, May 1910).
27. Ibid.: 5–6, 52–53.
28. Ibid.: front page.
29. *"1915" Boston Exposition. Official Catalogue and the Boston-1915 Year Book*, ed. Thomas N. Carver. (Boston: "1915" Boston Exposition Company [1910]).
30. Hegemann, *City Planning: Housing*. Vol. 1: *Historical and Sociological*. (New York: Architectural Book Publishing Co., 1936), 206–8.
31. Hegemann, 1915 Boston Exposition. Public Buildings. Division I of Department I, The Visible City. September 9, 1909. Typewritten, 16 pages. *HP*.

32. *Official Catalogue*: 19–21, and passim.
33. Lincoln Steffens Papers, Columbia University, Rare Books and Manuscript Library.
E. A. Filene to L. Steffens, June 8, July 1, 1908. Dec. 13, 1909.
L. Steffens, "Preliminary Memorandum." (1908?)
L. Steffens, *An Autobiography of Lincoln Steffens*, "A Successful Failure," "The Muck I Raked in Boston," (New York: Harcourt Brace & Company, Inc, 1931), 598–627.
34. Collins, "City Planning Exhibitions and Civic Museums: Werner Hegemann and Others." *The City after Patrick Geddes*, ed. Volker M. Welter and James Lawson. (New York: P. Lang, 2000), 113–30.
Leopold Katscher, "Die sogenannten 'Sozial-Museen': Museen für Arbeiterwohlfahrt und Sozialpolitik und das Pariser 'Musée social' als Vorbild." *Sozialer Fortschritt* 14 (1904): 1–16.
Francis G. Peabody, "The Social Museum as an Instrument of University Teaching," Department of Social Ethics, No. 4, Harvard University (1911).
"The Social Museum: A Place in the Inductive Teaching of the University." *The Harvard Bulletin*, 10.21. (Feb. 26, 1908). Reprinted from *Internationale Wochenschrift* (Nov. 23, 1907).
Lorna Beth Ellis, "The Department of Social Ethics at Harvard," MS, Harvard University Archives.
35. Peabody, "Social Museum."
36. James Ford, *The Housing Problem: A Summary of Conditions and Remedies*. (Cambridge, MA: Dept. of Social Ethics, Harvard University, 1911).
37. Hegemann, *City Planning: Housing*, 207.

2: A New Discipline

1. *Anregungen zur Erlangung eines Grundplanes für die Städtebauliche Entwicklung von Gross-Berlin, gegeben von der Vereinigung Berliner Architekten und dem Architektenverein zu Berlin*. (Berlin: Ernst Wasmuth, 1907).
The Ernst Wasmuth Verlag, the leading publisher for architecture, art, and city planning, brought out all publications related to the Greater Berlin movement and the exhibitions. The periodicals *Der Städtebau* and *Wasmuths Monatshefte für Baukunst* also carried its imprint.
2. Ibid. and *Programm-Skizze für den Wettbewerb zur Erlangung eines Grundplanes für Gross-Berlin*. (Berlin: n.d.)
3. On "Boston 1915" see Chapter I. 2.
Mansel G. Blackford, *The Lost Dream: Businessmen and City Planning on the Pacific Coast, 1890–1920* (Columbus, OH: 1993), 1 and passim.
4. *Anregungen . . .* ibid.
Herrmann Jansen, "Der Wettbewerb für Gross-Berlin," *Der Baumeister*, 7, no. 2 (Nov. 1908): 13–23.
5. W. Hegemann, "Die grossen städtebaulichen Wettbewerbe und städtebaulichen Ausschüsse." *Bauwelt*, Nr. 108 [1911]. Off-print without page numbers or date. HP.
6. Raymond Unwin, "The Berlin Exhibition of Town Planning," *The Builder* 99 (July 2, 1910): 17–19.
7. Typescript dated January 1916. *HP*.
Hegemann, "Die Ausstellung für Städtebau und Städtische Kunst in New York (3–16 Mai 1909)." *STB* 6 (1909): 10, 127–31, and Conclusion; 11, 146–48.
8. Documentation of direct contacts between Otto March and/or the steering committee in Berlin and Hegemann in Boston in the form of correspondence has not been located.
9. Ibid. Typescript of Hegemann letter to Ford.
10. Hegemann, "Plans for City Planning Exhibitions," n.d. Typescript. *HP*.
11. "Städtebau-Ausstellung in Berlin 1910," listed in the section "Chronik," *STB* 6 (1909): 11. The committee included Eberstadt, Goecke, Heimann, Jansen, Muthesius, and Stübben, with Otto March as chairman.

12. *Allgemeine Städtebau-Ausstellung in Berlin im Mai und Juni 1910*. Dritter Bericht. *STB*. (Berlin: Wasmuth, 1910).
13. Correspondence in the *Burnham Papers*, The Ryerson & Burnham Library, The Chicago Art Institute.
    The Plan of Chicago: An Exhibition of the Burnham Library of Architecture. Chicago: The Chicago Art Institute, 1979), 28, note 32.
14. S. D. Adshead, "The Town Planning Conference of the Royal Institute of British Architects: The Exhibition," *Town Planning Review* 1, no. 3 (Oct. 1910): 178–90.
15. W. Hegemann, *Der neue Bebauungsplan für Chicago*. (Berlin: Wasmuth [1911]).
    Plan of Chicago: Daniel H. Burnham, Edward H. Bennett. Ed. Charles Moore. Introduction by Kristen Schaffer. (New York: 1993).
16. W. Hegemann, *Ein Parkbuch—Amerikanische Parkanlagen: Zierparks, Nutzparks, Aussen—und—Innenparks, Nationalparks, Park—Zweckverbände*. (Berlin: Wasmuth, 1911). The publication was sponsored by Jakob Ochs, Gartenbau, Hamburg. An appendix is included in the pamphlet: "Deutsche Neuzeitliche Gärten von Jakob Ochs, Gartenbau, Hamburg. Künstlerische Leitung: Leberecht Migge." An exhibition based on the contents was shown in Frankfurt a. M., Bremen, Cologne, and Dresden.
17. Some are included in Hegemann's volumes documenting the exhibitions in Berlin and in Düsseldorf.
    A set of sixteen photographs of housing exhibited in Berlin and/or Düsseldorf, made available by George B. Ford (perhaps taken by him) are preserved in the Frances Loeb Library (Special Collections) of the Graduate School of Design, Harvard University. They were intended for James Ford, who was organizing a housing exhibition at the Harvard Museum of Social Ethics for May 1911.
18. *Führer durch die Allgemeine Städtebau-Ausstellung in Berlin 1910*. Präsident Kirschner, Oberbürgermeister von Berlin. Ernst Wasmuth A. G., Berlin.
19. Werner Hegemann, *Der Städtebau nach den Ergebnissen der Allgemeinen Städtebau-Ausstellung in Berlin nebst einem Anhang: Die Internationale Städtebau-Ausstellung in Düsseldorf*. 600 Wiedergaben des Plan-Materials der Beiden Ausstellungen. Herausgegeben im Auftrage der Arbeitsausschüsse von Dr. Werner Hegemann, Generalsekretär der Städtebau-Ausstellungen in Berlin und Düsseldorf (City Planning according to the Results of the Universal City Planning Exhibition in Berlin with an Addition: The International City Planning Exhibition in Düsseldorf. 600 reproductions of the plans in both exhibitions. Published at the request of the Working Committees by Dr. Werner Hegemann, General Secretary of the City Planning Exhibitions in Berlin and Düsseldorf), vol. 1 (Berlin: Ernst Wasmuth, 1911), vol. 2 (1913). (Henceforth cited as Werner Hegemann, *Der Städtebau nach den Ergebnissen*).
    The illustration showing the entrance hall with the Vienna model is in vol. 2, Abb.167.
20. Raymond Unwin, "The Berlin Exhibition of Town Planning," *The Builder* 99 (July 2, 1910): 17–19.
21. Joseph Brix and Felix Genzmer, *Grundplan für die Bebauung von Gross-Berlin*. (Berlin: 1911), 3, 68.
22. Op. cit., 18.
23. Dietrich Neumann, *"Die Wolkenkratzer kommen!" Deutsche Hochhäuser der zwanziger Jahre; Debatten, Projekte, Bauten*. (Braunschweig/Wiesbaden: 1995), 22, 159, and passim.
24. Op. cit., 19.
25. Raymond Unwin, "Town Planning in Berlin," *Town Planning and Housing: Supplement to The Architectural Review* 28 (Aug. 1910): 93–102.
26. Ibid. Note 13. Author's emphasis. Adshead refers to the exhibitions in New York and Boston the previous year, and the conference on housing held in Vienna.
27. Ursula v. Petz, "Robert Schmidt and the Public Park Policy in the Ruhr District, 1900–1930," *Planning Perspectives* 14 (1999): 163–82.
28. W. Hegemann, Untitled lecture, Düsseldorf, Sept. 29, 1910. Typescript. Stadtarchiv Duisburg. Rep100A, 1208. I am grateful to v. Petz for providing a copy of this document.
29. *Wettbewerb zur Erlangung eines Bebauungsplanes der Stadt Düsseldorf*. n.d. pamphlet.
30. *Neudeutsche Bauzeitung* 7 (1911): 707.

31. *Führer durch die Internationale Städtebau-Ausstellung Düsseldorf 1910.* Präsident Marx, Oberbürgermeister. (Düsseldorf: 1910), 146–47.
32. *Schweizerische Bauzeitung* 56, no. 10 (Sept. 3, 1910): 132; no. 13 (Sept. 17, 1910): 158. *Verhandlungen des Ersten Kongresses für Städtewesen, Düsseldorf 1912.* (Düsseldorf: 1913).
33. *Günther Wasmuth zum achtzigsten Geburtstag gewidmet von seinen Freunden, Kollegen und Autoren* (Tübingen: Ernst Wasmuth, 1968).
125 Jahre Wasmuth: Eine Firmenchronik von 1872–1997 (Tübingen/Berlin: Ernst Wasmuth Verlag GmbH & Co., 1997/98).
Neither publication mentions Wasmuth's involvement with the Greater-Berlin movement, the exhibition, and the two large volumes documenting it and authored by Werner Hegemann. In 1922 Hegemann became editor of the periodicals *Wasmuth's Monatshefte für Baukunst* and *Der Städtebau*, which were later combined. The economic crisis of 1931 brought serious difficulties for the company. In November 1943 allied bombing totally destroyed Wasmuth's headquarters and archives. After the war, Wasmuth resumed publishing in Tübingen and later on again in Berlin, continuing into the present.
More on Hegemann's not always smooth relations with Wasmuth in later chapters.
34. George R. and Christiane Crasemann Collins, *Camillo Sitte: The Birth of Modern City Planning.* With a translation of the 1889 Austrian edition of his *City Planning According to Artistic Principles.* (New York: Rizzoli 1986), 365–66.
35. Joseph Brix and Felix Genzmer, eds. *Städtebauliche Vorträge aus dem Seminar für Städtebau an der Königlichen Technischen Hochschule zu Berlin*, vol. 1 (Berlin: Wilhelm Ernst & Sohn, 1908). Later volumes published by Wasmuth.
36. Collins, *Camillo Sitte*, 359–60 and passim, 91–99.
37. Ibid. and Giorgio Piccinato, *Städtebau in Deutschland 1871–1914: Genese einer wissenschaftlichen Disziplin.* (Vieweg, 1983), 52–53 and passim.
38. Theodor Goecke, "Der Siebente Jahrgang," *STB* 7, no. 1 (1910): 1–2.
39. Theodor Goecke, "Gross-Berlin: Ein Program für die Plannung der neuzeitlichen Grossstadt. Von Professor Rud. Eberstadt, a.d. Kgl. Universität, Professor Bruno Möhring, Architekt und Oberingenieur Rich. Petersen," *STB* 7, no. 4 (1910): 58.
40. Theodor Goecke, "Allgemeine Städtebau-Ausstellung Berlin 1910," *STB* 7, no. 7/8 (1910): 73–92.
41. W. Hegemann, *Ein Parkbuch.* In a preview of the "Allgemeine Städtebau-Ausstellung Berlin 1910," *Neudeutsche Bauzeitung* 6 (1910): 85, Hegemann gave an overview of the American park movement, especially the park system of Greater Boston, before briefly mentioning some other recent additions to the exhibition.
42. *STB* 8, no. 1 (1911): 1–2. "Vorwort," presumably written by Goecke, but not signed.
43. *Neudeutsche Bauzeitung: Organ des Bundes Deutscher Architekten e.V.* 6 (1910).
44. Walter Kornick, "Die Städtebauausstellung Berlin 1910," *Neudeutsche Bauzeitung: Organ des Bundes Deutscher Architekten e.V.* 6 no. 27 (1910): 237–39, 328–37.
45. W. Hegemann, "Die Städtebauausstellung und ihre Lehren," *Die Woche: Moderne Illustrierte Zeitschrift.* Berlin (May 28, 1910): 901–903.
46. W. Hegemann, "Die grossen städtebaulichen Wettbewerbe und städtebauliche Ausschüsse," *Bauwelt* no. 108 (1911?)
47. In connection with her research on Joseph Hudnut, partner of Hegemann from 1916–1922, and admiring friend, later Dean of the GSD at Harvard (1936–1953), Jill Pearlman writes that " . . . Hudnut was inspired by Hegemann to fashion himself as a public intellectual or educator . . . reaching out beyond the university to a far broader public." Pearlman letter to the author, April 27, 1997.
48. Miron Mislin, "Internationale Städtebau-Ausstellung 1910: Was könnten die Erfahrungen von 1910 der IBA '84 lehren? Zum 100. Geburtstag von Werner Hegemann." *Baukultur* (April 1983): 4–9.
49. S. D. Adshead, "The Town Planning Conference of the Royal Institute of British Architects," *Town Planning Review* 1, no. 3 (Oct. 1910): note 20.
Volker M. Welter, "Stages of an Exhibition: The Cities and Town Planning Exhibition of Patrick Geddes," *Planning History*, 20, no. 1 (1998): 25–35.
50. Raymond Unwin, "The Berlin Exhibition of Town Planning," *The Builder* 99 (July 2, 1910): 17–19.

51. Raymond Unwin, *Town Planning in Practice: An Introduction to the Art of Designing Cities and Suburbs* (London: 1909), 2nd. ed. with a new introduction (London: 1934).
52. Raymond Unwin, "Town Planning in Berlin," *Town Planning and Housing: Supplement to The Architectural Review* 28 (Aug. 1910): 93–102.
53. Town Planning Conference, London, Oct.10–15, 1910. *Transactions*. Brief comments by the "Vice-Chairman, Dr. Hegemann (of Berlin)" on radial "Ausfallstrassen" and radiating parks in the Berlin proposals, 239–40.
54. Ibid., 313–33.
55. R. Eberstadt, *Handbuch des Wohnungswesens und der Wohnungsfrage*. (Jena, 1909, 1910).
56. W. Hegemann, *City Planning: Housing Vol. I. Historical and Sociological; Vol. II. Political Economy and Civic Art; Vol. III. A Graphic Review of Civic Art, 1922–1937*. (New York: 1936, 1937, 1938).
57. George B. Ford, "City Planning Exhibition in Berlin," *The American City*. 3, no. 3 (Sept. 1910): 120–24.
58. George B. Ford, "The Ninth International Housing Congress in Vienna," *The American City* 3, no. 2 (1910): 81–83.
59. See p. 12, note 14.
60. James Ford, "The Housing Problem: A Summary of Conditions and Remedies," prepared to accompany the "Housing Exhibit" in May 1911. Publication of the Department of Social Ethics at Harvard University, no. 5 (1911). The exhibition included international examples, some shown in Berlin. On the Museum of Social Ethics at Harvard, see pp. 30–31.
61. Bertel Jung, "Allgemeine Städtebau-Ausstellung in Berlin 1910," *Arkitekten* V, no. 4: 89–92. Translated from the Swedish original by Anja Kervanto Nevanlinna (1997). Bertel Jung's review of Hegemann's volumes documenting the exhibitions are discussed later in this chapter.
62. C. Crasemann Collins, "City Planning Exhibitions and Civic Museums: Werner Hegemann and Others," *The City after Patrick Geddes*. Volker M. Welter and James Lawson, eds. (Oxford, Bern, 2000), 113–30.
63. Cipriano (Cebriá de) Montoliu, (1873–1923). *Las Modernas Ciudades y sus Problemas á la luz de la Exposición de Construcción Cívica de Berlin (1910) con un Apéndice sobre otros Certámenes Análogos etc.* (Barcelona: Sociedad Cívica, La Ciudad Jardín, 1913). The author is grateful to Manuel Ribas i Piera, Francesc Roca, and Arturo Soria i Puig for providing assistance in researching Montoliu.
64. Francesc Roca, "Cebriá de Montoliu y la 'ciencia cívica'," *Cuadernos de Arquitectura y Urbanismo*, no. 80 (Jan./Feb. 1971): 41–46.
    Francesc Roca, ed. *Cebriá Montoliu* (1873–1923). Collecció Gent de la Casa Gran, 7. (Barcelona: Ayuntamiento de Madrid, 1986).
    Manuel de Torres i Capell, "Urbanística, Gestion y Cultura, Barcelona, 1917" *Gestión Urbanística Europea 1920–1940* (Madrid, 19??), passim.
65. On early Le Corbusier, see: H. Allen Brooks, *Le Corbusier: Formative Years*. (Chicago: University of Chicago Press, 1997). Giuliano Gresleri, *Le Corbusier, Viaggio in Oriente: Gli inediti di Charles Edouard Jeanneret, fotografo e scrittore* (Paris: Fondation Le Corbusier; Venice: Marsilio Editore, 1984). *Charles Edouard Jeanneret/Le Corbusier, Les voyages d'Allemagne Carnets: Skizzen- und Reisetagebücher, Deutschland 1910/11*. (Paris: Fondation Le Corbusier; Milan: Electa; Munich: Bangert, 1994). G. Gresleri, "Die Carnets über Deutschland; 'triomphe de l'ordre' und 'heureuse évolution.'" Rosario De Simone, *Ch.E. Jeanneret-Le Corbusier: Viaggio in Germania 1910–1911*. (Rome: Officina Edizioni, 1989).
    I am grateful to Francesco Passanti for his generous help regarding Jeanneret/Le Corbusier research.
66. A. Brooks, "Jeanneret and Sitte," 282–83 and passim.
67. C. C. Collins, "Urban Interchange in the Southern Cone: Le Corbusier (1929) and Werner Hegemann (1931) in Argentina," *Journal of the Society of Architectural Historians* 54, no. 2 (June 1995).
    Werner Oechslin, "Le Corbusier und Deutschland; 1910/1911," in *Le Corbusier im Brennpunkt; Vorträge an der Abteilung für Architektur ETHZ* (1988).

68. Charles-Edouard Jeanneret (Le Corbusier), *Étude sur le mouvement d'art décoratif en Allemagne*. (La Chaux-de-Fonds, 1912), 35–36.
69. Lewis Mumford, "Form and Personality" (1930), cited in Robert Wojtowicz, *Lewis Mumford and American Modernism: Utopian Theories for Architecture and Urban Planning*. (New York: Cambridge University Press, 1996), 136 and passim.
70. Donatella Calabi, "Marcel Poëte: pioneer of l'urbanisme and defender of 'histoire des villes,'" *Planning Perspectives* 11, no. 4 (1996): 413–36. *Parigi anni venti: Marcel Poete e le origini della storia urbana*. (Venice: Marsilio, 1997).
71. ibid., *Marcel Poëte ...*, 420.
72. W. Hegemann, *Der Städtebau nach den Ergebnissen der Allgemeinen Städtebau-Ausstellung in Berlin nebst einem Anhang: Die Internationale Städtebau-Ausstellung in Düsseldorf*. 600 Wiedergaben des Bilder-und Plan-Materials der Beiden Ausstellungen. Herausgegeben im Auftrage der Arbeitsausschüsse von Dr. Werner Hegemann, Generalsekretär der Städtebau-Ausstellungen in Berlin und Düsseldorf. (Berlin: Ernst Wasmuth vol. 1, 1911; vol. 2, 1913). Verkehrswesen—Freiflächen. Paris, Wien, Budapest, München, Cöln, London, Stockholm, Chicago, Boston. Erweitert durch das Material der Städteausstellung Düsseldorf 1912.
    Despite the importance of this publication no new edition has been issued, and there is only one translation: Werner Hegemann, *Catalogo delle Exposizioni Internazionali di Urbanistica, Berlino 1910, Düsseldorf 1911–12*. Antologia a cura de Donatella Calabi e Marino Folin. Note introduttive di D. Calabi e M. Folin. Traduzione di Elfi Perkhofer. (Milan: Il Saggiatore, 1975).
73. op. cit.
74. Obituaries: *New York Times*, Feb. 28, 1948. *Herald Tribune*, Feb. 27, 1948. "Dr. Devine Hailed for Welfare Work," *New York Times*, May 4, 1937. The Columbiana Collection, Columbia University.
75. *HP*. Undated. Exists in a German and English version.
76. W. C. Behrendt, "Neue Bücher: Über Baukunst," *Kunst und Künstler* XI, no. 2 (1913): 484.
77. Bertel Jung, "Der Städtebau nach den Ergebnissen der Allgemeinen Städtebau-Ausstellung in Berlin von Dr. Werner Hegemann," *Architekten* (Helsinki) V (1912): 83–85. Translated from the Swedish by Anja Kervanto Nevanlinna.
78. Hegemann, *Der Städtebau*, vol. I, 7.
79. ibid., 10.
80. The title page of Volume II refers to "600 Wiedergaben des Bilder-und Plan-Materials der beiden Ausstellungen."
81. Volume II. Gustav von Schmoller, "The propertied classes have to be roused from their sleep; they must finally realize, that although it would mean great sacrifice, this would only be a moderate insurance fee to guard them against epidemics and social revolutions, which will certainly take place, if we do not stop to condemn the lower classes in our cities with their housing conditions to a living standard of barbarity and bestiality."
    Rudolf Eberstadt, "Berlin must be conquered first; then other cities can also be improved .... We represent a universal national cause. And our goal must be the highest that is presently foisted on our country: To elevate our people from the class and convictions of the proletarian to the rank of citizen."
82. Vol. II, 151–52.
83. idem., 156, cited by Hegemann.
84. idem., 222, illus. 144 and 145. In his article on "City Planning Competitions" (1911?), Hegemann comments on the origin and trajectory of the Napoleon/Haussmann plan, which was influenced by one proposed by the Parisian Artists Commission in 1793.
    I am grateful to Rosa Tamborrino, Venice, for calling my attention to this important plan and its disappearance. Letter to the author, 1996.
    Rosa Tamborrino, "Le plan Haussmann en 1864," *Genéses 15: Sciences sociales et histoire* (March 1994): 130–41.
85. idem., 162, note 126. Among those cited are Eugen Hénard, Marcel Pöete, and Georges Benoit-Levy.
86. W. Hegemann, *Ein Parkbuch—Amerikanische Parkanlagen: Zierparks, Nutzparks, Aussen-und Innenparks, Nationalparks, Park-Zweckverbände* (Berlin: Wasmuth, 1911).

Sponsored by Jakob Ochs, Gartenbau, Hamburg. An appendix included in the pamphlet: "Deutsche Neuzeitliche Gärten von Jakob Ochs, Gartenbau, Hamburg. Künstlerische Leitung: Leberecht Migge."
See Vol. II, 337. Some of the photographs were made for the exhibitions from slides taken by Hegemann, and enlarged to 1–2 qm by the Neue Photographische Gesellschaft Steglitz in Berlin.

87. H. Kayser, "Nordamerikanische Parkanlagen," *STB* 9 (1905): 113–23.
88. Ursula v. Petz, "Robert Schmidt and the Public Park Policy in the Ruhr District, 1900–1930," *Planning Perspectives* 14, no. 2 (April 1999): 163–82.
I am most grateful to Ursula v. Petz for providing me with a copy of Hegemann's lecture, which only exists in a typescript. See also note 24.
W. Hegemann, Untitled lecture of Sept. 29, 1910; Typescript, 10 pp. Stadtarchiv Duisburg, Rep. 100 A, 1208.
89. Stadtarchiv Duisburg, Rep. 100 A 1208.
Hegemann recognized the unique importance of the SVR and followed its progress. In his lectures in Argentina in 1931, he showed plans of the SVR, recommending it as an exemplary model for a regional plan for Buenos Aires, especially for its open space provisions. C. C. Collins, "Urban Interchange in the Southern Cone . . . " op. cit.
90. Hegemann, *Der Städtebau nach den Ergebissen,* Vol. II, 348.
91. Arminius, *Die Grossstädte in ihrer Wohnungsnot und die Grundlagen einer durchgreifenden Abhilfe.* (Leipzig: 1874).
92. Hegemann, *Der Städtebau* Vol. II, 362.
93. C. C. Collins, Review of *Leberecht Migge, 1881–1935: Gartenkultur des 20. Jahrhunderts* (Worpswede, 1981) *JSAH*, XLI, no. 4, (Dec. 1982): 358–59.
94. W. Hegemann, "Zweckverband Gross-Boston," *Berliner Neueste Nachrichten.* Morgenausgabe. (Feb. 11, 1911).
95. Mitteilung. *STB* 9, no. 3 (1912): 35.
96. *Für Gross-Berlin: Decentralized Developments of Healthy Single-Family Homes. Extension of the Rapid-Transit Railroad Network and Cheap Fares. Accessible Parks and Playgrounds. Forest and Meadow Rings.* Published by the Propaganda-Ausschuss. (Pamphlet 1). (Charlottenburg: Feb. 1912).
Für Gross-Berlin. Dernburg, Naumann, Südekum. The Development of Greater-Berlin in Pictures. (Pamphlet 2). (Charlottenburg: March 1912).
Only two pamphlets were published.
97. W. Hegemann, "600,000 Gross Berliner in übervölkerten Wohnungen," *Soziale Praxis und Archiv für Volkswohlfahrt* 21, no. 21 (1912): 1–4.
98. Lincoln Steffens, *The Shame of the Cities* (1903, 1960). A collection of articles reprinted from *McClure's Magazine.*
Harvey Swados, ed. *Years of Conscience: The Muckrakers: An Anthology of Reform Journalism* (New York: Meridian Books, 1962).
Thomas C. Leonard, "How 'Muckraking', Born 80 Years Ago, Altered U.S. Politics." *New York Times*, April 19, 1986. T. C. Leonard writes that the term "muckraking" was brought to public attention when President Theodore Roosevelt used it in April 1906, referring to journalists exposing political scandal.
99. Werner Weisbach, "Die Städtebau-Ausstellung und Gross-Berlin," *Preussische Jahrbücher* 148 (April-June 1912): 109–124.
100. Weisbach, *"Und alles ist zerstoben": Erinnerungen aus der Jahrhundertwende* Vol. I (Vienna: Anton Schroll Co., 1937).
Geist und Gewalt Vol. II (Vienna: 1956).
101. Ibid. Vol. II, 71–77.
102. Galerie St. Etienne, New York. *Käthe Kollwitz: The Power of Print.* With an essay by Jane Kallir. (1987).
Käthe Kollwitz. *Für Gross Berlin (For Greater Berlin).* 1912. Lithograph poster on cream woven paper. Signed lower left. 72.4 x 95.9 cm. Klipstein 119/I.
103. Lothar Uebel, *Viel Vergnügen: Die Geschichte der Vergnügungsstätten rund um den Kreuzberg und die Hasenheide* (Berlin: Dirk Nishen, 1985), 106–120.
Alfred Döblin, *Berlin Alexanderplatz: Die Geschichte vom Franz Biberkopf* (1929), contains a vivid description of the Hasenheide Neue Welt as an amusement and dance hall

on pages 65–69. The Nazis would also hold their public harangues at the Neue Welt. In 1931, eighteen years after the "Propaganda Ausschuss" meeting, Hitler gave a speech in the same locale, which Hegemann and his wife attended and left horrified. (*Für Gross-Berlin* no. 2 (March 12, 1912): 76–77, 88).

104. Hegemann, "Aufruf an die Haus- und Grundbesitzer in Gross-Berlin," signed Hans Biedermann, Hausbesitzer und Bauspekulant. Typewritten manuscript. 6 pages. *HP*. "Biedermann" literally means "honest man," but ironically designates a philistine. It is comparable to the name "Franz Biberkopf," chosen by Alfred Döblin for the protagonist of his novel *Berlin Alexanderplatz: Die Geschichte vom Franz Biberkopf* (1929).
105. Karl Scheffler, "Der Staat und die Wohnungspolitik Berlins," *Vossische Zeitung*, Berlin (Sept. 19, 1913).
106. Hermann Kötschke, *Die Berliner Waldverwüstung und verwandte Fragen*. Herausgegeben vom Ansiedlungsverein Gross Berlin in Schöneberg. (1910)
107. W. Hegemann, "Drei Hauptstücke grossstädtischer Parkpolitik." *Bauwelt*, no. 89 (August 1911);
    "Das Problem der Umgestaltung des Universitätsviertels." *Bauwelt* (1912?).
108. W. Hegemann, "Protest 'alter Herren' der Berliner Universität und des Berliner Waldschutzvereins gegen die geplante Vernichtung des Universitätsgartens," Berlin, Sept. 1912. "Der unverletzliche Universitätsgarten," Berlin, Dec. 18, 1912. Announcement of lecture, "Moderne Parks und Spielplätze," Berlin, Feb. 27, 1912. *HP*.
109. ibid.
110. *75 Jahre Ideal: Gemeinnütziges Wohnungsunternehmen e. G. 1907–1982*. (Berlin: Baugenossenschaft Ideal, 1982).
111. Paul Westheim, "Das Viermillionenchaos," *Sozialistische Monatshefte*, no. 6 (1912): 360–66.
112. W. Hegemann, *Der Städtebau nach den Ergebissen*, op. cit., Vol. I, 26, illus. 28.
113. Nicholas Bullock and James Read, *The Movement for Housing Reform in Germany and France 1840–1914* (1985). "Part One: The Movement for Housing Reform in Germany 1840–1914" provides an excellent overview of this very complex subject.
    Brian Ladd, *Urban Planning and Civic Order in Germany 1860–1914*. (1990). With a wider scope than the above, Ladd integrates housing into the urban planning in Germany.
114. *75 Jahre Ideal.*
115. "Einige Angaben über die Gartenvorstadt in Britz," *STB* 9, no. 10: 120.
116. *The Opinions of Recognized City Planning Authorities Regarding the Single-house Project in Rixdorf by the Cooperative Building Association Ideal on the 3200 Square [Rute?] on the Hannemann- and Franz Körner Street in Britz*. Above the title: "No more Rental Barracks! Everybody their own House! The Beginning of a radical Change in Greater Berlin Housing!" (1912/13?) Photocopy in the Vertical Files of the Loeb Library, Harvard University. Note: Gift of Mrs. George B. Ford.
117. W. Hegemann, "Heinrich Mann? Hitler? Gottfried Benn? Oder Goethe?" *Tagebuch* (April 11, 1931): 580–88.

3: New Worlds

1. C. Crasemann Collins, "Werner Hegemann: Formative Years," op. cit. "Werner Hegemann's American Lecture Tour of 1913." Lecture delivered at the Society of Architectural Historians Meeting, Boston 1990.
2. Ruth Nanda Anshen, "Introduction: A Biographical Note," W. Hegemann, *City Planning: Housing*. Vol. 2 (1937), 13–22. Anshen mentions Mayor Adickes of Frankfurt a. M. and Mayor Marx of Düsseldorf.
3. Frederic C. Howe, *The Confessions of a Reformer* (New York: The People's Institute, 1925), 240–51.
4. Frederic C. Howe, Managing Director, The People's Institute. "Important Announcement" (1912).
5. Frederic C. Howe, "Suggestions to Dr. Hegemann" (1912/13). Two-page ms. *HP*.

6. Werner Hegemann, Untitled Manuscript, 15 pages (1913). *HP*.
7. Werner Hegemann, "European City Plans and Their Value to the American City-Planner," *Landscape Architecture* 4 (April 1914): 89–103.
8. James Russell Lowell, "Don't Imitate Europe, Says Expert to City Planners." *New York Times*, April 26, 1914.
9. "German City Plan Expert Criticizes Sky-scrapers Here. Dr. Werner Hegemann of Berlin heard at University Club and the City Club. Praise for some things." *Brooklyn Daily Eagle*, March 30, 1913.
   "Our Big Terminals Ugly, Says Expert. Dr. Hegemann, Berlin city planner, criticizes stations we're so proud of." *New York Sun*, March 30, 1913.
10. "Berlins dritte Dimension." *Berliner Morgenpost*, Nov. 16, 23, 27, 1912. Survey regarding the structural development of the "city" of Berlin.
11. W. Hegemann, "Soll Berlin Wolkenkratzer bauen?" *Berliner Illustrirte Zeitung*, Jan. 26, 1913, 69–71.
12. "Day of Skyscraper is Passing. Borough President McAneny tells City Club it may soon be prohibited by law. Plans for City Beautiful." *New York Times*, March 30, 1913, 11: 1 (Section II).
13. *Brooklyn Eagle*, op. cit.
14. Edward Marshall, "Vaster Skyscrapers Inevitable Says German Expert" *New York Times*, April 6, 1913. V, 6: 1.
15. "Dr. Hegemann Presents Practical Plan for Philadelphia. Beautiful blocks of small houses at less cost than present monotony." "Foul congested subways vs. airy, artistic elevateds." *Philadelphia Public Ledger*, April 8, 1913.
16. B. Antrim Haldeman, Philadelphia, to John Nolen, Cambridge, MA. April 18, 1913. Department of Manuscripts & University Archives, Cornell University, Ithaca, NY. Nolen Papers, Box 6.
17. "Dr. Hegemann Arrives." *Baltimore American*, April 15, 1913.
   "For 'City Practical'. Dr. Hegemann not looking for beauty, but real conditions." *The Sun*, Baltimore. April 19, 1913.
   "Expert Tells How to Plan Fine City; Dr. Hegemann says Baltimore needs civic center." *Baltimore News*, April 20, 1913.
   "Baltimore's Civic Imperfections as Seen by Dr. Hegemann. Fallsway plan was mistake, says expert." *Baltimore News*, April 22, 1913.
   "Resent Criticism of the Fallsway; Mayor and Mr. Hendrick reply to Berlin expert, unfamiliar with problem." *Baltimore American*, April 23, 1913.
   "Hegemann Is Sure He Is Right." *The Evening Sun*, April 23, 1913.
18. W. Hegemann, "The Commercial Necessity of City-Planning." Undated two-page ms. *HP*.
19. W. Hegemann, "The City Planning Situation of Syracuse," presented at the invitation of the Chairman of the City Planning Committee, Mr. C. W. Andrews. May 1–2, 1913. Thirteen-page typewritten report with extensive penciled notations. A three-page typewritten manuscript that may be the summary of one of his lectures composed by another person. *HP*.
20. "Beautify City in New River Plan; Cost Same, Says Expert." "Expect Crowd at Hegemann Lecture." *Columbus Citizen*, May 3, 1913. *HP*.
21. *Proceedings of the Fifth National Conference on City Planning*. Chicago, Illinois, May 5–7, 1913. (Boston/Cambridge: University Press, 1913).
22. "Program of City Plan Experts." *Construction News* 35, no. 15 (April 12, 1913): 8.
23. "Editorials," *The City Plan* 2, no. 1 (April 1916): 1.
24. "Tells Chicago to Copy London. Expert City Planner Declares Berlin and Paris Are Not Good Models."
   "Tell Values of Through Routes; New York and German Experts Explain Step in City Planning Idea." *Chicago Daily Tribune*, May 7 and 8, 1913.
25. *Proceedings . . .* , 222–43.
26. W. Hegemann, *Der neue Bebauungsplan für Chicago*. (Berlin: Wasmuth, 1911).
27. W. Hegemann, *Ein Parkbuch; Amerikanische Parkanlagen: Zierparks, Nutzparks, Aussen-und Innenparks, Nationalparks, Park-Zweckverbände. Zur Wanderausstellung von Bildern und Plänen amerikanischer Parkanlagen*. (Berlin: Wasmuth, 1911). The

publication received financial support from the garden design firm Jakob Ochs, Hamburg.

28. Among the many publications by and about Jane Addams, and the so-called "stormy years" in Chicago, only a select few will be mentioned here.
Jane Addams, *Twenty Years at Hull-House with Autobiographical Notes* (New York: MacMillan, 1910).
The Second Twenty Years at Hull-House, September 1909 to September 1929; With a Record of a Growing World Consciousness (New York: Macmillan, 1930).
Garry Wills, "Sons and Daughters of Chicago," *The New York Review* (June 9, 1994): 52–59.
Joan E. Draper, "Country Clubs for the Poor: Chicago's Small Parks of 1903." Paper presented at the Society of Architectural Historians conference, 1982.
Christine Stansell, "What a Woman Could Do," Review of Jean Bethke Elshtain, *Jane Addams and the Dream of American Democracy* (New York: Basic, 2002). *New York Times Book Review*, January 27, 2002.
29. "Never Saw Any Side Streets Quite So Bad; Dr. Hegemann says Williamsport is in class by itself in this; . . . The smoke nuisance." *Gazette and Bulletin*, Williamsport, PA. April 8, 1913. *HP*.
30. *Proceedings of the Eighth National Conference on City Planning*, Cleveland, June 5–7, 1916: 262–64.
31. "Designer of Cities Tells How to Better 'Our Town'. Parks, gardens, boulevards and playgrounds needed in heart of every city. Dr. Hegemann also advises building laws making for more light." *Minneapolis Morning Tribune*, May 9, 1913.
"Minneapolis' Opportunity in City Planning Shown." *Minneapolis Journal*, May 9, 1913. *HP*.
32. "Ancient Depot in Cleveland Stuns Planning Expert; Dr. Hegemann, Berlin authority, amazed at use of 50-year-old structure; Attacks grip of railroads." *Cleveland Leader*, May 16, 1913.
"Asks City to Save Euclid Ave. Beauty; Expert declares rules should control building lines." *Cleveland Plain Dealer*, May 17, 1913.
"Elevate Streets, Expert Suggests; Dr. Hegemann would raise Euclid Ave. and Ontario Str. at Public Square." op. cit. May 20, 1913.
"Keep Natural Beauty, Urges Civic Expert; Dr. Hegemann pleads for preservation of distinctive architecture style on Euclid Ave.; Condemns copying of foreign ideas." *Cleveland Leader*, May 17, 1913.
33. "Hiring a Planner" Editorial. "Oppose Hiring of German to Plan Our City." *The Cleveland News*, June 20, 1917.
34. "City Beauty Specialist Will Address Meeting at Lima Club at 8 O'clock Tonight." *Times Democrat*, Lima, Ohio. May 29, 1913.
35. W. Hegemann, "Gewitter 1913." Typewritten ms., eight pages. *HP*.
36. "Berlin City Expert Has No Love for Modern Flats and Skyscrapers." *The Denver Times*, June 7, 1913.
37. "City Planning Expert Arrives." *Sacramento Bee*, June 10, 1913. All in *HP*.
"Dr. Hegemann Ready to Lend Experience for City Betterment." op. cit., June 11, 1913.
"Hegemann Suggests Ways of Beautifying: more playgrounds, trees on business streets and improvements of water front, urged by expert." op. cit., June 12, 1913.
"Hegemann to Address Catholics." op. cit. June 13, 1913.
"German Expert Urges Municipal Lodging Houses; Dr. Hegemann also favors industrial zones in cities." op. cit., June 13, 1913.
"Expert Advice This City Should Follow." op. cit., June 14, 1913.
"Waterfront Big Asset, Says Expert." op. cit., June 17, 1913.
"Housing Problems Interest Visitor . . . Is Not Here to Beautify." *Sacramento Union*, June 13, 1913.
38. Mel Scott, *The San Francisco Bay Area: A Metropolis in Perspective* (Berkeley: University of California Press, 1985).
Mansel G. Blackford, *The Lost Dream: Businessmen and City Planning on the Pacific Coast, 1890–1920.* (Columbus, Ohio: Ohio State University Press, 1993).
39. Beth Bagwell, *Oakland: The Story of a City.* (Oakland: Oakland Heritage Alliance, 1982).

40. Mel Scott, op. cit., 160–65.
American City Planning Since 1890. (Berkeley: U. of CA, 1969), 149–69 and passim.
Fukuo Akimoto, "Charles H. Cheney of California," *Planning Perspectives* 18, no. 3 (July 2003): 253–75.
41. "Ideal Oakland to Be Reality; City-Planning Expert Here; Beautification of Municipality to Receive Careful Study." *Oakland Tribune*, Oct. 5, 1913.
42. Charles Henry Cheney, "Makes Study of Plans for City: Dr. Werner Hegemann is engaged to point way for betterments; What may be accomplished for Oakland outlined in forecast." *Oakland Tribune*, Oct. 10, 1913.
"City Planning Affects All Classes: Work of Dr. Hegemann is beginning of plan affecting future metropolis; Will furnish basis for systematic control of city's expansion." ibid., Oct. 11, 1913.
"Capitalizing Attractions of City; Will prescribe only beautifying Oakland where it will pay; Fine buildings stamp the city." ibid., Oct. 13, 1913.
"Planning New City Great Problem; Noted expert to aid in traffic question of City of Oakland; Report of Hegemann to take up big projects ahead." ibid., Oct. 15, 1913.
43. Werner Hegemann, *Report on a City Plan for the Municipalities of Oakland & Berkeley*. (Municipal Governments of Oakland and Berkeley, The Supervisors of Alameda County, The Chamber of Commerce and Commercial Club of Oakland, The Civil Art Commission of the City of Berkeley, The City Club of Berkeley, 1915).
44. "Col. Rees Reports on Western Waterfront." *Oakland Tribune*, Oct. 30, 1913.
"Why Not Island Parks? East shore cities may have most beautiful system in the world at little cost." *Oakland Review*, Nov. 8, 1913. *HP*.
45. C. C. Collins, "Oscar Prager (Leipzig, Sajonia 1876—Santiago, Chile 1962): Jardines en el paisaje." *ARQ* 37 (Nov. 1997): 6–66.
46. "City Planning Expert Talks to U. C. Students." *Oakland Tribune*, Oct. 24, 1913.
"Berkeley Plans Annual Banquet." *San Francisco Chronicle*, Oct. 17, 1913.
"City-planning Expert to Make His Report." *San Francisco Examiner*, Dec. 6, 1913.
"Berkeleyans to Hear Hegemann's Report." [n.a.] n.d.
"City Planning. I. The Introduction to the Report of Dr. Werner Hegemann to be made to the City Club and the City Council is presented in this bulletin." *Berkeley Civic Bulletin* 2, no. 6 (Jan. 15, 1914).
47. George B. Ford in American Institute of Architects, Committee on Town Planning, *City Planning Progress in the United States* (1917), 15: "This is one of the most studious city planning reports which America has produced."
Anthony Sutcliffe, *Toward the Planned City: Germany, Britain, the United States and France 1780–1914*. (New York: St. Martin's, 1981), 121 and passim: "a plan which broke firmly away from aesthetic preoccupations and established a mode of intervention which might fairly be described as comprehensive."
48. W. Hegemann, *Report*, op. cit.
49. W. Hegemann & Elbert Peets, *The American Vitruvius: An Architects' Handbook of Civic Art* (New York: Princeton Architectural Press, 1988).
50. "City Planning Show Draws Thousands." *Oakland Tribune*, March 14, 1914.
"Berkeleyans Take Part at Exhibit." *Berkeley Gazette*, March 17, 1914.
51. W. Hegemann, *Diary* of [1915], includes a list of "Dates" from 1896 to July 1915, listing places and events (birthdays and Christmas). It was probably composed as a reminder for himself of the numerous places he had visited and events during the first 34 years of his life. *HP*.
52. Minister for Home Affairs, Australia, to Werner Hegemann, Menzies Hotel, Melbourne, July 10, 1914. Commonwealth of Australia, Federal Parliament House Competition Programme. *HP*.
53. "Extraordinary Opportunities for American Cities Interested in Town Planning. Town Planning Surveys and Lectures." The People's Institute Lecture Bureau, 1915/16.
54. Duncan McDuffie to Werner Hegemann, July 2, 1915. *HP*.
55. Bagwell, op. cit., 189–200.
56. W. Hegemann to Professor Ford, Cambridge, MA. January 1916. Three-page typewritten manuscript. *HP*.
57. W. Hegemann, *City Planning for Milwaukee: What It Means and Why It Must Be*

Secured. A report submitted to The Wisconsin Chapter of the American Institute of Architects, The City Club, The Milwaukee Real Estate Association, Westminster League, South Side Civic Association. (Milwaukee: Feb. 1916).

58. City Planning Commission of the City of Milwaukee, *Preliminary Reports.* (November 1911).
59. A. R. Alanen and Th. J. Peltin, "Kohler, Wisconsin: Planning and Paternatism in a Model Industrial Village." *Journal of the American Institute of Planners* 44 (1978): 145–59.
A. R. Alanen, "Elbert Peets: Classicism and Iconoclasm in the Midwest," in *Shaping Heartland Landscapes: Landscape Architects in the Midwest.* Baltimore: Johns Hopkins.
A. R. Alanen's sharing of copies of letters exchanged between Mr. Kohler and Hegemann from the Kohler Company files is gratefully acknowledged.
J. M. Ellias, "Kohler, Wisconsin: A Model Industrial Community." Research paper, Columbia Univ. (1977). This is the most thorough study of the Kohler Village and Hegemann & Peets's contribution, based on extensive research into various archives and on-site investigation. I thank J. M. Ellias for providing me with the results of her research and for photographs and plans.
C. Crasemann Collins, "Hegemann and Peets: Cartographers of an Imaginary Atlas," in W. Hegemann and E. Peets, *The American Vitruvius: An Architects' Handbook of Civic Art* (New York: Princeton Architectural Press, 1988), xii–xxii, op. cit.
C. Crasemann Collins, "Werner Hegemann (1881–1936): Formative Years in America," *Planning Perspectives* 11 (1996): 1–21.
60. Barry Parker from Letchworth signed Hegemann's diary in 1916, perhaps while discussing the Kohler proposal.
61. W. J. Kohler to W. Hegemann (Oakland, CA), Jan. 15, 1917. p. 3. Kohler Company Archives.
This letter is part of the scant documentation of an interchange between W. J. Kohler and Hegemann. J. M. Ellias credits C. Shillaber with the rediscovery of this material in connection with her research on Elbert Peets, in 1974. She was aided by Dick Limmerhirt, the public affairs officer at the Kohler Company.
62. *On the Art of Designing Cities: Selected Essays of Elbert Peets.* Edited by Paul D. Speiregen. (Cambridge, MA: MIT Press, 1968).
C. Shillaber, "Elbert Peets, Champion of the Civic Form." *Landscape Architecture* 72, no. 6 (Nov. 1982): 54–100.
63. W. Hegemann, untitled typescript. (November, 1916). Sixteen pages. Kohler Company Archives.
64. Hegemann's interest in prefabricated and self-built homes, which were prevalent in Scandinavian countries, continued, and he wrote about them as a solution for low-cost housing.
On the Aladdin Company see also Dolores Hayden, *Building Suburbia; Green Fields and Urban Growth, 1820–2000* (New York: 2003), 102–103, 110–11, 116.
65. W. Hegemann (San Francisco /Santa Barbara) to W. J. Kohler, Dec. 20, 1916 and Jan. 8, 1917.
W. J. Kohler to W. Hegemann (Oakland), Jan. 15 and Jan. 16, 1917. Kohler Company Archives.
66. Marylin Bender, "The Kohlers of Wisconsin." *New York Times*, May 6, 1973.
67. C. Shillaber, *Elbert Peets*, op. cit., 58–59.
68. W. Hegemann, *Amerikanische Architektur & Stadtbaukunst. Ein Überblick über den heutigen Stand der amerikanischen Baukunst in ihrer Beziehung zum Städtebau.* (Berlin: Wasmuth, 1925/26), 125.
69. Richter, Dick, & Reuteman, *Washington Highlands* (Milwaukee: 1917).
70. Washington Highlands Co., *Owners Restrictions and Protections, Articles of Incorporation and By-Laws of Washington Homes Association* (Milwaukee, WI: 1919).
71. Wauwatosa County, Milwaukee, Wisconsin, Washington Highlands Historic District, Milwaukee, WI. (1988). I am grateful to A . R. Alanen for providing me with a copy of this thoroughly researched report.
72. W. Hegemann, *Amerikanische Architektur.* op. cit., 125.
73. J. B. Groy, "Lake Forest, The Lost City (Madison, Wisconsin): One of Wisconsin's first totally planned communities." BSc thesis, Landscape Architecture, University of Wisconsin, 1981.

A. Alanen, "Elbert Peets: Classicism and Iconoclassm in the Midwest," in *Shaping Heartland Landscapes; Landscape Architects in the Midwest*, op. cit.

74. W. Hegemann, *Amerikanische Architektur*, op. cit., 127.
    Hegemann & Peets, *American Vitruvius*, op. cit., 283.
75. ibid., 127.
    ibid., 223.
76. ibid., 252–53.
    ibid., 29.
77. W. Hegemann, *Amerikanische*, op. cit., 140.
    Hegemann & Peets, *American Vitruvius*, op. cit., 217.
78. W. Hegemann, *Amerikanische*, op. cit., 143.
    Hegemann & Peets, *American Vitruvius*, op. cit., 224, 218.
79. Otto Luening, *The Odyssey of an American Composer: The Autobiography of Otto Luening* (New York: Charles Scribner & Sons, 1980), 3–78.
    Otto Luening's conversations with the author 1985–1986; he provided copies of Hegemann's plans and sketches for the house and related correspondence.
80. W. Hegemann, "Erinnerungen an einen Amerikanischen Garten. Architekten: Werner Hegemann und Elbert Peets." *WMB* (1926): 194–207.
81. Keith N. Morgan, Charles A. Platt; *The Artist as Architect*. The Architectural History Foundation, New York. (Cambridge: MIT, 1985).
82. "Tercentennial Pilgrim City Association, Inc. Nineteen Hundred and Twenty Dinner," Boston 31, 1916.
    "Dine by Plymouth Rock. Representative Boston Men, Meeting at Somerset, Talk Pilgrim Tercentenary Celebration Plans." *Boston Evening Transcript*, April 1, 1916. *HP*.
83. A. Alanen, "Elbert Peets," op. cit.
    On the Art of Designing Cities: Selected Essays of Elbert Peets. Paul D. Speiregen, ed. (Cambridge: MIT, 1968), biographical resume of Elbert Peets, 226–27.
84. W. Hegemann, Diary (Feb. 14, 1918). *HP*.
85. Frank Koester, New York, Dec. 20, 1916, to W. Hegemann. *HP*.
86. Hegemann & Peets, *Wyomissing Park: The Modern Garden Suburb of Reading, Pennsylvania, A Stepping Stone towards Greater Reading*. Report and Plans for the Development of the Land under the Control of The Wyomissing Development Company. (Wyomissing, PA: 1919).
87. op. cit., 8–10 and passim.
88. Hegemann & Peets, *American Vitruvius*, 281–83.
    W. Hegemann, *Amerikanische*, 128–33.
89. Lauren Weiss Bricker, "American Backgrounds: Fiske Kimball's Study of Architecture in the United States," in Craig High Smyth and Peter M. Lukehart, eds. *The Early Years of Art History in the United States* (Princeton: 1993), 123–32.
    L. W. Bricker's information regarding her research on F. Kimball is gratefully acknowledged.
90. Fiske Kimball Papers, Philadelphia Museum of Art, Archives. Series 7, Correspondence Fiske Kimball–Werner Hegemann. Sept. 26, Oct. 1, 9, 11, 17, 22, 28, Dec. 24, 1918; Jan., March 6, 1919.
91. Biographical information on Werner and Ida Belle Hegemann and their family is contained in the *Family Saga* by I. B. Hegemann, based on her recollections, their letters and diaries. ca. 300 manuscript pages. See also "Sources."
92. W. Hegemann, Chicago, Feb. 22, 1919, to I. B. Guthe. Copied in *Family Saga*.
93. W. Hegemann, California, Feb. 1920, to I. B. Guthe. Copied in *Family Saga*.
94. *San Francisco Chronicle*, Feb. 21, 1920.
    W. Hegemann, "Expressions of a European City Planner on the New San Francisco Real Estate Development." Typewritten three-page ms. *HP*.
95. Hegemann & Peets, *American Vitruvius*, op. cit., 160, 272.
    W. Hegemann, Amerikanische, op. cit., 115.
96. "A Note from the Office of Hegemann & Peets, Landscape Architects." (1920). *HP*.
97. W. Hegemann to I. B. Guthe. Spring 1920. *Family Saga*.
98. W. Hegemann and E. Peets, *The American Vitruvius: An Architects' Handbook of Civic Art* (New York: Architectural Book Publishing Company, 1922).

Reprint edition with an Introduction by Alan J. Plattus. Preface by Leon Krier. Introductory Essay by Christiane Crasemann Collins. (New York: Princeton Architectural Press, 1988).
For reprint editions in Germany and Spain, see Bibliography.

99. Ibid., 1.
100. R. Unwin, "An Architect's Handbook of Civic Art," *Journal of the Royal Institute of British Architects*. Series 3, 30. (May 12, 1923): 416–17.
101. E. Peets, "Differentiating Features of Cities as Seen from the Air," (1944). Unpublished article. Cornell University Libraries. 2772: 2: 96.
102. Hegemann & Peets, *American Vitruvius*, op. cit., 2–3, 147.
103. ibid., 148–49.
104. C. Crasemann Collins, "Hegemann and Peets: Cartographers of an Imaginary Atlas," op. cit., xii–xxii.
105. "The American Vitruvius: An Architects' Handbook of Civic Art, by Werner Hegemann and Elbert Peets." *Landscape Architecture* 13, no. 1 (Oct. 1922): 76–78.
106. C. Crasemann Collins, op. cit.

4: Theory and Criticism

1. John H. D'Arms, *Romans on the Bay of Naples: A Social and Cultural Study of the Villas and Their Owners from 150 B.C. to A.D. 400* (Cambridge: Harvard University Press, 1970).
2. R. T. Günther, *Pausilypon, The Imperial Villa near Naples* (Oxford, 1913), 145. Cited by J. H. D'Arms, ibid., 44.
3. Manfred Maria Ellis, *Deutsche Schriften, gesammelt in drei Bänden von Werner Hegemann*. 2nd ed. (Berlin: Sanssouci-Verlag, 1924). Vol.1, part 1, *Iphigenie, Ein Lustspiel*, with eleven drawings by Markos Zavitzianos. Part 2, *Das Königsopfer: Sieben Gespräche . . .* Part 3, *Das vierte Gespräch: Friedrich II . . . , Gespräche* 5, 6, 7. (The sequence is confusing.)
W. Hegemann, *Fridericus oder das Königsopfer* (Hellerau: Jakob Hegner, 1925, 1926).
Der gerettete Christus oder Iphigenies Flucht vor dem Ritualopfer (Potsdam: Kiepenheuer, 1928).
4. op. cit. Vol.1, Part 2, 166.
5. Walter Benjamin, Hermann Kesten, Arnold Zweig.
W. Hegemann, "Achsialität und Wohnungspolitik," *WMB* (1926): 31–33. W.H. lists admiring comments on *Deutsche Schriften/Iphigenie* by Franz Blei, Hermann Bahr, Hermann Hesse, Hugo v. Hofmannsthal, and Jakob Wassermann.
6. W. Hegemann, "Achsialität und Wohnungspolitik/An den Schriftleiter der 'Schweizerischen Bauzeitung'," *WMB* (1926): 31–33.
7. Review in *Frankfurter Zeitung* (Oct. 21, 1924).
W. Hegemann, "Manfred Maria Ellis," *Weltbühne* (Oct. 1924).
8. "Ellis" was perhaps derived from Hegemann's mother's name, Elise, or from Ellis Island, the point of entry for immigrants arriving in America.
9. W.H. to Fiske Kimball. New York, June 7, 1934. HP.
10. op. cit., 216–217.
11. Joseph Hudnut, Statement on Werner Hegemann to serve as Preface for the 2nd. volume of Hegemann's *City Planning: Housing* (1937), but not published in its entirety. Dated July 29,1936. Pusey Archive, Harvard University, UA V 322.7.
12. Hermann Kesten, "Stilisten: Werner Hegemann," *Weltbühne* VII, 16 (1929): 97–98.
13. *Deutsche Schriften*, op. cit., 643–46.
14. op. cit., 555–601.
15. op. cit., 564. The passage is from Johann Peter Eckermann, *Gespräche mit Goethe in den letzten Jahren seines Lebens*, (Leipzig: H. Barsdorf, 1895), vol. 3, 156 (1830).
16. W. Hegemann, "H. G. Wells," *Weltbühne* (Apr. 28, 1929): 636–38, and a sequence, "Theegespräch mit Wells," *Neue Zürcher Zeitung* (May 10, 1929).

17. Roland Jaeger, *Heinrich de Fries und sein Beitrag zur Architekturpublizistik der Zwanziger Jahre* (Berlin: 2001).
"Aus dem Lebenswerke eines Architekturpublizisten: Heinrich de Fries (1887–1938)," *Architektur Jahrbuch/Architecture Annual*, Victorio Magnago Lampugnani, Andrea Gleiniger eds. (Deutsches Architektur-Museum, Frankfurth a. M. München, Prestel, 1992), 166–82.
Correspondence between de Fries and Hegemann has not survived.
R. Jaeger has generously shared his information on H. de Fries with the author. His help is gratefully acknowledged.
18. Heinrich de Fries, "Gross-Berlin: Städtebau-Siedlungswesen," *STB* 17, no. 9/10 (1920): 100.
19. Walter Lehweiss, "Die Städtebauliche Tätigkeit des Verbandes Grossberlin," *Stadtbaukunst alter und neuer Zeit* 1, no. 17 (1920): 263–66.
20. Bruno Möhring, "Zur Wahl des Städtebaudirektors," idem. 1, no. 13 (1921): 203–204.
21. "Chronik," *STB* 18, no. 9/10 (1920): 107.
22. Hegemann may have been intrigued by the prospect of working for *STB*.
23. Bruno Möhring, Berlin, letter to Werner Hegemann, Milwaukee, May 7, 1920. *HP*.
24. Ida Belle Hegemann, *Family Saga*. She quotes from Werner Hegemann's letters to her, but not all the original letters are contained in the *HP*.
25. It is illustrated in *WMB* (1926): 199, and in H. de Fries, *Moderne Villen und Landhäuser* (Berlin: Wasmuth, 1924), 124–27. More on the Hegemanns' life and home in Nikolassee in Chapt. V.
26. *International Cities and Town Planning Exhibition: Jubilee Exhibition Gothenburg, Sweden 1923*. English Catalogue, ed. Werner Hegemann (Gothenburg: Zachrissons, 1923).
27. ibid. Gustav Linden, "Town Planning in Sweden after 1850," 250–61.
Hans Bjur, "Genesis of Modern Town Planning in Sweden," *Planning History: Bulletin of the Planning History Group* 12, no. 1 (1990): 26–28.
Riitta Nikula, *Harmonious Townscape 1900–1930: On the Ideals and Aims of Urban Construction in Finland*. Dissertation, Helsinki 1981. Engl Transl.
Heleni Porfyriou, "Artistic Urban Design and Cultural Myths: The Garden City Idea in Nordic Countries, 1900–1925," *Planning Perspectives* 7, no. 3 (1992): 263–303.
28. Werner Hegemann, *Amerikanische Architektur & Stadtbaukunst: Ein Überblick über den heutigen Stand der amerikanischen Baukunst in ihrer Beziehung zum Städtebau.* 550 Abbildungen ausgewählt und erläutert von Werner Hegemann (Berlin: Wasmuth, 1925, 1927).
29. ibid., 9.
30. *Stadtbaukunst* 3, no. 1 (1922): 1.
31. I am grateful to Anthony Alofsin for generously sharing his knowledge regarding F. L. Wright with me.
Anthony Alofsin, *Frank Lloyd Wright—The Lost Years, 1910–1922: A Study of Influence* (Chicago: University of Chicago Press, 1993).
A. Alofsin, ed. *Frank Lloyd Wright: Europe and Beyond* (Berkeley and Los Angeles: University of California Press, 1999).
A. Alofsin, "Frank Lloyd Wright and Modernism," in *Frank Lloyd Wright, Architect.* Terence Riley with Peter Reed, eds. (New York: The Museum of Modern Art, 1994), 32–57.
Heidi Kief-Niederwöhrmeier, *Frank Lloyd Wright und Europa: Architekturelemente, Naturverhältnis, Publikationen, Einflüsse* (Stuttgart, 1983).
32. Frank Lloyd Wright, *Ausgeführte Bauten und Entwürfe* . . . op. cit.
Frank Lloyd Wright Chicago. Achtes Sonderheft der Architektur des zwanzigsten Jahrhunderts. European edition. Introduction by Charles Robert Ashbee, "Frank Lloyd Wright. Eine Studie zu seiner Würdigung." (Berlin: Wasmuth, 1911). Various American editions.
33. Alofsin, *F. L. Wright: Lost Years*, 33–34. Möhring's lecture took place Feb. 16, 1910. Hegemann could have met Wright during his involvement with *Berlin 1910*. Alofsin does not believe that Wright visited the city planning exhibition.
34. Ludwig Hilberseimer and Udo Rukser, "Amerikanische Architektur," *Kunst und Künstler* XVIII, no. 12 (Sept. 1920): 537–45.

35. ibid., 538.
36. This topic has been probed by Werner Oechslin, "Between America and Germany: Werner Hegemann's Approach to Urban Planning," in *Berlin/New York: Like and Unlike: Essays on Architecture and Art from 1870 to the Present*, Josef Paul Kleihues ed. (New York: Rizzoli, 1993), 281–95.
37. Daniel T. Rodgers, *Atlantic Crossings: Social Politics in a Progressive Age* (Cambridge: Harvard University Press, 1998). This study explores the context of these premises in great depth.
38. *Ausgeführte Bauten und Entwürfe von Frank Lloyd Wright* and *Frank Lloyd Wright: Ausgeführte Bauten* (Berlin: Wasmuth, 1910–1911). The latter is often called the "Little Wasmuth."
39. Dietrich Neumann, *"Die Wolkenkratzer kommen!": Deutsche Hochhäuser der Zwanziger Jahre*; Debatten—Projekte—Bauten. (Braunschweig/Wiesbaden: Vieweg, 1995).
Fritz Neumeyer, "Manhattan Transfer: The New York Myth and Berlin Architecture in the Context of Ludwig Hilberseimer's High-Rise City," in *Berlin/New York: Like and Unlike*. op. cit., 315–30.
C. C. Collins, "A Visionary Discipline: Werner Hegemann and the Quest for the Pragmatic Ideal," *Center, Modernist Visions and the Contemporary American City* 5 (1989): 81 and passim.
Hegemann's involvement in the skyscraper debate in Germany and exchanges with Le Corbusier are also discusssed in other chapters.
40. W. Hegemann, "Die Gefahren des Hochhauses; Der Wolkenkratzer Unsinn," *Berliner Illustrirte Zeitung* 28, no. II (1924): 1124–27.
41. W. Hegemann, *Amerikanische Architektur*, 33.
42. Raymond Unwin, "Higher Buildings in Relation to Town Planning," *Journal of the Royal Institute of British Architects*, 3rd Series, XXXI, no. 5 (1924): 1–26.
43. Carol Willis, "Zoning and Zeitgeist: The Skyscraper City in the 1920s," *Journal of the Society of Architectural Historians* 45, no. 1 (March 1986): 47–59.
44. *STB*, no.1–2 (1925): 65.
45. With minor changes, Hegemann's "Schlussbemerkung" was published as "Amerikanische Baukunst" in *Der Cicerone* 17, no. 12 (1925): 592–99.
46. Adolf Rading, "Buchbesprechung: Werner Hegemann, *Amerikanische Architektur u. Stadtbaukunst*," *Die Baugilde* (Zeitschrift des Bundes Deutscher Architekten: BDA) 7, no. 1 (1925): 37. Roland Jaeger's information regarding H. de Fries and A. Rading is gratefully acknowledged.
47. Heinrich de Fries, "Reisebilder aus Holland," *Die Baugilde*, BDA 15 (1924): 269–72.
48. W. Hegemann, "Holland, Wright, Breslau," *WMB* 9, no. 4 (1925): 165–67.
49. [W.H.], "Aus der Amsterdamer Schreckenskammer," von unserm Sonderberichtserstatter. *WMB* 9 (1925): 147–51.
Richard Konwiarz, "Neue Baukunst in Breslau," *WMB* 9 (1925): 152–64.
50. W. Hegemann, "Holland, Wright, Breslau" op. cit., 166.
51. Margo Stipe, "Wright and Japan," in Alofsin, *Frank Lloyd Wright; Europe and Beyond*. op. cit., 24–44. cited p. 27.
52. Conversation with A. Alofsin.
53. Nigel Pennick, *The Ancient Science of Geomancy: Man in Harmony with the Earth*, (Sebastopol, CA: CRCS, 1988), 7.
54. Heinrich de Fries, *Frank Lloyd Wright: Aus dem Lebenswerke eines Architekten* (Berlin: Ernst Pollak Verlag, 1926).
55. ibid., 30, 10.
56. "Amerikanische Architektur und Stadtbaukunst," replies by W. Hegemann and by A. Rading, *Baugilde* 7, no. 4 (1925): 206–210.
57. Hegemann, "Holland, Wright, Breslau," op. cit., 167.
58. W. Hegemann, "Bemerkungen. Baumeister Frank Lloyd Wright," *Die Weltbühne* 25, no. 26 (June 25, 1929): 982.
59. W. Hegemann, "Exotik und 'Amerikanismus'," *WMB* 9, no. 3 (1925): 119. More on this article further on.
60. Em. Henvaux, "Modernistische Baukunst in Belgien ausserhalb Gross-Brüssels," *WMB* (1927): 12–23. Hegemann's comments on pp. 16 and 23.

61. Fiske Kimball, "Alte und neue Baukunst in Amerika: Der Sieg des jungen Klassizismus über den Funktionalismus der neunziger Jahre," *WMB* 9 (1925): 225–39.
62. Lauren Weiss Bricker, "American Backgrounds: Fiske Kimball's Study of Architecture in the United States," in *The Early Years of Art History in the United States*, Craig Hugh Smyth and Peter M. Lukehart, eds. (Princeton, NJ: Princeton University Press, 1993), 123–32.

    Correspondence between Fiske Kimball and Werner Hegemann, Philadelphia Museum of Art Archives, and *HP*.
63. ibid. in PMAA, Various letters, W. H. and F. K., Spring 1925.
64. W.H., "Vergleiche, Fragen und Reisenotizen," *WMB* 9 (1925): 240–52.
65. L. Sullivan, "The Tall Office Building Artistically Considered," *Lippincotts Magazine* (March 1896).

    The Autobiography of an Idea (1924), the American Institute of Architects.
66. Kimball to Hegemann, May 13, 1925. PMAA, ibid. This passage is also cited, somewhat abbreviated, by Hegemann in his article op. cit., 252. The reference is to Oud's article in *WMB*.
67. Detlev J. K. Peukert, *The Weimar Republic: The Crisis of Classical Modernity* (New York: Farrar Straus & Giroux, 1992), 178 and passim.
68. Hilde Heynen, *Architecture and Modernity, A Critique*, (Cambridge: MIT, 1999).
69. Kathleen James, *Erich Mendelsohn and the Architecture of German Modernism.* (Cambridge: Cambridge University Press, 1997). This excellent study of Mendelsohn unfortunately repeats the established interpretation of Hegemann as reactionary and firmly aligned with the status quo. He is often quoted out of context.
70. The Contents note that all articles without an author's name are by Hegemann.
71. *Wasmuths Monatshefte für Baukunst* 8, no. 1/2 (1924): 1–66.
72. ibid., no. 2/3, 68–86.
73. Walter Gropius, "Idee und Aufbau des staatlichen Bauhauses," in *Staatliches Bauhaus Weimar 1919–1923*, [1923].
74. op. cit. The wording of Hegemann's citation is not exactly the same as it appears in the Bauhaus book.
75. Ida Belle Hegemann, *Family Saga*. W.H. to I.B.H., Munich, May 27, 1922.
76. The Wasmuth/Hegemann correspondence was destroyed during World War II in the bombing of Berlin.
77. Letters to Ida Belle Hegemann, Vienna, n.d., apparently written on two consecutive days in the first week of June, 1924. *HP*.
78. Robert Schmidt, "Landesplanung," *STB* 8 (1926): 127–31.
79. [W. Hegemann], "Aus der Amsterdamer Schreckenskammer," von unserem Berichterstatter. *WMB* 9, no. 4 (1925): 147–51. More in "The Pitfalls of Criticism."
80. *WMB* 8, no. 9/10 (1924): 296–312.
81. "Siedlungen" is a term applied to planned housing settlements of the 1920s in Germany; it is best left in German, as there is no equivalent in English or any other language.
82. Ibid. no. 11/12, 333–45.
83. Werner Hegemann, "Randbebauung des Tempelhofer Feldes," *WMB* 5 (1925): 205–208.
84. *STB*, 20, no. 1/2 (1925). Compare his Introduction to *Amerikanische Architektur*, op. cit., and Walter Lehweiss, op. cit.
85. K. James, op. cit., 57–70.
86. Heinrich Straumer, "Der Bau des Hauses der Deutschen Funkindustrie," *WMB* 9, no. 3 (1925): 103.
87. W. Hegemann, "Exotik und 'Amerikanismus': Betrachtungen über die Bilder auf Seite 120 bis 124 und über die Ausführungen Herrn Professor Straumers auf Seite 103 bis 111." ibid., 112–19.
88. F. Kimball, "Alte und neue Baukunst in Amerika...", op. cit.
89. Erich Mendelsohn, "Frank Lloyd Wright," *WMB* 10 (1926): 244–46. Also in *Wendingen, The Life-Work of Frank Lloyd Wright* (Amsterdam: 1925, reprint ed. 1965), 96–100. A note/subtitle explains, "Das Nachstehende entspringt einer Diskussion mit Mr. Fiske Kimball—Philadelphia, der in Wasmuth- Monatsheften Heft 6/1925 über den 'Sieg des jungen Klassizismus über den Funktionalismus der 90er Jahre' schrieb."

90. ibid.
91. Leo Adler, "Zuschriften an die Herausgeber: F. L. Wrights neue Baukunst und Mendelsohns neue Logik." Note: "Zu Erich Mendelsohns Aufsatz über Frank Lloyd Wright im vorigen Heft erhielten wir die nachfolgende Zuschrift." *WMB* 10 (1926): 308–309.
92. James, op. cit. Chapt. 4, "An Architecture for the Metropolis," pp. 108-139, and passim.
93. W. Hegemann, "Die Krystallische Form Gotischer Kirchen und ihre Vorplätze: Betrachtungen zum Ulmer Münsterplatz-Wettbewerb," *STB* XX no. 3/4 (1925): 29–63.
94. James, op. cit., 111–15.
95. W. Hegemann, "Eine wichtige Berliner Stadtbaufrage: Erich Mendelsohns Herpich-Umbau in der Leipziger Strasse: Eine Erklärung des Schriftleiters." *STB* 20, no. 9–10 (Sept./Oct. 1925): 156–57.
96. W. Hegemann, "Zum 'Linden' Wettbewerb: Die Strasse als Einheit." *STB* 20, no. 5–8 (May/August 1925): 95–107.
97. James, op. cit. p. 111–15.
98. W. Hegemann. *Facades of Buildings: Fronts of Old and Modern Business and Dwelling Houses* (Berlin: Wasmuth, 1929).
99. ibid., 23.
100. ibid., 27.
101. W. Hegemann, *Das steinerne Berlin: Geschichte der grössten Mietskasernenstradt der Welt* (Berlin: Kiepenheuer, 1930), 480, 252–53.
102. W. Hegemann, "Erich Mendelsohn's Kaufhaus Schocken-Chemnitz." *WMB* (1930): 345–50.
Charles du Vinage, "Erich Mendelsohn's Skizzen." ibid., 350–53.
E. Mendelsohn, "Baubeschreibung des Architekten." ibid., 354–55.
103. W. Hegemann, Typewritten manuscript, untitled, undated, probably 1932/33. *HP*.
104. W. Hegemann, "Mendelsohn-Haus und Goethe-Haus," *WMB/STB* 16, no. 5 (May 1932): 221–27.
"Der Schöpferische Sinn der Krise," *WMBS* 16, no. 5, 11 (Nov. 1932): 548.
"Der Schöpferische Sinn der Krise," Manuscript with penciled additions, 5 pages. *HP*.
E. Mendelsohn, *Der Schöpferische Sinn der Krise* (Berlin: Cassirer, 1932).
105. W. Hegemann, "Baut euer eigen Heim sehr schlicht . . . , Wohnstil, Städtebau und Landesplanung," Das Deutsche Sparta: Ein Notprogramm der deutschen Lebensgestaltung für das kommende Jahrzehnt; Ein Jahrzehnt des Aufstiegs. *Kölnische Zeitung, Zweite Beilage zur Neujahrs-Ausgabe* no. 1 (January 1, 1931).
106. Raymond Unwin to Christy Booth, Holland, Sept. 14, 1930. Courtesy of Mervyn Miller.
107. Gustav Adolf Platz, *Die Baukunst der neuesten Zeit* (1927). Title of Section II, 80.
108. C. C. & G. R. Collins, *Camillo Sitte: The Birth of Modern City Planning*. (New York: Rizzoli, 1986).
109. W. Hegemann & E. Peets, *The American Vitruvius: Civic Art* (1922), (New York: Princeton Architectural Press, 1988), 7–28, 266.
110. W.H., "Camillo Sitte und die 'Fischerschule'," *STB* 20, no. 3/4 (1925): 39–45. W.H. referred to responses to this article in his comments to W. Kreis, "Aus der Amsterdamer Schreckenskammer," *WMB* 9, no. 5 (1925): 210–11; W.H., 212.
W.H. "Die Krystallische Form Gotischer Kirchen und ihre Vorplätze:Betrachungen zum Ulmer Münsterplatz-Wettbewerb," and "Camillo Sitte und die 'Fischerschule'," *STB* 20, no. 3/4 (1925): 29–39, 39–47. Also in this issue of *STB*, "Aus dem Ulmer Federkrieg um den Münsterplatz," by various authors with comments by W.H., pp. 48–63.
W.H. "Neues vom Münsterplatz," *STB*, no. 9/10 (1925): 159–61.
W.H. and P. Schmitthenner, "Der Ulmer Münsterplatz-Entwurf von Paul Schmitthenner," *STB*, no. 11/12 (1925): 167–73.
Various commentaries on the Ulmer Münsterplatz competition by W. H. and others in *WMB* (1925): 398–415.
W. H. "Achsialität und Wohnungspolitik/An den Schriftleiter der 'Schweizerischen Bauzeitung'," *WMB* (1926): 31–33.
111. Katharina Medici-Mall, *Im Durcheinander der Stile: Architektur und Kunst im Urteil von Peter Meyer (1894–1984)*, (Berlin: Birkhäuser, 1998).

Simone Rümmele, *Peter Meyer: Architekt und Theoretiker; Peter Meyers Beitrag zur Architekturdiskussion der Zwischenkriegszeit.* Ph.D. dissertation, Univ. of Zürich, 1999.

112. Peter Meyer, "Über Axe und Symmetrie. Ein Beitrag zu der Polemik der 'Ostendorfschule' gegen die 'Fischerschule'," *Schweizerbauzeitung* 85 (1925): 205– n.a., 216– n.a., 231– n.a.
P. M. "Axiale Architektur," *Baugilde* 7 (1925): 1177– n.a., 1587– n.a.
On Ostendorf see Chapter V, 2.
113. C. C. Collins & G. R. Collins, op. cit., 207 and passim.
114. G. A. Platz, op. cit., 137–40.
115. C. C. & G. R. Collins, *Sitte*, op. cit., 189–91 and passim.
116. W.H. op. cit. *STB*, no. 3/4 (1925): 39–51 and passim.
117. W.H. "Achsialität und Wohnungspolitik/An den Schriftleiter der 'Schweizer Bauzeitung,'" *WMB* (1926): 31–33. "Die Architekturkritiker Peter Meyer und Karl Scheffler," p. 80. "Kleinigkeiten: Die Architekturkritiker Meyer und Scheffler," p. 208.
118. Roland Jaeger, *Heinrich de Fries und sein Beitrag zur Architekturpublizistik der Zwanziger Jahre* (Berlin: Gebr. Mann, 2001), 62–63. Jaeger's generously sharing information on de Fries with the author is gratefully acknowledged.
119. W.H. "Der Berliner Stadtbaumeister," *WMB* (1926): 34.
120. "Eine Rechtfertigung für Herr Dr. Hegemann in der Stadtbaufrage Berlin. Eine Berichtigung der Stadtbauratfrage," *Bauwarte*, no. 8 (1926): 82–83.
121. [W. H.] "Potsdamer Platz-Phantasien," *STB* (1925): 176–77.
122. *Mitteilungen der Freien Deutschen Akademie des Städtebaues.*
123. *STB* 20, no. 1–2 (Jan.–Feb. 1925): 25. *WMB* 9, no. 5 (May 1925): 217–18.
124. Erich Karweik, "Westachse," *WMB*, op. cit., 218.
125. *STB* 20, no. 5/8 (May–Aug. 1925): Part 2, 67–69 and passim.
126. W.H. "Die Architektonische Rückeroberung Berlins: Berliner Neubauten, Umbauten und Aufstockungen," *WMB* 8, no. 5/6 (1924): 133–48.
127. Paul Spencer Byard, *The Architecture of Additions: Design and Regulation* (New York: W. W. Norton, 1998).
128. ibid., 144.
129. ibid., 95–107.
130. *STB* 20, no. 5–6 (1925): Part 1: *Unter den Linden 1680 bis 1980.* Ergebnisse des Wettbewerbs "Wie soll Berlins Hauptstrasse sich im 20. Jahrhundert gestalten?" Veranstaltet von den Monatsschriften *Städtebau* und *Wasmuths Monatshefte für Baukunst* herausgegeben von Werner Hegemann. Hegemann adds a "Schlusswort des Herausgebers," p. 48, dated Fall 1927, explaining that the publication of the above was intentionally delayed to acknowledge the continued interest in the result of the competition by the city authorities eager to implement some of the suggestions.
131. The author gratefullly acknowledges Franziska Bollerey's sharing information on C. van Eesteren.
Franziska Bollerey, *Cornelis van Eesteren: Urbanismus zwischen 'de Stijl' und C.I.A.M.* (Vieweg: Wiesbaden, 1999).
132. "Die Sieger im 'Linden'-Wettbewerb, ein wahrhaft internationaler Wettbewerb," *WMB* (1925): 495.
133. "Van Eesterens 'Kurze Erklärung' zu seinem Preisgekrönten Entwurf," op. cit., 18–19.
134. W. Hegemann, "Zur Beurteilung des van Eesterenschen Entwurfes," *STB*, no. 2 (1926): 27–28, 31–32. In *STB* 20, no. 5–6, Part 1, pages 31–32 of Hegemann's remarks are not inluded.
135. C. van Eesteren, *The Idea of the Functional City: A Lecture with Slides 1928*, with an Introduction by Vincent van Rossem (Rotterdam, Netherlands: Netherlands Architecture Institute; The Hague, EFL Publications, 1997), 15 and passim. "Eine Stunde Städtebau: A Lecture with Slides; An Urban Detail," 60–77.
136. op. cit. cited on p. 17. Letter of Nov. 20, 1924. Van Eesteren Archives. Netherlands Architecture Institute.
137. Bollerey, op. cit.
138. van Rossem, op. cit., 23, 25.
139. W. Hegemann, *Report on a City Plan for the Municipalities of Oakland & Berkeley* (Oakland/Berkeley: 1915), 18. (See Chapter III, 1).

140. van Rossem, op. cit., 39 and passim.
141. Roland Jaeger, *Heinrich de Fries und sein Beitrag zur Architekturpublizistik der Zwanziger Jahre*, op. cit., 7, 147.
Haila Ochs, *Adolf Behne: Architekturkritik in der Zeit und über die Zeit hinaus*, Texte 1913–1946 (Basel, Berlin, Boston: 1994), 7 and passim.
142. Adrian Forty, *Words and Buildings: A Vocabulary of Modern Architecture* (New York: Thames & Hudson, 2000).
Rosemarie Haag Bletter, "Introduction" in Adolf Behne, *The Modern Functional Building* (tr. of *Der moderne Zweckbau*, 1923), (Getty Research Institute, 1996), 1–84.
143. Haila Ochs, *Adolf Behne*, op.cit.
Adolf Behne, *The Modern Functional Building*, op. cit.
Walter Curt Behrendt, *The Victory of the New Building Style*, Introduction by Detlef Mertins, (Los Angeles: Getty, 2000).
R. Jaeger, *Heinrich de Fries*. op. cit.
Gustav Adolf Platz und sein Beitrag zur Architekturhistoriographie der Moderne, (Berlin: 2000).
Katharina Medici-Mall, *Im Durcheinandertal der Stile: Architektur und Kunst im Urteil von Peter Meyer (1894–1984)*, (Basel, Boston, Berlin: 1998).
Robert Wojtowicz, *Sidewalk Critic: Lewis Mumford's Writings on New York* (New York: Princeton Architectural Press, 1998).
Lewis Mumford and American Modernism: Utopian Theories for Architecture and Urban Planning (Cambridge: Cambridge University Press, 1996).
144. W. Hegemann, typewritten manuscript, untitled, undated, probably 1932/33. *HP*. See also Chapter IV, 4.
145. The assistance of Cor Wagenaar, who generously shared valuable insights and copies of J. J. P. Oud's letters with me, is gratefully acknowledged.
The Netherlands Architecture Institute, Rotterdam, and the Netherlands Letterkundig Museum, The Hague, are the sources for the Oud correspondence and Hegemann's letters to him. The archives of the Wasmuth Verlag were lost in the bombing of Berlin.
146. W.H., Chronik, *WMB* 8, no. 5/6 (1924): 196.
147. W.H. to J. J. P. Oud, Jan. 23, 1925.
148. J. J. P. Oud, "Ja und Nein: Bekenntnisse eines Architekten," *WMB* 9, no. 4 (1925): 140–46. The essay was reprinted from the almanac *Europa* (Potsdam: Kiepenheuer, 1925).
149. W.H., "Aus der Amsterdamer Schreckenskammer" von unserem Berichterstatter. *WMB*, op. cit., 147–51.
150. W.H. to J. J. P. Oud, April 11, 1925. Oud to W.H., May 27, 1925. Oud expressed himself awkwardly in German.
151. W.H. editorial note. *WMB* 9, no. 8 (1925): 352.
152. Nancy Stieber, "Beyond 'Mendicant America': Berlage's Assessment of Urban Planning in the United States." Talk delivered at the Annual Conference of the Society of Architectural Historians, Boston, 1989. Session "In Search of a Transatlantic Culture: European Travel Accounts of American Buildings and Civic Spaces, 1900–1925." Stieber's study is based on H. P. Berlage, *Amerikaansche Reiseerinneringen* (Rotterdam: 1913).
153. Wilhelm Kreis, "Aus der Amsterdamer Schreckenskammer," *WMB* 9, no. 5 (1925): 210–12.
154. The J. J. P. Oud Correspondence, op. cit. is a well-organized and accessible resource, whereas other primary documentation disappeared during World War II.
155. Adolf Behne letters to J. J. P. Oud, Dec. 19 and 31, 1925; Jan. 21, 1926. Copy of Adolf Behne letter to W. Hegemann, Dec. 31, 1925. Netherlands Letterkundig Museum, The Hague.
156. A. Behne is referring to several articles in *WMB* 9 (1925).
Theo van Doesburg, "Die Neue Architektur und ihre Folgen," no. 12, 502–518, with a note by W. Hegemann.
W. Hegemann, "A. und G. Perret, Architekten in Eisenbeton," no. 8, 322–37. It discussed the theater des Champs Elysées (1913) and the theater at the Werkbund Exposition of 1914, both claimed by Henry van de Velde based on his designs, which the Perrets denied.

W. Hegemann, "Van de Velde, Chaos und die Dänen," no. 12, 518–23, addressed the issues raised in the article on the Perrets, citing letters in defense of van de Velde and accusing the Perrets of "*Plagiat.*"

157. A. Behne, *The Modern Functional Building*, Introduction by Rosemarie Haag Bletter. Translation by Michael Robinson (Getty Research Institute, 1996), 1.
158. Erich Mendelsohn to W. Hegemann, Feb. 1, 1926. Replies by W. H., March 11 and June 2, 1926.
E. Mendelsohn to J. J. P. Oud, June 6, 1926.
J. J. P. Oud to E. Mendelsohn, June 19 and 22, 1926.
159. *Hugo Häring: Schriften, Entwürfe, Bauten.* Heinrich Lauterbach, Jürgen Joedicke, eds. (Stuttgart: 1965), 153 and passim, note 17 cites the Ring's announcement with the names of its fifteen members in *Die Form* (1926): 225.
160. Hugo Häring to J. J. P. Oud, June 18, 1926.
161. J. J. P. Oud to E. Mendelsohn, June 19 and 22, 1926.
162. E. Mendelsohn, "Frank Lloyd Wright," *WMB* 10, no. 6 (1926): 244–46.
Zuschriften an die Herausgeber: Leo Adler, "F. L. Wright's neue Baukunst und Mendelsohn's neue Logik," op. cit., no. 7, 308–309.
163. J. J. P. Oud, "The Influence of Frank Lloyd Wright on the Architecture of Europe," in *The Life-Work of Frank Lloyd Wright*, reprint ed. of the 1925 ed. by T. Th. Wijdeveld (Amsterdam: 1965), 5–89.
164. Theo van Doesburg, "Die neue Architektur und ihre Folgen," *WMB* 9, no. 12 (1925): 502–518.
W.H., "Van de Velde, Chaos und die Dänen," 518–23.
165. W.H. to J. J. P. Oud, January 12, 1926.
166. J. J. P. Oud to W. Hegemann, Rotterdam, Sept. 19, 1926.
167. *Dr. Werner Hegemann zum fünfzigsten Geburtstage.* A testimonial volume. (Berlin: June 1931). *WHA.* Oud wrote in somewhat awkward German.
168. W.H. to J. J. P. Oud, June 22, 1931.
169. Fondation Le Corbusier, Paris. I am grateful to Francesco Passanti for his assistance regarding Le Corbusier.
170. Hegemann to Le Corbusier, October 19, 1923. FLC, Paris, A1(4), E2(7)II. [Author's translation].
See Francesco Passanti, "The Skyscrapers and the Ville Contemporaine," *Assemblage* 4 (Oct. 1987): 52–65.
For Hegemann and the skyscraper debate, see C. C. Collins, "Hegemann & Peets: Cartographers of an Imaginary Atlas," in Hegemann & Peets, *The American Vitruvius*, ibid., xii–xxii. Also "A Visionary Discipline: Werner Hegemann and the Quest for the Pragmatic Ideal," *Center 5 Modernist Visions and the Contemporary American City* (1989): 74–85. School of Architecture, University of Texas, Austin.
171. Le Corbusier to Hegemann, March 12, 1924. FLC, Paris, A1(4).
Mardges Bacon, *Le Corbusier in America; Travels in the Land of the Timid* (Cambridge, MA: 2001).
172. W. Hegemann, "Kritik des Grosstadt-Sanierungs-Planes Le Corbusiers," *STB* (1927): 69–74.
173. ibid., 70.
174. Marion Schnerb Liévre to the author, Paris, Dec. 18, 1984. The daughter of Pierre Liévre (1882–1939) reports that her father obtained a "doctor in law," was a timber merchant, and had strong literary interests. He wrote many short stories and novels, while managing his timber business. She remembered several visits from Hegemann. During the Nazi occupation the family, who was Jewish, considered it safer to burn the correspondence with Hegemann.
175. Steen Eiler Rasmussen, "Le Corbusier; Die kommende Baukunst?" *WMB* 9 (1926): 378–93. The title refers to Le Corbusier's book *Vers une Architecture* (1923), published in a German translation by Hans Hildebrandt as *Kommende Baukunst* (1926).
176. St. E. Rasmussen, London: *The Unique City I* (in Danish, 1934; Cambridge: 1974).
Towns and Buildings, Described in Drawings and Words (in Danish, 1949; Cambridge: 1973).
Experiencing Architecture (in Danish, 1959; Cambridge, 1962).

"First Impressions of London: or, Sir Edwin in Wonderland," AA Files 20, 1990. Introductory note and translation by Andrew Saint, pp. 16–21. Original published in *WMB* 12 (1928): 304–13.

177. Rasmussen, "Peking," *STB* 8 (1926): 121–26.
178. Steen Eiler Rasmussen kindly arranged for the Royal Library of Copenhagen to send photocopies of Werner Hegemann's letters to the author. In a letter by Rasmussen to the author, February 22, 1985, he writes: "Our interesting discussions have almost solely been face to face in Nicolassee or in Copenhagen."
179. Rasmussen in op. cit. *WHA*.
180. Kurt W. Forster, "Antiquity and Modernity in the La Roche-Jeanneret Houses of 1923," *Oppositions* 15/16: Le Corbusier 1905–1933 (Winter/Spring 1979): 131–58.
181. Rasmussen, "Le Corbusier: Die kommende Baukunst?" op. cit., 381.
182. Some passages from Rasmussen's article and Le Corbusier's comments are cited in Peter Serenyi, ed. *Le Corbusier in Perspective* (Englewood Cliffs, NJ: Prentice Hall, 1975), 90–91.
183. Hegemann to Rasmussen, July 22, 1926.
184. "Le Corbusier über Pessac," op. cit., 433.
185. Chronik: "Le Corbusier-Ausstellung in Berlin," *STB* (1926): 176.
186. Elbert Peets (Cleveland, Ohio), "Away from Architecture," unpublished, 4-page manuscript. Department of Manuscripts & University Archives, Conell University, Ithaca, NY. *Elbert Peets Papers*, Box 3, Folder 9.
187. Hegemann to Rasmussen, Oct. 27 and Nov. 8, 1926.
188. Hegemann to Rasmussen, Oct. 15 and 27, 1926. Hegemann singles out a passage on p. 380.
189. Günter Hirschel-Protsch, "Zuschrift an die Herausgeber," *WMB* 10, no. 10 (1926): 435–36.
190. Leo Adler, "Vorbericht zum Wettbewerb des Völkerbundes in Genf," *WMB* (1927): 345–52.
W. Vetter, "Der Entwurf von A. und G. Perret für das Völkerbundsgebäude in Genf," 416–19.
Leo Adler, "Wettbewerb des Völkerbundes in Genf; II. Bericht," 419–23.
Konrad Hippenmeier and W. Hegemann, "Wettbewerb des Völkerbundes in Genf; III. Bericht," 452–59.
Leo Adler, "Wettbewerb des Völkerbundes in Genf; IV. Bericht," 501–503.
191. W. Hegemann, *Napoleon, oder "Kniefall vor dem Heros."* (Hellerau: Jakob Hegner, 1927).
Hegemann's historical writings will be discussed in another chapter.
192. George R. and Christiane Crasemann Collins, "Monumentality: A Critical Matter in Modern Architecture," *The Harvard Architecture Review IV, Monumentality and the City* (Spring 1984): 15–35.
193. W.H. op. cit., 452–53.
194. W. Hegemann, "Berliner Neubauten und Ludwig Hoffmann," *WMB* (1927): 185–97.
Editorial Note to Börries von Münchhausen's letter to the above article, 341–43.
"Künstlerische Tagesfragen beim Bau von Einfamilienhäusern. Die Nachfolge Messels/Schultze-Naumburg und Ernst May/Flaches und Schiefes Dach," 106–127.
195. Börries von Münchhausen (1874–1945), known for his historical ballads, was a descendant of an ancient noble family. One of his ancestors is known as the author of tall tales describing the fictional adventures of the Baron Münchhausen.
196. op. cit., 343.
197. op. cit.
198. Richard Pommer, "The Flat Roof: A Modernist Controversy in Germany," *Art Journal* 43, no. 2 (Summer 1983): 158–69.
199. Hegemann, ibid., 120–27; illus., 144.
Walter Gropius, "Das flache Dach; Internationale Umfrage über die technische Durchführbarkeit horizontal abgedeckter Dächer und Balkone," *Bauwelt*, no. 8 (1926): 162–68, and no. 9 (1926): 223–27.
Paul Schultze-Naumburg, "Zur Frage des schrägen und des flachen Daches bei unserem Wohnhausbau," *Deutsche Bauzeitung*, nos. 94 and 96 (1926).

"Die Wirtschaftlichkeit der Dachformen und Ein Gutachten über die Wirtschaftlichkeit der Dachformen," Sonderabdruck *Deutsches Dachdecker-Handwerk*, nos. 52 and 26 (1926).

200. [W. Hegemann], "Die Überwindung des Daches: Sechs Aufnahmen gesammelt auf einem Aschermittwochspaziergang im Wilden Westen Berlins," *WMB* (1927): 144.

201. Richard Pommer and Christian F. Otto, *Weissenhof 1927 and the Modern Movement in Architecture* (Chicago: 1991). This study will remain unsurpassed for some time for its insightfulness and scope.

202. W. Hegemann, "Stuttgarter Schildbürgerstreiche und Berliner Bauaustellung 1930," *WMB* (1928): 8–12.
"Schmitthenner, Bruno Taut u.s.w.: Sklaven eines falsch verstandenen Klassizismus? Grundriss-Analysen im Geiste Alexander Kleins," idem., 345–48.
Edgar Wedepohl, "Die Weissenhof-Siedlung der Werkbundausstellung 'Die Wohnung' Stuttgart 1927," idem. (1927): 391–402.
Leo Adler, "Modernistische in Italien, Stuttgart und so weiter," idem., 402–406. This is a sequence to Wedepohl's article by the "Schriftleiter" and colleague of Hegemann, sometimes considered his mouthpiece.
Konrad Nonn, "Unabänderliches im Kleinwohnungsbau," idem., 406–408.
Other articles, etc., on Weissenhof in *WMB* will be mentioned further on.

203. W. Hegemann, "Kritisches zu den Wohnbauten der Stadt Wien." *WMB* (1926): 362–68. For an overview of Hegemann's ideas on housing, summarized in his late work, *City Planning: Housing*, three vols., 1936, 1937, 1938; see Chapter VI, 4.

204. C. C. Collins, "Urban Interchange in the Southern Cone . . . ," op. cit., 211.

205. Katharina Medici-Mall, *Im Durcheinander der Stile: Architektur und Kunst im Urteil von Peter Meyer (1894–1984)*. (Basel: 1998). Medici-Mall perceptively comments on Hegemann's position, especially on pp. 139–40.

206. W. Hegemann, "Stuttgarter," op. cit.

207. "Stuttgart, Breslau und der Werkbund: Zuschrift von P. Bonatz, P. Schmitthenner," *WMB* (1928): 109.
R. Pommer and C. Otto, *Weissenhof 1927*, op. cit., 147 and 266.

208. Leo Adler, "Neue Arbeiten von J. J. P. Oud—Rotterdam," *WMB* (1927): 294–95.
Alexander Klein, "Versuch eines graphischen Verfahrens zur Bewertung von Kleinwohnungsgrundrissen," idem., 296–98.

209. Correspondence in Netherlands Architecture Institute.

210. Wedepohl, "Die Weissenhof Siedlung," op. cit.

211. R. Pommer and C. Otto, *Weissenhof 1927*, op. cit., 147 and 266.

212. Letter, W.H. to I.B.H., Cairo, Jan. 25, 1928, cited in *Family Saga*.

213. "Stuttgart, Breslau und der Werkbund: Zuschrift von P. Bonatz, P. Schmitthenner," *WMB* (1928): 109.

214. L. Adler, "Paul Bonatz," *WMB* (1928): 1–5.
P. Schmitthenner, "Neue Arbeiten von Paul Schmitthenner," idem., 13–31.

215. R. Heiligenthal, "Wettbewerb für einen Bebauungsplan des Messe- und Ausstellungsgeländes in Berlin," *WMB* (1926): 44–58.
R. Heiligenthal, "Offener Brief an die technischen Preisrichter im Messe-Wettbewerb Berlin," *STB* (1926): 1–2.
R. Heiligenthal, "Studien für den Ausbau des Messe- und Ausstellungsgeländes in Berlin," *STB* (1927): 113–18.
"Wettbewerb der deutschen Bauausstellung Berlin 1930," *STB* (1928): 59.
"Aufruf zur fruchtbaren Kritik am Wettbewerbe für die Bau-Ausstellung Berlin 1930," *STB* (1928): 79–88. Reprints of the controversial exchange of letters between him and Martin Wagner.
"Aufruf zur fruchtbaren Kritik am Wettbewerbe für die Bau-Ausstellung Berlin 1930," signed by W. Hegemann and L. Adler for *STB*. *WMB* (1928): 141–43.
Dr. Coerper, "Bau-Ausstellung Berlin 1930," idem., 182–83.
W. Hegemann, "In eigener Sache: Wozu der Berliner Stadtbaurat Zeit hat." idem., 272–73.

216. Leo Adler, "Die Bauausstellung in Berlin 1930," *WMB* (1927): 506–507.

217. C. Crasemann Collins, "City Planning Exhibitions and Civic Museums: Werner Hegemann and Others," in *The City after Patrick Geddes*. Volker M. Welter and James

Lawson, eds. (Peter Lang, 2000), 113–30.
218. [W. Hegemann], "Deutsche Bauausstellung Berlin 1930," *STB* (1927): 198.
219. op. cit., 12.
220. Cited in "Bau-Ausstellung Berlin 1930," *WMB* (1928): 183.
221. "Aufruf," *STB* (1928): 79–81.
222. W. Hegemann to Hans Poelzig, May 18, 1928. Draft in *HP*.
223. Bruno Taut to J. J. P. Oud, March 26, 1928. *Netherlands Architecture Institute*, Rotterdam.
224. W. Hegemann to J. J. P. Oud, March 15, 17, 22, 1928.
W. Hegemann to Hans Poelzig, March 22, 1928.
Mrs.Oud to W. Hegemann, March 23, 1928.
Correspondence in *Netherlands Architecture Institute*, Rotterdam.
225. "Ein offener Brief: Herrn Dr. Werner Hegemann, Schriftleitung des 'Städtebau', Berlin," *Bauwelt*, no. 19 (May 10, 1928): 443–44.
226. Hegemann to Paulsen, May 12, 1928. Includes his reply to Wagner. Copy in *HP*.
"Erwiderung zum offenen Brief. Dr. Hegemann an Stadtbaurat Wagner," "Der Standpunkt Stadtbaurat Wagners," *Bauwelt*, no. 20 (1928): 467.
227. F. Paulsen, "In eigener Sache," *Bauwelt*, no. 29 (1928): 675–76.
228. W. Hegemann, "Vergleich zwischen Martin Wagner und Werner Hegemann," *STB*, no. 2 (1929): 56.
229. Johannes Cramer/Niels Gutschow, "Berlin 1931: Deutsche Bauausstellung auf dem Austellungsgelände am Funkturm vom 16. Mai–3. August," in *Bauausstellungen: Eine Architekturgeschichte des 20. Jahrhunderts* (Stuttgart: 1984), 163–67.
230. Martin Wagner, "Eine Studie über die Gestaltung des Berliner Ausstellungsgeländes," *WMB* 1 (1931): 33–40.
W. Hegemann, "Die Berliner Bauausstellung," WMB 5 (1931): 193–99.
231. "Von der deutschen Bauausstellung Berlin 1931," *WMB* 6 (1931): 241–47.
232. *La Ciudad Lineal; Formula española de Ciudad Jardín como sistema de arquitectura de ciudades y de colonización de campos. Memoria presentada al XIII Congreso Internacional de la Habitación y de Urbanismo por la Compañía Madrileña de Urbanización.* (Madrid: Imprenta de la Cindad Lineal, 1931). German translation of the Spanish text in the same volume.
233. "Bauen und Weltfrieden; Zwiegespräch zwischen Dr. Werner Hegemann u. Dr. Lutz Weltmann." Manuscript in *HP*, 1931.
Jean Giraudoux, "Berlin, nicht Paris!" *Der Querschnitt* XI, no. 5 (1931): 295–96.
234. W. Hegemann, "Bauausstellung," Zürich [1931] Undated offprint in *HP*.
235. The Architectural Association, *Exhibition of Modern German Architecture* arranged in Conjunction with a lecture by Werner Hegemann, editor of Wasmuths *Monatshefte für Baukunst*. April 30th to May 19th, 1928. (London: 1928).
236. W. Hegemann to Hans Poelzig, May 18, 1928. *HP*.
237. "Deutsche Baukunst in England," *Vossische Zeitung*, June 22, 1928. *HP*.
W. Hegemann, "Bonatz, Hertlein, Schumacher in London," *WMB* (1928): 246–48.
238. Howard Robertson, "Architekturstudium in England," *WMB* (1928): 297–300.
239. op. cit., 318
240. W. Hegemann to I. B. Hegemann, Berlin, July 12 and 13, 1928.
241. *Baukunst* 4 (1928): 128. The text is cited in Christian F. Otto, "Modern Environment and Historical Continuity: The *Heimatsschutz* Discourse in Germany," *Art Journal* 43, no. 2 (Summer 1983): 148–57. Note 71, p. 157.
242. Wolfgang Voigt, "Zwischen Weissenhof-Streit und Pour le mérite: Paul Schmitthenner im Architekturstreit der zwanziger bis fünfziger Jahre," in W. Voigt und Hartmut Frank, *Paul Schmitthenner 1884–1972* (Tübingen/Berlin: Wasmuth, 2003), 67–99. Voigt maintains that Hegemann joined the "Block" briefly, as did Poelzig. I am grateful to Voigt for sharing his research on the Block.
243. "Die Architektur-Schule Stuttgart," *WMB* XII no. 11 (1928): 473–22.
W. Voigt, "Die 'Stuttgarter Schule' und die Alltagsarchitektur des Dritten Reiches," ARCH+ 68, May 1983, pp. 64-71. "Die Stuttgarter Bauschule," in *Das Dritte Reich in Baden und Württemberg*, Stuttgarter Symposion, vol. 1, 1988. pp. 250-325.
244. Walter Curt Behrendt, *Der Sieg des neuen Baustils* (Stuttgart: 1927). English edition, *The*

Victory of the New Building Style (Los Angeles: Getty, 2000); Introduction by Detlef Mertins.

245. W. Hegemann, "Nachwort über die Arbeiten von Bonatz und Scholer und: Renaissance des Mittelalters?" *WMB* (1928): 153–65.

246. Hartmut Frank, "Der Fall Schmitthenner," *ARCH+* 68 (1983): 68–69.
"Schiffbrüche der Arche: Introduction to Paul Schmitthenner's Baugestaltung" in Paul Schmitthenner, *Das Deutsche Wohnhaus*, 4th ed. (Stuttgart: Deutsche Verlags Anstalt, 1984, 1st ed. 1932).
Barbara Miller Lane, *Architecture and Politics in Germany*, 1918–1945 (Cambridge, MA: 1968), passim.
Wolfgang Voigt, "Die Stuttgarter Bauschule" in *Das Dritte Reich in Baden und Württemberg*, ed. Otto Borst (Stuttgart: Stuttgarter Symposien 1, 1988), 250–325.
W. Voigt and Hartmut Frank, eds. *Paul Schmitthenner* 1884–1972, op cit.
These are only a few of many discussions of P. Schmitthenner.

247. Paul Schultze-Naumburg, *Kulturarbeiten.*

248. W.H. "Schräges oder flaches Dach," *WMB* (1927): 120–27, on Schultze-Naumburg, 120–21.
Schultze-Naumburg, "Zur Frage des schrägen und des flachen Daches bei unserem Wohnhausbau," *Deutsche Bauzeitung*, no. 94, 96 (1926).

249. W. Hegemann, "Kunst oder Kitsch zu Ehren unserer Sechzigjährigen?" *WMB* (1929): 265–73.

250. W. C. Behrendt, n.t., *Frankfurter Zeitung* (April 30, 1929).

251. W.H., typewritten drafts, titled variously: "Rasse—Rembrandt—schwarzROTgold oder Gegen den Kulturbolschewismus," "Scharzrotgold." "Rasse—Rembrandt—Schwarzrotgold: I Rasse, II Rembrandt, III Schwartzrotgold." "Kunst versöhnt die Rassen," unpaged, undated, probably 1932. *HP*.
W. Hegemann, "Kunst versöhnt die Rassen: Auseinandersetzung mit Schultze-Naumburg," *Vorwärts* (August 8, 1932).

252. W.H. "Nazisturm aufs Dessauer Bauhaus," *Generalanzeiger*, Dortmund (Sept. 23, 1932).
"Nazi-Reue über Dessau," *Die Weltbühne* (Sept. 6, 1932).

253. Julius Langbehn, *Rembrandt als Erzieher, Von einem Deutschen. 1890.* (Weimar, 1928), with an Introduction by H. Kellermann. A copy in *HP* contains numerous penciled notes by Hegemann.

254. W. Hegemann, "Hitler plaudert mit Nietzsche über die Juden," *Aufbau, Streitschrift für Menschenrechte*, Prag III, no. 16 (Sept. 15, 1933): 24–26. On the cover the title is given as "Hitler und Nietzsche über Antisemitismus." It was also published in Warshaw in Polish, and in Paris. The manuscript version in English, dated 1934, bears a note stating that the article caused the confiscation of the author's house. All in *HP*.

255. W.H. to the editor of *The Milwaukee Herold*, Milwaukee, WI (April 18, 1920). *HP*.

256. Ernst Kretschmer, *Körperbau und Charakter: Untersuchungen zum Konstitutions-Problem und zur Lehre von den Temparamenten.* 7th and 8th enl. ed. (Berlin: Springer, 1929).

257. On "Kulturbolschewismus" see B. Miller Lane, op. cit., 140–43 and passim.
W. Voigt, op. cit., 260–61.
Peter Meyer, "Kulturbolschewismus," *Das Werk* XIX (1932): 120–1.

258. Paul Renner, *Kulturbolschewismus?* (Munich/Leipzig: Eugen Rentasch Verlag, 1932).

259. W. Hegemann, "Kathedralen, Bodenwucher und das Kollektiv," *Die Weltbühne* 27, no. I (1931): 692–96. Typewritten manuscript in *HP*. Reprinted in *Ausstellungs-Zeitung* (Nov. 10, 1985): 6.

260. Peter Meyer, "I Situation Anfang 1933, II Schmitthenner: Das deutsche Wohnhaus, III Die Architektur im dritten ReichIV Bausünden und Baugeldvergeudung," *Das Werk* 20 (Feb. 1933): 56–64. Of interest here are parts I and II, pp. 56–61.

261. W. Hegemann, "Stuttgarter Werkbund-Ausstellung und Paul Schmitthenner," *Die Horen* 4 (1927/1928): 233–42.

262. Paul Mebes, *Um 1800; Architektur und Handwerk im letzten Jahrhundert ihrer traditionellen Entwicklung*, with an Introduction by Walter Curt Behrendt (Munich: F. Bruckmann A.-G., 1908; 3rd. ed. 1920).

263. Paul Schmitthenner, *Baugestaltung; Erste Folge: Das Deutsche Wohnhaus* (Stuttgart:

Konrad Wittwer, 1932). A copy of this book formerly owned by Hegemann was purchased in 1942 by the Avery Architectural Library of Columbia University. It is copiously annotated in pencil by Hegemann. Some of his writing is barely legible.

264. Hartmut Frank, "Schiffbrüche der Arche," Introductory essay to Paul Schmitthenner, *Das Deutsche Wohnhaus; Baugestaltung: Erste Folge*. New edition of the 1932 ed., (Stuttgart: Deutsche Verlagas Anstalt, 1984), v-xvii.
W. Voigt, "Die Stuttgarter Bauschule," 1988, op. cit.
Barbara Miller Lane, *Architecture and Politics in Germany, 1918–1945*, op.cit. remains the pioneering study of this period.

265. W. Hegemann, "*Das Deutsche Wohnhaus*" (Letter to "Lieber Herr Schmitthenner), *WMB* (1932): 559–66.
Paul Schmitthenner, "*Das Deutsche Wohnhaus* von Paul Schmitthenner; Eine Entgegnung an Werner Hegemann," *WMB* (1933): 137–38.
W. Hegemann, "Hierzu schreibt Werner Hegemann," *WMB* (1933): 138.
Manuscript copies of both published letters by Hegemann in *HP*.
W. Hegemann letters to René Schickele: 19.XI. (1932), 5.XII. (1932), n.d. XII. (1932) or I. (1933), 14.I. (1933). Letter by Annette Kolb is cited in Hegemann's undated letter to René Schickele. Correspondence in Deutsches Literaturarchiv Marbach a. N., Handschriften Abteilung.

266. "Neue Arbeiten von Paul Schmitthenner und seinen Schülern," comments by Hegemann; "Die Arche über Stuttgart," by René Schickele; "Fachwerkbau," by P. Schmitthenner; "Auf das von Schmitthenner gebaute Haus," by Annette Kolb; "Der Hausherr über sein Haus," by Fritz Wertheimer; "Das fabrizierte Fachwerkhaus," "Fabrikhallen," "Schmitthenner's 'Schüler'," by Schmitthenner. *WMB* (1929): 353–400.

267. References are to Schmitthenner, *Das deutsche Wohnhaus* (1932), op. cit. Copy formerly owned by W. Hegemann.

268. Peter Meyer, "I Situation Anfang 1933"; "II Schmitthenner: Das deutsche Wohnhaus," *Das Werk* XX (1933): 56–61.

269. W. Hegemann, "Schinkelscher Geist in Südamerika," *WMB/STB* 7 (1932): 333–41.
C. Crasemann Collins, "Urban Interchange in the Southern Cone: Le Corbusier (1929) and Werner Hegemann (1931) in Argentina," *JSAH* 54, no. 2 (June 1995): 208–227.
See also Chapter V, 2.

270. W. Hegemann, *WMB/STB* (1933): 137.

271. W. Hegemann, "Internationale Architektur," *WMB* (1928): 375.

272. Albert Leon Guérard (1880–1959), *L'avenir de Paris: Urbanisme francais et urbanisme americain* (Paris: 1929).
Letter by A. L. Guérard to W. Hegemann, Nov. 20, 1931; to I. B. Hegemann, April 27, May 25, 1936; *HP*. Letters by W.H. to A. L. Guérard, May 27, Oct. 22, 1931; March 1, 1932, in Stanford University Libraries, Department of Special Collections. Letter by A. L. Guérard to Abraham Flexner, recommending W.H. for The Institute for Advanced Study in Princeton, Dec. 6, 1934; *HP*.
A. L. Guérard, "*Werner Hegemann: Entlarvte Geschichte*: Aus Nacht zum Licht, von Arminius bis Hitler, Hegner" (1933). Manuscript of unpublished review. *HP*.
A. L. Guérard Papers at Stanford University Libraries, Department of Special Collections.
Letters by Albert J. Guérard (son) to the author, Feb. 8 and 26,1995. CCCC.

5: Life in Ideological Times

1. Ida Belle Hegemann, letter to her mother, July 27, 1922, from *Family Saga*.
2. Ibid.
3. H. de Fries, *Moderne Villen und Landhäuser* (Berlin: Wasmuth, 1924), 124–27.
W. Hegemann, "Schmitthenner, Bruno Taut u. s. w.: Sklaven eines falsch verstandenen Klassizismus? Grundriss-Analysen im Geiste Alexander Kleins," *WMB* (1928): 345–48. Hegemann's house plans and comments, 347–48.
4. I. B. Hegemann to C. C. Collins, Putney, VT, Sept. 4, 1979.

5. Ellis Feer Devereux, Honolulu, Hawaii, to C. C. Collins, Feb. 11, 1985.
6. George F. Kennan interview with C. C. Collins, Institute for Advanced Studies, May 17, 1985.
   Kennan soon took up a position at the American consulate in Riga and became an astute observer of developments in Russia.
7. Elisabeth Wehrmann, "Grosser Verleger des deutschen Exils; Gründer des deutschsprachigen Querido-Verlages in Amsterdam, Fritz Landshoff," *Die Zeit*, no. 11–12 (March 1982).
   Fritz Landshoff conversation with C. C. Collins, New York, Oct. 11, 1982. Letters to C. C. Collins, June, 1982; April, June, 1983. Fritz Landshoff died in The Netherlands, March 1988, at the age of 86.
8. I am most grateful to David R. Midgley for sharing information on Arnold Zweig, including his paper, "Fearing for the Past and Hoping for the Future: Arnold Zweig and Werner Hegemann," presented at the IVth International Arnold Zweig Symposium, Duke University, Durham, NC, Sept. 1996.
   Arnold Zweig, "Meine Nachbarn," in *Über Schriftsteller* (Berlin: 1967), 50–54.
   A. Zweig, "Auch Werner Hegemann . . . ," *Neue Weltbühne* 21, no. 6 (1936): 639–42.
   A. Zweig to W. Hegemann, Haifa, 26. 5. 35. *HP*.
   A. Zweig to I. B. Hegemann, Haifa, 8. V. 36. *HP*.
   Beatrice Zweig to I. B. Hegemann, Haifa, 7. V. 36. *HP*.
9. W. Hegemann, *Entlarvte Geschichte* (Hildesheim: Gerstenberg, 1979).
10. Lene Shulof, London, to C. C. Collins, April 27, 1981.
11. Margret Ohlischlaeger von Bismarck to I. B. Hegemann, May 25, 1936. *HP*.
12. M. Ohlischlaeger von Bismarck, Munich, to C. C. Collins, Dec. 21, 1984.
13. I. B. Hegemann, *Family Saga*.
    Dr. Werner Hegemann zum fünfzigsten Geburtstage. Commemorative album in *HP*. The Album contains signed sheets and telegrams from congratulators and copies of W. Hegemann's thank-you letters.
    "Glückwünsche aus aller Welt," *WMB/StdB* (July 1931): 335–36.
14. Copies of the letter by the Ausschuss and the dedication, with a note regarding the numbers sent out and replies received, are in the *HP*.
15. W. Hegemann to Mendelsohn, June 26, 1931. Copy in the album.
16. The measles episode must have impinged on the birthday celebrations, and Hegemann mentioned it in several thank-you letters.
17. Eric P. Mumford, *The CIAM Discourse on Urbanism, 1928–1960* (Cambridge, MA: MIT, 2000), 56.
18. *WMB/STB* 15, no. 7 (July 1931): 335–36.
19. The corrections are penciled in Hegemann's handwriting on a proof sheet enclosed in the album. His activities during those years and the difference between the "Zweckverband" and the "Propaganda-Ausschuss" are described in Chapter II, 5.
20. W. Hegemann, "Luckhardt's and Erich Mendelsohn's Neubauten am Potsdamer Platz," *WMB/STB*, no. 5 (1931): 226–32.
21. C. C. Collins, "Urban Interchange in the Southern Cone: Le Corbusier (1929) and Werner Hegemann (1931) in Argentina," *Journal of the Society of Architectural Historians* 54, no. 2 (June 1995): 208–27. This article was also published in a Spanish translation. It may be considered seminal for the ensuing interest in Hegemann by scholars in Argentina, who have based their publications extensively on this and other essays by C. C. Collins.
22. Several articles published in *Obras, Revista de Construcción*. Madrid, 1932, 1933, 1934. See W. Hegemann Bibliography.
23. W. Hegemann to I. B. Hegemann, August 10, 17, 18, 23, 1931. Letters also copied selectively into the *Family Saga*.
24. C. C. Collins, op. cit. This article discusses extensively Le Corbusier's stay in Buenos Aires and its repercussions for the architect and for South American architecture and urbanism. The essay has become the source for publications by Argentinian and Chilean authors, especially with regard to Hegemann, who was scarcely known prior to C. C. Collins's article.
25. W. Hegemann to I. B. Hegemann, Sept. 15, 1931. Cited in *Family Saga*.

26. Los Amigos de la Ciudad, "Informe de la Secretaría General sobre la Visita del Urbanista Alemán Arqto. Dr. Werrner Hegemann."
27. CCCC.
28. Adrián Gorelik, *La grilla y el parque: Espacio público y cultura urbana en Buenos Aires, 1887–1936* (Universidad Nacional de Quilmes, 1998). Also a lecture, "Werner Hegemann en la otra América: Buenos Aires, 1931," delivered at the Ibero-American Institute, Berlin, March 2001. From Gorelik's exclusive perspective and knowledge of the complex political history of Argentina, he disagrees with C. C. Collins's interpretations, which are based on her background in international city planning and in particular, her extensive study of Hegemann.
29. W. Hegemann, "Als Städtebauer in Südamerika [1]," *WMB/STB* 16, no. 3 (1932): 141–48. "Gemeinnützige Kleinwohnungsbauten in Buenos Aires," and "Als Städtebauer in Südamerika, 2," *WMB/STB* 16, no. 4 (1932): 185–96. "Als Städtebauer in Südamerika, 3: Der Sieg der Randsiedlung über die Mietskaserne," *WMB/STB* 16, no. 5 (1932): 247–51. "Schinkelscher Geist in Südamerika," *WMB/STB* 16, no. 7 (1932): 333–41. "Südamerikanische Verkehrsnöte," *Monatshefte für Baukunst und Städtebau* (formerly *WMB/STB*) 17, no. 2 (1933): 89–94.
W. Hegemann, "Ein deutscher Städtebauer in Südamerika," *Berliner Tageblatt* (July 5, 1932). "Ein deutscher Städtebauer in Südamerika, 2: Wohnt man in Buenos Aires besser als in Berlin?" *BT* (July 14, 1932). "Ein deutscher Städtebauer in Südamerika, 3: Argentinien am Scheideweg—Paris oder Berlin?" *BT* (August 8, 1932).
30. W. Hegemann, "Mar del Plata: El balneario y el urbanismo moderno," Conferencia del urbanista y arquitecto Dr. Werner Hegemann, pronunciada el 11 de noviembre de 1931 en el Teatro Odeon de Mar del Plata. Buenos Aires, 1931.
W. Hegemann, "Problemas urbanos de Rosario," Conferencias del urbanista Dr. W. Hegemann. Rosario, 1931.
31. "En el Instituto Popular de Conferencias hablará hoy el doctor Werner Hegemann," and "En los Salones de los Amigos de Arte fué inaugurada la exposición de urbanismo; El doctor Hegemann pronunció una conferencia sobre el desarrrollo de la urbanización moderna," *La Prensa* (Oct. 6, 1931).
32. "Die Entwicklung von Buenos Aires und anderer Grossstädte; Der erste Vortrag Werner Hegemanns," *Argentinische Tageblatt*, Buenos Aires (Sept. 19, 1931).
W. Hegemann, "Die Stadtbaukunst in Buenos Aires und in anderen grossen Städten der Welt," *Deutsche La Plata Zeitung*, Buenos Aires. Part I, Sept. 27, 1931; Part II, Sept. 28, 1931. The byline identifies Hegemann as publisher of *WMB/STB*.
33. op. cit., 8. See also C. C. Collins, "Le Corbusier and Hegemann in Argentina," 223–24.
34. Municipalidad de Rosario, *Plan Regulador y de Extensión*. Proyectistas Carlos M. della Paolera, Adolfo P. Farengo, Angel Guido. (Rosario: 1935).
35. W. Hegemann to I. B. Hegemann, Buenos Aires, Dec. 2, 3, 1931.
I. B. Hegemann to W. Hegemann, Berlin, Dec. 2, 1931.
36. W. Hegemann to I. B. Hegemann, Cap Arcona/Paris, Dec. 28, 30, 1931.
37. W. Hegemann to I. B. Hegemann, Buenos Aires, August 30, 1931.
38. Hermann Kesten, "Stilisten: Werner Hegemann," *Weltbühne* (June 16, 1929): 97–98.
39. *125 Jahre Wasmuth: Eine Firmenchronik von 1872–1997* (Tübingen/Berlin: 1998).
Europäische Moderne: Buch und Graphik aus Berliner Kunstverlagen 1890–1933 (Berlin: Kunstbibliothek Berlin, Staatliche Museen Preussischer Kulturbesitz, 1989).
Roland Jaeger, *Neue Werkkunst: Architekturmonographien der zwanziger Jahre.* Mit einer Basis-Bibliographie deutschsprachiger Architekturpublikationen 1918–1933. Gebr. (Mann, Berlin: 1998).
Neue Werkkunst Reprint Edition of the originals with the addition of new commentaries.
40. For *Neue Werkkunst* volumes with Hegemann's Introductions, see Bibliography.
41. *Die Architekten Brüder Gerson*, Introduction by W. Hegemann. *Neue Werkkunst.* (Berlin: Hübsch, 1928).
42. Wolfgang Voigt, *Hans und Oskar Gerson; Hanseatische Moderne*, With contributions by Hartmut Frank and Ulrich Höhns (Hamburg: Dölling und Galitz, 2000).
43. H. and O. Gerson, "Hamburgs Neues Büroviertel," *WMB* XIII, no. 4 (1929): 137–229. Commentary by W. Hegemann, 230.

H. and O. Gerson, "Bauten der Brüder Gerson, Hamburg," *WMB* XIII no. 7 (1929): 279–83.

44. Ernst Gerson, "Reise-Eindrücke in Nordamerika," *STB* 11 (1929): 293–300.
"Amerikanische Geschäftsbauten und Wohnhäuser," *WMB/StB* XIV (1930): 22–34.

45. Adolf Goetz, H. and O. Gerson, "Die Erweiterung der Hamburgischen City und das Messehausprojekt," *STB* 9/10 (1925): 121–34.

46. Olaf Bartels, *Altonaer Architekten; Eine Stadtbaugeschichte in Biographien* (Hamburg: Junius, 1997), 63–69.

47. *Neue Warenhausbauten der Rudolf Karstadt A.-G. von Architekt Philipp Schaefer, Hamburg*, Introduction by W. Hegemann, *Neue Werkkunst* (Berlin: Hübsch, 1929).

48. *Klophaus, Schoch, Zu Putlitz*, Introduction by W. Hegemann, *Neue Werkkunst* (Berlin: Hübsch, 1930).

49. *German Bestelmeyer*, Introduction by W. Hegemann, *Neue Werkkunst* (Berlin: Hübsch, 1929).
Otto Kohtz, Introduction by W. Hegemann, *Neue Werkkunst* (Berlin: Hübsch, 1930).
Dietrich Neumann, *"Die Wolkenkratzer kommen!" Deutsche Hochhäuser der zwanziger Jahre: Debatten—Projekte—Bauten.* (Vieweg, Braumschweig Wiesbaden, 1995).

50. Neumann, op. cit., 21–22; 37, note 62.

51. W. Hegemann, "Das Hochhaus als Verkehrsstörer und der Wettbewerb der Chicago Tribune, mittelalterliche Enge und neuzeitliche Gotik," *WMB* VIII, no. 9/10 (1924): 296–309. Illustrations, including those of the *Chicago Tribune* competition, are from his book.

52. Steen Eiler Rasmussen, "Le Corbusier: Die kommende Baukunst?" *WMB* (1926): 378–93.
W. Hegemann to S. E. Rasmussen, Oct. 15 and 27, 1926.

53. W. Hegemann and Leo Adler, "Warnung vor 'Akademismus' und 'Klassizismus'," *WMB* (1927): 1–11.

54. W. Hegemann, "Zu Schinkels 150. Geburtstag," *WMB/STB* 4 (1931): 157–58.

55. W. Hegemann, "Anmerkung des Schriftleiters zu Joseph Gantner," "Randbemerungen zu den neuen Büchern Brinckmanns," and "Randbemerkungen zum neuen Buche Gantners," *WMB* (1926): 24–31. The comment on *Sitte* is on p. 25.

56. W. Hegemann, "Romanticismo y realismo en la arquitectura moderna," *Obras: Revista de Construcción* (June 1932): 143–48. The Spanish version is slightly abbreviated from the German draft in *HP*.

57. Gustav Adolf Platz, *Die Baukunst der neuesten Zeit* (Berlin: Propyläen Verlag, 1927), 102–107.

58. Georg Kolbe, "Neues Bauen gegen Plastik? Ein Bildhauer spricht," *WMB/STB* 8 (August 1932): 381.
W. Hegemann, "Der Bildhauer als Teufelsbeschwörer der Architektur. Ein Gespräch mit Rudolf Belling," ibid., 382–88.

59. Peter Meyer, *Moderne Architektur und Tradition* (Zürich: 1928), 33.

60. Walter Curt Behrendt, "Einleitung," in Paul Mebes, *Um 1800: Architektur und Handwerk im letzten Jahrhundert ihrer traditionellen Entwicklung*, 3rd. ed. (Munich: Bruckmann, 1920), 7–12.

61. Friedrich Ostendorf, *Sechs Bücher vom Bauen.* Vol. 1 (Berlin: Wilhelm Ernst & Sohn, 1913); later volumes and new editions, 1914–1922. New editions heavily edited and with additions by Walther Sackur.
Hegemann owned Vol. 1, 4th ed. (1922), Vol. 2 (1919), and Vol. 3 (1920). Robert C. Weinberg bought them from I. B. Hegemann in 1936 and gifted them to G. R. and C. C. Collins in 1969.
Werner Oechslin, "Entwerfen heisst, die einfachste Erscheinungsform zu finden: Missverständnisse zum Zeitlosen, Historischen, Modernen und Klassischen bei Friedrich Ostendorf," in *Moderne Architektur in Deutschland 1900 bis 1950: Reform und Tradition*, Vittorio Lampugnani and Romana Schneider, eds. (Stuttgart: Gerd Hatje, 1992): 29–53.

62. Hans Detlef Rösiger, "Friedrich Ostendorf," *WMB* (1926): 281–91.
Edgar Wedepohl, "Aufgaben und Grenzen architektonischer Theorie," ibid., 291–92.
"Arbeiten von Karl Gruber—Danzig und die Einheitlichkeit städtebaulicher Anlagen,"

ibid., 293–301.
63. CCCC.
64. Ostendorf, op. cit., 96. Hegemann's notes.
65. ibid., 222.
66. W. Hegemann, *Das steinerne Berlin. Geschichte der grössten Mietskasernenstadt der Welt* (Berlin: G. Kiepenheuer, Jakob Hegner, 1930). For later editions see Bibliography.
W. Hegemann, *La Berlino di Pietra: Storia della piú grande cittá die caserne d'affitto*, (Milano: G. Mazzotta, 1975).
67. Walter Benjamin, "Ein Jakobiner von heute. Zu Werner Hegemanns 'Das steinerne Berlin'," *Frankfurter Zeitung, Literaturblatt* (Sept. 14, 1930).
W. Benjamin, *Gesammelte Schriften*, vol. 3, Kritiken und Rezensionen (Frankfurt: Suhrkamp, 1972), 260–65.
Also in W. Hegemann, op. cit., 4th. ed. (Braunschweig, 1988).
68. Franziska Bollerey, "*Das steinerne Berlin*," *Der Architekt* 4 (1995): 195–99.
Hans Stimmann, "*Das steinerne Berlin*—ein Missverstandnis," *Der Architekt* 3 (1997): 164–69, 185.
69. C. C. Collins, "City Planning Exhibitions and Civic Museums: Werner Hegemann and Others," in *The City after Patrick Geddes*, Volker M. Welter & James Lawson, eds. (Oxford: Peter Lang, 2000), 113–33.
70. See Chapter II, 6.
71. Guenter Hirschel-Protsch, "Die Gemeindebauten der Stadt Wien," *WMB* (1926): 357–62.
W. Hegemann, "Kritisches zu den Wohnbauten der Stadt Wien," ibid., 362–69.
Eve Blau, *The Architecture of Red Vienna 1919–1934* (Cambridge, MA: MIT, 1999). Presents a superb overview of the social democratic housing program as developed in Vienna. Blau's references to Hegemann's article are indicative of its value.
More on Vienna's housing policies in Chapter VI, 4.
72. Wilhelm Abegg, "Das steinerne Berlin. Gedanken zu einem Buch von Werner Hegemann. *Berliner Tageblatt* 29, no. 7 (1930) (Nr. 353).
73. David Midgley, *Writing Weimar: Critical Realism in German Literature 1918–1933* (Oxford: 2000). Especially "The City and the Country," pp. 260–303 and passim.
74. Karl Scheffler, *Berlin, ein Stadtschicksal* (Berlin: 1910, revised 1931).
Alfred Döblin, *Berlin Alexanderplatz: Die Geschichte vom Franz Biberkopf* (Berlin: 1929).
75. Walter Benjamin, "Berliner Kindheit um Neumzehuhmdert," *Beroliniana*. Berlin: Koeler & Amelang, 2001. pp. 7–122.
The Arcades Project (Passagen-Werk) tr. by Howard Eiland and Kevin McLaughlin, (Cambridge, MA: Belknap /Harvard, 1999).
"*Ein Jakobiner von heute . . .* " op. cit.
76. Joseph Roth, "Das steinerne Berlin," *Das Tagebuch* 5, no. 7 (1930).
77. W. Hegemann, "Selbstanzeige. Werner Hegemann: *Das steinerne Berlin*. Verlag Gustav Kiepenheuer, Berlin," *Das Tagebuch* 11 (1930): 633–34.
78. Ernst Kaeber, "Werner Hegemanns Werk: '*Das steinerne Berlin*. Geschichte der grössten Mietskasernenstadt der Welt' oder: Der alte und der neue Hegemann," *Mitteilungen des Vereins für die Geschichte Berlins* 47, no. 1 (1930): 101–114.
Joachim Lachmann, "Ernst Kaeber zum Gedächtnis," *Der Bär von Berlin. Jahrbuch des Vereins für die Geschichte Berlins* 14 (Folge, 1965). Festschrift zum 100-jährigen Bestehen des Vereins, 313–24.
79. W. Hegemann, "Zu Schinkels 150. Geburtstag," *WMB*/STB 4 (April 1931): 155–62.
80. W. Hegemann, "Schinkel als Fassadenkünstler," *WMB* 7 (1932): 332–33.
81. op. cit., Chapter XIX, 241–58.
82. W. Hegemann, "Schinkel und das Reichsehrenmal: Zu Schinkels 150. Geburtstag," *Neue Rundschau* 42, Part 1 (April 1931): 539–46.
"Das Reichsehrenmal," *Das Tagebuch* (July 9, 1932): 1073–1076.
"Zum Reichsehrenmal Wettbewerb," *WMB/STB* (Sept. 1932).
"Reichsehrenmal für die 'Bekannten Soldaten,'" typewritten manuscript in *HP*. Note in pencil: "Zurück 23, II *Tagebuch*."
83. C. C. and G. R. Collins, "Monumentaility: A Critical Matter in Modern Architecture." *The Harvard Architecture Review*. IV. 1984. Monumentality and the City. Cambridge:

MIT Press. pp. 14–35.

84. W. Hegemann, "Luckhardt's und Erich Mendelsohn's Neubauten am Potsdamer Platz," *WMB & STB* 5 (1931): 226–32.
    E. Mendelsohn, "Das Columbushaus in Berlin," *Bauwelt* 4 (1933): 1–8.
85. "Potsdamer Platz–Phantasien," *StB* 11–12 (Nov.–Dec. 1925): 176–77.
    W. Hegemann, *Das steinerne Berlin*, 171–72, 258.
86. op. cit., 196.
    "Die Berliner Staatsoper für 2500 statt 1600 Zuschauer: Rettungsversuch mit Skizzen von W. Hegemann und L. Adler," *STB* (1926): 88–89.
87. W. Hegemann, "Zu der bürokratischen Anarchie am Berliner Opernplatz und in Kaiserslautern," *WMB* (1926): 354–[356 not numbered].
88. W. Hegemann, *Das steinerne Berlin*, 450–51.
89. Christoph Gradmann, *Emil Ludwig, Werner Hegemann und die "Historische Belletristik,"* Populäre Geschichtsschreibung zwischen Politik, Wisenschaft und Gesellschaft in der Weimarer Republik.
    Ph.D. dissertation, Hanover University, 1990.
    Historische Belletristk; Populäre historische Biographien in der Weimarer Republik, (Frankfurt/New York: Campus, 1993).
    "Geschichte, Fiktion und Erfahrung–kritische Anmerkungen zur neuerlichen Aktualität der historischen Biographie," *Internationales Archiv für Sozialgeschichte der deutschen Literatur* 17, no. 2 (1992).
90. op. cit. See Chapter IV, 1
91. W. Hegemann, *Fridericus, oder das Königsopfer* (Hellerau: Hegner, 1926).
    Paul Claudel, *Proteus; Satyrspiel in zwei Aufzügen. Nach der französischen Dichtung deutsch von Werner Hegemann* (Hellerau: Hegner, 1926).
    W. Hegemann, *Napoleon, oder "Kniefall vor dem Heros"* (Hellerau: Hegner, 1927).
    Der gerettete Christus, oder Iphigenies Flucht vor dem Ritualopfer (Potsdam: Kiepenheuer, 1928).
    Das Jugendbuch vom grossen König, oder Kronprinz Friedrichs Kampf um die Freiheit (Hellerau: Hegner, 1930).
    Das steinerne Berlin; Geschichte der grössten Mietskasernenstadt der Welt (Berlin: Kiepenheuer, 1930).
    Entlarvte Geschichte (Leipzig: Hegner, 1933). It will be discussed in the following chapter.
92. *The HP* contain extensive documentation that was transported to the United States when the family left Berlin in 1933.
93. op. cit., 682–736. This section was also published as a separate "*Sonderdruck*" with a brief introductory note by the Verlag Jakob Hegner.
94. Veit Valentin, "Kampf um Friedrich den Grossen," *Frankfurter Zeitung, Erstes Morgenblatt* (April 27, 1927). Second part, "Schluss."
    "Schlusswort," op. cit. (June 29, 1927).
    W. Hegemann, "Der Kampf um Friedrich den Grossen," Eine Entgegnung. ibid. (June 1, 1927).
    Letter to the Editor, July 30, 1927.
    On the *Fridericus* controversies, see the extensive analysis in Gradmann, op. cit., 52–67.
95. W. Hegemann, "Die 'geheimen Testamente' des 'ersten Nationalsozialisten', Friedrich's des Grossen," typewritten manuscript, 7 pages, n. d.
    "Die 'geheimenen Testamente' des 'ersten Nationalsozialisten', Friedrichs des Grossen," *General-Anzeiger für Dortmund und das gesamte Ruhrgebiet* (July 30, 1932).
    Also in *Der Abend, Spezialausgabe des Vorwärts* (Berlin: July 30, 1932). *Arbeiter-Zeitung* (Vienna: July 28, 1932). *Neue Zürcher Zeitung* (July 31, 1932).
    W. Hegemann, "Alter Fritz—der erste Nazi . . . Wie Adolf Hitler seinem Potsdamer Vorbild gleicht," *Abendblatt* (July 29, 1932).
96. Lothar Müller, "Wie neide ich meinen Opfern ihren Tod. Deutschland erinnert sich an Preussen und den grossen König Friederich, aber die Literatur verwahrt die Erinnerung an seine Grausamkeit," *Frankfurter Allgemeine Zeitung* (January 18, 2001). I am grateful to Sabine Sellschopp for calling my attention to this essay.
97. op. cit., 9–24.

98. op. cit., 11.
99. op. cit., 9–13.
100. W. Hegemann, *Der gerettete Christus oder Iphigenies Flucht vor dem Ritualopfer* (Potsdam: Gustav Kiepenheuer, 1928).
Christ Rescued (Der gerettete Christus). Translated by Gerald Griffin (London: Skeffington, 1933).
101. W. Hegemann, *Napoleon oder "Kniefall vor dem Heros"* (Hellerau: Hegner, 1927).
102. W. Hegemann, *Frederick the Great*, Translated from the German by Winifred Ray (New York: A. A. Knopf, 1929), author's Foreword to the English Translation.
103. W. Hegemann, *Napoleon*, 9–10.
104. The author is most grateful to Jan Ellen Kurth for generously sharing her unpublished paper "Authority and the City Planner: Werner Hegemann's *Frederick the Great* and *Napoleon*," and some of her research material.
105. Bruno Taut, *Auflösung der Städte* (1918); *Alpine Architecture* (1919).
106. W. Hegemann, *Napoleon*, Chaps. 1–2 and passim.
107. op. cit., 27–43 and passim.
108. "Das Land in dem ich leben möchte: Umzugsgedanken," *Die Literarische Welt* 18 (1932): 3–4, 7; vol. 21, p. 3.
109. op. cit., 43.
110. op. cit., Ch. 14, "Napoleon und Friedrich die [sic] Grossen und die Malerei, Baukunst und Musik," 232–44.
111. W. Hegemann, *Der gerettete Christus oder Iphigenies Flucht vor dem Ritualopfer*, (Potsdam: Kiepenheuer, 1929).
112. Günther Dehn, "Der gerettete Christus," *Eckart: Blätter für evangelische Geisteskultur* 5, no. 2 (Feb. 1929): 67–71.
113. *Karl Barth [1886–1968] and Radical Politics*, George Hunsinger, ed. and trans. (Westminster Press, 1976). On Gunther Dehn, 75–76.
114. C. C. Collins, "City Planning Exhibitions and Civic Museums: Werner Hegemann and Others," in *The City after Patrick Geddes*, Volker M. Welter and James Lawson, eds. (Bern: P. Lang, 2000), 113–30.
Francis G. Peabody, *The Social Museum as an Instrument of University Teaching* (Cambridge, MA: Harvard University, 1911).
115. W. Hegemann, op. cit., 36.
116. Rita Nakashima Brock and Rebecca Ann Parker, "Violence and Doctrine," *UUWorld* (March/April 2002).
Erik Walker Wikstrom, "Jesus and the Modern Seeker," idem. (Jan./Feb. 2004).
117. W. Hegemann, "Entwurf zu einer Einleitung." Typescript, 3 pages, incomplete. (1933?) *HP*.
118. W. Hegemann, "Christentum, Landwirtschaft und Wohnungsnot," *Neue Leipziger Zeitung*. Section: "Glaube und Weltgestaltung: Wie sieht das religiöse Erlebnis unserer Zeit aus?" (Dec. 25–26, 1928).
Also in *Die Warte*, Section: "Glaube, Weltgestaltung und Bauen," (Sept. 15, 1929).
119. W. Hegemann, "Christliche Schülertragödie," *Weltbühne* (Aug. 7, 1928): 207–10.
120. W. Hegemann, "Die Festfreude der Kinder," *8-Uhr-Abendblatt der National-Zeitung*, no. 122 (May 26, 1928).
121. W. Hegemann, *Deutsche Schriften*, vol. 3, 604–42.
122. W. Hegemann, *Christ Rescued (Der gerettete Christus)*, Gerald Griffin, trans. (London: Skeffington & Son, 1933).
123. W. Hegemann to Bernard Shaw, Geneva, May 14, 1933. Copy in *HP*. Shaw's letter not preserved.
124. opus. cit., 27–31.
125. Thomas Mann, *Deutsche Ansprache: Ein Appell an die Vernunft* (Berlin: S. Fischer, 1930), 8–9.
126. Conversations with the author at the home of Eva Maria Hegemann Ladd in Wakefield, R. I., June 6, 1989.
127. "Taktische Wendung der KPD," Berlin, *Unabhängiger Zeitungsdienst* (December 15, 1934). *HP*.
128. Correspondence copied into I. B. Hegemann, *Family Saga*.

129. op. cit., xviii.
130. Arnold Berney, "Friedrich 'der Grosse'?" *Frankfurter Zeitung* (Feb. 28, 1931).
W. Hegemann, "Das Jugendbuch vom Grossen König, Eine Entgegnung," *F. Z.* (April 22, 1932).
131. Celsus, "Der junge Fridericus," *Weltbühne* (1930): 948–50.
132. W. Hegemann, *Entlarvte Geschichte* (Leipzig: Hegner, 1933). For later editions see Bibliography.
133. What Hegemann published in periodicals such as *Weltbühne*, *Tagebuch*, and others is easier to locate than what appeared in publications that did not survive Nazi cleansing.
134. Einhart Vorster [W. Hegemann], "Ritterlichkeit; Hindenburgs Mahnung an Hitler," *Berliner Montagspost* (August 22, 1932).
"Aber die Nerven . . . ," ibid. (August 29, 1932).
"Zwei Volkstribunen; Die Brüder Strasser," ibid. (September 5, 1932).
"Politik in der Familie," ibid. (September 12, 1932).
"Der betrogene Liebhaber," ibid. (September 19, 1932).
"Parlaments-Reform tut not!" ibid. (September 26, 1932).
"Was wird aus dem dritten Reich? " ibid. (October 3, 1932).
135. W. Hegemann, "Volkstümliches aus Hitlers Sportpalast," *Neue Zürcher Zeitung* (Nov. 2, 1932). Also a draft in *HP*.
136. W. Hegemann, "Weimarer Bauhaus und Ägyptische Baukunst," *WMB* (1924): 68–86. See Chapter IV, 4.
137. W. Hegemann, "Nazisturm aufs Dessauer Bauhaus," *General-Anzeiger für Dortmund* (Sept. 23, 1932). Also a draft/manuscript in *HP*.
"Nazi-Reue über Dessau," *Weltbühne* (Sept. 6, 1932).
Barbara Miller Lane, *Architecture and Politics in Germany, 1918–1945* (Cambridge, MA: Harvard University Press, 1969). Chaps. 5–7 provide a detailed, well-documented account of the controversies regarding architecture within the Nazi party. She does not refer to Hegemann.
138. W. Hegemann, "'Die Nation greift an!'" *Vorwärts* (Nov. 23, 1932).
139. Hegemann's lecture was published as "Grosstädtisches Wohnungselend und die Gartenstadt," *Deutsche Werkmeister-Zeitung* (May 3, 1929), with a cartoon of an editor under police supervision, and a note on the *Rundfunkzensur*. The sections censored out are included and highlighted.
"Lächerliche Zensur des Berliner Rundfunks," "Berliner Rundfunkzensur," *Frankfurter Zeitung* (April 3, 10, and May 14, 1929).
"Die Praxis der Rundfunkzensur; Ein aufschlussreicher Briefwechsel," *Kölnische Zeitung* (April 11, 1929).
"Der Rundfunk-Zensor lässt wieder 'nichts passieren'. Keine Kritik an der Berliner Strassenbaupolitik erlaubt. Der Schutzengel des Landrates." *Neue Berliner Zeitung* (May 10, 1929).
"Immer wieder Rundfunkzensur; Der Verantwortliche bleibt immer unsichtbar." *Die Welt am Abend* (April 12, 1929).
140. W. Hegemann, "Gestern: 2. Diskussions-Abend des Pen-Klubs/Freiheit und Schriftsteller. Das Gewissen der Zeit." *Berliner Zeitung am Mittag* (Feb. 23, 1931).
141. W. Hegemann, "Heinrich Mann? Hitler? Gottfried Benn? oder Goethe?" *Tagebuch* (April 11, 1931): 580–88.
Gottfried Benn mit Selbstzeugnissen und Bilddokumenten dargestellt von Walter Lennig, (Rowohlt, 2000), 94–99.
142. Quoted in Rita Reiff, "Einstein and Freud on War," in a note on an auction at Sotheby's in New York, offering letters by Freud and Einstein written at the request of the International Committee on Intellectual Cooperation of the League of Nations in 1932, and printed by the organization in an edition of fewer than 200, under the title "Why War?" *The New York Times* (Nov. 30, 1990).
143. "Streiflichter," *Berliner Börsenzeitung* (Feb. 17, 1933).
Will Vesper, "Gemeinschaft der geistig Schaffenden?" *Völkischer Beobachter*, München (March 27, 1933).
"Gemeinschaft der geistig schaffenden Deutschlands. Eine Rundfrage zum 'Tag des Buches'," *Literarische Welt*, no. 11/12 (1933): 3–4, 7.

144. Hellmuth Langenbucher, "Die 'Literarische Welt' derer von gestern." *Völkischer Beobachter* (March 23, 1933).
W. Hegemann, "Rückkehr zu Novalis." *Völkischer Beobachter* (Feb. 3, 1933). Also, manuscript in *Hegemannn Papers*.
145. Author's interview with George F. Kennan, Institute for Advanced Studies, Princeton, NJ, May 1985. It was not clear if Kennan was present at the open houses in 1932 or on earlier occasions.
Author's interview with Fritz H. Landshoff, New York, NY, Oct. 1982. Exchange of letters between F. H. Landshoff and C. C. Collins regarding the possibility of reprinting some of Hegemann's publications, May–June 1983.
See also Chapter V, 1.
146. Istvan Deak, *Weimar Germany's Left-Wing Intellectuals: A Poltical History of the Weltbühne and Its Circle* (University of California Press, 1968).
Berthold Jacob, *Weltbürger Ossietzky; Ein Abriss seines Werkes zusammengestellt und mit einer Biographie Ossietzkys versehen von Berthold Jacob. Vorwort von Wickham Steed* (Paris: Editions du Carrefour, 1937). A copy of this book dedicated to Mrs. Hegemann by Berthold Jacob is preserved in the *HP*.
147. Francis X. Clines, "Wiesel, Accepting the Nobel, Asks the Living to Remember." *The New York Times* (Nov. 11, 1986).
148. op. cit. Chapter VIII and passim.
149. Wilhelm Michel, "Die Fridericus-Legende," *Weltbühne* (Feb. 24, 1925): 259–60.
150. W. Hegemann, "Christliche Schülertragödie," *Weltbühne* (Aug. 7, 1928): 207–10.
151. W. Hegemann, *Entlarvte Geschichte* (History unmasked) (Leipzig: Hegner, 1933). This first edition has become quite rare, as many copies were destroyed. A second edition, newly edited and expanded by the author, was published by Prag, Soziologische Verlagsanstalt, 1934.
For later editions, mostly based on the 1934 edition, and translations see the Bibliography.
152. I. B. Hegemann, *Family Saga*.
153. W. Hegemann, "Entlarvte Geschichte: I. Marschall Vorwärts; II. Undank dem Feldmarschall?; III. and IV. Martin Luther?; V. Der 'Heilige Bernhard'; VI. Hermann der Befreier? [Arminius]," *8-Uhr-Abendblatt der National-Zeitung* (Dec. 3, 12, 20, 30, 1932; Jan. 27, 14, 1933). (VI was published prior to V.)
154. Hellmuth Langenbucher, "Entlarvter Geschichtsklitterer," *Völkischer Beobachter*, (March 15, 1933).
155. "Das Pamphlet von Werner Hegemann," Buchbesprechung von L. H. van Elhorst in "De Groene Amsterdammer (6. Mai 1933.) Der letzte Mohikaner," in W. Hegemann, ibid., 194–95. German translation of "Het pamflet van Werner Hegemann," Boekbespreking L. H. van Elhorst.
156. *Prager Presse* (May 12, 1933). *HP*.
157. W. Hegemann, "The Books the Nazis Ban; An Author in Prison," and "Firespells: Nazi Incantations at the Book Bonfire," Letters dated June 16 and 24. *The Manchester Guardian* (June 21 and 29, 1933). *HP*.
158. XYZ to Monsieur Lancy, Berlin, April 4, 1933. *HP*.
159. I. B. Hegemann to Carl E. Guthe, Ann Arbor, Michigan. April 28, 1933. *HP*.
160. W. Hegemann, "Präsident Masaryk im Gespräch," "Masaryk und Schleicher: Gespräch über Dienstzeit und Milizsystem," *Vossische Zeitung* (January 22 and 29, 1933).
Various manuscripts of variations of these articles in *HP*.
161. W. Hegemann, "Der verkannte Hitler," *Basler Nachrichten* (March 16, 1933). Also, manuscript in *HP*.
162. W. Hegemann, "Ein neuer Sieg Hitlers?"; "Hitler erobert Paris"; "Zwei Gespräche mit Guglielmo Ferrero: I. Die Werkzeuge der Diktatur. II. Über die Illegimität der Diktatur." Manuscripts in *HP*.
163. W. Hegemann, "Adolf Hitler und die Frauen. Ein Gespräch mit der Delegierten Englands in Genf." *HP*, 9 pages.
On Margery Corbett-Ashby (1882–1981) see *Women in World History: A Biographical Encyclopedia*, vol. 4 (1999), 112–13.
164. Fiske Kimball to W. Hegemann, July 26, 1933. *HP*.

165. W. Hegemann and Alvin Johnson correspondence. August 29, Sept. 21 and 24, Oct. 1 and 18, 1933. *HP*.

6: Exile

1. Bruce Bliven, "Thank you, Hitler!" *The New Republic* (Nov. 10, 1937): 11–12.
   Anthony Heilbut, *Exiled in Paradise; German Refugee Artists and Intellectuals in America, from the 1930s to the Present* (New York:Viking, 1983).
   The Muses Flee Hitler; Cultural Transfer and Adaptation 1930–1945, Jarrell C. Jackman and Carla Borden, eds. (Washington, DC: Smithsonian, 1983).
2. Claus-Dieter Krohn, *Intellectuals in Exile; Refugee Scholars and the New School for Social Research* (Amherst, MA: University of Massachusetts Press, 1993).
   Peter M. Rutkoff, William B. Scott, *New School: A History of the New School for Social Research* (New York: Free Press, 1986).
3. W. Hegemann (New York) to Rudolf Olden (London), June 21, 1934. *HP*.
4. Rutkoff, Scott, op. cit., 106–107 and passim.
5. W. Hegemann. Typewritten outline. 1 page. n.d. Text of lecture. Typewritten, 15 pages. *HP*.
6. *New School for Social Research Catalogues and Announcements* (1933–1935/36).
7. Alvin Johnson to W. Hegemann, March 19, 1936. *HP*.
8. *NewYork American*, *New York Sun*, and *New York Herald Tribune* (Nov. 1933–Feb., March, 1934).
9. W. Hegemann, "The Books the Nazis Ban; An Author in Prison," *The Manchester Guardian* (June 21, 1933).
   "Firespells: Nazi Incantations at the Book Bonfire," idem. (June 29, 1933).
10. A comparable interpretation is expressed by the Holocaust survivor and Nobel Prize–winning author Imre Kertesz in an interview with Alan Riding. *The New York Times* (Dec. 4, 2002).
11. *Nazism: An Assault on Civilization*, Pierre Van Paassen and James Waterman Wise, eds. (New York: Smith & Hass, 1934).
    W. Hegemann, "The Debasement of the Professions," pp. 59–75.
12. Charles A. Beard, "Hitlerism and Our Liberties," the New School for Social Research (April 10, 1934).
13. Lewis J. Edinger, *German Exile Politics: The Social Democratic Executive Committee in the Nazi Era* (Berkeley: University of California Press, 1956), 205 and passim.
14. "Hitler Downfall Foreseen by Exile." Interview with W. Hegemann upon his arrival in New York. *The New York Times* (Nov. 6, 1933).
15. "Organisation des Kampfes gegen den deutschen Nationalismus." Typewritten manuscript, 12 pages. *HP*.
16. W. Hegemann's correspondence from his exile years is preserved in the *HP*.
17. *Neue Volkszeitung* (June 15, 1935). *Neue Weltbühne* (June 27, 1935).
18. Copy in *Family Saga*.
19. Announcements in *HP*. Information on the Wendekreis has not been located.
20. Handwritten drafts of the lectures in *HP*.
21. On Hegemann's influence on Joseph Hudnut, and the latter's role at the Graduate School of Design at Harvard, see Jill Pearlman, "Joseph Hudnut's Other Modernism at the 'Harvard Bauhaus,'" *Journal of the Society of Architectural Historians* 56, no. 4 (1997): 452–77. And "Joseph Hudnut and the Unlikely Beginnings of Post-modern Urbanism at the Harvard Bauhaus," *Planning Perspectives* 15 (2000): 201–39.
    For a thorough history of the modern movement at Harvard, see Anthony Alofsin, *The Struggle for Modernism, Architecture, Landscape Architecture, and City Planning at Harvard* (New York: Norton, 2002).
22. C. Crasemann Collins, "Josep Luis Sert, the Architect of Urban Design 1953–1969." Review of the exhibition at Harvard Graduate School of Design (Sept. 13–Nov. 19, 2003). JSAH, December 2004.
23. W. Hegemann, *City Planning Housing*, vol. 1: *Historical and Sociological*; vol. 2: *Political Economy and Civic Art*; vol. 3: *A Graphic Review of Civic Art 1922–1937*, William W. Forster and Robert C. Weinberg, eds. (New York: Architectural Book

Publishing, 1936, 1937, 1938).
24. Charles A. Beard to W. Hegemann Nov. 27, 1934. *HP*.
25. W. Hegemann to Charles A. Beard. Nov. 18, 1934. *HP*.
26. Sverre Pedersen to Abraham Flexner, Dec. 3, 1934. Albert Guerard to Abraham Flexner, Dec. 6, 1934. Copies in *HP*.
27. Fiske Kimball to W. Hegemann, June 5, 8, 12, Nov. 13, 1934.
W. Hegemann to Fiske Kimball, June 7, 1934.
W. Hegemann to Wilbur K. Thomas, Carl Schurz Foundation, May 23, 1934.
Copies in *HP*.
28. New York Public Library, Humanities and Social Sciences Library, Manuscripts and Archives Division.
Emergency Committee in Aid of Foreign Scholars. Box 13.
29. *The Making of an Architect: 1881–1981*. Richard Oliver, ed. (New York: Columbia University Press, 1981). Especially: Rosemarie Haag Bletter, "Modernism Rears Its Head—The Twenties and Thirties," pp. 103–18; and Judith Oberlander, "History IV: 1933–1935," pp. 119–36.
Columbia University, New York. University Archives and Columbiana Library. Central Files.
30. ibid., J. Hudnut to F. D. Fackenthal, Feb. 6, 1934.
31. M. Uebelhoer, "'Urbanisme' in Frankreich," *STB* 3 (1929): 82.
32. ibid., J. Hudnut to The President and Trustees of The Carnegie Corporation, Nov. 19, 1934.
33. opus cit. J. Hudnut to E. R. Murrow, Feb. 21, May 1 and 23, 1935.
34. opus cit. Columbia University Archives.
35. Henry Wright, "City Planning in Relation to the Housing Problem," *Proceedings of the Twenty-Fourth National Conference on City Planning, Pittsburgh, PA* (1932): 17–22.
Henry Wright, *Rehousing Urban America* (New York: 1935).
36. C. Crasemann Collins, "City Planning Exhibitions and Civic Museums: Werner Hegemann and Others," in *The City after Patrick Geddes*, Volker M. Welter and James Lawson, eds. (Oxford: Oxford University Press, 2000), 112–30.
37. W. Hegemann to Professor Ford, Cambridge, MA, Jan. 1916. 3-page typescript. *HP*.
38. *Columbia University Bulletin of Information*. Announcement of the School of Architecture for the Winter and Spring Sessions 1935–1936, pp. 4, 22, 26, 27, 31.
39. W. Hegemann, "Prepared New Course for First Year: The Architecture of New York City and the Growth of New York City" [1935/1936]. 4-page typescript, *HP*.
40. Robert C. Weinberg, New York, to Joseph Hudnut, GSD, Harvard, June 23, 1936. CCCC.
41. "A Small Residential Park for Inexpensive Houses. A Study of 53 Acres in a Metropolitan Area, by Students and Instructors in the Graduate School of Architecture, Columbia University." W. Hegemann, "The Planning of Greyrock." William L. Drewry Jr., "Design and Construction," *The Architectural Forum* 62, no. 5 (May 1935): 478–98.
Greyrock on Sound Development Corp., "Greyrock Park on Sound: A Beautiful and Secluded Modern Residential Park in Rye-Port Chester."
42. W. Hegemann, *City Planning: Housing*. op. cit. vol. III, 151.
43. *Architectural Forum* 64, 65 (Feb., Apr., Sept., Nov., 1936).
44. opus cit. pp. 484–85.
Howard T. Fischer, "General Houses, Inc., Chicago: New Housing Designs and Construction Systems," Technical News and Research, *Architectural Record* (Jan. 1934): 18–19.
Editors of Fortune, *Housing America* (New York: 1932). "Industry's Answer: General Houses, Inc. The General Motors of the New Industry of Shelter," 118–31.
A Guide to the Professional Papers of Robert C. Weinberg. Albert Fein and Elliott S. M. Gatner, eds. A. Fein, "Biographical Essay." Sponsored by the Vinmont Foundation. The Department of Urban Studies, Long Island University, Brooklyn Center, Brooklyn, NY, 1984.
"Robert C. Weinberg, Regional Planner: Vinmont Project Architect and Consultant Dies, 72," *The New York Times* (Jan. 26, 1974).
R. C. Weinberg gave most of his papers pertaining to W. Hegemann to the author; they form part of the CCCC.

45. A. Lawrence Kocher and Albert Frey, "New Materials and Improved Construction Methods," *Architectural Record* (Apr. 1933): 281–88 and passim.
46. R. C. Weinberg to H. T. Fischer, "Professional Discussion in New York," April 14, 1934. *R. C. Weinberg Papers*. Box CXIX, Folder 2.
47. Exchange of letters between R. C. Weinberg, H. T. Fischer and W. Hegemann. A fragment of Hegemann's draft for the article is dated June 1934. "The Progress of the Modern House Abroad," undated 4-page draft intended for General Houses. CCCC.
48. W. Hegemann, "The Progress of the Modern House Abroad," *Our Homes* (General Houses, Inc., 1934), 6–8.
49. Anthony Alofsin, *The Struggle for Modernism: Architecture, Landscape Architecture and City Planning at Harvard* (New York: Norton, 2002).
50. "Internationaler Städtebaukongress in Wien 1926," *STB* (1926): 175, 198–200.
W. Hegemann, "Kritisches zu den Wohnbauten der Stadt Wien," *WMB* 10 (1926): 362–69.
Guenter Hirschel-Protsch, "Die Gemeindebauten der Stadt Wien," idem., 357--62.
For a thorough discussion of housing in Vienna, see Eve Blau, *The Architecture of Red Vienna 1919–1934* (Cambridge: MIT Press, 1999). Blau refers extensively to the above articles.
51. Riitta Nikula, *Harmonious Townscape 1900–1930: The Ideals and Aims of Urban Construction in Finland* (in Finnish). Doctoral dissertation, University of Helsinki, 1981.
Heleni Porfyriou, "Artistic Urban Design and Cultural Myths: The Garden City Idea in Nordic Countries, 1900–1925," *Planning Perspectives* 7, no. 3 (1992): 263–302.
52. Steen Eiler Rasmussen, "Kleinwohnungen und Wohnviertel: Die gegenwärtigen Wohnungsverhältnisse als Grundlagen der Planung," *STB* (1927): 75–80, 86–88.
Axel Dahlberg, "Kleinhaus-Siedlungen in Stockholm," *STB* (1928): 241–52.
W. Hegemann, "Stockholmer Kleinhäuser," *WMB/STB* 6 (1931): 279–85.
53. W. Hegemann, "The Shelter Famine," *Survey Graphic* 14, no. 5 (Feb. 1929). The New Germany: 1919–1929.
54. Catherine K. Bauer, *Modern Housing* (Boston/New York: Houghton Mifflin, 1934).
55. Eugenie Ladner Birch, "Woman-made America: The Case of Early Public Housing Policy," and "From Civic Worker to Civic Planner: Women and Planning, 1890–1980," in *The American Planner, Biographies and Recollections*, Donald A. Krueckeberg, ed. (New Brunswick, NJ: Rutgers University Center for Urban Policy Research, 1983), 149–75, 396–427. Birch does not mention Hegemann in her thorough study.
56. P. M. Rutkoff and W. B. Scott, *New School*, op. cit., 120–27 and passim.
57. W. Hegemann. Typewritten drafts. 8 fragments of pages. undated. *HP*.
58. "Hegemann and Aronovici to Give Housing Views," *New York Herald Tribune* (March 8, 1934).
National Public Housing Conference Luncheon, Nov. 25, 1934.
W. Hegemann, "Political Economy in German Housing Today," in Carol Aronovici, ed. *America Can't Have Housing* (New York: Committee on the Housing Exhibition by the Museum of Modern Art, 1934), 44–47.
59. W. Hegemann, "Are the United States ahead of the Soviet Union in Planning for Low-Cost Housing?" Radio Address, April 15, 1934. Draft, 4 pages. *HP*.
60. W. Hegemann, "With Hammer and Trowel," *Survey Graphic* (Nov. 1934): 553–57, 573.
Florence Loeb Kellogg to W. Hegemann, July 12, 1934. *CCCC*.
61. W. Hegemann to Henri Sellier, Sept. 28, 1934.
W. Hegemann to Madame A. Bonnaud, Jan. 7, 1935. Thanking for the receipt of the "Renseignements pour M. Hegemann." *CCCC*.
Nicholas Bullock and James Reid, *The Movement for Housing Reform in Germany and France 1840–1914* (Cambridge, MA: 1985), 365–73 and passim.
62. The Wagner–Steagall Act establishing the United States Housing Authority was passed in August 1937.
Eugenie Ladner Birch, op.cit., 163–70 and passim.
63. *Housing America*. The Editions of Fortune. New York, 1932. 109–70 and passim.
64. Henry Wright, *Rehousing Urban America* (New York: Columbia Univ. Press,1935).
65. ibid., 12.
66. "New Homes for a New Deal." I. Albert Mayer, "Slum Clearance—But How?" II. [miss-

ing?]. III. Lewis Mumford, "The Shortage of Dwellings and Direction." IV. Albert Mayer, Henry Wright, and Lewis Mumford, "A Concrete Program." *The New Republic* (Feb. 14, 28, March 7, 1934).

67. W. Hegemann, *City Planning: Housing*, Vol. I, *Historical and Sociological*, op. cit., 11.
68. Alan Mather, "At Large in the Library: *City Planning: Housing* by Dr. Werner Hegemann," *Pencil Points* (Feb. 1939).
    W. M. McRortie to *Pencil Points*. Reply to a review by Alan Mather of W. Hegemann, *City Planning: Housing* in the February issue of the journal. *Pencil Points* (March 1939). Professional Papers of Robert C. Weinberg, Brooklyn Center, Long Island University, Brooklyn, New York. Box CXV, Folder 9.
69. W. Hegemann, *City Planning: Housing*, op. cit. Vol. I, 1.
70. Charles A. Beard's note on Walter A. Agard's review, "*City Planning and Housing*, vol. I, by Werner Hegemann," *New York Herald Tribune Books*, May 31, 1936. *Weinberg Papers*, Box CXV, Folder 6.
71. W. Hegemann, op. cit., 67 and passim.
72. ibid., 79.
73. ibid., 83–84.
74. ibid., 87–88.
75. R. Weinberg, "*City Planning—Housing* by Werner Hegemann," Typescript. Weinberg Papers, Box CXX, Folder 6. [1936].
76. "Books: *City Planning and Housing: Historical and Sociological*. By Werner Hegemann," *Architectural Forum* (July 1936): 28.
    Frederick Ackerman, "City Planning: Yesterday, Today and Tomorrow," *The New York Times Book Review* (June 21, 1936): 11, 25.
77. Carol Aronovici, "How We Grew: *City Planning: Housing*, by Werner Hegemann," *The Survey* (May 1936): 191–92.
    "Housing and the American Tradition. *City Planning and Housing: Historical and Sociological* by Werner Hegemann." *Architectural Forum* (July 1936).
78. Joseph Hudnut's statement on Werner Hegemann. This was to have served as the Preface for Volume II of W. Hegemann, *City Planning: Housing*. Dated July 29, 1936, signed by Joseph Hudnut. Harvard University, Pusey Archive: UA V 322.7. Subseries I: Deans' General Correspondence and Travel Records, Box 3, IB. Dean Hudnut, 1932–1942.
    The author gratefully acknowledges Jill Perlman for bringing this document to her attention.
79. A thick folder of Weinberg's international correspondence on behalf of the illustrations testifies to his contribution to the publication. CCCC.
80. Pedro Martínez Inclán, Havana, Cuba. "*City Planning: Housing*," Vol. III by Werner Hegemann, W. W. Forster, R. C. Weinberg. undated.
    "*City Planning: Housing*, Vol. III, by Werner Hegemann, W. W. Forster, R. C. Weinberg," *South African Architectural Record* (Oct. 1938).
    Both typewritten manuscripts in CCCC.
81. "*City Planning: Housing*, Vol. III," *Town Planning Review* (Dec. 1938). Typescript. CCCC.
82. *City Planning: Housing*. Vol. III. op. cit., 14.
    J. Nolen to W. Hegemann, June 22, 1934. W. Hegemann to J. Harold De Nike (Harvard), March 6, 1935. CCCC.
83. "Houses for Needle Workers Designed by Architect Kastner, Blessed by Scientist Einstein, Built by the U.S. An Experiment in Cooperatives," *Architectural Forum* (July 1936): 76–77.
84. John Nolen to W. Hegemann, June 22, 1934. CCCC.
    "The Carl Mackley Houses, A Community Development for Hosiery Workers in Philadelphia." CCCC.
    City Planning: Housing, op. cit. Vol. III , 143.
    Ursula Cliff, "Oskar Stonorov: Public Housing Pioneer," *Design and Environment* 2, no. 3 (1971): 50–57.
85. W. Hegemann to Henri Sellier, Sept. 28, 1934.
    W. Hegemann to Madame A. Bonnaud, Jan. 7, 1935. Thanking her for the receipt of the "Renseignements pour M. Hegemann." CCCC.

Nicholas Bullock and James Reid, *The Movement for Housing Reform in Germany and France 1840–1914* (Cambridge: Cambridge Univ. Press, 1985), 365–73 and passim.

86. W. Hegemann to Steen Eiler Rasmussen, Dec. 13, 1935. *HP*.
87. I. B. Hegemann, *Family Saga*. The following description of Hegemann's illness and death is based on Ida Belle Hegemann's narrative and the cited excerpts from her letters.
88. Without I. B. Hegemann's knowledge, the hospital bill was paid by Henry Morgenthau Sr.
89. A. Johnson to I. B. Hegemann, April 17, 1936. *HP*.
90. A. Johnson, typescript, dated April 13, 1936. "In Memoriam. Werner Hegemann, 1881–1936." Printed. *HP*.
91. I. B. Hegemann, *Family Saga*, letter to Tante Martha and Onkel Oscar, May 28, 1936.
92. I. B. Hegemann investigated teaching positions and initially accepted one at the Bancroft School in Worcester, MA. Her teaching career proceeded to other private schools in Massachusetts, and she was the headmistress at Dana Hall Junior School in Wellesley for several years before retiring to Putney, Vermont.
93. Robert C. Weinberg introduced C. C. and George R. Collins to I. B. Hegemann around 1962. Weinberg furthered the author's interest in studying Hegemann's work and career and presented her with his material on Hegemann to form part of the CCCC.
94. "Dr. Hegemann, City Planning Expert is Dead," *New York Herald Tribune* (April 13, 1936).
    "Werner Hegemann, City Planner is Dead," *New York Times* (April 13, 1936).
    "Dr. Hegemann is Dead at 54," *New York Sun* (April 13, 1936).
    "City Plan Expert Buried; Exile of Reich Lived Here," *Standard Star*, New Rochelle, N.Y. (April 14, 1936).
95. "Werner Hegemann," *Survey* 25, no. 5 (June 1936): 357.
96. Flavel Shurtleff, "A Challenge to the Younger Men in the Planning Profession," *The American City* (August 1936): 64.
97. Elbert Peets, untitled two-page typewritten fragment. (1936?) CCCC.
98. Arnold Zweig, "Meine Nachbarn," 1936, reprinted in *Über Schriftsteller* (Berlin: 1967), 50–54.
99. I am grateful to David Midgley for sharing with the author his knowledge of Arnold Zweig as a literary figure, and providing me with his essay "Fearing for the Past and Hoping for the Future: Arnold Zweig and Werner Hegemann," delivered at the Fourth International Arnold Zweig Symposium, Duke University, Durham, North Carolina, 1996.
100. Beatrice Zweig to I. B. Hegemann, Haifa, May 7, 1936. Arnold Zweig to I. B. Hegeimann, Haifa, May 8, 1936. *HP*.
101. A. Zweig, "Auch Werner Hegemann . . . ," *Neue Weltbühne* (June 21, 1936): 639–42. Reprinted as Introduction to a new edition of W. Hegemann, *Entlarvte Geschichte*, Exilliteratur, vol. 5 (Hildesheim, 1979). A draft of the obituary corrected and annotated was sent by Zweig to I. B. Hegemann. *HP*.
102. D. Midgley, "Fearing for the Past . . . ," op. cit., 1.
103. Rudolf Olden, "Werner Hegemann, Dem Freund und dem Kämpfer!" *Pariser Tageblatt* (later *Pariser Tageszeitung*), no. 866 (April 1936): 3. Olden to I. B. Hegemann, Apr. 27, 1936. *HP*.
104. "Werner Hegemann," *Das Neue-Tagebuch* (April 25, 1936): 391–92.
105. Albert Guerard to I. B. Hegemann, April 27 and May 25, 1936. *HP*.
106. Mary Simkhovitch to I. B. Hegemann, May 14 [1936], and n.d. Edith Elmer Wood to I. B. Hegemann, April 18, 1936.
     Frieda Wunderlich to I. B. Hegemann, April 12, 1936. *HP*.
107. Harold S. Buttenheim, Welfare Council of New York CIty, to I. B. Hegemann, May 27, 1936. Allen H. Seed, The City Club of New York, April 21, 1936. *HP*.
108. Mrs. Frederick Pabst to I. B. Hegemann, April 20, 1936. Cora B. Cheney to I. B. Hegemann, May 1, 1936. *HP*.
109. Albert Lilienberg to I. B. Hegemann, May 5, 1936. Sverre Pedersen to I. B. Hegemann, May 2, 1936. *HP*.
110. Joseph Roth, "The Auto-da-Fé of the Mind," *Cahiers Juifs* (Paris: Sept./Nov. 1933). Reprinted in *What I Saw: Reports from Berlin, 1920–1933*, Michael Hoffmann, trans.

Bibliography

Selected Works by Werner Hegemann

"Mexikos Übergang zur Goldwährung: Ein Beitrag zur Geschichte des mexikanischen Geldwesens (1867–1906)." Ph.D. diss., University of Munich, 1908. Volkswirtschaftliche Studien 86, edited by Lujo Brentano and Walther Lotz. Stuttgart: Cotta, 1908.

Der Neue Bebauungsplan für Chicago. Berlin: Wasmuth, [1910].

Ein Parkbuch: Amerikanische Parkanlagen—Zierparks, Nutzparks, Aussen- u. Innenparks, Nationalparks, Park-Zweckverbände. Berlin: Wasmuth, 1911.

Der Städtebau nach den Ergebnissen der allgemeinen Städtebau-Ausstellung in Berlin nebst einem Anhang: Die Internationale Städtebau-Ausstellung in Düsseldorf. Vols. 1 and 2. Berlin: Wasmuth, 1911, 1913.

Für Gross-Berlin: Was erwarten wir vom Zweckverband? Publication of the Propaganda-Ausschuss 1. Edited by Werner Hegemann. Charlottenburg: Vita, Deutsches Verlagshaus, 1912.

Für Gross-Berlin: Dernburg, Naumann, Südekum; Das Tempelhofer Feld in Bildern; Das Wachsen Gross-Berlins in Bildern. Publication of the Propaganda-Ausschuss 2. Edited by Werner Hegemann. Charlottenburg: Vita, Deutsches Verlagshaus, 1912.

"Report on a City Plan for the Municipalities of Oakland & Berkeley." Berkeley, Calif, 1915.

"City Planning for Milwaukee: What It Means and Why It Must Be Secured." Milwaukee, 1916.

Washington Highlands. Drawings by Elbert Peets. Richter, Dick & Reuteman, Planners and Developers. Milwaukee, [1916].

"Wyomissing Park, the Modern Garden Suburb of Reading, Pennsylvania: A Stepping Stone Toward a Greater Reading." Wyomissing, Pa: 1919.

The American Vitruvius: An Architects' Handbook of Civic Art. [With Elbert Peets.] New York: The Architectural Book Publishing Co. Paul Wenzel & Maurice Krakow, 1922. Reprint, New York: Princeton Architectural Press, 1988.

International Cities and Town Planning Exhibition. English Catalog of the Jubilee Exhibition, Gothenburg, Sweden, 1923.

Ellis Manfred Maria [pseud.]. *Deutsche Schriften*. Collected in three volumes by W. Hegemann. Drawings by Markos Zavitzianos. Berlin, 1922. Reprint, Berlin: Sanssouci Verlag des Deutschen Verlagsinstituts, 1924.

Amerikanische Architektur & Stadtbaukunst: Ein Überblick über den heutigen Stand der Amerikanischen Baukunst in ihrer Beziehung zum Staedtebau. Der Staedtebau nach den Ergebnissen der Internationalen Staedtebau-Ausstellung Gothenburg. Vol. 1, *Amerikanische Architektur & Stadtbaukunst*. Berlin: Wasmuth, 1925–26.

Introduction to Ahlberg, Hakon. *Moderne Schwedische Architektur*. Berlin: Wasmuth, 1925.

Frederick the Great. Translated by Winifred Ray. New York: Alfred A. Knopf, 1929. Originally published as *Fredericus oder das Königsopfer*. Hellerau: Jakob Hegner, 1926.

Claudel, Paul. *Proteus [Protée]*. Satyrspiel in zwei Aufzügen, nach der französischen Dichtung von Paul Claudel (. . .). Hellerau: Jacob Hegner, 1926.

Napoleon or "Prostration before the Hero." New York: Alfred A. Knopf, 1931. Originally published as *Napoleon oder "Kniefall vor dem Heros."* Hellerau: Jakob Hegner, 1927.

Christ Rescued. Translated by Gerald Griffin. London: Skeffington, 1933. Originally published as *Der gerettete Christus oder Iphigenies Flucht vor dem Ritualopfer*. Illustrated with woodcuts after Dürer. Potsdam: Gustav Kiepenheuer, 1928.

Reihenhausfassaden, Geschäfts- und Wohnhäuser aus alter und neuer Zeit. 500 illustrations collected by W. Hegemann. Berlin: Wasmuth, 1929.

Neue Werkkunst Series of Monographs on Architects. Edited with Introductions by W. Hegemann. Berlin: Friedrich Ernst Hübsch. *Die Architekten Brüder Gerson* (1928); *German Bestelmeyer* (1929); *Hans Herkommer* (1929); *Neue Warenhausbauten der Rudolph Karstadt A.-G. von Architekt Philipp Schaefer, Hamburg* (1929); *Pinno und Grund* (1929); *Architekten Lossow & Kühne, Dresden* (1930); *Benno Franz Moebus* (1930); *Zerbe und Harder* (1930); *Paul Zimmerreimer* (1930).

Herrenhaus Hohenhorst bei Bremen, erbaut 1928–1929; Architekt Otto Blendermann. Introduction by W. Hegemann. Berlin: Wasmuth, [1930].

Das Jugendbuch vom Grossen König oder Kronprinz Friedrichs Kampf um die Freiheit. Hellerau: Jakob Hegner, 1930.

Das steinerne Berlin: Geschichte der grössten Mietskasernenstadt der Welt. Berlin, Kiepenheuer, 1930. Reprint (abridged) Berlin: Ullstein, 1988, and Braunschweig: Birkhäuser/Vieweg, 1992.

Hermann Distel: Krankenhäuser. Edited with an introduction by W. Hegemann. Hellerau: Jakob Hegner, 1931.

Mar del Plata, El Balneario y el Urbanismo Moderno. Conferencia del Urbanista y Arquitecto Dr. Werner Hegemann pronunciada el 11 de Niviembre en el Teatro Odeon de Mar del Plata. Buenos Aires: L. J. Rosso, 1931.

Problemas Urbanos de Rosario. Conferencias del Urbanista Doctor Werner Hegemann. Municipalidad de Rosario, 1931.

Revised and expanded edition. Prague: Soziologische Verlagsanstalt, 1934.

Reprint of the Prague edition including Arnold Zweig, "Auch Werner Hegemann . . ." Hildesheim, Gerstenberg, 1979.

History Unmasked. London. Originally published as *Entlarvte Geschichte*. Leipzig: Jakob Hegner, 1933).

City Planning: Housing. Vol. 1, *Historical and Sociological*. Vol. 2, *Political Economy and Civic Art*, edited by Ruth Nanda Anshen, Preface by Joseph Hudnut; chapter on Washington by Elbert Peets. Vol. 3, *A Graphic Review of Civic Art 1922–1937*, edited by William W. Forster and Robert C. Weinberg. Foreword by Raymond Unwin. New York: Architectural Book Publishing Co., Inc., 1936, 1937, 1938.

Index

G

H

U

V

W

Y

Z